Drugs, Society & Human Behavior

Seventeenth Edition

Carl L. Hart
Columbia University

Charles Ksir
University of Wyoming

Mc
Graw
Hill
Education

DRUGS, SOCIETY & HUMAN BEHAVIOR, SEVENTEENTH EDITION

Published by McGraw-Hill Education, 2 Penn Plaza, New York, NY 10121. Copyright © 2018 by McGraw-Hill Education. All rights reserved. Printed in the United States of America. Previous editions © 2015, 2013, and 2011. No part of this publication may be reproduced or distributed in any form or by any means, or stored in a database or retrieval system, without the prior written consent of McGraw-Hill Education, including, but not limited to, in any network or other electronic storage or transmission, or broadcast for distance learning.

Some ancillaries, including electronic and print components, may not be available to customers outside the United States.

This book is printed on acid-free paper.

3 4 5 6 7 8 9 LCR 21 20 19

ISBN 978-1-259-91386-0
MHID 1-259-91386-4

Portfolio Manager: *Jamie Laferrera*
Product Developer: *Francesca King*
Marketing Manager: *Meredith Leo*
Content Project Managers: *Rick Hecker and George Theofanopoulos*
Buyer: *Susan Culbertson*
Design: *Egzon Shaqiri*
Content Licensing Specialists: *Lori Slattery*
Cover Image: ©Rayhart (http://www.rayhart.com/)
Compositor: *Lumina Datamatics, Inc.*

All credits appearing on page or at the end of the book are considered to be an extension of the copyright page.

Library of Congress Cataloging-in-Publication Data

Names: Hart, Carl L., author. | Ksir, Charles, author.
Title: Drugs, society & human behavior [electronic resource] / Carl L. Hart, Charles Ksir.
Other titles: Drugs, society, and human behavior
Description: Seventeenth edition. | New York, NY: McGraw-Hill Education,
    [2018] | Includes bibliographical references and index.
Identifiers: LCCN 2017028977 (print) | LCCN 2017030020 (ebook) | ISBN 9781260240924 (Web) |
    ISBN 9781259913860 (pbk. : alk. paper) | ISBN 1259913864 (pbk. : alk. paper)
Subjects: | MESH: Psychotropic Drugs—pharmacokinetics | Substance-Related
    Disorders—complications | Behavior—drug effects | Social Behavior Disorders—etiology
Classification: LCC RM316 (ebook) | LCC RM316 (print) | NLM QV 77.2 | DDC
    362.29—dc23
LC record available at https://lccn.loc.gov/2017028977

The Internet addresses listed in the text were accurate at the time of publication. The inclusion of a website does not indicate an endorsement by the authors or McGraw-Hill Education, and McGraw-Hill Education does not guarantee the accuracy of the information presented at these sites.

mheducation.com/highered

Brief Contents

Contents

List of Boxes

Drugs in the Media

Taking Sides

Drugs in Depth

Targeting Prevention

Unintended Consequences

Myth Buster

Life Saver

DSM-5

Focus on Drug Policy

Focus on Treatment

About the Authors

Dr. Hart is the chair of the Department of Psychology and Dirk Ziff Professor in Psychiatry at Columbia University. He has published extensively in the area of neuropsychopharmacology and continues to lecture on the topic of psychoactive drug use throughout the world.

Dr. Ksir is professor emeritus of psychology and neuroscience at the University of Wyoming. Now retired after 35 years of research and teaching, he has authored or coauthored *Drugs, Society and Human Behavior* since 1984. He continues to teach a class based on this text via the Internet.

Preface

Today's media-oriented college students are aware of many issues relating to drug use. Nearly every day we hear new concerns about the "opioid crisis" legal pharmaceuticals, and the effects of tobacco and alcohol, and most of us have had some personal experience with these issues through family, friends, or co-workers. This course is one of the most exciting students will take because it will help them relate the latest information on drugs to their effects on society and human behavior. Students will not only be in a better position to make decisions to enhance their own health and well-being, but they will also have a deeper understanding of the individual problems and social conflicts that arise when others misuse and abuse psychoactive substances.

Much has changed in the 40 plus years since *Drugs, Society and Human Behavior* was first published. The 1970s were a period of widespread experimentation with cannabis and psychedelics, while the 1980s brought increased concern about illegal drugs and conservatism, along with decreased use of alcohol and all illicit drugs. Not only did drug-using behavior change, but so did attitudes and knowledge. And, of course, in each decade the particular drugs of immediate social concern have changed: LSD gave way to angel dust, then to heroin, then to cocaine. In the 1990s, we saw increased use of LSD and cannabis, but not to the levels of the 1970s.

Recent Trends

The most alarming trend in recent years has been the increased misuse of heroin and prescription opioid pain relievers such as Oxycontin and Vicodin. This class of drug has now replaced cocaine as the leading cause of drug overdose deaths in the United States (not counting alcohol overdoses), and it inspired a new White House task force on opioid addiction.

Meanwhile, our old standbys, alcohol and tobacco, remain with us and continue to create serious health and social problems. Regulations undergo frequent changes, new scientific information becomes available, and new approaches to prevention and treatment are being tested, but the reality of substance use and abuse always seems to be with us.

This text approaches drugs and drug use from a variety of perspectives—behavioral, pharmacological, historical, social, legal, and clinical—which will help students connect the content to their own interests.

Special Features

Updated Content in the Seventeenth Edition

Throughout each chapter, we have included the very latest information and statistics, and—the Drugs in the Media feature has allowed us to comment on breaking news right up to press time. In addition, we have introduced many timely topics and issues that are sure to pique students' interest and stimulate class discussion.

The following are just some of the new and updated topics in the seventeenth edition.

- Statistics on drug use trends, new drug treatments, and drug-related mortality statistics from National Survey on Drug Use and Health and DAWN (Chapter 1 and throughout)

- Toxicity data from the Drug Abuse Warning Network (Chapter 2)

- Information on the cost of current drug control strategies (Chapter 3)

- Introduction to the concept of neuropeptides (Chapter 4)

- Information on how racial discrimination persists today in the enforcement of cocaine laws (Chapter 6)

- Updated tables containing information on antipsychotic and antidepressant medications (Chapter 8)

- Updated statistics on per-capita ethanol consumption by beverage type (Chapter 9)

- Presentation of tips that may be useful in preventing opioid overdoses (Chapter 13)

- Updated information on the number of states that allow the medical and/or recreational use of cannabis (Chapter 15)

- New chapter on drug policies that work (Chapter 18)

Focus Boxes

Boxes are used in *Drugs, Society and Human Behavior* to explore a wide range of current topics in greater detail than is possible in the text itself. The boxes are organized around key themes.

 Drugs in the Media Our world revolves around media of all types—TV, films, radio, print media, and the Web. To meet students on familiar ground, we have included Drugs in the Media boxes, which take an informative and critical look at these media sources of drug information. Students can build their critical thinking skills while reading about such topics as alcohol advertising, media coverage of prescription drugs, and the presentation of cigarette smoking in films.

 Taking Sides These boxes discuss a particular drug-related issue or problem and ask students to take a side in the debate. This thought-provoking material will help students apply what they learned in the chapter to real-world situations. Taking Sides topics include potential medical uses of marijuana, current laws relating to drug use, and the issue of government funding for research on psychedelics.

 Targeting Prevention The Targeting Prevention boxes offer perspective and provoke thought regarding which drug-related behaviors we, as a society, want to reduce or prevent. Topics include syringe exchange programs, criminal penalties for use of date rape drugs, and nondrug techniques for overcoming insomnia. These boxes help students better evaluate prevention strategies and messages.

 Drugs in Depth These boxes examine specific, often controversial, drug-related issues such as the extrapolation of animal studies to humans, and the growing number of people in prison for drug-related offenses. Drugs in Depth boxes are a perfect starting point for class or group discussion.

 Life Saver These boxes provide simple and specific information that can reduce many negative effects associated with drug use harms, such as avoiding the combination of sleeping pills with alcohol or opioids and getting sufficient amounts of sleep if taking amphetamines. Life Saver boxes are concise harm reduction tips.

 Unintended Consequences Students quickly learn that drugs have multiple effects, including unwanted negative ones. The same is true for drug policy. The Unintended Consequences boxes highlight unexpected negative consequences of policies aimed at controlling drug use and/or sales. These boxes provide students with opportunities to think critically about such topics as whether restricting the sale of hypodermic needles and syringes increase the risk for contracting a blood-borne disease.

Myth Buster There are many misconceptions about psychoactive drugs use. The Myth Buster boxes present a popular drug use myth and systematically dissect it using the best available empirical information.

These boxes provide an excellent example of how to think through information critically. Topics covered include the "meth mouth" phenomenon and the "real" performance-enhancing drug in Major League Baseball.

 Focus on Drug Policy These boxes examine drug policies from around the globe that successfully strike a balance between individual freedom and public health and safety. Focus on Drug Policy boxes provide excellent examples of how local governments work to solve local problems.

 Focus on Treatment Focus on Treatment boxes provide up-to-date information on treatment strategies used for specific drug addictions. These boxes help students to understand the available treatments for addiction.

Check Yourself! Activities

These self-assessments, found at the end of most chapters, help students put health concepts into practice. Each Check Yourself! activity asks students to answer questions and analyze their own attitudes, habits, and behaviors. Self-assessments are included in such areas as sleep habits, daily mood changes, alcohol use, caffeine consumption, and consideration of consequences.

Attractive Design and Illustration Package

The inviting look, bold colors, and exciting graphics in *Drugs, Society and Human Behavior* draw the reader in with every turn of the page. Sharp and appealing photographs, attractive illustrations, and informative tables support and clarify the chapter material.

Pedagogical Aids

Although all the features of *Drugs, Society and Human Behavior* are designed to facilitate and improve learning, several specific learning aids have been incorporated into the text:

- **Chapter Objectives:** Chapters begin with a list of objectives that identify the major concepts and help guide students in their reading and review of the text.

- **Definitions of Key Terms:** Key terms are set in boldface type and are defined in corresponding boxes. Other important terms in the text are set in italics for emphasis. Both approaches facilitate vocabulary comprehension.

- **Chapter Summaries:** Each chapter concludes with a bulleted summary of key concepts. Students can use the chapter summaries to guide their reading and review of the chapters.

- **Review Questions:** A set of questions appears at the end of each chapter to aid students in their review and analysis of chapter content.

- **Appendices:** The appendices include handy references on brand and generic names of drugs and on drug resources and organizations.

- **Summary Drugs Chart:** A helpful chart of drug categories, uses, and effects appears on the back inside cover of the text.

Supplements

The seventeenth edition of *Drugs, Society and Human Behavior* is now available online with Connect, McGraw-Hill Education's integrated assignment and assessment platform. Connect also offers SmartBook for the new edition, which is the first adaptive reading experience proven to improve grades and help students study more effectively. All of the title's website and ancillary content is also available through Connect, including:

- A full Test Bank of multiple-choice questions that test students on central concepts and ideas in each chapter.

- An Instructor's Manual for each chapter with full chapter outlines, sample test questions, and discussion topics.

- Lecture Slides for instructor use in class.

 **connect®**

McGraw-Hill Connect® is a highly reliable, easy-to-use homework and learning management solution that utilizes learning science and award-winning adaptive tools to improve student results.

Homework and Adaptive Learning

- Connect's assignments help students contextualize what they've learned through application, so they can better understand the material and think critically.

- Connect will create a personalized study path customized to individual student needs through SmartBook®.

- SmartBook helps students study more efficiently by delivering an interactive reading experience through adaptive highlighting and review.

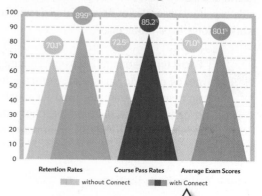

Connect's Impact on Retention Rates, Pass Rates, and Average Exam Scores

- Retention Rates: 70.1%, 89.9%
- Course Pass Rates: 72.5%, 85.2%
- Average Exam Scores: 71.0%, 80.1%

without Connect / with Connect

Using **Connect** improves retention rates by **19.8%**, passing rates by **12.7%**, and exam scores by **9.1%**.

Over **7 billion questions** have been answered, making McGraw-Hill Education products more intelligent, reliable, and precise.

73% of instructors who use **Connect** require it; instructor satisfaction **increases** by 28% when **Connect** is required.

Quality Content and Learning Resources

- Connect content is authored by the world's best subject matter experts, and is available to your class through a simple and intuitive interface.

- The Connect eBook makes it easy for students to access their reading material on smartphones and tablets. They can study on the go and don't need internet access to use the eBook as a reference, with full functionality.

- Multimedia content such as videos, simulations, and games drive student engagement and critical thinking skills.

Robust Analytics and Reporting

©Hero Images/Getty Images

- Connect Insight® generates easy-to-read reports on individual students, the class as a whole, and on specific assignments.

- The Connect Insight dashboard delivers data on performance, study behavior, and effort. Instructors can quickly identify students who struggle and focus on material that the class has yet to master.

- Connect automatically grades assignments and quizzes, providing easy-to-read reports on individual and class performance.

Impact on Final Course Grade Distribution

without Connect		with Connect
22.9%	A	31.0%
27.4%	B	34.3%
22.9%	C	18.7%
11.5%	D	6.1%
15.4%	F	9.9%

More students earn **As** and **Bs** when they use **Connect**.

Trusted Service and Support

- Connect integrates with your LMS to provide single sign-on and automatic syncing of grades. Integration with Blackboard®, D2L®, and Canvas also provides automatic syncing of the course calendar and assignment-level linking.

- Connect offers comprehensive service, support, and training throughout every phase of your implementation.

- If you're looking for some guidance on how to use Connect, or want to learn tips and tricks from super users, you can find tutorials as you work. Our Digital Faculty Consultants and Student Ambassadors offer insight into how to achieve the results you want with Connect.

www.mheducation.com/connect

Acknowledgments

We would like to express our appreciation to the following instructors who reviewed the previous edition and helped lay the groundwork for the improvements and changes needed in the seventeenth edition:

Kwangseog Ahn
University of Wisconsin-Whitewater

Perry Fuchs
University of Texas Arlington

Julie Gast
Utah State University

Devin Jordan
Western Michigan University

Tina Lamb
Kishwaukee College

Jeanie McCarville Kerber
Des Moines Area Community College

Timothy McQuade
Erie Community College

Robert Metzger
University of Iowa

James Myers
Genesee Community College

Kerry J. Redican
Virginia Tech

Diane Sevening
University of South Dakota

Amy H. Smith
Virginia Tech

Sokoyama K. Songu-Mbriwa
Prince Georges Community College

James H. Taylor, III
J. Sargeant Reynolds Community College

Kelly B. Wingo
University of Alabama

We'd also like to thank Malakai Hart for detailed comments and suggestions on the glossary section.

Carl L. Hart

Charles Ksir

Drug Use in Modern Society

The interaction between drugs and behavior can be approached from two general perspectives. Certain drugs, the ones we call "psychoactive", have profound effects on behavior. Part of what a book on this topic should do is describe the effects of these drugs *on behavior*, and later chapters do that in some detail. Another perspective, however, views drug taking *as behavior*. The psychologist sees drug-taking behaviors as interesting examples of human behavior that are influenced by many psychological, social, and cultural variables. In the first section of this text, we focus on drug taking as behavior that can be studied in the same way that other behaviors, such as aggression, learning, and human sexuality, can be studied.

1   Drug Use: An Overview
Which drugs are being used and why?

2   Drug Use as a Social Problem
Why does our society want to regulate drug use?

3   Drug Policy
What are the regulations, and what is their effect?

1 Drug Use: An Overview

©Ryan McVay/Getty Images RF

"The Drug Problem"

Drug use is an issue that affects individuals, families, communities, and all levels of government, not just in the United States, but around the world. Of course, the simple term *drug use* represents a complex mix of behaviors, scientific questions, legal issues, moral dilemmas, and more. In fact, this entire book provides an opportunity to examine the many kinds of substances involved, the biology underlying their effects, the psychology of various drug-using behaviors, and societal influences on drug use and reactions to drug issues. As we discuss these topics, our aim is to report evidence that is based on empirical data, derived from scientific studies. This stands in contrast to anecdotal evidence, which is typically based on one person's casual observation or perception. What we began by calling *drug use* is not a simple thing at all. In this first chapter, as we take an overview of drug use, there are some general principles that we can always rely on.

Objectives

When you have finished this chapter, you should be able to:

- Develop an analytical framework for understanding any specific drug-use issue.

- Apply five general principles of psychoactive drug use to any specific drug-use issue.

- Explain the differences between misuse, abuse, and dependence.

- Describe the general trends of increases and decreases in drug use in the United States since 1975.

- Remember several correlates and antecedents of adolescent drug use.

- Describe correlates and antecedents of drug use in the terminology of risk factors and protective factors.

- Discuss motives that people may have for illicit and/or dangerous drug-using behavior.

Use Is Not Abuse

Most users of any given substance do not use it in ways that can be defined as either abuse or dependence (see definitions on page 5). We know that many people drink alcohol in ways that do not cause problems for them or their families, but about 10 percent of drinkers do have significant problems such as missing work due to a hangover or having multiple arrests for driving under the influence, and some require treatment for alcohol dependence. The same principle applies to all drugs. The single most common type of illicit drug use is marijuana smoking, and the vast majority of those users are what some have called "recreational" or "social" or "casual" users. The last

Our concern about the use of a substance often depends on who is using it, how much is being used, and when, where, and why it is being used. ©Emma Lee/Life File/Getty Images RF (*left*), ©Getty Images RF (*right*)

three U.S. presidents and at least one current member of the U.S. Supreme Court have admitted to using marijuana when they were young. A small fraction of marijuana users seek admission to treatment programs because they want to quit and have not been able to do so without help. Even for drugs such as heroin, crack cocaine, and methamphetamine, which the media consistently portray as producing "instant addiction," the actual experiences of most users of those substances do not support such claims. We will learn much more about these drugs and their use in later chapters. Some have argued that if a substance like methamphetamine is illegal, then any use at all should be considered abuse. Not only does that not fit the accepted definition of abuse, it ignores and trivializes one of the most important questions about substance abuse: Why do some people develop serious problems while most avoid them?

Every Drug Has Multiple Effects

Although a user might be seeking only one effect (relaxation, or alertness, or feeling "high"), every psychoactive drug acts at multiple sites, both in the brain and on other organs. So relaxation might be accompanied by slower reaction time, or alertness might be produced along with an increase in heart rate.

Amount Matters

This may seem obvious, but it's important to point out that large doses, frequent doses, or taking the

drug by a method that results in a lot of the drug getting to the brain quickly can produce very different effects, and generally more problems, than taking the same drug in a single lower dose. Not only are a drug's effects often increased with higher drug concentrations, but additional effects tend to show up as well. This principle is easily illustrated with alcohol, as the increased talkativeness of low doses becomes accompanied by slower reaction times, then slurred speech and difficulty walking, and eventually unconsciousness as blood alcohol rises.

Psychoactive Drug Effects Are Powerfully Influenced by the User's History and Expectations

Experienced users may react differently than new users, for example, showing less disruption in a driving simulator test after drinking alcohol (the same happens with marijuana). Experienced users may also report more of the positive effects of a drug, partly because of associations from their prior use. But even people who have never used a substance have learned a lot about what they are supposed to expect from it, and those expectations can influence what they do experience. It's easy to imagine that if someone has to take a drug for medical reasons but has been told that it will produce an unpleasant side effect, that person might be fearful and have a much worse reaction than if he or she had not been warned. But you probably didn't know

Unintended Consequences

Reporting on the "Drug du Jour"

One of the most common types of drug stories appearing in news media has to do with prescription drug abuse. Over the years there have been several "waves" of drug topics that grow to dominate the news media for a period of time and then slowly give way to the next wave. The hot topic in the 1980s was crack cocaine, which gave way to stories on ecstasy, then GHB, and methamphetamine. More recent waves of publicity have focused on "spice," "flakka," carfentanil, and U-47700 ("pink"). Although there is overlap, it almost seems that at any given time the news media all tend to be focused on the *drug du jour* (drug of the day).

One question that doesn't get asked much is this: What role does such media attention play in popularizing the current drug fad, perhaps making it spread farther and faster than would happen without the publicity? About 40 years ago, in a chapter titled "How to Create a Nationwide Drug Epidemic," journalist E. M. Brecher described a sequence of news stories that he believed were the key factor in spreading the practice of sniffing the glues sold to kids for assembling plastic models of cars and airplanes (see *volatile solvents* in Chapter 7). He argued that, without the well-meant attempts to warn people of the dangers of this practice, it would probably have remained isolated to a small group of youngsters in Pueblo, Colorado. Instead, sales of model glue skyrocketed across America, leading to widespread restrictions on sales to minors.

Thinking about the kinds of things such articles often say about the latest drug problem, are there components of those articles that you would include if you were writing an advertisement to promote use of the drug? Do you think such articles actually do more harm than good, as Brecher suggested? If so, does the important principle of a free press mean there is no way to reduce the impact of such journalism?

For an interesting look at the 2014 wave of media reports on the "flesh-eating Zombie drug" Krokodil, see http://www.forbes.com/sites/jacobsullum/2014/01/10/krokodil-crock-how-rumors-of-a-flesh-eating-zombie-drug-swept-the-nation/.

Box icon credit: ©Adam Gault/age fotostock RF

this: The more a person believes that alcohol makes people more sociable, the more talkative and friendly that person will become after drinking even a small amount.

Drugs, Per Se, Are Not Good or Bad

There are no "bad drugs." When drug abuse, drug dependence, and deviant drug use are talked about, it is the behavior, the way the drug is being used, that is being referred to. This statement is controversial to many, and even offensive to some. It therefore requires some defense. To a chemist, it is difficult to view the drug, the chemical substance itself, as somehow possessing evil intent. It sits there in its bottle and does nothing until we put it into a living system. Ascribing morality to the substance—a pure chemical—seems illogical. On the other hand, a psychologist who has spent years treating drug users, or a police officer whose job it is to arrest them, finds it difficult to imagine what good there might be in a drug like heroin or cocaine or methamphetamine, and easily views the substance as an enemy of the good work he or she is trying to perform. The truth is that any drug that produces effects might produce some benefit when used carefully and has the potential to produce harm when abused. For example, heroin is a perfectly good painkiller, as effective as any of the widely prescribed opioid analgesics, and it is used medically in many countries. Cocaine is a good local anesthetic and is still used for medical procedures, even in the United States. Methamphetamine is available as a prescription drug in the United States, approved to treat ADHD and obesity. Each of these drugs can also produce bad effects when people abuse them. In the cases of heroin and cocaine, our society has weighed its perception of the risks of bad consequences against the potential

Drugs in Depth

Important Terms—and a Caution!

Some terms that are commonly used in discussing drugs and drug use are difficult to define with precision, partly because they are used so widely for many different purposes. For each of the following terms, we have pointed out some of the "gray areas" that help us to clarify our understanding of the term, as well as to make us leery of hard-and-fast labeling of someone's behavior.

The word **drug** will be defined as "any substance, natural or artificial, other than food, that by its chemical nature alters structure or function in the living organism." One obvious difficulty is that we haven't defined *food*, and how we draw that line can sometimes be arbitrary. Alcoholic beverages, such as wine and beer, may be seen as drug, food, or both. Are we discussing how much sherry wine to include in beef Stroganoff, or are we discussing how many ounces of wine can be consumed before becoming intoxicated? Since this is not a cookbook but, rather, a book on the use of psychoactive chemicals, we will view all alcoholic beverages as drugs.

Illicit drug is a term used to refer to a drug that is unlawful to possess or use. Many of these drugs are available by prescription, but when they are manufactured or sold illegally they are illicit. Traditionally, alcohol and tobacco have not been considered illicit substances even when used by minors, probably because of their widespread legal availability to adults. Common household chemicals, such as glues and paints, take on some characteristics of illicit substances when people inhale them to get "high."

Deviant drug use is drug use that is not common within a social group *and* that is disapproved of by the majority, causing members of the group to take corrective action when it occurs. The corrective action may be informal (making fun of the behavior, criticizing the behavior) or formal (incarceration, treatment). Some examples of drug use might be deviant in the society at large but accepted or even expected in particular subcultures. We still consider this behavior to be deviant, since it makes more sense to apply the perspective of the larger society.

Drug misuse generally refers to the use of prescribed drugs in greater amounts than, or for purposes other than, those prescribed by a physician or dentist. For nonprescription drugs or chemicals such as paints, glues, or solvents, misuse might mean any use other than the use intended by the manufacturer.

Abuse consists of the use of a substance in a manner, amounts, or situations such that the drug use causes problems or greatly increases the chances of problems occurring. The problems may be social (including legal), occupational, psychological, or physical. Once again, this definition gives us a good idea of what we're talking about, but it isn't precise. For example, some observers would consider any use of an illicit drug to be abuse because of the possibility of legal problems, but the majority of marijuana users do not meet the clinical criteria for substance abuse. Also, the use of almost any drug, even under the orders of a physician, has at least some potential for causing problems. The question might come down to how great the risk is and whether the user is recklessly disregarding the risk. For someone to receive a diagnosis of having a *substance use disorder* (see the DSM-5 feature in Chapter 2), the use must be recurrent, and the problems must lead to significant impairment or distress.

Addiction is a controversial and complex term that has **different** meanings for different people. Some people want to reserve the term only for those whose lives have been completely taken over by substance use, whereas others will apply the term broadly to anyone who is especially interested in watching television, reading, running, skiing, or any other activity. When it comes to substance use, we will use *addiction* only to refer to cases in which people have struggled to control their use and have suffered serious negative consequences from that use.

Drug **dependence** refers to a state in which the individual uses the drug so frequently and consistently that it appears that it would be difficult for the person to get along *without* using the drug. For some drugs and some users, there are clear withdrawal signs when the drug is not taken, implying a *physiological dependence*. Dependence can take other forms, as shown in the DSM-5 feature in Chapter 2. If a great deal of the individual's time and effort is devoted to getting and using the drug, if the person often winds up taking more of the substance than he or she intended, and if the person has tried several times without success to cut down or control the use, then the person meets the behavioral criteria for dependence. This behavioral dependence is what we mean when we use the term *addiction*.

Box icon credit: ©Ingram Publishing/SuperStock RF

The effects of drugs are influenced by the setting and the expectations of the user. ©Brand X Pictures RF

benefits and decided that we should severely restrict the availability of these substances. It is wrong, though, to place all of the blame for these bad consequences on the drugs themselves and to conclude that they are simply "bad" drugs. Many people tend to view some of these substances as possessing an almost magical power to produce evil. When we blame the substance itself, our efforts to correct drug-related problems tend to focus exclusively on eliminating the substance, perhaps ignoring all of the factors that led to the abuse of the drug.

How Did We Get Here?

Drug use is not new. Humans have been using alcohol and plant-derived drugs for thousands of years—as far as we know, since *Homo sapiens* first appeared on the planet. A truly "drug-free society" has probably never existed, and might never exist. Psychoactive drugs were used in rituals that we could today classify as religious in nature, and Chapter 14 provides several examples of hallucinogenic drugs reported to enhance spiritual experiences. A common belief in many early cultures was that illness results from invasion by evil spirits, so in that context it makes sense that psychoactive drugs were often used as part of a purification ritual to rid the body of those spirits. In these early cultures the use of drugs to treat illness likely was intertwined with spiritual use so that the roles of the "priest" and that of the "shaman" (medicine

man) often were not separate. In fact, the earliest uses of many of the drugs that we now consider to be primarily recreational drugs or drugs of abuse (nicotine, caffeine, alcohol, and marijuana) were as treatments for various illnesses.

Psychoactive drugs have also played significant roles in the economies of societies in the past. Wine was a significant trade item among Greek, Turkish, Egyptian, and Italian people via the Mediterranean Sea over 2,000 years ago. Chapter 10 describes the importance of tobacco in the early days of European exploration and trade around the globe as well as its importance in the establishment of English colonies in America; Chapter 6 discusses the significance of the coca plant (from which cocaine is derived) in the foundation of the Mayan empire in South America; and Chapter 13 points out the importance of the opium trade in opening China's doors to trade with the West in the 1800s.

One area in which enormous change has occurred over the past 100-plus years is in the development and marketing of legal pharmaceuticals. The introduction of vaccines to eliminate smallpox, polio, and other communicable diseases, followed by the development of antibiotics that are capable of curing some types of otherwise deadly illnesses, laid the foundation for our current acceptance of medicines as the cornerstone of our health care system. The introduction of birth control medications in the early 1960s was important not only for the enormous implications they had for women's opportunities to pursue educational and career goals, but also because millions of young, healthy people were taking drugs for reasons other than illness. During this same time period, mental health treatment began to shift dramatically as new drugs were introduced to reduce symptoms of schizophrenia, anxiety, mania, and depression (Chapter 8).

Another significant development in the past 100 years has been government efforts to limit access to certain kinds of drugs that are deemed too dangerous or too likely to produce dependence to allow them to be used in an unregulated fashion. The enormous growth, both in expenditures and in

Focus on Drug Policy

Is There Really a "War on Drugs"?

"War on drugs" is not an official term but rather a short-hand way to refer to the efforts by the United States and other governments to reduce or eliminate certain kinds of drug use. It is often attributed to U.S. president Richard Nixon, who in 1971 declared that drug abuse was "public enemy number one." The term has been used for many years, mostly by people critical of drug-control efforts. Two of the terms defined on page 5 are relevant for understanding these government efforts. *Deviant drug use* is drug use that is disapproved of by a social group, and which the group acts to correct when it occurs. In this case, the important group is the governing body (e.g., Congress in the United States, or parliament in some other countries). The corrective actions taken by these governments are formalized and may include some form of punishment, or treatment offered as an alternative to punishment. Therefore, these examples of deviant drug use also comprise *illicit drug use* (use of a drug that is illegal). It is important to understand that the deviant and illicit quality of these acts depends both on the drug-using behavior and on the government's response to that behavior. For example, 50 years ago interracial dating and marriage were considered by many to be deviant behaviors and were even outlawed in several U.S. states

prior to a 1967 Supreme Court decision. The same type of behavior now is neither illicit nor deviant in the eyes of most Americans. As marijuana use becomes increasingly acceptable to more Americans, it is less likely to be considered deviant, at least at the level requiring formal legal correction. Many U.S. states have reduced or eliminated penalties for possession and use, and pressure is being put on Congress to take similar steps at the federal level.

The origins of today's war on drugs are described in Chapter 3, but for now we need to understand that a great deal of money is spent and many peoples' jobs depend on these efforts worldwide. The United States is considered by most to be the leading governmental factor, both in terms of the amount of money spent and its influential role in convincing other nations to pass similar laws and to participate in international drug control efforts.

In subsequent chapters we will examine the effects of this so-called war on drugs on the lives of users, service providers, and other participants, whether willing or unwilling.

U.S. President Richard Nixon, 1971

Box icon credit: ©Edward.J.Westmacott/Alamy Images RF

the breadth of substances now controlled, has led many to refer to this development as a "war on drugs." These laws are also outlined in Chapter 3, but we will trace their effect throughout the chapters on different drug classes, and the chapters on prevention and treatment of drug abuse and dependence.

With both of these developments, the proportion of our economy devoted to psychoactive drugs, both legal and illegal, and to their regulation, has also expanded considerably. Drug use would be an important topic for us to understand if only for that fact. In addition, drug use and its regulation are reflective of changes in our society and in how we as individuals interact with that society. Also, drug problems and our attempts to solve them have in turn had major influences on us as individuals and

on our perceptions of appropriate roles for government, education, and health care. Therefore, the topic of psychoactive drugs provides a window through which we can study our own current psychology, sociology, and politics.

Drugs and Drug Use Today

Extent of Drug Use

In trying to get an overall picture of drug use in today's society, we quickly discover that it's not easy to get accurate information. It's not possible to measure with great accuracy the use of, let's say, cocaine in the United States. We don't know exactly how much is imported and sold, because most of it is illegal. We don't know exactly how many cocaine users there are in the country, because none of the measures we do have (survey results, arrest data, admissions to treatment programs) captures every single one. For some substances, such as prescription drugs, tobacco, and alcohol, we have a wealth of sales information and can make much better estimates of rates of use. Even there, however, our information might not be complete (home-brewed beer would not be counted, for example, and prescription drugs might be bought and then left unused in the medicine cabinet).

Just because we can't get precise answers to these questions doesn't mean that we should give up and conclude that we don't know anything about how much drug use is going on. We do have information about which drugs are more widely used than others and also whether the use of a particular drug is increasing or decreasing. So let's look at some of the kinds of information we do have. A large number of survey questionnaire studies have been conducted in junior highs, high schools, and colleges, partly because this is one of the easiest ways to get a lot of information with a minimum of fuss. Researchers have always been most interested in drug use by adolescents and young adults, because drug use usually begins and reaches its highest levels in this age group.

This type of research has a couple of drawbacks. The first is that we can use this technique only on the students who are in classrooms. We can't get this information from high school dropouts. That causes a bias, because those who skip school or have dropped out are more likely to use drugs.

A second limitation is that we must assume that most of the self-reports are done honestly. In most cases, we have no way of checking to see if Johnny really did smoke marijuana last week, as he claimed on the questionnaire. Nevertheless, if every effort is made to encourage honesty (including assurances of anonymity), we expect that this factor is minimized. To the extent that tendencies to over-report or underreport drug use are relatively constant from one year to the next, we can use such results to reflect trends in drug use over time and to compare relative reported use of various drugs.

Table 1.1

Percentage of College Students One to Four Years beyond High School Reporting Use of Eight Types of Drugs (2015)

Drug	Ever Used	Used in Past 30 Days	Used Daily for Past 30 Days
Alcohol	81	63	3.1
Cigarettes	NA	11	4.2
E-cigarettes	26	8.8	NA
Marijuana/hashish	50	21	4.6
Inhalants	3	0.2	0.0
Amphetamines	14	4.2	0.0
Hallucinogens	7	1.4	0.0
Cocaine (all)	6	1.5	0.0
Crack	0.5	0.0	0.0

Source: Monitoring the Future Project, University of Michigan 2016.

Let's look first at the drugs most commonly reported by young college students in a recent nationwide sample. Table 1.1 presents data from one of the best and most complete research programs of this type, the Monitoring the Future Project at the University of Michigan.[1] Data are collected each year from more than 15,000 high school seniors in schools across the United States, so that nationwide trends can be assessed. Data are also gathered from 8th- and 10th-graders and from college students. Three numbers are presented for each drug: the percentage of college students (one to four years beyond high school) who have *ever* used the drug, the smaller percentage who report having used it within the past *30 days,* and the still smaller percentage who report *daily* use for the past 30 days. Note that most of these college students have tried alcohol at some time in their lives. Half have tried marijuana, about one-third have tried cigarettes or e-cigarettes, and most students report never having tried the rest of the drugs listed. Also note that daily use of any of these drugs may be considered rare.

Populations of Users

One very important thing to remember about the people who use a particular substance is that there is a wide range of rates and amounts of use, even within the using population. Look again at Table 1.1. Starting with alcohol, we can see that over 80 percent of college students have used alcohol at some time in their lives, and about two-thirds report drinking within the month prior to the survey. The difference between those two figures includes some who might have tried drinking at one time but never plan to drink again, but a larger number who have no real objection to drinking but only do so on rare occasions throughout a given year, such as at a wedding or on New Year's Eve. Then there is a big drop in numbers down to the 3 percent or so who reported daily drinking. So,

when we think about those who have reported drinking in the past 30 days, some of them might have had only one drink in that month. Others might have one or two drinks in a typical week. Others might have a few drinks on one occasion and then not drink again for a month. Others might regularly have two or three drinks on Friday and Saturday nights and not drink at all during the week. Others might start their weekend on Wednesday or Thursday and drink pretty heavily several nights each week, but still not drink daily. Most of us have some familiarity with this wide range of behavior when it comes to alcohol, because we probably know some people in each of these categories: never used, used at one time but won't use again, use rarely, use regularly but in small amounts, and so on.

What is harder for most people to understand is that the same wide range of behavior is found among users of every psychoactive drug. Not every marijuana user, crack smoker, or heroin user is the same. Given the wide range of human behavior when it comes to everything else in life, this should not be a surprise, but we often forget that there are many types of users of any kind of drug. Look at Table 1.1 for amphetamines. The 14 percent who report ever using includes what? In these surveys, we exclude the legitimate use of prescribed amphetamines for treating ADHD, for example. But, if you have a friend who has a prescription and she gives you an Adderall pill to stay awake and study, then that nonmedical use would be included in this figure, along with someone who was smoking or injecting methamphetamine. As we dig more specifically into even the use of illicit methamphetamine, we find the same range of users: Some have tried it and will never use again, some might use it on rare occasions, some might use it more regularly but in small doses, and a fairly small percentage of users will meet the criteria for dependence. When we ask college students about daily (nonmedical) use of amphetamines, the percentage drops to virtually zero.

This range of users has important implications for our prevention efforts, treatment efforts, and law enforcement, and must be kept in mind when

Drugs in Depth

Determining the Extent of Substance Use and Abuse

Imagine that you have been asked to participate in a task force in the community where you are living. This group is specifically looking into substance abuse, and one of the group members, a parent of two teenagers, has heard that high-school students have been using *Salvia divinorum*, also called diviner's sage. We will learn more about this substance and its effects in Chapter 14, but for now let's just ask ourselves how your group can get an idea of the actual extent of its use. What kinds of agencies would you turn to for information? What kinds of information would each of them be likely to have? What else could your task force do to gather even more information? Given all these sources, how close do you think you could come to estimating the size of the problem in your community?

we discuss the nature of dependence. We are going to look at more data on the proportions of users of various substances, but remember this wide variety of behavior as we look at trends over time.

Trends in Drug Use

The Monitoring the Future study, which has now been conducted annually for almost 40 years, allows us to see changes over time in the rates of drug use. Figure 1.1 displays data on marijuana use among 12th-graders.[2] Look first at the line labeled "Use." In 1975, just under 30 percent of high school seniors reported that they had used marijuana in the past 30 days (an indication of "current use"). This proportion rose each year until 1978, when 37 percent of 12th-graders reported current marijuana use. Over the next 14 years, from 1979 to 1992, marijuana use declined steadily so that by 1992 only 12 percent of 12th-graders reported current use (about one-third as many as in 1978). Then the

trend reversed, with rates of current use climbing back to 24 percent of 12th-graders by 1997. Changes over the past 20 years have been small, with the 2015 rate at 21 percent. Because marijuana is by far the most commonly used illicit drug, we can use this graph to make a broader statement: Illicit drug use among high school seniors has not changed a great deal in the past 20 years. Currently, marijuana use is about half as common among 12th-graders as it was in 1978, but it is more common than it was at its lowest point 25 years ago. This is important because there always seem to be people trying to say that drug use is increasing among young people, or that people are starting to use drugs at younger and younger ages, but the best data we have provide no support for such statements (e.g., data from 8th-graders show the same trends as for 12th-graders).

How can we explain these very large changes in rates of marijuana use over time? Maybe marijuana

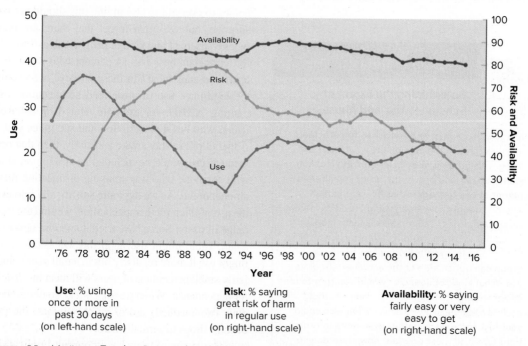

Use: % using
once or more in
past 30 days
(on left-hand scale)

Risk: % saying
great risk of harm
in regular use
(on right-hand scale)

Availability: % saying
fairly easy or very
easy to get
(on right-hand scale)

Figure 1.1 Marijuana: Trends in Perceived Availability, Perceived Risk of Regular Use, and Prevalence of Use in the Past 30 Days for 12th-Graders

SOURCE: Monitoring the Future Study, The University of Michigan.

was easier to obtain in 1978, less available in 1992, and so on. Each year the same students were asked their opinion about how easy they thought it would be to get marijuana if they wanted to do so. Looking at the "Availability" line, and using the scale on the right-hand side of Figure 1.1, we can see that back in 1975 about 90 percent of the seniors said that it would be fairly easy or very easy for them to get marijuana.[2] The interesting thing is that this perception has not changed much, remaining above 80 percent for 40 years. Thus, the perceived availability does NOT appear to explain differences in rates of use over time. This is important because it implies that we can have large changes in rates of drug use even when the supply of the drug does not appear to change much.

There is another line on Figure 1.1, labeled "Risk" (and also tied to the right-hand scale). In 1975, about 40 percent of 12th-graders rated the risk of harm from regular marijuana use as "great risk of harm." The proportion of students reporting great risk declined over the same time that use was increasing (up to 1978). Then, as use dropped from 1979 to 1992, perceived risk increased. Perceived risk declined during the 1990s when use was again increasing, and then didn't change a great deal in recent years. You should be able to see from Figure 1.1 that as time goes by, the line describing changes in perception of risk from using marijuana is essentially a mirror image of the line describing changes in rates of using marijuana. This is important because it seems to say that the best way to achieve low rates of marijuana use is by convincing students that it is risky to use marijuana, whereas efforts to control the availability of marijuana ("supply reduction") might have less of an influence. However, we must keep in mind that a cause and effect relationship has not been proven. Changes in both rates of use and perceptions of risk could be caused by something else that we are not directly measuring.

In addition to the surveys of students, broad-based self-report information is also gathered through house-to-house surveys. With proper sampling techniques, these studies can estimate the drug use in most of the population, not just among students. This technique is much more time-consuming and expensive, it has a greater rate of refusal to participate, and we must suspect that individuals engaged in illegal drug use would be reluctant to reveal that fact to a stranger on their doorstep. The National Survey on Drug Use and Health is a face-to-face, computer-assisted interview done with more than 68,000 individuals in carefully sampled households across the United States. Figure 1.2 displays the trends in reported past month use of marijuana for two different age groups.[3] This study shows the same pattern as the Monitoring the Future study of 12th-graders: Marijuana use apparently grew throughout the 1970s, reaching a peak in about 1980, and then declining until the early 1990s, when it increased again. The 18–25 age group does show a slow but steady increase in use over the past 20 years, whereas the 12–17 age group has been more stable.

We have seen fairly dramatic trends over time in marijuana use, but what about other substances? Figure 1.3 shows rates of current use of alcohol and cocaine alongside marijuana use for Americans between 18 and 25 years of age.[3] Many more people are current users of alcohol (about two-thirds of adults), and many fewer use cocaine in any given year. But overall, the trends over time are generally similar, with the peak year for all three substances around 1980, lower rates of use in the early 1990s, and less dramatic changes in recent years.

Finding such a similar pattern in two different studies using different sampling techniques gives us additional confidence that these trends have been real and probably reflect broad changes in American society over this time. Political observers will be quick to note that Ronald Reagan was president during most of the 1980s, when use of marijuana and other drugs was declining, while Bill Clinton was in office during most of the 1990s, when these rates rose. Were these changes in drug use the result of more conservative drug-control policies under the Reagan administration and more liberal policies under the Clinton administration? There are two reasons to think that is not the answer.

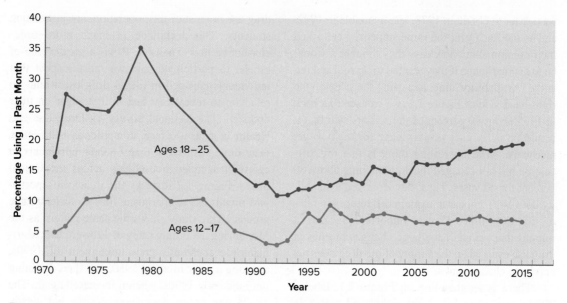

Figure 1.2   Trends in Marijuana Use among Persons Ages 12–25, by Age Group
SOURCE: National Survey on Drug Use and Health.

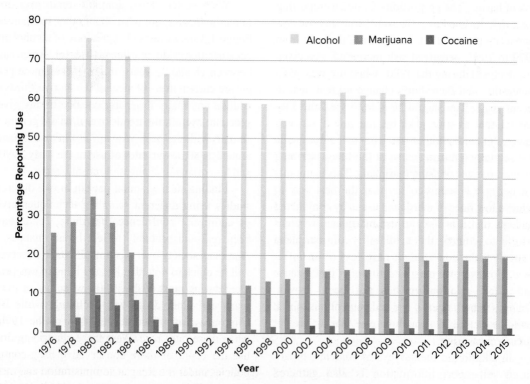

Figure 1.3   Trends in Reported Drug Use within the Past 30 Days for Young Adults Ages 18 to 25
SOURCE: National Survey on Drug Use and Health.

Marijuana is the most commonly used illicit drug, and major surveys including the Monitoring the Future study and the National Survey on Drug Use and Health track trends in its usage. ©McGraw-Hill Education/Gary He, photographer

First, the timing is not quite right. President Reagan was elected in 1980, took office in 1981, and didn't begin focusing on the "Just Say No" antidrug messages until 1983. Most of the important legislation was passed in 1986. All of this was after the downward trend in drug use had already begun. It seems more likely that the Reagan administration recognized the opportunity provided by an underlying change in attitude among the general public. The government's policies might have helped to amplify the effects of this underlying social change, but they did not create it. The same timing problem is associated with trying to link increased drug use to the Clinton presidency: The election was in 1992, and increased use was already beginning in 1993, during the first year of the Clinton administration. Also, the Clinton administration can hardly be accused of having liberal drug-control policies—drug-control budgets and arrests for drug violations were higher than in any previous administration. Finally, if the country was in a more conservative mood during the George W. Bush years (2000–2008) and then shifted to a more liberal mood in 2008 when Barack Obama was elected, the corresponding changes in marijuana use are not very apparent in Figure 1.2.

If we can't point to government policies as causes of these substantial changes in drug use, how can we explain them? The short answer is that for now, we can't. We are left with saying that changes in rates of illicit drug use and in alcohol use probably reflect changes over time in a broad range of attitudes and behaviors among Americans—what we can refer to as "social trends." As of now, we can't explain why the use of a particular drug increases and decreases over time, any more than we can explain why people wore loud bell-bottom trousers in the 1970s or why people in the current decade have more tattoos than previous generations. This isn't much of an explanation, and that is somewhat frustrating. After all, if we understood why these changes were taking place it might allow us to influence rates of substance use among the general population, or at least to predict what will happen next. Perhaps some of today's college students will be the ones to develop this understanding over the next few years.

Let's summarize the kinds of things we do and don't know from these studies: We can determine which kinds of substances are most widely used (alcohol, cigarettes, and marijuana are much more widely used than the other substances), and we can follow some fairly significant overall trends in substance use (not much change over the past decade, somewhat higher than in the early 1990s, but much lower use than in 1980). And, while there have been ups and downs in the use of marijuana and other illicit drugs, we should be skeptical of claims that a slight downward trend means that government efforts are "working," or of claims that a slight upward trend signals a new "epidemic."

Correlates of Drug Use

Once we know that a drug is used by some percentage of a group of people, the next logical step is to ask about the characteristics of those who use the drug, as compared with those who don't. Often the same questionnaires that ask each person which drugs they have used also include several questions about the persons completing the questionnaires. The researchers might then send their computers "prospecting" through the data to see if certain personal characteristics can be correlated with drug

---

Table 1.2
Risk and Protective Factors Associated with Marijuana Use by Adolescents

Risk Factors (in order of importance):	Protective Factors (in order of importance):
1. Having friends who use marijuana or other substances	1. Perceiving that there are strong sanctions against substance use at school
2. Engaging in frequent fighting, stealing, or other antisocial activities	2. Having parents as a source of social support
3. Perceiving that substance use is prevalent at your school	3. Being committed to school
4. Knowing adults who use marijuana or other substances	4. Believing that religion is important and frequently attending religious services
5. Having a positive attitude toward marijuana use	5. Participating in two or more extracurricular activities

---

use. But these studies rarely reveal much about either very unusual or very common types or amounts of drug use. For example, if we send a computer combing through the data from 1,000 questionnaires, looking for characteristics correlated with heroin use, only one or two people in that sample might report heroin use, and you can't correlate much based on one or two people. Likewise, it would be difficult to identify the distinguishing characteristics of the people who have "ever tried" alcohol, because that group usually represents more than 90 percent of the sample.

Much of the research on **correlates** of drug use has used marijuana smoking as an indicator, partly because marijuana use has been a matter of some concern and partly because enough people have tried it so that meaningful correlations can be done. Other studies focus on early drinking or early cigarette smoking.

Risk and Protective Factors

Increasingly, researchers are analyzing the correlates of drug use in terms of *risk factors* and *protective factors*. Risk factors are correlated with higher rates of drug use, while protective factors are correlated with lower rates of drug use. A study based on data obtained from the National Survey on Drug Use and Health examined risk and protective factors regarding use of marijuana among

adolescents (ages 12–17).[4] This large-scale study provides some of the best information we have about the correlates of marijuana use among American adolescents. The most significant factors are reported in Table 1.2.

In some ways, the results confirm what most people probably assume: The kids who live in rough neighborhoods, whose parents don't seem to care what they do, who have drug-using friends, who steal and get into fights, who aren't involved in religious activities, and who don't do well in school are the most likely to smoke marijuana. The same study analyzed cigarette smoking and alcohol use, with overall similar results.

There are some surprising results, however. Those adolescents who reported that their parents frequently monitored their behavior (e.g., checking homework, limiting TV watching, and requiring chores) were actually a little more likely to report using marijuana than adolescents who reported less parental monitoring. This finding points out the main problem with a correlational study: We don't know if excessive parental monitoring makes adolescents more likely to smoke marijuana, or if adolescents' smoking marijuana and getting in fights makes their parents more likely to monitor them (the latter seems more likely).

Another example of the limitation of correlational studies is the link between marijuana

Table 1.3
Drug Use among 18- to 25-Year-Olds: Percentage Reporting Use in the Past 30 Days

Drug	Male	Female	White	African American	Hispanic	American Indian	Asian	High School Graduate	College Graduate
Alcohol	60	57	64	50	51	52	48	50	81
Tobacco	40	26	38	30	25	51	16	37	22
Marijuana	23	16	21	23	18	17	9	19	16
Cocaine	2	1.3	2.0	0.8	1.1	1.6	0.9	1.3	2.2

Source: National Survey on Drug Use and Health, 2015 data, available at http://www.samhsa.gov/data.

smoking and poor academic performance. Does smoking marijuana cause the user to get lower grades? Or is it the kids who are getting low grades anyway who are more likely to smoke marijuana? One indication comes from the analysis of risk and protective factors for cigarette smoking in this same study. The association between low academic performance and cigarette smoking was even stronger than the association between low academic performance and marijuana smoking. This leads most people to conclude that it's the kids who are getting low grades anyway who are more likely to be cigarette smokers, and the same conclusion can probably be reached about marijuana smoking.

Deviant Drug Use

The overall picture that emerges from studies of risk and protective factors is that the same adolescents who are likely to smoke cigarettes, drink heavily, and smoke marijuana are also likely to engage in other deviant behaviors, such as vandalism, stealing, fighting, and early sexual behaviors, and to not do well in school. It can be useful to simply consider adolescent drug use as one of a cluster of deviant behaviors. Calling early use of cigarettes, alcohol, or marijuana deviant behavior does nothing to explain why these behaviors appear in some people, but it does change our perspective a bit. Rather than asking whether one of these behaviors causes the other (i.e., Does marijuana

cause poor school performance?), we can understand that either of these behaviors indicates that an adolescent's conduct is less influenced by society's expectations than most others of the same age, and that in such cases a variety of deviant behaviors might appear. From this perspective, drug use, stealing, fighting, and poor school performance are all indicators that the individual's conduct is not conforming to the norms of society. If we now look again at Table 1.2, instead of thinking of these entries as factors that either help to cause or prevent marijuana use, we can see that they are the characteristics of people who are more or less likely to conform to social norms in general.

Race, Gender, and Level of Education

Table 1.3 shows how demographic variables are related to current use of some drugs of interest.[3] The first thing to notice is something that has been a consistent finding over many kinds of studies for many years: Males are more likely to drink alcohol, use tobacco, smoke marijuana, and use cocaine than are females. This probably doesn't surprise most people too much, but it is good to see that in many cases the data do provide support for what most people would expect.

correlate (*core a let*): a variable that is statistically related to some other variable, such as drug use.

Expectations regarding ethnic and racial influences on drug use are more likely to clash with the data from the National Survey on Drug Use and Health. For example, overall, whites are more likely to drink alcohol, use tobacco, or use cocaine than are African Americans and Hispanics, and these three groups are about equally likely to use marijuana. These results do not conform to many peoples' stereotypes, so let's remind ourselves that we are talking about household surveys that cut across socioeconomic and geographic lines and attempt to examine American society at large. Also, remember that we are getting data simply about recent use of these substances, which for most people means relatively low-level and infrequent use. Why then, do we have such a strong stereotyped image of drug use being highly prevalent in black and Latino communities? This stereotype likely comes from the poorest neighborhoods, where crime rates are high and therefore police presence is more concentrated.[5] These neighborhoods are often characterized by limited educational and economic opportunities, and in these circumstances there is less incentive to adhere to the social norms of the overall society. We therefore do see somewhat higher rates of various types of deviant behavior, including drug use. But perhaps more important is that the selling of drugs in these neighborhoods often occurs openly on the street, and this combines with heavy police presence to result in high arrest rates. It is important for us to understand that the majority of black and Latino citizens do not live in these neighborhoods and also that people in these neighborhoods are much more likely to be arrested for selling drugs than people living in other areas of the same cities where there are fewer police and drug sales take place behind closed doors. In other words, overall drug use is not much influenced by one's ethnic grouping, but arrest rates for drug crimes are higher in high-crime neighborhoods. We do see from Table 1.3 that the group labeled American Indian has somewhat higher rates of tobacco and marijuana use, and across Asian groups there is a generally lower rate of use of all these substances.

Education level is powerfully related to two common behaviors: Young adults with college degrees (compared to those who completed only high school) are much more likely to drink alcohol and much less likely to use tobacco.

Personality Variables

The relationships between substance use and various indicators of individual differences in personality variables have been studied extensively over the years. In general, large-scale survey studies of substance use in the general population have yielded weak or inconsistent correlations with most traditional personality traits as measured by questionnaires. So, for example, it has been difficult to find a clear relationship between measures of self-esteem and rates of using marijuana. More recently, several studies have found that various ways of measuring a factor called *impulsivity* can be correlated with rates of substance use in the general population.[6] Impulsivity is turning out to be of much interest to drug researchers but also is hard to pin down in that different laboratories have different ways of measuring it. In general, it seems to relate to a person's tendency to act quickly and without consideration of longer-term consequences. We can expect to see more research on this concept over the next few years.

Instead of looking at any level of substance use within the general population, we can look for personality differences between those who are dependent on substances and a "normal" group of people. When we do that, we find many personality differences associated with being more heavily involved in substance abuse or dependence. The association with impulsivity, for example, is much stronger in this type of study. Likewise, if we look at groups of people who are diagnosed with personality disorders, such as conduct disorder or antisocial personality disorder, we find high rates of substance use in these groups. Overall, it seems that personality factors may play a small role in whether someone decides to try alcohol or marijuana but a larger role in whether that use develops into a serious problem. Because the main focus of this first chapter is on rates of drug use in the general population, we will put off further discussion of personality variables to Chapter 2.

Genetics

There is increasing interest in genetic influences on drug use. Again, studies looking across the general population and asking simply about recent use are less likely to produce significant results than studies that focus on people diagnosed with substance use disorders. Genetic factors probably play a small role in whether someone tries alcohol or marijuana but a larger role in whether that use develops into a serious problem. Studies of genetic variability in impulsivity and related traits are beginning to show clear association with substance use disorders.[7] Genetic factors in dependence are discussed further in Chapter 2.

Antecedents of Drug Use

Finding characteristics that tend to be associated with drug use doesn't help us understand causal relationships very well. For example, do adolescents first become involved with a deviant peer group and then use drugs, or do they first use drugs and then begin to hang around with others who do the same? Does drug use cause them to become poor students and to fight and steal? To answer such questions, we might interview the same individuals at different times and look for **antecedents,** characteristics that predict later initiation of drug use. One such study conducted in Finland found that future initiation of substance use or heavy alcohol use can be predicted by several of the same risk factors we have already discussed: aggressiveness, conduct problems, poor academic performance, "attachment to bad company," and parent and community norms more supportive of drug use.[8] Because these factors were measured *before* the increase in substance use, we are more likely to conclude that they may be *causing* substance use. But some other, unmeasured, variables might be causing both the antecedent risk factors and the subsequent substance use to emerge in these adolescents' lives.

Gateway Substances

One very important study from the 1970s pointed out a typical sequence of involvement with drugs.[9] Most of the high-school students in that group started their drug involvement with beer or wine. The second stage involved hard liquor, cigarettes, or both; the third stage was marijuana use; and only after going through those stages did the students try other illicit substances. Not everyone followed the same pattern, but only 1 percent of the students began their substance use with marijuana or another illicit drug. It is as though they first had to go through the **gateway** of using alcohol and, in many cases, cigarettes. The students who had not used beer or wine at the beginning of the study were much less likely to be marijuana smokers at the end of the study than the students who had used these substances. The cigarette smokers were about twice as likely as the nonsmokers to move on to smoking marijuana.

One possible interpretation of the gateway phenomenon is that young people are exposed to alcohol and tobacco and that these substances somehow make the person more likely to go on to use other drugs. Because most people who use these gateway substances do not go on to become cocaine users, we should be cautious about jumping to that conclusion. More likely is that early alcohol use and cigarette smoking are common indicators of the general deviance-prone pattern of behavior that also includes an increased likelihood of smoking marijuana or trying cocaine. A large cross-cultural study compared patterns of drug initiation across 17 countries and reported many differences in the most common order of drugs used, implying that the gateway phenomenon is not due to a direct chemical effect but instead is heavily influenced by social and cultural factors.[10]

---

antecedent (ant eh *see* dent): a variable that occurs before some event such as the initiation of drug use.

gateway: one of the first drugs (e.g., alcohol or tobacco) used by a typical drug user.

Males who are aggressive in early elementary school are more likely to be drug users as adults. ©Don Hammond/ Design Pics RF

Because beer and cigarettes are more widely available to a deviance-prone young person than marijuana or cocaine, it is logical that beer and cigarettes would most often be tried first. The socially conforming students are less likely to try even these relatively available substances until they are older, and they are less likely ever to try the illicit substances. Let's ask the question another way: If we developed a prevention program that stopped all young people from smoking cigarettes, would that cut down on marijuana smoking? Most of us think it might, because people who don't want to suck tobacco smoke into their lungs probably won't want to inhale marijuana smoke either. Would such a program keep people from getting D averages or getting into other kinds of trouble?

Probably not. In other words, we think of the use of gateway substances not as the *cause* of later illicit drug use but, instead, as an early indicator of the basic pattern of deviant behavior resulting from a variety of psychosocial risk factors.

Motives for Drug Use

To most of us, it doesn't seem necessary to find explanations for normative behavior; we don't often ask why someone takes a pain reliever when she has a headache. Our task is to try to explain the drug-taking behavior that frightens and infuriates—the deviant drug use. We should keep one fact about human conduct in mind throughout this book: Despite good, logical evidence telling us we "should" avoid certain things, we all do some of them anyway. We know that we shouldn't eat that second piece of pie or have that third drink on an empty stomach. Cool-headed logic tells us so. We would be hard pressed to find good, sensible reasons why we should smoke cigarettes, drive faster than the speed limit, go skydiving, sleep late when we have work to do, flirt with someone and risk an established relationship, or use cocaine. Whether one labels these behaviors sinful or just stupid, they don't seem to be designed to maximize our health or longevity.

But humans do not live by logic alone; we are social animals who like to impress each other, and we are pleasure-seeking animals. These factors help explain why people do some of the things they shouldn't, including using drugs.

The research on correlates and antecedents points to a variety of personal and social variables that influence our drug taking, and many psychological and sociological theorists have proposed models for explaining illegal or excessive drug use. We have seen evidence for one common reason that some people begin to take certain illegal drugs: Usually young, and somewhat more often male than female, they have chosen to identify with a deviant subculture. These groups frequently engage in a variety of behaviors not condoned by the larger society. Within that group, the use of a particular drug might not be deviant at all but might, in fact,

People who use drugs and who identify with a deviant subculture are more likely to engage in a variety of behaviors not condoned by society. ©fmajor/E+/Getty Images RF

be expected. Occasionally the use of a particular drug becomes such a fad among a large number of youth groups that it seems to be a nationwide problem. However, within any given community there will still be people of the same age who don't use the drug.

Rebellious behavior, especially among young people, serves important functions not only for the developing individual but also for the evolving society. Adolescents often try very hard to impress other people and may find it especially difficult to impress their parents. An adolescent who is unable to gain respect from people or who is frustrated in efforts to "go his or her own way" might engage in a particularly dangerous or disgusting behavior as a way of demanding that people be impressed or at least pay attention.

One source of excessive drug use may be found within the drugs themselves. Many of these drugs are capable of *reinforcing* the behavior that gets the drug into the system. **Reinforcement** means that, everything else being equal, each time you take the drug you increase slightly the probability that you will take it again. Thus, with many psychoactive drugs there is a tendency to increase the frequency or amount of use. Some drugs (such as intravenous heroin or cocaine) appear to be so reinforcing that this process occurs relatively rapidly. For other drugs, such as alcohol, the process seems to be slower. In many people, social factors, other

reinforcers, or other activities prevent an increase. For some, however, the drug-taking behavior does increase and consumes an increasing share of their lives.

Most drug users are seeking an altered state of consciousness, a different perception of the world than is provided by normal, day-to-day activities. Many of the high-school students in the nationwide surveys report that they take drugs "to see what it's like," or "to get high," or "because of boredom." In other words, they are looking for a change, for something new and different in their lives. This aspect of drug use was particularly clear during the 1960s and 1970s, when LSD and other perception-altering drugs were popular. We don't always recognize the altered states produced by other substances, but they do exist. A man drinking alcohol might have just a bit more of a perception that he's a tough guy, that he's influential, that he's well liked. A cocaine user might get the seductive feeling that everything is great and that she's doing a great job (even if she isn't). Many drug-abuse prevention programs have focused on efforts to show young people how to feel good about themselves and how to look for excitement in their lives without using drugs.

Another thing seems clear: Although societal, community, and family factors (the outer areas of Figure 1.4) play an important role in determining whether an individual will first *try* a drug, with increasing use the individual's own experiences with the drug become increasingly important. For those who become seriously dependent, the drug and its actions on that individual become central, and social influences, availability, cost, and penalties play a less important role in the continuation of drug use.

> **reinforcement:** a procedure in which a behavioral event is followed by a consequent event such that the behavior is then more likely to be repeated. The behavior of taking a drug may be reinforced by the effect of the drug.

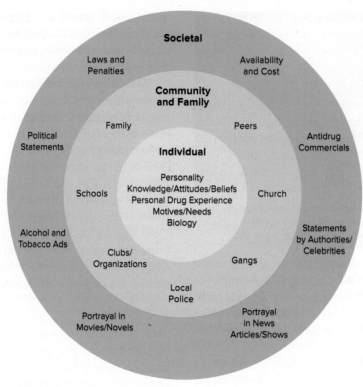

Figure 1.4   Influences on Drug Use

Summary

- The users of every type of drug include some who have tried it but won't use it again, some who use it infrequently, some who use it more often but in small amounts, and some who use frequently and in greater amounts. This is as true for users of heroin and crack cocaine as it is for users of alcohol and marijuana.

- No drug is entirely good or bad, and every drug has multiple effects. The size and type of effect depends on the dose of the drug and the user's history and expectations.

- Deviant drug use includes those forms of drug use not considered either normal or acceptable by the society at large. Drug misuse is using a drug in a way that was not intended by its manufacturer. Drug abuse is drug use that causes problems. (If frequent and serious, then a diagnosis of substance use disorder is applied.) Drug dependence involves using the substance more often or in greater amounts than the user intended, and having difficulty stopping or cutting down on its use.

- Among American college students, almost 65 percent can be considered current users of alcohol, less than 20 percent current smokers of tobacco cigarettes, or marijuana, and less than 2 percent current users of cocaine.

- Both alcohol and illicit drug use reached an apparent peak around 1980, then decreased until the early 1990s, with a slower increase after that. Current rates of use are lower than at the peak.

- Adolescents who use illicit drugs (mostly marijuana) are more likely to know adults who use drugs, less likely to believe that their parents would object to their drug use, less likely to see their parents as a source of social support, more likely to have friends who use drugs, less likely to be religious, and more likely to have academic problems.

- A typical progression of drug use starts with cigarettes and alcohol, then marijuana, then other drugs such as amphetamines, cocaine, or heroin. However, there is no evidence that using one of the "gateway" substances causes one to escalate to more deviant forms of drug use.

- People may use illicit or dangerous drugs for a variety of reasons: They may be part of a deviant subculture, they may be signaling their rebellion, they may find the effects of the drugs to be reinforcing, or they may be seeking an altered state of consciousness. The specific types of drugs and the ways they are used will be influenced by the user's social and physical environment. If dependence develops, then these environmental factors may begin to have less influence.

Review Questions

1. Besides asking a person the question directly, what is one way a psychologist can try to determine why a person is taking a drug?

2. What two characteristics of a drug's effect might change when the dose is increased?

3. In about what year did drug use in the United States peak?

4. About what percentage of college students use marijuana?

5. What do the results of the National Survey on Drug Use and Health tell us about the overall rates of marijuana and cocaine use among whites compared to African Americans and Hispanics in the United States?

6. How does having a college degree influence rates of drinking alcohol? Using tobacco?

7. Name one risk factor and one protective factor related to the family/parents.

8. How does impulsivity relate to rates of drug use in the general population? How does impulsivity relate to substance dependence?

References

1. Johnston, L. D., P. M. O'Malley, J. G. Bachman, J. E. Schulenberg and R. A. Meich. *Monitoring the Future National Survey Results on Drug Use, 1975–2015.* Volume II: *College Students and Adults Ages 19–55.* Ann Arbor: Institute for Social Research, The University of Michigan, 2016. Available at http://monitoringthe future.org/pubs.html#monographs.

2. Miech, R. A., L. D. Johnston, P. M. O'Malley, J. G. Bachman, and J. E. Schulenberg. *Monitoring the Future National Survey Results on Drug Use, 1975–2015. Volume I: Secondary School Students.* Ann Arbor: Institute for Social Research, The University of Michigan, 2016. Available at http://monitoringthe-future.org/pubs.html#monographs.

3. Substance Abuse and Mental Health Services Administration. 2015 National Survey on Drug Use and Health: Detailed Tables, 2016. Available at www.samhsa.gov/data.

4. Wright, D., and M. Pemberton. *Risk and Protective Factors for Adolescent Drug Use: Findings from the 1999 National Household Survey on Drug Abuse* (DHHS Publication No. SMA 04-3874, Analytic Series A-19). Rockville, MD: Substance Abuse and Mental Health Services Administration, Office of Applied Studies, 2004.

5. Corsaro, N. "The High Point Drug Market Intervention: Examining Impact across Target Areas and Offense Types." *Victims & Offenders* 8 (2013), pp. 416–45.

6. Vangsness, L., B. H. Bry, and E. W. LaBouvie. "Impulsivity, Negative Expectancies, and Marijuana Use. A Test of the Acquired Preparedness Model." *Addictive Behaviors* 30 (2005), pp. 1071–76.

7. Kreek, M. J., D. A. Nielsen, E. R. Butelman, and K. S. LaForge. "Genetic Influences on Impulsivity, Risk Taking, Stress Responsivity and Vulnerability to Drug Abuse and Addiction." *Nature Neuroscience* 8 (2005), pp. 1450–57.

8. Poikolainen, K. "Antecedents of Substance Use in Adolescence." *Current Opinion in Psychiatry* 15 (2002), pp. 241–45.

9. Kandel, D., and R. Faust. "Sequence and Stages in Patterns of Adolescent Drug Use." *Archives of General Psychiatry* 32 (1975), pp. 923–32.

10. Degenhardt, L., L. Dierker, W. T. Chiu, M. E. Medina-Mora, Y. Neumark, N. Sampson, J. Alonso, et al. "Evaluating the Drug Use 'Gateway' Theory Using Cross-National Data: Consistency and Associations of the Order of Initiation of Drug Use among Participants in the WHO World Mental Health Surveys." *Drug and Alcohol Dependence* 108 (2010), pp. 84–97.

Check Yourself

Name _____   Date _____

Do Your Goals and Behaviors Match?

One interesting thing about young people who get into trouble with drugs or other types of deviant behavior is that they often express fairly conventional long-term goals for themselves. In other words, they want or perhaps even expect to be successful in life but then do things that interfere with that success. One way to look at this is that their long-term goals don't match up with their short-term behavior. Everyone does this sort of thing to some extent—you want to get a good grade on the first exam, but then someone talks you into going out instead of studying for the next one. Or perhaps you hope to lose 5 pounds but just can't pass up that extra slice of pizza.

Make yourself a chart that lists your long-term goals down one side and has a space for short-term behaviors down the other side, like the one below.

Write in your goal under each category as best you can. Then think about some things you do occasionally that tend to interfere with your achieving that goal and put a minus sign next to each of those behaviors. After you have gone through all the goals, write down some short-term behaviors that you could practice to assist you in achieving each goal, and put a plus sign beside each of those behaviors.

How do your goals and behaviors stack up? Are there some important goals for which you have too many minuses and not enough pluses? If study skills and habits, relationship problems, or substance abuse appear to be serious roadblocks for your success, consider visiting a counselor or therapist to get help in overcoming them.

	Goals (Long-Term)	Behaviors (Short-Term)
Educational		
Physical health and fitness		
Occupational		
Spiritual		
Personal relationships		

2

Drug Use as a Social Problem

Objectives

When you have finished this chapter, you should be able to:

- **Distinguish between the federal government's regulatory approach before the early 1900s and now.**

- **Distinguish between acute and chronic toxicity and between physiological and behavioral toxicity.**

- **Describe the two types of data collected in the DAWN system and know the top four drug classes for emergency room visits and for mortality.**

- **Understand why the risks of HIV/AIDS and hepatitis are higher among injection drug users.**

- **Define tolerance, physical dependence, and behavioral dependence.**

- **Understand how the scientific perspective on substance dependence has changed in recent years.**

- **Differentiate between substance abuse and substance dependence using diagnostic criteria.**

- **Debate the various theories on the cause of dependence.**

- **Describe four ways that drug use might cause an increase in crime.**

©sakhorn38/iStock/Getty Images RF

As we look into the problems experienced by society as a result of the use of psychoactive drugs, we need to consider two broad categories. The first category is the problems directly related to actually taking the drug, such as the risk of developing dependence or of overdosing. Second, because the use of certain drugs is considered a deviant act, the continued use of those drugs by some individuals represents a different set of social problems, apart from the direct dangers of the drugs themselves. These problems include arrests, fines, jailing, and the expenses associated with efforts to prevent misuse and to treat abuse and dependence. We begin by examining the direct drug-related problems that first raised concerns about cocaine, opium, and other drugs. Problems related to law enforcement, prevention, and treatment will be examined more thoroughly in Chapters 3, 17, and 18.

Land of the Free?

In the 1800s, the U.S. government, like the majority of countries around the world, had virtually no laws governing the sale or use of most drugs. Many modern-day Libertarians would like to see us return to something like that, either allowing each state to regulate drugs or simply allowing people to choose what to use, as long as they don't harm others. Others believe that approach would be taking too much of a risk. The tension between freedom and safety plays out in many arenas, whether we're talking about security screening at airports, regulating air and water pollution, or the use of drugs like marijuana or heroin. This chapter will explain why people came to believe that unregulated access to drugs led to serious social problems, with the result that the United States now spends billions of dollars each year trying to control access to and use of hundreds of controlled substances, making 1.5 million arrests each year for drug-law violations. We will also discuss the costs and consequences to society of maintaining the current approach to drug regulation. What happened to cause the leaders of the "land of the free" to believe it was necessary to create especially restrictive regulations for some drugs?

Three main concerns aroused public interest: (1) *toxicity:* some drug sellers were considered to be endangering the public health and victimizing individuals because they were selling dangerous, toxic chemicals, often without labeling them or putting appropriate warnings on them; (2) *dependence:* some sellers were seen as victimizing individuals and endangering their health by selling them habit-forming drugs, again often without appropriate labels or warnings; and (3) *crime:* the drug user came to be seen as a threat to public safety—the attitude became widespread that drug-crazed individuals would often commit horrible, violent crimes. In Chapter 3, we will look at the roots of these concerns and how our current legal structures grew from them. For now, let's look at each issue and develop ground rules for the discussion of toxicity, dependence, and drug-related crime.

Toxicity

Categories of Toxicity

The word **toxic** means "poisonous, deadly, or dangerous." All the drugs we discuss in this text can be toxic if misused or abused. We will use the term to refer to those effects of drugs that interfere with normal functioning in such a way as to produce dangerous or potentially dangerous consequences. Seen in this way, for example, alcohol can be toxic in high doses because it suppresses respiration—this can be dangerous if breathing stops long enough to induce brain damage or death. But we can also consider alcohol to be toxic if it causes a person to be so disoriented that, for them, otherwise normal behaviors, such as driving a car or swimming, become dangerous. This is an example of something we refer to as **behavioral toxicity.** We make a somewhat arbitrary distinction, then, between behavioral toxicity and "physiological" toxicity—perhaps taking advantage of the widely assumed mind-body distinction, which is more convenient than real. The only reason for making this distinction is that it helps remind us of some important kinds of toxicity that are special to psychoactive drugs. This kind of behavioral impairment due to drug or alcohol intoxication is potentially dangerous not only to the user but also to others if the user is an airline pilot or is driving a car or performing surgery. This danger has led to special laws to reduce these risks.

Why do we consider physiological toxicity to be a "social" problem? One view might be that if an individual chooses to take a risk and harms his or her own body, that's the individual's business. But impacts on hospital emergency rooms, increased health insurance rates, lost productivity, and other consequences of physiological toxicity mean that social systems also are affected when an individual's health is put at risk, whether by drug use or failure to wear seat belts.

Another distinction we make for the purpose of discussion is **acute** versus **chronic.** Most of the time when people use the word *acute,* they mean "sharp" or "intense." In medicine an acute condition is one that comes on suddenly, as opposed to a chronic or long-lasting condition. When talking about drug effects, we can think of the acute effects as those that result from a single administration of a drug or that are a direct result of the presence of the drug in the system at the time. For example, taking an overdose of a prescription painkiller can slow your respiration rate to dangerously low levels. By

Drugs in Depth

Drugged Driving

From the 2016 National Survey on Drug Use and Health (Chapter 1), it is estimated that over 10 million Americans reported driving under the influence of some illicit drug during the past year. Given the frequency of reported use of various drugs, we expect that most of those had been smoking marijuana. When combined with concerns about driving under the influence of legal prescription and nonprescription drugs, the National Highway Traffic Safety Administration (NHTSA) has put increased emphasis on impaired driving caused by a variety of drugs. One of their efforts has been supporting the training of police officers to become **drug recognition experts (DREs).**

When a police officer suspects impaired driving, he or she will usually conduct a field sobriety test. These tests include nystagmus (jerky movements as the eyes track a moving target), walk and turn, and one-legged stand, and have been demonstrated to detect intoxication due to alcohol and some classes of drugs. If the person is arrested based on this test, many police departments are now able to conduct a more detailed examination using trained DREs, who check pulse rates, pupil dilation, and several other factors. Based on the results, these DREs can usually determine which major class of drugs is responsible for the impairment.

Proving impairment in court is a complex and often difficult task. State laws vary considerably regarding blood testing, setting limits for some drugs, and reliance on behavioral testing.

Box icon credit: ©Ingram Publishing/SuperStock RF

---

contrast, the chronic effects of a drug are those that result from long-term exposure and can be present whether or not the substance is in the system at a given point. For example, smoking cigarettes is a major cause of high blood pressure. After you develop high blood pressure, that condition is there when you wake up in the morning and when you go to bed at night, and whether your most recent cigarette was five minutes ago or five days ago doesn't make much difference. Another important example is that chronic exposure to large amounts of alcohol can cause both neurological and liver damage.

Drug Abuse Warning Network

In an effort to monitor the toxicity of drugs other than alcohol, the U.S. government set up the Drug Abuse Warning Network (**DAWN**). This system collected data on drug-related emergency room visits from hospital emergency departments in major metropolitan areas around the country. The DAWN system was discontinued in 2011, so we are presenting the last data collected. A new data system is being developed by the National Center for Health Statistics, but no results have yet been released.

When an individual went to an emergency room with any sort of problem related to drug misuse or abuse, each drug involved (up to six) was recorded. The visit could be for a wide variety of reasons, such as injury due to an accident, accidental overdose, a suicide attempt, or a distressing panic reaction that was not life-threatening to the patient. If someone was in an automobile accident after drinking alcohol, smoking marijuana, and

toxic: poisonous, dangerous.
behavioral toxicity: toxicity resulting from behavioral effects of a drug.
acute: referring to drugs, the short-term effects of a single dose.
chronic: referring to drugs, the long-term effects from repeated use.
drug recognition expert (DRE): a police officer trained to examine intoxicated individuals to determine which of several classes of drugs caused the intoxication.
DAWN: Drug Abuse Warning Network. System for collecting data on drug-related deaths or emergency room visits.

using cocaine, rather than trying to say which one of these substances was responsible for the accident, each of them was counted as being involved in that emergency room visit.

Not every emergency room in the United States participated in the DAWN system, so the numbers for emergency room visits for 2011 shown in Table 2.1 are the totals from the sampled hospitals.[1]

Alcohol was treated somewhat differently than other drugs in the sample. An emergency room visit related only to alcohol use by an adult was not tracked by the DAWN system. Alcohol-related problems were counted when alcohol and some other drug were involved (alcohol-in-combination). Notice that alcohol-in-combination was in first place for emergency room visits, a place it held for many years. In fact, if alcohol were counted alone, its numbers would be large enough to make the other drugs seem much less important comparatively. This seems to indicate that alcohol is a fairly

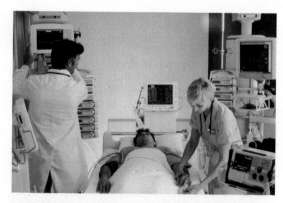

The Drug Abuse Warning Network (DAWN) used data from hospital emergency rooms to monitor drug toxicity.
©Martin Barraud/AGE Fotostock RF

toxic substance. It can be, but remember that about half of all adult Americans drink alcohol at least once a month, whereas only a small percentage of the adult population uses cocaine, the drug that came in second. The DAWN system did not correct for differences in rates of use, but rather gave us an idea of the relative impact of a substance on medical emergencies. Prescription opioids, including the widely prescribed hydrocodone (Vicodin) and oxycodone (Oxycontin), have become increasingly important over the past two decades in causing medical emergencies, and by 2016 might have passed cocaine. Other groups of prescription drugs, such as benzodiazepine sedatives (e.g., Xanax) and sleeping pills (e.g., Halcion) and the antidepressants, are relatively important. Marijuana was mentioned in a large number of ER visits, largely because it is such a widely used drug and its presence is easily detected in blood or urine samples.

It is more difficult to determine how many people actually die as a result of using a particular type of drug, but some evidence is available. The Centers for Disease Control and Prevention (CDC) compiles data from death certificates and in most of these a cause of death is recorded. A recent analysis of data from 2012 found about 40,000 drug overdose deaths, and 39 percent of those (16,007) involved prescription opioids.[2] The next largest contributor was the benzodiazepines, followed by heroin and cocaine.

Table 2.1
Toxicity Data from the Drug Abuse Warning Network (DAWN)

DRUG-RELATED EMERGENCY ROOM VISITS, NATIONAL ESTIMATES (2011)

Rank	Drug	Number
1	Alcohol-in-combination	606,653
2	Cocaine	505,224
3	Prescription opioids	488,004
4	Marijuana	455,668
5	Benzodiazepines	357,836
6	Heroin	258,482
7	Methamphetamine	102,961
8	Antidepressants	88,965
9	PCP	75,538
10	Antipsychotics	61,951

Source: Drug Abuse Warning Network.

How Dangerous Is the Drug?

Now that we have some idea of the drugs contributing to the largest numbers of toxic reactions, let's see if we can use that information to ask some questions about the relative danger to a person taking one drug versus another. We mentioned that the DAWN data do not correct for frequency of use. However, in Chapter 1 we reviewed other sets of data that provide information on the relative rates of use of different drugs, such as the National Survey on Drug Use and Health discussed on pages 11–15. The populations and sampling methods are different, so we're not going to be able to make fine distinctions with any degree of accuracy. But we know, for example, that roughly eight times as many people report current use of marijuana as report current use of cocaine. An older (2009) DAWN mortality report found almost 10 times as many cocaine-related deaths as marijuana-related deaths. If one-eighth as many users experience 10 times as many deaths, can we say that the risk of death to an individual cocaine user is 80 times the risk of death to an individual marijuana user? That's too precise an answer, but it seems pretty clear that cocaine is relatively much more toxic than marijuana.

We will see in Chapter 9 that we have good estimates as to the increased risk of an alcohol-related accident with increasing blood alcohol concentration, so for alcohol we can get a statistical estimate based on that increased risk. The same is true for cigarette smoking and heart disease. So, when we say that alcohol use is responsible for about 100,000 total U.S. deaths annually (Chapter 9) and cigarettes for over 400,000 (Chapter 10), those are fairly good estimates of the mortality that results from using those substances. We do not have similar data for cocaine, heroin, marijuana, and so on, but the total numbers of deaths caused by these substances is much lower than the deaths caused by either alcohol or tobacco.

Blood-Borne Diseases

One specific toxicity concern for users who inject drugs is the potential for spreading blood-borne diseases, such as **HIV, AIDS,** and the life-threatening liver infections hepatitis B and hepatitis C. These viral diseases can be transmitted through the sharing of needles. Reported rates of these diseases vary widely from one city to another, and have changed over time. For example, one large drug detoxification program in New York City found HIV infections in more than 50 percent of injecting drug users in the early 1990s. However, education programs and an aggressive syringe exchange program have led to a steady reduction in those rates to just over 10 percent. In this population, sexual transmission is now more important than needle-sharing as far as transmitting new cases of HIV.[3]

This type of drug-associated toxicity is not due to the action of the drug itself, but is incidental to the sharing of needles, no matter which drug is injected or whether the injection is intravenous or intramuscular. An individual drug user may inject 1,000 times a year, and that represents a lot of needles. In several states and cities, drug paraphernalia laws make it illegal to obtain syringes or needles without a prescription, and the resulting shortage of new, clean syringes increases the likelihood that drug users will share needles. One response to this has been the development of syringe exchange programs, in which new, clean syringes are traded for used syringes. Although the U.S. Congress had prohibited the use of federal funds to support these programs, based on the theory that they provide moral encouragement for illegal drug use, exchange programs were funded by state and local governments, and many other countries support such programs. Evidence shows that given the opportunity, drug injectors increase their use of clean syringes, rates of infection are lowered, and the programs more than pay for themselves in the long run. In 2008 it was reported that the incidence of new HIV infections associated with intravenous drug use had declined by 80 percent in the past 20 years.[4]

HIV: human immunodeficiency virus.
AIDS: acquired immunodeficiency syndrome.

Focus on Drug Policy

"Purple Drank"

Fear is a useful emotion. Being afraid of something that threatens you helps you to avoid the real dangers that do exist in our world. But, of course, fear also can be irrational, far out of proportion to any real threat. When that happens, as individuals we might be hampered by being unable to use elevators or ride in airliners, or fear of contamination might seriously interfere with our social lives. Fear is also a favorite tool of many politicians. If they can convince us that there is a real threat of some kind and they offer to protect us from it, we are likely to elect them and to give them the power or funding they seek to provide that protection. Again, this is a rational and perfectly appropriate governmental response to the extent that the threat is both real and likely to harm us, but sometimes it is difficult to get it right. Maybe the U.S. government has underestimated the threat of global climate change. Maybe because of the horrible televised images of a terrorist attack in some faraway place we

overestimate the actual risk of being killed by terrorists in our own community. Raising fears about specific types of drugs has been a staple of politics and government in the United States for more than 100 years, from the age of "demon rum" through heroin, marijuana, LSD, PCP, cocaine, MDMA (Ecstasy), and methamphetamine. How do we get it right?

Recently there has been quite a bit of media publicity about "purple drank," which seems to have first appeared in Houston, Texas, and then became more widely known after being mentioned in some rap songs. The major ingredient in this drink is prescription cough syrup containing codeine and promethazine. Codeine is an opioid (Chapter 13) and promethazine is an antihistamine (Chapter 12). Each of these drugs can suppress respiration, and when taken in high doses and if alcohol is also consumed, there is a risk of death from respiratory depression.

Box icon credit: ©Edward.J.Westmacott/Alamy Images RF

Unintended Consequences

Syringes and the Harm-Reduction Approach

In the early days of concern about drug addiction (1911), New York was the first state to require a prescription to obtain hypodermic syringes. This was done in the belief that limiting access to syringes would reduce the number of injecting drug users. They certainly could not have foreseen one apparent consequence of that law when more than 70 years later, HIV began to spread rapidly among drug users who shared their syringes. Several studies have found that providing clean syringes reduces the spread of HIV, and that cities with over-the-counter sales of syringes have lower rates of HIV infection among drug users.[3] Several states have modified their syringe laws in recent years to allow for either syringe exchanges or nonprescription purchase of syringes, in an effort to reduce the spread of HIV and hepatitis. This is a clear example of something called the *harm-reduction approach*. This approach

recognizes that in spite of efforts to control drug use, there will still be users, and if there are ways to reduce the harm to the users and others, that is the right thing to do.

We will see other examples of harm-reduction efforts throughout this book, but one other example will be of interest to college students. In the United States it is illegal for college students under the age of 21 to drink alcohol, yet most do. College administrators mostly recognize that trying to prevent all underage drinking in this population is unrealistic. Therefore, in spite of the illicit nature of underage drinking, freshmen are taught about responsible drinking, avoiding driving under the influence, and preventing alcohol poisoning, sexual assault, and impaired grades due to overindulgence.

Box icon credit: ©Adam Gault/age fotostock RF

Needles are collected through an exchange program in an effort to prevent the spread of HIV among intravenous drug users. ©Time & Life Pictures/Getty Images

The authors pointed out that intravenous drug users have been acquiring clean needles from pharmacies and syringe exchange programs, and also limiting the number of people sharing their needles. In response to all the evidence favoring syringe exchange, in 2009 the U.S. Congress voted to lift the more than 20-year federal ban on funding for such programs.

Substance Dependence: What Is It?

All our lives we have heard people talk about "alcoholics" and "addicts," and we're sure we know what we're talking about when one of these terms is used. Years ago when people first became concerned about some people being frequent, heavy users of cocaine or morphine, the term *habituation* was often used. If we try to develop scientific definitions, terms such as *alcoholic* or *addict* are actually hard to pin down. For example, not everyone who is considered an alcoholic drinks every day—some drink in binges, with brief periods of sobriety in between. Not everyone who drinks every day is

considered an alcoholic—a glass of wine with dinner every night doesn't match most people's idea of alcoholism. The most extreme examples are easy to spot: the homeless man dressed in rags, drinking from a bottle of cheap wine, or the heroin user who needs a fix three or four times a day to avoid withdrawal symptoms. No hard-and-fast rule for quantity or frequency of use can help us draw a clear line between what we want to think of as a "normal drinker" or a "recreational user" and someone who has developed a dependence on the substance, who is compelled to use it, or who has trouble controlling his or her use of the substance. It would be nice if we could separate substance use into two distinct categories: In one case, the individual controls the use of the substance; in the other case, the substance seems to take control of the individual. However, the real world of substance use, misuse, abuse, and dependence does not come wrapped in such convenient packages.

Three Basic Processes

The extreme examples mentioned above, of the homeless alcohol drinker or the frequent heroin user, typically exhibit three characteristics of their substance use that distinguish them from first-time or occasional users. These appear to represent three processes that may occur with repeated drug use, and each of these processes can be defined and studied by researchers interested in understanding drug dependence.

Tolerance **Tolerance** refers to a phenomenon seen with many drugs, in which repeated exposure to the same dose of the drug results in a lesser effect. There are many ways this diminished effect can occur, and some examples are given in Chapter 5. For now, it is enough for us to think of the body as developing ways to compensate for the chemical imbalance caused by introducing a drug into the system. As the individual experiences less and less

tolerance: reduced effect of a drug after repeated use.

of the desired effect, often the tolerance can be overcome by increasing the dose of the drug. Some regular drug users might eventually build up to taking much more of the drug than it would take to kill a nontolerant individual.

Physical Dependence Physical dependence is defined by the occurrence of a **withdrawal syndrome.** Suppose a person has begun to take a drug and a tolerance has developed. The person increases the amount of drug and continues to take these higher doses so regularly that the body is continuously exposed to the drug for days or weeks. With some drugs, when the person stops taking the drug abruptly, a set of symptoms begins to appear as the drug level in the system drops. For example, as the level of heroin drops in a regular user, that person's nose might run and he or she might begin to experience chills and fever, diarrhea, and other symptoms. When a drug produces a consistent set of these symptoms in different individuals, we refer to the collection of symptoms as a withdrawal syndrome. These withdrawal syndromes vary from one class of drugs to another. Our model for why withdrawal symptoms appear is that the drug initially disrupts the body's normal physiological balances. These imbalances are detected by the nervous system, and over a period of repeated drug use the body's normal regulatory mechanisms compensate for the presence of the drug. When the drug is suddenly removed, these compensating mechanisms produce an imbalance. Tolerance typically precedes physical dependence. To continue with the heroin example, when it is first used it slows intestinal movement and produces constipation. After several days of constant heroin use, other mechanisms in the body counteract this effect and get the intestines moving again (tolerance). If the heroin use is suddenly stopped, the compensating mechanisms produce too much intestinal motility. Diarrhea is one of the most reliable and dramatic heroin withdrawal symptoms.

Because of the presumed involvement of these compensating mechanisms, the presence of a withdrawal syndrome is said to reflect physical (or

Frequent drug use, craving for the drug, and a high rate of relapse after quitting indicate psychological dependence.
©McGraw-Hill Education/Gary He, photographer

physiological) dependence on the drug. In other words, the individual has come to depend on the presence of some amount of that drug to function normally; removing the drug leads to an imbalance, which is slowly corrected over a few days.

Psychological Dependence Psychological dependence (also called *behavioral dependence*) can be defined in terms of observable behavior. It is indicated by the frequency of using a drug or by the amount of time or effort an individual spends in drug-seeking behavior. Often it is accompanied by reports of *craving* the drug or its effects. A major contribution of behavioral psychology has been to point out the scientific value of the concept of **reinforcement** for understanding psychological dependence.

The term *reinforcement* is used in psychology to describe a process: A behavioral act is followed by a consequence, resulting in an increased tendency to repeat that behavioral act. The consequence may be described as pleasurable or as a "reward" in some cases (e.g., providing a tasty piece of food to someone who has not eaten for a while). In other cases, the consequence may be described in terms of escape from pain or discomfort. The behavior itself is said to be strengthened, or *reinforced,* by its consequences. The administration of certain drugs can reinforce the behaviors that led to the drug's administration. Laboratory rats and monkeys have been trained to press levers when the only consequence of lever pressing is a small intravenous injection of heroin, cocaine, or another drug. Because some drugs but not others are capable of serving this function, it is possible to refer to some drugs as having "reinforcing properties" and to note that a general correlation exists between those drugs and the ones to which people often develop psychological dependence.

Changing Views of Addiction

Until the 20th century, the most common view was probably that alcoholics and addicts were weak-willed, lazy, or immoral (the "moral model"). Then medical and scientific studies began of users of alcohol and opioids. It seemed as if something more powerful than mere self-indulgence was at work, and the predominant view began to be that dependence is a drug-induced illness.

Early Medical Models If heroin dependence is induced by heroin, or alcohol dependence by alcohol, then why do some users develop dependence and others not? An early guess was simply that some people, for whatever reasons, were exposed to large amounts of the substance for a long time. This could happen through medical treatment or self-indulgence. The most obvious changes resulting from long exposure to large doses are the withdrawal symptoms that occur when the drug is stopped. Both alcohol and the opioids can produce rather dramatic withdrawal syndromes. Thus, the problem came to be associated with the presence of physical dependence (a withdrawal syndrome), and enlightened medically oriented researchers went looking for treatments based on reducing or eliminating withdrawal symptoms. According to the most narrow interpretation of this model, the dependence itself was cured when the person had successfully completed withdrawal and the symptoms disappeared.

Pharmacologists and medical authorities continued into the 1970s to define *addiction* as occurring only when physical dependence was seen. Based on this view, public policy decisions, medical treatment, and individual drug-use decisions could be influenced by the question "Is this an addicting drug?" If some drugs produce dependence but others do not, then legal restrictions on specific drugs, care in the medical use of those drugs, and education in avoiding the recreational use of those drugs are appropriate. The determination of whether a drug is or is not "addicting" was therefore crucial.

In the 1960s, some drugs, particularly marijuana and amphetamines, were not considered to have well-defined, dramatic, physical withdrawal syndromes. The growing group of interested scientists began to refer to drugs such as marijuana, amphetamines, and cocaine as "merely" producing psychological dependence, whereas heroin produced a "true addiction," which includes physical dependence. The idea seemed to be that psychological dependence was "all in the head," whereas physical dependence involved bodily processes, subject to physiological and biochemical analysis and possibly to improved medical treatments. This was the view held by most drug-abuse experts in the 1960s.

Positive Reinforcement Model In the 1960s, a remarkable series of experiments began to appear in the scientific literature—experiments in which

---

physical dependence: drug dependence defined by the presence of a withdrawal syndrome, implying that the body has become adapted to the drug's presence.
withdrawal syndrome: a consistent set of symptoms that appears after discontinuing use of a drug.
psychological dependence: behavioral dependence; indicated by a high rate of drug use, craving for the drug, and a tendency to relapse after stopping use.
reinforcement: a procedure in which a behavioral event is followed by a consequent event such that the behavior is then more likely to be repeated. The behavior of taking a drug may be reinforced by the effect of the drug.

DSM-5

Psychiatric Diagnosis of Substance Use Disorders

A problematic pattern of substance use leading to clinically significant impairment or distress, as manifested by at least two of the following, occurring within a 12-month period:

1. The substance is often taken in larger amounts or over a longer period than was intended.
2. There is a persistent desire or unsuccessful efforts to cut down or control substance use.
3. A great deal of time is spent in activities necessary to obtain the substance.
4. Craving, or a strong desire or urge to use the substance.
5. Recurrent substance use resulting in a failure to fulfill major role obligations.
6. Continued substance use despite having persistent or recurrent social or interpersonal problems caused or exacerbated by the effects of the substance.
7. Important social, occupational, or recreational activities are given up or reduced because of substance use.
8. Recurrent substance use in situations in which it is physically hazardous.
9. Substance use is continued despite knowledge of having a persistent or recurrent physical or psychological problem that is likely to have been caused or exacerbated by the substance.
10. Tolerance, as defined by either of the following:
    a. A need for markedly increased amounts of the substance to obtain the desired effect.
    b. A markedly diminished effect with continued use of the same amount of the substance.
11. Withdrawal, as manifested by either of the following:
    a. The characteristic withdrawal syndrome for the substance.
    b. The substance (or a closely related substance) is taken to relieve or avoid withdrawal symptoms.

Adapted from *Diagnostic and Statistical Manual of Mental Disorders*, 5th edition (DSM-5).

laboratory monkeys and rats were given intravenous tubes connected to motorized syringes and controlling equipment so that pressing a lever would produce a single brief injection of morphine, an opioid very similar to heroin. In the initial experiments, monkeys were exposed for several days to large doses of morphine, allowed to experience the initial stages of withdrawal, and then connected to the apparatus to see if they would learn to press the lever, thereby avoiding the withdrawal symptoms. These experiments were based on the predominant view of drug use as being driven by physical dependence. The monkeys did learn to press the levers.

As these scientists began to publish their results and as more experiments like this were done, interesting facts became apparent. First, monkeys would begin pressing and maintain pressing without first being made physically dependent. Second, monkeys who had given themselves only fairly small doses and who had never experienced withdrawal symptoms could be trained to work very hard for their morphine. A history of physical dependence and withdrawal didn't seem to have much influence on response rates in the long run. Clearly, the small drug injections themselves were working as positive reinforcers of the lever-pressing behavior, just as food can be a positive reinforcer to a hungry rat or monkey. Thus, the idea spread that drugs can act as reinforcers of behavior and that this might be the basis of what had been called psychological dependence. Drugs such as amphetamines and cocaine could easily be used as reinforcers in these experiments, and they were known to produce strong psychological dependence in humans. Animal experiments using drug self-administration are now of central importance in determining which drugs are likely to be used repeatedly by people, as well as in testing new drugs that might be used to treat drug addiction.[5]

Which Is More Important, Physical Dependence or Psychological Dependence?

The animal research that led to the positive reinforcement model implies that psychological dependence is more important than physical dependence in explaining repeated drug use, and this has led people to examine the lives of heroin users from a different perspective. Stories were told of users who occasionally stopped taking heroin, voluntarily going through withdrawal so as to reduce their tolerance level and get back to the lower doses of drug they could more easily afford. When we examine the total daily heroin intake of many users, we see that they do not need a large amount and that the agonies of withdrawal they experience are no worse than a case of intestinal flu. We have known for a long time that heroin users who have already gone through withdrawal in treatment programs or in jail have a high probability of returning to active heroin use. In other words, if all we had to worry about was users' avoiding withdrawal symptoms, the problem would be much smaller than it actually is.

Psychological dependence, based on *reinforcement,* is increasingly accepted as the real driving force behind repeated drug use, and tolerance and physical dependence are now seen as related phenomena that sometimes occur but probably are not critical to the development of frequent patterns of drug-using behavior.

Researchers and treatment providers rely heavily on the definitions of *substance use disorder* developed by the American Psychiatric Association and presented in their *Diagnostic and Statistical Manual,* 5th edition (DSM-5).[6] These are presented in outline form on the previous page. We have provided a generic version using the word *substance,* but in fact there are 10 separate diagnoses, defined for each class of drug (e.g., alcohol, sedatives, cannabis, stimulants, tobacco, hallucinogens, opioids).Notice that

the diagnosis is complex, and the exact set of behaviors seen may vary from person to person. The severity of the disorder is characterized as mild if two or three of the symptoms are present, moderate if there are four or five, and severe if the person exhibits six or more. Also, note that 9 of the 11 symptoms describe behaviors, such as taking more of the substance than was intended or giving up other important activities because of substance use. This again points out that these substance use disorders are seen primarily as behavioral in nature, with tolerance and physical dependence being less important.

Broad Views of Addiction

If we define drug addiction not in terms of withdrawal but in more behavioral or psychological terms, as an overwhelming involvement with getting and using the drug, then might this model also be used to describe other kinds of behavior? What about a man who visits prostitutes several times a day; someone who eats large amounts of food throughout the day; or someone who places bets on every football and basketball game, every horse race or automobile race, and who spends hours each day planning these bets and finding money to bet again? Shouldn't these also be considered examples of addiction? Do the experiences of overeating, gambling, sex, and drugs have something in common—a common change in physiology or brain chemistry or a common personality trait that leads to any or many of these compulsive behaviors? Are all of these filling an unmet social or spiritual need? More and more, researchers are looking for these common threads and discussing "addictions" as a varied set of behavioral manifestations of a common process or disorder.

Is Addiction Caused by the Substance?

Especially with chemical dependence, many people speak as though the substance itself is the cause of the addiction. Certainly some drugs are more likely than others to result in dependence. For example, it is widely believed that heroin and cocaine are both likely to lead to compulsive use. In contrast, most

Alcohol causes dependence in some drinkers.
©McGraw-Hill Education/Jill Braaten, photographer

Table 2.2 Dependence Potential of Alcohol, Nicotine, Cocaine, and Marijuana			
Probability of Transition to Dependence			
	After 1 year of use	**After 10 years of use**	**Lifetime estimate**
Alcohol	2.0%	11.0%	22.7%
Nicotine	2.0%	15.6%	67.5%
Cocaine	7.1%	14.8%	20.9%
Marijuana	2.0%	5.9%	8.9%

users of marijuana report occasional use and little difficulty in deciding when to use it and when not to. We also know that some methods of taking a drug (e.g., intravenous injection) are more likely to result in repeated use than other methods of taking the same drug (by mouth, for instance). There have been estimates of the relative dependence liability of different drugs based on the judgments of panels of experts in the field, but even experts are not always objective about such things. The most scientific approach to date is based on a survey study starting with more than 40,000 participants, who answered questions about their first use of several substances and also questions designed to determine whether they met the criteria for dependence, either currently or in the past.[7] The authors then determined the probability that someone who had used marijuana, for example, would have developed a marijuana dependency at different time points after their first use. The results for nicotine, alcohol, marijuana, and cocaine are shown in Table 2.2. We can see that one year after the initial use, there was only about a

2 percent chance that dependence would develop for alcohol, nicotine, or marijuana, but a 7.1 percent chance for cocaine to produce dependence within one year. Over time, these risks grew at different rates, so that the estimated lifetime risk is 67.5 percent for nicotine, just over 20 percent for alcohol and cocaine, and under 10 percent for marijuana. So yes, some substances are more "addictive" than others, but as we will see, many other factors influence dependence. Thus, the substance itself cannot be seen as the entire cause of the problem, even though some people would like to put all the blame on "demon rum" or on heroin or crack cocaine.

When we extend the concept of addiction to other activities, such as gambling, sex, or overeating, it seems harder to place the entire blame on the activity, again because many people do not exhibit compulsive patterns of such behaviors. Some activities might be more of a problem than others—few people become dependent on filling out income tax forms, whereas a higher proportion of all those who gamble become overwhelmingly involved. Still, it is wrong to conclude that any activity is by its nature always "habit forming."

When a chemical is seen as causing the dependence, there is a tendency to give that substance a personality and to ascribe motives to it. When we listen either to a practicing user's loving description of his interaction with the drug or to a recovering alcoholic describe her struggle against the bottle's attempts to destroy her, the substance seems to take on almost human characteristics. We all realize that is going too far, yet the analogy is so powerful that it pervades our thinking. **Alcoholics Anonymous (AA)** members often describe alcohol as being "cunning, baffling, and powerful" and admit that they are powerless against such a foe. And those seeking the prohibition of alcohol, cocaine, marijuana, heroin, and other drugs have over the years tended to demonize those substances, making them into powerful forces of evil. The concept of a "war on drugs" reflects in part such a perspective—that some drugs are evil and war must be waged against the substances themselves.

It might be emotionally satisfying to put the blame for dependence on a chemical, and for most people it makes sense to simply treat heroin or methamphetamine as something to be avoided at all cost. But in reality these drugs do have beneficial uses, and dependence does not develop in every user. Placing all the blame on the drug itself is not only illogical, but it also has caused the U.S. government to put most of its drug abuse control funding into efforts to prevent access to the drugs and too little into teaching people how to live in a world in which such drugs will continue to exist.

Is Dependence Biological?

In recent years, interest has increased in the possibility that all compulsive behaviors might have some common physiological or biochemical action in the brain. For example, many theorists have recently focused on dopamine, one of the brain's important neurotransmitters, which some believe to play a large role in positive reinforcement. The idea is that any drug use or other activity that has pleasurable or rewarding properties spurs dopamine activity in a particular part of the brain. This idea is discussed more fully in Chapter 4. Although this theory has been widely tested in animal models and much evidence is consistent with it, considerable evidence also shows that this model is too simple and that other neurotransmitters and other brain regions are also important.

A great deal of attention has been given to reports from various brain-scanning experiments done on drug users. Although these studies show some of the physiological *consequences* produced by cocaine or by even thinking about cocaine, they have not yet been useful in examining the possible biological *causes* of dependence. One important question that remains is whether the brains of people who have used cocaine intermittently show different responses, compared with the brains of dependent cocaine users. Ultimately, the strongest demonstration of the power of such techniques would be if it were possible to know, based on looking at a brain scan, whether a person had developed dependence. However, that has not been demonstrated (and might never be).

Numerous studies in both animals and humans have shown that there are genetic influences on drug use, effects, and dependence. One study examined over 2,000 twins with a history of substance dependence.[8] Comparisons between monozygotic (identical) and dizygotic (fraternal) twins were used to estimate genetic versus environmental influences. The researchers also looked for "comorbidity," that is, people who developed dependencies on more than one substance. Using a complex statistical technique, they estimated that heritability (genetics) could explain 38 percent of alcohol dependence, 55 percent of tobacco dependence, and 19 percent of marijuana dependence. It was estimated that for alcohol and nicotine, about half of this heritability was due to a common factor increasing risk for any type of substance, and the other half to genetic factors specific to that substance. So, while we have evidence that genetic factors do play a role in determining which people become dependent, we do not know the specific genes involved, nor do we know the biological mechanisms by which the genes influence these behaviors.

Alcoholics Anonymous (AA): a worldwide organization of self-help groups based on alcoholics helping each other achieve and maintain sobriety.

These biological studies are fascinating and perhaps someday will lead to a better understanding of, or better treatments for, specific addictions. For now, we recommend caution when someone tries to give you a biological explanation of addiction, since none has yet become widely accepted or truly useful.

Is There an "Addictive Personality"?

Perhaps the explanation for why some people become dependent but others do not lies in the personality—that complex set of attributes and attitudes that develops over time, partly as a result of particular experiences. Is there a common personality factor that is seen in compulsive drug users but not in others? We've known for some time that people who are diagnosed with certain types of personality disorders, such as antisocial personality or conduct disorder, are more likely to also have one of the substance use disorder diagnoses. We've also known that people who have a long history of alcohol dependence or heroin dependence will demonstrate a variety of differences from the normal population on personality tests. But neither of these findings tells us anything about what caused these relationships. Conduct disorder and antisocial personality disorder reflect a general tendency for a person to violate social norms. Perhaps drug use is just one of many ways this person might choose to break the rules? And someone who has been drinking heavily for many years, has had health problems, perhaps lost a job and family, might well have developed personality differences due to the consequences of years of substance abuse. So we have not had much good information until fairly recently about personality differences that might predispose individuals to develop a substance use disorder.

One personality trait that has frequently been associated with greater risk for abuse of stimulants such as amphetamine or cocaine is called *sensation-seeking*. The sensation-seeking scale measures the person's preference for variety, risk, and various physical sensations. People who score higher on this scale tend to report a greater "high" and a greater "liking" for the drug when given amphetamine in a laboratory setting.[9]

Another, possibly related, personality factor is often referred to as *impulsivity*—the tendency to act quickly without as much regard to long-term consequences. The relationships between impulsivity and drug use are complex, and researchers are becoming more sophisticated in trying to understand the relationships among impulsivity, specific types of drug use, and the setting in which the drug is used. In other words, being impulsive might have more to do with whether a person drinks too much at a party than it does with whether a person has a glass of wine with dinner.[10]

Is Dependence a Family Disorder?

Although few scientific studies have been done, examination of the lives of alcohol-dependent individuals reveals some typical patterns of family adaptation to the problem. A common example in a home with an alcohol-dependent father is that the mother enables this behavior, by calling her husband's boss to say he is ill or by making excuses to family and friends for failures to appear at dinners or parties and generally by caring for her incapacitated husband. The children might also compensate in various ways, and all conspire to keep the family secret. Thus, it is said that alcohol dependence often exists within a dysfunctional family—the functions of individual members adjust to the needs created by the presence of excessive drinking. This new arrangement can make it difficult for the drinker alone to change his or her behavior, because doing so would disrupt the family system. Some people suspect that certain family structures actually enhance the likelihood of alcohol abuse or dependence developing. For example, the "codependent" needs of other family members to take care of someone who is dependent on them might facilitate drunkenness.

Much has been written about the effects on children who grow up in an "alcoholic family," and there is some indication that even as adults these individuals tend to exhibit certain personality characteristics. The "adult children of alcoholics" are then perhaps more likely to become involved in dysfunctional relationships that increase the likelihood of alcohol abuse, either in themselves or in another family member. Again, the evidence indicates that such influences are statistical tendencies and are not all-powerful. It is perhaps unfortunate that some people with alcoholic parents have adopted the role of "adult children" and try to explain their entire personalities and all their difficulties in terms of that status.

Is Substance Dependence a Disease?

The most important reason for adopting a disease model for dependence is based on the experiences of the founders of AA and is discussed in Chapter 9. Psychiatrists had commonly assumed that alcohol dependence was secondary to another disorder, such as anxiety or depression, and often attempted to treat the presumed underlying disorder while encouraging the drinker to try to "cut down." The founders of AA believed that alcohol dependence itself was the primary problem and needed to be recognized as such and treated directly. This is the reason for the continued insistence that alcohol dependence is a disease—that it is often the primary disturbance and deserves to stand in its own right as a recognized disorder requiring treatment.

Peele[11] and others have argued, by contrast, that substance dependence does not have many of the characteristics of some classic medical diseases, such as tuberculosis or syphilis: We can't use an X-ray or blood test to reveal the underlying cause, and we don't have a way to treat the underlying cause and cure the symptoms—we don't really know that there is an underlying cause, because all we have are the symptoms of excessive involvement. Furthermore, if substance dependence itself is a disease, then gambling, excessive sexual involvement, and overeating should also be seen as diseases. This in turn weakens our normal understanding of the concept of disease. The disease model is perhaps best seen as an analogy—substance dependence is *like* a disease in many ways, but that is different from insisting that it *is* a disease. One reason for the conflict over the disease model of dependence may be differences in how we think of the term *disease*. For example, many would agree that high blood pressure is considered a disease—it's certainly viewed as a medical disorder. We know that high blood pressure can be produced by genetic factors, cigarette smoking, diet, lack of exercise, or other medical conditions. In that context, the idea that alcohol or drug dependence is like a disease doesn't seem so far-fetched. This is taking a broad, **biopsychosocial** perspective that dependence might be related to dysfunctions of biology, personality, social interactions, or a combination of these factors.

Crime and Violence: Does Drug Use Cause Crime?

It might seem obvious to a reader of today's newspapers or to a viewer of today's television that drugs and crime are linked. There are frequent reports of killings attributed to warring gangs of drug dealers. Our prisons house a large population of people convicted of drug-related crimes, and several reports have revealed that a large fraction of arrestees for nondrug felonies have positive results from urine tests for illicit substances.

The belief that there is a causal relationship between many types of drug use and criminality probably forms the basis for many of our laws concerning drug use and drug users. The relationship between crime and illegal drug use is complex, and only recently have data-based statements become possible. Facts are necessary because laws are enacted on the basis of what we believe to be true.

The basis for concern was the belief that drug use *causes* crime. The fact that drug users engage in robberies or that car thieves are likely to also use illicit drugs does not say anything about

> **biopsychosocial:** a theory or perspective that relies on the interaction of biological, individual psychological, and social variables.

There are more than 1.5 million drug-related arrests in the United States each year. ©Michael Matthews/Police Images/ Alamy Stock Photo

causality. Both criminal activity and drug use could well be caused by other factors, producing both types of deviant behavior in the same individuals. There are several senses in which it might be said that drugs cause crime, but the most frightening possibility is that drug use somehow *changes the individual's personality in a lasting way,* making him or her into a "criminal type." For example, during the 1924 debate that led to prohibition of heroin sales in the United States, a testifying physician asserted, regarding users, that heroin "dethrones their moral responsibility." Another physician testified that some types of individuals will have their mental equipment "permanently injured by the use of heroin, and those are the ones who will go out and commit crimes." Similar beliefs are reflected in the introductory message in the 1937 film *Reefer Madness,* which referred to marijuana as "The Real Public Enemy Number One!" and described its "soul-destroying" effects as follows:

> emotional disturbances, the total inability to direct thought, the loss of all power to resist physical emotions, leading finally to acts of shocking violence … ending often in incurable insanity.

Such verbal excesses seem quaint and comical these days, but the underlying belief that drug use changes people into criminals still can be detected in much current political rhetoric. You should remember from Chapter 1 that research on children and adolescents has led to the conclusion that indicators of criminal or antisocial behavior usually occur before the first use of an illicit drug. The interaction over time between developing drug-use "careers" and criminal careers is complex and interactive, but it is incorrect to conclude that using any particular drug will turn a person into a criminal.[12]

A second sense in which drug use might *cause* criminal behavior is when the person is *under the influence* of the drug. Do the acute effects of a drug make a person *temporarily* more likely to engage in criminal behavior? There is little good evidence for this with most illicit substances. In most individuals, marijuana produces a state more akin to lethargy than to crazed violence (see Chapter 15), and heroin tends to make its users more passive and perhaps sexually impotent (see Chapter 13). Stimulants such as amphetamine and cocaine can make people paranoid and "jumpy," and this can contribute to violent behavior in some cases (see Chapter 6). The hallucinogen PCP causes disorientation and blocks pain, so users are sometimes hard to restrain (see Chapter 14). This has led to a considerable amount of folklore about the dangerousness of PCP users, although documented cases of excessive violence are either rare or nonexistent. A study of U.S. homicide cases found that every year about 5 percent are considered to be drug-related. However, most of these are murders that occur in the context of drug trafficking, so it cannot be said that increased violence results from the pharmacological actions of the drugs.[13]

Although there is some question as to whether the direct influence of illicit drugs produces a person more likely to engage in criminal or violent behavior, there has been less doubt about one commonly used substance: alcohol. Many studies indicate that alcohol is clearly linked with violent crime. In many assaults and sexual assaults, alcohol is present in both assailant and victim. Most homicides are among people who know each other—and alcohol use is associated with half or more of all murders. Drinking at the time of the offense was reported in about 25 percent of assaults and more than one-third of all rapes and sexual assaults, with drinking rates closer to two-thirds for cases of domestic violence.[14] Victims of violent crime report that they believe the offender had been using alcohol in 25 percent of the cases, compared to about 5 percent of the cases in which they believe the offender had been using drugs other than alcohol.[12] Even with such strong correlational evidence linking alcohol use with crime and violence, there is still debate about how much of the effect is related to the "disinhibitory" pharmacological action of alcohol, and how much is related to other factors. For example, several studies that have controlled for age, sex, and a generalized tendency to engage in problem behaviors have concluded that both drinking and criminal violence are associated with young males who exhibit a range of antisocial behaviors, and that the immediate contribution of being intoxicated might be small.

A third sense in which drug use may be said to cause crime refers to *crimes carried out for the purpose of obtaining money* to purchase illicit drugs. Among jail inmates who had been convicted of property crimes, about one-fourth reported that they had committed the crime to get money for drugs. Also, about one-fourth of those convicted of drug crimes reported that they had sold drugs to get money for their own drug use.[13]

From 1987 through 2003, and then beginning again in 2007, the U.S. Justice Department collected data on drug use from people arrested and booked into jails for serious crimes. All interviews and urine tests were anonymous; about 90 percent of arrestees who were asked agreed to an interview, and about 90 percent of those agreed to provide urine specimens. In 2013, in five sites around the country, between 60 and 80 percent of the adult male arrestees tested positive for the presence of at least one of the 10 drugs of interest. Marijuana was the drug detected most frequently (34–59 percent), followed by cocaine (7–33 percent). Methamphetamine detection varied considerably from site to site, and was as high as 50 percent in Sacramento,

California.[15] This level of drug use among those arrested for nondrug crimes is quite high; how can we account for it? First, those who adopt a deviant lifestyle might engage in both crime and drug use. Second, because most of these arrests were for crimes in which profit was the motive, the arrestees might have been burglarizing a house or stealing a car to get money to purchase drugs.

The commission of crimes to obtain money for expensive illicit drugs is due to the artificially high cost of the drugs, not primarily to a pharmacological effect of the drug. The inflated cost results from drug controls and enforcement. Both heroin and cocaine are inexpensive substances when obtained legally from a licensed manufacturer, and it has been estimated that if heroin were freely available it would cost no more to be a regular heroin user than to be a regular drinker of alcohol. The black-market cost of these substances makes the use of cocaine or heroin consume so much money.

The fourth and final sense in which drug use causes crime is that *illicit drug use is a crime.* At first that may seem trivial, but there are two senses in which it is not. First, we are now making more than 1.5 million arrests for drug-law violations each year, and more than half of all federal prisoners are convicted on drug charges. Thus, drug-law violations are one of the major types of crime in the United States. Second, it is likely that the relationship between drug use and other forms of deviant behavior is strengthened by the fact that drug use is a crime. A person willing to commit one type of crime might be more willing than the average person to commit another type of crime. Some of the people who are actively trying to impress others by living dangerously and committing criminal acts might be drawn to illicit drug use as an obvious way to demonstrate their alienation from society. To better understand this relationship, imagine what might happen if the use of marijuana were legalized throughout the U.S. Presumably, a greater number of otherwise law-abiding citizens might try using the drug, thus reducing the correlation between marijuana use and other forms of criminal activity.

Focus on Drug Policy

Should Pregnant Drug Users Keep Their Children?

Several popular media outlets reported on the case of Cleveland's Hollie Sanford, who used marijuana tea to treat morning sickness and sciatic nerve pain.[16] On September 26, 2015, she gave birth to a healthy baby girl. A drug test of mother and child revealed marijuana metabolites. Despite no evidence of physical or emotional abnormalities, the child was removed from her mother's custody shortly after birth. The court determined that removal was necessary because Ms. Sanford's marijuana use during pregnancy was an indication of "immediate or threatened physical or emotional harm."

This court decision is consistent with a disturbing trend in legal actions and policies that criminalize the use by pregnant women of certain substances thought to produce adverse perinatal outcomes. Currently, 18 states consider substance abuse during pregnancy to be child abuse under civil child-welfare statutes, and Tennessee allows criminal assault charges to be filed against a pregnant woman who uses certain substances, including marijuana.[17] In such cases, the child is placed in foster care if a suitable relative is unavailable.

Although legal action against pregnant women who use substances is taken with the intent to protect the child, removal from the family may also put the child at risk. For example, there is an increased risk of negative outcomes associated with foster care, including physical and sexual abuse and increased risk of incarceration.[18] Women who use substances, including cannabis, might avoid prenatal medical care, fearing the social and legal consequences associated with being identified as a substance user.

As we will see in Chapter 15, most of the published evidence shows that the cognitive performance of children and adolescents exposed to cannabis prenatally is nearly identical to that of individuals who were not exposed to cannabis during pregnancy. Therefore, the actual risk to an individual child from exposure to marijuana is uncertain at best. And, in Chapter 6 we will learn that the consequences of prenatal exposure to cocaine and methamphetamine have also been overstated in popular media.

Given all these uncertainties about the consequences of leaving the child with a marijuana-using mother versus removing the child to live with a relative or in foster care, what do you feel should be our society's stance on this complex issue? Should hospitals request permission from patients before conducting drug screening on blood samples collected for other purposes? Should positive drug tests obtained in this way be used as a basis for taking civil action to remove children from their mothers' care? Should some evidence of actual harm to the child be required before legal action is taken?

The concern over possibly increased drug use is, of course, one major argument in favor of maintaining legal controls on the illicit drugs.

Why We Try to Regulate Drugs

We can see that there are reasonable concerns about the potential toxicity and habit-forming nature of some drugs and even the criminality of some drug users. But the drugs that have been singled out for special controls, such as heroin, cocaine, and marijuana, are not unique in their association with toxicity, dependence, or criminal behavior.

Tobacco, alcohol, and many legally available prescription drugs are also linked to these same social ills. At the beginning of the chapter, we mentioned, another important source of social conflict over drug use. Once a substance is regulated in any way, those regulations will be broken by some. This produces enormous social conflict and results in many problems for society. From underage drinking to injecting heroin, from Internet sales of prescription narcotics to "date-rape" drugs, the conflicts resulting from particular kinds of drug use lead to additional costs to American society (police, courts, prisons, treatment, etc.) beyond the direct drug effects of toxicity, dependence, and links to other kinds of criminal behavior. Our current laws do not represent a rationally devised plan to counteract the most realistic of these concerns in the most effective manner. In fact, most legislation is passed in an atmosphere of emotionality, in response to a specific set of concerns. Often the problems have been there for a long time, but public attention and concern have been recently aroused and Congress must respond. Sometimes members of Congress or government officials play a major role in calling public attention to the problem for which they offer the solution: a new law, more restrictions, and a bigger budget for some agency. As we will see in Chapter 3, often the justification for these government interventions includes a lot of emotion-arousing rhetoric that borders on the irrational, and sometimes the results of this inflamed rhetoric and the ensuing legislation are unexpected and undesirable.

- The idea that opioid drugs or marijuana can produce violent criminality in their users is an old and largely discredited idea. Opioid users seem to engage in crimes mainly to obtain money, not because they are made more criminal by the drugs they take. One drug that is widely accepted as contributing to crimes and violence is alcohol.

- There are more than 1.5 million arrests each year in the United States for drug-law violations.

- Laws that have been developed to control drug use have a legitimate social purpose, which is to protect society from the dangers caused by some types of drug use. Whether these dangers have always been viewed rationally, and whether the laws have had their intended results, can be better judged after we have learned more about the drugs and the history of their regulation.

Summary

- American society has changed from being one that tolerated a wide variety of individual drug use to being one that attempts to exert strict control over some types of drugs. This has occurred in response to social concerns about drug toxicity, dependence potential, and drug-related crime and violence.

- *Toxicity* can refer either to physiological poisoning or to dangerous disruption of behavior. Also, we can distinguish acute toxicity, resulting from the presence of too much of a drug, from chronic toxicity, which results from long-term exposure to a drug.

- Heroin and cocaine have high risks of toxicity per user, but their overall public health impact is low compared to tobacco and alcohol.

- Prescription drugs are also important contributors to overall drug toxicity figures.

- Drug dependence does not depend solely on the drug itself, but the use of some drugs is more likely to result in dependence than is the use of other drugs.

Review Questions

1. What three major concerns about drugs led to the initial passage of laws controlling their availability?

2. Long-term, heavy drinking can lead to permanent impairment of memory. What type of toxicity is this (acute or chronic; physiological or behavioral)?

3. What two kinds of data were recorded by the DAWN system?

4. What drugs other than alcohol were mentioned most often in both parts of the DAWN system?

5. Why has AIDS been of particular concern for users of illicit drugs?

6. What drugs and methods of using them are considered to have very high dependence potential?

7. What is the apparent dependence potential of marijuana?

8. What are four ways in which drug use might theoretically cause crime?

9. About how many arrests are made each year in the United States for violations of drug laws?

References

1. Substance Abuse and Mental Health Services Administration. *Drug Abuse Warning Network, 2011: National Estimates of Drug-Related Emergency Department Visits.* HHS Publication No. (SMA) 13-4760. DAWN Series D-39. Rockville, MD: Substance Abuse and Mental Health Services Administration, 2013.

2. Ruhm, C. J. "Drug Poisoning Deaths in the United States, 1999–2012: A Statistical Adjustment Analysis." *Population Health Metrics* 14 (December 2016).

3. Des Jarlais, D. C., K. Arasteh, and S. R. Friedman. "HIV among Drug Users at Beth Israel Medical Center, New York City, the First 25 Years." *Substance Use and Misuse* 46(2/3) (2011), pp. 131–39.

4. Hall, H. I., and others. "Estimation of HIV Incidence in the United States." *Journal of the American Medical Association* 300 (2008), pp. 520–29.

5. Gerak, L. R., G. T. Collins, and C. P. France. "Effects of Lorcaserin on Cocaine and Methamphetamine Self-Administration and Reinstatement of Responding Previously Maintained by Cocaine in Rhesus Monkeys." *Journal of Pharmacology and Experimental Therapeutics* 359 (2016): pp. 383–91.

6. American Psychiatric Association. *Diagnostic and Statistical Manual of Mental Disorders,* 5th ed. Washington, DC: American Psychiatric Association, 2013.

7. Lopez-Quintero, C., and others. "Probability and Predictors of Transition from First Use to Dependence on Nicotine, Alcohol, Cannabis, and Cocaine: Results of the National Epidemiological Survey on Alcohol and Related Conditions (NESARC)." *Drug and Alcohol Dependence* 115 (2011), pp. 120–30.

8. Palmer, R. H. C., and others. "Genetic Etiology of the Common Liability to Drug Dependence: Evidence of Common and Specific Mechanisms for DSM-IV Dependence Symptoms." *Drug and Alcohol Dependence* 123S (2012), pp. S24–S32.

9. Kelly, T. H., and others. "Individual Differences in Drug Abuse Vulnerability: d-Amphetamine and Sensation-Seeking Status." *Psychopharmacology* 189 (2006), pp. 17–25.

10. White, T. L., D. Lott, and H. de Wit. "Personality and the Subjective Effects of Acute Amphetamine in Healthy Volunteers." *Neuropsychopharmacology* 31 (2006), pp. 1064–74.

11. Peele, S. *Recover!* Boston: Da Capo Press, 2014.

12. Simpson, M. "The Relationship between Drug Use and Crime. A Puzzle Inside an Enigma." *International Journal of Drug Policy* 14 (2003), pp. 307–19.

13. Bureau of Justice Statistics. *Drugs and Crime Facts.* (Pub. No. NCJ 165148). Washington, DC: U.S. Department of Justice, 2004.

14. National Institute on Alcohol Abuse and Alcoholism. *Tenth Special Report to the U.S. Congress on Alcohol and Health.* (Pub. No. 00-1583). Bethesda, MD: National Institutes of Health, 2000.

15. Arrestee Drug Abuse Monitoring Program II, 2013 Report. Washington, DC: Office of National Drug Control Policy, January 2014. Available at: www.whitehouse.gov/ondcp.

16. Sullum, J. "Consuming Marijuana during Pregnancy Does Not Make a Mother Unfit." *Forbes.* November 19, 2015. Available at http://www.forbes.com/sites/jacobsullum/2015/11/19/consuming -marijuana-during-pregnancy-does-not-make-a-mother-un-fit/#3e30b45743b9.

17. Guttmacher Institute. *Substance Abuse during Pregnancy.* March 1, 2016. Available at https://www.guttmacher.org/sites/default/files/pdfs/spibs/spib_SADP.pdf.

18. Leve, L. D., G. T. Harold, P. Chamberlain, J. A. Landsverk, P. A. Fisher, and P. Vostanis. "Practitioner Review: Children in Foster Care—Vulnerabilities and Evidence-Based Interventions That Promote Resilience Processes." *Journal of Child Psychology and Psychiatry* 53 (2012), pp. 1197–211.

Check Yourself

Name _____ Date _____

Are You Hooked on an Activity?

Think of an activity other than substance use that you either really enjoy or find yourself doing a lot. This can be a hobby, such as playing video games or watching movies; something more energetic, such as skiing or mountain biking; or something that involves spending money, such as buying books, CDs, or clothing or shopping on the Internet or TV shopping channels. It can be sexual behavior or gambling, or it can even be working longer hours than most people. Now, with the most "addictive" of those activities in mind, go through the DSM-5 diagnostic criteria one by one and ask whether your nondrug "habit" meets each criterion, obviously substituting the behavior in question for the words *the substance* and *substance use*. Probably the most informative questions in this context are the following (note the words in italics):

- Have you *often* done more of the behavior or for a longer period than you intended?
- Have you *persistently* tried to cut down or control the behavior?
- Have you given up *important* social, occupational, or recreational activities because of this behavior?
- Is the behavior continuing despite recurrent physical or psychological problems *caused or made worse* by the behavior?

If you answered yes to all four questions, then whether or not you agree that you meet the criteria for a disorder, you should consider talking to a behavioral health professional to obtain some assistance in reducing the impact of this behavior on your life.

What's Your Risk of Drug Toxicity?

Any drug that has the ability to affect you in any way also has the potential to be toxic if used in too great a quantity or in the wrong combination with other drugs. If you use alcohol or other drugs, use the following assessment to estimate the risk of toxicity to which your drug use exposes you:

1. When you take over-the-counter medications, including headache remedies, do you read the instructions carefully and make sure not to exceed the recommended dose?
2. If you are already taking some sort of medication on a regular basis, do you always check with your doctor or pharmacist about the safety of taking any additional drug along with your regular medication?
3. Do you check the expiration dates of drugs in your medicine cabinet before using them?
4. If you drink alcohol, do you drink only in moderation and check to make sure the alcohol won't interact with a drug you are also taking?
5. Do you avoid taking drugs prescribed for someone else and avoid the use of street drugs of unknown strength and purity?

If you answered yes to all these questions, you are probably a responsible consumer of alcohol, prescription drugs, and over-the-counter drugs, and you are unlikely to suffer from drug toxicity.

3

Drug Policy

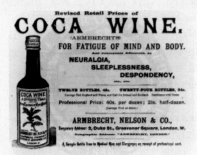

Source: National Library of Medicine

Objectives

When you have finished this chapter, you should be able to:

- **Discuss the role of reformist attitudes and social concerns in moving the U.S. government toward drug regulations.**

- **Understand the major purposes and influence of the 1906 Pure Food and Drugs Act.**

- **Understand the evolution, major purposes, and influence of the 1914 Harrison Act.**

- **Describe the process of approval for new pharmaceuticals.**

- **Describe drugs and dietary supplements as defined by the FDA.**

- **Describe the historical sequence of controls on opioids, cocaine, marijuana, and other controlled substances.**

- **Understand controlled substance schedules (I–V).**

- **Explain the impact of mandatory minimum sentencing.**

- **Compare and contrast the major types of drug testing.**

- **Explain how drug-control efforts affect the federal budget, international relations, and the criminal justice systems.**

Once upon a time in the United States, there weren't any federal regulations about drug use. That lasted for about two years. In 1791, Congress passed an excise tax on whiskey, which resulted in a disagreement that historians call the Whiskey Rebellion. West of the Appalachian Mountains, where most whiskey was made, the farmers refused to pay the tax and tarred and feathered revenue officers who tried to collect it. In 1794, President George Washington called in the militia, which occupied counties in western Pennsylvania and sent prisoners to Philadelphia for trial. The militia and the federal government carried the day. The Whiskey Rebellion was an important test for the new government because it clearly established that the federal government had the power to enforce federal laws within the states.

There are two important classes of drug laws: One group of laws regulates the practices of pharmaceutical companies, pharmacists, physicians, dentists, veterinarians, and others who manufacture or dispense "legal" drugs. These regulations are similar to laws that regulate the safety of other kinds of products, such as automobiles, furnaces, and toys. The other class of laws are those that have resulted in the criminalization of certain types of drug use, possession, and sales. Again there are other examples of behavior that have become criminalized, such as gambling, prostitution, and stalking. The processes by which a society comes to criminalize behaviors that were previously legal is very complex,[1] but it is worth noting that when laws are passed that criminalize a behavior such as drug use, there are two kinds of impacts. Sociologists have labeled these *symbolic* and *instrumental*. The people who promote such laws gain immediate social status, first by being identified as supporting goodness, morality, and decency, and then when the law passes by being on the winning side. Those who continue to support and defend these laws continue to benefit from these symbolic associations with good and with political power. These are the *symbolic* results of the legislation and provide status benefits to the supporters of criminalization regardless of how effectively the laws are enforced. The *instrumental* impacts of criminalization refer to the consequences to those affected by the implementation of the laws: effects on local, state, and federal budgets; effects on the lives of those who are arrested and their families; and effects on the police agencies, prosecutors, prison guards, and others whose livelihood may depend upon the implementation of the laws. Our laws concerning drug use resemble a patchwork quilt reflecting the many social changes that have occurred in this country. If we want to understand our current drug laws, we must see how they have evolved over the years in response to one social crisis after another.

The Beginnings

Reformism

Current federal approaches to drug regulation in the United States can be traced to three pieces of legislation passed between 1906 and 1918. The 1906 Pure Food and Drugs Act regulated pharmaceutical manufacturing and sales. The 1914 Harrison "Narcotics" Act regulated opioids and cocaine. Finally, alcohol prohibition was ratified in 1918 and implemented in 1919. The nation was moving out of the gilded age of free-market capitalism into the reform area, in which legislation was passed regulating business and labor practices, meatpacking, and food production. This general movement toward improvement of our nation's moral character led by 1918 to a constitutional amendment prohibiting the sale of alcoholic beverages. America's "Noble Experiment" with federal alcohol prohibition during the 1920s played an important role in how the nation approached other substances associated with the social problems described in Chapter 2.

Also, the period between 1890 and 1920 has been called the "nadir" (lowest point) of race relations in the United States. During the Civil War, many Northerners had favored the integration of blacks into society. After the Civil War, blacks moved north to take jobs in factories; the U.S. Army battled Native Americans in the West; Chinese immigrants came in large numbers to build the intercontinental railroads and to work in mines; Mexican laborers came to the South and Southwest to work in the fields; and immigrants from Italy, Ireland, and other parts of Europe also came to contribute labor to all these efforts. For some, this was just too much social change in too short a time period. Racism became more widespread and open across the entire country, and was targeted against all these groups. Many of the first labor unions were openly racist, trying to protect jobs for "real" Americans. For many Americans, concerns about drunkenness, crime, drug misuse, and other forms of deviant behavior came to be associated with minority racial groups, fueling not just beliefs about the immorality of members of those races but also the desire to pass tough laws regulating these undesirable behaviors. The legacy of those beliefs and those laws remains with us today.

Issues Leading to Legislation

The trend toward reform was given direction and energy by the public discussion of several drug-related problems, and those first federal drug laws reflected the specific problems that prompted their passage. In the early 1800s, opium (see Chapter 13) was the medical doctor's most reliable and effective medicine, used for a variety of conditions but most notably as a pain reliever. Physicians prescribed various forms of opium liberally and with only limited concern about patients developing dependence. Commercial production of pure **morphine** from opium in the 1830s was followed by the

Drugs in the Media

Fentanyl

The synthetic opioid drug fentanyl has been in the news quite a bit recently. Fentanyl is often given intravenously as a pain reliever during surgery. Because the drug is readily absorbed, it is also available as a skin patch and in an oral "lollipop." Fentanyl and its various derivatives have also been produced and sold illicitly for recreational use over the past 30 years. However, in recent years there have been news reports about an apparent increase in the number of overdose deaths involving fentanyl. Chapter 13 has more information about opioid-related deaths, but you should be aware that in most cases more than one substance is involved in those deaths (often alcohol or a sedative in combination with the opioid).

The news reports about fentanyl refer to its high potency, as it is estimated to be 50 to 100 times as potent as morphine. Chapter 5 discusses the concept of potency in more depth, but in brief, *potency* refers to the dose required to produce an effect, not to how "powerful" the effect is. In other words, fentanyl has similar effects to morphine, but a lot less fentanyl is required to produce the same effect.

In June 2016, the U.S. Drug Enforcement Agency issued a warning to police departments to take care when examining potential drug evidence (https://www.dea.gov/divisions/hq/2016/hq061016.shtml). Citing the high potency of fentanyl and its ability to be absorbed through the skin, the warning made reference to the experience of two New Jersey police officers who accidentally inhaled powdered fentanyl and were rushed to the hospital, where they were treated with naloxone, a narcotic antagonist. Both recovered quickly, but they reported being disoriented and having difficulty breathing. The DEA recommended that officers not attempt to do field tests on suspected heroin or cocaine but instead submit the samples to a lab for analysis.

Fentanyl is certainly a potent and potentially dangerous substance when misused or mishandled, but reports of a drug's high potency or the risks of its misuse should not be employed to "demonize" the substance and portray the drug itself as the culprit when things go wrong. Fentanyl is used safely and frequently in legitimate medicine, but that doesn't appear in the news.

Box icon credit: ©Glow Images RF

introduction of the hypodermic syringe in the 1850s, and this more potent delivery method led to increasing medical recognition of the negative aspects of "morphinism," analogous to the term *alcoholism.* By the start of the 20th century, most physicians were aware of the dangers of morphine overuse, but many patients had developed morphine dependence under their doctor's care and relied upon their physicians and pharmacists for a regular supply. Physicians debated whether their morphine-dependent patients had developed a medical disorder requiring continued treatment, or whether they were merely weak-willed or simply seeking pleasure in the drug's effects. More than a hundred years later, those two perspectives on addiction still produce arguments over how best to deal with dependent users.

Patent Medicines The broadest impact on drug use in this country came from the widespread legal distribution of **patent medicines.** Patent medicines were dispensed by traveling peddlers and were readily available at local stores for self-medication. Sales of patent medicines increased from $3.5 million in 1859 to $74 million in 1904.

morphine: a narcotic, the primary active chemical in opium. Heroin is made from morphine.
patent medicines: medicines sold directly to the public under various trademark names. Primarily associated with the period before 1906.

Within the United States, conflict increased between the steady progress of medical science and the therapeutic claims of the patent medicine hucksters. The alcohol and other habit-forming drug content of the patent medicines was also a matter of concern. One medicine, Hostetter's Bitters, was 44 percent alcohol, and another, Birney's Catarrh Cure, was 4 percent cocaine. In October 1905, *Collier's* magazine culminated a prolonged attack on patent medicines with a well-documented, aggressive series titled "Great American Fraud."[2]

Opium and the Chinese The roots of Chinese opium smoking and the history of the Opium Wars are discussed in Chapter 13. In the mid-1800s, many British and some American merchants were engaged in the lucrative sale of opium to the Chinese, and many reformers and world leaders disapproved. In 1833, the United States signed its first treaty agreeing to control international trade in opium, and a regulatory tax on crude opium imported into this country was legislated in 1842.

The United States imported Chinese workers after the Civil War, mainly to help build the rapidly expanding railroads, and some of these people brought with them the habit of smoking opium. As always happens when a new pleasure is introduced into a society, the practice of opium smoking spread rapidly. Also, as always happens, the new practice upset the status quo and caused society to react. A contemporary report in 1882 described both the spread of opium smoking in San Francisco and the reactions it elicited:

> The practice spread rapidly and quietly among this class of gamblers and prostitutes until the latter part of 1875, at which time the authorities became cognizant of the fact, and finding ... that many women and young girls, as also young men of respectable family, were being induced to visit the dens, where they were ruined morally and otherwise, a city ordinance was passed forbidding the practice under the penalty of a heavy fine or imprisonment, or both. Many arrests were made, and the punishment was prompt and thorough.[3]

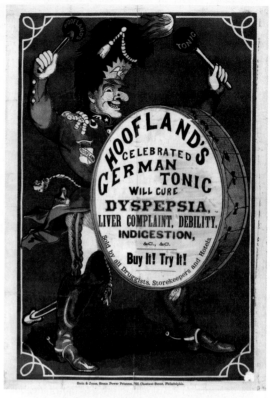

Many patent medicines contained habit-forming drugs. This tonic from the 1860s was about 30 percent alcohol.
Source: Library of Congress Prints and Photographs Division [LC-USZ62-9194]

This 1875 San Francisco ordinance was the first U.S. law forbidding opium smoking. In 1882, New York State passed a similar law aimed at opium use in New York City's expanding Chinatown. An 1890 federal act permitted only American citizens to import opium or to manufacture smoking opium in the United States. Although this law is sometimes viewed as a racist policy, it was partly in response to an 1887 agreement with China, which also forbade American citizens from engaging in the Chinese opium trade.

As more states and municipalities outlawed opium dens, the cost of black-market opium increased, and many of the lower-class opium users took up morphine or heroin, which were readily available and inexpensive. As the old saying goes, "Those who cannot remember the past are condemned to repeat it." We have recently seen a similar phenomenon as some people who are addicted to prescription painkillers have turned to purchasing illicit heroin if they have been unable to obtain further prescription opioids or if they cannot afford the high cost of the prescription drugs.

Cocaine Pure **cocaine** (see Chapter 6) became available in the mid-1800s, and its use increased over time. By 1900, its presence in many patent medicines and tonics (including the original Coca-Cola), and its ready availability by mail order and in pharmacies led medical experts to be increasingly concerned about the effects of overuse. In the early 1900s, drug reformers repeatedly raised this public issue: Cocaine sniffing had supposedly become widespread among southern "negroes," and it was claimed to be responsible for an increase in violent crimes perpetrated by "lower class" blacks in the South. The widespread distribution of this largely unsubstantiated fear was especially important in building support for federal drug-control laws among southern senators and congressmen despite their typical "states' rights" opposition to increasing federalism.[4]

1906 Pure Food and Drugs Act

President Theodore Roosevelt recommended in 1905 that a law be enacted to regulate interstate commerce in misbranded and adulterated foods, drinks, and drugs. The 1906 publication of Upton Sinclair's *The*

Opium smoking spread widely following its introduction in the 19th century. Source: Library of Congress Prints and Photographs Division [LC-USZ62-103376]

Jungle, exposing the horribly unsanitary conditions in the meatpacking industry, shocked Congress and America. Five months later, the Pure Food and Drugs Act was passed. This 1906 act prohibited interstate commerce in adulterated or misbranded foods and drugs, bringing the federal government full force into the drug marketplace. Subsequent modifications have built on it. A drug was defined as "any substance or mixture of substances intended to be used for the cure, mitigation, or prevention of disease." Of particular importance was the phrasing of the law with respect to misbranding. Misbranding referred *only to the label, not to general advertising,* and covered

> "any statement, design, or device regarding … a drug, or the ingredients or substances contained therein, which shall be false or misleading in any particular."
>
> Federal Food and Drugs Act of 1906

The act specifically referred to alcohol, morphine, opium, cocaine, heroin, *Cannabis indica*, and several other agents. Each package was required to state how much (or what proportion) of these drugs was included in the preparation. This meant, for example, that the widely sold "cures" for alcohol or morphine dependence had to indicate that they contained another habit-forming drug. However, as long as the ingredients were clearly listed on the label, any drug could be sold and bought with no federal restrictions. The goal was to protect people from unscrupulous merchants, not from themselves. The 1906 Pure Food and Drugs Act provided the rootstock on which all our modern laws regulating pharmaceuticals have been grafted.

Harrison Act of 1914

In 1908, President Theodore Roosevelt appointed Dr. Hamilton Wright to a post as United States Opium Commissioner, and he helped to organize the International Opium Conference in Shanghai, China, in 1909. After that, he and President William Taft hoped to gain favored trading status with China

cocaine: a stimulant; the primary active chemical in coca.

by leading international efforts to aid the Chinese in their attempts to reduce opium importation. At the request of the United States, an international conference met in 1912 to discuss controls on the opium trade. Great Britain, which was giving up a very lucrative business, wanted morphine, heroin, and cocaine included as well, because, as opium was being controlled, these German products were replacing it.[5] Eventually, several nations agreed to control both international trade and domestic sale and use of these substances. In response, Dr. Wright drafted a bill, which was submitted by Senator Harrison of New York, titled "An Act to provide for the registration of, with collectors of internal revenue, and to impose a special tax upon all persons who produce, import, manufacture, compound, deal in, dispense, or give away opium or coca leaves, their salts, derivatives, or preparations, and for other purposes."[6] With a title like that, it's no wonder that this historic law is usually referred to as the Harrison Act.

For the first time, dealers and dispensers of the opioids and cocaine had to register annually, pay a small tax, and use special order forms provided by the Bureau of Internal Revenue. Physicians, dentists, and veterinary surgeons were named as potential lawful distributors if they registered. In 1914, there would have been no support and no constitutional rationale for a federal law prohibiting an individual from possessing or using these drugs. Congress would not have considered such a law; if it had, the Supreme Court would probably have declared it unconstitutional. The Harrison Act was a tax law, constitutionally similar to the whiskey tax. It was not a punitive act, penalties for violation were not severe, and the measure contained no reference to users of "narcotics."

During congressional debate, some concern was expressed about the tax law's inconvenience to physicians and pharmacists, and it is doubtful that such a law would have been passed in the United States if its purpose had been merely to meet the rather weak treaty obligations of the 1912 Hague Conference. It was not meant to replace existing laws and, in fact, specifically supported the continuing legality of the 1906 Pure Food and Drugs Act and the 1909 Opium Exclusion Act. Dr. Wright had written and lectured extensively, waging an effective, emotional, and in some instances outright racist public campaign for additional controls over these drugs. For example, his claims about the practice of "snuffing" cocaine into the nose, which he said was popular among southern blacks, caused a great deal of concern and fear.[7] Dr. Wright testified before Congress that this practice led to the raping of white women. Combining this depiction with the racially tinged fears about "those immoral Chinese opium dens" added the necessary heat to make the difference, and the Harrison Act passed and was signed into law in 1914. This law was the seed, which has since sprouted into all of our federal controlled-substance regulations. However, it is important to remember that individual use or possession of any drug was not criminalized by this law, and that physicians were still free to prescribe heroin, cocaine, or any other available drug.

Two Bureaus, Two Types of Regulation

By 1914, two basic federal laws had been passed that would influence our nation's drug regulations up to the current time. The Pure Food and Drugs Act was administered within the Department of Agriculture, whereas the Harrison Act was administered by the Treasury Department—two different federal departments administering two different laws. Many of the drugs regulated by the two laws were the same, but the political issues to which each agency responded were different. The Agriculture Department was administering a law aimed at ensuring that drugs were pure and honestly labeled. By contrast, the Treasury Department's experience was in taxing alcohol, and it would soon be responsible for enforcing Prohibition. The approach taken by each bureau was further shaped by court decisions, so that the effect of each law became something a bit different from what seems to have been intended.

Regulation of Pharmaceuticals

The pharmaceutical industry has grown into one of the most important sources of commerce in the world, with the U.S. market of more than $180 billion representing almost half the estimated total. Prescription and nonprescription drugs are subject to a complex set of regulations, but in the United States they all grew out of the Pure Food and Drugs Act. The 1906 law called for the government to regulate the purity of both foods and drugs, and evidence had been presented during the congressional debate that thousands of products in both categories were at fault. Because the public was most concerned about food safety, most of the first federal cases under this new law dealt with food products.

Purity

Most large drug manufacturers made efforts to comply with the new law, although they were not given specific recommendations as to how this should be accomplished. The manufacturer of Cuforhedake Brane-Fude modified its label to show that it contained 30 percent alcohol and 16 grains of a widely used headache remedy. The government took the manufacturer to trial in 1908 on several grounds: The alcohol content was a bit lower than that claimed on the label, and the label seemed to claim that the product was a "cure" and food for the brain, both misleading claims. After much arguing about different methods of describing alcohol content and about the label claims, the manufacturer was convicted by the jury, probably because of the "brane-fude" claim, and paid a fine of $700.[8]

The Food and Drug Administration (**FDA**) went on testing products and pursuing any that were adulterated or didn't properly list important ingredients, but they also went after many companies on the basis of their therapeutic claims. In 1911, government action against a claimed cancer cure was overturned by arguing that the ingredients were accurately labeled and that the original law had not covered therapeutic claims, only claims about the nature of the ingredients. Congress rapidly passed the 1912 Sherley Amendment, which outlawed "false and fraudulent" therapeutic claims on the label. Even so, it was still up to the government to prove that a claim was not only false but also fraudulent in that the manufacturer knew it to be false. In a 1922 case, the claim that "B&M External Remedy" could cure tuberculosis was ruled not to be fraudulent because its manufacturer, who had no scientific or medical training, truly believed that its ingredients (raw eggs, turpentine, ammonia, formaldehyde, and mustard and wintergreen oils) were effective.[8] This seemed like an encouragement for the ignorant to become manufacturers of medicines!

From its beginning, the FDA had adopted the approach of encouraging voluntary cooperation, which it could obtain from most of the manufacturers through educational and corrective actions rather than through punitive, forced compliance. As more and more cases were investigated, FDA officials determined that many of the violations of the 1906 law were unintentional and caused primarily by poor manufacturing techniques and an absence of quality-control measures. The FDA began developing assay techniques for various chemicals and products and collaborated extensively with the pharmaceutical industry to improve standards.

Despite these improvements, many smaller companies continued to bring forth quack medicines that were ineffective or even dangerous. The Great Depression of the 1930s increased competition for business, and the Franklin Roosevelt administration took a more critical view of the pharmaceutical industry. FDA surveys in the mid-1930s showed that more than 10 percent of the drug products studied did not meet the standards of the *United States Pharmacopoeia* or *The National Formulary*. Several attempts were made during the early 1930s to enact major reforms, but opposition by drug manufacturers prevented these changes from happening.

FDA: The United States Food and Drug Administration.

Safety

The 1930s had seen an expansion in the use of "sulfa" drugs, which are effective antibiotics. In searching for a form that could be given as a liquid, a chemist found that *sulfanilamide* would dissolve in diethylene glycol. The new concoction looked, tasted, and smelled fine, so it was bottled and marketed in 1937. Diethylene glycol causes kidney poisoning, and within a short time 107 people died from taking "Elixir Sulfanilamide." The federal government could not intervene simply because the mixture was toxic—there was no legal requirement that medicine be safe. The FDA seized the elixir on the grounds that a true elixir contains alcohol, and this did not. The chemist committed suicide, the company paid the largest fine ever under the 1906 law, and a public crisis arose, which led to passage of the 1938 Food, Drug, and Cosmetic Act.[8]

A critical change in the 1938 law was the requirement that *before* a new drug could be marketed its manufacturer must test it for toxicity. The company was to submit a "new drug application" (**NDA**) to the FDA. This NDA was to include

> "full reports of investigations which have been made to show whether or not such a drug is safe for use."
>
> 21 U.S. Code § 355

If the submitted paperwork was satisfactory, the application was allowed to become effective.

The new drug application provision was important in two ways: First, it changed the role of the FDA from testing and challenging some of the drugs already being sold to that of a gatekeeper, which must review every new drug before it is marketed. This increased power and responsibility led to a great expansion in the size of the FDA. Second, the requirement that companies conduct safety research before marketing a new drug greatly reduced the likelihood of new drugs being introduced by small companies run by untrained people.

The 1938 act also stipulated that drug labels either give adequate directions for use or state that the drug is to be used only on the prescription of a physician. Thus, the federal law now recognized a difference between drugs that could be sold over the counter and prescription-only drugs.

Effectiveness

In the late 1950s, the U.S. Senate began a series of hearings investigating high drug costs and marketing collaboration between drug companies. One major concern was that some of the most widely sold over-the-counter medications were probably ineffective. For example, Carter's Little Liver Pills consisted of small bits of candy-coated dried liver. It was accurately labeled and made no unsubstantiated therapeutic claims on the label—if you concluded that it was supposed to help your liver, that wasn't the company's fault. And no law required the medicines to actually do anything. Amendments to the Food, Drug, and Cosmetic Act were written but were bottled up in committee. Again it took a disaster that raised public awareness and congressional concern before major reforms were implemented.

Thalidomide, a sedative and sleeping pill, was first marketed in West Germany in 1957. The drug was used by pregnant women because it reduced nausea and vomiting associated with morning sickness experienced early in pregnancy. An American company submitted an NDA in 1960 to market thalidomide, but luckily the FDA physician in charge of the application did not approve it quickly. In 1961 and early 1962, it became clear that thalidomide had been responsible for birth defects. In West Germany, hundreds of children had been born with deformed limbs. The American company had released some thalidomide for clinical testing, but, because its NDA was not approved, a major disaster was avoided in the United States.[8]

The 1962 Kefauver-Harris Amendments added several important provisions, including the requirement that companies seek approval of any testing to be done with humans before clinical trials are conducted. Another provision required advertisements for prescription drugs (mostly in medical journals) to contain a summary of information about adverse reactions to the drug.

The most important change was one requiring that every new drug be demonstrated to be *effective* for the illnesses mentioned on the label. As with the details of safety testing required by the 1938 law, this research on effectiveness was to be submitted to the FDA. The FDA was also to begin a review of the thousands of products marketed between 1938 and 1962 to determine their effectiveness. Any that were found to be ineffective were to be removed from the market. In 1966, the FDA began the process of evaluating the formulations of prescription drugs. In the next eight years, the FDA removed from the market 6,133 drugs manufactured by 2,732 companies.

Marketing a New Drug

The basic rules for introducing a new drug have been in place for more than 50 years. Companies are required to demonstrate, through extensive chemical, biological, animal, and human testing, that the new drug they want to sell is both safe and effective. According to the pharmaceutical industry, the entire research and approval process now takes on average more than 10 years and costs more than $2 billion.[9]

The FDA formally enters the picture only when a drug company is ready to study the effects of a compound on humans. At that time the company supplies to the FDA a "Notice of Claimed Investigational Exemption for a New Drug" (**IND**); it is also required to submit all information from preclinical investigations, including the effects of the drug on animals.

As minimum evidence of safety, the animal studies must include acute, one-time administration of several dose levels of the drug to different groups of animals of at least two species. There must also be studies in which the drug is given regularly to animals for a period related to the proposed use of the drug in humans. For example, a drug to be used chronically requires two-year toxicology studies in animals. The method of drug administration and the form of the drug in these studies must be the same as that proposed for human use.

In addition to these research results, the company must submit a detailed description of the proposed clinical studies of the drug in humans. The company must also certify that the human research participants will be told they are receiving an

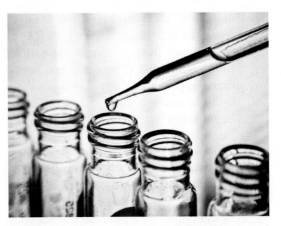

A new drug must move through three phases of clinical investigation before it reaches the market. ©Totojang/ iStock/Getty Images RF

investigational compound. Finally, the company must agree to forward annually a comprehensive report and to inform the FDA immediately if any adverse reactions arise in either animals or humans receiving the investigational drug.

If the FDA authorizes the testing of the drug in humans, the company can move into the first of *three phases of clinical investigation:*

1. *Phase One* encompasses studies with relatively low doses of the drug on a limited number of healthy people—typically, 20 to 80 company employees, medical school personnel, and others who volunteer for such trials. At this stage the researchers are primarily interested in learning how their drug is absorbed and excreted in healthy people, as well as the side effects it may trigger.

2. *Phase Two* of the human studies involves patients who have the condition the candidate drug is designed to treat. These studies involve a few hundred patients who are chosen because the new agent might help them.

NDA: new drug application. Must be approved before a drug is sold.
IND: application to investigate a new drug in human clinical trials.

3. *Phase Three* administers the drug to larger numbers of individuals (typically, 1,000 to 5,000) with the disease or symptom for which the drug is intended. If the compound proves effective in phase three, the FDA balances its possible dangers against the benefits for patients before releasing it for sale to the public.

There have been a few changes to this basic procedure since 1962. In 1983, Congress passed the Orphan Drug Act, offering tax incentives and exclusive sales rights for a guaranteed seven years for any company developing a drug for rare disorders afflicting no more than 200,000 people. Up to that time, companies had stayed away from much research on rare disorders because they couldn't earn enough to recover the enormous research costs. By 2016, more than 360 drugs developed under this act had received FDA approval.[9] However, because of the limited market, many of these orphan drugs are extremely expensive, with some costing more than $100,000 per patient per year.

On the "drug war" front, the Prescription Drug Marketing Act of 1987 tightened the procedures whereby drug company salespeople could provide free samples to physicians, after Congress had heard testimony about widespread diversion of samples. Also, because counterfeit and adulterated drugs had found their way into the U.S. market from abroad as shipments of "American goods returned," new regulations were added covering the transfer and reimportation of drugs. During the 2009 debate over health care reform, members of Congress pointed out that U.S. manufactured drugs sold in Canada could be much less expensive, and moved to again allow licensed drugs to be purchased in other countries and brought into the United States. However, the U.S. pharmaceutical industry stopped this, arguing that costs could be kept down without allowing drugs' reimportation. By 2016, it seems clear that that promise has not exactly come true, with several companies raising prices at rates much higher than inflation.[10]

The 1997 FDA Modernization Act made several more procedural adjustments, including guidelines for annual postmarketing reporting by the companies of adverse reactions to some medications (so-called Phase IV reporting). Also, the act allowed companies to distribute information to physicians about other, less well-researched, uses for an approved medication. One example of such "off-label" prescribing is the drug carbamazepine, which was originally tested and approved for use as an anticonvulsant. Based on published research as well as clinical experience, the drug is also widely prescribed as a mood stabilizer (see Chapter 8) even though it has not received FDA approval for that use.

There is one big, continually debated issue surrounding the FDA drug approval system: Why does it take so long? The issue is not just of concern to the sick individual. Pharmaceutical manufacturers have a 20-year patent on a new drug. They usually patent the chemical as soon as there is some evidence that it is marketable. The manufacturers claim that, by the time a drug is cleared for marketing, they have only a few years left on the patent. From the mid-1980s to the late 1990s, the average approval time was reduced from 32 months to 12 months—but the increased speed of the FDA's approval process has been offset by an increased amount of time spent by companies in clinical trials—an average of almost seven years. The bottom line is that this is a high-risk, high-reward business. In any given year, there are about 3,000 drug compounds undergoing some type of study, and about 30 new ones will be approved and marketed. Of those that are marketed, the industry claims that only about one in five will earn back all the development costs.[9]

Dietary Supplements

Certain druglike products, such as vitamin pills, are not drugs but, rather, are considered dietary supplements and treated more as foods. They don't need to be proved to be effective for a specific intended purpose. Many questions arose about whether such new products needed to be reviewed for safety before marketing them and whether some of the beneficial claims made by people selling them constituted mislabeling. The 1994 Dietary Supplement Health and Education Act cleared up many of those issues. It broadened the definition of dietary supplements to include not only vitamins, minerals, and proteins but also herbs and herbal extracts. The labels are not allowed to make unsubstantiated direct claims, such as "cures cancer," but they are permitted to make general statements about the overall health and "well-being" that can be achieved by consuming the dietary ingredient. The label must then say, "This statement has not been evaluated by the Food and Drug Administration. This product is not intended to diagnose, treat, cure, or prevent any disease." Nevertheless, growth in sales of herbal products and other dietary supplements has been enormous, probably in large part because many consumers don't distinguish between the vague, general claims made by supplements and the specific, demonstrated effectiveness required of drugs.

One issue that should be of concern for users of dietary supplements is that, rather than the company demonstrating the safety of the supplement before it is marketed, the FDA must prove that the product is unsafe before its sale can be stopped. For example, the FDA became concerned in 1997 about *ephedra* (see Chapter 12), found in many herbal weight-loss products. In high doses, this herbal product can cause dangerous increases in blood pressure and interfere with normal mechanisms for reducing body heat during exercise. It took seven years and the well-publicized deaths of some athletes before *ephedra* was banned in 2004.

Controlled Substances

To most Americans, the word *narcotics* means drugs that are manufactured and sold illegally. Pharmacologically, the term refers only to drugs having certain effects, with the prototype being the narcotic analgesics derived from opium, such as morphine and heroin. Although the 1914 Harrison Act controlled opioids, which are narcotics, and cocaine, which is not, the enforcement effort

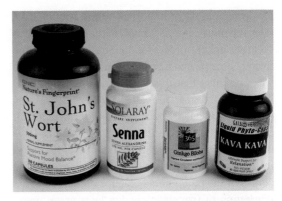

Dietary supplements are not regulated in the same way as drugs. They do not have to be proven safe and effective before they are marketed. ©McGraw-Hill Education/Jill Braaten, photographer

focused so much on the opioids that eventually the enforcement officers became known as narcotics officers, the office within the Treasury Department officially became the Narcotics Division, and people began to refer to the "Harrison Narcotics Act," though the word *narcotics* was not in the original title. The meaning of the term changed so much in political use that later federal laws incorrectly classified cocaine and then marijuana as narcotics.

After the Harrison Act

In 1914, it was estimated that about 200,000 Americans—1 in 400—were dependent on opium or its derivatives. One way to administer the Harrison Act would have been to allow a continued legal supply of opioids to those individuals through registered physicians and to focus enforcement efforts on the smugglers and remaining opium dens. After all, the Harrison Act stated that an unregistered person could purchase and possess any of the taxed drugs if they had been prescribed or administered by a physician "in the course of his professional practice and for legitimate medical purposes." Until the 1920s, most users continued to receive opioids quietly through their private physicians, and in most large cities public clinics dispensed morphine to users who could not afford private care.

Early enforcement efforts focused on smugglers and did not result in a large number of arrests.

However, one very important arrest was to have later repercussions. It seems that a Dr. Webb was taking telephone orders for opioids, including some from people he had never seen in person. Evidence was presented that this physician would prescribe whatever amount the caller requested. He was arrested, convicted, and appealed the conviction all the way to the U.S. Supreme Court, which in 1919 upheld his conviction on the grounds that his activity did not constitute a proper prescription in the course of the professional practice of medicine. It's interesting to speculate whether fears about unexpected uses for the telephone, which most people did not yet have in their homes, might have contributed to Dr. Webb's prosecution. There is a parallel with today's Internet pharmacies, some of which provide medical consultation and prescription through home computers.

The single most important legislation that has shaped the federal government's approach to controlled substances wasn't a "drug law" at all but, rather, the 18th Amendment prohibiting alcohol. That law was also to be enforced by the Treasury Department, and a separate Prohibition unit was established in 1919. The Narcotics Division was placed within that unit, and Colonel Levi G. Nutt was appointed the first director, with 170 agents at his disposal.[5] Although the Harrison Act had not changed, the people enforcing it had. Just as with alcohol, these people believed that the cure for narcotic dependence was to prevent the user from having access to the drug (in other words, opioid "prohibition," at least for those who were dependent). The new enforcers interpreted the Webb case to mean that any prescription of a habit-forming drug to a dependent user was not a "legitimate medical purpose," and they began to charge many physicians under the Harrison Act.

Arresting Physicians and Pharmacists The Internal Revenue Service (IRS) moved to close municipal narcotics clinics in more than 30 cities from coast to coast. From 1919 to 1929, the Narcotics Division arrested about 75,000 people, including 25,000 physicians and druggists.[5] The American Medical Association supported the view that reputable physicians would not prescribe morphine or other opioids to dependent users. Because there was then no legal way to obtain the drug, the user was forced either to stop using drugs or to look for them in the illegal market. Thus, this new method of enforcing the Harrison Act resulted in the growth of an illicit drug trade, which charged users up to 50 times more than the legal retail drug price. Opioid dependence came increasingly to be viewed as a police, rather than a medical, problem. The Narcotics Division also concluded that users in possession of heroin, morphine, opium, or cocaine who could not produce a valid prescription must have obtained the drug illegally, and they began to charge individual users with violating the Harrison Act. Thus, the use of the drugs was effectively criminalized for the first time, not because that was the intent of the 1914 Harrison Act, but because of the Narcotics Division's interpretation of it. Whether this would have happened eventually without the prohibitionist enforcement approach that resulted from alcohol prohibition being administered by the same agency is open to debate, but it almost certainly would not have happened as soon as 1919.

Stiffer Penalties Partly in response to the growing illicit market, in 1922 Congress passed the Jones-Miller Act, which more than doubled the maximum penalties for dealing in illegally imported drugs to $5,000 and 10 years of imprisonment. Included also was the stipulation that the mere possession of illegally obtained opioids or cocaine was sufficient basis for conviction, thus officially making the user a criminal. Because illegal opioids were so expensive, many users came to prefer the most potent type available, heroin. In 1924, another act prohibited importing opium for the manufacture of heroin. Already by this time several important trends had been set: Users were criminals at odds with the regulatory agency, the growth of the illicit market was responded to with greater penalties and more aggressive enforcement, and the focus was on attempting to eliminate a substance (heroin) as though the drug itself were the problem. In the

1925 Linder case, the U.S. Supreme Court declared it could be legal for a physician to prescribe opioids for a dependent user if it were part of a curing program and did not transcend "the limits of that professional conduct with which Congress never intended to interfere."[6] However, the damage had been done, and most physicians would have nothing to do with drug-dependent patients.

Prison versus Treatment   By 1928, individuals sentenced for drug violations made up one-third of the total population in federal prisons. Even though the 1920s was the period of alcohol prohibition, during those years twice as many people were imprisoned for drug violations as for liquor violations.[11] In 1929, Congress viewed this enormous expenditure for drug offenders as an indicator that something was wrong and decided that users should be cured rather than repeatedly jailed. It voted to establish two "narcotic farms" for the treatment of persons dependent on habit-forming drugs (including marijuana and peyote) who had been convicted of violating a federal law. The farm in Lexington, Kentucky, opened in 1935 and generally held about a thousand patients, two-thirds of whom were prisoners.

The Bureau of Narcotics   Answering the call for new approaches to dependence, and in response to the end of Prohibition and to charges of corruption in the previous Narcotics Division, in 1930 Congress formed a separate Bureau of Narcotics in the Treasury Department. Harry Anslinger became the first commissioner of that bureau in 1932 and took office with a pledge to stop arresting so many users and instead to go after the big dealers. Anslinger became the first "drug czar," although he wasn't called that at the time. To some extent, he followed the lead of J. Edgar Hoover, director of the Federal Bureau of Investigation (FBI). Each of these men was regularly reappointed by each new president, and each built up a position of considerable power and influence. Anslinger had almost total control of federal efforts in drug education, prevention, treatment, and enforcement for

30 years, from 1932 to 1962. No federal or state drug-control law was passed without his influencing it, and he also represented U.S. drug-control interests to international organizations, including the United Nations.

The end of Prohibition, combined with Depression-era cutbacks, had reduced the number of agents available for enforcement, but not for long. After newspaper reports linked marijuana smoking with crime, Anslinger adopted this new cause and began writing, speaking, testifying, and making films depicting the evils of marijuana. This effort succeeded in bringing public attention to the fight his bureau was waging against drugs and resulted in the 1937 passage of the Marijuana Tax Act. Marijuana came under the same type of legal control as cocaine and the opiates, in that one was supposed to register and pay a tax to legally import, buy, or sell marijuana. From 1937 until 1970, marijuana was referred to in federal laws as a narcotic.

Narcotic Control Act of 1956

World War II had caused a decrease in the importation of both legal and illegal drugs. With the end of the war and the resumption of easy international travel, the illegal drug trade resumed and increased every year, despite the 1951 Boggs Amendment to the Harrison Act, which established mandatory minimum sentences for drug offenses. Testimony before a subcommittee of the Senate Judiciary Committee in 1955 included the statement that inducing drug dependence in U.S. citizens was one of the ways Communist China planned to demoralize the United States. Remember that this was the height of the so-called McCarthy era, during which a mere hint by Senator Joseph McCarthy that someone associated with "known Communists" was enough to ruin that person's career. One interesting bit of history from that time was revealed years later. Anslinger and Hoover were aware that McCarthy, in addition to his widely known alcohol abuse, was dependent on morphine. Anslinger secretly arranged for McCarthy to

Focus on Drug Policy

Alternative Approaches: Portugal, Uruguay, and Thailand

In 2001, a new law went into effect in Portugal. While drug trafficking is still illegal, drug possession has been decriminalized. This is true not only for marijuana but for all drugs, including cocaine and heroin. If a person is caught using or possessing, they are required to meet with a local "Commission for Dissuasion of Drug Addiction," consisting of a lawyer, a physician, and a social worker. After interviewing the user, the Commission might require the user to enroll in a treatment program or to attend an educational or counseling session, or might prohibit the individual from engaging in certain activities that have been associated with drug-using problems for him or her. Overall, the country has been spending more money than before on prevention and treatment, and less on criminal prosecution and imprisonment.

How is this working for them? A recent economic analysis estimated that there had been an 18 percent reduction in "social costs" over an 11-year period, mostly from reduced costs in the legal system, but also in reduced health-related costs.[13]

Uruguay completely legalized marijuana beginning in 2013, including the right of people over the age of 18 to grow their own. This has resulted in a plentiful supply of inexpensive marijuana, which should practically eliminate the illegal trade. For those who do not wish to grow their own, the government is opening dispensaries, selling each person up to 40 grams per month at a cost no greater than $1 per gram.

Meanwhile, Thailand seems poised to change its highly restrictive laws, basing its approach on treatment rather than punishment.[14] It will be interesting to follow the experience of these and other countries over the next few years to see whether drug-related problems increase or decrease.

Box icon credit: ©Edward.J.Westmacott/Alamy Images RF

---

obtain a regular supply of his drug from a Washington, D.C., pharmacy without interference from narcotics officers.[5] Meanwhile, Congress waged its public fight against both crime and communism by passing the 1956 Narcotic Control Act, with the toughest penalties yet. Under this law, any offense except first-offense possession had to result in a jail term, and no suspension, probation, or parole was allowed. Anyone caught selling heroin to a person younger than 18 could receive the death penalty. Anslinger commented on that particular provision by saying, "I'd like to throw the switch myself on drug peddlers who sell their poisons to minors."[12]

Drug Abuse Control Amendments of 1965

The early 1960s saw not only an increase in illegal drug use but also a shift in the type of drugs being used illegally. The trend was for the new drug users to be better educated and to emphasize drugs that alter mood and consciousness, such as amphetamines, barbiturates, and hallucinogens. Some hospitals in large cities reported that up to 15 percent of their emergency room calls involved individuals with adverse reactions to these drugs. Although amphetamines and barbiturates were legal prescription drugs, it was felt that they should be under the same types of controls as opioids, cocaine, and marijuana. The 1965 Drug Abuse Control Amendments referred to these as dangerous drugs and included hallucinogens, such as LSD. The Bureau of Narcotics became the Bureau of Narcotics and Dangerous Drugs. Thus, the 1960s saw a number of major changes for this agency. Anslinger had retired, the bureau had new classes of drugs to control, and it was facing widespread disregard of the drug laws by large numbers of young people who were not members of the underprivileged and criminal classes.

Comprehensive Drug Abuse Prevention and Control Act of 1970

By the late 1960s, it was clear that the patchwork of laws and amendments that had built up over the years since the 1914 Harrison Act could use some major reform. For one thing, the existing system was a legal and bureaucratic mess, based originally on tax law (Treasury Department), with later modifications based on interstate commerce (Commerce Department) and international treaty (State Department), but with increasing focus on federal law enforcement (Justice Department). Also, indications were that drug use and abuse continued to increase in spite of the harsh penalties that were sometimes imposed. The 1970 law threw out everything that went before and started with a clean slate, based on current research and a rational approach that attempted to balance public health concerns with law enforcement issues. Part of the law gave increased funding to the Department of Health, Education, and Welfare (now the Department of Health and Human Services) for research, treatment, and prevention efforts. The other major part established that certain drugs were to be controlled directly rather than through tax or interstate commerce laws. The responsibility for this enforcement was transferred to the Justice Department's new Drug Enforcement Administration (**DEA**).

Several aspects of this law could be seen as a more liberal approach to the issue, even on the law enforcement side. Mandatory minimum penalties were done away with, as was the death penalty. Decisions about how best to control specific drugs were to be taken out of the political arena and based on the best available evidence from both a health and law enforcement perspective. Five "schedules" of controlled substances were established, and initially the secretary of health was in charge of deciding which substances to control under which schedule, based on objective evidence balancing potential medical uses against abuse potential. A person convicted for the first time of possessing a small amount of a substance could be allowed a year's probation and, if no violation occurred during that year, the conviction could be "erased." Penalties for making or selling controlled substances were greater than for simple possession, but in the original law, no sentence greater than 15 years was provided for a first offense of distribution.

The basic structure of this law remains in place, including the five schedules, which are summarized in Table 3.1 The most important issue to arise out of this has to do with the difference between Schedule I (the most restrictive) and all the other schedules. The key point is that Schedule I drugs have "no currently acceptable medical use in treatment in the United States." Physicians are not allowed to prescribe Schedule I drugs, and they are not found in pharmacies. Drugs on Schedules II–V are available by prescription. Initially this system made it clear that there would be absolutely no legal access to Schedule I drugs such as heroin, LSD, or marijuana. Forty years later, this Schedule I distinction seems problematic. For about 30 years, the drugs causing the most concern have not been Schedule I drugs (cocaine, methamphetamine, oxycodone, etc., are all available by prescription and therefore are not on Schedule I). Meanwhile, many states have passed medical marijuana laws that allow marijuana to be dispensed on a physician's recommendation. But marijuana remains on Schedule I under federal law, meaning no prescriptions are allowed and there is no legal method to provide marijuana. With cannabis now considered to be legal for medical purposes in more than half the states, the DEA considered several petitions asking them to reschedule marijuana to Schedule II, but in August of 2016 they announced that it would remain on Schedule I, continuing the conflict between state and federal laws.

The 1970 reform was widely greeted as an improvement, both by people concerned about the overly harsh and punitive nature of previous laws

DEA: Drug Enforcement Administration, a branch of the Department of Justice.

Table 3.1
Summary of Controlled Substance Schedules

Schedule	Criteria	Examples
Schedule I	*a.* High potential for abuse *b.* No currently acceptable medical use in treatment in the United States *c.* Lack of accepted safety for use under medical supervision	Heroin Marijuana MDMA (Ecstasy)
Schedule II	*a.* High potential for abuse *b.* Currently accepted medical use *c.* Abuse may lead to severe psychological or physical dependence	Morphine Cocaine Methamphetamine
Schedule III	*a.* Potential for abuse less than I and II *b.* Currently accepted medical use *c.* Abuse may lead to moderate physical dependence or high psychological dependence	Anabolic steroids Most barbiturates Dronabinol (THC)
Schedule IV	*a.* Low potential for abuse relative to III *b.* Currently accepted medical use *c.* Abuse may lead to limited physical or psychological dependence relative to III	Alprazolam (Xanax) Fenfluramine Zolpidem (Ambien)
Schedule V	*a.* Low potential for abuse relative to IV *b.* Currently accepted medical use *c.* Abuse may lead to limited physical or psychological dependence relative to IV	Mixtures having small amounts of codeine or opium

and by law enforcement people looking for a more logical and consistent framework. However, subsequent events have led to amendments that have reversed most of these benefits and once again resulted in a system that is both very complex and quite punitive in nature.

Anti-Drug Abuse Acts of 1986 and 1988

As we saw in Chapter 1, marijuana use continued to increase during the 1970s, and we began to get documented evidence from annual surveys that were developed as a result of the research and prevention components of the 1970 law. Cocaine became popular during the 1970s, and there was growing concern that federal drug laws were not adequately addressing these problems. However, it was the introduction of crack cocaine in the early 1980s and the fearful, emotional response generated by the media and politicians that led to significant

amendments to the 1970 Controlled Substances Act. The 1986 law stiffened penalties for selling drugs, and reinstituted mandatory minimum sentences and sentences without parole. Congress established specific amounts of drugs in possession that would trigger the higher "trafficking" penalties (the logic is that if you are caught with an ounce of marijuana, it could be for personal use, but if you have several pounds in your possession, you're no doubt planning to sell most of it). One aspect of this 1986 law was that 500 grams of powdered cocaine—but only 5 grams of crack cocaine—were required to trigger a mandatory five-year prison term. This was clearly a political reaction to the widespread fears about crack cocaine's dependence potential and association with violence, because there was no pharmacological justification for such a wide discrepancy. This discrepancy has proved to be controversial in recent years and led to an important 2007 Supreme Court decision (see Chapter 6 for details). Overall, the longer sentences, mandatory minimums, and no-parole provisions of the 1986 law have contributed greatly to a huge growth in prison populations over the past 20 years (see "Americans in Prison," box).

In 1988, additional amendments were designed to provide even more "teeth" for federal prosecutions. Components of this new law included more restrictions on aircraft registrations, requiring banks to report all transactions over $10,000 or other "suspicious activities," restricting firearms sales, and restricting chemicals used in the manufacture of drugs. The death penalty came back, this time for drug-related murders. A further amendment in 1994 extended the death penalty to so-called drug kingpins (leaders of large-scale drug-distributing organizations). One noteworthy change in the 1988 law was a toughening of approaches toward drug users, aimed at reducing the *demand* for drugs (as opposed to efforts to control the drug *supply*).

Scheduling A 1984 law allowed the Justice Department to "trump" the secretary of health by immediately placing a drug on Schedule I, pending later review. This provision was used right away to place the hallucinogen MDMA (Ecstasy) on Schedule I. Since then, the DEA has had the major voice in determining which drugs to schedule and at what level. In an even greater overturning of the original logic of the scheduling system, in 2000 Congress itself mandated that GHB, which had surfaced as a date-rape drug, be placed on Schedule I.

Sentencing The original law had only a few categories of sentences, based mainly on possession versus distribution, and also on whether this was a first offense or a repeat offense. Since then, not only has Congress gotten directly involved (as in the crack versus powder cocaine controversy discussed further in Chapter 6), but the sentencing guidelines developed by the U.S. Sentencing Commission have become based on a point system so complicated that it cannot be meaningfully summarized here.[15] Additional complexities were provided by congressional

amendments in 2005 related to Homeland Security (importation of methamphetamine or precursors) and in 2006 to Internet sales of date-rape drugs. Overall, the sentencing system has once again evolved into a bureaucratic nightmare.

Before the Anti-Drug Abuse Acts, there were few penalties and little interest in convicting users for possessing small (personal-use) amounts of controlled substances. Under the new laws, these are some of the unpleasant possibilities if convicted of possession:

- A civil fine of up to $10,000

- Forfeiture of the car, boat, or plane conveying the substance

- Loss of all federal benefits, including student loans and grants, for up to one year after the first offense and for up to five years after a second offense

The 1988 law also removes from public housing the entire family of anyone who engages in criminal activity, including drug-related activity, on or near public-housing premises.

Asset Forfeiture Long-standing legal precedents allow governments to seize property that they have reason to believe is associated with the commission of a crime. In the 1980s, the federal government began to use this power aggressively against suspected drug dealers, targeting large sums of cash, airplanes, boats, automobiles, houses, and farms. A 1984 law allowed the federal government to share up to 80 percent of the proceeds with state and local law enforcement agencies, which encouraged local police to cooperate with the federal government in investigating suspected drug dealers. One important aspect of this is that the concept of "innocent until proven guilty" does not hold, since these are not criminal charges. The government seizes the assets based on reasonable suspicion, and then the burden is on the previous owner of the assets to hire an attorney and go to court to try to get the property returned. Over the past 30 years, billions of dollars worth of property has been seized from suspected

Under laws enacted in 1986, penalties for small amounts of crack cocaine (*left*) were much higher than those for powdered cocaine (*right*). ©Jodi Cobb/National Geographic/Getty Images(*left*), ©Doug McLean/Shutterstock.com RF (*right*)

drug dealers, and there have been complaints that the process has been abused. Some states have changed their own laws so that property may not be kept unless the person is convicted of a criminal offense, but in most states that is not required.

Office of National Drug Control Policy To better coordinate all these federal efforts, the 1988 law established the cabinet-level position of director of national drug control policy (commonly referred to as a "drug czar"). This individual is ordered by the legislation to prepare a national drug-control strategy and an annual consolidated drug-control budget for all federal agencies involved, to advise the National Security Council, and to report directly to the president. The Office of National Drug Control Policy was reauthorized and given additional authority in 1998.

Designer Drugs The term *designer drug* was coined in the 1980s to refer to chemicals that are close relatives of controlled substances but not themselves listed on one of the schedules. At that time, chemists were making minor changes to the structure of some opioids (fentanyl and meperidine) and selling these drugs as "synthetic heroin." Congress passed the Controlled Substance Analogue Enforcement Act in 1986, saying that any drug or any chemical intended for human use that is substantially similar to a controlled substance is also controlled under the same schedule. However, the law was overturned on the grounds of being too vague. The rise of newer designer drugs, such as synthetic marijuana derivatives (Chapter 15), stimulants sold as "bath salts" (Chapter 6), and several hallucinogens in the "2C" family (Chapter 14) have led to their being listed as Schedule I drugs, and alpha-fentanyl was added in 2015.

State and Local Regulations

It is impossible to describe here all of the varied drug laws in the 50 states. Most states and many local communities had laws regulating sales of drugs before the federal government got into the act in 1906. Aspects of those old laws might still be in effect in some areas. Regarding the legal sales of prescription and over-the-counter drugs, there is considerable uniformity across the states, but some details do differ. For example, in some states licensed physician's assistants or psychologists are allowed to prescribe many types of medication, and in a few states pharmacists are now allowed to prescribe a few types of drugs that had previously required prescription by a physician or dentist.

Drugs in Depth

Americans in Prison

Fueled largely by the increases in drug-law arrests, the number of people held in state and local prisons in the United States reached record levels in 2007. From the 1920s through the mid-1970s, about 1 person was in prison for every 1,000 people in the U.S. population. There were peaks and valleys, with the highest peak in 1939 (the end of the Depression) at 1.39 per 1,000 population. From 1974 to 1985, the rate doubled, from 1 to 2 per 1,000. By 2008, the imprisonment rate had more than doubled again to 5 per 1,000 population. Increased

awareness of the cost of this high incarceration rate has resulted in some adjustments in sentencing procedures, and prison populations have declined slightly since then. One change has been that the number of people admitted to prison for drug offenses or parole violation has decreased. In spite of this small decline, the United States still has a greater proportion of its own citizens in prison than does any other country.

Box icon credit: ©Ingram Publishing/SuperStock RF

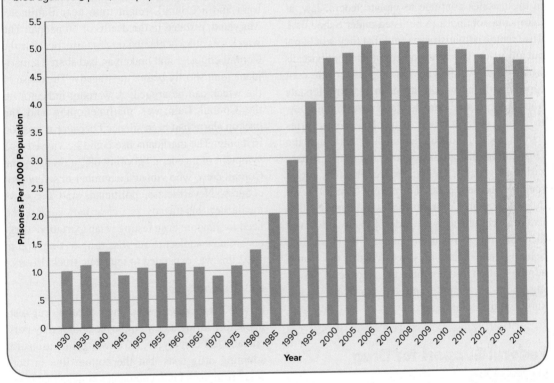

After the passage of the federal 1970 Controlled Substances Act, states began to adopt the *Uniform Controlled Substances Act,* a model state law recommended by the DEA. The majority of states have adopted the same five schedules as in the federal law, but six states have a different breakdown of schedules (four, six, or seven categories), and three states have a

completely different method of categorizing illicit drugs that is not based on "schedules." Although the basic scheduling is similar in most states, there are large differences in the penalties. For example, possession of a small amount of cocaine can result in a maximum prison sentence ranging from less than 1 year up to 15 years, depending on the state.[16]

Violations of illicit drug laws may lead either to federal charges or to state charges, and this is important because federal mandatory minimum laws often mean much longer sentences than if the individual is convicted under most state laws.

State versus Federal Marijuana Laws The greatest discrepancy between state and federal laws is now in the realm of marijuana regulation. Twenty-eight states now have some sort of allowance for the medical use of marijuana (Chapter 15). And as of 2016, six of these states also allow for recreational use of marijuana under state law. The interesting thing is that both users and dispensers of marijuana in these states continue to violate federal law, as marijuana continues to be listed under Schedule I. The Obama administration said that they would not put any effort into arresting or charging individuals who operate within state laws, but they were concerned with the possibility of increased interstate trafficking in marijuana to states that do not allow it. Even state-licensed marijuana dispensaries remain in violation of federal law. Although the Obama administration stopped raiding the dispensaries in general, federal prosecutors may target specific problem areas. For example, in 2011, all dispensaries in Colorado that were within 1,000 feet of a school zone were ordered to close down or face federal prosecution under the Drug-Free Schools and Communities Act. Whether the Trump administration will continue the practice of allowing states to regulate and sell marijuana is not known at this time.

Federal Support for Drug Screening

Military and Federal Employees

It wasn't until the 1970s that relatively inexpensive screening tests were invented that could detect a variety of abused substances or their metabolites in urine. The Navy, followed by the other armed forces, was the first to use random urine screening on a large scale. Soon to follow were tests of people in various high-risk or high-profile positions, oil-field workers, air traffic controllers, and professional athletes. In 1986, President Reagan first declared that random urine tests should be performed on all federal employees in "sensitive" jobs. He also urged companies doing business with the federal government to begin testing their employees if they had not already done so. Since then, most federal employees have become subject to at least the possibility of being asked to provide a random urine sample, although such tests are rare in most federal occupations.

Transportation Workers

In 1987, a collision between an Amtrak passenger train and a Conrail freight train near Baltimore, Maryland, resulted in the deaths of 16 people. The wreck was quickly blamed on drug use, because the Conrail engineer and brakeman had shared a marijuana joint shortly before the tragedy. The cause of the wreck can be argued: A warning indicator on the Conrail train was malfunctioning and the backup alarm had been silenced because it was too irritating. The marijuana use could be viewed as a symptom of a general "goofing off" attitude by the Conrail crew, who violated a number of safety procedures. Nevertheless, politicians and the news media saw this tragedy as a clear indication of the need for random drug testing. Transportation workers are now subject to surprise drug testing, and in 1992 this was expanded to interstate truck drivers.

Private Employers

Private corporations, which may require drug testing before hiring a new employee and/or may periodically test employees, have two main reasons for adopting drug tests, but the bottom line in both cases is money. First, companies believe that drug-free workers will be absent less often, will make fewer mistakes, will have better safety records, and will produce more and better work. Second, by spending relatively few dollars on drug tests, they protect the company against negligence suits that might follow if a "stoned" employee hurt someone on the job or turned out a dangerously faulty product. Companies doing business with the federal

Taking Sides

Drug Tests for Welfare Recipients?

By 2015, 13 of the 50 state legislatures had passed laws requiring a urine sample for people receiving welfare, unemployment assistance, job training, food stamps, or public housing. Several other states were considering doing the same, with the expressed hope of saving money.

Opponents of these laws have produced data showing the high cost of administering the testing programs compared to the relatively small number of positive drug tests found. For example, according to ThinkProgress.org, in one year Oklahoma spent just over $230,000 on a program that gave urine tests to about 1,300 welfare applicants for whom they had "reasonable suspicion" of drug use. There were 138 positive results, just over 10 percent. Others have reported that in all these programs the rate of positive urine tests is lower than the rate of self-reported illicit drug use in the overall population, suggesting that welfare applicants or recipients have a lower than average likelihood of being drug users.

Proponents of these laws argue that drug testing is not uncommon in the workplace, and since welfare assistance, unemployment assistance, and job training are all intended to provide a transition to employment, these policies make sense. However, one opponent was quoted as saying,

> "All this does is perpetuate the stereotype that low-income people are lazy, shiftless drug addicts and if all they did was pick themselves up by the bootstraps then the country wouldn't be in the mess it's in."

> Quoted in A.G Sulzberger States Adding Drug Test as Hurdle for Welfare, *Newyork times*

What do you think? Is this a reasonable type of policy to impose during a time of high government expenditures? Is it unreasonable, particularly in a time of high unemployment?

Imagine a specific example of a single mother with two young children. Previously employed at a low-paying job, she is receiving unemployment payments while attending a community college, and she also has been receiving food stamps. If she smokes marijuana and fails the urine test, should this assistance be stopped?

Box icon credit: ©Nova Development RF

government have an additional reason—they are required to have drug-free workplace rules in place.

Public Schools

Giving urine tests to high-school students seems like a great idea to some parents and community officials. After all, society is most concerned about substance use and abuse among the young, and the belief is that if the students know testing is a possibility they will be less likely to use drugs in the first place. But many believe that such testing is an invasion of privacy, and to test students randomly without some evidence pointing to likely drug use by a particular individual destroys any sense of trust that might exist between the students and school officials. With all the concern about drug use by athletes, the first groups of students to be widely subjected to urine screening for drugs were those involved in team sports. In a legal challenge to this

process, the U.S. Supreme Court in 1995 allowed drug testing of athletes, based partly on evidence from the school in question that its student athletes were at a higher than average risk for drug use. Many schools have since adopted policies that include other extracurricular activities, and a 2002 Supreme Court case upheld those programs as well. Students are required by law to attend school up to a certain age, but extracurricular activities are voluntary. Therefore, if a student wants to participate in football, band, or the debate team, he or she might have to agree to random urine screening as a condition of being part of that activity. In 2003, President George W. Bush endorsed random testing of all students, and provided federal funds to assist school districts in implementing these programs. However, as of 2012, the legality of random, suspicionless urine testing for all public-school students has not been established at the federal level.

Testing Methods

With so many pilots, truck drivers, federal workers, hospital employees, athletes, and students being tested, selling testing kits and lab analysis has become a big business. New methods for analyzing urine have combined with test kits for saliva, hair, and other kinds of samples to make a wide variety of choices available. What are the apparent advantages and disadvantages of the different kinds of samples? Urine testing, the standard method for many years, is said to be capable of detecting most kinds of drugs for up to three days, as the drug, or its metabolites, clears the system. But that depends on how much drug was used and on the detection levels set for triggering a positive result: The higher the amount required for a positive result, the shorter the detection time. Setting a lower threshold for a positive result makes the test sensitive for a longer period of time, but it increases the rate of false-positive results. The metabolites of marijuana can be detected in the urine for five days or more. For someone who has been smoking a lot of marijuana for a long time, urine tests may be positive for a couple of weeks or more after the last dose. One concern employers and officials have about urine testing is whether a drug user can beat the test, by substituting a clean urine sample from someone else, by diluting the urine, or by ingesting something that will mask the presence of a drug in the urine. With proper monitoring to avoid sample substitution or dilution, concerns about masking drug use do not seem to be too great. Although Internet companies offer a variety of products that are supposed to help users mask the drug in their urine, the value of these products is questionable.

Hair testing has increased in popularity in recent years. Hair samples are theoretically capable of detecting drug use (based on levels incorporated into the hair as it grows) for up to 90 days. That means that an occasional drug user will be more easily detected with this sampling method. Also, it seems less invasive to ask to take a small sample of someone's hair than to have someone watch while they "pee into the cup." Saliva samples also seem less invasive and are easy to collect. However, they detect only fairly recent drug use, up to one day, in most cases.

Although many employers treat the results of these tests as absolute proof of drug use, there should always be concern about their accuracy. In a large workplace testing program, proper procedure would call for splitting the sample and keeping half for a retest, and submitting known positive samples and known negative samples to the lab along with the actual samples. The biggest practical concern is the rate of false-positive results (the test results indicate drug use when the person did not actually take the drug being tested for). False positives can be caused by legal drugs, or even by some foods (e.g., poppy seeds contain trace amounts of opioids). If 4 percent of those tested actually use methamphetamine, and the test has a 5 percent false-positive rate, then a positive result is more likely due to an error than to actual drug use! The FDA has worked with reputable testing companies over the years to improve the accuracy of their tests, but none is perfect.

Most test kits look for marijuana, opioids, amphetamines, and cocaine. Often one or two other drugs (PCP, MDMA, benzodiazepines) may be included. These drug screens can detect the presence of a drug or its metabolite, but they can't tell anything about the state of impairment of the individual at the time of the test. One person might show up at work Monday morning with a terrible hangover from drinking the night before, be unable to perform well on the job, and pass the drug screen easily. Another person might have smoked marijuana on Friday night, have experienced no effect for the past day and a half, and yet fail the screen. The general idea of the screens seems to be to discourage illicit drug use more than to detect impairment of performance.

The Impact of Drug Enforcement

We can examine the current efforts at enforcing federal drug laws by asking ourselves three questions. What exactly are we doing to enforce drug laws? How much is it costing? How effective is it? Although there had been previous "wars" on illicit drugs, the largest efforts to date began in 1982, when President Reagan announced a renewed and reorganized effort to combat drug trafficking and organized crime. For the first time, all federal agencies were to become involved, including the DEA; FBI; IRS; Alcohol, Tobacco and Firearms Bureau; Immigration and Naturalization; U.S. Marshals; U.S. Customs Service; and Coast Guard. In some regions, Defense Department tracking and pursuit services were added. This last item had been legalized earlier in the Reagan administration and had signaled an important change in the role of the military. The idea of using our military forces to police our population had long been abhorrent to Americans, who had insisted that most police powers remain at the state and local levels. Because of the success of smugglers, we now use Air Force radar and aircraft and Navy patrol boats to detect and track aircraft and boats that might be bringing in drugs. These efforts have continued to expand, and now include unmanned drone aircraft and tethered balloons with video cameras, particularly along the southwestern border with Mexico.

Budget

A good overview of the widespread federal efforts can be obtained from the National Drug Control Strategy review and budget prepared each year by the White House. Budgeting methods changed during both the George W. Bush and the Obama administrations, so it has been difficult to track the overall budget over time. However, the request for FY 2016 was for $27.6 billion. No matter how you measure it, that's a big increase from less than $1 billion in 1980.[17]

International Programs

International efforts aimed at reducing the drug supply include State Department programs that provide aid to individual countries to help them with narcotics controls, usually working in conjunction with the DEA. The DEA has agents in more than 40 countries, and they assist local authorities in eradicating drug crops, locating and destroying illicit laboratories, and interfering with the transportation of drugs out of those countries. The State Department's Bureau of International Narcotics and Law Enforcement Affairs budget includes direct aid tied to drug enforcement and loans and support for countries in Central and South America and in the Middle East to develop alternative crops and industries. The United States is providing increased military aid in the form of helicopters, "defensive" weapons, uniforms, and other supplies to be used in combating drug trafficking, plus military training to both army and police agencies. This program is supposedly restricted to countries that do not engage in a "consistent pattern of gross violations" of human rights.

In a challenge to the international ban on drug trafficking, Uruguay became the first nation to completely legalize the sale and use of marijuana. Some have hailed this move as beneficial to peace in the Americas and even nominated Uruguay's president Mujica for the Nobel Peace Prize. But the chief of the United Nations' Narcotics Control Board has criticized him for violating international treaties.

Other Federal Agencies

Efforts within the United States have broadened to include activities related to drug trafficking. The Department of Homeland Security allocates about $2 billion, or 20 percent of its overall budget, to drug-control efforts, primarily to interdiction efforts by Customs and Border Patrol agents. The Federal Aviation Administration is involved not only in the urine testing of pilots and other airline workers but also in keeping track of private aircraft and small airports that might be used for transporting drug shipments. The Department of Agriculture, Bureau of Land Management, and National Park Service are on the lookout for marijuana crops planted on federal land.

Other Costs

Besides the direct budget for drug-control strategies, there are other costs, only some of which can be measured in dollars. We are paying to house a large number of prisoners: 250,000 drug-law violators in state prisons and local jails and more than 90,000 in federal prisons.[18] Add to this the cost of thousands on probation or parole, plus various forms of juvenile detention. We should also add the cost of crimes committed to purchase drugs at black-market prices and the incalculable price of placing so many of our state and local police, DEA, FBI, and other federal agents in danger of losing their lives to combat the drug trade, as some have done. A price that has been paid by many law enforcement agencies over the years is the corruption that is ever-present in drug enforcement. Because it is necessary for undercover officers to work closely with and to gain the trust of drug dealers, they must sometimes ignore an offense in hopes of gaining information about more and bigger deals in the future. They may even accept small favors from a drug dealer, and some officers have found it necessary to use drugs along with the suspects. Under those circumstances, and given the large amounts of money available to some drug dealers and the small salaries paid to most law officers, the possibility of accepting too large a gift and ignoring too many offenses is always there, and there might be no obvious "line" between doing one's job and becoming slightly corrupted.[19]

There are costs on the international level, too. The United States and most other countries work together to restrict international drug trafficking. However, there have been times when our interest in controlling illicit drug supplies is in conflict with national security issues and one or the other must be compromised. One example would be in Afghanistan, which has a long tradition of growing opium poppies and since 1992 has been the world's leading producer of opium. In May 2001, the U.S. Secretary of State announced a $43 million grant to the Taliban government as a reward for the crackdown on opium production in Afghanistan. Four months later, we were at war against the Taliban government following the attack on the World Trade Center. After the fall of the Taliban and the institution of a government friendly to the United States, opium production increased. This trend has

continued, with 2016 opium production estimated to be 10 percent higher than the previous year, according to the United Nations Office of Drugs and Crime. Politicians in the United States have often tried to characterize this opium production as being conducted primarily in areas controlled by "known terrorist groups," but the truth is that opium production occurs throughout the country and is an important source of income to farmers in government-controlled areas as well. Due to our concerns about supporting the Afghan government, the United States has not concerned itself much with the opium issue in recent years.

Our drug-control efforts sometimes find us providing help to repressive governments, and it has been charged that some of our previous drug-control aid has been used for political repression, in both Latin America and Southeast Asia. To the extent that narcotics-control efforts place additional strains on our foreign policy needs in the East, the Caribbean, and Latin America, this also represents a significant cost to our country.

Finally, there is an unquantifiable cost in the loss of individual freedom that is inevitable when the government acquires increased powers. Because of increased drug-control efforts, American citizens are subjected to on-the-job urine tests; searches of homes, land, and vehicles; computer-coded passports that record each international visit; and increased government access to financial records. Americans are also threatened with seizure of their property and loss of federal benefits.

Given this effort and these costs, are our drug-enforcement efforts effective? Do they work? Critics have pointed out that, despite escalating expenditures, more agents, and an increasing variety of supply-reduction efforts, the supplies of cocaine, heroin, and marijuana have not dried up; in fact, they may have increased. Although there have been record-breaking seizures of cocaine year after year, the price of cocaine has actually decreased since the 1980s. The U.S. government made a decision in 1924 to make heroin completely unavailable to users in this country, and after more than 80 years we can say only that it has been consistent in its

Afghanistan is the largest producer of opium poppies in the world. ©Jan Herodes/123RF RF

failure to accomplish that goal. Our effort to eradicate illegal coca fields in South America was described as a failure by the General Accounting Office, which pointed out that many more new acres were being planted in coca each year than were being destroyed by our program.[20] An economic analysis indicated that, even if eradication and interdiction efforts could result in massive disruption of a particular source country's production, it would take only about two years for the market to push production back to the previous levels.[21]

Illicit drug trade remains a big business, even if most people avoid these substances. The United Nations estimates that only about 5 percent of the world's population uses illicit drugs, yet that amounts to about 250 million people, and a total market value in the hundreds of billions of dollars.[22]

Effectiveness of Control

The laws do work at one level. It is estimated that 10 to 15 percent of the illegal drug supply is seized by federal agencies each year. In 2012, for example, the DEA reported seizing 354,000 kg of marijuana, 36,000 kg of cocaine, 3,900 kg of methamphetamine, and 934 kg of heroin. These efforts have made it difficult and expensive to do business as a major importer. Evidence that supply is restricted can be found in the high prices charged on the streets. The price is many times more than the cost of the drug itself if sold legally. It is likely that the high cost influences the amount taken by some of

these users. Local efforts make a difference, too. Small pushers forced to work out of sight are less able to contact purchasers, and both the buyer and the seller have a higher risk of being hurt or cheated in the transaction. This not only raises the cost of doing business, but it also probably deters some people from trying the drugs. Another kind of success is reported by many of those who are in treatment or who have completed treatment: They probably would not have stopped using when they did if they had not been arrested and offered treatment as an alternative to jail. And, yes, treatment can still work even when people are coerced into going (see Chapter 18).

Summary

- In the early 1900s, two federal laws were passed on which our current drug regulations are based.

- The 1906 Pure Food and Drugs Act, requiring accurate labeling, was amended in 1938 to require safety testing and in 1962 to require testing for effectiveness.

- A company wishing to market a new drug must first test it on animals, then file an IND. After a three-phase sequence of human testing, the company can file the NDA.

- The 1914 Harrison Act regulated the sale of opioids and cocaine.

- The Harrison Act was a tax law, but after 1919 it was enforced as a prohibition against providing drugs to dependent users.

- As drugs became more scarce and their price rose on the illicit market, the illicit market grew. Harsher penalties and increased enforcement efforts, which were the primary strategies of Commissioner of Narcotics Harry Anslinger, failed to reverse the trend.

- Marijuana was added to the list of controlled drugs in 1937, and in 1965 amphetamines, barbiturates, and hallucinogens were also brought under federal control.

- The Controlled Substances Act of 1970 first provided for direct federal regulation of drugs, not through the pretense of taxing their sale.

- Controlled substances are placed on one of five schedules, depending on medical use and dependence potential.

- Amendments in 1988 were aimed at increasing pressure on users, as well as on criminal organizations and money laundering.

- Federal support for drug screening began in the military and has since spread to other federal agencies, nonfederal transportation workers, and many private employers.

- Current federal enforcement efforts involve thousands of federal employees and include activities in other countries, along our borders, and within the United States.

- Most states have adopted some version of the DEA's recommended Uniform Controlled Substances Act.

- Federal, state, and local enforcement limits the supply of drugs and keeps their prices high, but the high prices attract more smugglers and dealers. It will never be possible to eliminate illicit drugs.

Review Questions

1. What four kinds of habit-forming drug use at the start of the 20th century caused social reactions leading to the passage of federal drug laws?

2. What were the two fundamental pieces of federal drug legislation passed in 1906 and 1914?

3. In about what year did it first become necessary for drug companies to demonstrate to the FDA that new drugs were effective for their intended use?

4. What three phases of clinical drug testing are required before a new drug application can be approved?

5. What historic piece of federal legislation did the most to shape our overall approach to the control of habit-forming drugs in the United States?

6. On which of the five schedules is each of these drugs listed: heroin, marijuana, cocaine, methamphetamine?

7. What is the important difference between a Schedule I and a Schedule II controlled substance?

8. What are the limitations of urine screening versus hair sample analysis?

9. Approximately how much is the United States spending per year on federal drug-control efforts?

References

1. Jenness, V. "Explaining Criminalization: From Demography and Status Politics to Globalization and Modernization," *Annual Review of Sociology* 30 (2004), pp. 147–71.
2. Adams, S. H. "The Great American Fraud," *Collier's,* six segments, October 1905 to February 1906.
3. Kane, H. H. *Opium-Smoking in America and China.* New York: G.P. Putnam's Sons, 1882.
4. Musto, D. F. *The American Disease: Origins of Narcotic Control,* 3rd ed. New York: University Press, 1999.
5. Latimer, D., and J. Goldberg. *Flowers in the Blood: The Story of Opium,* New York: Franklin Watts, 1981.
6. Terry, C. E., and M. Pellens. *The Opium Problem.* New York: Bureau of Social Hygiene, 1928.
7. Courtwright, D. T. *Dark Paradise: Opiate Addiction in America before 1940.* Cambridge, MA: Harvard University Press, 1982.
8. Young, J. H. *The Medical Messiahs: A Social History of Health Quackery in Twentieth-Century America.* Princeton, NJ: Princeton University Press, 1967.
9. 2016 *profile.* Washington, DC: Pharmaceutical Manufacturers Association, 2016. Available at: http://phrma.org/sites/default/files/pdf/biopharmaceutical-industry-profile.pdf.
10. Tuttle, B. "Prescription Drug Prices in America Are Rising Like No Other Industry," *Money,* July 14, 2016. Available at: http://time.com/money/4406167/prescription-drug-prices-increase-why/.
11. Schmeckebier, L. F. *The Bureau of Prohibition.* Service Monograph No. 57, Institute for Government Research, 1929, Brookings Institute. Cited in R. King, "Narcotic Drug Laws and Enforcement Policies," *Law & Contemporary Problems* 22, no. 122 (1957).
12. *U.S. News & World Report* 41, no. 22 (1956).
13. Gonçalves, R, A. Lourenço, and S. N. da Silva. "A Social Cost Perspective in the Wake of the Portuguese Strategy for the Fight against Drugs." *International Journal on Drug Policy* 26, no. 2 (2015), pp. 199–209.
14. Paungsawad, G., A. Aramrattana, J. Sintunava, G. Lai, A. Fordham, P. Jinawat, C. Angkurawaranon, J. Jaturapataraporn, A. Wodak, and C. L. Hart. "Bangkok 2016: From Overly

Punitive to Deeply Humane Drug Policies." *Drug and Alcohol Dependence*, in press (2016).

15. United States Sentencing Commission, Guidelines Manual, §3E1.1 (November 2016)

16. Impacteen Illicit Drug Team. *Illicit Drug Policies: Selected Laws from the 50 States.* Berrien Springs, MI: Andrews University, 2002.

17. Office of National Drug Control Policy. *National Drug Control Strategy.* Washington, DC: The White House, 2013.

18. Carson, E. A. *Prisoners in 2014.* Bureau of Justice Statistics, U.S. Department of Justice Bulletin NCJ248955, September 2015.

19. Gray, J. P. *Why Our Drug Laws Have Failed and What We Can Do about It.* Philadelphia: Temple University Press, 2001.

20. Culhane, C. "U.S. Fails in South American Drug War," *U.S. Journal of Drug and Alcohol Dependence,* January 1989.

21. Riley, K. J. *Snow Job?* New Brunswick, NJ: Transaction, 1996.

22. United Nations Office on Drugs and Crime. *World Drug Report 2016.* Available at: https://www.unodc.org/wdr2016/.

Check Yourself

Consider the Consequences

One of the most damaging things that can occur to a person who is working toward a successful and happy life is to get into trouble with the law and establish a criminal record. Many people have done a few things for which they could have been apprehended and either fined or arrested. Perhaps it is only parking illegally for a few minutes or driving a few miles over the speed limit. We all know that we don't get caught every time, or perhaps even most of the time, so there's a certain amount of luck involved. Also, of course, the seriousness of the violation and the ensuing consequence vary quite a bit. Most people can afford to pay a parking fine and it is not considered much of a blemish on their record. However, some people seem to tempt fate more often than others and for higher stakes—in other words, they do things that risk more serious consequences, and they do those things more often. Many of the risks that people take involve the use of substances, and often it seems they have not considered the possible consequences. Create a confidential list of such behaviors in the following table. For each behavior, indicate how often you have done it; whether you have been caught; if so, what the consequences were; and how the consequence or lack of consequence influenced your likelihood of doing it again.

	Behavior			
	Underage smoking	Underage drinking	Driving while intoxicated	Using an illegal drug
Done it? (How often?)				
Caught? (Y/N)				
Consequence				
Influence on future behavior: +, —, none				

How Drugs Work

A drug is nothing but a chemical substance until it comes into contact with a living organism. In fact, that's what defines the difference between drugs and other chemicals—drugs have specific effects on living tissue.

Because this book is about psychoactive drugs, the tissue we're most interested in is the brain. We want to understand how psychoactive drugs interact with brain tissue to produce effects on behavior, thoughts, and emotions.

Obviously, we don't put drugs directly into our brains; usually we swallow them, inhale them, or inject them. In Section Two, we will find out how the drugs we take get to the brain, and what effects they might have on the other tissues of the body.

4

The Nervous System

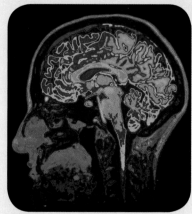

©SpeedKingz/Shutterstock.com RF

Drugs are psychoactive, for the most part, because they alter ongoing functions in the brain. To understand how drugs influence behavior and psychological processes, it is necessary to have some knowledge of the normal functioning of the brain and other parts of the nervous system and then to see how drugs can alter those normal functions. Our goal in this chapter is to introduce basic concepts and terminology that will help you understand the effects of psychoactive drugs on the brain and, ultimately, on behavior. The knowledge acquired here should also help you understand the limitations of applying an exclusively biological approach to the study of psychoactive drug effects.

Objectives

When you have finished this chapter, you should be able to:

- **Understand how psychoactive drugs alter communication among the billions of cells in the human brain.**

- **Explain the concept of homeostasis.**

- **Know the general properties of glia and neurons.**

- **Understand and describe the action potential.**

- **Describe the roles of the sympathetic and parasympathetic branches of the autonomic nervous system and associated neurotransmitters.**

- **Be able to associate important neurotransmitters with key brain structures and chemical pathways, and describe the major functions of the neurotransmitters.**

- **Describe the life cycle of a neurotransmitter molecule.**

- **Understand the importance of receptor subtypes in determining the action of a neurotransmitter at a particular site in the brain.**

- **Give examples of a drug that alters neurotransmitter availability and of a drug that interacts with neurotransmitter receptors.**

Homeostasis

Since the first multicellular organisms oozed about in their primordial tidal pools, some form of cell-to-cell communication has been necessary to ensure the organism's survival. Those first organisms probably needed to coordinate only a few functions, such as getting nutrients into the system, distributing them to all of the cells, and then eliminating wastes. At that level of organization, perhaps one cell excreting a chemical that could act on neighboring cells was all that was necessary. As more complex organisms evolved with multicellular systems for sensation, movement, reproduction, and temperature regulation, the sophistication of these communication mechanisms increased markedly. It became necessary for many types of communication to go on simultaneously and over greater distances.

Although those early organisms were at the mercy of the sea environment in which they lived, we carry our own seawater-like cellular environment around with us and must maintain that internal environment within certain limits. This process is known as **homeostasis.** This word can be loosely translated as "staying the same," and it describes the fact that many biological factors are maintained at or near certain levels. For example, most of the biochemical reactions basic to the maintenance of life are temperature dependent, in that these reactions occur optimally at temperatures near 37°C (98.6°F). Because we cannot live at temperatures too much above or below this level, our bodies have many mechanisms to either raise or lower temperature: perspiring, shivering, altering blood flow to the skin, and others. Similar homeostatic mechanisms regulate the acidity, water content, and sodium content of the blood; glucose concentrations; and other physical and chemical factors that are important for biological functioning.

Psychoactive drugs can also influence homeostasis. For example, alcohol inhibits the release of the **antidiuretic** hormone vasopressin, which causes an increase in the excretion of urine. Two lines of evidence suggest that homeostatic processes mobilize to counteract some alcohol-related effects: (1) Following consumption of alcohol, heavy drinkers have less urine output than do infrequent drinkers; and (2) during alcohol withdrawal, heavy drinkers exhibit an increased vasopressin release, resulting in greater water retention.[1]

Components of the Nervous System

The body's tissues and organs are composed of cells. The specific functions and interactions of these cells determine the functions of organs. The brain is the organ of most interest for our purpose—the study of psychoactive drugs. Here we focus on the structure of the two types of cells found throughout the nervous system: (1) *neurons,* sometimes referred to as nerve cells and (2) *glia,* also called glial cells.

Neurons

Neurons are the primary elements of the nervous system responsible for analyzing and transmitting information. Everything that we see and understand as behavior is dependent upon the functioning of these cells. The nervous system contains more than 100 billion neurons, and each can influence or be influenced by hundreds of other neurons and glia. Before we can understand how neurons produce behavior, we must first become familiar with a few basic facts. Each neuron is contained within a single **membrane** that separates the inside of the neuron from the outside. All have four morphologically defined regions: (1) **cell body,** (2) **dendrites,** (3) **axon,** and (4) **axon terminals** (see Figure 4.1). These regions contribute to the neuron's ability to communicate with other neurons. The cell body contains the processes that maintain the life of the

---

homeostasis: maintenance of an environment of body functions within a certain range (e.g., temperature, blood pressure).

antidiuretic: the suppression of urine production.

membrane: a thin, limiting covering of a cell.

cell body: the central region of a neuron, which is the control center.

dendrites: branchlike structures that extend from the cell body and specialize in receiving signals from other neurons.

axon: a thin tube that extends from the cell body and specializes in transmitting signals to other neurons.

axon terminals: the end region of the axon.

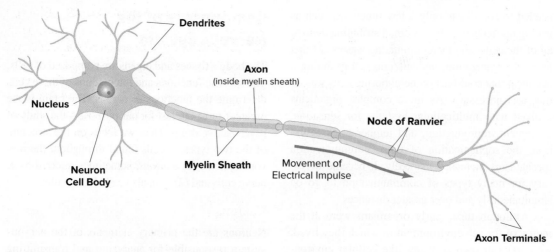

Figure 4.1   Every Neuron Has Four Regions: Cell Body, Dendrites, Axon, and Axon Terminals

neuron, including the nucleus, which stores the genetic material of the cell, as well as the endoplasmic reticulum, where the cell's proteins are made. Extending from one end of the cell body are branchlike projections called dendrites; the other end contains one long, tubular structure called an axon. Dendrites are the main mechanism through which incoming signals from other neurons are received. Located within their membranes are **receptors,** specialized structures that recognize and respond to specific chemical signals. Axons, by contrast, specialize in transmitting signals to other neurons. Located at the end of the axons are bulbous structures called axon terminals. **Neurotransmitters** are stored in the terminals in small, round packages known as **synaptic vesicles**.

Glia

About 90 percent of the cells in the human brain are glia.[2] The word *glia* derives from the Greek word meaning "glue," which provides some insight into how early neuroscientists viewed the role of these cells. Indeed, glia provide several important functions that help to ensure the survival of the organism, including providing firmness and structure to the brain, getting nutrients in the system, eliminating waste, and forming **myelin**. Myelin is a white fatty substance that is wrapped around the axons of some

neurons to form a myelin sheath, which increases the information-processing speed of these neurons. The **autoimmune disease multiple sclerosis** results from a loss of myelin wrappings.

Another important function of glia is to create the **blood-brain barrier,** a barrier between the blood and the fluid that surrounds neurons. This **semipermeable** structure protects the brain from potentially toxic chemicals circulating in the blood. For a drug to be psychoactive, its molecules must be capable of passing through the blood-brain barrier.

Many neuroscientists thought the role of glia was limited to the functions described above. This simplistic view has been challenged because mounting evidence demonstrates that glia also have communication capabilities. Nonetheless, we remain confident that neurons perform the majority of information processing in the brain. Therefore, we focus the bulk of our attention on neurons.

Neurotransmission

Have you ever wondered how local anesthetics, such as those used by dentists, block the perception of pain? After a brief discussion of the basic concepts of **neurotransmission,** you will be better able to understand how local anesthetics and other drugs work to alter perception, mood, and behavior.

Action Potential

The production of even simple behavioral acts requires complex interactions between the individual's environment and nerve cells. Here we focus on only one element of this complex interaction—the communication between neurons. Such communication is accomplished through a highly specialized, precise, and rapid method. An essential process for neuronal communication is the **action potential** (see Figure 4.2). This electrical signal initiates a chain of events that allows one neuron to communicate with another through the release of neurotransmitters. The action potential occurs as a result of the opening of **ion channels** that allow electrically charged particles called **ions** to move inside of the cell. This change moves the cell's membrane away from its **resting potential** to a more positively charged voltage. When the cell membrane is at rest, there is an uneven distribution of ions between the inside and outside of the cell. Specifically, there are more potassium (K^+) ions and negatively charged organic anions on the inside of the cell, while there are more sodium (Na^+) and chloride (Cl^-) ions on the outside of the cell. The uneven distribution of ions and opened K^+ channels are the sources of the negative resting potential across the membrane. In this state, the neuron is **hyperpolarized.**

A sequential opening and closing of ion channels in the neuron's membrane generates the action potential. As Na^+ channels open, Na^+ ions rapidly move across the membrane into the cell. As a result, the cell is **depolarized.** If the cell is depolarized to the threshold of excitation, an all-or-none action potential will occur. We refer to the action potential as all-or-none because once initiated it will travel to the axon terminal without decrement. During the action potential, additional Na^+ channels open, allowing the influx of even more Na^+ ions. Near the peak of the action potential, more K^+ channels now open, while Na^+ channels close. The now positive internal state of the cell causes K^+ ions to exit the cell, which causes the membrane potential to become even more negative than it is at rest. Once K^+ channels close, the cell will return to its normal resting level.

Suppose we selectively blocked Na^+ channels? What would be the effect? Selective blockade of Na^+ channels prevents the action potential and thus disrupts communication between neurons. Selective blockade of Na^+ channels is the mechanism through which drugs such as cocaine and other local anesthetics reduce pain. Cocaine was the first

receptors: recognition mechanisms that respond to specific chemical signals.

neurotransmitter: chemical messengers released from axon terminals.

synaptic vesicles: small bubbles of membrane that store neurotransmitters.

myelin: a fatty white substance that is wrapped around portions of the axons.

autoimmune disease: a condition that occurs when the immune system mistakenly attacks and destroys healthy body tissue.

multiple sclerosis: an autoimmune disease caused by damage to the myelin sheath that wraps axons. A wide range of symptoms can accompany this disorder including muscle spasms, vision loss, severe pain, dizziness, fatigue, and intestinal problems.

blood-brain barrier: the structure that prevents many drugs from entering the brain.

semipermeable: allowing some, but not all, chemicals to pass.

neurotransmission: the process of transferring information from one neuron to another at a synapse.

action potential: the electrical signal transmitted along the axon when a neuron fires.

ion channels: pores formed in the cell membrane that allow the passage of ions from one side of the membrane to the other.

ion: an atom or molecule that has a net electrical charge because of a difference in the number of electrons and protons.

resting potential: the voltage maintained by a cell when it is not generating action potentials. The resting potential of neurons is about −65 mV.

hyperpolarized: when the membrane potential is more negative.

depolarized: when the membrane potential is less negative.

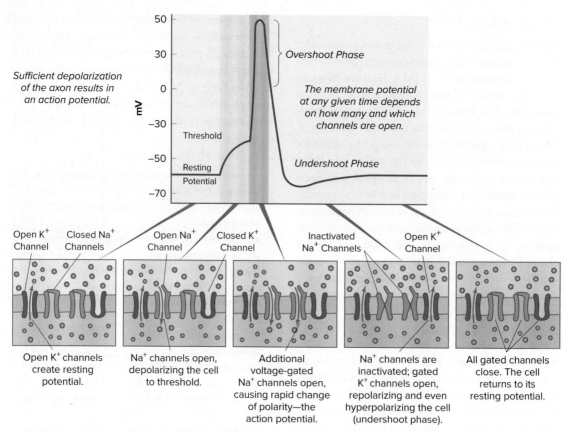

Figure 4.2 Action Potential
SOURCE: Rosenzweig et al.: *Biological Psychology,* Second Edition, Sinauer Associates, Inc., Sunderland, MA (1999).

local anesthetic, although it has been largely replaced by newer drugs for this purpose. Newer local anesthetics are simple modifications of the cocaine molecule. Slight chemical alterations of the cocaine structure can yield compounds that do not readily cross the blood-brain barrier and therefore do not produce cocainelike psychoactive effects.

The Nervous System(s)

Somatic Nervous System

The nerve cells that are on the "front lines," interacting with the external environment, are referred to as the *somatic* system. These peripheral nerves carry sensory information into the central nervous system and carry motor (movement) information back out. The cranial nerves that relate to vision, hearing, taste, smell, chewing, and movements of the tongue and face are included, as are spinal nerves carrying information from the skin and joints and controlling movements of the arms and legs. We think of this system as serving voluntary actions. For example, a decision to move your leg results in activity in large cells in the motor cortex of your brain. These cells have long axons, which extend down to the spinal motor neurons. These neurons also have long axons, which are bundled together to form nerves, which travel out directly to the muscles. The neurotransmitter at neuromuscular junctions in the somatic system is **acetylcholine,** which acts on receptors that excite the muscle.

Table 4.1
Sympathetic and Parasympathetic Effects on Selected Structures

Structure or Function	Sympathetic Reaction	Parasympathetic Reaction
Pupil	Dilation	Constriction
Heart rate	Increase	Decrease
Breathing rate	Fast and shallow	Slow and deep
Stomach and intestinal glands	Inhibition	Activation
Stomach and intestinal wall	No motility	Motility
Sweat glands	Secretion	No effect
Skin blood vessels	Constriction	Dilation
Bronchi	Relaxation	Constriction

Autonomic Nervous System

Your body's internal environment is monitored and controlled by the **autonomic** nervous system (ANS), which regulates the visceral, or involuntary, functions of the body, such as heart rate and blood pressure. Many psychoactive drugs have simultaneous effects in the brain and on the ANS. The ANS is also where chemical neurotransmission was first studied. If the vagus nerve in a frog is electrically stimulated, its heart slows. If the fluid surrounding that heart is then withdrawn and placed around a second frog's heart, it, too, will slow. This is an indication that electrical activity in the vagus nerve causes a chemical to be released onto the frog's heart muscle. We now know that this is acetylcholine, the same chemical that stimulates muscle contraction in our arms and legs. Because a different type of receptor is found in the heart, acetylcholine inhibits heart muscle contraction. An important lesson here is that the same neurotransmitter can have different effects depending on the receptor being activated.

The ANS is divided into **sympathetic** and **parasympathetic** branches. The inhibition of heart rate by the vagus nerve is an example of the parasympathetic branch; acetylcholine is the neurotransmitter at the end organ. In the sympathetic branch, **norepinephrine** is the neurotransmitter at the end organ. Table 4.1 gives examples of parasympathetic and sympathetic influences on various systems. Note that often, but not always, the two systems oppose each other.

Because the sympathetic system is interconnected, it tends to act more as a unit, to open the bronchi, reduce blood supply to the skin, increase the heart rate, and reduce stomach motility. This has been called the "fight-or-flight" response and is elicited in many emotion-arousing circumstances in humans and other animals. Amphetamines, because they have a chemical structure that resembles

acetylcholine (eh see till co leen): neurotransmitter found in the parasympathetic branch in the cerebral cortex.
autonomic: the part of the nervous system that controls "involuntary" functions, such as heart rate.
sympathetic: the branch of the autonomic system involved in fight-or-flight reactions.
parasympathetic: the branch of the autonomic system that stimulates digestion, slows the heart, and has other effects associated with a relaxed physiological state.
norepinephrine: neurotransmitter that may be important for regulating waking and appetite.

norepinephrine, stimulate these functions in addition to their effects on the brain. Those drugs that activate the sympathetic branch are referred to as sympathomimetic drugs.

Central Nervous System

The **central nervous system (CNS)** consists of the brain and spinal cord. These two structures form a central mass of nervous tissue, with sensory nerves coming in and motor nerves going out. This is where most of the integration of information, learning and memory, and coordination of activity occur.

The Brain

Chemical Pathways Implicated in Reward

Although many neurotransmitters have been identified, we are concerned mostly with those few we believe to be associated with the actions of the psychoactive drugs we are studying. Those neurotransmitters include dopamine, acetylcholine, norepinephrine, serotonin, GABA, and glutamate. We will also discuss a few **neuropeptides** that are involved in the actions of psychoactive drugs.

Dopamine In some cases, groups of cells in a particular brain region contain a particular neurotransmitter, and axons from these cells are found grouped together and terminating in another brain region. We think of many psychoactive drug actions in terms of a drug's effect on one of these chemical pathways. For example, we know that cells in the **nucleus accumbens** receive input from **dopamine** fibers that arise in the **ventral tegmental area** in the midbrain to form the **mesolimbic dopamine pathway** (see Figure 4.3). This pathway has been proposed to mediate some types of psychotic behavior such as those seen in **schizophrenia.** That is, overactivation of dopamine neurons in this pathway produces hallucinations, which are attenuated by dopamine-blocking drugs. This example highlights an important point and provides the basis for many neurochemical theories of behavior: *Malfunctions of neurotransmitter systems lead to disease states, which can be treated with drugs that target the affected system.*

The most prominent neurochemical theory of drug abuse is based on the idea that all rewarding drugs, from alcohol to methamphetamine, stimulate

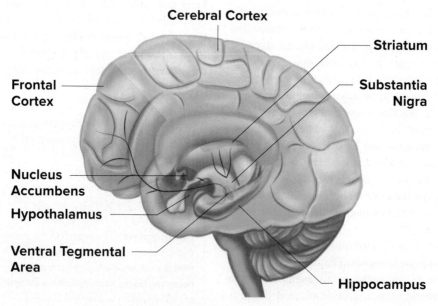

Figure 4.3 Mesolimbic and Nigrostriatal Dopamine Pathways

dopamine neurons in the mesolimbic pathway. This same pathway is proposed to be activated by the electrical stimulation that some animals apparently find rewarding. According to this major theory, drugs lead to abuse because they stimulate this reward system, which is responsible for telling the rest of the brain "that's good—do that again."

Over the past decade, mounting contradictory evidence has challenged this simplistic view of reward. For example, although initial depletion of dopamine in the nucleus accumbens produces reductions in cocaine self-administration by rodents, cocaine self-administration is reinstated long before restoration of nucleus accumbens dopamine levels.[3] In addition, several studies using human research volunteers show that drugs that block dopamine activity do not reduce euphoria produced by cocaine.[4] Together, these are just some of the findings that suggest that nondopamine mechanisms play a role in the rewarding effects of psychoactive drugs. Further, they call into question the simplistic view of dopamine's role in drug reward.

Another important dopamine pathway also begins in the midbrain—the **nigrostriatal dopamine pathway.** Cells from the **substantia nigra** course together past the **hypothalamus,** and terminate in the **striatum** to form this pathway. Substantial loss of cells along this pathway leads to **Parkinson's disease;** as a result, Parkinson's disease can be defined as a dopamine-deficiency disorder. Accordingly, treatment of Parkinson's disease consists of administering the dopamine **precursor** *L*-dopa. Once in the brain, *L*-dopa is rapidly converted to dopamine, temporarily restoring brain dopamine concentrations and relieving many symptoms related to Parkinson's disease. Dopamine itself is not administered as a treatment because it does not readily cross the blood-brain barrier.

Acetylcholine Pathways containing acetylcholine arise from cell bodies in the **nucleus basalis** in the lower part of the brain and project widely throughout the **cerebral cortex.** Nucleus basalis–cortex projections have been implicated in learning and memory. Cells in this region are damaged in patients

with **Alzheimer's disease.** The cortex of these patients has also been observed to contain lower levels of acetylcholine. This observation, coupled with

central nervous system (CNS): brain and spinal cord.

neuropeptides: small proteinaceous substances produced and released by neurons that act on neural targets.

nucleus accumbens: a collection of neurons in the forebrain that plays an important role in reward and emotional reactions to events.

dopamine (*dope ah meen*): neurotransmitter found in the basal ganglia and other regions.

ventral tegmental area: a group of dopamine-containing neurons located in the midbrain whose axons project to the forebrain, especially the nucleus accumbens and cortex.

mesolimbic (meh zo *lim* bick) dopamine pathway: one of two major dopamine pathways; may be involved in psychotic reactions and in drug reward.

schizophrenia: a mental disorder characterized by chronic psychosis.

nigrostriatal dopamine pathway: one of two major dopamine pathways; damaged in Parkinson's disease.

substantia nigra: a dopamine-rich midbrain structure that projects to the striatum.

hypothalamus: a structure found near the bottom of the forebrain. It participates in the regulation of hunger, thirst, sexual behavior, and aggression.

striatum: a term used to describe the caudate nucleus and putamen. Located in the forebrain, it is involved in the initiation of body movements and procedural memory.

Parkinson's disease: a movement disorder involving damage to and/or loss of dopamine neurons along the nigrostriatal dopamine pathway. Major symptoms include tremors, rigidity of the limbs, postural instability, and difficulty initiating movements.

precursors: chemicals that are acted on by enzymes to form neurotransmitters.

nucleus basalis: a group of neurons of the basal forebrain that send projections throughout the cortex.

cerebral cortex: the outermost layer of the brain.

Alzheimer's disease: a progressive brain disease that destroys memory and thinking skills.

evidence showing that acetylcholine blockers impair memory, suggest that replenishing acetylcholine functioning would be a useful treatment strategy for Alzheimer's disease. Of the five available treatment medications, all but one enhance the function of acetylcholine.

Norepinephrine Pathways arising from the *locus ceruleus* in the brain stem have numerous branches and project both up and down in the brain, releasing norepinephrine and influencing the level of arousal and attentiveness. It is perhaps through these pathways that stimulant drugs induce wakefulness. Norepinephrine pathways play an important role in the initiation of food intake, although other transmitter systems are also involved in the very important and therefore very complex processes of controlling energy balance and body weight.

Serotonin Serotonin-containing pathways arise from the brain-stem **raphe nuclei** and have projections both upward into the brain and downward into the spinal cord. Animal research has suggested one or more roles for serotonin in the complex control of food intake and the regulation of body weight. The diet drug sibutramine produces its weight-reducing effects by blocking the reuptake of serotonin and norepinephrine.[5] Research on aggressiveness and impulsivity has also focused on serotonin. In studies with monkeys, low levels of serotonin metabolites in the blood have been associated with impulsive aggression, as well as with excessive alcohol consumption. And recent studies indicate a role for serotonin system dysfunction in individuals who commit suicide.[6] The success of selective serotonin reuptake inhibitors, such as Prozac, in treating major depressive disorder has also led to theories linking serotonin to depression. In all these cases (food intake and weight control, aggression and impulsivity, alcohol use, and depression), environmental influences play important roles, and other drugs that work through different neurotransmitter systems can also influence these behaviors. Therefore, it is much too simple to attribute these behavioral problems to low serotonin

levels alone. In Chapter 14, we will discuss the role played by serotonin receptors in the actions of some hallucinogenic drugs.

GABA (γ-amino butyric acid) GABA is one neurotransmitter that is *not* neatly organized into discrete pathways or bundles. GABA is found in most areas of the CNS and exerts generalized inhibitory functions. Many sedative drugs act by enhancing GABA inhibition (see Chapter 7). The recreational drug GHB (γ-hydroxy butyrate) is a close chemical relative of the neurotransmitter GABA. Interfering with normal GABA inhibition, such as with the GABA-receptor-blocking drug strychnine, can lead to seizures resembling those seen in epilepsy.

Glutamate Glutamate, like GABA, is found throughout the brain, and nearly all neurons have receptors that are activated by it. But, unlike GABA, stimulation of receptors that respond to glutamate makes cells more excitable. Thus, glutamate is often referred to as the brain's major excitatory neurotransmitter. In recent years, increasing amounts of evidence indicate that specific glutamate pathways may be important for the expression of some psychoactive drug effects. For instance, abnormal glutamate transmission, caused by prolonged chronic cocaine use, in the projection from the prefrontal cortex to the nucleus accumbens has been hypothesized to mediate relapse to cocaine use following a period of drug abstinence.[7] Nearly all of the data supporting this hypothesis have been obtained using laboratory animals. Therefore, clinical implications of altered glutamate transmission in substance abuse remain unclear.

Neuropeptides and Other Neuroactive Substances
Neurotransmitters are not the only neuroactive substances found in the brain. Neuropeptides are small protein-like substances produced in the cell body, whereas neurotransmitters are mainly produced in the axon terminal. The study of neuropeptides is particularly important because some have been implicated in pleasure and pain, areas of direct interest for our purposes.

Several neuropeptides in the brain produce effects similar to those of morphine and other drugs derived from opium. The term **endorphin** was coined in reference to endogenous (coming from within) morphinelike substances. These substances are known to play a role in pain relief, but they are found in several places in the brain as well as circulating in the blood, and not all their functions are known. Although it is tempting to theorize about the role of endorphins in drug abuse or dependence, the actual evidence linking dependence to endorphins has not been strong, and other neurotransmitter systems (particularly dopamine and serotonin systems) have also been shown to influence behaviors related to drug abuse.

Oxytocin has been suggested to facilitate social bonding. Indirect evidence has been obtained from studies showing that 3,4-methylenedioxymethamphetamine (MDMA) increased participants' ratings on sociability and plasma oxytocin levels.

The brain also has chemicals that produce effects similar to those produced by **Δ**9-tetrahydrocannabinol (THC), the main psychoactive component of cannabis. These endogenous neuroactive substances are called **endocannabinoids** and are widely distributed throughout the brain. Endocannabinoids do not act as standard neurotransmitters, which influence the activity of the postsynaptic cell (see Figure 4.4). Endocannabinoids influence the firing rate of the presynaptic cell.

Structures

Knowing about a few structures can also make it easier to understand some of the effects of psychoactive drugs. When looking at the brain of most mammals, and especially of a human, much of what one can see consists of *cortex,* a layer of tissue that covers the top and sides of the upper parts of the brain. Some areas of the cortex are known to be involved in processing visual information; other areas are involved in processing auditory or somatosensory information. Relatively smaller cortical areas are involved in the control of muscles (motor cortex), and large areas are referred to as association areas. Higher mental processes, such as

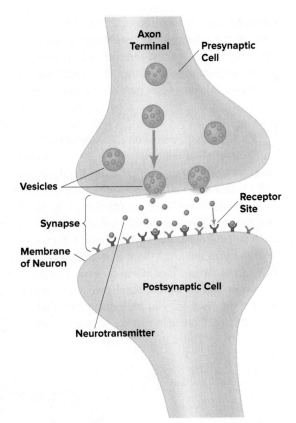

Figure 4.4   Schematic representation of the release of neurotransmitter molecules from synaptic vesicles in the axon terminal of one neuron and the passage of those molecules across the synapse to receptors in the membrane of another neuron.

serotonin (sehr o *tone* in): neurotransmitter found in the raphe nuclei; may be important for impulsivity, depression.

raphe nuclei: a group of serotonin-containing neurons found in the brain stem and project widely throughout the brain.

GABA: inhibitory neurotransmitter found in most regions of the brain.

glutamate: excitatory neurotransmitter found in most regions of the brain.

endorphin: opiate-like chemical that occurs naturally in the brain of humans and other animals.

endocannabinoids: cannabis-like chemicals that occur naturally in the brains of humans and other animals.

reasoning and language, occur in the cortex. In an alert, awake individual, arousal mechanisms keep the cortex active. When a person is asleep or under the influence of sedating drugs, the cortex is much less active, whereas other parts of the brain might be equally active whether a person is awake or asleep.

Underneath the cortex on each side of the brain and hidden from external view are the **basal ganglia.** A primary component of the basal ganglia is the striatum, which is a part of the nigrostriatal dopamine pathway. Thus, one function of the basal ganglia is to help maintain proper muscle tone. Too much output from these structures results in muscular rigidity in the arms, legs, and facial muscles. This can occur as a side effect of some psychoactive drugs that act on the basal ganglia, or it can occur if the basal ganglia are damaged by Parkinson's disease. Note also that the striatum receives

widespread projections from cells in the cortex and serves as the primary source of basal ganglia input. Given that a major function of the cortex is to facilitate cognitive operations, it is not surprising that the basal ganglia are critical for specific aspects of learning.[8]

The *hypothalamus* is a small structure near the base of the brain just above the pituitary gland (see Figure 4.5). The hypothalamus is an important link between the brain and the hormonal output of the pituitary and is thus involved in feeding, drinking, temperature regulation, and sexual behavior.

The *limbic system* consists of a number of connected structures (e.g., amygdala, hippocampus) that are involved in emotion, memory for location, and level of physical activity. Together with the hypothalamus, the limbic system involves important mechanisms for behavioral control at a more primitive level than that of the cerebral cortex.

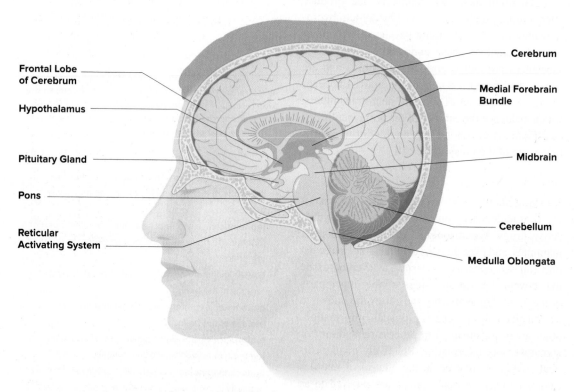

Figure 4.5   Cross Section of the Brain: Major Structures

The midbrain, pons, and medulla are the parts of the brain stem that connect the larger structures of the brain to the spinal cord. Within these brain-stem structures are many groups of cell bodies (nuclei) that play important roles in sensory and motor reflexes as well as coordinated control of complex movements. Within these brain-stem structures also lie the nuclei that contain most of the cell bodies for the neurons that produce and release the neurotransmitters dopamine, norepinephrine, and serotonin. Virtually all of the brain's supply of these important neurotransmitters is produced by a relatively small number of neurons (a few thousand for each neurotransmitter) located in these brain-stem regions.

The lower *brain stem* contains a couple of small areas of major importance. One such area is the medulla oblongata (see Figure 4.5). Within the medulla oblongata is a region called the **area postrema**; this region is also referred to as the vomiting center. Often when the brain detects foreign substances in the blood, such as alcohol or opioids, this center is activated, and vomiting results. It is easy to see the survival value of such a system to animals, including humans, who have it. Another medulla oblongata center regulates the rate of breathing. Sedatives, opioids, and other drugs can suppress the respiratory center, causing respiratory depression, which can lead to death.

Drugs and the Brain

A drug is carried to the brain by the blood supply. How does each drug know where to go once it gets into the brain? The answer is that the drug goes everywhere. But, because the drug molecules of LSD, for example, have their effect by acting on serotonin systems, LSD affects the brain systems that depend on serotonin. The LSD molecules that reach other types of receptors appear to have no particular effect. Because the brain is so well supplied with blood, an equilibrium develops quickly for most drugs, so that the drug's concentration in the brain is about equal to that in the blood and the number of molecules leaving the blood is equal to the number leaving the brain to enter the blood. As the drug is removed from the blood (by the liver or kidneys) and the concentration in the blood decreases, more molecules leave the brain than enter it, and the brain levels begin to decrease.

We are currently able to explain the mechanisms by which many psychoactive drugs act on the brain. In most of these cases, the drug has its effects because the molecular structure of the drug is similar to the molecular structure of one of the neurotransmitter chemicals. Because of this structural similarity, the drug molecules interact with one or more of the stages in the life cycle of that neurotransmitter chemical. We can therefore understand some of the ways drugs act on the brain by looking at the life cycle of a typical neurotransmitter molecule.

Life Cycle of a Neurotransmitter

Neurotransmitter molecules are made inside the cell from which they are to be released. If they were just floating around everywhere in the brain, then the release of a tiny amount from a nerve ending wouldn't have much information value. However, the precursors from which the neurotransmitter will be made are found circulating in the blood supply and generally in the brain. A cell that is going to make a particular neurotransmitter needs to bring in the right precursor in a greater concentration than exists outside the cell, so machinery is built into that cell's membrane for active **uptake** of the precursor. In this process, the cell expends energy to bring the precursor into the cell, even though the concentration inside the cell is already higher than that outside the cell. Obviously, this uptake mechanism must be selective and must recognize the

basal ganglia: subcortical brain structures controlling muscle tone.

area postrema: a region of the brain stem, located in the medulla oblongata, that is important for triggering nausea and vomiting.

uptake: an energy-requiring mechanism by which selected molecules are taken into cells.

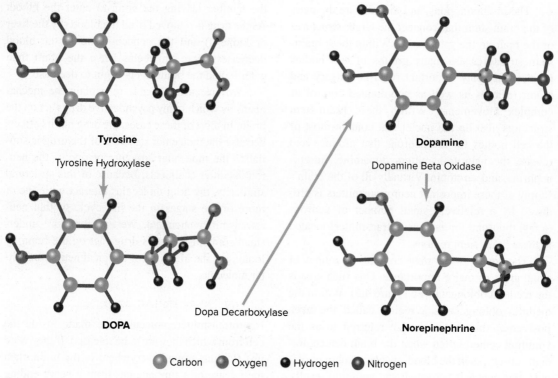

Figure 4.6 Neurons Use Enzymes to Synthesize the Neurotransmitters Dopamine and Norepinephrine

precursor molecules as they float by. Many of the precursors are amino acids that are derived from proteins in the diet, and these amino acids are used in the body for many things besides making neurotransmitters. In the example diagram of the life cycle of the neurotransmitter norepinephrine in Figure 4.6, the amino acid tyrosine is recognized by the norepinephrine neuron, which expends energy to take it in.

After the precursor molecule has been taken up into the neuron, it must be changed, through one or more chemical reactions, into the neurotransmitter molecule. This process is called **synthesis.** At each step in the synthetic chemical reactions, the reactions are helped along by **enzymes.** These enzymes are themselves large molecules that recognize the precursor molecule, attach to it briefly, and hold it in such a way as to make the synthetic chemical reaction occur. Figure 4.7 provides a schematic

representation of such a synthetic enzyme in action. In our example diagram of the life cycle of the catecholamine neurotransmitters dopamine and norepinephrine (Figure 4.6), the precursor tyrosine is acted on first by one enzyme to make DOPA and then by another enzyme to make dopamine. In dopamine cells the process stops there, but in our norepinephrine neuron, a third enzyme is present to change dopamine into norepinephrine.

After the neurotransmitter molecules have been synthesized, they are stored in synaptic vesicles near the terminal from which they will be released. This storage process also calls for recognizing the transmitter molecules and concentrating them inside the vesicles.

The arrival of the action potential in the presynaptic terminals causes calcium (Ca^{2+}) channels to open. Calcium enters the cells and assists the movement of the small vesicles filled with

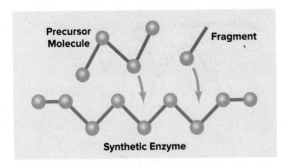

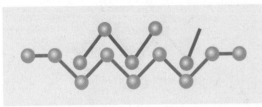

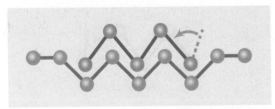

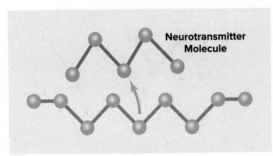

Figure 4.7   Schematic representation of the action of a synthetic enzyme. A precursor molecule and another chemical fragment both bind to the enzyme. The fragment has a tendency to connect with the precursor, but the connection is made much more likely because of the way the enzyme lines up the two parts. After the connection is made, the new transmitter molecule separates from the enzyme.

neurotransmitter toward the axon terminal membrane so that the neurotransmitter is released into the **synapse.** Several thousand neurotransmitter molecules are released at once, and it takes only microseconds for these molecules to diffuse across

the synapse. Once neurotransmitters are released into the synapse, they may bind with receptors on the membrane of the next neuron, sometimes referred to as the postsynaptic cell (see Figure 4.4). This receptor is the most important recognition site in the entire process, and it is one of the most important places for drugs to interact with the natural neurotransmitter. In the process of binding, the neurotransmitter distorts the receptor, so that a tiny passage is opened through the membrane, allowing ions to move through the membrane. As a result, the postsynaptic cell can either become more or less excitable, and thus more or less likely to initiate an action potential.

Whether the effect of a neurotransmitter is excitatory or inhibitory depends on the type of receptor. There are specific receptors for each neurotransmitter, and most neurotransmitters have more than one type of receptor in the brain. For example, the neurotransmitter GABA has at least three receptor subtypes—$GABA_A$, $GABA_B$, and $GABA_C$—and stimulation of all seem to make the cell less excitable. Therefore, GABA is often called an inhibitory neurotransmitter. Many of the sedative-like effects produced by drugs such as barbiturates and benzodiazepines are dependent upon their binding to the $GABA_A$ receptors. Acetylcholine also acts at multiple receptors in the brain: muscarinic and nicotinic. At least five muscarinic receptor subtypes and at least 11 nicotinic receptor subtypes have been identified, and acetylcholine's action can be either excitatory or inhibitory, depending on the receptor stimulated.

Because signaling in the nervous system occurs at a high rate, once a signal has been sent in the form of neurotransmitter release, it is important to terminate that signal, so that the next signal can be transmitted. Thus, the thousands of

synthesis: the forming of a neurotransmitter by the action of enzymes on precursors.

enzyme: a large molecule that assists in either the synthesis or metabolism of another molecule.

synapse: the space between neurons.

neurotransmitter molecules released by a single action potential must be removed from the synapse. Two methods are used for this. The neurons that release the monoamine neurotransmitters serotonin, dopamine, and norepinephrine have specific **transporters** built into their terminals. The serotonin transporter recognizes serotonin molecules and brings them back into the releasing neuron, thus ending their interaction with serotonin receptors. The dopamine transporter and norepinephrine transporter are specific to their neurotransmitters, also. With other neurotransmitters, enzymes in the synapse **metabolize,** or break down, the molecules (see Figure 4.8). In either case, as soon as neurotransmitter molecules are released into the synapse, some of them are removed or metabolized and never get to bind to the receptors on the other neuron. All neurotransmitter molecules might be removed in less than one-hundredth of a second from the time they are released. In the case of our example neurotransmitter, norepinephrine, those molecules are rapidly taken back up into the neuron from which they were released. Once inside the neuron, the norepinephrine molecules are metabolized by an enzyme found in the cell.

Examples of Drug Actions

It is possible to divide the actions of drugs on neurotransmitter systems into two main types. Through actions on synthesis, storage, release, reuptake, or metabolism, drugs can alter the *availability of the neurotransmitter in the synapse.* Perhaps one of the most interesting mechanisms is interference with the transporters that clear neurotransmitters, such as dopamine, norepinephrine, and serotonin, from the synapse by bringing them back into the neuron from which they were just released. Cocaine and most antidepressant drugs block one or more of these transporters and cause the normally released neurotransmitter to remain in the synapse longer than usual.

The second main way a drug can exert its effects is *directly on the receptor.* A drug can act as an **agonist** by mimicking the action of the neurotransmitter and directly activating the receptor, or

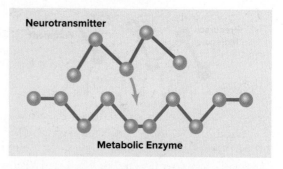

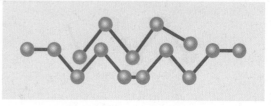

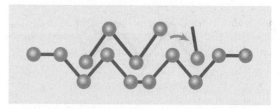

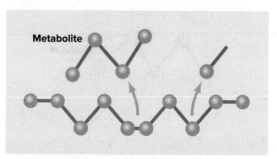

Figure 4.8   Schematic representation of the action of a metabolic enzyme. The transmitter molecule binds to the enzyme in such a way that the transmitter molecule is distorted and "pulled apart." The fragments then separate from the enzyme.

it can act as an **antagonist** by occupying the receptor and preventing the neurotransmitter from activating it. The opioid agonist, heroin, mimics the action of endorphins at opioid receptors and produces many of the same behavioral and physiological effects. By contrast, the opioid antagonist, naloxone, binds to the same opioid receptors but does not stimulate these receptors. Instead, it simply prevents endorphins and other opioid agonists from activating the receptors.

Chemical Theories of Behavior

Drugs that affect existing neurochemical processes in the brain often affect behavior, and this has led to many attempts to explain normal (not drug-induced) variations in behavior in terms of changes in brain chemistry. For example, differences in personality between two people might be explained by a difference in the chemical makeup of their brains, or changes in an individual's reactions from one day to the next might be explained in terms of shifting tides of chemicals. The ancient Greek physician Hippocrates believed that behavior patterns reflected the relative balances of four *humors:* blood (hot and wet, resulting in a sanguine or passionate nature); phlegm (cold and wet, resulting in a phlegmatic or calm nature); yellow bile (hot and dry, resulting in a choleric, bilious, or bad-tempered nature); and black bile (cold and dry, resulting in a melancholic or gloomy nature). The Chinese made do with only two basic dispositions: *yin,* the moon, representing the cool, passive, "feminine" nature; and *yang,* the sun, representing the warm, active, "masculine" nature. Thus, any personality could be seen as a relative mixture of these two opposing forces. Unfortunately, most of the chemical-balance theories that have been proposed based on relative influences of different neurotransmitters have not really been more sophisticated than these yin-yang and humoral notions of ancient times. For example, the major theory guiding the treatment of clinical depression proposes that too little activity of the **monoamine** neurotransmitters can cause depression and too much can cause a manic state. Because the rationale underlying the treatment of some psychopathologies—including depression, schizophrenia, and Alzheimer's disease—is based on correcting a neurochemical abnormality, it is tempting to speculate that depressed individuals differ from "normal" people in terms of neurochemical levels or functioning. Two important points should be noted here. First, drug treatments for the vast majority of psychopathologies are *not* cures; they only provide relief from disease-related symptoms, indicating that much of the complexities associated with many psychopathologies have yet to be elucidated. Second, to date, no single neurochemical theory of depression (or schizophrenia) has yet obtained sufficient experimental support to be considered an explanation. The most prominent theory was proposed in the 1960s when there were only a few known neurotransmitters. Today, there are more than 100, but the neurochemical theory of mood has not been appreciably modified.

Brain Imaging Techniques

Nowadays, it's difficult to read an article about drug abuse without some reference to the brain. This is, in part, because of the advances made in brain-imaging techniques in recent years. It is also because many believe that using brain pictures to represent brain activity increases the credibility of the science and findings. Indeed, one study found that presenting brain images with articles resulted in greater acceptance of the scientific arguments made in those articles, as compared to articles accompanied by other forms of data representation (e.g., bar graphs).[9] Given this situation, we thought it might be helpful to describe a few commonly

---

transporter: mechanism in the nerve terminal membrane that removes neurotransmitter molecules from the synapse by taking them back into the neuron.

metabolize: to break down or inactivate a neurotransmitter (or a drug) through enzymatic action.

agonist: a substance that facilitates or mimics the effects of a neurotransmitter on the postsynaptic cell.

antagonist: a substance that prevents the effects of a neurotransmitter on the postsynaptic cell.

monoamine: a class of chemicals characterized by a single amine group; monoamine neurotransmitters include dopamine, norepinephrine, and serotonin.

Unintended Consequences

Viewing Addiction as a Brain Disease Facilitates Social Injustice

Many neuroscientists view drug addiction (or substance use disorder) as a brain disease, and this idea is rarely questioned. On the surface, this perspective is appealing, in part because it appears to remove blame from the afflicted individual and offers hope for treatment through chemical manipulations. But a closer look raises concerns. For example, although cocaine and other recreational drugs temporarily alter the functioning of specific neurons in the brains of all who ingest the drugs, the vast majority of users never become addicted. And regarding the relatively small percentage of individuals who do become addicted, co-occurring psychiatric disorders and socioeconomic factors account for a substantial proportion of these addictions. Most important, to date, there has been no identified biological marker to differentiate nonaddicted persons from addicted individuals.

So the notion that drug addiction is a brain disease is compelling, but it is not supported by the evidence: There are virtually no data from human studies indicating that addiction is a disease of the brain, in the way that, for instance, Huntington's or Parkinson's are diseases of the brain. With these illnesses, one can look at the brains of affected individuals and make accurate predictions about the disease involved and the associated symptoms.

We are nowhere near being able to distinguish the brains of persons who meet criteria for a substance use disorder from those of individuals who do not.

Even so, the "diseased brain" perspective has outsized influence on research funding and direction, as well as on how drug use and addiction are viewed in society. For example, the recently initiated multimillion-dollar Adolescent Brain Cognitive Development longitudinal study seeks primarily to gather neuroimaging data to better understand drug use and addiction among adolescents. It measures drug use, genetic information, and academic achievement but lacks careful consideration of important social factors. Notably, there has never been such an ambitious funding effort focused on psychosocial determinants or consequences (e.g., socioeconomic status, employment status, racial discrimination, neighborhood characteristics, policing) of drug use or addiction.

This situation contributes to unrealistic, costly, and harmful drug policies. If the real problem with drug addiction, for example, is the interaction between the drug itself and an individual's brain, then the solution to this problem lies in one of two approaches. Either remove the drug from society through policies and law enforcement (e.g., drug-free societies) or focus exclusively on the "addicted" individual's brain as the problem. In either case, there is no need to understand the role of socioeconomic factors in maintaining drug use or mediating drug addiction, nor is there any interest in doing so.

The detrimental effects of using law enforcement as a primary means to deal with drug use are

continued

used brain-imaging techniques, explaining what they can and cannot tell us.

For centuries, neuroscientists have investigated the structure of the brain by removing it from the skull and dissecting it section by section. Although much was learned by using this approach, there was at least one obvious limitation: The brain under study was dead. With advances made in imaging technologies, we can now view the living human brain while an individual is at rest or engaged in activities such as complex problem solving. Imaging techniques used in the study of drug effects are usually divided into

two categories: structural and functional imaging. An example of a structural imaging technique is magnetic resonance imaging (MRI). This technology can be extremely valuable for detecting brain structural abnormalities such as brain tumors. Two commonly used functional imaging techniques are positron-emission tomography (PET) and functional MRI (fMRI). These techniques provide us with brain activity information (e.g., neurotransmission) that is not available by simple inspection of the brain's anatomy. Here we briefly describe each procedure with some attention paid to its merits and limitations.

Unintended Consequences

Viewing Addiction as a Brain Disease Facilitates Social Injustice—*continued*

well documented. Millions are arrested each year for simple drug possession, and the abhorrent practice of racial discrimination flourishes in the enforcement of such policies. In the United States, for example, cannabis possession accounts for nearly half of the 1.5 million annual drug arrests, and blacks are four times more likely to be arrested for cannabis possession than whites, even though both groups use cannabis at similar rates (see Chapter 15).

An implicit and pernicious assumption of the diseased brain theory is that any use of certain drugs (e.g., crack, heroin, methamphetamine) is considered pathological, even the nonproblematic, recreational use that characterizes the experience of the overwhelming majority who ingest these drugs. For example, in the Meth Project's popular U.S. antidrug campaign, "The Deep End," young people are told that one hit of methamphetamine is enough to cause irrevocable damage (http://www.methproject.org/ads/tv/deep-end.html).

In the mid1980s, crack cocaine use was blamed for everything from extreme violence to high unemployment rates to premature death to child abandonment. Even more frightening, addiction to the drug was said to occur after only one hit. Drug experts with neuroscience leanings weighed in. "The best way to reduce demand," Yale University psychiatry professor Frank Gawin was quoted as saying, "would be to have God redesign the human brain to change the way cocaine reacts with certain neurons."[10]

Frank Gawin quoted in *Newsweek* (June 16, 1986).

"Neuro" remarks made about drugs with no foundation in evidence were insidious: They helped to shape an environment in which there was an unwarranted and unrealistic goal of eliminating certain types of drug use at any cost to marginalized citizens. In 1986, the U.S. Congress passed now-infamous legislation setting penalties that were literally a hundred times harsher for crack than for powder cocaine violations. More than 80 percent of those sentenced for crack cocaine offenses are black, despite the fact that the majority of users of the drug are white (see Chapter 6). Today, many people find the crack and powder cocaine laws repugnant because they exaggerate the harmful effects of crack and are enforced in a racially discriminatory manner, but few critically examine the role played by the scientific community in propping up the assumptions underlying these laws.

Many in the scientific community have virtually ignored the shameful racial discrimination that occurs in drug law enforcement, abetted by arguments poorly grounded in scientific evidence. This situation illustrates that we cannot ignore psychosocial factors in our narrow pursuit of a neural understanding of drug addiction. Otherwise, we run the risk of facilitating unintended consequences such as racial discrimination and other negative effects.

Box icon credit: ©Adam Gault/age fotostock RF

Structural Imaging

Magnetic Resonance Imaging (MRI) is a technique that uses powerful magnets to determine the amount of hydrogen atoms at different locations in the body. It has become one of the most important tools for providing a detailed view of the brain. Here's an abbreviated version of how it works. The human body contains a lot of water, which means it also has a lot of hydrogen atoms. Normally, these atoms are randomly aligned in the brain. When radio frequency pulses are applied during MRI, the magnetic field aligns all the atoms. Once all the atoms are aligned in the same

direction, the radio frequency pulse is turned off and the time it takes for the atoms to go back to random alignment is measured. Since atoms in different tissues take different amounts of time to return to random alignment, this information can be used to create an image of the brain. The most important merits of this technique are that it provides a high-resolution image of the brain's anatomy and it is noninvasive. It is said to be noninvasive because, until like PET imaging, no radioactive chemicals are injected in the person being examined. An important limitation associated with

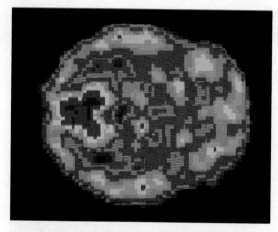

Example of an image of the brain using positron-emission tomography (PET). ©Hank Morgan/Science Source

MRI is that it provides no information about brain functioning. So, using this technique, we cannot determine anything about brain activity or how well or poorly the brain is functioning.

Functional Imaging

Positron-Emission Tomography (PET) With this technique, a radioactively labeled chemical is injected into the bloodstream, and a computerized scanning device then maps out the relative amounts of the chemical in various brain regions. The radioactively labeled chemical is usually a form of glucose or a drug that binds to specific neurotransmitter receptors. The rationale for using radioactively labeled glucose is that all neurons in the brain rely on blood glucose for their energy and the most active neurons use more glucose. Thus, the radioactively labeled glucose accumulates in the area of the brain most metabolically active. The radioactive glucose eventually decays, and the emitted positrons and electrons produce gamma rays, which are then detected by a computerized scanning device. The end result is a colored statistical map indicating which parts of the brain were most active. Of course, the regions that are most active vary depending on what the person is doing. Similarly, blood flow to a particular brain region reflects the activity there, and labeled oxygen or other gases can map regional cerebral

blood flow, which also changes depending on what the person is doing. More recently, labeled drugs that bind to neurotransmitter receptors have been used, and it is therefore possible to see the extent to which binding occurs in the living human brain. For example, one might predict that years of drug abuse cause a decrease in dopamine neurons, including lower dopamine receptor availability. If so, we would expect these individuals to show less binding of the radioactive dopamine-binding drug. A major benefit of PET is that it provides us with a direct measure of brain activity and an indirect measure of potential toxicity to specific neurons. We say indirect measure of toxicity because neuron toxicity cannot be definitely determined in PET studies alone. Additional procedures or techniques are needed because changes in radioactive binding may reflect adaptation of the neuron and not toxicity. The most important limitation of PET is that it requires the injection of radioactive chemicals, which can limit its use in some individuals. In addition, PET does not provide any information about brain structures.

Functional MRI (fMRI) fMRI uses the same machine as MRI, but provides real-time information about changes in brain blood flow as an individual tells us about their mood or performs behavioral or cognitive tasks. fMRI measures the blood oxygen level

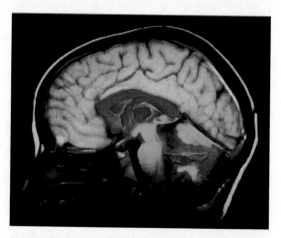

Example of an image of the brain using magnetic resonance imaging (MRI). Source: National Cancer Institute Visuals Online

Drugs in the Media

Don't Be Fooled by Pretty Pictures

"This Is Your Brain on Meth: A 'Forest Fire' of Damage." That was the title of an article printed in *The New York Times* on July 20, 2004. The author wrote, "People who do not want to wait for old age to shrink their brains and bring on memory loss now have a quicker alternative—abuse methamphetamine . . . and watch the brain cells vanish into the night."[1] This conclusion was based on a recent study using magnetic resonance imaging (MRI) to compare brain sizes of methamphetamine abusers with healthy control subjects. The researchers also assessed the correlation between memory performance and several brain structural sizes. They found that the right cingulate gyrus and hippocampus were smaller in methamphetamine users than in control participants (by 11 and 8 percent, respectively). Memory performance on only one of four tests was correlated with hippocampal size (i.e., individuals with larger hippocampal volume performed better). As a result, the study investigators concluded, "chronic methamphetamine abuse *causes* a selective pattern of cerebral deterioration that contributes to impaired memory performance." This interpretation, as well as the one printed in *The New York Times* article, is inappropriate for several reasons. First, brain images were collected at only one time point for both groups of participants. This makes it virtually impossible to determine whether methamphetamine use *caused* "cerebral deterioration," as preexisting differences between the two groups cannot be ruled out. Second, the functional significance of the structural differences is unclear because an 11 percent difference between individuals, for example, may be within the normal range of brain structure sizes. Third, there were no data comparing methamphetamine users with controls on any memory task. This precludes the researchers from making statements regarding impaired memory

performance caused by methamphetamine. Finally, control subjects had significantly higher levels of education than methamphetamine users (15.2 vs. 12.8 years, respectively); it is well established that higher levels of education lead to better memory performance.

Sandra Blakeslee, This Is Your Brain on Meth: A 'Forest Fire' of Damage, The New York Times, July 20, 2004.

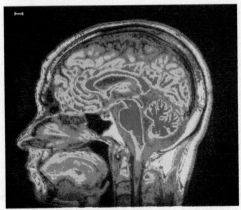

©CNRI/Science Photo Library/Getty Images

This example is not unique. There has been a growing number of media reports drawing causal conclusions about psychiatric illnesses based on inappropriate interpretations of brain-imaging findings. Although most science editors of major news outlets are careful not to make logical errors like the ones pointed out here, it is important for you to read the original sources cited in the article. In this way, you can see how the study was conducted, with the entire dataset and the potential limitations of the findings. Many original sources can be obtained through your college library online resources.

Box icon credit: ©Glow Images RF

---

dependent signal (BOLD signal), which can then be used to create a colored statistical map of brain regions active during task activity. The rationale behind this approach is that as brain activity increases, so does oxygen consumption. This, in turn, leads to an increase in blood flow. During this process, oxyhemoglobin levels rise, while deoxyhemoglobin levels decrease. The result is an increased BOLD signal. These changes in blood flow reflect changes in brain activity in specific regions, making it possible to determine, for example, what brain regions are activated when a person is experiencing the euphoric effects of methamphetamine or is completing a memory test. An obvious benefit of this technique is that it gives us real-time information about changes in brain blood flow. These changes in blood flow provide an indirect measure of neuron activity in specific brain regions. Another benefit is that, unlike PET, fMRI is noninvasive in that it does not require the injection of radioactive chemicals. The drawback associated with this technique is that it does not provide information about the anatomy of the brain.

Word of Caution

Brain imaging is an exciting technological advance that offers a glimpse into the working of the living human brain, but it is not without limitations. For example, the production of a brain image involves many assumptions and complicated statistical analysis, which are often not standardized from one laboratory or hospital to the next. In addition, color-coding of various amounts of brain activity can be arbitrary, and some researchers may use a color scheme that gives an illusion of enormous differences, when only small differences actually exist. These limitations make it difficult, if not impossible, to compare brain scans collected in one laboratory with those from another in any meaningful manner.

Finally, a growing number of studies have combined cognitive testing and brain-imaging techniques to examine differences between drug users and non-users. In general, several researchers have found some brain differences between the groups but no group differences in cognitive performance (see Drugs in the Media).[12] Despite such findings, many investigators still conclude that drug users are cognitively impaired based solely on the imaging data. Such interpretations are inappropriate for two reasons: (1) It's unclear whether observed brain differences are within the normal range of human variability; and (2) the brain differences in the majority of studies were not predictive of cognitive performance.

The point here is not to give precedence to behavioral over brain-imaging data, but to emphasize the need to carefully examine and interpret the most relevant functional outcome—in this case, cognitive functioning. This careful approach allows us to understand the functional consequences of brain activity. If we omit, discard, or ignore behavioral data, we may be enticed to make unwarranted speculations about the neural basis of behavior.

Summary

- Chemical signals in the body are important for maintaining homeostasis. The two types of chemical signals are hormones and neurotransmitters.

- Neurotransmitters act over brief time periods and very small distances because they are released into the synapse between neurons and are then rapidly cleared from the synapse.

- Receptors are specialized structures that recognize neurotransmitter molecules and, when activated, cause a change in the electrical activity of the neuron.

- The nervous system can be roughly divided into the central nervous system, the somatic system, and the autonomic system.

- The autonomic system, with its sympathetic and parasympathetic branches, is important because so many psychoactive drugs also have autonomic influences on heart rate, blood pressure, and so on.

- Specialized chemical pathways contain the important neurotransmitters dopamine, acetylcholine, norepinephrine, and serotonin.

- The nigrostriatal dopamine system is damaged in Parkinson's disease, leading to muscular rigidity and tremors.

- The mesolimbic dopamine system is thought by many to be a critical pathway for the dependence produced by many drugs.

- The neurotransmitter GABA is inhibitory and the neurotransmitter glutamate is excitatory; both are found in most parts of the brain.

- The life cycle of a typical neurotransmitter chemical involves uptake of precursors, synthesis of the transmitter, storage in vesicles, release into the synapse, interaction with the receptor, reuptake into the releasing neuron, and metabolism by enzymes.

- Psychoactive drugs act either by altering the availability of a neurotransmitter at the synapse or by directly interacting with a neurotransmitter receptor.

Review Questions

1. What are some examples of homeostasis in the human body?

2. What are the similarities and differences between glia and neurons?

3. Describe the process of neurotransmitter release and receptor interaction.

4. Give some examples of the opposing actions of the sympathetic and parasympathetic branches of the autonomic nervous system. What is the neurotransmitter for each branch?

5. What is the function of the basal ganglia, and which neurotransmitter is involved?

6. What is the proposed role of the mesolimbic dopamine system in drug dependence?

7. Alzheimer's disease produces a loss of which neurotransmitter from which brain structure?

8. What neurotransmitter seems to have only inhibitory receptors?

9. After a neurotransmitter is synthesized, where is it stored while awaiting release?

10. What are the two main ways in which drugs can interact with neurotransmitter systems?

11. PET and MRI are two examples of what technology?

References

1. Brunton, L. L., J. S. Lazo, and K. L. Parker, eds. *Goodman & Gilman's The Pharmacological Basis of Therapeutics.* 11th ed. New York: McGraw-Hill, 2006, p. 596.

2. Allen, N. J., and B. A. Barres. "Neuroscience: Glia—More Than Just Brain Glue." *Nature* 457 (2009), pp. 675–77.

3. Sizemore, G. M., and others. "Time-Dependent Recovery from the Effects of 6-Hydroxydopamine Lesions of the Rat Nucleus Accumbens on Cocaine Self-Administration and the Levels of Dopamine in Microdialysates." *Psychopharmacology* 171 (2004), pp. 413–20.

4. Hart, C. L., and W. J. Lynch. "Developing Pharmacotherapies for Cannabis and Cocaine Use Disorders." *Current Neuropharmacology* 3 (2005), pp. 95–114.

5. Ryan, D. H. "Clinical Use of Sibutramine." *Drugs Today* 40 (2004), pp. 41–54.

6. Lin, P. Y., and G. Tsai. "Association Between Serotonin Transporter Gene Promoter Polymorphism and Suicide: Results of a Meta-Analysis." *Biological Psychiatry* 55 (2004), pp. 1023–30.

7. Kalivas, P. W. "Glutamate Systems in Cocaine Addiction." *Current Opinions in Pharmacology* 4 (2004), pp. 23–29.

8. Shohamy, D., C. E. Myers, J. Kalanithi, and M. A. Gluck. "Basal Ganglia and Dopamine Contributions to Probabilistic Category Learning." *Neuroscience and Biobehavior Review* 32 (2008), pp. 219–36.

9. McCabe, D. P., and A. D. Castel. "Seeing Is Believing: The Effect of Brain Images on Judgments of Scientific Reasoning." *Cognition* 107 (2008), pp. 343–52.

10. Quoted in Tom Morganthau and others, "Crack and Crime," *Newsweek* (1986, June 16), pp. 16–20.

11. This and other statements put forth were based on conclusions drawn from a paper published in the prestigious *Journal of Neuroscience* that compared cognitive performance and brain structure sizes of methamphetamine abusers with those of healthy control participants. *See* Thompson P. M., and others. "Structural Abnormalities in the Brains of Human Subjects Who Use Methamphetamine." *Journal of Neuroscience* 24 (2004), pp. 6028–36.

12. Hart, C. L. et al. "Is Cognitive Functioning Impaired in Methamphetamine Users? A Critical Review." *Neuropsychopharmacology* 37 (2012), pp. 586–608.

The Actions of Drugs

Objectives

When you have finished this chapter, you should be able to:

- Explain why plants produce so many of the chemicals we use as drugs.

- Distinguish among generic, brand, and chemical names for a drug.

- Understand and describe the typical effects of drugs in each of six categories.

- Understand the importance of placebo effects and the necessity of double-blind studies.

- Define and explain dose-response relationship, ED_{50}, LD_{50}, and therapeutic index.

- Explain why pharmacological potency is not synonymous with effectiveness.

- Compare and contrast the most important routes of drug administration.

- Explain the potential influence of protein binding on interactions between different drugs.

- Describe ways psychoactive drugs interact with neurons to produce effects in the brain.

- Explain the role of homeostatic mechanisms in pharmacodynamic tolerance and withdrawal symptoms.

©Universal Images Group/Universal Images Group/Superstock

Sources and Names of Drugs

Sources of Drugs

Most of the drugs in use 50 years ago originally came from plants. Even now, most of our drugs either come from plants or are chemically derived from plant substances. Why do plants produce so many drugs? Suppose a genetic mutation occurred in a plant so that one of its normal biochemical processes was changed and a new chemical was produced. If that new chemical had an effect on an animal's biochemistry, when the animal ate the plant the animal might become ill or die. In either case, that plant would be less likely to be eaten and more likely to reproduce others of its own kind. Such a selection process must have occurred many thousands of times in various places all over the earth. Many of those plant-produced chemicals have effects on the intestines or muscles; others alter brain functioning. In large doses the effect is virtually always unpleasant or dangerous, but in controlled doses those chemicals might alter the neurochemistry just enough to produce interesting or even useful effects. In earlier cultures, the people who learned about these plants and how to use them safely were important figures in their communities. Those medicine men and women were the forerunners of today's pharmacists and physicians, as well as being important religious figures in their tribes.

Today the legal pharmaceutical industry is one of the largest and most profitable industries in the United States, with sales totaling $300 billion a year.[1] With such extensive sales, many people expect that there are zillions of drugs. Not so. More than half of all prescriptions are filled with only 200 drugs.

Names of Drugs

Commercially available compounds have several kinds of names: *brand, generic,* and *chemical.* The *chemical* name of a compound gives a complete chemical description of the molecule and is derived from the rules of organic chemistry for naming any compound. Chemical names of drugs are rarely used except in a laboratory situation where biochemists or pharmacologists are developing and testing new drugs.

Generic names are the official (i.e., legal) names of drugs and are listed in the *United States Pharmacopoeia (USP).* Although a generic name refers to a specific chemical, it is usually shorter and simpler than the complete chemical name. For example, amphetamine is a generic name and is contained in several medications used to treat attention-deficit/hyperactivity disorder (**ADHD**; discussed in Chapter 6). Generic names are in the public domain, meaning they cannot be trademarked.

The *brand* name of a drug specifies a particular formulation and manufacturer, and the trademark belongs to that manufacturer. A brand name is usually quite simple and as meaningful (in terms of the indicated therapeutic use) as the company can make it. For example, the name **Adderall (combination of amphetamine and dextroamphetamine)** was chosen for an ADHD drug to indicate that it would help patients to be more attentive and alert. However, brand names are controlled by the U.S. Food and Drug Administration, and overly suggestive ones are not approved.

When a new chemical structure, a new way of manufacturing a chemical, or a new use for a chemical is discovered, it can be patented. Patent laws in the United States now protect drugs for 20 years, and after that time the finding is available for use by anyone. Therefore, for 20 years a company that has discovered and patented a drug can manufacture and sell it without direct competition. After that, other companies can apply to the FDA to sell the "same" drug. Brand names, however, are copyrighted and protected by trademark laws. Therefore, the other companies have to use the drug's generic name or their own brand name. The FDA requires these companies to submit samples to demonstrate that their version is chemically equivalent and to do studies to demonstrate that the tablets or capsules they are making will dissolve appropriately and result in blood levels similar to those of the original drug. When a drug "goes generic," the original manufacturer might reduce the price of the brand name product to remain competitive. It may also develop new formulations of the drug. For example, in 2009, competitor companies were allowed to produce and sell a generic form of Adderall. As a result, the original manufacturer developed a slightly different version of the drug and called it **Vyvanse (lisdexamfetamine dimesylate)**. Like Adderall, Vyvanse is approved to treat ADHD but has patent protection through 2023.

Categories of Drugs

Physicians, pharmacologists, chemists, lawyers, psychologists, and users all have drug classification schemes that best serve their own purposes. A drug such as amphetamine might be categorized as a weight-control aid by a physician, because it reduces food intake for a period of time. It might be classed as a phenylethylamine by a pharmacologist, because its basic structure is a phenyl ring with an ethyl group and an amine attached. The chemist says amphetamine is 2-amino-1-phenylpropane. To the lawyer, amphetamine might be only a controlled substance falling in Schedule II of the federal drug

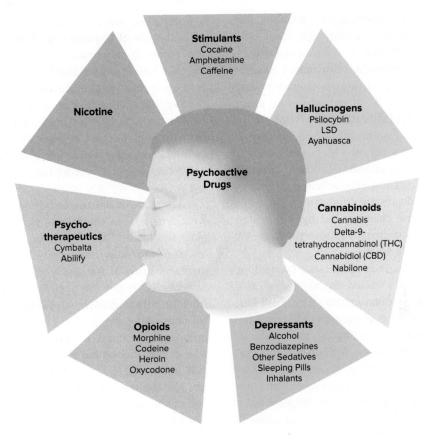

Figure 5.1   Classification of Psychoactive Drugs

law, whereas the psychologist might say simply that it is a stimulant. The person taking the drug might call it a diet pill or an upper. Any scheme for categorizing drugs has meaning only if it serves the purpose for which the classification is being made.

The scheme presented here organizes the drugs according to their effects on the user, with first consideration given to the psychological effects. The basic organization and examples of each type are given in Figure 5.1, but it is worthwhile to point out some of the defining characteristics of each major grouping.

At moderate doses, *stimulant drugs* produce wakefulness and a sense of energy and well-being. The more powerful stimulants, such as cocaine and amphetamines, can at high doses produce a manic state of excitement combined with paranoia and hallucinations if large doses of the drugs are taken over extended periods of time, especially without sleep and proper nutrition.

If you know about the behavioral effects of alcohol, then you know about the *depressant drugs*.

generic (juh *ner* ic): a name that specifies a particular chemical but not a particular brand.

ADHD: attention-deficit/hyperactivity disorder.

Adderall (combination of amphetamine and dextro-amphetamine): a medication used to treat ADHD and narcolepsy.

Vyvanse (lisdexamfetamine dimesylate): a slightly different version of Adderall, approved to treat ADHD.

At low doses they appear to depress inhibitory parts of the brain, leading to disinhibition or relaxation and talkativeness that can give way to recklessness. As the dose is increased, other neural functions become depressed, leading to slowed reaction times, uncoordinated movements, and unconsciousness. Stimulants and depressants do not entirely counteract one another. Although it may be possible to keep a person who is intoxicated on alcohol awake with caffeine or cocaine, he or she would still be reckless, uncoordinated, and so on. Regular use of depressant drugs can lead to a withdrawal syndrome characterized by restlessness, shakiness, hallucinations, and sometimes convulsions, which cause death.

Opioids are a group of analgesic (painkilling) drugs that produce a relaxed, dreamlike state; moderately high doses often induce sleep. Pharmacologically, this group is also known as the narcotics, and it is important to distinguish them from the "downers," or depressants. With opioids there is a clouding of consciousness without the reckless abandon, staggering, and slurred speech produced by alcohol and other depressants. Regular use of any of the opioids followed by abrupt discontinuation of use can lead to a withdrawal syndrome different from that of depressants and characterized by diarrhea, cramps, chills, and profuse sweating.

The *hallucinogens* produce altered perceptions, including unusual visual sensations and quite often changes in the perception of one's own body.

The *psychotherapeutic drugs* include a variety of drugs prescribed by psychiatrists and other physicians for the control of mental problems. The *antipsychotics,* such as aripiprazole (Abilify), are also called neuroleptics. They can calm psychotic patients and over time help them control hallucinations and illogical thoughts. The *antidepressants,* such as duloxetine (Cymbalta), help some people recover more rapidly from seriously depressed mood states. Lithium is used to control manic episodes and to prevent mood swings in bipolar disorder.

As with any classification system, some things don't seem to fit into the classes. Nicotine and cannabis are two such drugs. Nicotine is often thought of as being a mild stimulant, but it also seems to have some of the relaxant properties of a low dose of a depressant. Cannabinoids is often thought of as a relaxant, depressive type of drug, but it doesn't share most of the features of that class. It is sometimes listed among the hallucinogens because at high doses it can produce altered perceptions, but that classification doesn't seem appropriate for the way most people use it.

There are many reasons to identify exactly what drug is represented by a tablet, capsule, or plant substance. The *Physician's Desk Reference (PDR)* has for many years published color photographs of many of the legally manufactured pharmaceuticals.[2] In this way a physician can determine from the pills themselves what drugs a new patient has been taking and in what doses. More critically, in emergency rooms it is possible to determine what drugs a person has just taken, if some of the pills are available for viewing. Police chemistry labs also use the *PDR* to get a preliminary indication of the nature of seized tablets and capsules. Nowadays one can also search the Internet to determine a pill's identity.

Even illicit drugs can sometimes be identified by visual appearance. Often the makers of illicit tablets containing amphetamines such as MDMA (3,4-methylenedioxymethamphetamine) mark them, however crudely, in a consistent way, so that they can be recognized by their buyers. Such visual identification is far from perfect, of course. Cocaine or heroin powder can also be wrapped and labeled in a consistent way by street dealers. Some plant materials, such as psilocybin mushrooms, peyote cactus, or coca or marijuana leaves, can be fairly easy to identify visually, although again not with perfect accuracy.

If a case involving illicit drugs is to be prosecuted in court, the prosecution will usually be expected to present the testimony of a chemist indicating that the drug had been tested and identified using specific chemical analyses.

Drug Effects

No matter what the drug or how much of it there is, it can't have an effect until it is taken. For there to be a drug effect, the drug must be brought together with a living organism. After a discussion of the basic concepts of drug movement in the body, you will be better able to understand such important issues as blood alcohol level, the addictive potential of crack cocaine, and urine testing for marijuana use.

Nonspecific (Placebo) Effects

The effects of a drug do not depend solely on chemical interactions with the body's tissues. With psychoactive drugs in particular, the influences of expectancy, experience, and setting are also important determinants of the drug's effect. For example, a good "trip" or a bad trip on LSD seems to be highly dependent on the experiences and mood of the user before taking the drug. Even the effect of alcohol depends on what the user expects to experience. *Nonspecific* effects of a drug are those that derive from the user's unique background and particular perception of the world. In brief, the nonspecific effects include anything except the chemical activity of the drug and the direct effects of this activity. Nonspecific effects are also sometimes called **placebo** effects, because they can often be produced by an inactive chemical (placebo) that the user believes to be a drug.

The effects of a drug that depend on the presence of the chemical at certain concentrations in the target tissue are called *specific* effects. One important task for psychopharmacologists is to separate the specific effects of a drug from the nonspecific effects.

Suppose you design an experiment with two conditions: One group of people receives the drug you're interested in testing, in a dose that you have reason to believe should work. Each person in the second condition, or control group, receives a capsule that looks identical to the drug but contains no active drug molecules (a placebo). The people must

be randomly assigned to the groups and be treated and evaluated identically except for the active drug molecules in the capsules for the experimental group. For this reason, tests for the effectiveness of a new drug must be done using a **double-blind procedure.** Neither the experimental participant nor the person evaluating the drug's effect knows whether a particular individual is receiving a placebo or an experimental drug. Only after the experiment is over and the data have all been collected is the code broken, so that the results can be analyzed.

Placebo effects have been shown to be especially important in two major kinds of therapeutic effects: treating pain and treating major depression. The size of the placebo response in studies of depression has led to some recent controversy about just how effective the "real" antidepressants are. It has been known for the past 50 years that at least one-third of psychologically depressed patients treated with placebos show improvement—in some published studies the rates of placebo response have been even higher. One group of scientists reviewed all the data submitted to the FDA between 1987 and 2004 in support of new drug applications for 12 of the most popular antidepressant medications on the U.S. market.[3] They concluded about 80 percent of the effectiveness attributed to the antidepressant drugs could be obtained from a placebo!

Nonspecific effects are not caused by the chemicals in drugs, but they are still "real" effects that in some cases might have a biological basis. A recent review concluded that placebo effects are caused by a range of processes, including learning and expectations; they can change physiological measures—such as brain signals—as well as behavioral measures—such as decrease in pain response.[4]

---

placebo (pluh *see* bo): an inactive drug.

double-blind procedure: an experiment in which neither the doctor nor the patient knows which drug is being used.

Dose-Response Relationships

Perhaps the strongest demonstration of the specific effects of a drug is obtained when the dose of the drug is varied and the size of the effect changes directly with the drug dose. A graph showing the relationship between the dose and the effect is called a **dose-response curve.** Typically, at very low doses no effect is seen. At some low dose, an effect on the outcome measure (e.g., reaction time, alertness) is observed. This dose is the *threshold,* and as the dose of the drug is increased, there are more molecular interactions and a greater effect on the outcome measure. At the point where the measure shows maximal response, further additions of the drug have no effect.

In some drug-response interactions, the effect of the drug is all or none, so that when there is a response, it is maximal. There can also be variability among individuals in their response to the drug dose such that as the dose is increased, a larger percentage of individuals respond to the drug.

It is also important to note that outcome measures may be differentially affected by the drug dose. That is, some outcome measures have higher dose thresholds than others. Figure 5.2 shows a series of dose-response curves for three different effects of alcohol. As the dose increases from the low end, first a few and then more and more of the individuals show a slowing of their reaction times. If we also have a test for **ataxia** (staggering or inability to walk straight), we see that, as the alcohol dose reaches the level at which most individuals are showing slowed reaction times, a few are also beginning to show ataxia. As the dose increases further, more people show ataxia, and some become **comatose** (they pass out and cannot be aroused). At the highest dose indicated, all of the individuals would be comatose. We could draw curves for other effects of alcohol on such a figure; for example, at the high end we would begin to see some deaths from overdose, and a curve for lethality could be placed to the right of the coma curve.

In the rational use of drugs, four questions about drug dosage must be answered. First, what is the effective dose of the drug for a desired goal? For example, what dose of morphine is necessary

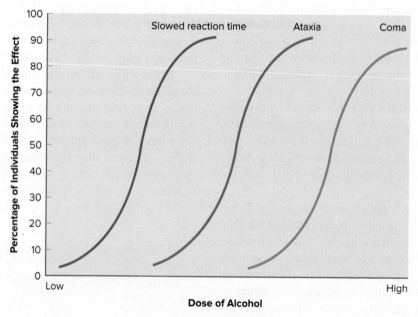

Figure 5.2   Relationship between Alcohol Dose and Multiple Responses

Taking Sides

Attention-Deficit/Hyperactive Disorder and Stimulant Medications: Who Benefits?

Increased recognition of ADHD as a psychiatric disorder has led to the destigmatization of severely hyperactive and impulsive children, who were once shunned as dim-witted and unruly. Over the past two decades, the number of children diagnosed with ADHD has risen steadily, and the Centers for Disease Control and Prevention (CDC) now estimates that as many as 10 percent of children ages 5 to 17 have the diagnosis.

Some observers view these changes as positive developments: Troubled children are no longer ostracized but instead are diagnosed and treated. Indeed, most individuals diagnosed with ADHD are prescribed stimulant medications to treat their symptoms, and the medications are generally effective at relieving, at least, some of these symptoms. It should be noted, though, that behavior therapies are the recommended first line of treatment for young children. On the other hand, critics raise concerns about the dramatic increases in ADHD prevalence and caution that this should lead us to question the validity of the diagnosis or, at least, question the ease with which the diagnosis is given. Most individuals are not diagnosed by mental health specialists—such as psychologists or psychiatrists—but by primary care physicians.

Another concern is the fact that the number of children taking medication for the disorder has increased dramatically to more than 4 million from 600,000 in 1990. Furthermore, the average age of those prescribed medication for ADHD is 7 years old, which raises concerns about over-prescribing and medication-related developmental disruptions. More immediate side effects associated with stimulant medications include restlessness, insomnia, significant appetite suppression, and mood swings, all of which could have detrimental effects on academic performance.

Equally troubling, to some, is the fact that pharmaceutical companies intensely publicize the disorder and vigorously promote the pills not only to physicians but also to the public. And, perhaps not surprising, the rise of ADHD diagnoses and prescriptions for stimulants over the years coincided with a successful two-decade campaign by pharmaceutical companies. Together, these observations raise a couple of questions. Is it possible that the number of individuals meeting criteria for ADHD has been exaggerated to justify the large quantity of stimulant medication prescriptions? Or could it be that we have become better at identifying symptoms of ADHD, thus explaining the rise in the number of people who have the disorder and are being treated with stimulants?

Box icon credit: ©Nova Development RF

---

to reduce pain? What amount of marijuana is necessary for an individual to feel euphoric? How much aspirin will make the headache go away? The second question is what dose of the drug will be toxic to the individual? Combining those two, the third question is what is the safety margin—how different are the effective dose and the toxic dose? Finally, at the effective dose level, what other effects, particularly adverse reactions, might develop? Leaving aside for now this last question, a discussion of the first three deals with basic concepts in understanding drug actions.

Estimating the safety margin is an important part of the preclinical (animal) testing that is done on any new drug before it is tried in humans.

To determine an *effective dose (ED),* it is necessary to define an effect in animals that is meaningful in terms of the desired human use, although in some cases this is difficult. Say we will test a new sleeping pill (hypnotic), on several groups of 20 mice each. Each group will receive a different dose, and an hour later we will check to see how many mice in each group are sleeping. Let us assume that at the

> **dose-response curve:** a graph comparing the size of response to the amount of drug.
> **ataxia (ay *tax* ee ah):** uncoordinated walking.
> **comatose (co mah tose):** unconscious and unable to be aroused.

lowest dose we tested, only 1 of the 20 mice was asleep, and at the highest doses all were asleep, with other values in between. By drawing a line through these points, we can estimate the dose required to put half of the mice to sleep (the ED_{50} or the effective dose for 50 percent of the animals).

Before a drug is marketed, toxicity is usually measured in at least one animal study by determining how many animals die as a result of the drug. Sticking with the same experiment, let's say we check each cage the next day to see how many mice in each group died. From such a study we can estimate the LD_{50} (lethal dose for 50 percent of the mice). The **therapeutic index (TI)** is defined as LD_{50}/ED_{50}. Since the *lethal dose* should be larger than the *effective dose,* the TI should always be greater than 1. How large should the TI be if the company is going to go forward with expensive clinical trials? It depends partly on the TIs of the drugs already available for the same purpose. If the new drug has a greater TI than existing drugs, it is likely to be safer when given to humans.

This approach of estimating the dose to affect 50 percent of the mice is used in early animal tests because it is statistically more reliable to estimate the 50 percent point using a small number of mice per group than it is to estimate the 1 percent or 99 percent points. However, with humans we don't do LD_{50} experiments. Also, with some disorders, perhaps the best drugs we have can help only half of the people. What we ultimately want is to estimate the dose that will produce a desired effect in most patients and the lowest dose producing some unacceptable toxic reaction. The difference between these doses would be called the **safety margin.**

Most of the psychoactive compounds have an LD_1 well above the ED_{95} level, so the practical limitation on whether or not, or at what dose, a drug is used is the occurrence of **side effects.** With increasing doses there is usually an increase in the number and severity of side effects—the effects of the drug that are not relevant to the treatment. If the number

of side effects becomes too great and the individual begins to suffer from them, the use of the drug will be discontinued or the dose lowered, even though the drug may be very effective in controlling the original symptoms. The selection of a drug for therapeutic use should be made on the basis of effectiveness in treating the symptoms with minimal side effects.

Potency

The **potency** of a drug is one of the most misunderstood concepts in the area of drug use. Potency refers only to the *amount of drug* that must be given to obtain a particular response. The smaller the amount needed to get a particular effect, the more potent the drug. Potency does not necessarily relate to how effective a drug is or to how large an effect the drug can produce. *Potency* refers only to relative effective dose; the ED_{50} of a potent drug is lower than the ED_{50} of a less potent drug. For example, it has been said that LSD is one of the most potent psychoactive drugs known. This is true in that hallucinogenic effects can be obtained with 50 micrograms (μg), compared with several milligrams (mg) required of other hallucinogens (a μg is 1/1,000 of a mg, which is 1/1,000 of a gram [g]). However, the effects of LSD are relatively limited—it doesn't lead to overdose deaths the way heroin and alcohol do. Alcohol has a greater variety of more powerful effects than LSD, even though in terms of the *dose* required to produce a psychological effect LSD is thousands of times more *potent*.

Time-Dependent Factors in Drug Actions

In the mouse experiment, we picked one hour after administering the drug to check for the sleeping effect. Obviously, we would have had to learn a bit about the **time course** of the drug's effect before picking one hour. Some very rapidly acting drug might have put the mice to sleep within 10 minutes and be wearing off by one hour, and we would pick a 20- or 30-minute time to check the effect of that drug. The time course of a drug's action

Life Saver

Keeping Inexperienced Users Safe

Experienced drug users tend to use via routes that get drugs to the brain fast. Smoking and intravenous injections are popular among this group. Not only do these routes produce the most intense high, but they also require less amounts of the drug to produce the desired effects. Given these apparent appealing features, why should novices be discouraged from smoked and intravenous drug use, at least initially? Inexperienced users will not have developed tolerance. This means that smaller doses are likely to produce greater toxic effects, including overdose. Because the smoked and intravenous routes produce more potent effects, the likelihood of deleterious consequences is increased with these routes. Alternatively, taking a drug by mouth (oral) is usually

safer than other ways of consuming drugs because the stomach can be pumped in case of an overdose, something that is not possible to do with smoked or injection overdoses. In addition, when a drug is taken by mouth, some of it is broken down before reaching the brain, which means that the total drug dose and potential drug-related negative outcomes are reduced. In part, this is why experienced drug users seeking intense highs tend to avoid eating their drugs or swallowing them as pills. In short, inexperienced users should (1) avoid using via routes that increase a drug's potency (e.g., smoked and intravenous) and (2) use lower doses than experienced users.

Box icon credit: ©McGraw-Hill Education

depends on many things, including how the drug is administered, how rapidly it is absorbed, and how it is eliminated from the body.

Figure 5.3 describes one type of relationship between administration of a drug and its effect over time. Between points *A* and *B* there is no observed effect, although the concentration of drug in the blood is increasing. At point *B* the threshold concentration is reached, and from *B* to *C* the observed drug effect increases as drug concentration increases. At point *C* the maximal effect of the drug is reached, but its concentration continues increasing to point *D*. Although deactivation of the drug probably begins as soon as the drug enters the body, from *A* to *D* the rate of absorption is greater than the rate of deactivation. Beginning at point *D* the deactivation proceeds more rapidly than absorption, and the concentration of the drug decreases. When the amount of drug in the body reaches *E*, the maximal effect is over. The action diminishes from *E* to *F*, at which point the level of the drug is below the threshold for effect, although the drug is still in the body up to point *G*.

If the relationship described in Figure 5.3 is true for a particular drug, then increasing the dose of the drug will not increase the magnitude of its effect. Aspirin and other headache remedies are probably the most misused drugs in this respect—if two are good, four should be better, and six will really stop this headache. No way! When the maximum possible therapeutic effect has been reached,

ED$_{50}$: effective dose for half of the animals tested.

LD$_{50}$: lethal dose for half of the animals tested.

therapeutic index (TI): ratio of LD$_{50}$ to ED$_{50}$.

safety margin: dosage difference between an acceptable level of effectiveness and the lowest toxic dose.

side effects: unintended effects that accompany therapeutic effects.

potency: measured by the amount of drug required to produce an effect.

time course: timing of the onset, duration, and termination of a drug's effect.

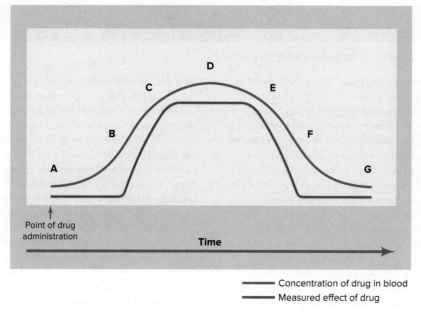

Point of drug
administration

Time

———— Concentration of drug in blood
———— Measured effect of drug

Figure 5.3   Possible Relationship between Drug Concentration in the Body and Measured Effect of the Drug

increasing the dose primarily adds to the number of side effects.

The usual way to obtain a prolonged effect is to take an additional dose at some time after the first dose has reached its maximum concentration and started to decline. The appropriate interval varies from one drug to another. If doses are taken too close together, the maximum blood level will increase with each dose and can result in **cumulative effects.**

One of the important changes in the manufacture of drugs is the development of time-release preparations. These compounds are prepared so that after oral ingestion the active ingredient is released into the body over a 6- to 10-hour period. With a preparation of this type, a large amount of the drug is initially made available for absorption, and then smaller amounts are released continuously for a long period. The initial amount of the drug is expected to be adequate to obtain the response desired, and the gradual release thereafter is designed to maintain the same effective dose of the drug even though the drug is being continually

deactivated. In terms of Figure 5.3, a time-release preparation would aim at eliminating the unnecessarily high drug level at *C–D–E* while lengthening the *C–E* time interval.

Getting the Drug to the Brain

A Little "Chemistry"

The chemistry of the drug molecules determines if some drugs act quickly and others more slowly. One of the most important considerations is the **lipid solubility** of the molecules. Shake up some salad oil with some water, let it stand, and the oil floats on top. When other chemicals are added, sometimes they "prefer" to be concentrated more in the water or in the oil. For example, if you put sodium chloride (table salt) in with the oil and water and shake it all up, most of the salt will stay with the water. If you crush a garlic clove and add it to the mix, most of the chemicals that give garlic its flavor will remain in the oil. The extent to which a chemical can be dissolved in oils and fats is called its lipid solubility. Most psychoactive drugs dissolve to some extent in

Drugs in the Media

Marijuana Brownie Overdose?

In April 2006, a Michigan police officer and his wife attempted to get "high" by eating brownies laced with marijuana that he had confiscated from criminal suspects. Approximately 90 minutes after eating the brownies, the officer made the following panicked 911 emergency call:

Officer: I think I'm having an overdose and so's my wife . . .
Dispatcher: Overdose of what?
Officer: Marijuana. I don't know if there was something in it . . . Can you please send rescue?
Dispatcher: Do you guys have a fever or anything?
Officer: No, I'm just . . . , I think we're dying.
Dispatcher: How much did you guys have?
Officer: Uh, I don't know we made brownies and I think we're dead. I really do . . . Time is going by really, really, really, really slow.

Listeners to an audio transcript of the call found it hilarious, despite the officer's clear distress. One reason that many were amused is because they recognized the likelihood of death following marijuana consumption is low. They might have also understood some basic facts about routes of drug administration, which is most germane to our discussion in this chapter.

Like most drugs, marijuana can be ingested in several ways, including orally. The oral route is convenient (no special equipment is needed), but the time that it takes to feel "high" using this route is often delayed and the effects tend to last longer. Inexperienced users might become impatient after several minutes without feeling a recognizable change in mood. This can lead to the immediate consumption of even more drug in hopes of bringing about an effect. With a drug like marijuana, this would be a mistake, because not only can the onset of drug actions be delayed for up to an hour after ingestion, but also the effects can be quite intense if a large dose was taken. The point here is that knowing a few basic pharmacology facts might help one minimize drug-related harms and avoid the panic and public humiliation experienced by the officer in this example.

Box icon credit: ©Glow Images RF

Absorption of a drug into the bloodstream through the gastrointestinal tract is a complicated process. ©Corbis/VCG/ Getty Images RF

either water or lipids, and in our oil-and-water experiment some fraction of the drug would be found in each. The importance of lipid solubility will become clear as we see how molecules get into the brain.

Routes of Administration

We rarely put chemicals directly into our brains. All psychoactive drugs reach the brain tissue by way of the bloodstream. Most psychoactive drugs are taken by one of four routes: by mouth, **insufflation,** injection, or inhalation. Table 5.1 compares some characteristics of the major routes used to get drugs in the bloodstream.

Oral Administration Most drugs begin their grand adventure in the body by entering through the mouth. Even though oral intake might be the

> **cumulative effects:** effects of giving multiple doses of the same drug.
> **lipid solubility:** tendency of a chemical to dissolve in fat, as opposed to in water.
> **insufflation:** to take a drug through the nose.

Table 5.1
Some Characteristics of Routes of Drug Administration

Route	Advantages	Disadvantages
Oral	Usually more safe Convenient	Absorption rate can be unpredictable Slow onset of drug effects
Insufflation	Liver metabolism avoided Rapid drug effects Reliable and convenient	Potential for nasal necrosis

Intravenous injection	Liver metabolism avoided
	Rapid drug effects
		Suitable for irritating substances
		Increased risk of adverse effects
		    Direct (e.g., overdose)
		    Indirect (e.g., potential for blood-borne diseases)
		Potential for collapsed veins

Subcutaneous injection	Drug absorption can be slow and constant providing a sustained drug effect	Potential for pain and necrosis from irritating substances
Intramuscular injection	Drug effects are more rapid than subcutaneous route	Suitable for irritating substances Drug absorption can be unpredictable or unusual in very obese and emaciated individuals
Smoked	Liver metabolism avoided Rapid drug effects	Increased risk of direct adverse effects Potential for lung toxicity

simplest way to take a drug, absorption from the gastrointestinal tract is the most complicated way to enter the bloodstream. A chemical in the digestive tract must withstand the actions of stomach acid and digestive enzymes and not be deactivated by food before it is absorbed. The antibiotic tetracycline provides a good example of the dangers in the gut for a drug. This antibiotic readily combines with calcium ions to form a compound that is poorly absorbed. If tetracycline is taken with milk (calcium ions), blood levels will never be as high as if it were taken with a different beverage.

The drug molecules must next get through the cells lining the wall of the gastrointestinal tract and into the blood capillaries. If taken in capsule or tablet form, the drug must first dissolve and then, as a liquid, mix into the contents of the stomach and intestines. However, the more other material there is in the stomach, the greater the dilution of the drug and the slower it will be absorbed. The drug must be water soluble for the molecules to spread throughout the stomach. However, only lipid-soluble and very small water-soluble molecules are readily absorbed into the capillaries surrounding the small intestine, where most absorption into the bloodstream occurs.

Once in the bloodstream, the dangers of entering through the oral route are not over. The veins from the gut go first to the liver (see Figure 5.4). If the drug is the type that is metabolized rapidly by the liver (nicotine is one example), very little may get into the general circulation. Thus, nicotine is much more effective when inhaled than when swallowed.

Insufflation Drugs can be insufflated (snorted or sniffed) through the nose. The mucous membranes of the nose contain a rich supply of blood vessels that line the nasal cavity. This ensures quick access to the general blood circulation while bypassing the liver, which means that the onset of drug effects is faster than it is for oral administration. For

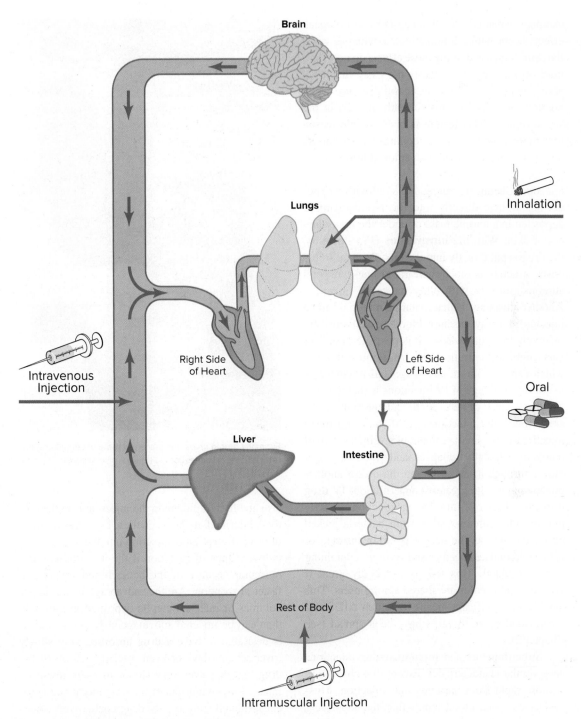

Figure 5.4   Distribution of Drugs through the Body

example, when cocaine is taken intranasally, peak effects occur within a few minutes, whereas when the drug is ingested orally these effects do not occur until 30 minutes after ingestion. A key drawback associated with repeated intranasal drug use is the potential for nasal necrosis (death of cells in the septal region). This feature is one possible reason that more experienced and committed drug users move on to the intravenous or smoked route.

Injection Chemicals can be delivered with a hypodermic syringe directly into the bloodstream or deposited in a muscle mass or under the upper layers of skin. With the **intravenous (IV)** injection, the drug is put directly into the bloodstream, so the onset of action is much more rapid than with oral administration or with other means of injection. Another advantage is that irritating material can be injected this way, because blood vessel walls are relatively insensitive. Also, it is possible to deliver very high concentrations of drugs intravenously, which can be both an advantage and a danger. A major disadvantage of IV injections is that the vein wall loses some of its strength and elasticity in the area around the injection site. If there are many injections into a small segment of a vein, the wall of that vein eventually collapses, and blood no longer moves through it, necessitating the use of another injection site. The greatest concern about IV drug use is the danger of introducing infections directly into the bloodstream, either from bacteria picked up on the skin as the needle is being inserted or from contaminated needles and syringes containing traces of blood. This risk is especially great if syringes and needles are shared among users. This has been a significant means by which AIDS and other blood-borne diseases have been spread (see Chapter 2).

Subcutaneous and **intramuscular** injections have similar characteristics, except that absorption is more rapid from intramuscular injection. Muscles have a better blood supply than the underlying layers of the skin and thus more area over which absorption can occur. Absorption is most rapid when the injection is into the deltoid muscle of the

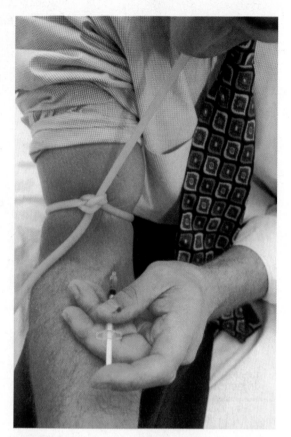

For many heroin users, the preferred route of administration is by intravenous injection. ©Ingram Publishing/Ingram Publishing/Getty Images RF

arm and least rapid when the injection is in the buttock. Intermediate between these two areas in speed of drug absorption is injection into the thigh. There is less chance of irritation if the injection is intramuscular because of the better blood supply and faster absorption. Another advantage is that larger volumes of material can be deposited in a muscle than can be injected subcutaneously. Sometimes it is desirable to have a drug absorbed very slowly (over several days or even weeks). A form of the drug that dissolves very slowly in water might be injected into a muscle, or the drug might be microencapsulated (tiny bits of drug coated with something to slow its absorption).

One disadvantage of subcutaneous injection is that, if the material injected is extremely irritating to the tissue, the skin around the site of injection might die and be shed. This method of injection is not very common in medical practice but has long been the kind of injection used by beginning opioid users. This is commonly called "skin popping."

Inhalation Inhalation is the drug delivery system used for smoking nicotine, marijuana, and crack cocaine, and for "huffing" gasoline, paints, and other inhalants; it is used medically with various anesthetics. It is an efficient way to deliver a drug. Onset of drug effects is quite rapid because the capillary walls are accessible in the lungs, and the drug thus enters the blood quickly. For psychoactive drugs, inhalation can produce more rapid effects than even intravenous administration. This is because of the patterns of blood circulation in the body (review Figure 5.4). The blood leaving the lungs moves fairly directly to the brain, taking only five to eight seconds to do so. By contrast, blood from the veins in the arm must return to the heart, then be pumped through the lungs before moving on to the brain, and this takes 10 to 15 seconds. Aerosol dispensers have been used to deliver some drugs via the lungs, but three considerations make inhalation of limited value for medical purposes. First, the material must not be irritating to the mucous membranes and lungs. Second, control of the dose is more difficult than with the other drug delivery systems. Last, and perhaps the prime advantage for some drugs and disadvantage for others, there is no depot of drug in the body. This means the drug must be given as long as the effect is desired and that, when drug administration is stopped, the effect decreases rapidly.

Other Routes Topical application of a drug to the skin is not widely used because most drugs are not absorbed well through the skin. However, for some drugs this method can provide a slow, steady absorption over many hours. For example, a skin patch results in the slow absorption of nicotine over an entire day. This patch has been found to help prevent relapse in people who have quit smoking. Application to mucous membranes results in more

Inhalation is a very effective means of delivering a drug to the brain. ©Igor Stevanovic/123RF RF

rapid absorption than through the skin because these membranes are moist and have a rich blood supply. Both rectal and vaginal suppositories take advantage of these characteristics, although suppositories are used only rarely. The mucosa of the oral cavity provide for the absorption of nicotine from chewing tobacco directly into the bloodstream without going through the stomach, intestines, and liver.

intravenous (IV) (in trah _vee_ nuss): injection directly into a vein.

subcutaneous (sub cue _tay_ nee us): injection under the skin.

intramuscular: injection into a muscle.

Transport in the Blood

When a drug enters the bloodstream, often its molecules will attach to one of the protein molecules in the blood, albumin being the most common protein involved. The degree to which drug molecules bind to plasma proteins is important in determining drug effects. As long as there is a protein-drug complex, the drug is inactive and cannot leave the blood. In this condition, the drug is protected from inactivation by enzymes.

An equilibrium is established between the free (unbound) drug and the protein-bound forms of the drug in the bloodstream. As the unbound drug moves across capillary walls to sites of action, there is a release of protein-bound drug to maintain the proportion of bound to free molecules. Considerable variation exists among drugs in the affinity that the drug molecules have for binding with plasma proteins. Alcohol has a low affinity and thus exists in the bloodstream primarily as the unbound form. In contrast, most of the molecules of THC, the active ingredient in marijuana, are bound to blood proteins, with only a small fraction free to enter the brain or other tissues. If two drugs were identical in every respect except protein binding, the one with greater affinity for blood proteins would require a higher dose to reach an effective tissue concentration. On the other hand, the duration of that drug's effect would be longer because of the "storage" of molecules on blood proteins.

Because different drugs have different affinities for the plasma proteins, one might expect that drugs with high affinity would displace drugs with weak protein bonds, and they do. This fact is important because it forms the basis for one kind of drug interaction. When a high-affinity drug is added to blood in which there is a weak-affinity drug already largely bound to the plasma proteins, the weak-affinity drug is displaced and exists primarily as the unbound form. The increase in the unbound drug concentration helps move the drug out of the bloodstream to the sites of action faster and can be an important influence on the effect the drug has. At the very least, the duration of action is shortened.

More about the Blood-Brain Barrier

The brain is very different from the other parts of the body in terms of drugs' ability to leave the blood and move to sites of action. As described in Chapter 4, the blood-brain barrier keeps certain classes of compounds in the blood and away from brain cells. Thus, some drugs act only on neurons outside the central nervous system—that is, only on those in the peripheral nervous system—whereas others may affect all neurons.

The blood-brain barrier is not well developed in infants; it reaches complete development only after one or two years of age in humans. Although the nature of this barrier is not well understood, several factors are known to contribute to the blood-brain barrier. One is the makeup of the capillaries in the brain. They are different from other capillaries in the body, because they contain no pores. Even small water-soluble molecules cannot leave the capillaries in the brain; only lipid-soluble substances can pass the lipid capillary wall.

In general, only small **lipophilic** molecules enter the brain. This feature has important implications for the effects of some psychoactive drugs on the brain and, ultimately, on behavior. Take, for example, the opioid drugs morphine and heroin. Heroin (also known as diacetylmorphine) was synthesized by adding two acetyl groups to the morphine chemical. This slight modification of the morphine structure made the new chemical more lipophilic, thereby facilitating its movement across the blood-brain barrier and into the brain. As a result, heroin has a more rapid onset of effects and is about three times as potent as morphine.

If a substance can move through the capillary wall, another barrier unique to the brain is met. About 85 percent of the capillaries are covered with glial cells; there is little extracellular space next to the blood vessel walls. With no pores and close contact between capillary walls and glial cells, almost certainly an active transport system is needed to move chemicals in and out of the brain. In fact, known transport systems exist for some naturally occurring agents.

A final note on the mystery of the blood-brain barrier is that cerebral trauma can disrupt the barrier and permit agents to enter that normally would be excluded. Concussions and cerebral infections frequently cause enough trauma to impair the effectiveness of this screen, which normally permits only selected chemicals to enter the brain.

Mechanisms of Drug Actions

Many types of actions are suggested in Chapters 6 to 16 as ways in which specific drugs can affect physiochemical processes, neuron functioning, and ultimately thoughts, feelings, and other behaviors. It is possible for drugs to affect all neurons, but many exert actions only on very specific presynaptic or postsynaptic processes.

Effects on All Neurons

Chemicals that have an effect on all neurons must do so by influencing some characteristic common to all neurons. One general characteristic of all neurons is the cell membrane. It is semipermeable, meaning that some agents can readily move in and out of the cell, but other chemicals are held inside or kept out under normal conditions. The semipermeable characteristic of the cell membrane is essential for the maintenance of an electric potential across the membrane. It is on this membrane that some drugs seem to act and, by influencing the permeability, alter the electrical characteristics of the neuron.

Most of the general anesthetics have been thought to affect the central nervous system by a general influence on the cell membrane. The classical view of alcohol's action on the nervous system was that it has effects similar to the general anesthetics through an influence on the neural membrane. However, evidence has pointed to more specific possible mechanisms for alcohol's effects (see Chapter 9), and even the gaseous anesthetics might be more selective in their action than was previously thought. Thus, the entire notion that some drugs act nonspecifically through altering the nerve membrane's electrical properties is in dispute.[5]

Effects on Specific Neurotransmitter Systems

The various types of psychoactive drugs (e.g., opioids, stimulants, depressants) produce different types of effects primarily because each type interacts in a different way with the various neurotransmitter systems in the brain. Chapter 4 pointed out that the brain's natural neurotransmitters are released from one neuron into a small space called a *synapse,* where they interact with receptors on the surface of another neuron. Psychoactive drugs can alter the *availability* of a neurotransmitter by increasing or decreasing the transmitter chemical's rate of synthesis, metabolism, release from storage vesicles, or reuptake into the releasing neuron. Or the drug might act directly on the *receptor,* either to activate it or to prevent the neurotransmitter chemical from activating it. With the existence of more than 100 known neurotransmitters, and considering that different drugs can interact with several of these in different combinations, and given the variety of mechanisms by which each drug can interact with the life cycle of a natural neurotransmitter, the potential exists for an endless variety of drugs with an endless variety of actions. However, all of these actions are nothing more mysterious than a modification of the ongoing (and quite complex) functions of the brain.

Drug Deactivation

Before a drug can cease to have an effect, one of two things must happen to it. It may be excreted unchanged from the body (usually in the urine), or it may be chemically changed so that it no longer has the same effect on the body. Although different drugs vary in how they are deactivated, the most common way is for enzymes in the liver to act on the drug molecules to change their chemical

---

lipophilic: the extent to which chemicals can be dissolved in oils and fats.

Drugs in Depth

Drug Interactions

Various drugs can interact with one another in many ways: They may have similar actions and thus have additive effects, one may displace another from protein binding and thus one drug may enhance the effect of another even though they have different actions, one drug may stimulate liver enzymes and thus reduce the effect of another, and so on.

Even restricting ourselves to psychoactive drugs, there is such a variety of possible interactions that it would not make sense to try to catalog them all here. Instead, a few of the most important interactions are described.

Respiratory Depression (Alcohol, Other Depressants, Opioids)

The single most important type of drug interaction for psychoactive drugs is the effect on respiration rate. All depressant drugs (sedatives such as Valium and Xanax, barbiturates, sleeping pills), alcohol, and all narcotics tend to slow down the rate at which people breathe in and out, because of effects in the brain stem. Combining any of these drugs can produce effects that are additive and in some cases may be more than additive. Respiratory depression following drug combinations (two or more

sedatives) is the most common type of drug overdose death: People simply stop breathing.

Stimulants and Depressants

It might seem that the "uppers" and "downers" would simply counteract one another, but it's a little more complicated than that when it comes to human behavior. The combination of an upper (e.g., methamphetamine) and a downer (e.g., alcohol) produces a profile of effects that is different from either drug alone. Methamphetamine lessens alcohol-related disruptive effects on performance, whereas alcohol reduces the sleep disruptions caused by methamphetamine. Furthermore, the drug combination produces greater increases in heart rate and euphoria than either drug alone. This constellation of effects is probably why the upper–downer combination is popular. A word of caution is in order, however. Some individuals might underestimate their level of alcohol-related impairment when taking the drug combination, which could allow them to undertake risky behaviors, such as driving while intoxicated.

Box icon credit: ©Ingram Publishing/SuperStock RF

structure. This usually has two effects: one, the **metabolite** no longer has the same action as the drug molecule; two, the metabolite is more likely to be excreted by the kidneys.

The kidneys operate in a two-stage process. In the first step, water and most of the small and water-soluble molecules are filtered out. Second, most of the water is reabsorbed, along with some of the dissolved chemicals. The more lipid-soluble molecules are more likely to be reabsorbed, so one way in which the liver enzymes can increase the elimination of a drug is by changing its molecules to a more water-soluble and less lipid-soluble form.

The most important drug-metabolizing enzymes found in the liver belong to a group known as the CYP450 family of enzymes. The CYP450 enzymes seem to be specialized for inactivating

various general kinds of foreign chemicals that the organism might ingest. This is not like the immune system, in which foreign proteins stimulate the production of antibodies for that protein—the CYP450 enzymes already exist in the liver and are waiting for the introduction of certain types of chemicals. Various plants have evolved the ability to produce chemicals that do nothing directly for the plant but kill or make ill any animals that eat the plant. In defense, apparently many animals have evolved CYP450 enzymes for eliminating these toxic chemicals once they are eaten.

Although the CYP450 enzymes are always available in the liver, the introduction of drugs can alter their function. Many drugs, including alcohol and the barbiturates, have been shown to induce (increase) the activity of one or more of these drug-metabolizing enzymes. Once the body's cells detect the presence of these foreign molecules, they produce more of the enzyme that breaks down that molecule, in an effort to normalize the cell's chemistry (homeostasis—see Chapter 4). Enzyme induction has important potential not only for tolerance to that particular drug, but also for interactions with other drugs that might be broken down by the same enzyme. The increased rate of metabolism could mean that a previously effective dose of an antibiotic or heart medicine can no longer reach therapeutic levels. The enzyme activity typically returns to normal some time after the inducing drug is no longer being taken. For example, the FDA has warned that the herbal product Saint John's wort can decrease blood concentrations of several drugs, presumably by inducing CYP450 enzymes. Other drugs, including fluoxetine (Prozac) and other modern antidepressant drugs, have a high affinity for one of the CYP450 enzymes and "occupy" the enzyme molecules, so that they effectively inhibit the enzyme's action on any other drug. Now a previously safe dose of blood-pressure medication or cough suppressant results in much higher blood levels that could be dangerous. Prescribing physicians have to be aware of the potential for these types of drug interactions, either to avoid using certain drugs together or to adjust doses upward or downward to compensate for enzyme induction or inhibition.

Not all of the metabolites of drugs are inactive. Both diazepam (Valium) and marijuana have **active metabolites** that produce effects similar to those of the original (parent) drug and prolong the effect considerably. In fact, so-called **prodrugs** are being developed that are inactive in the original form and become active only after they are altered by the liver enzymes.

Mechanisms of Tolerance and Withdrawal Symptoms

The phenomena of tolerance and withdrawal symptoms have historically been associated with drug dependence. *Tolerance* refers to a situation in which repeated administration of the same dose of a drug results in gradually diminishing effects. There are at least three mechanisms by which a reduced drug response can come about: drug disposition tolerance, behavioral tolerance, and pharmacodynamic tolerance.

Sometimes the use of a drug increases the drug's rate of metabolism or excretion. This is referred to as **drug disposition tolerance,** or pharmacokinetic tolerance. For example, phenobarbital induces increased activity of the CYP450 enzymes that metabolize the drug. Increased metabolism reduces the effect of subsequent doses, perhaps leading to increased dosage. But additional amounts of the drug increase the activity of the enzymes even more, and the cycle continues. Another possible mechanism for increased elimination has to do with the pH (acidity) of the urine. Amphetamine is excreted unchanged in the urine, and the rate of excretion can be increased by making the urine more acidic. Both amphetamine itself and the decreased food intake that often accompanies heavy amphetamine use tend to make the urine more acidic. Amphetamine is excreted 20 times as rapidly in urine with a pH of 5 as in urine with a pH of 8.

Particularly when the use of a drug interferes with normal behavioral functions, individuals may learn to adapt to the altered state of their nervous system and therefore compensate somewhat for the impairment. In some ways, this is analogous to a person who breaks a wrist and learns to write with the nonpreferred hand— the handwriting probably won't be as good that way, but with practice the disruptive effect on

> **metabolite (muh *tab* oh lite):** product of enzyme action on a drug.
> **active metabolites:** metabolites that have drug actions of their own.
> **prodrugs:** drugs that are inactive until acted on by enzymes in the body.
> **drug disposition tolerance:** tolerance caused by more rapid elimination of the drug.

writing will be reduced. A person who regularly drives a car after drinking alcohol will never be as good a driver as he or she would be sober, but with experience the impairment may be reduced. In this type of tolerance, called **behavioral tolerance,** the drug may continue to have the same biochemical effect but with a reduced effect on behavior.

In many cases the amount of drug reaching the brain doesn't change, but the sensitivity of the neurons to the drug's effect does change. This is best viewed as an attempt by the brain to maintain its level of functioning within normal limits (an example of homeostasis). There are many possible mechanisms for this. For example, if the central nervous system is constantly held in a depressed state through the regular use of alcohol or another depressant drug, the brain might compensate by reducing the amount of the inhibitory neurotransmitter GABA that is released, or by reducing the number of inhibitory GABA receptors (many studies show that the brain does regulate the numbers of specific types of receptors). This adjustment might take several days, and after it occurs the depressant drug doesn't produce as much CNS depression as it did before. If more drug is taken, the homeostatic mechanisms might further decrease the release of GABA or the number of GABA receptors. If the drug is abruptly stopped, the brain now does not have the proper level of GABA inhibition, and the CNS becomes overexcited, leading to wakefulness, nervousness, possibly hallucinations, and the sensation that something is crawling on the skin. In severe cases, brain activity becomes uncontrolled and seizures can occur. These withdrawal symptoms are the defining characteristic of physical dependence. Thus, **pharmacodynamic tolerance** leads not only to a reduced effectiveness of the drug but also to these withdrawal reactions. After several days the compensating homeostatic mechanisms return to a normal state, the withdrawal symptoms cease, and the individual is no longer as tolerant to the drug's effect.

Summary

- Most drugs are derived directly or indirectly from plants.

- The legal pharmaceutical industry is one of the largest and most profitable industries in the United States.

- Brand names belong to one company; the generic name for a chemical may be used by many companies.

- Most psychoactive drugs can be categorized as stimulants, depressants, opioids, hallucinogens, or a psychotherapeutic agent.

- Drugs can be identified by the appearance of commercial tablets or capsules, in some cases by the packaging or appearance of illicit drugs, or by a variety of chemical assays.

- Specific drug effects are related to the concentration of the chemical; nonspecific effects can also be called placebo effects.

- Because each drug is capable of producing many effects, many dose-effect relationships can be studied for any given drug.

- The ratio of LD_{50} to ED_{50} is called the therapeutic index and is one indication of the relative safety of a drug for a particular use or effect.

- The potency of a drug is the amount needed to produce an effect, not the importance of the effect.

- The time course of a drug's effect is influenced by many factors, including route of administration, protein binding in the blood, and rate of elimination.

- Virtually all psychoactive drugs have relatively specific effects on one neurotransmitter system or more, either through altering availability of the transmitter or by interacting with its receptor.

- The liver microsomal enzyme system is important for drug deactivation and for some types of drug interactions.

- Drug tolerance can result from changes in distribution and elimination, from behavioral adaptations, or from changes in the responsiveness of the nervous system caused by compensatory (homeostatic) mechanisms. Physical dependence (withdrawal) can be a consequence of this last type of tolerance.

Review Questions

1. Morton's makes table salt, also known as sodium chloride. What is the chemical name, what is the generic name, and what is the brand name?
2. Into which major category does each of these drugs fall: heroin, cocaine, alcohol, LSD, Prozac?
3. Why might nonspecific factors influence psychoactive drug effects more than the effect of an antibiotic?
4. Why should LD_{50} always be greater than ED_{50}?
5. Why do people say that LSD is one of the most potent psychoactive drugs?
6. Which route of administration gets a drug to the brain most quickly?
7. If an elderly person has less protein in the blood than a younger person, how would you adjust the dose of a drug that has high protein binding?
8. How might two drugs interact with each other through actions on the CYP450 enzyme system?
9. Which type of tolerance is related to physical dependence, and why?

References

1. *Biopharmaceutical Research Industry Profile 2016*, Washington, DC: Pharmaceutical Research and Manufacture of America.
2. *Physician's Desk Reference.* Oradell, NJ: Medical Economics Company.
3. Turner, E. H., A. M. Matthews, E. Linardatos, R. A. Tell, and R. Rosenthal. "Selective Publication of Antidepressant Trials and Its Influence on Apparent Efficacy." *New England Journal of Medicine* 358 (2008), pp. 252–60.
4. Wager, T. D., and Atlas, L. Y. "The Neuroscience of Placebo Effects: Connecting Context, Learning and Health." *Nature Reviews Neuroscience* 16 (2015), pp. 403–18.
5. Hu, H., and M. Wu. "Mechanism of Anesthetic Action: Oxygen Pathway Perturbation Hypothesis." *Medical Hypotheses* 57 (2001), p. 619.

behavioral tolerance: tolerance caused by learned adaptation to the drug.

pharmacodynamic tolerance: tolerance caused by altered nervous system sensitivity.

ACROSS

3. Space between two neurons
5. Cause for tobacco dependence
7. Brain part for integration of information, planning
8. Chemical signal carried through the blood
9. Amount of drug given
11. Fastest way to get a drug to the brain
12. Agency responsible for regulating pharmaceuticals
15. Where most drugs are broken down
16. Transmitter in the sympathetic branch
20. Transmitter in the mesolimbic system
21. Most widely used depressant
22. Axons, dendrites are part of the nerve _____.
23. Most rapid method of injection is into a _____.
24. Potent CNS drugs must be _____ soluble.
25. Type of modern brain scan using radioactive chemicals

DOWN

1. Reduced effect of a drug after repeated use
2. Opiate-like substance found in the brain
4. Nervous system controlling heart, pupils of the eye, etc.
6. Chemical that affects a living organism
7. Powerful stimulant derived from a South American plant
10. An _____ signal travels along the axon.
13. Drug that makes you drowsy, drunk, uncoordinated
14. Drug name used by several companies
17. Inactive or "fake" drug
18. Common term for opium, morphine, heroin, etc.
19. Neuron part that carries electrical signals to the terminals
20. Neuron part that picks up signals from other neurons
25. Hallucinogen

Uppers and Downers

We start our review of drugs by studying two types that have straightforward actions on behavior. Stimulants generally excite the central nervous system, whereas depressants generally inhibit it. In Section Three, we find that most drugs used in

treating mental disorders are not simply uppers or downers—their action is more complicated. However, this can best be appreciated by comparing them with the stimulants and depressants. Antidepressant drugs, used in treating psychological depression, are not stimulants. When taken for several weeks they can help raise a depressed mood into the normal range, but they don't produce excited, sleepless effects as stimulants do. Likewise, the tranquilizers used in treating psychotic behavior are not depressants and do not always produce the drowsiness that sedatives and sleeping pills do.

6

Stimulants

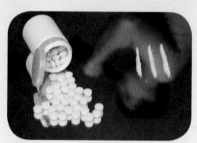

©Janne Tervonen/Alamy Atock Photo RF

Stimulants are the drugs that can keep you going, both mentally and physically, when you should be tired. There have been lots of claims about the other things these drugs can do for (and to) people. Do they really make you smarter, faster, or stronger? Can they sober you up? Improve your sex life? Do they produce dependence?

We can divide the stimulants somewhat arbitrarily: The readily available stimulants nicotine and caffeine are discussed in Chapters 10 and 11, and the restricted stimulants cocaine and the amphetamines are covered in this chapter. Since the widespread introduction of cocaine into Western Europe and the United States in the 19th century, a fair-sized minority of individuals has always been committed to the regular recreational use of the stimulants, but neither cocaine nor the amphetamines have ever achieved widespread social acceptance as recreational drugs.

Objectives

When you have finished this chapter, you should be able to:

- Discuss the history of cocaine and amphetamine use and how their rates of use are related.

- Describe how cocaine hydrochloride and crack cocaine are processed from coca.

- Describe early psychiatric uses of cocaine and its current use for local anesthesia.

- Explain the concerns about the selective racial impact of federal sentencing requirements for crack vs. powder cocaine.

- Compare and contrast the mechanism of action and route of administration of cocaine and amphetamine.

- Discuss the dependence potential of cocaine and amphetamines.

- Compare and contrast the supply sources for illicit cocaine and illicit methamphetamine.

- Compare the chemical structure of amphetamine to the catecholamine neurotransmitters and to ephedrine.

- Discuss the medical uses and names of new stimulant drugs.

- Compare and contrast acute and chronic toxicity concerns associated with cocaine and amphetamines.

Cocaine

History

The origin of the earliest civilization in the Americas, the beginning around 5,000 B.C. of what was to become the Inca Empire in Peru, has been traced to the use of **coca**. Natives of the Andes mountains in Bolivia and Peru today still use coca as their ancestors did: chewing the leaves and holding a ball of coca leaf almost continually in the mouth. The freedom from fatigue provided by the drug is legendary in allowing these natives to run or to carry large bundles great distances over high mountain trails. The psychoactive effects can be made stronger by adding some calcified lime to raise the alkalinity inside the mouth—this increases the extraction of **cocaine** and allows greater absorption into the blood supplying the inside of the mouth. It appears that humans in the Andes first settled down and formed communities around places where this calcified lime could be mined.[1] Eventually they took up the planting and harvesting of crops in the nearby fields—and one of those important crops was, of course, coca.

Erythroxylon coca seems to thrive at elevations of 2,000 to 8,000 feet (600 to 2,400 meters) on the Amazon slope of the mountains, where more than 100 inches (254 centimeters) of rain fall annually. The shrub is pruned to prevent it from reaching the normal height of 6 to 8 feet (1.8 to 2.4 meters), so that the picking, which is done three or four times a year, is easier to accomplish. The shrubs are grown in small, two- to three-acre patches called cocals, some of which are known to have been under cultivation for over 800 years.

Before the 16th-century invasion by Pizarro, the Incas had built a well-developed civilization in Peru. The coca leaf was an important part of the culture, and although earlier use was primarily in religious ceremonies, coca was treated as money by the time the conquistadors arrived. The Spanish adopted this custom and paid coca leaves to the native laborers for mining and transporting gold and silver. Even then the leaf was recognized as increasing strength and endurance while decreasing the need for food.

Early European chroniclers of the Incan civilization reported on the unique qualities of this plant, but it never interested Europeans until the last half of the 19th century. At that time the coca leaf contributed to the economic well-being and fame of three individuals. They, in turn, brought the Peruvian shrub to the notice of the world.

Coca Wine

The first of the individuals was Angelo Mariani, a French chemist. His contribution was to introduce the coca leaf indirectly to the general public. Mariani imported tons of coca leaves and used an extract from them in many products. You could suck on a coca lozenge, drink coca tea, or obtain the coca leaf extract in any of a large number of other products. It was Mariani's coca wine, though, that made him rich and famous. Assuredly, it had to be the coca leaf extract in the wine that prompted the pope to present a medal of appreciation to Mariani.

Local Anesthesia

Coca leaves contain, besides the oils that give them flavor, the active chemical cocaine (up to almost 2 percent). Cocaine was isolated before 1860, but there is still debate over who did it first and exactly when. Simple and inexpensive processing of 500 kilograms of coca leaves yields 1 kilogram of cocaine. An available supply of pure cocaine and the newly developed hypodermic syringe improved the drug delivery system, and in the 1880s physicians began to experiment with it. In the United States, the second famous cocaine proponent, Dr. W. S. Halsted, who was later referred to as "the father of modern surgery," experimented with the ability of cocaine to produce local anesthesia.

Early Psychiatric Uses

The third famous individual to encourage cocaine use was Sigmund Freud, who studied the drug for its potential as a treatment medication in a variety of ailments including depression and morphine

coca: a bush that grows in the Andes and produces cocaine.
cocaine: the active chemical in the coca plant.

Drugs in the Media

How the Myth of the "Negro Cocaine Fiend" Helped Shape American Drug Policy

NEGRO COCAINE "FIENDS" ARE A NEW SOUTHERN MENACE. That was the headline of an article that appeared in *The New York Times* on February 8, 1914. You may not be surprised to know that it was once acceptable to print such blatantly racist words in respectable papers. But, you may be disturbed by how similar such writings were to modern media coverage of illegal drugs and how, from early on, the racialized discourse on drugs served a larger political purpose.

The author of *The New York Times* piece, a distinguished physician, wrote, "[The Negro fiend] imagines that he hears people taunting and abusing him, and this often incites homicidal attacks upon innocent and unsuspecting victims." And he continued, "the deadly accuracy of the cocaine user has become axiomatic in Southern police circles. . . . The record of the 'cocaine nigger' near Asheville who dropped five men dead in their tracks using only one cartridge for each, offers evidence that is sufficiently convincing."

Cocaine, in other words, made black men uniquely murderous and better marksmen. But that wasn't all. It also produced "a resistance to the 'knock down' effects of fatal wounds. Bullets fired into vital parts that would drop a sane man in his tracks, fail to check the 'fiend.'"

Preposterous? Yes, but such reporting was not the exception. Between 1898 and 1914, numerous articles appeared exaggerating the association of heinous crimes and cocaine use by blacks. In some cases, suspicion of cocaine intoxication by blacks was reason enough to justify lynchings. Eventually, it helped influence legislation.

Around this time, Congress was debating whether to pass the Harrison Narcotics Tax Act, one of the country's first forays into national drug legislation. This unprecedented law sought to tax and regulate the production, importation, and distribution of opium and coca products. Proponents of the law saw it as a strategy to improve strained trade relations with China by demonstrating a commitment to controlling the opium trade. (China was experiencing an opium addiction problem, which its leaders claimed was weakening its technological and economic superiority.) Opponents, mostly from southern states, viewed it as an intrusion into states' rights and had prevented passage of previous versions.

By 1914, however, the law's proponents had found a convenient scapegoat in their quest to get it passed: The mythical "negro cocaine fiend," which prominent newspapers, physicians, and politicians readily exploited. Indeed, at congressional hearings, "experts" testified that "most of the attacks upon white women of the South are the direct result of a cocaine-crazed Negro brain." When the Harrison Act became law, proponents could thank the South's fear of blacks for easing its passage.

With this as background, drug policy in the decades following takes on a sharper focus. Although the Harrison Act did not explicitly prohibit the use of opiates or cocaine, enforcement of the new law quickly became increasingly punitive, helping set the stage for passage of the Eighteenth Amendment (alcohol prohibition) in 1919 and, ultimately, all our narcotics policy until 1970. As important, the rhetoric that laced those early conversations about drug use didn't just evaporate; it continued and evolved, reinventing itself most powerfully in the mythology of crack cocaine.

continued

dependence. In 1884, Freud wrote to his fiancée that he had been experimenting with "a magical drug." He wrote, "If it goes well I will write an essay on it and I expect it will win its place in therapeutics by the side of morphium, and superior to it. . . . I take very small doses of it regularly against depression and against indigestion, and with the most brilliant success." He urged his fiancée, his sisters, his colleagues, and his friends to try it, extolling the drug as a safe exhilarant, which he himself used and recommended as a treatment for morphine dependence. For emphasis he wrote in italics, *"inebriate asylums can be entirely dispensed with."*[2]

Drugs in the Media

How the Myth of the "Negro Cocaine Fiend" Helped Shape American Drug Policy—*continued*

From its earliest appearance in the 1980s, crack was steeped in a narrative of race and pathology. While powder cocaine came to be regarded as a symbol of luxury and associated with whites, crack was portrayed as producing uniquely addictive, unpredictable, and deadly effects and was associated with blacks. By this time, of course, references to race in such a context were no longer acceptable. So problems related to crack were described as being prevalent in "poor," "urban," or "troubled" neighborhoods, "inner cities" and "ghettos," terms that were codes for "blacks" and other undesired people.

A March 7, 1987, *New York Times* article, "New Violence Seen in Users of Cocaine" offers a potent example. It describes an incident in which "a man apparently using cocaine held four people hostage for 30 hours in an East Harlem apartment." That cocaine use was never confirmed was minimized; and since East Harlem was almost exclusively black and Latino, there was no need to mention the suspect's race. The message was clear: Crack makes poor people of color crazy and violent.

Over the next few years, a barrage of similar articles connected crack and its associated problems with black people. Entire specialty police units were deployed to "troubled neighborhoods," making excessive arrests and subjecting the targeted communities to dehumanizing treatment. Along the way, complex economic and social forces were reduced to criminal justice problems; resources were directed toward law enforcement rather than neighborhoods' real needs, such as job creation, education, and/or other opportunities.

In 1986, Congress passed the infamous Anti-Drug Abuse Act, setting penalties that were 100 times harsher for crack than for powder cocaine convictions. We now know that an astonishing 85 percent of those sentenced for crack cocaine offenses were black, even though the majority of users of the drug were, and are, white. We also know that the effects of crack were greatly exaggerated; crack is no more harmful than powder cocaine. On August 3, 2010, President Barack Obama signed legislation that reduced the sentencing disparity between crack and powder cocaine from 100:1 to 18:1. This is an important step, but any sentencing disparity is inconsistent with the data.

Black males are no longer lynched for violating drug laws, but they are killed. (Ramarley Graham, the unarmed Bronx teen who was chased into his bathroom and shot because police officers believed he had drugs, is just one recent example.) More common is the insidious damage inflicted on black men by the selective enforcement of drug laws. Arrested, incarcerated, and placed under criminal justice supervision, they wind up marginalized and deprived of an education. Incredibly, one in three black males born today will spend time in prison if this country doesn't alter its current approach.

One hundred years after the myth of the "Negro cocaine fiend" helped sell the Harrison Act to Congress, its legacy lives on. The next time that you read about illegal drugs in your local newspaper, see if you can detect biases aimed at poorly regarded groups.

Box icon credit: ©Glow Images RF

In an 1885 lecture before a group of psychiatrists, Freud commented on the use of cocaine as a stimulant, saying, "On the whole it must be said that the value of cocaine in psychiatric practice remains to be demonstrated, and it will probably be worthwhile to make a thorough trial as soon as the currently exorbitant price of the drug becomes more reasonable"—the first of the consumer advocates!

Freud was more convinced about another use of the drug, however, and in the same lecture said,

We can speak more definitely about another use of cocaine by the psychiatrist. It was first discovered in America that cocaine is capable of alleviating the serious withdrawal symptoms observed in subjects who are abstaining from morphine and of suppressing their craving for morphine. . . . On the basis of my experiences with the effects of cocaine, I have no hesitation in recommending the administration of cocaine for such withdrawal cures in subcutaneous injections of 0.03–0.05 g per dose, without any fear of increasing the dose. On several occasions, I have even seen cocaine quickly eliminate the manifestations of intolerance that appeared after a rather large dose of morphine, as if it had a specific ability to counteract morphine.[3]

Even great people make mistakes. The realities of life were harshly brought home to Freud when he used cocaine to treat a close friend, Fleischl, for morphine dependence. Increasingly larger doses were needed, and eventually Freud spent a frightful night nursing Fleischl through an episode of cocaine psychosis. After that experience, he generally opposed the use of drugs in the treatment of psychological problems.

Although physicians were well aware of the dangers of using cocaine in large doses regularly, nonmedical and quasimedical use of cocaine was widespread in the United States around the start of the 20th century. It was one of the secret ingredients in many patent medicines and elixirs but was also openly advertised as having beneficial effects. The Parke-Davis Pharmaceutical Company noted in 1885 that cocaine "can supply the place of food, make the coward brave, and silent eloquent" and called it a "wonder drug."[4]

Early Legal Controls on Cocaine

With so much going for cocaine, and its availability in a large number of products for drinking, snorting, or injection, it may seem strange that, between 1887 and 1914, 46 states passed laws to regulate the use and distribution of cocaine. One historian provided extensive documentation and concluded

> All the elements needed to insure cocaine's outlaw status were present by the first years of the 20th century: it had become widely used as a pleasure drug, and doctors warned of the dangers attendant on indiscriminate sale and use; it had become identified with despised or poorly regarded groups—blacks,

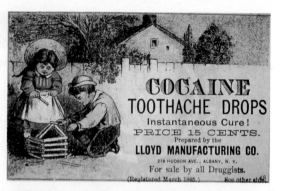

Cocaine was an ingredient in many patent medicines in the United States. Source: National Library of Medicine

lower-class whites, and criminals; it had not been long enough established in the culture to insure its survival; and it had not, though used by them, become identified with the elite, thus losing what little chance it had of weathering the storm of criticism.[5]

Many articles were written—both in the popular press and medical journals—connecting heinous crimes to black men under the influence of cocaine (see Drugs in the Media, pages 122–123). Despite the questionable veracity of such accounts, they were recounted often. During congressional hearings regarding the control of cocaine and opium, for instance, a report from President William Howard Taft was read: "It has been

Users of cocaine hydrochloride, the most common form of pure cocaine, either "snort" the drug or inject it intravenously. ©McGraw-Hill Education/Gary He, photographer

authoritatively stated that cocaine is often the direct incentive to the crime of rape by the negroes of the South . . . the cocaine vice, the most serious that has to be dealt with, has proved to be a creator of criminals and unusual forms of violence, and it has been a potent incentive in driving the humbler negroes all over the country to abnormal crimes."[6]

Such negative publicity was a major influence on the passage of the 1914 Harrison Act, which taxed the importation and sale of coca and cocaine along with opium. These efforts contributed to a decline in cocaine use, although cocaine never completely disappeared.

Forms of Cocaine

As a part of the process of making illicit cocaine, the coca leaves are mixed with an organic solvent, such as kerosene or gasoline. After thorough soaking, mixing, and mashing, the excess liquid is filtered out to form a substance known as **coca paste**. In South America, this paste is often mixed with tobacco and smoked. The paste can be made into **cocaine hydrochloride**, a salt that mixes easily in water and is so stable that it cannot be heated to form vapors for inhalation. Recreational users of this form of cocaine either "snort" (sniff) or inject the drug intravenously. Some users who wanted to smoke cocaine used to convert it into **freebase** by extracting it into a volatile organic solvent, such as ether. The freebase can be heated and the vapors inhaled. This method of smoking cocaine can be very dangerous because the combination of fire and ether fumes is extremely explosive. The popularity of this form of freebasing began to decline in the mid-1980s when it was discovered that mixing cocaine with simple household chemicals, including baking soda and water, and then drying it resulted in a lump of smokable cocaine (**crack** or **rock**). As was pointed out in Chapter 5, it is important to understand *how* a drug is taken when determining the potential effects of that drug. Cocaine can be taken by mouth, insufflation, injection, or inhalation. The onset of drug effects (and therefore intensity of effect) varies depending on the route of administration. Drug effects are more intense following intravenous injection and inhalation compared with oral or intranasal administration. Despite this, it is crucial to emphasize that the effects produced by cocaine are qualitatively similar despite the route of administration. Stated another way, powder and crack cocaine are qualitatively the same drug. In addition, because powder cocaine can be dissolved in water or saline and injected intravenously, the onset and intensity of effects produced by both powder and crack cocaine are similar. More important, cocaine base is responsible for all cocaine-related effects, and it is the active ingredient in all forms of cocaine.

Contemporary Legal Controls on Cocaine

Little concern was given to cocaine until the end of the 1960s, when amphetamines became harder to obtain and cocaine use again began to increase. As had occurred nearly a century before, the virtues of cocaine were again being touted. Some medical experts even argued that as strong a case could be made for legalizing it as for legalizing marijuana due to cocaine's apparent benign side effect profile.[7,8] One reason the drug was perceived as being relatively innocuous is related to its street cost. Cocaine was usually sold in bulk amounts that were expensive. This restricted access of the drug to those with substantial resources, potentially masking negative consequences related to cocaine use. Money has a way of insulating people from harmful consequences.

Cocaine use before 1985 had come to symbolize wealth and fame. By the mid- to late-1980s,

---

coca paste: a crude extract containing cocaine in a smokable form.

cocaine hydrochloride: the most common form of pure cocaine, it is stable and water soluble.

freebase: a method of preparing cocaine as a chemical base so that it can be smoked.

crack: a street name for a simple and stable preparation of cocaine base for smoking.

rock: another name for crack.

enterprising dealers began selling crack cocaine. The cocaine experience was now available to anyone with $5 to $10, a lighter, a pipe, and access to a dealer. As the accessibility of crack cocaine increased, so did the income and racial diversity of cocaine users. For example, use increased among black Americans, especially among the poor, although absolute use by this group never exceeded use by white Americans. Because the majority of crack cocaine sold by street-level dealers is considerably **adulterated,** it can be more expensive than powder cocaine.

Media reports changed from glorifying cocaine and its users to vilifying both. In the months leading up to the 1986 congressional elections, more than 1,000 stories appeared about cocaine in the national media, including five cover stories in *Time* and *Newsweek*.[9] And when Len Bias, the 22-year-old college basketball star, died on June 19, 1986, the media frenzy seemed to reach an even higher pitch. Initially, he was believed to have died from smoking crack cocaine, but later it was discovered that he had used powder. Bias was celebrating having been selected as the second overall pick in the NBA draft by the Boston Celtics. His death had an outsized impact because the then–Speaker of the House, Democrat Tip O'Neill, was from the Boston area and a committed Celtics fan.

The cocaine-attributed death of Don Rogers, the 23-year-old Cleveland Browns defensive back, eight days later only made matters worse. The closely timed deaths of these two young athletes in their prime contributed to the public belief that cocaine's effects were dangerously unpredictable. Of course, the cocaine-related deaths were not placed in the context of the millions who had used or were using the drug without such effects.

In response to concerns about cocaine, President Ronald Reagan issued a proclamation designating October 1986 as "Crack/Cocaine Awareness Month"; Congress passed the Anti-Drug Abuse Act of 1986. The new law supposedly targeted high-level crack cocaine dealers and manufacturers

(kingpins). It created a 100:1 quantity ratio between the amounts of powder and crack cocaine needed to trigger certain mandatory minimum sentences for trafficking cocaine. An individual convicted of selling 5 grams of crack cocaine would be required to serve a *minimum* sentence of five years in prison. To receive the same sentence for trafficking in powder cocaine, that individual would need to possess 500 grams of cocaine—100 times the 5 gram crack cocaine amount. Two years later, the law was modified so that it applied to individuals convicted of simple possession of 5 grams of crack cocaine, even first-time offenders. Simple possession of any other illicit drug, including powder cocaine, by a first-time offender carries a *maximum* penalty of one year in prison.

By the mid-1990s, it was well known in the scientific community that crack and powder cocaine were essentially the same drug. But, forces other than scientific—mainly political—greatly influence drug policies. Politicians feared being labeled soft on crime and many laypersons held the belief that crack was considerably more dangerous than other forms of cocaine. As a result, the federal cocaine law went unchanged.

This inaction occurred despite the fact that many people raised concerns about the selective enforcement of the law. Blacks accounted for an extraordinarily high percentage of those convicted under these laws (see Table 6.1). As a result of concerns of **racial discrimination**, Congress directed the U.S. Sentencing Commission to study this issue. The commission found that (1) penalties' severity mostly impacted blacks; (2) the penalties exaggerated the relative harmfulness of crack cocaine; (3) the penalties sweep too broadly and were applied most often to lower-level offenders; and (4) quantity-based penalties overstated the seriousness of most crack cocaine offenses and failed to provide adequate proportionality.[10]

After more than 20 years without corrective action by Congress, President Obama on August 3, 2010, signed the Fair Sentencing Act that reduced—but

Table 6.1
Racial Characteristics of Federal Cocaine Offenders

	1992		2000		2006		2010		2014	
	Number	Percent	Number	Percent	Number	Percent	Number	Percent	Number	Percent
Crack Cocaine										
Black	2,096	91.4	4,069	84.7	4,411	81.8	3,723	78.7	1,973	83.4
Hispanic	121	5.3	434	9.0	452	8.4	615	13.0	203	8.6
White	74	3.2	269	5.6	474	8.8	345	7.3	154	6.5
Other	3	0.1	33	0.7	56	1.0	47	1.1	36	1.5

Source: U.S. Sentencing Commission, Fair Sentencing Act Datafiles. www.ussc.gov/search/site/cocaine

did not eliminate—the sentencing disparity between crack and powder cocaine from 100:1 to 18:1. Under the new law, the amount of crack cocaine required to trigger a five-year sentence is at least 28 grams. The change to the law was an important acknowledgement of an inappropriate drug policy; but it is also important to point out that *any* sentencing disparity for crack and powder is not in line with pharmacological evidence. Of course, drug laws are rarely made on the basis of pharmacology.

Mechanism of Action

The chemical structure of cocaine is shown in Figure 6.1. This is a fairly complicated molecule, which doesn't resemble any of the known neurotransmitters in an obvious way. In fact, the structure of cocaine doesn't give us much help at all in understanding how the drug works on the brain.

The more we learn about cocaine's effects on the brain, the more complex the drug's actions seem. Cocaine blocks the reuptake of dopamine, norepinephrine, and serotonin, causing a prolonged effect of these neurotransmitters. The observation that the blockage of dopamine receptors or the destruction of dopamine-containing neurons lessened the amount of cocaine that laboratory animals

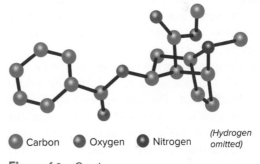

Carbon   Oxygen   Nitrogen   *(Hydrogen omitted)*

Figure 6.1   Cocaine

self-administered led many researchers to focus on dopamine neurons. After several years of intense scientific research, enthusiasm regarding dopamine's exclusive role in cocaine-related behaviors has been tempered, in part, because drugs that block only dopamine reuptake do not produce the same behavioral effects as cocaine. Additionally,

adulterated: to make something poorer in quality by adding another substance. With regards to street drugs, also known as "cut" or "stepped on."

racial discrimination: an action that results in unjust or unfair treatment of persons from a specific racial group.

these drugs have been unsuccessful in treating cocaine addiction. Because cocaine is a complex drug, affecting many neurotransmitters, the latest bet is that cocaine's behavioral effects depend on an interaction of multiple neurotransmitters, including dopamine, serotonin, GABA, and glutamate.

Absorption and Elimination

People can, and do, use cocaine in many ways. Chewing and sucking the leaves allows the cocaine to be absorbed slowly through the mucous membranes. This results in a slower onset of effects and much lower blood levels than are usually obtained via snorting, the most common route by which the drug is used recreationally. In snorting, the intent is to get the very fine cocaine hydrochloride powder high into the nasal passages—right on the nasal mucosa. From there it is absorbed quite rapidly and, through circulatory mechanisms that are not completely understood, reaches the brain rather quickly.

The intravenous use of cocaine delivers a very high concentration to the brain, producing a rapid and brief effect. For that reason, intravenous cocaine used to be a favorite among compulsive users, many of whom switched from intranasal to intravenous use. However, the smoking of crack is now preferred by most compulsive users because this route is less invasive (no needles) and the onset of its effects is just as fast.

The cocaine molecules are metabolized by enzymes in the blood and liver, and the activity of these enzymes is variable from one person to another. In any case, cocaine itself is rapidly removed, with a half-life of about one hour. The major metabolites, which are the basis of urine screening tests, have a longer half-life of about eight hours. It takes about three days for complete elimination of cocaine metabolites from the urine following moderate use of the drug.

Beneficial Uses

Local Anesthesia The local anesthetic properties of cocaine—its ability to numb the area to which it is applied—were discovered in 1860 soon after its

isolation from coca leaves. It was not until 1884 that this characteristic was used medically; the early applications were in eye surgery and dentistry. The use of cocaine spread rapidly because it apparently was a safe and effective drug. The potential for misuse soon became clear, though, and a search began for synthetic agents with similar anesthetic characteristics but little or no potential for misuse. This work was rewarded in 1905 with the discovery of procaine (Novocain), which is still in wide use.

Many drugs have been synthesized since 1905 that have local anesthetic properties similar to those of cocaine but have little or no ability to produce CNS stimulation. Those drugs have largely replaced cocaine for medical use. However, because cocaine is absorbed so well into mucous membranes, it remains in use for surgery in the nasal, laryngeal, and esophageal regions.

Other Claimed Benefits Because cocaine produces a feeling of increased energy and well-being, it continues to enjoy an important status among certain individuals who self-prescribe it to overcome fatigue. Athletes, entertainers, and politicians are only a few of the people who may use the drug in an effort to consistently perform at their peak. Cocaine has not been used medically for its CNS effects for many years, in part because its effects are brief, but mostly because of concern about the development of addiction.

Causes for Concern

Acute Toxicity There is no evidence that occasional use of small amounts of cocaine is a threat to the individual's health. However, some people have increased the amount they use to the point of toxicity. Acute cocaine poisoning can lead to profound CNS stimulation, progressing to convulsions, which can lead to respiratory or cardiac arrest. This is in some ways similar to amphetamine overdose. But it is important to remember that whether a drug produces a desired or toxic effect is largely dependent on the dose taken. Potential toxicity increases with larger doses. It is equally important to know that illicit cocaine is often adulterated (or cut with other chemicals in order to maximize dealers' profits. Some adulterants may be more toxic than cocaine itself. In the past, a substantial proportion of the cocaine in North America was cut with levamisole, a drug approved to treat cancer and used to deworm animals. Levamisole can reduce a person's white blood cell count, making them more susceptible to infections. In severe cases, this can be fatal.

It was reported in 1992 that the combination of cocaine and alcohol (ethanol) in the body could result in the formation of a chemical called **cocaethylene,** which was subsequently shown to be more toxic than cocaine in mice. However, studies in humans have shown that cocaethylene is less potent than cocaine with respect to its cardiovascular and subjective effects.[11]

Chronic Toxicity Use of cocaine in a binge, during which the drug is taken repeatedly and at increasingly high doses, can lead to a state of increasing irritability, restlessness, and paranoia. In severe cases, this can result in a full-blown paranoid psychosis, in which the individual loses touch with reality and experiences auditory hallucinations.[12] This experience is disruptive and quite frightening. However, most individuals seem to recover from the psychosis as the drug leaves the system.

Addictive Potential Cocaine can produce addiction in some users. But it's important to emphasize that the majority of cocaine users use the drug without becoming addicted. Nonetheless, virtually every species of laboratory animal, when given the opportunity, will readily self-administer cocaine. Humans will also perform rigorous tasks in order to receive a dose of cocaine,[13] and each year, the drug accounts for one of the largest proportions of admission for drug treatment in the United States.[14] Thus, it's clear that cocaine use can cause disruptions in functioning for some users.

Throughout the 1970s, the importance of this addiction went unrecognized because drug addiction was linked to the presence of physical withdrawal symptoms. After prolonged daily cocaine

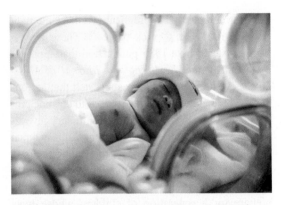

It seems clear that the early negative effects of prenatal cocaine exposure were overstated in media accounts, but it remains unwise to use cocaine during pregnancy. ©Naypong/Shutterstock.com RF

administration in animals, there were no obvious withdrawal signs (e.g., no diarrhea or convulsions), and many scientists concluded that cocaine produces no physical dependence and is therefore not an addictive drug. More recent experience has led to a different way of looking at this issue. The addictive potential of a drug is no longer defined solely by the presence of physical withdrawal symptoms during drug abstinence. As was discussed in Chapter 2, a person may be diagnosed with a cocaine use disorder if he or she exhibits a set of maladaptive behaviors listed in the *DSM-5,* which may or may not include physical withdrawal symptoms. Following abrupt cessation of several days of cocaine use (a binge), a constellation of withdrawal symptoms may be present, including cocaine craving, irritability, anxiety, depressed mood, increased appetite, and exhaustion. However, these symptoms vary greatly among individuals, with some individuals exhibiting little or no symptoms.

Crack Babies When crack cocaine first appeared in late 1984, media reports claimed the drug was taking over U.S. cities, and that it was having especially

cocaethylene (co cah *eth* eh leen): a chemical formed when ethanol and cocaine are co-administered.

devastating effects on pregnant women and their developing fetuses ("crack babies"). These reports were bolstered by a 1985 publication that appeared in the influential *New England Journal of Medicine*.[15] Authors of the report suggested that serious harm would come to infants exposed to cocaine prenatally. Despite the fact that this preliminary investigation was based on only 23 cocaine-using women and their babies—which meant that caution should have been exercised before applying the findings broadly—many sounded the alarm that we should prepare for a generation of children whose lives would be characterized by drug addiction, extreme suffering, physical and developmental disabilities, and intellectual inferiority. Pediatrician Ira Chasnoff, lead author of the *New England Journal of Medicine* article, went so far as to advise parents of cocaine-exposed infants not to make eye contact with their babies because this, he claimed, overwhelmed the child. (Note that this advice conflicted with the major theories on parent-child bonding.) At the same time, it was frequently reported that the number of babies addicted to cocaine as a result of prenatal exposure was extraordinary high, as many as 400,000 babies per year.

By the time the dust had settled and data from well-controlled studies were in, it was clear that earlier reports overstated both the number of such children and the expected long-term effects. It turned out that most of the women who gave birth to infants with reported fetal cocaine exposure were also malnourished, drinking alcohol heavily, and using multiple drugs during pregnancy, in addition to using cocaine. Almost all of the expectant mothers in the studies also smoked tobacco cigarettes. Many of these women were living in intensely stressful situations—sometimes with a violent partner or lacking reliable housing—and few received prenatal care. Not surprisingly, many of their children were born prematurely; the symptoms touted as characterizing "classic crack babies" such as tremoring limbs and low birth weight were most likely symptoms of prematurity.

The data had also indicated that there were no consistent negative associations between prenatal

cocaine exposure and several developmental measures, including physical growth, test scores, and language development.[16] By the time this information was widely known, however, a tremendous amount of damage had already been done. Policies were passed that severely punished pregnant women who used cocaine, and considerable stigmas were associated with crack use. In some cases, children were separated from their mothers, and some mothers were incarcerated. We are not implying that use of cocaine during pregnancy is a good idea. It is not. There are real and immediate problems associated with cocaine use during pregnancy, including increased risk for spontaneous abortion (miscarriage) and torn placenta. It is important, however, to remember that misunderstandings of the relationship between prenatal cocaine exposure and subsequent health can lead to an oversimplification of the complex relationships between socioeconomic factors and the functioning of an individual, whether drug use is involved or not. These misunderstandings can sometimes have worse consequences than cocaine itself.

Supplies of Illicit Cocaine

Cocaine is readily available on the illicit market in all major U.S. metropolitan areas, despite the fact that most of it originates in South America. Illicit cocaine comes to the United States primarily from three South American countries: Peru, Bolivia, and Colombia. Each year, about 1,000 tons of cocaine hydrochloride are produced in South America. Bolivia typically produces about half as much coca as Peru, and Colombia twice as much as Peru. In all of these countries, attempts to control production are complex: U.S. DEA agents assist local police, who may be in conflict with army units fighting against local guerrillas. Often the price and availability of coca in these countries are determined more by local politics than by the DEA's eradication and interdiction efforts. Although we might pay some farmers to grow alternative crops, the high profits from growing illicit cocaine draw others to plant new fields. An economic analysis of the impact of eradication efforts indicates that even the most successful projects result in at best only temporary shortages.[17]

Large shipments of cocaine were traditionally routed by boat or plane to any of hundreds of islands in the Caribbean, and from there to Miami or other ports in the eastern United States, again by small boat or airplane. Although sea routes continue to be important, the pressure brought by Navy, Air Force, and Coast Guard interdiction efforts has shifted trafficking somewhat more to land routes through Central America and Mexico. Now, more than half of the cocaine smuggled into the United States crosses the U.S.–Mexico border.

Current Patterns of Cocaine Use

Throughout the early 1980s, the National Survey on Drug Use and Health (see Chapter 1) found that 7 to 9 percent of young adults reported use of cocaine within the past month. In 2015, the comparable figure was less than 1 percent (corresponding to about 1.9 million people), and the use of cocaine had dropped significantly in the general population. Data from the Monitoring the Future study (Chapter 1) show that cocaine use decreased substantially among high school seniors between 1985 and 1994. Although the number reporting use increased somewhat during the mid-1990s, less than 3 percent now report use in the past year, compared to 12 percent at the peak of cocaine use in the early 1980s.

Amphetamines

History

Development and Early Uses For centuries the Chinese have made a medicinal tea from herbs they call *ma huang,* which American scientists classify in the genus *Ephedra.* The active ingredient in these herbs is called **ephedrine,** and it is used to dilate the bronchial passages in asthma patients. Bronchial dilation can be achieved by stimulating the sympathetic branch of the autonomic nervous system, and that is exactly what ephedrine does (it is referred to as a **sympathomimetic** drug). This drug

The active ingredient in the herb *ma huang* is ephedrine, which is chemically similar to amphetamine. ©Spike Mafford/ Getty Images RF

also has other effects related to its sympathetic nervous system stimulation, such as elevating blood pressure. In the late 1920s, researchers synthesized and studied the effects of a new chemical that was similar in structure to ephedrine: **Amphetamine** was patented in 1932.

All major effects of amphetamine were discovered in the 1930s, although some of the uses were developed later. Amphetamine's first use was as a replacement for ephedrine in the treatment of asthma. Quite early it was shown that amphetamine was a potent dilator of the nasal and bronchial passages and could be efficiently delivered through inhalation. The Benzedrine (brand name) inhaler was introduced as an over-the-counter (OTC) product in 1932 for treating the stuffy noses caused by colds.

---

ephedrine (eh *fed* rin): a sympathomimetic drug used in treating asthma.

sympathomimetic (sim path o mih *met* ick): a drug that stimulates the sympathetic branch of the autonomic nervous system.

amphetamine: a synthetic CNS stimulant and sympathomimetic.

Some of the early work with amphetamine showed that the drug would awaken anesthetized dogs. As one writer put it, amphetamine is the drug that won't let sleeping dogs lie! This effect didn't go unnoticed by students and truck drivers. Students used amphetamine because it helped them stay awake and study longer. Truck drivers used amphetamine to stay awake during long hauls. The wake-promoting effect of amphetamine led to testing it for the treatment of **narcolepsy** in 1935. Narcolepsy is a condition in which the individual spontaneously falls asleep as many as 50 times a day. Amphetamine enables these patients to remain awake and function almost normally. Other beneficial effects of amphetamine noticed in the 1930s included appetite suppression and reduction of activity in hyperactive children. Even today the drug remains in use for these purposes.

Wartime Uses In 1939, amphetamine went to war. There were many reports that Germany was using amphetamines to increase the efficiency of its soldiers. Such statements provided the basis for several other countries, including the United States, to evaluate the utility of amphetamines. A 1944 report in the *Air Surgeon's Bulletin,* titled "Benzedrine Alert," stated, "This drug is the most satisfactory of any available in temporarily postponing sleep when desire to sleep endangers the security of a mission."[18]

The "Speed Scene" of the 1960s Most of the misuse of amphetamines until the 1960s was through the legally manufactured and legally purchased oral preparation. When the amphetamines became so widely available after World War II, some people discovered that they could get a cocaine-like high if they injected amphetamine. By the 1960s, amphetamines had become so widely available at such a low price that more IV drug users were using them, either in combination with heroin or alone. Although they were prescription drugs, it was not difficult to obtain a prescription to treat depression or obesity.

The most desired drug on the streets was methamphetamine, which was available in liquid form in ampules for injection. Hospital emergency rooms sometimes used this drug to stimulate respiration in patients suffering from overdoses of sleeping pills (no longer considered an appropriate treatment), and physicians also used injectable amphetamines intramuscularly to treat obesity.

Because some heroin users would inject amphetamines alone when they could not obtain heroin, some physicians also felt that methamphetamine could serve as a legal substitute for heroin and thus be a form of treatment. In those days, amphetamines were not considered to produce dependency, so these physicians were quite free with their prescriptions.[19] Reports of those abuses led to federal regulation of amphetamines within the new concept of dangerous drugs in the 1965 law. Although the speed scene of the late 1960s was relatively short-lived and only a small number of people were directly involved, it was the focus of a great deal of national concern, and it helped change the way the medical profession and society at large viewed these drugs, which had been so widely accepted.

As the abuse of amphetamines began to be recognized, physicians prescribed less of the drugs. Their new legal status as dangerous drugs put restrictions on prescriptions and refills, and in the 1970s the total amount of these drugs that could be manufactured was limited. Thus, within less than a decade, amphetamines went from being widely used and accepted pharmaceuticals to being less widely used, tightly restricted drugs associated in the public mind with drug-abusing hippies.

The Return of Methamphetamine One reaction to limited amphetamine availability was an increase in the number of illicit laboratories making methamphetamine, which acquired the name **crank.** Most illicit methamphetamine consumed in the United States is produced in small "stovetop laboratories," which might exist for only a few days in a remote area before moving on. The process for making methamphetamine has been on the streets since the 1960s, and illicit laboratories have been raided every year. By the late 1990s, however, the number of illicit methamphetamine laboratories confiscated by the authorities increased dramatically. One

Myth Buster

Meth Mouth: Fact or Fiction?

You may have seen the dramatic pictures showing the extreme tooth decay associated with methamphetamine abuse, the so-called "meth mouth." One effect of methamphetamine is the restriction of salivary flow, which could lead to dryness of the mouth. Because dryness of the mouth can increase the likelihood of plaque and tooth decay, some have speculated that this condition underlies the dramatic pictures of meth mouth seen in the popular media. Dryness of the mouth is a relatively common side effect associated with many widely used medications, including the popular antidepressant duloxetine (Cymbalta) and the ADHD medication *d*-amphetamine (Adderall: combination of amphetamine and *d*-amphetamine mixed salts). Despite the fact that these medications are used daily and frequently prescribed (each year both are among the top 100 most prescribed drugs in the United States), there are no published reports of dental problems associated with their use. Given the structural and pharmacological similarities of methamphetamine and *d*-amphetamine, this suggests that the phenomenon of meth mouth has less to do with the direct pharmacological effects of methamphetamine and more to do with nonpharmacological factors, ranging from poor dental hygiene to media sensationalism. In fact, much of the evidence linking methamphetamine abuse and tooth decay is anecdotal and not scientific; detailed investigations of the impact of methamphetamine abuse on dental health with suitable oral health assessments are lacking. Thus, meth mouth is probably more fiction than fact.

Box icon credit: ©McGraw-Hill Education

reason that the number of laboratories has increased is said to be related to the relative ease by which methamphetamine can be produced. A quick search of the Internet can provide the surfer with dozens of "How to make meth" recipes within minutes. According to these recipes and law enforcement personnel, methamphetamine can be "easily" made from a few common products, the most important of which is the over-the-counter cold medication pseudophedrine. Examples of some other ingredients used are iodine, phosphorus, and various organic solvents, including starting fluid, lye (Drano), paint thinner, and antifreeze. You might have noticed that some of these solvents can be quite caustic, flammable, and toxic. In the final stages of the synthesis process, however, the harsh components and solvents are washed away. Thus, methamphetamine users are not ingesting Drano or antifreeze per se, as is sometimes reported by less than knowledgeable sources. Nonetheless, performing a successful synthesis resulting in pure methamphetamine is a much more difficult task than what is portrayed in the popular media. In the early 2000s, a wave of stories appeared attesting to the destructive effects associated with methamphetamine use. The reports were similar to those about the "crack scare" of the 1980s. Some claimed that use of methamphetamine had reached epidemic proportions, whereas others detailed the apparent terrible consequences of using the drug, including immediate addiction, cognitive impairments, extreme tooth decay (see Myth Buster box), and even physical unattractiveness.

But, like with the reporting on crack, the evidence showed many of these accounts to be wildly exaggerated. The number of methamphetamine users, for example, has always been considerably lower than the number of users of drugs such as cocaine, opioids, and marijuana. Even during the peak methamphetamine use years, there were never more than a million people who had used the drug in the past 30 days. This number is considerably

narcolepsy: a disease that causes people to fall asleep suddenly.
crank: street name for illicitly manufactured methamphetamine.

Ice is a smokable form of methamphetamine. Source: Drug Enforcement Administration

lower than the 2.5 million cocaine users, the 4.4 million illegal prescription opioid users, or the 15 million marijuana smokers during the same period. The number of methamphetamine users has never come close to exceeding the number of users of these other drugs. In 2015, approximately 900,000 individuals reported current methamphetamine use. This figure represents 0.3 percent of the U.S. population aged 12 or older.

With regard to the addictiveness of methamphetamine, less than 15 percent of those who have ever used the drug will become addicted, indicating that the overwhelming majority of users use the drug without problems of addiction.[20] And the supposition that methamphetamine use leads to cognitive impairments is not supported by research. Finding from a critical review of the scientific literature evaluating the long-term effects of methamphetamine in humans indicated that methamphetamine users' cognitive functioning and their brain structures were generally normal.[21]

Basic Pharmacology

Chemical Structures Figure 6.2 illustrates some similarities in the structures of amphetamines and related drugs. First, note the likeness between the molecular structures of the catecholamine neurotransmitters (dopamine and norepinephrine) and the basic amphetamine molecule. It appears that amphetamine produces its effects because it is recognized as one of these catecholamines at many

sites in both the central and the peripheral nervous systems.

Next, look at the methamphetamine molecule, which simply has a methyl group added to the basic amphetamine structure. This methyl group seems to make the molecule cross the blood-brain barrier more readily and thus further increase the CNS potency. (If more of the molecules get into the brain, then fewer total molecules have to be given.) However, the behavioral significance of this in humans seems limited, as studies directly comparing the two compounds report no difference on many measures, including abuse potential, euphoria, and cardiovascular activity.[22] Notice the structures for ephedrine, the old Chinese remedy that is still used to treat asthma, and for phenylpropanolamine (PPA). Before 2000, PPA was an ingredient in OTC weight-control preparations and in many of the look-alikes. Both of these molecules have a structural addition that makes them not cross the blood-brain barrier as well; therefore, they produce peripheral effects without as much CNS effectiveness.

Mechanism of Action Like cocaine, amphetamines increase the activity of monoamine neurotransmitters (dopamine, norepinephrine, and serotonin), although amphetamines accomplish this effect via a different mechanism. Amphetamines augment the activity of these neurotransmitters by stimulating release rather than by inhibiting reuptake. Findings from studies of laboratory animals strongly

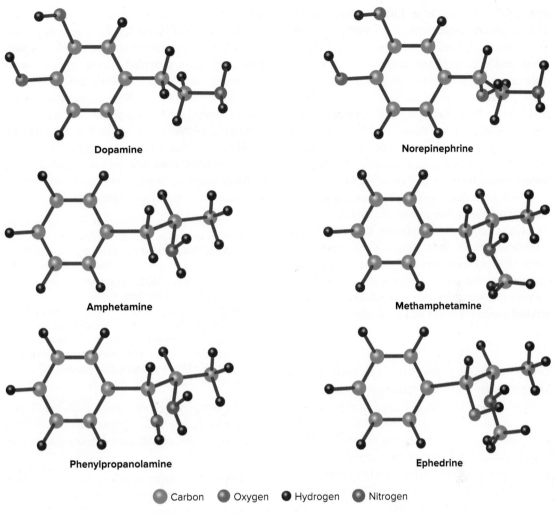

Dopamine

Norepinephrine

Amphetamine

Methamphetamine

Phenylpropanolamine

Ephedrine

⬤ Carbon   ⬤ Oxygen   ⬤ Hydrogen   ⬤ Nitrogen

Figure 6.2   Molecular Structures of Neurotransmitters and Stimulants

implicate dopamine in mediating amphetamine-related reinforcement. For example, researchers have reported that amphetamines produce substantial increases in dopamine levels in nucleus accumbens, a brain region thought to be important for drug-related reinforcement. In humans, while amphetamine-induced euphoria and brain dopamine elevations have been positively correlated, dopamine antagonists do not block the euphoria produced by amphetamine.[23] These observations suggest that exclusive focus on dopamine might be too simplistic.

Recent evidence shows that amphetamines are more potent releasers of norepinephrine than of dopamine and serotonin. As a result, some researchers speculate that norepinephrine activity mediates the euphoric effects of amphetamines.[24] Nevertheless, it is unlikely that complex drug effects, such as subjective effects and drug taking, are mediated via one neurotransmitter system. As we are learning from our experience with cocaine, amphetamine-related effects are probably the result of interactions with multiple neurotransmitters.

Absorption and Elimination Like cocaine, amphetamines are consumed through a variety of routes: oral, intranasal, intravenous, and smoked. When taken orally, peak effects occur about 1.5 hours after ingestion. In contrast, intranasal peak effects occur between 5 and 20 minutes after administration; peak effects following the intravenous and smoked routes occur within 5 to 10 minutes. The half-life of amphetamines ranges from 5 to 12 hours. Virtually complete elimination of the drug occurs within two to three days of the last dose.

With high doses a tachyphylaxis (rapid tolerance) may be seen. Because amphetamine produces its effects largely by displacing the monoamine transmitters from their storage sites, with large doses the monoamines might be sufficiently depleted, so that another dose within a few hours may not be able to displace as much neurotransmitter, and a reduced effect will be obtained.

Beneficial Uses

Depression During the 1950s and early 1960s, amphetamines were the treatment of choice for depression and fatigue. As these drugs became more stigmatized in the late 1960s and newer antidepressants were developed, their use in this capacity was reduced. Today, amphetamines are still used in the treatment of depression but mostly as an **adjunctive therapy.** A major advantage of amphetamines is that their antidepressant effects occur rapidly (within a day or two) compared with standard antidepressant medications whose effects may not be observed for weeks. Of course, both clinicians and patients should be aware of concerns about the abuse potential associated with amphetamines. In the few controlled trials that have assessed amphetamines for their utility in treating depression, there was little evidence for such concerns.

Weight Control Probably the most common medical use for amphetamines through the mid-1960s was for weight control, even though only limited data showed the effectiveness of amphetamines for

this purpose. It's clear that amphetamines reduce appetite and food intake for short periods of time (i.e., a few weeks). Earlier studies as well as a more recent one have provided considerable evidence supporting this position. What's less clear, however, is the impact of amphetamines on long-term weight loss. Even though methamphetamine remains available as an adjunctive treatment for obesity, this uncertainty is apparent in the FDA-mandated statement that is included in the package insert for methamphetamine and related stimulant drugs used for weight control:

> The natural history of obesity is measured in years, whereas the studies cited are restricted to a few weeks duration; thus, the total impact of drug-induced weight loss over that of diet alone must be considered clinically limited. . . . Methamphetamine is indicated as a short-term (i.e., a few weeks) adjunct in a regimen of weight reduction based on caloric restriction, for patients in whom obesity is refractory to alternative therapy, e.g., repeated diets, group programs, and other drugs. The limited usefulness of methamphetamine tablets should be weighed against possible risks inherent in use of the drug.[25]

The other sympathomimetics available by prescription for short-term weight loss include diethylpropion, phentermine, phendimetrazine, and sibutramine.

Narcolepsy Narcolepsy is a sleep disorder in which individuals do not sleep normally at night and in the daytime experience uncontrollable episodes of muscular weakness and falling asleep. The best available treatment seems to be to keep the patient awake during the day with amphetamines or other stimulants such as modafinil and armodafinil.

Hyperactive Children Today, the most common use of amphetamines is for treating symptoms of attention-deficit/hyperactivity disorder (ADHD: see the DSM-5 box[26]). This class of drug has been shown to reduce activity levels and improve concentration in hyperactive children and adults. Despite this and the fact that hundreds of thousands of people are currently being treated with stimulants for this problem, there is controversy over the

DSM-5

Diagnostic Criteria for Attention-Deficit/Hyperactivity Disorder

A. Either (1) or (2):

1. Five (or more) of the following symptoms of inattention have persisted for at least six months to a degree that is maladaptive and inconsistent with developmental level:

Inattention

   a. Often fails to give close attention to details or makes careless mistakes
   b. Often has difficulty sustaining attention in tasks or play
   c. Often does not seem to listen when spoken to directly
   d. Often does not follow through on instructions and fails to finish schoolwork, chores, or duties
   e. Often has difficulty organizing tasks and activities
   f. Is often easily distracted by extraneous stimuli
   g. Is often forgetful in daily activities

2. Five (or more) of the following symptoms of hyperactivity-impulsivity have persisted for at least six months to a degree that is maladaptive and inconsistent with developmental level:

Hyperactivity

   a. Often fidgets with hands or feet or squirms in seat
   b. Often leaves seat in classroom or in other situations in which remaining seated is expected
   c. Often runs about or climbs excessively in situations in which it is inappropriate
   d. Often has difficulty playing or engaging in leisure activities quietly
   e. Is often "on the go" or often acts as if "driven by a motor"
   f. Often talks excessively

Impulsivity

   g. Often blurts out answers before questions have been completed
   h. Often has difficulty awaiting turn
   i. Often interrupts or intrudes on others

B. Some hyperactive-impulsive or inattentive symptoms that caused impairment were present before age seven years.

C. Some impairment from the symptoms is present in two or more settings.

D. There must be clear evidence of clinically significant impairment in social, academic, or occupational functioning.

E. The symptoms do not occur exclusively during the course of a Pervasive Developmental Disorder or other disorder and are not better accounted for by another mental disorder.*

---

*In making this diagnosis, children must have six or more symptoms of the disorder, whereas older teens and adults should have at least five symptoms.

Adapted from *Diagnostic and Statistical Manual of Mental Disorders*, 5th edition (DSM-5).

nature of the disorder being treated. We still don't understand what the drugs are doing to reduce hyperactivity, and we still don't have a widely accepted solution to the apparent paradox: Why does a "stimulant" drug appear to produce a "calming" effect?

The cause or causes of ADHD are not well understood. Data from twin studies indicate that genetic factors contribute substantially to the expression of ADHD. Findings from other studies suggest the disorder is associated with prefrontal cortex deficits, especially in catecholamine-rich regions.[27] The evidence demonstrating the

adjunctive therapy: a treatment used together with the primary treatment. Its purpose is to assist the primary treatment.

beneficial effects of amphetamines and **methylphenidate (Ritalin)** in the treatment of ADHD bolsters this latter theory. These medications increase brain catecholamine activity, which would, in theory, reverse catecholamine-associated deficits. Although this theory is plausible, there are other theories and none has yet been widely accepted.

One concern is that treatment with stimulant medications will lead to substance abuse, even though findings from controlled studies show that stimulant therapy is protective against substance abuse (i.e., the occurrence of substance use disorders is actually decreased). Despite this, an increasing number of nonstimulant medications are being assessed for utility. One such example is the drug atomoxetine (Strattera), which has been shown to be efficacious in the treatment of ADHD.[28] Atomoxetine's ability to increase catecholamines in the prefrontal cortex has been hypothesized to be the basis for these effects. Unlike stimulant therapies used to treat ADHD, atomoxetine does not increase dopamine transmission in the nucleus accumbens and does not appear to have abuse potential.

One of the more disturbing side effects of stimulant therapy is a suppression of height and weight increases during drug treatment. Amphetamine produces a slightly greater effect in most studies than methylphenidate. If drug treatment is stopped over the summer vacation, a growth spurt makes up for most of the suppressed height and weight gain.

"Smart Pills" Much research has been done on the role of stimulants in improving mental performance. One area of interest is performance that has been disrupted by fatigue and/or sleep deprivation. These symptoms are common in occupations that require extended work periods or abrupt changes in work schedules, for example, police officers and military personnel. As discussed earlier, militaries from several countries used (and continue to use) amphetamines for this purpose. Much of the information supporting the early use of amphetamines to attenuate disruptions cause by fatigue or sleep deprivation was anecdotal. Hart and colleagues developed a laboratory model of shift work in which participants work several days on the day and night shifts and are repeatedly switched between shifts. In a series of studies, they found that low oral doses of methamphetamine (5 and 10 mg) reduced shift-related performance disruptions and mood alterations.[29] Low doses of the stimulant modafinil have also been demonstrated to produce similar effects. Thus, it seems clear that stimulants administered at low doses can improve performance that had been disrupted by fatigue or sleep deprivation.

Life Saver

Amphetamine and Sleep

Adequate sleep is an essential physiological function for the health and survival of an individual. Deterioration of psychological functioning is one of the most noticeable and consistent manifestations of sleep loss. During prolonged sleep deprivation, there is an increase in fatigue and a decline in cognitive and perceptual ability. In severe cases, hallucinations and paranoia may also occur. Because amphetamine reliably reduces fatigue and offsets performance decrements, some people may repeatedly use this class of drug as a strategy to mitigate problems associated with sleep loss. Why would this approach be less than ideal? One of the most consistent effects of amphetamine use is the disruption of sleep, which means that repeated use could exacerbate problems related to sleep loss. Given the vital role that sleep plays in healthy functioning, regular users of amphetamine should be mindful of their sleep durations and make the appropriate adjustments (e.g., avoid drug use near the sleep period) to ensure that they get adequate amounts of sleep.

Box icon credit: ©McGraw-Hill Education

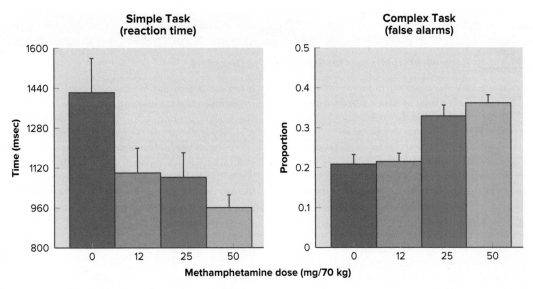

Figure 6.3   Effects of Methamphetamine on Performance

What are the effects of stimulants on performance that is not disrupted? Can stimulants improve the performance of healthy individuals seeking an edge? This issue has been the topic of much debate recently, especially as it relates to ethical concerns. For example, should the general public use stimulants routinely as "cognitive enhancers"? Because many of the ethical concerns assume that stimulants improve performance of healthy individuals, it might be helpful to look at the scientific evidence. The left panel of Figure 6.3 shows how methamphetamine affects performance on a simple reaction time task.[30] All three active doses improved reaction time with the largest dose producing the greatest effect. Now look at the right panel, which shows the effects of methamphetamine on the number of false alarms made during a metacognition task. On this more complicated task, performance is not improved by methamphetamine but is disrupted (i.e., more false alarms) by the two larger doses.[31] The bottom line is that the effects of amphetamines on performance of healthy individuals depend on the type of task and dose: Simple performance might be improved, but complex performance is likely to be disrupted at larger doses. (See Taking Sides, Chapter 16.)

Athletics   Under some conditions, the use of amphetamines or other stimulants at an appropriate dose can produce slight improvements in athletic performance. The effects are so small as to be meaningless for most athletes, but at the highest levels of competition even a 1 percent improvement can mean the difference between winning a medal or coming in sixth. The temptation has been strong for athletes to use amphetamines and other stimulants to enhance their performances, and this topic is discussed in more detail in Chapter 16.

Causes for Concern

Acute Toxicity   During the period of amphetamine intoxication with above-normal doses, the altered behavior patterns (acute behavioral toxicity) can cause some dangers. At higher doses, especially administered for extended periods, the user can become suspicious to the point of paranoia. Combine this with lack of sleep and poor nutrition, and there is

methylphenidate (Ritalin) (meth il *fen* ih date): a stimulant used in treating ADHD.

Focus on Treatment

Behavioral Treatments for Stimulant Use Disorders

Behavioral treatments are the predominant form of therapy used to treat stimulant use disorders because there has yet to be a medication that has received FDA approval for this purpose.

Cognitive-behavioral therapy (CBT) is probably the most widely used treatment for cocaine and amphetamine use disorders. This approach uses cognitive therapy techniques with behavioral-skills training. Individuals learn to identify and change behaviors that may lead to continued drug use, such as going out to previous drug-using locations or associating with drug-using friends.

Contingency management is an increasingly popular approach to treating stimulant use disorders. It provides rewards (e.g., cash or goods) to the individual for meeting specific goals such as abstaining from drug use. The value of the rewards is usually increased as the goals continue to be met.

Motivational enhancement, also known as motivational interviewing, is often used in combination with CBT or contingency management. It focuses on helping individuals accept the need for change as a result of drug use that has become disruptive. Strategies are developed for individuals to implement and maintain their efforts to change their own behavior.

Box icon credit: ©dencg/Shutterstock.com RF

even greater concern about the psychological and physical well-being of the person taking the drug.

Chronic Toxicity The development of a paranoid psychosis has long been known to be one of the effects of sustained amphetamine use. Laboratory studies in humans show that the paranoid psychosis after high-dose IV use of amphetamine is primarily the result of the drug. Evidence shows that the paranoid psychosis results from dopaminergic stimulation, probably in the mesolimbic system. In some cases in which paranoid psychoses have been produced by amphetamines, the paranoid thinking and loss of touch with reality have been slow to return to normal, persisting for days or even weeks after the drug has left the system. There is no good evidence for permanent behavioral or personality disruption.

Summary

- The stimulants can reverse the effects of fatigue, maintain wakefulness, decrease appetite, and temporarily elevate the mood of the user.

- Cocaine is derived from the coca plant. Coca leaves have been chewed for centuries.

- Cocaine's earliest uses in the United States were as a local anesthetic and in psychiatry.

- Coca paste and crack are smokable forms of illicit cocaine.

- Cocaine and amphetamines appear to act by interacting with several neurotransmitters, including dopamine, norepinephrine, and serotonin.

- Excessive cocaine or amphetamine use can result in a paranoid psychotic reaction.

- Cocaine and amphetamines can produce dependence.

- Use of cocaine has declined in the general population since 1985.

- Amphetamines are a synthetic sympathomimetic similar to ephedrine.

- The amphetamine-like drugs are similar in structure to dopamine and norepinephrine.

- Amphetamines are prescribed for short-term weight reduction, narcolepsy, and ADHD.

- Illicit methamphetamine is primarily made in small laboratories.

Review Questions

1. At about what periods in history did cocaine reach its first and second peaks of popularity, and when was amphetamine's popularity at its highest?
2. How did Mariani, Halsted, and Freud popularize the use of cocaine?
3. How are coca paste, freebase, and crack similar?
4. Following cocaine use, how long does it take for the drug (or its metabolites) to be eliminated from the body and not detected in the urine?
5. What similarities and what differences are there in the toxic effects of cocaine and amphetamine?
6. How would medical practice be affected if both cocaine and amphetamine were placed on Schedule I?
7. How does the chemical difference between methamphetamine and amphetamine relate to the behavioral effects of the two drugs?
8. Compare the dependence potential of cocaine with that of amphetamine.
9. Describe the effects of amphetamines on mental performance.

References

1. Dillehay, T. D., and others. "The Nanchoc Tradition: The Beginnings of Andean Civilization." *American Scientist* 85 (1997), pp. 46–55.
2. Taylor, N. *Flight from Reality.* New York: Duell, Sloan & Pearce, 1949.
3. Freud, S. *On the General Effect of Cocaine.* Lecture before the Psychiatric Union on March 5, 1885. Reprinted in *Drug Dependence* 5 (1970), p. 17.
4. Musto, D. F. "Opium, Cocaine and Marijuana in American History." *Scientific American,* July 1991, p. 40.
5. Ashley, R. *Cocaine: Its History, Uses and Effects.* New York: Warner Books, 1976.
6. Wright, H. "Report on the International Opium Commission and the Opium Problem as Seen Within the United States and Its Possessions." *61st Congress, 2nd Session, Senate Document No. 377,* February 21, 1910, pp. SO–SI.
7. Bourne, P. G. "The Great Cocaine Myth." *Drugs and Drug Abuse Education Newsletter 5* (1974).
8. Grinspoon, L., and others. *The Comprehensive Textbook of Psychiatry,* February 21, 1980, pp. 50–51.
9. Johnson, B. D., and others. "Careers in Crack, Drug Use, Drug Distribution, and Nondrug Criminality." *Crime and Delinquency* 41 (1995), p. 275.
10. United States Sentencing Commission. *Report to Congress: Cocaine and Federal Sentencing Policy,* May 2007.
11. Hart, C. L., and others. "Comparison of Intravenous Cocaethylene and Cocaine in Humans." *Psychopharmacology* 149 (2000), p. 153.
12. Brady, K. T., and others. "Cocaine-Induced Psychosis." *Journal of Clinical Psychiatry* 52 (1991), p. 509.
13. Haney, M., and others. "Effects of Pergolide on Intravenous Cocaine Self-administration in Men and Women." *Psychopharmacology* 137 (1998), p. 15.
14. Substance Abuse and Mental Health Services Administration, Center for Behavioral Health Statistics and Quality. *Treatment Episode Data Set (TEDS): 2001–2011. National Admissions to Substance Abuse Treatment Services.* BHSIS Series S-65, HHS Publication No. (SMA) 13-4772. Rockville, MD: Substance Abuse and Mental Health Services Administration, 2013.
15. Chasnoff, I. J., Burns, W. J., Schnoll, S. H., and Burns, K. A. "Cocaine Use in Pregnancy." *New England Journal of Medicine* 313 (1985), p. 666.
16. Frank, D. A., and others. "Growth, Development, and Behavior in Early Childhood Following Prenatal Cocaine Exposure: A Systematic Review." *Journal of the American Medical Association* 285 (2001), p. 1613; Frank, D. A., and others. "Level of Prenatal Cocaine Exposure and Scores on the Bayley Scales of Infant Development: Modifying Effects of Caregiver, Early Intervention, and Birth Weight." *Pediatrics* 110 (2002), pp. 1143–1152; Beeghly, M., and others. "Prenatal Cocaine Exposure and Children's Language Functioning at 6 and 9.5 Years: Moderating Effects of Child Age, Birthweight, and Gender." *Journal of Pediatric Psychology* 31 (2006), pp. 98–115; Lewis, B. A., and others. "The Effects of Prenatal Cocaine on Language Development at 10 Years of Age." *Neurotoxicology Teratology* 33 (2011), pp. 17–24; Betancourt, L. M., and others. "Adolescents with and without Gestational Cocaine Exposure: Longitudinal Analysis of Inhibitory Control, Memory and Receptive Language." *Neurotoxicology Teratology* 33 (2011), pp. 36–46.
17. Riley, K. J. *Snow Job?* New Brunswick, NJ: Transaction, 1996.
18. "Benzedrine Alert." *Air Surgeon's Bulletin* 1, no. 2 (1944), pp. 19–21.
19. Brecher, E. M. *Licit and Illicit Drugs.* Boston: Little, Brown, 1972.
20. O'Brien, M. S., and J. C. Anthony. "Extra-medical Stimulant Dependence among Recent Initiates." *Drug and Alcohol Dependence* 104 (2009), pp. 147–55.
21. Hart, C. L., and others. "Is Cognitive Functioning Impaired in Methamphetamine Users? A Critical Review." *Neuropsychopharmacology* 37 (2012) pp. 586–608.
22. Kirkpatrick, M. G., and others. "Comparison of Intranasal Methamphetamine and D-amphetamine Self-Administration by Humans." *Addiction* 107 (2012) pp. 783–91.
23. Brauer, L. H., and H. deWit. "High Dose Pimozide Does Not Block Amphetamine-Induced Euphoria in Normal Volunteers." *Pharmacology Biochemistry and Behavior* 56 (1997), p. 265.
24. Rothman, R. B., and others. "Amphetamine-Type Central Nervous System Stimulants Release Norepinephrine More

Potently Than They Release Dopamine and Serotonin." *Synapse* 39 (2001), p. 32.

25. *Physician's Desk Reference Medical Economies.* Ordell, NJ: Annual.

26. American Psychiatric Association. *Diagnostic and Statistical Manual of Mental Disorders,* 5th ed. Washington, DC: American Psychological Association, 2013.

27. Spencer, T. L., and others. "Overview and Neurobiology of Attention-Deficit/Hyperactivity Disorder." *Journal of Clinical Psychiatry* 63, Supplement 12 (2003).

28. Caballero, J., and M. C. Nahata. "Atomoxetine Hydrochloride for the Treatment of Attention-Deficit/Hyperactivity Disorder." *Clinical Therapeutics* 25 (2003), p. 3065.

29. Hart, C. L., A. S. Ward, M. Haney, J. Nasser, and R. W. Foltin. "Methamphetamine Attenuates Disruptions in Performance and Mood during Simulated Night Shift Work." *Psychopharmacology* 169 (2003), pp. 42–51.

30. Hart, C. L., and others. "Acute Physiological and Behavioral Effects of Intranasal Methamphetamine in Humans." *Neuropsychopharmacology* 33 (2008), pp. 1847–55.

31. Kirkpatrick, M. G., J. Metcalfe, M. J. Greene, and C. L. Hart. "Effects of Intranasal Methamphetamine on Metacognition of Agency." *Psychopharmacology* 197 (2008), pp. 137–44.

7

Depressants and Inhalants

©Pixtal/AGE Fotostock RF

Objectives

When you have finished this chapter, you should be able to:

- Give several examples of depressant drugs and describe the general set of behavioral effects common to them.

- Understand how concerns about barbiturate use led to acceptance of newer classes of sedative-hypnotics.

- Describe the differences in dose and duration of action that are appropriate for daytime anxiolytic effects as opposed to hypnotic effects of prescription depressants.

- Describe how the time of onset of a depressant drug relates to abuse potential and how duration of action relates to the risk of withdrawal symptoms.

- Describe the mechanism of action for barbiturates and benzodiazepines.

- Explain why it is not recommended that people use sleeping pills for more than a few days in a row.

- Describe several types of substances that are abused as inhalants.

- Describe GHB's typical dose range and behavioral effects, as well as its effects when combined with alcohol.

What is the most widely prescribed category of psychoactive medications? Downers, depressants, sedatives, hypnotics, anxiolytics: Known by many names, these prescription drugs have a widespread effect in the brain that can be summed up as decreased CNS activity. What are the behavioral effects? Most people have a good idea of the effects of alcohol, and these drugs have effects that are generally similar: Depending on the dose and the situation, people may experience relaxation, exhilaration, inebriation, or drowsiness, or they may become stuporous and uncoordinated. We consider these CNS **depressants** as a class because of those common effects. Alcohol is such an important substance that it is covered in its own chapter (Chapter 9). Beginning with the introduction of the **barbiturates** in the early 1900s, a series of prescription drugs have been marketed for two medical purposes. Many people have used low doses of these drugs to reduce anxiety, to keep them calm and relaxed. When prescription drugs are used in that way, we refer to them as **sedatives**. Current examples of popular sedatives include Xanax and Ativan, both members of the chemical class **benzodiazepines**. The other common medical use for the CNS depressants is to induce sleep. When these medications are used as sleeping pills, we refer to them as **hypnotics**. Current examples of popular sleep medications include Ambien and Lunesta, both examples of the newest type of nonbenzodiazepine hypnotics. In this chapter we also discuss the nonmedical use of various **inhalants** (e.g., glue, paint, solvents), because the typical effects of inhaling the fumes from these products also fall into the category of CNS depressant effects. Also included is the depressant drug **GHB** (gamma hydroxybutyric acid), which has attained notoriety as a date-rape drug.

History and Pharmacology

Before Barbiturates

Chloral Hydrate In the early 1900s a Chicago bartender named Mickey Finn became briefly famous when he was prosecuted for adding chloral hydrate to the drinks of some of his customers, after which they would become incapacitated and be robbed by one of his "house girls." The term *Mickey Finn* entered our language as slang for a drug added to someone's drink without his or her knowledge. This technique was used in several movie scripts, where it was referred to as "slipping" someone a "mickey." First synthesized in 1832, chloral hydrate was not used clinically until about 1870. It is rapidly metabolized to tri-chloroethanol, which is the active hypnotic agent. When taken orally, chloral hydrate has a short onset period (30 minutes), and 1 to 2 grams will induce sleep in less than an hour.

In 1869, Dr. Benjamin Richardson introduced chloral hydrate to Great Britain. Ten years later he called it "in one sense a beneficent, and in another sense a maleficent substance, I almost feel a regret that I took any part whatever in the introduction of the agent into the practice of healing."[1] He had learned that what humankind can use, some will abuse. Chloral hydrate abuse is a tough way to go; it is a gastric irritant, and repeated use causes considerable stomach upset.

Paraldehyde Paraldehyde was synthesized in 1829 and introduced clinically in 1882. Paraldehyde would probably be in great use today because of its effectiveness as a CNS depressant with little respiratory depression and a wide safety margin, except

for one characteristic: It has an extremely noxious taste and an odor that permeates the breath of the user. Its safety margin and its ability to sedate patients led to widespread use in mental hospitals before the 1950s. Anyone who worked in, was a patient in, or even visited one of the large state mental hospitals during that era remembered the odor of paraldehyde.

Barbiturates

Although the barbiturates have largely been replaced by more modern drugs, they were the first CNS depressant prescription medications to be widely used and abused. First introduced in 1903, the barbiturates became so important that eventually over 2,500 different examples of this chemical class were synthesized, and quite a few were marketed. Examples of once-popular barbiturates include phenobarbital, amobarbital, and secobarbital. The barbiturates are grouped according to their **duration of action** (how long the drug's effects last), which also happens to correspond to how quickly they act after being taken by mouth (time of onset). The short-acting barbiturates begin to produce effects in as little as 15 minutes, and have effects lasting only 2 or 3 hours, whereas the long-acting drugs may take an hour to produce effects, but they may last for 8 hours or more.

When these drugs were used during the daytime to reduce nervousness and anxiety, low doses (30–50 mg) of a long-acting barbiturate like phenobarbital were widely prescribed as sedatives. For use as sleeping pills, higher doses (100–200 mg) of a shorter-acting drug like secobarbital were prescribed.

Although the majority of people who took these medications did so without harm, the barbiturates were associated with overdose deaths, both accidental and intentional. As with other CNS depressants, the cause of death is typically respiratory depression (breathing slows and eventually stops) and in a great many cases this is due to the combined effects of alcohol and a depressant drug. Also, because these drugs produce effects similar to alcohol, sometimes people took barbiturates to get "high." Regular use of high doses, for either sleeping or intoxication, resulted in tolerance, and some people then increased the dose to several hundred milligrams per day. With these high daily doses, dangerous withdrawal symptoms could result if the person stopped the drug use abruptly (physical dependence).

During the heyday of barbiturate prescribing, neither overdose deaths nor dependence were big concerns among those being treated with sedatives (low doses of slow-acting drugs). The problems typically resulted from the prescriptions for sleeping pills (higher doses of fast-acting drugs). However, concerns about overdoses, psychological dependence, and physical dependence led to a bad reputation for all barbiturates, and by the 1950s the door was wide open for a safer substitute.

Meprobamate

Meprobamate (Miltown) was patented in 1952 and was believed to be a new and unique type of CNS depressant. The Food and Drug Administration approved its use in 1955, and it quickly became widely prescribed, based partly on a successful publicity campaign and partly on physicians' concerns about prescribing barbiturates.

It gradually became clear that meprobamate, like the barbiturates, can also produce both psychological and physical dependence. Physical dependence can result from taking a bit more than twice a normal daily dose. In 1970, meprobamate became a Schedule IV controlled substance, and although it is still available for prescriptions under several brand names, the benzodiazepines have largely replaced it.

In retrospect, it seems ironic that the medical community so readily accepted meprobamate as being safer than barbiturates. By deciding that the "barbiturates" were dangerous, the focus was on the chemical class, rather than on the dose and the manner in which the drug was used. Thus, a new, "safer" chemical was accepted without considering that its safety was not being judged under the same conditions. This mistake has occurred frequently with psychoactive drugs. It occurred again with methaqualone.

The risk of dependence on prescription sedatives depends on the timing of their effects and on the dose. ©Fancy Collection/ SuperStock RF

depressants: drugs that slow activity in the CNS.

barbiturates (bar *bitch er ates*): a chemical group of sedative-hypnotics.

sedatives: drugs used to relax, calm, or tranquilize.

benzodiazepines (ben zo die *ay* zah peens): a chemical grouping of sedative-hypnotics.

hypnotics: drugs used to induce sleep.

inhalants: volatile solvents inhaled for intoxicating purposes.

GHB: gamma hydroxybutyrate; chemically related to GABA; used recreationally as a depressant.

duration of action: how long a drug's effects last.

Methaqualone

With continued reports of overdoses and physical dependence associated with secobarbital and amobarbital sleeping pills, in the 1960s the market was wide open for a hypnotic that would be less dangerous. Maybe it was too wide open.

Methaqualone was synthesized in India and found to have sedative properties. Germany introduced methaqualone as an over-the-counter (nonprescription) drug in 1960, had its first reported methaqualone suicide in 1962, and discovered that 10 to 20 percent of the drug overdoses in the early 1960s resulted from misuse of methaqualone. Germany changed the drug to prescription-only status in 1963. From 1960 to 1964, Japan also had a problem with methaqualone abuse, which was the culprit in more than 40 percent of drug overdoses in that country. Japan placed strong restrictions on the prescribing of methaqualone, which reduced the number of subsequent overdoses.

Apparently no one in the United States was paying much attention to these problems in other countries, because in 1965, after three years of testing, Quaalude and Sopor, brand names for methaqualone, were introduced in the United States as prescription drugs with a package insert that read "Addiction potential not established."

In the early 1970s in this country, *ludes* and *sopors* were familiar terms in the drug culture and in drug-treatment centers. Physicians were overprescribing a hypnotic drug that they believed to be safer than the barbiturates. Sales zoomed, and front-page reporting of its effects when misused helped to build its reputation as a drug of abuse. In 1973, 8 years after it was introduced into this country, 4 years after American scientists began saying it produced dependence, and 11 years after the first suicide, methaqualone was put on Schedule II. By 1985, methaqualone was no longer available as a prescription drug, and it is now listed on Schedule I.

Benzodiazepines

The first of the benzodiazepines was chlordiazepoxide, which was marketed under the trade name Librium (possibly because it "liberates" one from anxieties).

Librium was marketed in 1960 as a more selective "antianxiety" agent that produced less drowsiness than the barbiturates and had a much larger safety margin before overdose death occurred in animals. Clinical practice bore this out: Physical dependence was almost unheard of, and overdose seemed not to occur except in combination with alcohol or other depressant drugs. Even strong psychological dependence seemed rare with this drug. The conclusion was reached that the benzodiazepines were as effective as the barbiturates and much safer. Librium became not only the leading psychoactive drug in terms of sales but also the leading prescription drug across the board. It was supplanted in the early 1970s by diazepam (Valium), a more potent (lower-dose) agent made by the same company. From 1972 until 1978, Valium was the leading seller among all prescription drugs. Since then, no single benzodiazepine has so dominated the market, but alprazolam is currently the most widely prescribed among this class of drugs.

As these drugs became widely used, reports of psychological dependence, occasional physical dependence, and overdose deaths appeared once again. Diazepam was one of the most frequently mentioned drugs in the DAWN system coroners' reports, although almost always in combination with alcohol or other depressants. What happened to the big difference between the barbiturates and the benzodiazepines? One possibility is that it might not be the chemical class of drugs that makes the big difference but the dose and time course of the individual drugs. *Overdose* deaths are more likely when a drug is sold in higher doses, such as those prescribed for hypnotic effects. *Psychological dependence* develops most rapidly when the drug hits the brain quickly, which is why intravenous use of heroin produces more dependence than oral use, and why smoking crack produces more dependence than chewing coca leaves. *Physical dependence* occurs when the drug leaves the system more rapidly than the body can adapt—one

Drugs in Depth

Seeking Tranquility

Humans have long sought to use substances to relax, to escape from anxious fears, and to sleep peacefully. Many people have tried to use alcohol for these purposes, and others have tried all the historical sedative-hypnotic agents as well as the currently popular benzodiazepine and nonbenzodiazepine pharmaceuticals. The strong desire to achieve these effects is a major reason this class of drugs is more widely prescribed than any other, more than antidepressants, opioids, or stimulants.

Perhaps the most extreme example of this search for chemically induced peace can be seen in the days leading up to the tragic 2009 death of pop superstar Michael Jackson. Before we go into that, we should point out that this is a single, and very unusual, case, and we are not offering this anecdote to represent the typical use of sedative drugs by most people.

The investigation of Jackson's death eventually led to the arrest and 2011 conviction of Conrad Murray, the physician who had administered intravenous propofol to Jackson the night he died. Propofol is a sedative-hypnotic agent that is administered intravenously to induce rapid anesthesia, usually by an anesthesiologist in a hospital setting (Murray's specialty was cardiology, but he had been hired by the promoter of Jackson's upcoming London concerts to serve as Jackson's personal physician). Jackson's associates and family members indicated that he had used this drug in the past and that during stressful concert tours, it was used to allow him to sleep. Although the focus of the news media was almost exclusively on propofol, Jackson also had significant blood levels of the benzodiazepine lorazepam and lower levels of several other drugs as well. The coroner's office attributed Jackson's death to the combination of drugs rather than to any single substance.

Although Jackson's case represents an unusual set of circumstances, in that most people cannot afford to hire a physician to administer intravenous drugs in their own homes, there are some elements that are common to many sedative-related overdoses. The most important is that these overdoses usually involve some combination of substances (sedatives, alcohol, opioids), any one of which alone would not have caused a medical emergency. Another is the dangerous practice of using a stimulant (or, perhaps in Jackson's case, steroids), to provide energy and alertness during part of the day and a sedative to induce sleep at night. Doing something like this once, for example, to counteract the disruptive effects of flying across several time zones, might not present much of a problem. But engaging in this cycle of drug-induced stimulation and depression on a daily basis is a dangerous recipe for tolerance, likely leading to increased dosing and a dependence on the medications to maintain the cycle.

"Death of Michael Jackson," https://en.wikipedia.org/wiki/Death_of_Michael_Jackson. Richards, M. *83 Minutes: The Doctor, the Damage, and the Shocking Death of Michael Jackson*. New York: St. Martin's Press, 2015.

Box icon credit: ©Ingram Publishing/SuperStock RF

way to reduce the severity of withdrawal symptoms is to reduce the dose of a drug slowly over time. Drugs with a shorter duration of action leave the system quickly and are much more likely to produce withdrawal symptoms than are longer-acting drugs.

The first benzodiazepine was chlordiazepoxide, which was sold in low doses for daytime use and has a slow onset of action and an even longer duration of action than phenobarbital. Chlordiazepoxide produced few problems with either compulsive use or withdrawal symptoms, and overdoses were almost unheard of. Diazepam has a more rapid onset than chlordiazepoxide, but because of slow metabolism and the presence of active metabolites, it also has a long duration of action. We might expect a drug with these characteristics to produce more psychological dependence than chlordiazepoxide but only rarely to produce withdrawal symptoms. This is exactly what happened. To summarize this pharmacology object lesson, there might be greater differences among the barbiturates and among the benzodiazepines than there are between these two classes.

As if to underscore the basic similarity that exists among all the depressant drugs, in the 1990s a new version of the "Mickey Finn" was popularized. **Rohypnol** (flunitrazepam), a benzodiazepine sold as a hypnotic in many countries around the world but not in the United States, hit the news when reports surfaced of its being put into the drinks of unsuspecting women by their dates. The combination of Rohypnol and alcohol was reputed to produce a profound intoxication, during which the woman would be highly suggestible and unable to remember what had happened to her. In reality, Rohypnol effects are not much different from the effects of other benzodiazepines (or any of the CNS depressants) when combined with alcohol, but popular folklore quickly established it as a "date-rape" drug (see the Targeting Prevention box). In 1997, the drug's manufacturer changed the formulation of the pill so that when it dissolves in a drink it produces a characteristic color.

Nonbenzodiazepine Hypnotics

The most recent additions to the class of depressant drugs do not have the chemical structure of the benzodiazepines, but they have similar effects. Zolpidem (Ambien) was introduced in 1993, followed later by zaleplon (Sonata) and eszopiclone (Lunesta).

Zopiclone, a close relative of eszopiclone, is available in Canada and the United Kingdom, but not in the United States. Because the generic names of these drugs are hard to pronounce, but all begin with the same letter, they are often informally referred to as the "Z-drugs." In general, they are very similar to the benzodiazepines but are called "nonbenzodiazepine" because they have a different chemical structure.

Zolpidem (Ambien) quickly became the most widely prescribed hypnotic drug on the market. It has a rapid onset and short duration of action,

Targeting Prevention

Date-Rape Drugs

You've all heard the stories about women having "roofies" (Rohypnol), GHB, or some other drug slipped into a drink while they weren't looking, and then being raped while they were incapacitated. There was a flurry of news and magazine articles about date-rape drugs in 1996, and in that year Congress passed the Drug-Induced Rape Prevention and Punishment Act, making it a federal crime punishable by up to 20 years in prison to give someone a controlled substance without the recipient's knowledge, with the intent of committing a violent crime. Notice that alcohol itself would not trigger the use of this law—it has to be a controlled substance, and it has to be administered without the recipient's knowledge. Actual prosecutions under this law have been rare, partly because rape is usually charged under state laws.

Studies have been done in the United States, the United Kingdom, Canada, and Australia, examining blood or urine samples from women who charged that they were given a drug without their knowledge. The most common finding was a high blood alcohol content, and in more than half the cases in each study, no other drug was detected. In some cases a drug might have been used that was not detected for some reason, but it also does appear that in many of these cases the date-rape drug was too much alcohol.[2] So, our advice for women would be to take all the precautions that you have read and heard about when you're out partying, but remember that while you're keeping your hand over your glass, the substance most likely to incapacitate you and make everything you do riskier might already be in that glass in the form of alcohol. And our advice for men is to remember that if she is incapable of giving her consent, it can be considered rape no matter how she became incapacitated.

Box icon credit: ©Medioimages/Alamy Images RF

similar to the short-acting barbiturates that were once so popular. It has been shown to help induce sleep, but because of its short duration, users didn't always remain asleep for 7 or 8 hours. This rapid, short action led to the introduction of an extended-release version (Ambien CR) to maintain longer sleep. However, taking advantage of the rapid onset, in 2011 the FDA approved a sublingual tablet (Intermezzo) to be taken when people awaken in the middle of the night. (Sublingual tablets are placed under the tongue, dissolve in the mouth, and often act more quickly than when swallowed.)

Although many initially hoped that the non-benzodiazepines would be more specific and avoid some of the problems of earlier drugs, there have been reports of withdrawal reactions and other complications with them as well. They are listed, along with the benzodiazepines, in Schedule IV, one step below the Schedule III classification of the barbiturates.

Mechanism of Action

An important key to understanding the effects of these sedative-hypnotic agents was found in 1977, when it was reported that diazepam molecules had a high affinity for specific receptor sites in brain tissue. Other benzodiazepine types of sedatives also bound to these receptors, and the binding affinities of these various drugs correlated with their behavioral potencies in humans and other animals. It was soon noticed that the benzodiazepine receptors were always near receptors for the amino acid neurotransmitter **GABA**. It now appears that when benzodiazepines (and their nonbenzodiazepine cousins) bind to their receptor site, they enhance the normally inhibitory effects of GABA on its receptors. The barbiturates act at a separate binding site nearby. The picture emerges of a GABA receptor *complex,* which includes the barbiturate binding site and the benzodiazepine receptor. Drug companies quickly began developing new drugs based on their ability to bind to these sites, leading to the development of the entire class of nonbenzodiazepine hypnotics, as well as other potentially useful compounds that are now being studied.[3]

Beneficial Uses
Anxiolytics

> Raze out the written troubles of the brain, and with some sweet oblivious antidote Cleanse the stuff'd bosom of that perilous stuff Which weighs upon the heart. . .
>
> William Shakespeare,
> *Macbeth* (Clarendon Press, 1876)

As these lines from Shakespeare's *Macbeth* reveal, humans have often sought a "sweet oblivious antidote" to the cares and woes of living. Alcohol has most frequently been used for that purpose, but the sedative drugs also play a major role in modern society. In the United States in recent decades, the barbiturates, then meprobamate, and then the benzodiazepines have been among the most widely prescribed medications. Four benzodiazepines are listed among the top 100 most commonly prescribed medications in the United States: alprazolam (Xanax), lorazepam (Ativan), clonazepam (Klonopin), and diazepam (Valium) (Table 7.1). These are all relatively long-lasting drugs used primarily as **anxiolytics** (to reduce anxiety).

Table 7.1
Some Popular Sedative-Hypnotics

Type	Half-Life (hours)
Anxiolytics	
Alprazolam (Xanax)	6 to 20
Chlordiazepoxide (Librium)	5 to 30
Clonazepam (Klonopin)	30 to 40
Diazepam (Valium)	20 to 100
Lorazepam (Ativan)	10 to 20
Hypnotics	
Temazepam (Restoril)	5 to 25
Zolpidem (Ambien)	1
Eszopiclone (Lunesta)	6

Rohypnol: a benzodiazepine; the "date-rape drug."

GABA: an inhibitory neurotransmitter.

anxiolytics: drugs, such as Valium, used in the treatment of anxiety disorders. Literally, "anxiety-dissolving."

The combined sales of these anxiolytics make them one of the most widely prescribed drug classes. Most physicians used to accept the widely held view that various types of dysfunctional behavior (e.g., phobias, panic attacks, obsessive-compulsive disorders, psychosomatic problems) result from various forms of psychological stress that can be lumped under the general classification of "anxieties." So if anxieties produce dysfunctional behavior and these drugs can reduce anxieties, then the drugs will be useful in reducing the dysfunctional behavior. Although this approach seems logical, in reality not all of these conditions respond well to antianxiety drugs. For specific phobias (e.g., fear of spiders), behavior therapy is a more effective treatment. And for obsessive-compulsive disorder and most of the official "anxiety disorders" (Chapter 8), certain antidepressant drugs seem to be most effective. Most of the prescriptions for antianxiety medications are not written by psychiatrists, nor are they written for patients with clearly defined anxiety disorders. In addition, many patients take the drugs daily for long periods. Galen, a 2nd-century Greek physician, estimated that about 60 percent of the patients he saw had emotional and psychological, as opposed to physical, illness. It is currently estimated that for a typical general practitioner, about half of the patients have no treatable physical ailment. Many of these patients who complain of nervousness, distress, or vague aches and pains will be given a prescription for an anxiolytic, such as alprazolam (Xanax). One way to look at this is that the patients may be suffering from a low-level generalized anxiety disorder, and the sedative is reducing the anxiety. A more cynical way of looking at it is that some patients are asking to be protected from the cares and woes of daily living. The physician prescribes something that can make the patient feel better in a general way. The patient doesn't complain as much and comes back for more pills, so everyone is happy.

Although most physicians would agree that the benzodiazepines are probably overprescribed,

Benzodiazepines are commonly prescribed for anxiety disorders. ©Ryan McVay/Getty Images RF

in any individual case it may be impossible to know whether the patient just enjoys getting a "feel-good pill" or feels better because of a specific antianxiety effect. Whatever the reason for each individual, based on history the market for prescription anxiolytics will continue to be very large and profitable.

Sleeping Pills

Although one or two beers might relax a person and reduce inhibitions a bit, the effect of larger amounts is more dramatic. If you consume several beers at an active, noisy party, you might become wild and reckless. But if you consume the same number of beers, go to bed, and turn off the lights, you will probably fall asleep fairly quickly. This is essentially the principle on which hypnotic drug therapy is based: A large enough dose is taken to help you get to sleep more quickly.

Insomnia is the term used to include several symptoms: trouble falling asleep, trouble staying asleep, or waking up too early. In a recent analysis of a large national health survey in the United States, among adults aged 20–39, almost 17 percent of women and about 9 percent of men reported one or more of these concerns (rates of insomnia are greater in older populations). In this sample of over 5,000 people, once the differences between men and women in rates of depression (Chapter 8) were accounted for, there was no longer a significant gender difference for insomnia.[4] What this means is that people who visit their doctors complaining of insomnia should probably be evaluated for depression. This could be especially important, because in controlled trials comparing placebo to the new nonbenzodiazepine hypnotics, there was a doubling of the risk of depression for the group given the active drug. So, taking these sleeping pills can worsen depression in some people.[5]

Previous research has shown that most people who are concerned about insomnia do not take prescription hypnotic drugs, and there are effective nonmedical ways of dealing with insomnia (see the next Drugs in Depth box). However, there is a large enough market for these drugs to encourage new drug development and quite a bit of television advertising.

About one-third of adults report trouble sleeping. ©vario images GmbH & Co.KG/Alamy Stock Photo

After 1976, the benzodiazepines displaced the barbiturates in the sleeping-pill market. By the early 1990s, triazolam (Halcion) sales had reached $100 million per year in the United States and $250 million worldwide. However, concerns were raised about the safety of the drug, and Upjohn, the drug's manufacturer, was sued by a woman who claimed the drug made her so agitated and paranoid that she had killed her own mother. That case was settled out of court, but it brought attention to the drug and to other claims that it produced an unusual number of adverse psychiatric reactions in patients. Halcion has been banned in five countries because of these side effects. It has survived two FDA reviews in the United States and remains on the market, but its sales have declined markedly.

The nonbenzodiazepine drug zolpidem (Ambien) binds selectively to the GABA-A receptor and has therefore been suggested to be a more specific hypnotic agent. Clinically it appears to be similar to Halcion, with rapid onset and short duration of action. Ambien has become the most-prescribed hypnotic drug in the United States, and several companies have been licensed to sell generic zolpidem as well. In spite of well-financed advertising campaigns by other nonbenzodiazepine competitors, zolpidem remains in the top spot. Concerns have been raised about sleepwalking, eating, and even driving while people are in a semi-waking state after taking these nonbenzodiazepine hypnotics. These concerns led the FDA to investigate such reports, and in 2008 all hypnotic drugs were required to attach a warning label about sleep-driving and other dangerous behaviors that might occur after taking these drugs.

We should be asking ourselves a few questions about the popularity of these new sleeping pills. Based on the history of hypnotic medications, every few years a new type of drug is marketed that promises to be safer than the old drugs. We then find out only after the new drugs have been widely accepted that they can produce the same old problems with overdose and dependence. This has happened with meprobamate, then methaqualone, and then the benzodiazepine hypnotics. Why should we be so ready to believe that these nonbenzodiazepine

Targeting Prevention

Falling Asleep without Pills

The following procedures are recommended ways of dealing with insomnia. If you occasionally have trouble sleeping, ask yourself which of these rules you typically follow, and which ones you often don't. Could you adopt some of these procedures?

- Establish and maintain a regular bedtime and a regular arising time. Try to wake up and get out of bed at the appointed time, even if you had trouble sleeping the night before. Avoid excessive sleep during holidays and weekends.
- When you get into bed, turn off the lights and relax. Avoid reviewing in your mind the day's stresses and tomorrow's challenges.
- Exercise regularly. Follow an exercise routine, but avoid heavy exercise late in the evening.
- Prepare a comfortable sleep environment. Too warm a room disturbs sleep; too cold a room does not solidify sleep. Occasional loud noises can disturb sleep without fully awakening you. Steady background noise, such as a fan, may be useful for masking a noisy environment.

- Watch what you eat and drink before bedtime. Hunger may disturb sleep, as may caffeine and alcohol. A light snack may promote sleep, but avoid heavy or spicy foods at bedtime.
- Avoid the use of tobacco.
- Do not lie awake in bed for long periods. If you cannot fall asleep within 30 minutes, get out of bed and do something relaxing before trying to fall asleep again. Repeat this as many times as necessary. The goal is to avoid developing a paired association between being in bed and restlessness.
- Do not nap during the day. A prolonged nap after a night of insomnia may disturb the next night's sleep.
- Avoid the chronic use of sleeping pills. Although sedative-hypnotics can be effective when used as part of a coordinated treatment plan for certain types of insomnia, chronic use is ineffective at best and can be detrimental to sound sleep.

hypnotics will be different? This is particularly interesting when we realize that these Schedule IV controlled substances not only are widely advertised on television ("Ask your doctor"!) but also are being promoted with "free trial" offers. Should companies be allowed to offer free trials of a drug that has a reasonable potential for leading to dependence? And, although it doesn't show up on our list of the top 10 drugs in the DAWN system in Chapter 2, a special DAWN report released in 2013 found that zolpidem (Ambien)-related emergency room visits more than tripled between 2005 and 2010.[6] Because use of nonbenzodiazepine hypnotics is still increasing, we can expect to see higher rates of drug-related emergencies in the future.

If you or someone you know has trouble sleeping, before resorting to the use of medication it would be wise to follow the suggestions given in the Drugs in Depth box. These tactics

will probably help most people deal with sleeplessness.

Anticonvulsants

A thorough description of seizure disorders (the **epilepsies**) is beyond the scope of this book. Both the barbiturates and the benzodiazepines are widely used for the control of epileptic seizures. Other antiepileptic drugs, such as valproic acid, carbamazepine, and lamotrigine, are usually prescribed in preference to benzodiazepines or barbiturates, but they may be used in combination. These other anticonvulsants are also widely used as mood stabilizers in psychiatric patients (Chapter 8).

Anticonvulsant medications are given chronically, so tolerance tends to develop. The dose should be kept high enough to control the seizures without producing undesirable drowsiness. Abrupt withdrawal of these drugs is likely to lead to seizures, so medication changes should be done carefully. Despite these problems, the sedative drugs are currently a necessary and useful treatment for epilepsy.

Causes for Concern

Dependence Liability

Psychological Dependence Most people who have used either barbiturates or benzodiazepines have not developed habitual use patterns. However, it was clear with the barbiturates that some individuals do become daily users of intoxicating amounts. Again, the short-acting barbiturates seemed to be the culprits. When Librium, the first benzodiazepine, was in its heyday, relatively little habitual use was reported. As Librium was displaced by the newer, more potent Valium, we saw increasing reports of habitual Valium use, perhaps because its onset, although slower than that of the short-acting barbiturates, is more rapid than that of Librium. Then Xanax, another rapid-acting benzodiazepine, became the most widely prescribed sedative, and reports of Xanax dependence appeared.

Animals given the opportunity to press a lever that delivers intravenous barbiturates will do so, and the short-acting barbiturates work best for this. Animals will also self-inject several of the benzodiazepines, but at lower rates than with the short-acting barbiturates. When human drug abusers were allowed an opportunity to work for oral doses of barbiturates or benzodiazepines on a hospital ward, they developed regular patterns of working for the drugs. When given a choice between pentobarbital and diazepam, the subjects generally chose pentobarbital.[7] These experiments indicate that these sedative drugs can serve as reinforcers of behavior but that the short-acting barbiturates are probably more likely to lead to dependence than are any of the benzodiazepines currently on the market.

Physical Dependence A characteristic withdrawal syndrome can occur after chronic use of large enough doses of any of the sedative-hypnotic drugs. This syndrome is different from the narcotic withdrawal syndrome and quite similar to the alcohol withdrawal syndrome. After chronic use of benzodiazepines, common side effects include anxiety, impaired concentration and memory, insomnia, nightmares, muscle cramps, increased sensitivity to touch and to light, and many others. More severe withdrawal symptoms occur after abrupt withdrawal from chronic use of larger doses, and may include delirium tremens, delusions, convulsions (may lead to death), and severe depression.[8]

This syndrome is nearly identical to the alcohol withdrawal syndrome and different in character from the narcotic withdrawal syndrome, longer lasting, and probably more unpleasant. In addition, withdrawal from the sedative-hypnotics or alcohol is potentially life-threatening, with death occurring in as many as 5 percent of those who withdraw abruptly after taking large doses.

Although it is said that withdrawal symptoms are less common after abrupt cessation of the newer nonbenzodiazepine hypnotics, there is at least one case report of a woman experiencing seizures during withdrawal after extended use of zolpidem.[9]

Because there is a cross-dependence among the barbiturates, the benzodiazepines, and alcohol, it is theoretically possible to use any of these drugs to halt the withdrawal symptoms from any other depressant. Drug treatment is often used, and a general rule is to use a long-acting drug, given in divided doses until the withdrawal symptoms are controlled. Typically, one of the benzodiazepines is used during detoxification from any of the CNS depressants, although one of the specific anticonvulsants may also be used effectively.[10]

Toxicity

The major areas of concern with these depressant drugs are the behavioral and physiological problems encountered when high doses of the drug are

epilepsies: disorders characterized by uncontrolled movements (seizures).

present in the body (acute toxicity). Behaviorally, all these drugs are capable of producing alcohol-like intoxication with impaired judgment and incoordination. Obviously, such an impaired state vastly multiplies the dangers involved in driving and other activities, and the effects of these drugs combined with alcohol are additive, so that the danger is increased further. On the physiological side, the major concern is the tendency of these drugs to depress the respiration rate. With large enough doses, as in accidental or intentional overdose, breathing ceases. Again, the combination of these depressants and alcohol is quite dangerous. Although benzodiazepines are usually quite high on the list of drugs associated with deaths in the DAWN coroners' reports, in almost every case the culprit is the drug in combination with alcohol or another drug, rather than the benzodiazepine alone (see Chapter 2).

Patterns of Abuse

Almost all of the abuse of the sedative-hypnotic agents has historically involved the oral use of legally manufactured products. Two characteristic types of abusers have been associated with barbiturate use, and these two major types probably still characterize a large fraction of sedative abusers. The first type of abuser is an older adult who obtains the drug on a prescription, either for daytime sedative use or as a sleeping pill. Through repeated use, tolerance develops and the dose is increased. Even though some of these individuals visit several physicians to obtain prescriptions for enough pills to maintain this level of use, many would vehemently deny that they are "drug abusers." This type of chronic use can lead to physical dependence.

The other major group tends to be younger and consists of people who obtain the drugs simply to get high. Sleeping pills might be taken from

---

Life Saver

Combining Depressants with Alcohol or Opioids

All of the CNS depressant drugs covered in this chapter (anxiolytics, sleeping pills, anticonvulsants, inhalants, and GHB) can produce two kinds of dangerous effects. For one, in high enough doses they produce an intoxication similar to alcohol, and that intoxication increases the dangerousness of many kinds of activities, from driving to sex to just about any active sport (see *behavioral toxicity*, Chapter 2).

The second danger lies in overdoses. As we saw in Chapter 2, each year there are several thousand deaths in the United States in which the use of benzodiazepine or nonbenzodiazepine drugs is mentioned. While it is theoretically possible to die from an overdose of any of these drugs alone, in practical terms this is very rare. In virtually every overdose death involving Valium, Xanax, or Ambien, some other substance is present. Most of the time it is alcohol. However, other combinations can be just as deadly, and as abuse of prescription opioids such as hydrocodone and oxycodone has increased, more opioid-sedative

combinations deaths are also occurring. For example, the Australian actor Heath Ledger's death in New York in 2008 was due to a combination of several benzodiazepines and opioids. No alcohol was reported in his case.

Clearly, some people must know that they are taking dangerous combinations of drugs. No single physician would have prescribed all the different medicines found in Ledger's blood, for example, and no pharmacist would have filled all of those prescriptions without warning of the dangers. But alcohol is such a common thing in some people's lives that they don't think about it when they also take a sleeping pill. Many might not know about the danger of combining opioid pain relievers with sleeping pills. One should always take care when combining two drugs or any drug with alcohol, and read and pay attention to warnings provided with any prescription drug.

Box icon credit: ©McGraw-Hill Education

the home medicine cabinet, or the drugs might be purchased on the street. These younger abusers tend to take relatively large doses, to mix several drugs, or to drink alcohol with the drug, all for the purpose of becoming intoxicated. With this type of use, the possibility of acute toxicity is particularly high.

Inhalants

Some people will do almost anything to escape reality. Gasoline, glue, paint, lighter fluid, spray cans of almost anything, nail polish, and Liquid Paper all contain volatile solvents that, when inhaled, can have effects that are similar in an overall way to those of the depressants. High-dose exposure to these fumes makes users intoxicated, often slurring their speech and causing them to have trouble walking a straight line, as if they were drunk on alcohol.

Although most people think first of the abuse of volatile solvents such as glues, paints, and gasoline, other types of substances can be abused through sniffing or inhaling in a similar manner (Table 7.2). Two major groups are the gaseous anesthetics and the nitrites, as well as volatile solvents.

Table 7.2
Some Chemicals Abused by Inhalation

Substances	Chemical Ingredients
Volatile solvents	
Paint and paint thinners	Petroleum distillates, esters, acetone
Paint removers	Toluene, methylene chloride, methanol, acetone
Nail polish remover	Acetone, ethyl acetate
Correction fluid and thinner	Trichloroethylene, trichloroethane
Glues and cements	Toluene, ethyl acetate, hexane, methyl chloride, acetone, methyl ethyl ketone, methyl butyl ketone, trichloroethylene, tetrachloroethylene
Dry-cleaning agents	Tetrachloroethylene, trichloroethane
Spot removers	Xylene, petroleum distillates, chlorohydrocarbons
Aerosols, propellants, gases	
Spray paint	Butane, propane, toluene, hydrocarbons
Hair spray	Butane, propane
Lighters	Butane, isopropane
Fuel gas	Butane, propane
Whipped cream, "whippets"	Nitrous oxide
Air duster (e.g., Dust-Off)	1,1 difluoroethane
Anesthetics	
Current medical use	Nitrous oxide, halothane, enflurane
Former medical use	Ether, chloroform
Nitrites	
Locker Room, Rush, poppers	Isoamyl, isobutyl, isopropyl nitrite, butyl nitrite

Gaseous Anesthetics

Gaseous anesthetics have been used in medicine and surgery for many years, and abuse of these anesthetics occurs among physicians and others with access to these gases. One of the oldest, nitrous oxide, was first used in the early 1800s and quite early acquired the popular name "laughing gas" because of the hilarity exhibited by some of its users. During the 1800s, traveling demonstrations of laughing gas enticed audience members to volunteer to become intoxicated for the amusement of others. Nitrous oxide is also one of the safest anesthetics when used properly, but it is not possible to obtain good surgical anesthesia unless the individual breathes almost pure nitrous oxide, which leads to suffocation through a lack of oxygen. Nitrous oxide is still used for light anesthesia, especially by dentists. It is also often used in combination with one of the more effective inhaled anesthetics, allowing the use of a lower concentration of the primary anesthetic. Nitrous oxide is also found as a propellant in whipping-cream containers and is sold in small bottles ("whippets") for use in home whipping-cream dispensers. Recreational users have obtained nitrous oxide from both sources.

Nitrites

Amyl nitrite was first introduced into medicine in the mid-1800s as a treatment for chest pain.

Chemicals abused by inhalation can be found in a variety of household products. ©McGraw-Hill Education/David Moyer, photographer

Inhaling the vapors of this drug relaxes blood vessels, including the coronary arteries. This increases blood flow but also briefly lowers blood pressure. Amyl nitrite is still used in emergency medicine as a treatment for cyanide poisoning. For much of the 20th century, amyl nitrite was sold in small glass vials that could be snapped in half or crushed to release the vapors under the nose. During the 1960s there was some recreational use of these "poppers." The increased blood flow created a sense of warmth, and increased blood flow to the sexual organs might have accounted for the street lore that nitrites can enhance sexual pleasure. At high doses there is also a brief sense of lightheadedness or faintness resulting from lower blood pressure. Although these glass vial "poppers" are much less available these days, the term *poppers* remains as the most common street name for illicitly sold nitrites. In addition to amyl nitrite, butyl, isopropyl, and isobutyl nitrite produce similar effects. These products have been used in various cleaning products, and some users have inhaled those products to achieve the same effect.

Volatile Solvents

The modern era of solvent abuse, or at least of widely publicized solvent abuse, can be traced to a 1959 investigative article in the Sunday supplement of a Denver, Colorado, newspaper. This article reported that young people in a nearby city had been caught spreading plastic model glue on their palms, cupping their hands over their mouths, and inhaling the vapors to get high. The article warned about the dangers of accidental exposure to solvent fumes, and an accompanying photograph showed a young man demonstrating another way to inhale glue vapors—by putting the glue on a handkerchief and holding it over the mouth and nose. The article described the effects as similar to being drunk.

That article both notified the police, who presumably began looking for such behavior, and advertised and described the practice to young people: Within the next six months, the city of Denver went from no previously reported cases of "glue-sniffing" to 50 cases. More publicity and warnings followed, and by the end of 1961 the juvenile authorities in Denver were seeing about "30 boys a month." The problem expanded further in Denver over the next several years, while similar patterns of publicity, increased use, and more publicity followed in other cities. In 1962, the magazines *Time* and *Newsweek* both carried articles describing how to sniff model glue and warning about its dangers, and the Hobby Industry Association of America produced a film for civic groups that warned about glue sniffing and recommended that communities make it illegal to sniff any substance with an intoxicating effect. Sales of model glue continued to rise as the publicity went nationwide.[11]

Since then, recreational use of various solvents by young people has occurred mostly as more localized fads. One group of kids in one area might start using cooking sprays, the practice will grow and then decline over a couple of years, and meanwhile in another area the kids might be inhaling a specific brand and even color of spray paint.

Although some "huffers" are adults (e.g., alcoholics without the funds to buy alcohol), most are young. The ready availability and low price of these solvents make them attractive to children. In the high-school senior class of 2015, 2 percent of the students reported having used some type of inhalant in the past year, whereas 4.6 percent of the eighth-graders reported using an inhalant within the past year.[12] Inhalant use has traditionally been more common among poor Hispanic youth and on Indian reservations.[13]

Because so many different solvents are involved, it is impossible to characterize the potential harm produced by abuse of glues, paints, correction fluids, and so on. Several of the solvents have been linked to kidney damage, brain damage, and peripheral nerve damage, and many of them produce irritation of the respiratory tract and result in severe headaches. However, several users of various inhalants have simply suffocated. Although most of the children who inhale solvents do so only occasionally and give it up as they grow older and have more access to alcohol, some become

dependent and a few will die. In recent years, difluoroethane (Dust-Off) abuse has been implicated in numerous automobile accidents, many of them fatal.

Laws to limit sales of these household solvents to minors or to make it illegal to use them to become intoxicated have been passed in some areas, but typically they have little effect. Too many products are simply too readily available. Look around your own home or on the shelves of a supermarket or discount store—how many products have a warning about using them in an enclosed place? These are the products containing volatile organic solvents that people sometimes use to get high.

Gamma Hydroxybutyric Acid

Gamma hydroxybutyrate (GHB) occurs naturally in the brain as well as in other parts of the body. Its structure is fairly close to that of the inhibitory neurotransmitter GABA. GHB has been known for some time to be a CNS depressant and has been used in other countries as an anesthetic. Because it appears to play a role in general cellular metabolism, for a time it was sold as a dietary supplement and taken (mostly in fairly low doses) by athletes and bodybuilders hoping to stimulate muscle growth. There is no good evidence that GHB is effective for this use, but its widespread availability in the 1980s led some to "rediscover" its powerful CNS depressant effects. Taking larger quantities of GHB alone, or combining GHB with alcohol, produces a combined depressant effect similar to what would be produced by combining alcohol with any of the other depressants discussed in this chapter, from chloral hydrate to the benzodiazepines.

The usual recreational dose of GHB taken alone ranges from 1 to 5 grams (1,000 to 5,000 mg). It has a fairly short half-life of about 1 hour. The behavioral effects are similar to alcohol, and higher doses produce muscular incoordination and slurring of speech. Increasing recreational use led the FDA to ban the inclusion of GHB in dietary supplements in 1990. Publicity about deaths

Unintended Consequences

Drugs and Capital Punishment

There is a long history of sentencing people to die for certain crimes, and although we no longer hang people for stealing horses, 31 of the U.S. states and the federal government still allow the death penalty for murder. In 1977, Oklahoma carried out the first execution using lethal injection of drugs, and since then it has become by far the most common technique. Most often, a three-drug combination is used: The first is a sedative used to make the person unconscious, followed by a paralytic drug that stops breathing, and then a drug to stop the heart. However, what may appear to some observers as a humane and sensible alternative to the more violent older methods has run into a number of both ethical and practical roadblocks.

For one thing, these drugs were developed, tested, and approved for other purposes; no drug has been approved by the FDA for causing death. The first sedative drug to be employed in this way was sodium pentothal, a very rapid-acting barbiturate. After the only U.S. supplier suspended production of this drug in 2009, states switched to phenobarbital, midazolam (a benzodiazepine), or the sedative propofol, which is only administered intravenously. All of these drugs are capable of rendering the person unconscious when administered, but their manufacturers are also opposed to their use for this purpose. States are not allowed to import drugs from other countries to use in lethal injection, and U.S. sources have become virtually nonexistent. In 2016, the drug company Pfizer announced new restrictions on seven of its products, to prevent them from being used in executions. This calls into question whether there is any legal source not only for the sedatives but also for the paralytic and heart-stopping substances that have been used. Some states have begun to turn to so-called compounding pharmacies, which are pharmacies that are allowed to prepare drugs without the same regulations imposed on regular manufacturers and distributors. However, the long-term viability of such relationships is not yet clear.

Consider the unintended consequences of adopting medically approved drugs and what is typically a medical procedure to end a person's life. Should physicians be involved? Can they justify doing so while still adhering to the Hippocratic oath to "do no harm"? What reasons do you think drug companies have for not wanting their products to be used for this purpose?

Box icon credit: ©Adam Gault/age fotostock RF

---

associated with the use of GHB and alcohol as a date-rape combination led in 2000 to congressional action directing that it be listed as a Schedule I controlled substance. Evidence from the Monitoring the Future survey indicated that, in 2012, only about 1.4 percent of high-school seniors reported using GHB in the past year, down from about 2 percent in 2000, the first year GHB use was studied.[12]

In 2000, Congress directed that GHB be placed on Schedule I. However, in 2002, the FDA approved Xyrem, an oral solution of GHB used to treat narcolepsy. For reasons that are not well understood, GHB tends to reduce the frequency of *cataplexy,* one common symptom of narcolepsy. Cataplexy refers to muscular weakness or paralysis, and in narcolepsy it is usually experienced as a brief, unpredictable episode. Thus, Xyrem, under the generic name sodium oxybate, is now available for prescription as a Schedule III controlled substance. Any other form of GHB remains listed on Schedule I.

Summary

- The barbiturates, benzodiazepines, inhalants, and other depressant drugs all have many effects in common with each other and with alcohol.

- Depressants may be prescribed in low doses for their sedative effect or in higher doses as sleeping pills (hypnotics).

- Over the past 40 years, the barbiturates have been mostly displaced by the benzodiazepines.

- The barbiturates and benzodiazepines increase the inhibitory neural effects of the neurotransmitter GABA.

- Drugs that have a rapid onset are more likely to produce psychological dependence.

- Drugs that have a short duration of action are more likely to produce withdrawal symptoms.

- Overdoses of these depressant drugs can cause death by inhibiting respiration, particularly if the drug is taken in combination with alcohol.

- The abused inhalants include gaseous anesthetics, certain nitrites, and volatile solvents.

- Abuse of inhalants, especially of the volatile solvents, can lead to organ damage, including neurological damage, more readily than with alcohol or other psychoactive substances.

Review Questions

1. What was the foul-smelling drug that was so widely used in mental hospitals before the 1950s?

2. Which use of a benzodiazepine (sedative vs. hypnotic) calls for a higher dose?

3. What is the relationship between psychological dependence and the time course of a drug's action?

4. The barbiturates and benzodiazepines act at which neurotransmitter receptor?

5. Why should hypnotic drugs usually be prescribed only for a few nights at a time?

6. What is zolpidem (Ambien)?

7. What are the characteristics of the sedative-hypnotic withdrawal syndrome?

8. What happens to a person who takes an overdose of a sedative-hypnotic?

9. How are the effects of the nitrites different from the effects of inhaled solvent fumes?

10. What are the effects of combining GHB with alcohol?

References

1. Richardson, B. W. "Chloral and Other Narcotics, I." *Popular Science* 15 (1879), p. 492.

2. Burgess, A., P. Donovan, and S. E. H. Moore. "Understanding Heightened Risk Perception of Drink 'Spiking.'" *British Journal of Criminology* 49 (2009), pp. 848–62.

3. Uwe, R., and K. Frederic. "Beyond Classical Benzodiazepines: Novel Therapeutic Potential of GABA-A Receptor Subtypes." *Nature Reviews Drug Discovery* 10 (2011), pp. 685–97.

4. Hale, L., and others. "Does Mental Health History Explain Gender Disparities in Insomnia Symptoms among Young Adults?" *Sleep Medicine* 10 (2009), pp. 1118–23.

5. Kripke, D. "Greater Incidence of Depression with Hypnotic Use Than with Placebo," *BMC Psychiatry* 7 (2007), pp. 42–45.

6. Substance Abuse and Mental Health Services Administration, Center for Behavioral Health Statistics and Quality. (May 1, 2013). *Emergency Department Visits for Adverse Reactions Involving the Insomnia Medication Zolpidem.* Rockville, MD.

7. Griffiths, R. R., G. Bigelow, and I. Liebson. "Human Drug Self-Administration: Double-Blind Comparison of Pentobarbital, Diazepam, Chlorpromazine and Placebo." *Journal of Pharmacology and Experimental Therapeutics* 210 (1979), pp. 301–10.

8. Lader M. "Benzodiazepines Revisited—Will We Ever Learn?" *Addiction* 106 (2011), pp. 2086–109.

9. Tripodianakis, J., and others. "Zolpidem-Related Epileptic Seizures: A Case Report." *European Psychiatry* 18 (2003), pp. 140–41.

10. Marin, M., and others. "New Agents for the Benzodiazepine Withdrawal Syndrome." *European Psychiatry* 25 (2010), p. 1286.

11. Brecher, E. M. *Licit and Illicit Drugs.* Boston: Little, Brown, 1972.

12. Meich, R. A., L. D. Johnston, P. M. O'Malley, J. G. Bachman, and J. E. Schulenberg. *Monitoring the Future National Survey Results on Drug Use, 1975–2015: Volume I, Secondary School Students.* Ann Arbor: Institute for Social Research, The University of Michigan (2016).

13. Beauvais, E., and others. "Inhalant Abuse among American Indian, Mexican American, and Non-Latino White Adolescents." *American Journal of Drug & Alcohol Abuse* 28 (2002), pp. 477–95.

8

Medication for Mental Disorders

©Comstock Images/PictureQuest RF

For most of today's mentally ill, the primary mode of therapy is drug therapy. Powerful psychoactive medications help control psychotic behavior, depression, and mania in thousands of patients, reducing human suffering and health care costs, yet these drugs are far from cures, and many have undesirable side effects. Should mental disorders be approached with chemical treatments? Do these treatments work? How do they work? What can these drugs tell us about the causes of mental illness? Although we don't yet have complete answers for any of these questions, we do have partial answers for all of them.

Objectives

When you have finished this chapter, you should be able to:

- Discuss the medical model of mental disorders and why many professionals oppose it.

- Describe the typical characteristics of anxiety disorders, schizophrenia, and mood disorders.

- Explain the historical context and the importance of the discovery of the phenothiazine antipsychotics.

- Recognize the names of a number of currently available antipsychotic drugs.

- Distinguish between conventional and atypical antipsychotics.

- Discuss theories of antipsychotic drug action and why it is difficult to understand the mechanism of action for these and other classes of psychoactive drugs.

- Explain the sales trend of antidepressants since 1987 and what is expected in the future.

- Explain why it is simplistic to say that antidepressant drugs work by restoring serotonin activity to normal.

- Describe how lithium and anticonvulsant drugs are used in treating bipolar disorder.

Mental Disorders

The Medical Model

The use of the term *mental illness* seems to imply a particular model for behavioral disorders or dysfunctions. The medical model has been attacked by both psychiatrists (who are medical doctors) and psychologists (who generally hold nonmedical doctorates such as a PhD or PsyD).

According to this model, the *patient* appears with a set of *symptoms,* and on the basis of these symptoms a *diagnosis* is made as to which *disease* the patient is suffering from. Once the disease is

161

known, its *cause* can be determined and the patient provided with a *cure*. In general terms, the arguments for and against a medical model of mental illness are similar to those for and against a medical model of dependence, presented in Chapter 2. For an infectious disease such as tuberculosis or syphilis, a set of symptoms suggests a particular disorder, but a specific diagnostic test for the presence of certain bacteria or antibodies is used to confirm the diagnosis, identify the cause, and clarify the treatment approach. Once the infection is cleared up, the disorder is cured.

For mental disorders, a set of behavioral symptoms is about all we have to define and diagnose the disorder. A person might be inactive, not sleep or eat well, and not say much, and what little is said might be quite negative. This behavior might lead us to call the person depressed. Does that mean the person has a "disease" called depression, with a biological cause and a potential cure? Or does it really only give a description of how he or she is acting, in the same way that we might call someone "crabby," "friendly," or "nerdy"? The behaviors that we refer to as indicating depression are varied and probably have many different causes, most of them not known. And we are far from being able to prescribe a cure for depression that will be generally successful in eliminating these symptoms.

Despite these attacks on the medical model, it still seems to guide much of the current thinking about behavioral disorders. The fact that psychoactive drugs can be effective in controlling symptoms, if not in curing diseases, has lent strength to supporters of the medical model. If chemicals can help normalize an individual's behavior, a natural assumption might be that the original problem resulted from a chemical imbalance in the brain—and that measurements of chemicals in urine, blood, or cerebrospinal fluid could provide more specific and accurate diagnoses and give direction to efforts at drug therapy. Although a lot of people have searched for many years, so far we have no direct evidence for a chemical imbalance causing depression or schizophrenia or anxiety disorders. And, although drug therapy is the first-line treatment for all these disorders, we don't have a clear biological understanding of how the drugs work to reduce the symptoms of these disorders.

Classification of Mental Disorders

Because human behavior is so variable and because we do not know the causes of most mental disorders, classification of the mentally ill into diagnostic categories is difficult. Nevertheless, some basic divisions are widely used and important for understanding the uses of psychotherapeutic drugs. In 2013, the American Psychiatric Association published the fifth edition of its *Diagnostic and Statistical Manual of Mental Disorders* (referred to as the *DSM-5*).[1] This manual provides criteria for classifying mental disorders into hundreds of specific diagnostic categories. Partly because this classification system has been adopted by major health insurance companies, its terms and definitions have become standard for all mental health professionals.

Anxiety is a normal and common human experience: Anticipation of potential threats and dangers often helps us avoid them. However, when these worries become unrealistic, resulting in chronic uneasiness, fear of impending doom, or bouts of terror or panic, they can interfere with the individual's daily life. Physical symptoms may also be present, often associated with activation of the autonomic nervous system (e.g., flushed skin, dilated pupils, gastrointestinal problems, increased heart rate, or shortness of breath). The *DSM-5* refers to these and other problems as **anxiety disorders** (see the DSM-5 box). Obsessive-compulsive disorder and posttraumatic stress disorder used to be included within this group, but the new manual gives each of these its own separate chapter.

Perhaps because these disorders all seem to have some form of anxiety associated with them, and perhaps because for many years psychiatrists classified benzodiazepines and other depressants as *antianxiety drugs* (see Chapter 7), we tend to think of anxiety not as a behavioral symptom but rather as an internal state that *causes* the disorders. That

Myth Buster

Using Drugs to "Cure" Mental Disorders

Psychoactive drugs have become by far the most common form of treatment for a wide variety of mental disorders, from attention-deficit/hyperactivity disorder to schizophrenia. No matter what the ailment, the first thing tried, and often the only thing tried, is to take a pill. And if that one doesn't work, try a different pill or perhaps two or three at once. Given our faith in these medications, what do they really do? The most important thing to realize is that there is no mental disorder that can be "cured" (i.e., eliminated) by any form of medication. For most of these disorders, there is evidence that, at least over a period of a couple of months, people who take the proper medication at the proper dose will have fewer symptoms of the disorder than people given a placebo. But it is also true that for most of these disorders the drugs only reduce, but do not eliminate, the symptoms. This kind of situation is not at all uncommon in medicine. For many chronic disorders, such as diabetes or high blood pressure, there is no cure. But for some of those disorders, we have long-term data showing that people who take their medications live longer or spend fewer days in the hospital.

Robert Whitaker published a book, *Anatomy of an Epidemic*,[2] which argued that for disorders such as depression, bipolar disorder, and schizophrenia, the reliance on psychoactive drugs may actually worsen long-term outcomes for many, if not most, individuals. His most important question is why the number of people on long-term disability for mental illness has tripled over the last two decades, during which time the rate of prescribing all these drugs has also skyrocketed. This is a complex issue, and the rate of disability can be influenced by many factors, such as changing admission criteria and increased public awareness of programs. Whitaker believes that the drugs themselves may be to blame, producing limited short-term improvements, but making their users function less well in the long run. The book has been quite controversial, of course, but we can hope that it will stimulate more research on the long-term effects of these drugs compared to non-drug treatments.

Box icon credit: ©McGraw-Hill Education

view fits well with the medical model, but we should guard against easy acceptance of the view that these disorders are caused by anxiety and that therefore we can treat them using antianxiety drugs. In recent years, psychiatrists have increasingly used selective reuptake inhibitors, classified as "antidepressants" to treat anxiety disorders.

Psychosis refers to a major disturbance of normal intellectual and social functioning in which there is loss of contact with reality. Not knowing the current date, hearing voices that aren't there, and believing that you are Napoleon or Christ are some examples of this withdrawal from reality. Many people refer to psychosis as reflecting a primary disorder of *thinking,* as opposed to mood or emotion.

Psychotic behavior may be viewed as a group of symptoms that can have many possible causes.

One important distinction is between the *organic* psychoses and the *functional* psychoses. An organic disorder is one that has a known physical cause. Psychosis can result from many things, including brain tumors or infections, metabolic or endocrine disorders, degenerative neurological diseases, chronic alcohol use, and high doses of stimulant drugs, such as amphetamine or cocaine. Functional disorders are simply those for which there is no known or obvious physical cause. A person suffering from a chronic (long-lasting) psychotic condition for which there is no known cause will probably

anxiety disorders: mental disorders characterized by excessive worry, fears, or avoidance.

psychosis (sy co sis): a serious mental disorder involving loss of contact with reality.

DSM-5

Anxiety Disorders

Specific Phobia
Specific phobia is excessive or unreasonable fear of a specific object or situation (e.g., elevators, flying, heights, or some type of animal).

Social Anxiety Disorder
Social phobia is a marked fear or anxiety about one or more social situations (meeting people, being observed by others, or performing in front of others).

Panic Disorder
Panic disorder is characterized by recurrent and unexpected panic attacks, which consist of an abrupt surge of intense fear or discomfort. During the attack a variety of symptoms may occur,

including pounding heart, sweating, trembling, or shortness of breath.

Agoraphobia
An agoraphobic is marked by fear or anxiety about two or more of these situations: using public transportation, being in open spaces, being in shops or theaters, standing in line, or being outside of the home alone.

Generalized Anxiety Disorder
Generalized anxiety disorder is excessive anxiety and worry about a number of events or activities, such as school or work performance or finances, lasting for a period of six months or longer.

Adapted from *Diagnostic and Statistical Manual of Mental Disorders, Text Revision*, DSM-5.

receive the diagnosis of **schizophrenia.** There is a popular misconception that schizophrenia means "split personality" or refers to individuals exhibiting multiple personalities. Instead, schizophrenia should probably be translated as *shattered mind.* See the DSM-5 box for the diagnostic criteria for schizophrenia.

Mood disorder refers to the appearance of depressed or manic symptoms. In simplistic terms, depression can be thought of as an abnormally low mood and mania as an abnormally high mood. The important distinction in the *DSM-5,* and in the drug treatment of mood disorders, is between **bipolar disorder,** in which at least one manic episode has occurred, perhaps alternating with periods of **depression,** and major depressive disorder, in which only depressive episodes are reported. See the DSM-5 box for diagnostic criteria for bipolar I disorder and major depressive disorder.

Individual human beings often don't fit neatly into one of these diagnostic categories, and in many

DSM-5

Schizophrenia

A. Characteristic symptoms: Two or more of the following, including at least one of the first three:

1. Delusions (irrational beliefs)
2. Hallucinations (e.g., hearing voices)
3. Disorganized speech (incoherent, frequent changes of topic)
4. Grossly disorganized behavior (inappropriate, unpredictable) or catatonic (withdrawn, immobile)
5. Negative symptoms (lack of emotional response, little or no speech, doesn't initiate activities)

B. Interference with social or occupational function

C. Duration of at least six months

Adapted from *Diagnostic and Statistical Manual of Mental Disorders, Text Revision*, DSM-5.

cases assigning a diagnosis and selecting a treat-ment are as much a matter of experience and art as they are of applying scientific descriptions. For example, it is common for people to experience symptoms of anxiety and depression at the same time, and different clinicians might view one or the other as the more important issue. Also, a person may be first seen when depressed, but a key issue is whether there might have been an unreported manic episode previous to the current problem.

Treatment of Mental Disorders

Before 1950

Over the centuries, mental patients have been sub-jected to various kinds of treatment, depending on the views held at the time regarding the causes of mental illness. Because we are concerned with drug therapy, a good place to begin our history is in 1917, when a physical treatment was first demon-strated to be effective in serious mental disease. In those days a great proportion of psychotic patients were suffering from *general paresis,* a syphilitic infection of the nervous system. It was noticed that the fever associated with malaria often produced marked improvement, and so in 1917 "malaria ther-apy" was introduced in the treatment of general paresis. The later discovery of antibiotics that could cure syphilis virtually eliminated this particular type of treatment.

In the 1920s, wealthier patients could afford a course of "narcosis therapy," in which barbiturates and other depressants were used to induce sleep for as long as a week or more. Another use for sedative drugs was in conjunction with psychotherapy: an intravenous dose of thiopental sodium, a rapid-acting barbiturate, would relax a person and pro-duce more talking during psychotherapy (see Chapter 7). The theory was that such a reduction in inhibitions would enable the patient to express repressed thoughts; thus, the term *truth serum* came to be used for thiopental sodium and for scopol-amine, an anticholinergic drug used similarly. Anyone who has ever listened to a person who has

Mental disorders are typically categorized by behavioral symptoms; for example, schizophrenia is characterized by delusions, hallucinations, and disorganized speech and behavior. ©McGraw-Hill Education/Lars A. Niki, photographer

drunk a good bit of alcohol will tell you that although the talk might be less inhibited, it isn't always more truthful. So-called truth serum apparently worked about as well.

In the 1930s, European physicians experi-mented with various chemicals to induce either a coma (insulin) or convulsions similar to epilepsy

schizophrenia (skitz o *fren* ee yah): a type of chronic psychosis.
bipolar disorder: a type of mood disorder also known as manic-depressive disorder.
depression: a major type of mood disorder.

DSM-5

Bipolar I Disorder

The key to a diagnosis of bipolar I is the presence of a manic episode, defined by:

A. Abnormally and persistently elevated, expansive, or irritable mood

B. At least three of the following:

1. Inflated self-esteem or grandiosity
2. Decreased need for sleep
3. More talkative than usual or pressure to keep talking
4. Flight of ideas or feeling that thoughts are racing
5. Distractibility
6. Increase in activity
7. Excessive involvement in pleasurable activities that have a high potential for painful consequences (shopping, sex, foolish investments)

C. Mood disturbance is sufficiently severe to cause marked impairment in functioning

Major Depressive Disorder

A. For two weeks or more, five or more of the following, including either No. 1 or No. 2:

1. Depressed mood most of the day, nearly every day
2. Markedly diminished interest or pleasure in most activities
3. Significant changes in body weight or appetite (increased or decreased)
4. Insomnia or hypersomnia nearly every day
5. Psychomotor agitation (increased activity) or retardation (decreased activity)
6. Fatigue or loss of energy
7. Feelings of worthlessness or excessive guilt
8. Diminished ability to think or concentrate
9. Recurrent thoughts of death or suicide, or a suicide attempt or plan for committing suicide

B. The symptoms cause clinically significant distress or impairment

C. Not due to a drug or medical condition and not a normal reaction to the loss of a loved one

Adapted from *Diagnostic and Statistical Manual of Mental Disorders, Text Revision*, DSM-5.

(camphor, Metrazol). At first this type of treatment was used in schizophrenia, and indeed the patients were calmer for at least a short while after the seizures were over. However, repeated treatments were problematic as the patients became quite agitated in the few minutes after the drug was administered and before the seizures began. In 1938 it was shown that electrical current could be used to induce immediate seizures, and so *electroconvulsive therapy (ECT)* replaced drug-induced seizures and came to be in widespread use in mental hospitals until the 1960s. While there proved to be no long-term benefits for schizophrenia, ECT turned out to be a rapid and effective way to reduce symptoms of depression. ECT is still used to treat severely depressed patients who do not respond to medication.[3]

By the 1950s, probably the major drug in use for severely disturbed patients in large mental hospitals was paraldehyde, a sedative (see Chapter 7). Although it produces little respiratory depression and therefore is safer than the barbiturates, the drug has a characteristic odor, which is still well remembered by those who worked in or visited the hospitals of that era. Sedation of severely disturbed patients by drugs that make them drowsy and slow them down has been referred to as the use of a "chemical straitjacket."

Antipsychotics

A number of people were involved in the discovery that a group of drugs called the **phenothiazines** had special properties when used with mental patients. Credit is usually given to a French surgeon, Henri Laborit, who first tested these compounds in conjunction with surgical anesthesia. He noted that the most effective of the phenothiazines, chlorpromazine, did not by itself induce drowsiness or a loss of consciousness, but it seemed to make the patients unconcerned about their upcoming surgery. He reasoned that this effect might reduce emotionality in psychiatric patients and encouraged his psychiatric colleagues to test the drug. The first report of these French trials of chlorpromazine in mental patients mentioned that not only were the patients calmed, but the drug also seemed to act on the psychotic process itself. This new type of drug action attracted a variety of names: In the United States the drugs were generally called tranquilizers, which some now think is an unfortunate term that focuses on the calming action and seems to imply sedation. Another term used was **neuroleptic,** meaning "taking hold of the nervous system," a term implying an increased amount of control. Although both of these terms are still in use, most medical texts now refer to this group of drugs as **antipsychotics,** reflecting their ability to reduce psychotic symptoms without necessarily producing drowsiness and sedation.

The tremendous impact of phenothiazine treatment on the management of hospitalized patients is clear from a 1955 statement by the director of the Delaware State Hospital:

> We have now achieved . . . the reorganization of the management of disturbed patients. With rare exceptions, all restraints have been discontinued. The hydrotherapy department, formerly active on all admission services and routinely used on wards with disturbed patients, has ceased to be in operation. Maintenance EST (electroshock treatment) for disturbed patients has been discontinued. . . . There has been a record increase in participation by these patients in social and occupational activities.
>
> These developments have vast sociological implications. I believe it is fair to state that pharmacology promises to accomplish what other measures have failed to bring about—the social emancipation of the mental hospital.[4]

Atypical Antipsychotic Drugs

In the years since 1950, many new phenothiazines were introduced and several completely new types of antipsychotic drugs have been discovered. Table 8.1 lists those on the U.S. market. We now refer to antipsychotic drugs as being either *conventional* antipsychotics (the phenothiazines and most of the other drug types introduced before the mid-1990s) or *atypical* (all antipsychotics introduced in the past 10 years are atypical antipsychotics). The atypical antipsychotics now dominate the market, with five of these drugs among the top 100 in prescription sales in 2010.

Mechanism of Antipsychotic Action   The first clue to the mechanism of action for antipsychotics was that virtually all of the phenothiazines and other conventional antipsychotics produce *pseudoparkinsonism.* Patients treated with these medications exhibit symptoms similar to Parkinson's disease (tremors and muscular rigidity). Because Parkinson's disease is known to be caused by a loss of dopamine neurons in the nigrostriatal dopamine pathway (see Chapter 4), scientists focused on the ability of antipsychotic drugs to block dopamine receptors. Although the conventional antipsychotics are generally fairly "dirty" drugs pharmacologically (they block other types of receptors as well), the doses required for the different drugs to produce antipsychotic effects do not correlate well with the ability of the different drugs to bind to any receptor except dopamine receptors (specifically, the D2 type of dopamine receptor). It is now well accepted that the initial effect of antipsychotic drugs is to block D2 dopamine receptors. However, this effect occurs with the first dose, but the antipsychotic effect of

phenothiazines (feen o *thigh uh* zeens): a group of drugs used to treat psychosis.

neuroleptic (noor o *lep* tick): a general term for antipsychotic drugs.

antipsychotics: a group of drugs used to treat psychosis; same as neuroleptic.

Table 8.1
Antipsychotic Drugs

Generic Name	Brand Name
Conventional antipsychotics	
fluphenazine	generic
haloperidol	generic
loxapine	Loxitane
mesoridazine	Serentil
molindone	Moban
perphenazine	generic
prochlorperazine	Compazine
thioridazine	generic
thiothixene	Navane
trifluoperazine	generic
Atypical antipsychotics	
aripiprazole	Abilify
asenaphine	Saphris
brexpiprazole	Rexulti
cariprazine	Vraylar
clozapine	Clozaril
iloperidone	Fanapt
lurasidone	Latuda
olanzepine	Zyprexa
paliperidone	Invega
pimavanserin	Nuplazid
quetiapine	Seroquel
risperidone	Risperdal
ziprasidone	Geodon

Source: www.pdrhealth.com

When clozapine was introduced, it differed from the other antipsychotics in two interesting ways. First, it produced much less pseudoparkinsonism than the other drugs. Second, some patients who had failed to improve with the other antipsychotics showed improvement when treated with clozapine. Clozapine was very promising, but it unfortunately has a risk of producing a deadly suppression of white blood cell production. The drug was withdrawn from the market but then made available again as long as patients have periodic blood samples taken to monitor their white cells. Clozapine produces effects on a wide range of receptor types, but eventually it was determined that its unique properties were probably related to its ability to block both D2 dopamine and 5HT2A serotonin receptors. Risperidone, olanzepine, and the other atypical antipsychotics were developed with these two actions in mind, and none of the newer drugs carries the risk of suppressing white blood cell production. The atypical antipsychotics are sometimes referred to as serotonin-dopamine antagonists. Pseudoparkinsonism is reduced because of serotonin-dopamine interactions in the nigrostriatal pathway.

Side Effects of Antipsychotics   Two positive aspects of the antipsychotics are that they do not produce drug dependence, and it is extremely difficult to use them to commit suicide. Allergic reactions might be noted, such as jaundice or skin rashes. Some patients exhibit photosensitivity, a tendency for the skin to darken and burn easily in sunlight. These reactions have a low incidence and usually decrease or disappear with a reduction in dosage. *Agranulocytosis,* low white blood cell count of unknown origin, can develop in the early stages of treatment. Because white blood cells are needed to fight infection, this disorder has a high mortality rate if not detected before a serious infection sets in. It is extremely rare with most of the antipsychotics other than clozapine.

The most common side effect of antipsychotic medication involves the nigrostriatal dopamine pathway (see Chapter 4). The major effects include

these drugs is not seen for at least 10 to 14 days (the "lag period"). Thus, the ultimate mechanism of antipsychotic action is some (as yet unknown) response of the nervous system to repeated administration of dopamine antagonists.

a wide range of movement disorders from facial tics to symptoms that resemble those of Parkinson's disease (tremors of the hands when they are at rest; muscular rigidity, including a masklike face; and a shuffling walk). As noted earlier, this pseudoparkinsonism is less of a problem with the newer atypical antipsychotics.

Tardive dyskinesia is the most serious complication of antipsychotic drug treatment. Although first observed in the late 1950s, it was not viewed as a major problem until the mid-1970s, 20 years after these drugs were introduced. The term *tardive dyskinesia* means "late-appearing abnormal movements" and refers primarily to rhythmic, repetitive sucking and smacking movements of the lips; thrusting of the tongue in and out ("fly-catching"); and movements of the arms, toes, or fingers. The fact that this syndrome usually occurs only after years of antipsychotic drug treatment, and that the symptoms persist and sometimes increase when medication is stopped, raised the possibility of irreversible changes. The current belief is that tardive dyskinesia is the result of supersensitivity of the dopaminergic receptors. Although reversal of the symptoms is possible in most cases, the best treatment is prevention, which can be accomplished through early detection and an immediate lowering of the medication level.

Based on results from a large international three-year study, it now appears that treatment with conventional antipsychotics produces pseudoparkinsonism in about 30 percent of psychotic patients, with tardive dyskinesia appearing in about 10 percent. Several of the atypical antipsychotics, including clozapine, olanzepine, and quetiapine, are in a lower-risk group that produces about one-third as many of each of these important side effects.[5]

Significant weight gain has been seen with many of the newer atypical agents, along with increased blood lipids and other indications of a "metabolic syndrome" that is associated with increased risk for diabetes. This is a significant public health concern because so many patients are now receiving these medications.

Long-Term Effectiveness   It was mentioned earlier that drug dependence is not a problem with these antipsychotic agents. In fact, it has long been known that even patients who clearly benefit from their use tend to dislike the drugs and often stop taking them. The drug trials that demonstrate the benefits of antipsychotics typically last six or eight weeks. This is a long enough time period to allow for some dosage adjustment and for the lag period for the antipsychotic effect to emerge, so these studies are optimal for the drug companies' purpose—to show that their drug works better than a placebo. But patients typically take these drugs for long periods of time—in many cases, for the remainder of their lives. The National Institute of Mental Health funded a long-term study, that followed 1,400 patients with chronic schizophrenia taking four different atypical antipsychotics and one conventional antipsychotic for up to 18 months.[6] The most surprising finding was that three-fourths of the patients quit taking the assigned medication before reaching 18 months of treatment. Some stopped because the drug did not appear to be helping and some stopped because the side effects became intolerable to them, but the biggest single reason for stopping was "patient's decision." In other words, in spite of short-term evidence of the efficacy of these drugs, their real-world effectiveness in treating chronic schizophrenia is considerably less than previously thought. The other surprising finding was that there was no clear evidence that the newer atypical agents worked any better than the conventional drugs, nor were there significant differences in extrapyramidal symptoms. A more recent meta-analysis of several long-term studies did report a slight advantage in relapse prevention for olanzepine, but the same drug caused greater weight gain.[7]

Antipsychotic Use in Children and the Elderly   Although almost all the research used to demonstrate the effectiveness of antipsychotic medications has been conducted on adults diagnosed with schizophrenia, once the drugs are marketed they can be prescribed for other populations and other uses. For example, in recent years there has been a large increase in the use of atypical antipsychotics in children, not only to treat psychotic disorders but also with diagnoses including ADHD and conduct disorder, for which they have not been approved. The reasoning seems to have been that because the newer drugs are less likely to produce the long-known and troublesome side effects of pseudoparkinsonism and tardive dyskinesia, they are "safer" than the older medications. However, several studies have now found an increased risk of both weight gain and metabolic changes combined with obesity, diabetes, and cardiovascular problems in children treated with the atypical antipsychotics.[8]

Likewise, elderly patients have been treated with antipsychotic drugs for years, often to control behavioral problems such as emotional outbursts or inappropriate sexual acting out in institutionalized patients. In many cases, these patients are suffering from dementia, and their uncontrolled behavior is a problem for their families, the staff, and the other patients. Evidence of a significant increase in death risk from cardiovascular and other problems in elderly patients treated with the atypical antipsychotics led the FDA in 2008 to require a "black box" warning regarding the use of these drugs for behavior management in elderly patients with dementia.

Antidepressants

Monoamine Oxidase Inhibitors The story of the antidepressant drugs starts with the fact that tuberculosis was a major chronic illness until about 1955. In 1952, preliminary reports suggested that a new drug, isoniazid, was effective in treating tuberculosis; isoniazid and similar drugs that followed were responsible for the emptying of hospital beds. One of the anti-tuberculosis drugs was iproniazid, which was introduced simultaneously with isoniazid but was withdrawn as too toxic. Clinical reports on its use in tuberculosis hospitals emphasized that there was considerable elevation of mood in the patients receiving iproniazid. These reports were followed up, and the drug was reintroduced as an antidepressant agent in 1955 on the basis of early promising studies with depressed patients.

Iproniazid is a **monoamine oxidase (MAO) inhibitor,** and its discovery opened up a new class of compounds for investigation. Although several MAO inhibitors have been introduced over the years, toxicity and side effects have limited their use and have reduced their number. Iproniazid was removed from sale in 1961 after being implicated in at least 54 fatalities. Currently two MAO inhibitors are on the U.S. market (see Table 8.2). A major limitation of the use of the MAO inhibitors is that

Table 8.2
Antidepressant Drugs

Generic Name	Brand Name
MAO inhibitors	
phenelzine	Nardil
tranylcypromine	Parnate
Tricyclics	
amitriptyline	Elavil
amoxapine	Asendin
desipramine	Norpramin
doxepin	Sinequan
imipramine	Tofranil
nortriptyline	Pamelor
protriptyline	Vivactil
Selective reuptake inhibitors	
citalopram	Celexa
desvenlafaxine	Pristiq
duloxetine	Cymbalta
escitalopram	Lexapro
fluoxetine	Prozac
paroxetine	Paxil
sertraline	Zoloft
venlafaxine	Effexor
Others	
bupropion	Wellbutrin
mirtazapine	Remeron
trazodone	Desyrel

they alter the normal metabolism of a dietary amino acid, tyramine, such that if an individual consumes foods with a high tyramine content while taking MAO inhibitors, a hypertensive (high blood pressure) crisis can result. Because aged cheeses are one source of tyramine, this is often referred to as the "cheese reaction." A severe headache, palpitations, flushing of the skin, nausea, and vomiting are some symptoms of this reaction, which has in some cases ended in death from a stroke (cerebrovascular accident). Besides avoiding foods and beverages that contain tyramine (aged cheeses, Chianti wine, smoked or pickled fish, and many others), patients taking MAO inhibitors must also avoid sympathomimetic drugs, such as amphetamines, methylphenidate, and ephedrine.

MAO is an enzyme involved in the breakdown of serotonin, norepinephrine, and dopamine, and its inhibition results in increased availability of these neurotransmitters at the synapse. This was the first clue to the possible mechanism of antidepressant action.

Tricyclic Antidepressants Sometimes when you are looking for one thing, you find something entirely different. The MAO inhibitors were found among antituberculosis agents, and the phenothiazine antipsychotics were found while looking for a better antihistamine. The **tricyclic** antidepressants were found in a search for better phenothiazine antipsychotics. The basic phenothiazine structure consists of three rings, with various side chains for the different antipsychotic drugs. Imipramine resulted from a slight change in the middle of the three rings and was tested in 1958 on a group of patients. The drug had little effect on psychotic symptoms but improved the mood of depressed patients. This was the first tricyclic antidepressant, and many more have followed (see Table 8.2). Although these drugs are not effective in all patients, most controlled clinical trials do find that depressive episodes are less severe and resolve more quickly if the patients are treated with one of the tricyclic antidepressants than if they are given a placebo.

The first tricyclics were discovered to interfere with the reuptake into the terminal of the neurotransmitters norepinephrine, dopamine, and serotonin. This results in an increased availability of these neurotransmitters at the synapse. Because MAO inhibition also results in increased availability of the same neurotransmitters, there has been considerable speculation that the antidepressant actions of both classes of drugs result from increased synaptic availability of one or more of these neurotransmitters. One of the effective antidepressants, desipramine, was found to have a much greater effect on the reuptake of norepinephrine than on the reuptake of either dopamine or serotonin, so for a time most theories of antidepressant action focused on norepinephrine.

Selective Reuptake Inhibitors The introduction in 1987 of fluoxetine (Prozac) ushered in the era of the *selective serotonin reuptake inhibitors* (**SSRIs**). Trazodone had already been available and was known to have a greater effect on serotonin than on norepinephrine reuptake, calling the norepinephrine theory into question. Prozac soon became the most widely prescribed antidepressant drug ever marketed. Prozac is safer than the tricyclic antidepressants in that it is less likely to lead to overdose deaths, so physicians felt more confident about prescribing it. Despite some reports in the early 1990s of unusual violent or suicidal reactions, sales of Prozac continued at a high rate, and several other SSRIs were introduced by other companies. Drugs have also been developed that are reuptake inhibitors for both serotonin and norepinephrine. In that sense they are similar to the older tricyclics, but these newer drugs are more selective (have fewer other actions than the tricyclics) and are thus referred to as selective serotonin and norepinephrine reuptake inhibitors

monoamine oxidase (MAO) inhibitor: a type of antidepressant drug.
tricyclic (try *sike* lick): a type of antidepressant drug.
SSRI: selective serotonin reuptake inhibitors, a type of antidepressant drug.

(SSNRIs). Effexor was the first of these, followed in 2004 by Cymbalta (see Table 8.2).

Add-On Medication   In 2007, the antipsychotic drug Abilify (aripiprazole) was approved by the FDA as an add-on treatment for those already taking antidepressant medication, because of some studies showing improvement in patients who had not responded to the antidepressant alone. Since then, sales of Abilify have increased dramatically to over $7 billion in 2016 (second in total dollar sales of all drugs). Abilify's patent ran out in 2014 and generic versions are expected soon, so Abilify's Japanese manufacturer Otsuka submitted a similar drug, brexpiprazol (Rexulti), which received FDA approval in 2015. We can expect a major advertising push to shift new prescriptions to this newly approved drug.

Although the worldwide value of antidepressant sales exceeded $15 billion in 2003, sales in the United States declined slightly in 2004 and 2005, primarily due to concerns about increased risk of suicide among children and adolescents.[9] Analysis of data submitted to the FDA for approval of nine drugs found higher rates of suicidal thoughts among the drug groups than among the placebo controls, so they began requiring a printed "black box" warning about the increased risk of suicidal tendencies in children and adolescents. Sales of selective reuptake inhibitors in the United States seemed back on track for further increases by 2006, led partly by their increasing use to treat generalized anxiety disorder. If we include the dollar value of sales for the add-on Abilify, total antidepressant sales have recovered quite well.

Another factor that perhaps should influence prescribing practices is the question of just how effective antidepressant medications are in general. It had been noticed in an earlier, not widely read Internet journal article that the data submitted to the FDA for approval of the SSRIs often showed very small, or sometimes no, differences between the tested drug and placebo. Because the FDA requires the company to submit records of all studies, even the unsuccessful ones, analysis of the overall set of results seemed to indicate that the

Depression is a serious, debilitating disorder that often responds to antidepressant medication. ©Yuri Arcurs/ Cutcaster RF

majority of the effectiveness produced by these drugs can be attributed to a placebo effect. A recent review of the research used to receive approval for the new antidepressant vortioxetine (Trintellix) pointed out a number of limitations in the results as well as in the FDA's process for evaluating effectiveness.[10] Overall, only about half of the 74 studies submitted to the FDA since 1987 in support of the new drug applications for 12 antidepressants found positive results in favor of the tested drug. The selective publication of only the positive findings means that practicing physicians who read the medical literature get an inflated picture of the overall effectiveness of this type of medication. At this point, the best evidence we have indicates that these antidepressant drugs are probably slightly better

Unintended Consequences

New Drugs Developed and Tested by Companies That Profit from Their Approval

As outlined in Chapter 3, the engine of drug discovery in the United States has always been the pharmaceutical companies themselves. These companies invest billions of dollars to develop and conduct research on a new drug in the hope that it will receive FDA approval and therefore bring in enough money from prescription sales to cover all those costs. The FDA scientists who review the information provided by the drug companies look at all the studies conducted on the new drug, but they appear to pay greater attention to results that appear in prestigious scientific journals. That seems like a good idea, since often those published papers are authored by researchers affiliated with academic institutions, and before being accepted for publication they are reviewed by other researchers who have examined the methods, statistics, and conclusions reported in the paper.

However, several recent studies of how this process actually works for antidepressant medications have reported that a new drug can meet the FDA's criteria for effectiveness even when many of the studies conducted have reported no difference between the drug and a placebo. The criteria for effectiveness chosen by those who designed the study might be only a small change in a depression rating scale, when such small changes do not reflect meaningful improvements in patients' clinical status. Also, there is no requirement that the new drug be compared to drugs already on the market to see if it provides better results. In addition, the language in the papers often overemphasizes the positive results while glossing over evidence for unwanted side effects.

Finally, a research report might appear to be written by academic scientists, but those scientists often have financial ties to the pharmaceutical company, or they acknowledge receiving assistance from the company in conducting the statistical analysis and even in writing the paper itself. In some cases, even the journal's editor receives grants or speaking fees from the company.[10]

To the extent that these reports influence the FDA's decision and are then used when discussing the new drug with prescribing physicians, the bottom line is that a new drug may be approved and widely prescribed even when it produces only small effects, is less helpful than other drugs on the market, and produces more unwanted side effects than is implied in the published research.

Box icon credit: ©Adam Gault/age fotostock RF

than placebos but are certainly not as effective overall as most people, including most physicians, have believed. However, if you are currently taking one of these medications yourself, please do not simply stop taking it abruptly. There are major withdrawal effects associated with abrupt cessation of most of these medications, so if you are trying to decide what to do about continued use, be sure to consult your physician.

Mechanism of Antidepressant Action It seems that most antidepressants work by increasing the availability of either norepinephrine or serotonin at their respective synapses. However, the antidepressant effect of MAO inhibitors, tricyclics, and SSRIs exhibits a "lag period": The patient must take the drug for about two weeks before improvement is seen, even though the biochemical effects on MAO or on reuptake occur in a matter of minutes. Although it has been suggested that some patients might benefit more from one type than from another, experiments have so far failed to reveal any rational basis for choosing among the drugs in any individual case, and overall the effectiveness of the drug does not seem to depend on which of the neurotransmitters is more affected.

Current theories of the antidepressant action of these agents focus less on the initial biochemical effects of the drugs than on the reaction of the neurons to repeated drug exposure. As is the case with antipsychotics, we do not yet know the complete story of how long-term exposure to antidepressant drugs eventually improves the symptoms of depression. In addition to the MAO inhibitors, tricyclics, and SSRIs, drugs such as Wellbutrin and Remeron act through somewhat different mechanisms. The fact that drugs with a wide variety of initial biochemical effects are all about equally effective (they reduce depressive symptoms for some people, but not for all) means it is possible that there is not a single biochemical mechanism to explain the effects of all these drugs.

Electroconvulsive Therapy

Probably the single most effective treatment for the depressed patient is electroconvulsive shock therapy (ECT). One report summarized the available good studies and showed that, in seven of eight studies, ECT was more effective in relieving the symptoms of depression than was placebo. Further, in four studies, ECT was more effective than the most effective class of antidepressant drugs, and in three other studies the two treatments were equal. One factor that makes ECT sometimes the clear treatment of choice is its more rapid effect than that found with current antidepressant drugs. Reversal of depression might not occur for two or three weeks with drug treatment, but with ECT results sometimes are noticed almost immediately. When there is a high risk of suicide, ECT is often considered necessary and it is possible to use both drug and ECT treatment simultaneously.[3]

Mood Stabilizers

In the late 1940s, two medical uses were proposed for salts of the element **lithium.** In the United States, lithium chloride, which tastes much like sodium chloride (table salt), was introduced as a salt substitute for heart patients. However, above a certain level lithium is quite toxic, and because there was no control over the dose, many users became ill and several died. This scandal was so great in the minds of American physicians that a proposed beneficial use published in 1949 by an Australian, John Cade, produced little interest in this country.

Cade had been experimenting with guinea pigs, examining the effects of lithium on urinary excretion of salts. Lithium appeared to have sedative properties in some of the animals, so he administered the compound to several disturbed patients. The manic patients all improved, whereas there seemed to be no effect on depressed or schizophrenic patients. This was followed up by several Danish studies in the 1950s and early 1960s, and it became increasingly apparent that the large majority of manic individuals showed dramatic remission of their symptoms after a lag period of a few days when treated with lithium carbonate or other salts.

Three factors slowed the acceptance of lithium in the United States. First was the salt-substitute poisonings, which gave lithium a bad reputation as a potentially lethal drug. Second, mania was not seen as a major problem in the United States. Manic patients feel energetic and have an unrealistically positive view of their own abilities, and such people are unlikely to seek treatment on their own. Also, patients who became quite manic and lost touch with reality would probably have been called schizophrenic in those days, perhaps at least partly because a treatment existed for schizophrenia. The antipsychotic drugs can control mania in most cases. The third and possibly most important factor is economic and relates to the way new drugs are introduced in the United States: by companies that hope to make a profit on them. Lithium is one of the basic chemical elements (number 3 on the periodic chart) and its simple salts had been available for various purposes for many years, so it would be impossible for a drug company to receive an exclusive patent to sell lithium. A company generally must go to considerable expense to conduct the research necessary to demonstrate safety and effectiveness to the FDA. If one company had done this, as soon as the drug was approved any other company could also have sold lithium, and it would have been impossible for the first company to recoup its research investment. After several years of frustration, the weight of the academically conducted research and the clinical experience in

Europe was such that several companies received approval to sell lithium in 1970.

Treatment with lithium requires 10 to 15 days before symptoms begin to change, and once again the ultimate mechanism for its action is not yet known. Lithium is both safe and toxic. It is safe because the blood level can be monitored routinely and the dose adjusted to ensure therapeutic, but not excessive, blood levels. Patients develop tolerances to the minor side effects of gastrointestinal disturbances and tremors. Excessively high levels in the blood cause confusion and loss of coordination, which can progress to coma, convulsions, and death if lithium is not stopped and appropriate treatment instituted.

Of primary importance in the therapeutic use of lithium is the realization that lithium acts as a mood-normalizing agent in individuals with bipolar illness. Lithium will prevent both manic and depressed mood swings. It has only moderate effects on unipolar depressions.

The biggest limitation to the usefulness of lithium is that patients simply do not like to take it and most will discontinue its use at some point. This high rate of noncompliance is the major reason why, although lithium is perhaps the single most effective psychotherapeutic agent available, alternative medications have been developed.

In addition to lithium, three drugs that were initially developed as anticonvulsants (to treat epileptic seizures) are being used as mood stabilizers (to treat bipolar disorder). Valproic acid (Depakote), carbamazepine (Tegretol), and lamotrigine (Lamictal) have received FDA approval for use in bipolar disorder, based on published evidence of their effectiveness. These drugs are particularly useful in people who might be susceptible to epileptic seizures. They are probably not quite as effective as lithium, but they have the advantage that monitoring of blood levels is not required. The mood-stabilizing anticonvulsants are also thought to be better accepted by patients than is lithium, but noncompliance is an issue with these drugs as well (perhaps not as much as with lithium). Patients with

bipolar disorder who clearly improve while on medication but who relapse because they stop taking it may go through this cycle repeatedly, often with tragic consequences (suicide, arrest, homelessness).

Consequences of Drug Treatments for Mental Illness

The use of modern psychopharmaceuticals, which began in the mid-1950s in the United States, has affected the lives of millions of Americans who have been treated with them. But the availability of these effective medications has also brought about revolutionary changes in our society's treatment of and relationship with our mentally ill citizens. Figure 8.1 depicts what happened to the population of our large mental hospitals from 1946 to 2014. These hospitals had grown larger and larger and held a total of over half a million people in the peak years of the early 1950s. The year in which chlorpromazine was introduced in the United States, 1955, was the last year in which the population of these hospitals increased. Since then the average population has continued to decline. The antipsychotics do not cure schizophrenia or other forms of psychosis, but they can control the symptoms to a great degree, allowing the patients to leave the hospital, live at home, and often earn a living. These drugs began the liberation of mental patients from hospitals, where many of them had previously stayed year after year, committed for an indefinite time.

The movement out of mental hospitals was accelerated by the 1963 Community Mental Health Act, which provided federal support to states to develop community-based mental health centers. The idea was to treat mental patients closer to home in a more natural environment, at lesser expense, and on an outpatient basis. The opportunity for such a

---

lithium (*lith* ee um): a drug used in treating mania and bipolar disorder.

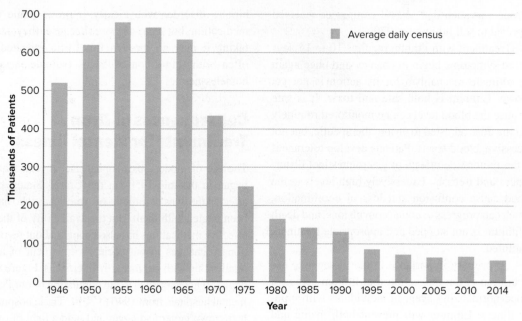

Figure 8.1 Number of Patients in Nonfederal Psychiatric Hospitals, 1946–2014

SOURCE: American Hospital Association, *Hospital Statistics, 2016.*

Prisons hold more mentally ill persons than do state mental hospitals. ©Sonny Timbelaka/AFP/Getty Images

program to work was greatly enhanced by the availability of the antipsychotics. The establishment of Medicare and Medicaid in 1965 moved thousands of elderly patients suffering from dementia out of mental hospitals and into nursing homes, further accelerating the decline in psychiatric hospital populations.

The mental health professions have been greatly affected by these drugs. The majority of psychiatrists in practice today spend less time doing psychotherapy than did their colleagues in the 1950s. In fact, for many psychiatrists the first issue is to establish an appropriate drug regimen, and only after the initial symptoms are controlled will they engage in much talk therapy. For some psychiatrists, the prescription pad has replaced the couch as their primary tool. This may be sensible in terms of overall cost effectiveness, but it has altered the doctor-patient relationship.

Along with the liberation of patients from hospitals and their return to the community came a concern for their civil rights. Indefinite commitment to a hospital was declared unconstitutional in

1975, and all states have since developed procedures to protect the rights of individual patients. Hearings are required before a person can be committed for treatment against his or her will, and it is usually necessary to demonstrate a clear and present danger to the patient's own person or to others. Periodic reviews of the patient's status are called for, and if at any time the immediate danger is not present, the patient must be released. No one would want to argue that mental patients should not have these rights, but the availability of psychoactive medications helps create difficult situations. A patient who is dangerously psychotic might be admitted for treatment and, after a few weeks on an antipsychotic drug, might be sufficiently in control to be allowed to leave the hospital. However, if the patient remains suspicious or simply doesn't like to take the medication, he or she will eventually stop taking it and again become psychotic. Or patients might be released into the community, perhaps functioning with medication or perhaps not, too sick to really take care of themselves but not sick enough to present an immediate danger. Often, the eventual result is violation of a law, leading to imprisonment. In fact, more mentally ill persons are jailed each year than are admitted to state mental hospitals. About one-third of all homeless people in the United States have some form of serious mental illness. The plight of our homeless, rootless, mentally ill citizens has been the subject of magazine and television reports, and efforts are being made to change the way these people are treated.

Summary

- The medical model of mental illness has been widely criticized, yet psychotherapeutic drugs are often discussed in the context of this model.
- Diagnosis of mental disorders is difficult and controversial, but the *DSM-5* provides a standard diagnostic approach for most purposes.
- The introduction of antipsychotics in the mid-1950s started a revolution in mental health care and increased interest in psychopharmacology.

- The antipsychotics reduce the symptoms of schizophrenia, but they often produce movement disorders, some of which resemble Parkinson's disease. Atypical antipsychotics are now widely prescribed for a variety of disorders.
- The major groups of antidepressant drugs are the MAO inhibitors, the tricyclics, and the selective reuptake inhibitors.
- The selective reuptake inhibitors are a major source of revenue for the pharmaceutical industry.
- Lithium is useful in treating mania and in preventing mood swings in bipolar disorder.
- The number of people occupying beds in mental hospitals has declined since 1955, partly because psychotherapeutic drugs allow people to be released after shorter stays.

Review Questions

1. Give two examples of anxiety disorder.
2. Is schizophrenia a functional or an organic psychosis?
3. Besides sadness, what are some other indicators of a major depressive episode?
4. What type of drug is chlorpromazine, and where was it first tested on patients?
5. What is tardive dyskinesia, and how does it respond to a reduction in the dose of an antipsychotic drug?
6. Which type of drug was discovered while testing an antituberculosis agent?
7. How do the selective reuptake inhibitors differ from the older tricyclics in terms of their actions in the brain?
8. What were two of the three reasons it took so long for lithium to be available for use in the United States?
9. If clozapine is so dangerous, why is it prescribed at all?
10. Why was Prozac the most widely prescribed antidepressant drug ever marketed?

References

1. American Psychiatric Association. *Diagnostic and Statistical Manual of Mental Disorders* (5th ed.). Washington, DC: 2013.
2. Whitaker, R. *Anatomy of an Epidemic: Magic Bullets, Psychiatric Drugs, and the Astonishing Rise of Mental Illness in America.* New York: Broadway Paperbacks, 2010.
3. Alves, L. P. C., T. F.V. Freire, M. P. A. Fleck, and N. S. Rocha. "A Naturalistic Study of High-Dose Unilateral ECT among Severely Depressed Inpatients: How Does It Work in the Clinical Practice?" *BMC Psychiatry* 16 (2016), pp. 1–8.
4. Freyhan, F. A. "The Immediate and Long-Range Effects of Chlorpromazine on the Mental Hospital." In Smith, Kline and French Laboratories, *Chlorpromazine and Mental Health.* Philadelphia: Lea & Febiger, 1955.
5. Baldessarini, R. J., and D. M. Gardner. "Incidence of Extrapyramidal Syndromes and Tardive Dyskinesia." *Journal of Clinical Psychopharmacology* 31 (2011), pp. 382–84.
6. Lieberman, J. A., and others. "Effectiveness of Antipsychotic Drugs in Patients with Chronic Schizophrenia." *New England Journal of Medicine* 353 (2005), pp. 1209–23.
7. Zhao, Y. J., L. Lin, M. Teng, A. L. Khoo, L. B. Soh, T. A. Furukawa, R. J. Baldessarini, B. P. Lim, and K. Sim. "Long-Term Antipsychotic Treatment in Schizophrenia: Systematic Review and Network Meta-Analysis of Randomised Controlled Trials." *British Journal of Psychiatry Open* 2, no. 1 (2016), pp. 59–66.
8. Galling, B., A. Roldán, R. E. Nielsen, J. Nielsen, T. Gerhard, M. Carbon, B. Stubbs, et al. "Type 2 Diabetes Mellitus in Youth Exposed to Antipsychotics: A Systematic Review and Meta-Analysis." *JAMA Psychiatry* 73 (2016), pp. 247–259.
9. Karanges, E., and I. S. McGregor. "Antidepressants and Adolescent Brain Development." *Future Neurology* 6 (2011), pp. 783–808.
10. Cosgrove, L., S. Vannoy, B. Mintzes, and A. F. Shaughnessy. "Under the Influence: The Interplay among Industry, Publishing, and Drug Regulation." *Accountability in Research* 23 (2016), pp. 257–279.

Check Yourself

Name _____ Date _____

Track Your Daily Mood Changes

Some days are better than others—we all experience that. Try using this psychological "instrument" to measure how your outlook on life changes on a day-to-day basis. Decide on a particular time to mark the scales and try to do them at the same time each day, because your mood also varies with time of day. Mark a spot on each vertical scale that corresponds to how you're feeling at the moment.

After you've finished the week, look back and see if you can relate the highs and lows to particular events or activities that happened at that time. Do all your scores tend to vary together, or are some areas unrelated to others?

If you find this useful, as an alternative to using paper, there are mobile mood-tracking apps as well as a free web-based tracker (www.medhelp.org/user_trackers/gallery/mood).

1. How optimistic do you feel about accomplishing something useful or meaningful in the next 24 hours?

	Day 1	Day 2	Day 3	Day 4	Day 5	Day 6	Day 7
Quite certain I will							
Probably will							
Not sure							
Probably won't							
Quite certain I won't							

2. How energetic do you feel at the moment?

	Day 1	Day 2	Day 3	Day 4	Day 5	Day 6	Day 7
Have lots of energy							
Fairly energetic							
About average							
Not much energy							
Almost no energy							

continued

3. How happy or sad are you today?

	Day 1	Day 2	Day 3	Day 4	Day 5	Day 6	Day 7
Very happy							
Happy							
Neither happy nor sad							
Sad							
Very sad							

4. How mentally sharp do you feel today (ability to remember things, ability to think)?

	Day 1	Day 2	Day 3	Day 4	Day 5	Day 6	Day 7
Quite sharp							
Pretty sharp							
Average							
A bit dull							
Very dull and slow							

5. How satisfied are you with yourself today?

	Day 1	Day 2	Day 3	Day 4	Day 5	Day 6	Day 7
Quite satisfied							
Fairly satisfied							
Not sure							
Fairly dissatisfied							
Quite dissatisfied							

Alcohol

Alcohol: social lubricant, adjunct to a fine meal, or demon
rum? People today are no different from people throughout
the centuries; many use alcohol,
and many others condemn its use. This love-hate relationship
with alcohol has been ongoing for a long time. The last two
decades have brought a slight swing of the pendulum: Health-
conscious Americans are opting for low-alcohol or no-alcohol
drinks, consumption of hard liquor is down, and we receive frequent reminders to use alcohol responsibly, not to drink and
drive, and not to let our friends drive if they've been drinking.
Let's take a closer look at the world's number one psychoactive
substance.

9 Alcohol
What is alcohol, and how does it affect the body and
brain? How does alcohol influence an individual's relationship with others, and what is its impact on society?

9

Alcohol

©Spike Mafford/Getty Images RF

Alcoholic Beverages

Fermentation and Fermentation Products

Many thousands of years ago, Neolithic humans discovered "booze." Beer and berry wine were known and used about 6400 BC and grape wine dates from 300 to 400 BC. Mead, which is made from honey, might be the oldest alcoholic beverage; some authorities suggest it appeared in the Paleolithic Age, about 8000 BC. Early use of alcohol seems to have been worldwide: Beer was drunk by the Native Americans whom Columbus met.

Fermentation forms the basis for all alcoholic beverages. Certain yeasts act on sugar in the presence of water, and this chemical action is fermentation. Yeast recombines the carbon, hydrogen, and oxygen of sugar into ethyl

Objectives

When you have finished this chapter, you should be able to:

- Understand the production and approximate alcohol content of the major beverage types.

- Relate the history and effectiveness of temperance and prohibition movements in the United States.

- Know recent alcohol consumption trends.

- Describe how alcohol is processed by the body.

- Understand how consumption rate and body size influence blood alcohol concentration, and know the legal BAC.

- Discuss the likely role of GABA in alcohol's mechanism of action.

- Explain the role of the balanced placebo study design in understanding alcohol's effects.

- Describe "alcohol myopia," acute alcohol poisoning, and alcohol withdrawal symptoms.

- Describe the impact of alcohol on traffic fatalities.

- Discuss the role of alcohol in sexual behavior and violence.

- Discuss alcohol exposure vs. malnutrition in the effects of chronic alcohol use on the brain and liver.

- Understand the role of Alcoholics Anonymous in promoting the disease model of alcohol dependence.

- Discuss genetic influences on the risk of developing alcohol dependence.

alcohol and carbon dioxide. Chemically, $C_6H_{12}O_6$ (glucose) is transformed into C_2H_5OH (ethyl alcohol) + CO_2 (carbon dioxide).

Most fruits, including grapes, contain sugar, and the addition of the appropriate yeast (which is pervasive in the air wherever plants grow) to a mixture of crushed grapes and water will begin the fermentation process. The yeast has only a limited tolerance for alcohol; when the concentration reaches 15 percent, the yeast dies and fermentation ceases. While up to 15 percent is theoretically possible, in practice the standard alcohol content for wine is about 12 percent.

Cereal grains can also be used to produce alcoholic beverages. However, cereal grains contain starch rather than sugar, and before fermentation can begin the starch must be converted to sugar. This is accomplished by making *malt,* which contains enzymes that convert starch into sugar. In American beer the primary grain is barley, which is malted by steeping it in water and allowing it to sprout. The sprouted grain is then slowly dried to kill the sprout but preserve the enzymes formed during the growth. This dried, sprouted barley is called malt, and when crushed and mixed with water, the enzymes convert the starch to sugar. Only yeast is needed then to start fermentation. The lower sugar content of these grain-based beverages results in somewhat lower alcohol content: The typical American commercial beer contains about 4 percent alcohol.

Distilled Products

To obtain alcohol concentrations above 15 percent, distillation is necessary. **Distillation** is a process in which the solution containing alcohol is heated, and the vapors are collected and condensed into liquid form again. Alcohol has a lower boiling point than water, so there is a higher percentage of alcohol in the distillate (the condensed liquid) than there was in the original solution.

There is still debate over who discovered the distillation process and when the discovery was made, but many authorities place it in Arabia around AD 800. The term *alcohol* comes from an Arabic word meaning "finely divided spirit" and originally referred to that part of the wine collected through distillation—the essence, or "spirit," of the wine. In Europe, only fermented beverages were used until the 10th century, when the Italians first distilled wine, thereby introducing "spirits" to the Western world. These new products were studied and used in the treatment of many illnesses, including senility. The initial feeling about their medicinal value is best seen in the Latin name given these condensed vapors by a 13th-century French professor of medicine: *aqua vitae,* "the water of life."

On the continent, Europeans distilled wine into "brandywine" (derived from the Dutch term "burnt wine"), while the Irish and Scots distilled their malted-grain beverages (beer) into whiskey (the Gaelic term *uisgebaugh* also means "water of life").

In the United States the alcoholic content of distilled beverages is indicated by the term **proof.** The percentage of alcohol by volume is one-half of the proof number: for instance, 90-proof whiskey is 45 percent alcohol. The word *proof* developed from a British Army procedure to gauge the alcohol content of distilled spirits before there were modern techniques. The liquid was poured over gunpowder and ignited. If the alcohol content was high enough, the alcohol would burn and ignite the gunpowder, which would go "poof" and explode. That was proof that the beverage had an acceptable alcohol content, about 57 percent. Typical distilled beverages sold commercially (whiskey, vodka, gin, etc.) range between 40 percent and 50 percent alcohol content (80 to 100 proof).

Beer

Beer is made by adding barley malt to other cereal grains, such as ground corn or rice. The enzymes in

---

fermentation (fer men *tay* shun): the production of alcohol from sugars through the action of yeasts.
distillation (dis ti *lay* shun): the evaporation and condensing of alcohol vapors to produce beverages with higher alcohol content.
proof: a measure of a beverage's alcohol content; twice the alcohol percentage.

Drugs in the Media

Alcohol in Movies

Alcohol is widely used in American society, so we would expect to find many examples of alcohol use being portrayed in popular films. The more interesting question is whether films portray alcohol in a realistic light. There is a long history of alcohol portrayal, even in movies designed for children. You can find a video including clips from some of these earlier films at https://www.youtube.com/watch?v=ZXA1AxQYhn8.

Think about some more recent films you have watched, and perhaps consider these questions while watching the next couple of movies you view. How often do you see alcohol use portrayed in the following three ways:

1. Responsible use by adults in a social setting.
2. Wild scenes of drunken behavior filled with excitement, fun, and sexuality.

3. The ravages of alcoholism, damaging social and professional relationships.

In real life, responsible social use is fairly common, but it is understandable that the entertainment industry would use alcohol for dramatic or comedic effect in movies to make them more interesting, so we would expect some overrepresentation of either wild party scenes or alcoholism. Which of the three types of portrayal seems to be the most common? Now consider the message these films deliver to young people even before they themselves first try alcohol. If someone's ideas about alcohol and its effects are derived partly from movies, what would a teenager expect to happen to him or her after drinking alcohol for the first time?

Box icon credit: ©Glow Images RF

the malt change the starches in these grains into sugar; then the solids are filtered out before the yeast is added to the mash to start fermentation. Hops (dried blossoms from only the female hop plant) are added with the yeast to give beer its distinctive, pungent flavor. Although there are many varieties of beer, they fall into two broad types: ale and lager. Most of the beer sold today in America is lager, from the German word *lagern,* meaning "to store." The fermentation process originally took place in alpine caves, where the cooler temperatures made for slower fermentation, and the yeasts tended to drop to the bottom of the mash. Over the years, this resulted in a selection process for types of yeast that work well as "bottom fermenters." So, modern lagers are made using bottom-fermenting yeasts, cool temperatures, and slower fermentation. Ale is made using a top-fermenting yeast and slightly warmer temperatures, and the shorter fermentation time results in more of the flavor of the malt being retained in the final product. In general, ales have a stronger taste and lagers the lighter taste favored by most American beer drinkers.

Because most American beer is sold in bottles or cans, the yeast must be removed to prevent it from spoiling after packaging. This is usually accomplished by heating it (pasteurization), but some brewers use microfilters to remove the yeasts while keeping the beer cold. The carbonation is added at the time of packaging. Standard brands of

Brewpubs have become increasingly popular, but most beer consumed in the United States is produced by the two largest brewers. ©Neil Beer/Getty Images RF

commercial American beer contain about 4 percent alcohol.

If you were asked to produce a "light" beer, with fewer calories, a lighter taste, and less alcohol, what would you do—add water? That's only part of the answer, because light beers have about 10 percent less alcohol and 25 to 30 percent fewer calories. The mash is fermented at a cooler temperature for a longer time, so that more of the sugars are converted to alcohol. *Then* the alcohol content is adjusted by adding water, resulting in a beverage with considerably less remaining sugar and only a bit less alcohol.

Two years after Prohibition ended there were 750 U.S. brewers, but by 1941 that number had dwindled to 507. The U.S. brewing picture has changed dramatically since 1960. The first phase, during the 1960s and 1970s, saw the fairly rapid disappearance of many local or regional breweries and increasing dominance by a smaller number of national brands. These traditional brewers have continued to close, consolidate, or be acquired by larger companies, so that in 2006 there were only 20 of the traditional breweries still in operation. The American brewing business has become even more consolidated, and less American, in recent years. The large Milwaukee-based Miller brewing company had already been bought by the London corporation SAB, and Coors had merged with the Canadian brewer Molson, before the 2007 merger that formed MillerCoors, with joint headquarters in Denver and London. This consolidation was planned to compete better with the true giant of American brewers, St. Louis-based Anheuser-Busch. However, in 2008 Anheuser-Busch was acquired by the Belgian company InBev, which had previously acquired large brewing operations in both Brazil and China. So now two "American" brewers, each a wholly owned subsidiary of an international corporation, account for 60 percent of all the beer sold in the United States. Beginning in the early 1980s, small "craft" breweries began to appear, followed later by the appearance of *micro-breweries,* or *brewpubs,* which make beer for sale only on the premises. The total number of these

craft breweries is now over 14,500. The distinction between the large brewers and craft brewers is becoming more blurred, as both of the giants also now produce craft-like brands, and Boston, the largest specialty brewer, produces several brands that together would rank right behind Busch in amount sold.

Table 9.1 points out a couple of interesting things about beer sales in the United States. First, Anheuser-Busch continues to dominate the U.S. market, making six of the top-selling brands. Bud Light sells more than twice as much beer as its nearest competitor, Coors Light. The increasing share held by light beers is also reflected here, with former industry leader Budweiser slipping to third place and six of the top brands falling into the light category. The two U.S. giants, Anheuser-Busch and MillerCoors, battle to retain their market shares with expensive advertising campaigns as well as by introducing a variety of specialty products. Most recently these include various fruit-flavored beers.

Imported beers have become increasingly popular in the past 20 years. The largest-selling imported beers are Corona and Modelo Especial,

Table 9.1
Largest-Selling Beer Brands (2016)

Brand	Market Share (percent)	Brewer
Bud Light	17.0 percent	Anheuser-Busch
Coors Light	7.9	MillerCoors
Budweiser	6.9	Anheuser-Busch
Miller Lite	6.2	MillerCoors
Corona Extra	3.9	Constellation
Natural Light	3.1	Anheuser-Busch
Busch Light	3.0	Anheuser-Busch
Modelo Especial	2.5	Constellation
Michelob Ultra	2.4	Anheuser-Busch
Busch	2.2	Anheuser-Busch

Source: Data from beerinsights.com, 2012.

both from Mexico. Imports now represent about 13 percent of total U.S. sales. The craft beers produced by new, small breweries combined with an increased variety of imports and no-alcohol beers add many new choices for the beer connoisseur, but Bud Light still dominates the mass market.

Wine

Wine is one of humankind's oldest beverages, a drink that for generations has been praised as a gift from heaven and condemned as a work of the devil. Although a large volume of wine is now produced in mechanized, sterilized wine "factories," many small wineries operate alongside the industry giants, and the tradition continues that careful selection and cultivation of grapevines, good weather, precise timing of the harvest, and careful monitoring of fermentation and aging can result in wines of noticeably higher quality.

There are two basic types of American wines. *Generics* usually have names taken from European land areas where the original wines were produced: Chablis, Burgundy, and Rhine are examples. These are all blended wines, made from whatever grapes are available, and during processing they are made to taste something like the traditional European wines from those regions. *Varietals* are named after one variety of grape, which by law must make up at least 51 percent of the grapes used in producing the wine. Chardonnay, merlot, and zinfandel are some examples. There are many varietal wines, and traditionally they have been sold in individual bottles and are more expensive than the generics. Most white wines are made from white grapes, although it is possible to use red grapes if the skins are removed before fermentation. Red wines are made from red grapes by leaving the skins in the crushed grapes while they ferment. "Blush" wines such as white zinfandel have become quite popular. With the zinfandel grape, which is red, the skins are left in the crushed grapes for a short while, resulting in a wine that is just slightly pink.

Besides red versus white and generic versus varietal, another general distinction is dry versus sweet. The sweeter wines are likely to have a "heavier" taste overall, with the sweetness balancing out flavors that might be considered harsh in a dry wine.

Because carbon dioxide is produced during fermentation, it is possible to produce naturally carbonated sparkling wines by adding a small amount of sugar as the wine is bottled and then keeping the bottle tightly corked. French champagnes are made in this way, as are the more expensive American champagnes, which might be labeled "naturally fermented in the bottle," or "methode Champagnoise." A cheaper method is used on inexpensive sparkling wines: Carbon dioxide gas is injected into a generic wine during bottling. Champagnes vary in their sweetness, also, with brut being the driest. Sweet champagnes are labeled "extra dry." The *extra* means "not," as in *extraordinary*.

Most wines contain about 12 percent alcohol. It was discovered many years ago in Spain that if enough brandy is added to a newly fermented wine the fermentation will stop and the wine will not spoil (turn to vinegar). Sealing the wine in charred oak casks for aging further refined its taste, and soon *sherry* was in great demand throughout Europe. Other fortified wines, all of which have an alcohol content near 20 percent, include port, Madeira, and Muscatel.

Wine consumption has increased considerably during the past 35 years. ©Andersen Ross/Getty Images RF

Distilled Spirits

Although brandy, distilled from wine, was probably the first type of spirits known to Europeans, the Celts of Ireland and the Scottish highlands were distilling a crude beverage known as *uisgebaugh* before 1500. If you try to pronounce that, you'll see that it was the origin of the word *whiskey* (spelled *whisky* in Scotland and Canada). Today's Scotch whisky is distilled from fermented barley malt (a strong beer).

In the Americas, one of the early distillers who established a good reputation was Elijah Craig, a Baptist minister living in what was then Bourbon County, Kentucky. He began storing his whiskey in charred new oak barrels, originating a manufacturing step still used with American bourbon whiskeys.

By the 17th century, improved distillation techniques had made possible the production of relatively pure alcohol. Today's standard product from many large commercial distilleries is 95 percent pure ethyl alcohol (ethanol) (190 proof). Into the process goes whatever grain is available at a cheap price and tank loads of corn syrup or other sources of sugars or starches. Out the other end come *grain neutral spirits,* a clear liquid that is essentially tasteless (except for the strong alcohol taste), which might be sold in small quantities as Everclear or for use in medicine or research. More often, it is processed in bulk in various ways. For example, large quantities of ethanol are added to gasoline to produce a less polluting fuel, which also helps out the American farmer. Besides other industrial uses for ethanol, such as in cleaners and solvents, bulk grain neutral spirits are also used in making various beverages, including blended Scotch whiskies. One of the first beverages to be made from straight grain neutral spirits was gin. By filtering the distillate through juniper berries and then diluting it with water, a medicinal-tasting drink was produced. First called "jenever" by the Dutch and "genievre" by the French, the British shortened the name to "gin." Gin became a popular beverage in England and now forms the basis for many an American martini.

Another major use for bulk grain neutral spirits is in the production of *vodka.* Many inexpensive

Bourbon whiskey is a distilled spirit first produced in the 18th century in Kentucky. Source: Library of Congress Prints and Photographs Division [LC-USZC4-6495]

vodkas are simply a mixture of grain neutral spirits and water, adjusted to the desired proof. More expensive vodkas are distilled to a lower proof and may retain more of the flavors of the original fermented grain or potatoes.

The proof at which distillation is carried out influences the taste and other characteristics of the liquor. When alcohol is formed, other related substances, known as **congeners,** are also formed. These may include alcohols other than ethanol, oils, and other organic matter. Luckily they are present only in small amounts, because some of them are quite toxic. Grain neutral spirits contain relatively few congeners and none of the flavor of the grains used in the mash. Whiskey is usually

congeners (*con* je nurz): other alcohols and oils contained in alcoholic beverages.

distilled at a lower proof, not more than 160, and thus the distillate contains more congeners and some of the flavor of the grain used. Whiskey accumulates congeners during aging, at least for the first five years, and the congeners and the grain used provide the variation in taste among whiskeys.

Until Prohibition almost all whiskey consumed in the United States was straight rye or bourbon manufactured in the United States. Prohibition introduced smuggled Canadian and Scotch whisky to American drinkers, and they liked them. World War II sent American men around the world, further exposing them to this different type of liquor. Scotch and Canadian whiskys are lighter than American whiskey, which means lighter in color and less heavy in taste. They are lighter because Canadian and Scotch whiskys are typically *blended* whiskys, made from about two-thirds straight whisky and one-third grain neutral spirits. After World War II, U.S. manufacturers began selling more blended whiskey. Seagram's 7-Crown has been one of the most popular blended American whiskeys.

Liqueurs, or cordials, are similar in some ways to the fortified wines. Originally the cordials were made from brandy mixed with flavorings derived from herbs, berries, or nuts. After dilution with sugar and water, the beverages are highly flavored, sweet, and usually about 20 to 25 percent alcohol. Some of the old recipes are still closely guarded secrets of a particular group of European monks. The late 20th century saw an increase in popularity for these drinks, which are usually consumed in small amounts and have only about half the alcohol content of vodka or whiskey. Many new types were introduced, from Bailey's Irish Cream to varieties of schnapps. Modern American peppermint, peach, and other types of schnapps are made from grain neutral spirits, which are diluted, sweetened, and flavored with artificial or natural flavorings.

Alcohol Use and "The Alcohol Problem"

Historians seem to agree that, at the time of America's revolution against the English in the late 1700s, most Americans drank alcoholic beverages and most people favored these beverages compared with drinking water, which was often contaminated. The per-capita consumption of alcohol was apparently much greater than current levels, and little public concern was expressed. Even the early Puritan ministers, who were moralistic about all kinds of behavior, referred to alcoholic drink as "the Good Creature of God." They denounced drunkenness as a sinful misuse of the "Good Creature" but clearly placed the blame on the sinner, not on alcohol itself.[1]

A new view of alcohol as the *cause* of serious problems began to emerge in America soon after the Revolution. That view took root and still exists as a major influence in American culture today. It is so pervasive that some people have a hard time understanding what is meant by the "demonization" of alcohol (viewing alcohol as a demon, or devil). The concept is important, partly because alcohol was the first psychoactive substance to become demonized in American culture, leading the way for similar views of cocaine, heroin, and marijuana in this century. We are referring to a tendency to view a substance as an *active* (sometimes almost purposeful) source of *evil,* damaging everything it touches. Whenever harmful consequences result from the use of something (firearms and nuclear energy are other possible examples), some people find it easiest to simply view that thing as "bad" and seek to eliminate it.

The Temperance Movement in America

The first writings indicating a negative view of alcohol itself are attributed to a prominent Philadelphia physician named Benjamin Rush, one of the signers of the Declaration of Independence. Rush's 1784 pamphlet, "An Inquiry into the Effects of Ardent Spirits on the Mind and Body," was aimed particularly at distilled spirits (*ardent* means "burning," "fiery"), not at the weaker beverages, such as beer and wine. As a physician, Rush had noticed a relationship between heavy drinking and jaundice (an indicator of liver disease), "madness" (perhaps the delirium tremens of withdrawal, or perhaps what we now call Korsakoff's psychosis), and "epilepsy" (probably the seizures seen during withdrawal). All of those are currently accepted and well-documented consequences of heavy alcohol use. However, Rush also concluded that hard liquor damaged the drinker's morality, leading to a variety of antisocial, immoral, and criminal behaviors. Rush believed that this was a direct toxic action of distilled spirits on the part of the brain responsible for morality. Rush then introduced for the first time the concept of "addiction" to a psychoactive substance, describing the uncontrollable and overwhelming desires for alcohol experienced by some of his patients. For the first time this condition was referred to as a *disease* (caused by alcohol), and he recommended total abstinence from alcohol for those who were problem drinkers.[1]

Other physicians readily recognized these symptoms in their own patients, and physicians became the first leaders of the **temperance** movement. What Rush proposed, and most early followers supported, was that everyone should avoid distilled spirits entirely, because they were considered to be toxic, and should consume beer and wine in a *temperate,* or moderate, manner. Temperance societies were formed in many parts of the country, at first among the upper classes of physicians, ministers, and businesspeople. In the early 1800s, it became fashionable for the middle classes to join the elite in this movement, and hundreds of thousands of American businesspeople, farmers, lawyers, teachers, and their families "took the pledge" to avoid spirits and to be temperate in their use of beer or wine.

In the second half of the 19th century, things changed. Up to this time there had been little consumption of commercial beer in the United States. It was only with the advent of artificial refrigeration and the addition of hops, which helped preserve the beer, that the number of breweries increased. The waves of immigrants who entered the country in this period provided the necessary beer-drinking consumers. At first, encouraged by temperance groups that preferred beer consumption to the use of liquor, breweries were constructed everywhere. However, alcohol-related problems did not disappear. Instead, disruptive, drunken behavior became increasingly associated in the public's mind with the new wave of immigrants—Irish, Italians, and eastern Europeans, more often Catholic than Protestant—and they drank beer and wine. Temperance workers now advocated total abstinence from all alcoholic beverages, and pressure grew to prohibit the sale of alcohol altogether.

Prohibition

It's difficult now to imagine how important the issue of alcohol prohibition became in American society, but it was one of the major "culture war" issues for almost 100 years, from before the Civil War until the Great Depression of the 1930s. As political power swung back and forth, states would pass and then sometimes later repeal laws intended to restrict access to alcoholic beverages. The first state prohibition period began in 1851 when Maine passed its prohibition law. Between 1851 and 1855, 13 states passed statewide prohibition laws, but by 1868 nine had repealed them. The National Prohibition Party and the Woman's Christian Temperance Union (WCTU), both organized in 1874, provided the impetus for the second wave of statewide prohibition, which developed in the 1880s. From 1880 to 1889 seven states adopted prohibition laws, but by 1896 four had repealed them.

In 1899, a group of educators, lawyers, and clergymen described the saloon as the "workingman's club, in which many of his leisure hours are spent, and in which he finds more of the things that approximate luxury than in his home. . . ." They went on to say: "It is a centre of learning, books, papers, and lecture hall to them. It is the clearinghouse for common intelligence, the place where their philosophy of life is worked out, and their political and social beliefs take their beginnings."[2] Truth lay somewhere between those statements and the sentiments expressed in a sermon:

> The liquor traffic is the most fiendish, corrupt and hell-soaked institution that ever crawled out of the slime of the eternal pit. It is the open sore of this land. . . . It takes the kind, loving husband and father,

temperance (temp a rance): the idea that people should drink beer or wine in moderation but drink no hard liquor.

smothers every spark of love in his bosom, and transforms him into a heartless wretch, and makes him steal the shoes from his starving babe's feet to find the price for a glass of liquor. It takes your sweet innocent daughter, robs her of her virtue and transforms her into a brazen, wanton harlot. . . .

The open saloon as an institution has its origin in hell, and it is manufacturing subjects to be sent back to hell.[3]

Prohibition was not just a matter of "wets" versus "drys" or a matter of political conviction or health concerns. Intricately interwoven with these factors was a middle-class, rural, Protestant, evangelical concern that the good and true life was being undermined by ethnic groups with a different religion and a lower standard of living and morality. One way to strike back at these groups was through prohibition. The temperance movement can be credited with strengthening the political power of women's groups, such as the WCTU. Acting as protectors of the family, women marched, organized letter-writing campaigns, raised money, and had a major influence on decisions to outlaw the sale of alcohol, even though U.S. women did not attain the right to vote until 1920.

Between 1907 and 1919, 34 states enacted legislation enforcing statewide prohibition, whereas only 2 states repealed their prohibition laws. By 1917, 64 percent of the population lived in dry territory, and between 1908 and 1917 over 100,000 licensed bars were closed.

But a state prohibition law did not mean that the residents did not drink. They did, both legally and illegally. They drank illegally in speakeasies and other private clubs. They drank legally from a variety of the many patent medicines that were freely available. A few of the more interesting ones were Whisko, "a nonintoxicating stimulant" at 55 proof; Colden's Liquid Beef Tonic, "recommended for treatment of alcohol habit" with 53 proof; and Kaufman's Sulfur Bitters, which "contains no alcohol" but was in fact 20 percent alcohol (40 proof) and contained no sulfur.

In August 1917, the U.S. Senate adopted a resolution, authored by Andrew Volstead, that submitted the national prohibition amendment to the states.

The U.S. House of Representatives concurred in December, and 21 days later, on January 8, 1918, Mississippi became the first state to ratify the 18th Amendment. A year later, January 16, 1919, Nebraska was the 36th state to ratify the amendment, and the deed was done.

As stated in the amendment, a year after the 36th state ratified it, national **Prohibition** came into effect—on January 16, 1920. The amendment was simple, with only two operational parts:

Section 1. After one year from the ratification of this article the manufacture, sale or transportation of intoxicating liquors within, the importation thereof into, or the exportation thereof from the United States and all territory subject to the jurisdiction thereof for beverage purposes is hereby prohibited.

Section 2. The Congress and the several States shall have concurrent power to enforce this article by appropriate legislation.

The beginning of Prohibition was hailed in a radio sermon by popular preacher Billy Sunday:

The reign of tears is over. The slums will soon be a memory. We will turn our prisons into factories and our jails into storehouses and corncribs. Men will walk upright now, women will smile, and the children will laugh. Hell will be forever for rent.[1]

The law did not result in an alcohol-free society, and this came as quite a surprise to many people. Apparently the assumption was that Prohibition would be so widely accepted that little enforcement would be necessary. Along with saloons, breweries, and distilleries, hospitals that had specialized in the treatment of alcohol dependence closed their doors, presumably because there would no longer be a need for them.

It soon became clear that people were buying and selling alcohol illegally and that enforcement was not going to be easy. The majority of the population might have supported the idea of Prohibition, but such a large minority insisted on continuing to drink that *speakeasies, hip flasks,* and *bathtub gin* became household words. Organized crime became both more organized and vastly more profitable as a result of Prohibition.

Prohibition Worked!

The popular conception is that Prohibition was a total failure, leading to its repeal. That is not the case. Prohibition did reduce overall alcohol intake. Hospital admissions for alcohol dependence and deaths from alcohol declined sharply at the beginning of Prohibition. But during the 1920s, it appears that the prohibition laws were increasingly violated, and the rates of alcohol dependence and alcohol-related deaths began to increase. However, even toward the end of the "noble experiment," as Prohibition was called by its detractors, alcohol dependence and alcohol-related deaths were still lower than before Prohibition.

Prohibition laws were frequently violated, and enforcement was an ongoing problem. Source: Library of Congress Prints and Photographs Division [LC-USZ62-96757]

Prohibition Is Repealed

If Prohibition did reduce alcohol-related problems, why was it repealed? In 1926, the Association Against Prohibition was founded by a small group of America's wealthiest men, including the heads of many of the largest corporations in America. Their primary concern seems to have been the income taxes they were paying. Historically, taxes on alcohol had been one of the primary sources of revenue for the federal government. The federal government relied heavily on alcohol taxes before the income tax was initiated in 1913. A major hope of the repeal supporters was that income taxes could be reduced. There was also fear that the widespread and highly publicized disrespect for the Prohibition law encouraged a sense of "lawlessness," not just among the bootleggers and gangsters but also in the public at large. The Great Depression, which began in 1929, not only made more people consider the value of tax revenues but also increased fears of a generalized revolt. If Prohibition weakened respect for law and order, it had to go. Although women's groups had played a big role in getting Prohibition passed and the WCTU lobbied against repeal, other women's groups (again acting as protectors of the family) argued that Prohibition's dangers were too great and supported repeal.

The 18th Amendment was repealed by the 21st Amendment, proposed in Congress on February 20, 1933, and ratified by 36 states by December 5 of that year. So ended an era. The 21st Amendment was also short and sweet:

> Section 1. The eighteenth article of amendment of the Constitution of the United States is hereby repealed.
>
> Section 2. The transportation or importation into any State, Territory, or possession of the United States for delivery or use therein of intoxicating liquors, in violation of the laws thereof, is hereby prohibited.

When national Prohibition ended, America did not return overnight to the pre-1920s levels of alcohol consumption. Sales increased until after World War II, at which point per-capita consumption was approximately what it had been before Prohibition. Thus, the prohibition of alcohol, much like the current prohibitions of marijuana and heroin, did work in that it reduced alcohol availability, alcohol use, and related problems. On the other hand, even at its best it did not allow us to close all the jails and mental hospitals, and it encouraged organized crime and created expensive enforcement efforts.

Regulation after 1933

After national Prohibition, control over alcohol was returned to the states. Each state has since had its own means of regulating alcohol. Although a few

Prohibition: laws prohibiting all sales of alcoholic beverages in the United States from 1920 to 1933.

states remained dry after national Prohibition, most allowed at least beer sales. Thus, the temperance sentiment that beer was a safer beverage continued to influence policy. In many cases, beer containing no more than 3.2 percent alcohol by weight was allowed as a "nonintoxicating" beverage.

Over the years the general trend was for a relaxation of laws: States that did not allow sales of liquor became fewer until in 1966 the last dry state, Mississippi, became wet. The minimum age to purchase alcoholic beverages was set at 21 in all states except New York and Louisiana before 1970, when the national voting age was lowered to 18. During the 1970s, 30 states lowered the drinking age to 18 or 19. Per-capita consumption rates, which were relatively stable during the 1950s, increased steadily from 1965 through 1980. However, times changed; pushed by concerns over young people dying in alcohol-related traffic accidents, in the 1980s Congress authorized the Transportation Department to withhold a portion of federal highway funds for any state that did not raise its minimum drinking age to 21. In 1988, the final state raised its drinking age, making 21 the uniform drinking age all across the United States.

Taxation

Federal taxes on alcoholic beverages are a significant means of gathering money for the federal government. Although most of the federal revenue comes from individual income taxes, taxes on alcohol produce about 1 percent of the total collections by the Internal Revenue Service ($9.6 billion in 2015). The states also collect over $6 billion each year in excise taxes and license fees for alcoholic beverages. When all these are added up, more than half the consumer's cost for an average bottle of distilled spirits is taxes. In 1991, after hearing arguments that taxes on alcoholic beverages had not kept up with inflation, Congress initiated a significant tax increase: The beer tax doubled to $18 per barrel, the tax on bottled wine increased sixfold to about 22 cents per bottle, and the tax on distilled spirits rose less than 10 percent to $13.50 per gallon of 100-proof liquor. There was some controversy

about how much such an increase would affect sales, especially because at the same time most producers increased their own prices by about 5 percent. The total increase in cost to the consumer (averaging about 10 percent more) did result in about a 2 percent decrease in sales of beer and liquor during the first half of the year. Domestic wine sales decreased even more, almost 9 percent. That such large price increases resulted in fairly modest declines in purchases might indicate that very large tax increases would be needed if part of the goal were to reduce alcohol intake significantly. These taxes have not changed since 1991.

Who Drinks? And Why?

Cultural Influences on Drinking

Comparing alcohol use in various cultures around the world allows us to look at ethnic and social factors that lead to differences in patterns of alcohol use. For example, both the Irish and the Russian cultures are associated with heavy drinking, especially of distilled spirits, and with high rates of intoxication and alcohol-related problems. By contrast, Mediterranean countries like Italy and Spain have been characterized by wine consumption, often in a family environment and associated with meals. In these cultures, children are introduced to wine drinking within the family at an early age, but drunkenness is discouraged. A report from the International Center for Alcohol Policies examined young people's attitudes toward drunkenness and their experience with drinking and becoming drunk in several countries around the world. They reported that 17-year-olds in Sweden and other northern European countries were five times as likely to report having been drunk, compared to 17-year-olds in Italy, France, and Greece.[4]

It is important to note that the culture of "extreme drinking" does not necessarily correlate well with overall alcohol consumption. The French and Italians may drink wine in moderation with their meals and in family settings, but they manage to drink a lot of wine. Luxembourg, France,

Ireland, and Italy are all among the top countries for total per-capita alcohol consumption, but the drinking patterns and alcohol-related problems vary considerably among these countries. It should be pointed out that these comparative statistics are based on reported sales, and Russia is not included because so much alcohol is sold on the black market in that country. As for beer consumption, the Czech Republic leads this list, followed by Seychelles, Germany, Austria, and Namibia with the United States in 17th place.[5]

Trends in U.S. Alcohol Consumption

Figure 9.1 shows trends in apparent alcohol consumption in the United States over more than two decades. This graph is based on the taxed sale of beer, wine, and spirits.[6] For comparison purposes, each beverage is calculated in terms of the amount of pure alcohol consumed. The figure shows that overall alcohol consumption, which had been rising

through most of the 1970s, peaked in 1981. Remember from Chapter 1 that this is about the same time that reported use of illicit drugs also reached a peak. Americans drink most of their alcohol in the form of beer. Just under 27 gallons of beer per person per year translates to more than 1 gallon of alcohol per person in that beer. The population consists of those age 14 and older, reflecting the long-known fact that the "drinking" population includes quite a few people who are not legally able to purchase alcohol. Although beer consumption has declined since 1981, the most obvious change was the decline in the consumption of spirits before 1995. Americans now consume just under three-fourths of a gallon of pure alcohol in the form of spirits, and about one-third of a gallon of alcohol per year in the form of wine, for a total from all three beverage types of a little over two gallons of pure alcohol per person per year, down more than half a gallon from the 1981 peak.

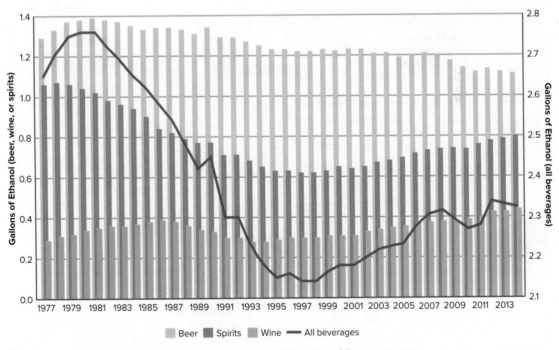

Figure 9.1   Per-Capita Ethanol Consumption by Beverage Type, United States, 1977–2013

SOURCE: NIAAA Surveillance Report #97, 2013.

Regional Differences in the United States

In the United States, about one-third of the adult population label themselves as abstainers. The two-thirds who use alcohol consume an amount that averages out to about three drinks per day. Most don't drink anything near that amount—in fact, another consistent finding is that half the alcohol is consumed by about 10 percent of the drinkers.

Whites are more likely to drink than blacks, northerners more than southerners, younger adults more than older, Catholics and Jews more than Protestants, nonreligious more than religious, urban more than rural, large-city dwellers more than small-city residents, and college-educated people more than those with only a high-school or grade-school education.

Figure 9.2 shows estimated overall alcohol consumption combining beer, wine, and distilled spirits (about half the total U.S. alcohol consumption comes from beer) for each state, based on sales.[6] New Hampshire has the highest per-capita sales, along with the District of Columbia. The District of Columbia is the leader in sales of wine, whereas New Hampshire and Nevada sell the most beer. Note the generally low consumption in the southern states and the generally higher consumption in the western states, with the notable exception of Utah, which has a large Mormon population. These differences in per-capita sales reflect differences in the degree of urbanization as well as some regional cultural differences. For example, the District of Columbia is completely urban, and a large proportion of the population of Nevada lives in either Las

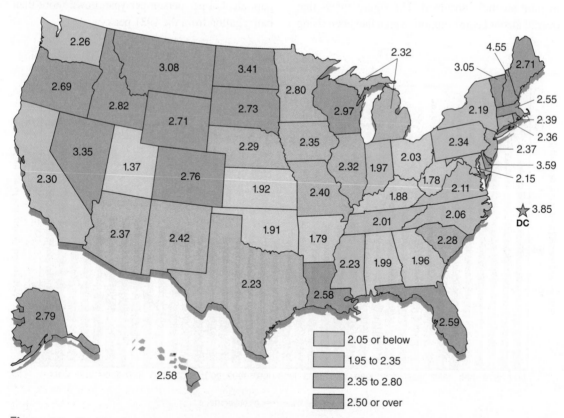

Figure 9.2   Total Per-Capita Consumption in Gallons of Ethanol by State, United States, 2014

SOURCE: NIAAA Surveillance Report #104, 2016.

Vegas or Reno. The outlier is New Hampshire, a low-population state. However, it has low alcohol taxes and more than half of all sales are to out-of state-buyers. In fact, a recent decrease in the alcohol tax in Massachusetts has slowed the growth of liquor sales in New Hampshire.[7]

Gender Differences

It will surprise no one that males are somewhat more likely to drink alcohol than females. The difference in proportions of those who have drunk alcohol in their lifetimes is not great, but 58 percent of males and 46 percent of females report current (past month) drinking. These results from the National Survey on Drug Use and Health are based on the U.S. population age 12 and older.[8] When "binge" drinking is defined as having five or more drinks on the same occasion, males are more likely than females to report binge drinking within the past 30 days (30 percent of males versus 16 percent of females). About 10 percent of males and 3.5 percent of females report "heavy" drinking, defined as binge drinking on five or more separate days during the past month. So, as we look at those who drink the most, as opposed to those who drink only occasionally, we find an increasing proportion of males among the heaviest drinkers.

Drinking among College Students

The college years have traditionally been associated with alcohol use, and in 2015 the proportion of drinkers was about 8 percent higher among 18- to 22-year-old college students than among others of that age (e.g., 58 percent of college students reported drinking within the past month, compared with 48 percent of other 18- to 22-year-olds in the National Survey on Drug Use and Health).[8] Many campuses have banned the sale or advertising of alcohol. Many fraternities have banned keg parties and the use of alcohol during "rush," partly out of concern for legal liability for the consequences if a guest becomes intoxicated and has an accident. Most colleges and universities have adopted a variety of prevention programs to reduce the negative consequences of excessive alcohol use (e.g.,

Alcohol abuse by college students usually occurs through binge drinking, which is defined as having five or more drinks in a row. ©McGraw-Hill Education/Gary He, photographer

education about blood alcohol levels, screening for alcohol use when students go to the health service or counseling center, teaching about helping someone who has had too much alcohol). There is some evidence that these activities are helping. In 2016, about one-third of college students reported binge drinking, as defined by five or more drinks at a sitting. This is down from about 40 percent in 2000. Even more impressive is the decrease from 30 percent to 10 percent in those who reported driving after drinking.[9]

Alcohol Pharmacology

Absorption

Some alcohol is absorbed from the stomach, but the small intestine is responsible for most absorption. In an empty stomach, the overall rate of absorption depends primarily on the concentration of alcohol. Alcohol taken with or after a meal is absorbed more slowly because the food remains in the stomach for digestive action, and the protein in the food retains the alcohol with it in the stomach. Plain water, by decreasing the concentration, slows the absorption of alcohol, but carbonated liquids speed it up. The carbon dioxide acts to move everything quite rapidly through the stomach to the small intestine. It is because of this emptying of the stomach and the more rapid absorption of alcohol in the intestine that champagne has a faster onset of action than noncarbonated wine.

Distribution

The relationship between **blood alcohol concentration** (BAC) and alcohol intake is relatively simple and reasonably well understood. When taken into the body, alcohol is distributed throughout the body fluids, including the blood. However, alcohol does not distribute much into fatty tissues, so a 180-pound lean person will have a lower BAC than a 180-pound fat person who drinks the same amount of alcohol.

Table 9.2 demonstrates the relationships among alcohol intake, BAC, and body weight for hypothetical, *average* females and males. The chart distinguishes between the sexes because the average female has a higher proportion of body fat and therefore, for a given weight, has less volume in which to distribute the alcohol. Understanding this table and trying one of the blood alcohol calculators on the Internet (see the Targeting Prevention box on page 198) could reveal how much you can probably drink to avoid going above a specified BAC.

Table 9.2 makes the simplifying assumption that all of the alcohol is absorbed quickly so that there is little opportunity for metabolism. If the 150-pound female had a tank of water weighing about 100 pounds (12.5 gallons, or 45 liters) and just dumped 1 ounce (28.3 g) into it and stirred it, the concentration would be about 0.6 g/liter, or 0.06 g/100 ml (0.06 percent). Figure 9.3 shows a schematic of such a tank. The 150-pound average male has a tank with more water in it, so his alcohol concentration after 1 ounce is about 0.05 percent. The major factor determining individual differences in BAC is the volume of distribution, so find your own weight on Table 9.2 and estimate how many drinks could be poured into your tank to obtain a BAC of 0.05 percent.

Notice that several beverages are equated to 0.5 ounce of absolute alcohol. A 12-ounce can or bottle of beer at about 4 percent alcohol contains $12 \times 0.04 = 0.48$ ounce of alcohol. The same amount is found in a glass containing about

4 ounces of wine at 12 percent alcohol, 1 ounce of 100-proof spirits, or 1.25 ounces of 80-proof spirits. Each of these can be equated as a standard "drink."

We have not yet considered metabolism, but we can do so with one more simple calculation. Alcohol is removed by the liver at a constant rate of 0.25 to 0.30 ounce of ethanol per hour. Most people fall within this range no matter what their body size or drinking experience, unless they have consumed so much alcohol that the liver is damaged. To be on the safe side, estimate that you can metabolize about 0.25 ounce per hour, and note that this is one-half of one of our standard drinks (1 beer, 1 shot, or 1 glass of wine). Over the course of an evening, if your rate of intake equals your rate of metabolism, you will maintain a stable BAC. If you drink faster than one drink every two hours, your BAC will climb.

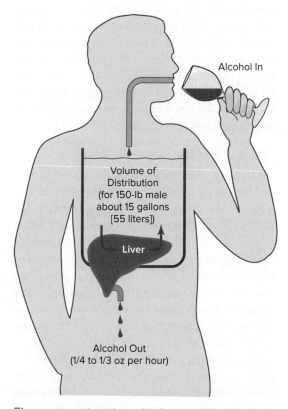

Figure 9.3   The Relationship between Blood Alcohol Concentration and Alcohol Intake

Table 9.2
Relationships among Gender, Weight, Alcohol Consumption, and Blood Alcohol Concentration

		BLOOD ALCOHOL CONCENTRATIONS (g/100 ml)					
Absolute Alcohol (ounces)	Beverage Intake*	Female (100 lb)	Male (100 lb)	Female (150 lb)	Male (150 lb)	Female (200 lb)	Male (200 lb)
1/2	1 oz spirits† 1 glass wine 1 can beer	0.05	0.04	0.03	0.03	0.02	0.02
1	2 oz spirits† 2 glasses wine 2 cans beer	0.09	0.08	0.06	0.05	0.05	0.04
2	4 oz spirits† 4 glasses wine 4 cans beer	0.18	0.15	0.12	0.10	0.09	0.07
3	6 oz spirits† 6 glasses wine 6 cans beer	0.27	0.22	0.18	0.15	0.13	0.11
4	8 oz spirits† 8 glasses wine 8 cans beer	0.36	0.30	0.24	0.20	0.18	0.15
5	10 oz spirits† 10 glasses wine 10 cans beer	0.45	0.37	0.30	0.25	0.22	0.18

*In one hour
†100-proof

Compared with men, women absorb a greater proportion of the alcohol they drink. Some metabolism of alcohol actually occurs in the stomach, where the enzyme alcohol dehydrogenase is present. Because this stomach enzyme is more active, on the average, in men than in women, women might be more susceptible to the effects of alcohol.[10]

Metabolism

Once absorbed, alcohol remains in the bloodstream and other body fluids until it is metabolized, and more than 90 percent of this metabolism occurs in the liver. A small amount of alcohol, less than 2 percent, is normally excreted unchanged—some in the breath, some through the skin, and some in the urine.

The primary metabolic system is a simple one: the enzyme *alcohol dehydrogenase* converts alcohol to *acetaldehyde*. Acetaldehyde is then converted fairly rapidly by aldehyde dehydrogenase to

blood alcohol concentration; also called blood alcohol level: a measure of the concentration of alcohol in blood, expressed in grams per 100 ml (percentage).

Targeting Prevention

Estimating Blood Alcohol Concentration

Table 9.2 is one way to estimate blood alcohol level based on gender, weight, and number of drinks. However, several more dynamic blood alcohol calculators are now available on the Internet. An Internet search for "blood alcohol calculator" turns up several. Whether or not you consume alcohol yourself, it is instructive to understand how your own body (and brain) will respond to various numbers of alcoholic drinks. Try a few of the Internet calculators to see how their results compare with each other and to Table 9.2. An important thing for you to learn is how many drinks it is likely to take to bring your BAC to 0.08, which is the legal limit for driving in all of the United States.

Box icon credit: ©Medioimages/Alamy Images RF

acetic acid. With most drugs a constant *proportion* of the drug is removed in a given amount of time, so that with a high blood level the amount metabolized is high. With alcohol, the *amount* that can be metabolized is constant at about 0.25 to 0.30 ounces per hour regardless of the BAC. The major factor determining the rate of alcohol metabolism is the activity of the enzyme alcohol dehydrogenase. Exercise, coffee consumption, and so on have no effect on this enzyme, so the sobering-up process is essentially a matter of waiting for this enzyme to do its job at its own speed.

Acetaldehyde might be more than just an intermediate step in the oxidation of alcohol. Acetaldehyde is quite toxic; though its blood levels are only one-thousandth of those of alcohol, this substance might cause some of the physiological effects now attributed to alcohol. One danger in heavy alcohol use might be in the higher blood levels of acetaldehyde.

The liver responds to chronic intake of alcohol by increasing the activity of metabolic enzymes (see Chapter 5). This gives rise to some interesting situations. In a person who drinks alcohol heavily over a long period, the activity of the metabolic enzymes increases. As long as there is alcohol in the system, alcohol gets preferential treatment and the metabolism of other drugs is *slower* than normal. When heavy alcohol use stops and the alcohol has disappeared from the body, the high activity level of the enzymes continues for four to eight weeks. During this time, other drugs are metabolized more *rapidly*. To obtain therapeutic levels of other drugs metabolized by this enzyme system (e.g., the benzodiazepines), it is necessary to administer less drug to a chronic heavy drinker and more drug to one who has recently stopped drinking. Thus, alcohol increases the activity of one of the two enzyme systems responsible for its own oxidation. The increased activity of this enzyme is a partial basis for the tolerance to alcohol that is shown by heavy users of alcohol.

Mechanism(s) of Action

Alcohol is like any other general anesthetic: It depresses the central nervous system. It was used as an anesthetic until the late 19th century, when nitrous oxide, ether, and chloroform became more widely used. However, it was not just new compounds that decreased the use of alcohol as an anesthetic; alcohol itself has some major disadvantages. In contrast to the gaseous anesthetics, alcohol metabolizes slowly. This gives alcohol a long duration of action that cannot be controlled. A second disadvantage is that the dose effective in surgical anesthesia is not much lower than the dose that causes respiratory arrest and death. Finally, alcohol makes blood slower to clot.

The exact mechanism for the CNS effect of alcohol is not clear. Until the mid-1980s, the most widely accepted theory was that alcohol acted on all neural membranes, perhaps altering their electrical excitability. However, with increased understanding of the role of the GABA receptor complex in the actions of other depressant drugs (see Chapter 7), researchers began to study the effects of alcohol on GABA receptors. As with the barbiturates and benzodiazepines, alcohol enhances the inhibitory effects of GABA at the GABA-A receptor. This would explain the similarity of behavioral effects among these three different kinds of chemicals. But alcohol has many other effects in the brain, so it has been very difficult to pin down a single mechanism. No matter what neurotransmitter or receptor or transporter is examined, alcohol appears to alter its function in some way. Because alcohol's ability to enhance GABA inhibition at the GABA-A receptor occurs at very low doses, this mechanism probably has special importance. Remember that GABA is a widespread inhibitory neurotransmitter, so alcohol tends to have widespread inhibitory effects on neurons in the brain. At higher doses, alcohol also blocks the effects of the excitatory transmitter glutamate at some of its receptors, so this may enhance its overall inhibitory actions.

Alcohol also produces a variety of effects on dopamine, serotonin, and acetylcholine neurons, and researchers continue to explore these various actions with an eye to understanding not only the acute intoxicating effects of alcohol, but also the long-term changes that occur when the brain is exposed to alcohol on a chronic basis. One of the oldest and chemically simplest psychoactive drugs also seems to have the most complicated set of effects on the nervous system.

Behavioral Effects

At the lowest effective blood levels, complex, abstract, and poorly learned behaviors are disrupted. As the alcohol dose increases, better learned and simpler behaviors are also affected. Inhibitions can be reduced, with the result that the overall amount of behavior increases under certain conditions. Even though alcohol can result in an increase in activity, most scientists would not call alcohol a stimulant. Rather, the increased behavioral output is usually attributed to decreased inhibition of behavior.

If the alcohol intake is "just right," most people experience euphoria, a happy feeling. Below a certain BAC there are no mood changes, but at some point we become uninhibited enough to enjoy our own "charming selves" and uncritical enough to accept the "clods" around us. We become witty, clever, and quite sophisticated, or at least it seems we are.

Life Saver

Signs of Alcohol Poisoning

Although most alcohol-related deaths among college students are due to accidents, every year we hear of tragedies involving college students who simply drink themselves to death. You might be in a position to save someone's life if you know the signs of alcohol poisoning and what to do.

Signs

1. The person is unconscious or semiconscious (unable to answer simple questions).
2. Breathing rate is slow (less than 8 breaths per minute) or irregular (10 seconds between any two breaths).
3. The person's skin is cold and clammy, is pale, or has a bluish tinge.
4. The person vomits and then loses consciousness.

What to Do

1. NEVER leave someone who is this drunk alone to "sleep it off."
2. Call 911 if the person is unconscious or incoherent.
3. If you have been drinking, try to get someone who is sober to help. BUT, don't be afraid to call for help yourself. Many colleges have formal "medical amnesty" policies, meaning you can't get in trouble for helping someone who is in a medical emergency. Even without such a policy, college officials will be happy that you took action.
4. Monitor breathing while waiting for help, and roll the person on his or her side to keep the person from drowning on vomit. If the person does vomit, be sure to clear the airway.

Adapted from the University of Arizona's StepUp program.

Box icon credit: ©McGraw-Hill Education

Another factor contributing to the feeling of well-being is the reduction in anxieties as a result of the disruption of normal critical thinking. The reduction in concern and judgment can range from not worrying about who'll pay the bar bill to being sure that you can take that next curve at 60 mph.

These effects depend on the BAC—also called blood alcohol level (BAL).

Before suggesting relationships between BAC and behavioral change, two factors must be mentioned. One is that the rate at which the BAC rises is a factor in determining behavioral effects. The more rapid the increase, the greater the behavioral effects. Second, a higher BAC is necessary to impair the performance of a chronic, heavy drinker than to impair a moderate drinker's performance.

Performance differences might reflect only the extent to which experienced drinkers have learned to overcome the disruption of nervous system functioning. Another explanation might be that the CNS in the regular drinker develops a tolerance to alcohol. It is established that neural tissue becomes tolerant to alcohol, and tolerance can apparently develop even when the alcohol intake is well spaced over time.

Table 9.3 describes some general behavioral effects of increasing doses of alcohol. These relationships are approximately correct for moderate drinkers. There are some reports that changes in nervous system function have been obtained at concentrations as low as 0.03 to 0.04 percent.

The surgical anesthesia level and the minimum lethal level are perhaps the two least precise points in the table. In any case, they are quite close, and the safety margin is less than 0.1 percent blood alcohol. Death resulting from acute alcohol intoxication usually is the result of respiratory failure when the medulla is depressed.

Scientific study of the behavioral effects of alcohol is made difficult by the importance of placebo effects. With a substance as pervasive as alcohol, we have a long history of learning about what to expect from this substance, even before taking a drink (and even for those who never drink). Culture passes along a rich set of ideas about how alcohol is

Table 9.3
Blood Alcohol Concentration and Behavioral Effects

Percent BAC	Behavioral Effects
0.05	Lowered alertness, usually good feeling, release of inhibitions, impaired judgment
0.10	Slower reaction times and impaired motor function, less caution
0.15	Large, consistent increases in reaction time
0.20	Marked depression in sensory and motor capability, intoxication
0.25	Severe motor disturbance, staggering, sensory perceptions, great impairment
0.30	Stuporous but conscious—no comprehension of what's going on
0.35	Surgical anesthesia; minimal level causing death
0.40	Estimated 50% mortality level

supposed to affect people, and we need to be sure which of the many behavioral changes we see after people drink are actually due to the pharmacological effects of having alcohol in the system. A number of laboratory studies have focused on alcohol effects using the *balanced placebo* design. Half the study participants are given mixed drinks that contain alcohol, while the other half get similar-tasting drinks without alcohol. Each of those groups is divided in half, with some being told they are getting alcohol (whether they are or not) and others being told they are testing a nonalcohol drink. By analyzing the behavioral effects seen in the four conditions, it is possible to determine which effects are actually produced by alcohol and which by the belief that one has consumed alcohol (alcohol expectancy effects). Many of the effects on social behavior (increased laughter, talkativeness, flirtation) are strongly influenced by expectancy even when no alcohol has been consumed, whereas such things as impairment in reaction times and driving simulators result from actual alcohol consumption even when the participant is not aware of the alcohol in the drink. Clearly such studies are limited to the effects of fairly low doses, because if enough alcohol is consumed the participants can detect its effects.

Time-Out

Many of the effects experienced by drinkers are based on what they expect to happen, which interacts somewhat with the pharmacological effects of alcohol. One important component of alcohol use is that drinking serves as a social signal, to the drinker and others, indicating a "time-out" from responsibilities, work, and seriousness. Sitting down with a drink indicates "I'm off duty now" and "Don't take anything I say too seriously." One hypothesis is that alcohol induces a kind of social and behavioral myopia, or nearsightedness. After drinking, people tend to focus more on the here and now and to pay less attention to peripheral people and activities, and to long-term consequences[11]. That might be why some people are more violent after drinking, whereas others become more helpful even if there is personal risk or cost involved. The idea is that alcohol releases people from their inhibitions, largely because the inhibitions represent concerns about what might happen, whereas the intoxicated individual focuses on the immediate irritant or the person who needs help right now.

Driving under the Influence

Attention was focused in the early 1980s on the large number of traffic fatalities involving alcohol. The total number of traffic fatalities in 1980 was over 50,000, but by 2015 that had dropped to just over 35,000, owing to safer cars and highways, seat belt laws, and decreases in driving while intoxicated.[12] It is difficult to estimate exactly how many of those fatalities are *caused* by alcohol, but we can obtain some relevant information. Many states mandate that the coroner measure blood alcohol in all fatally injured drivers. Based on those

The risk of crashes rises with increasing BAC, with a sharp increase at BACs above 0.10. ©wang Tom/123RF RF

measurements, estimates have been made of the number of alcohol-related traffic crash fatalities. From the peak of almost 60 percent in 1982, by 2004 the percentage had declined to less than 40 percent (see Figure 9.4).[13]

Several studies have demonstrated that the danger of combining alcohol with automobiles is dose-related. At a BAC of 0.08 percent the relative risk of being involved in a fatal crash is about three times as great as for a sober driver. A British study on younger, less experienced drivers (and drinkers) found that the relative risk at 0.08 percent was about five times as great. The risk rises sharply for all drivers with a BAC above 0.10. Similarly, the risk of involvement in a personal injury crash increases with BAC, as does the risk of involvement in a fatal pedestrian accident.

Other interesting facts have emerged from studies of alcohol and accidents. Alcohol-related traffic fatalities are not a random sample of all fatalities. Single-vehicle fatalities are more likely to involve alcohol than are multiple-vehicle fatalities. Alcohol-related fatalities are a greater proportion of the fatalities occurring during dark hours than of those occurring in daylight and are a greater proportion of fatalities occurring on the weekend than of those occurring during the week. Fatally injured drivers in accidents occurring between midnight and 3 AM are eight times as likely to have a BAC above 0.08 percent as drivers in accidents occurring between 9 AM and noon.[12]

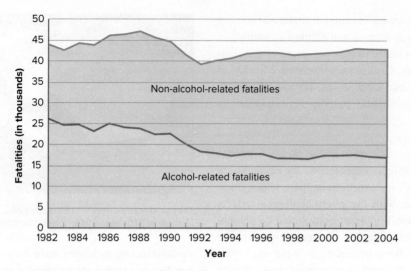

Figure 9.4 Alcohol-Related and Nonalcohol-Related Traffic Crash Fatalities for the United States, 1982–2004

SOURCE: H. Y. Yi and others, *NIAAA Surveillance Report #76: Trends in Alcohol-Related Traffic Fatalities in the United States, 1982–2004* (Bethesda, MD: USPHS, 2006).

When you hear that about 80 percent of all the fatally injured drivers who had been drinking were male, that sounds like a big difference, and it is. But it is important to remember that 70 percent of all fatally injured drivers are male, whether or not drinking is involved. That men are more likely to be involved in alcohol-related traffic fatalities reflects three important facts: Any given car is more likely to have a male than a female driver, men might take more chances when driving even when they're sober, and male drivers are more likely than female drivers to have been drinking.

Who is responsible for all these alcohol-related traffic accidents? One question is whether there are certain individuals, such as problem drinkers, responsible for much of the drunk driving. Problem drinkers, although a relatively small fraction of the drinking population, are more likely on a given day to be driving around with a high BAC. On the other hand, 90 percent of the intoxicated drivers involved in fatal crashes have never been convicted of DUI in the past. Therefore, whereas individual problem drinkers cause more than their share of traffic accidents, the majority of alcohol-related traffic accidents are caused by individuals who have not been identified as problem drinkers. Anyone who drinks and drives is a potential threat.

Younger drivers have more than their share of alcohol-related accidents. The highest rate of alcohol involvement in traffic fatalities is among 21- to 24-year-olds. In 2015, almost 30 percent of the fatalities in this age group were alcohol-related.[12]

What can be done about this problem? Current efforts focus mainly on three fronts: identifying repeat offenders and keeping them off the roads, publicizing in the mass media the dangers of drinking and driving, and targeting younger drinkers for special prevention efforts. Although it is impossible to determine the effectiveness of any one of these measures, Figure 9.4 indicates that the total effort has worked to reduce alcohol-related fatalities. In 2000, the U.S. Congress passed legislation requiring states to reduce the BAC for DUI conviction from 0.10 to 0.08.

What's a safe BAC? If you are going to drink and want to remain in reasonable control of your faculties, you should probably stay below 0.05 percent. Individuals differ considerably in their sensitivities to alcohol, however, so the best rule is to learn about your own sensitivity and not to feel compelled to keep up with anyone else's drinking. Alcohol-induced impairment is dose-related and depends on what you're trying to do. Carrying on bar conversation places fewer demands on your nervous system than driving on a crowded freeway during rush hour, where any alcohol at all might interfere.

BAC gives a good estimate of the alcohol concentration in the brain, and the concentration of alcohol in the breath gives a good estimate of the alcohol concentration in the blood. The concentration in the blood is almost 2,100 times the concentration in air expired from the lungs, making breath samples accurate indicators of BAC. Such breath samples are easily collected by police and can be the basis for conviction as a drunk driver in most states.

Sexual Behavior

No psychoactive substance has been as closely linked to sexuality as alcohol. Movies tell us that a romantic occasion is enhanced with wine or champagne, and the use of sexual attraction in beer ads on television is so common we are barely aware of it. The association has been noted for generations—400 years ago Shakespeare wrote about alcohol in Macbeth:

> "Lechery, sir, it provokes and unprovokes; it provokes the desire, but it takes away the performance."
>
> William Shakespeare, The Tragedy of Macbeth, 1606.

Was Shakespeare right? It certainly seems that alcohol does make people less inhibited, and more likely to desire sex, but can we demonstrate that this is a real effect? If so, how much of the enhancement of sexual interest after drinking is really due to the pharmacological effects of the alcohol, and how much is a placebo response based on our expectancies about alcohol's effects? The importance of understanding alcohol's ability to provoke

desire is enormous. On one hand, many people of both sexes for many generations and across many cultures have viewed alcohol's ability to enhance sexual interest and pleasure as a great benefit, and many will continue to do so. On the other hand, the use of alcohol is linked with risky sexual behavior (early sexual experience; unprotected sex) as well as with increased likelihood of sexual assault. The analogy to "playing with fire" is an apt one—under the right circumstances both fire and alcohol are beneficial, but both are risky and can lead to destructive outcomes.

And what about the other half of Shakespeare's statement, that alcohol takes away the performance? Anecdotal evidence shows that men with high BACs are unable to attain or maintain an erection, and there is clinical evidence that chronic alcohol abuse can lead to more permanent impotence in men. But are these effects consistent, and are they limited to high doses or long-term exposure?

Human sexual response is complex, but we can somewhat artificially divide our questions about sexuality into psychological effects (ratings of sexual arousal or interest) versus physiological effects (measurements of penile tumescence or vaginal blood volume; measurements of time to orgasm). Also, we should assume that men and women may differ considerably with respect to both dimensions of sexuality and alcohol's effects on them.

A review of the available literature on alcohol and sex points out some still unresolved questions, but also some reliable findings reported by different sets of researchers.[14] First, both men and women tend to agree with the expectancy statements that alcohol enhances or disinhibits sexuality. In balanced-placebo laboratory experiments, men who had stronger expectancies that alcohol would enhance sexuality also reported experiencing more arousal after being given a placebo drink. Therefore, at least some of the subjective arousal that men experience after drinking is a psychological reaction to the belief that alcohol enhances sexuality. There have been fewer such experiments with women, and the results have been inconsistent.

When men and women have been given alcohol in a laboratory setting and then exposed to erotic films, both sexes report more sexual arousal after alcohol, and there is a correlation between their ratings of feeling intoxicated and their self-reported arousal. These studies have not usually explored BACs above 0.15 percent, and most have used lower BACs. In men, physiological measures of penile tumescence are correlated with self-reports of arousal, whereas in women there is no consistent relation between self-reported arousal and vaginal blood volume.

Many studies have reported that alcohol reduces penile tumescence in men, sometimes even at fairly low doses. The long-standing assumption has been that this is a direct pharmacological effect on the physiological mechanisms responsible for penile erection. However, several studies have found no effect on this measure, even at fairly high doses. Studies on animals and on nocturnal penile tumescence in men who are asleep have generally not found that alcohol suppresses erection. Therefore, attention is now shifting to the idea that when men become less aroused at higher BACs it might be due to impaired attention to or processing of erotic information. Alcohol can also impair the ability to suppress an erection when men are instructed to avoid becoming aroused.

Several studies have reported that when men believe that a woman has been drinking, they rate her as being more interested in sex and more sexually available. A similar finding has been reported for women's perceptions of men who have been drinking.

Surveys typically find that people are more likely to have sex on a date (including first dates) when they drink on that date. With respect to risky sex, both men and women given alcohol in laboratory situations report more willingness to engage in unprotected sex, and more agreement with justifications for not using condoms.

We know that alcohol is a frequent presence in sexual assaults, and laboratory studies on college students have reported some related findings. When a date rape scene is described to either men or women, less blame is assigned to the perpetrator if he has been described as drinking before the rape, and more blame is assigned to the victim if she has been described as drinking. Men are generally more aroused by nonviolent erotic films than by erotic films that contain violence, but after consuming alcohol in the laboratory, they were less discriminating and more likely to be aroused by the violent films.

Many of these effects of alcohol on sexual behavior are consistent with the alcohol myopia theory mentioned previously—alcohol impairs information processing in such a way that people are more likely to attend to what's right in front of them at the time. In a conflicting sexual situation, the person affected by alcohol will be more likely to tend toward immediate gratification and less likely to be inhibited by concerns about outcomes that are uncertain or delayed.

Blackouts

Alcohol-induced blackouts are periods during alcohol use in which the drinking individual appears to function normally but later, when the individual is sober, he or she cannot recall any events that occurred during that period. The drinker might drive home or dance all night, interacting in the usual way with others. When the individual cannot remember the activities, the people, or anything else, that's a blackout. Most authorities include it as one of the danger signs suggesting excessive use of alcohol. The limited amount of recent research on this topic is probably related to ethical concerns about giving such high doses of alcohol to experimental subjects. An article from 1884 titled "Alcoholic Trance" referred to the syndrome:

> This trance state is a common condition in inebriety, where . . . a profound suspension of memory and consciousness and literal paralysis of certain brain-functions follow.
>
> This trance state may last from a few moments to several days, during which the person may appear and act rationally, and yet be actually a mere automaton, without consciousness or memory of his actual condition.[15]

Crime and Violence

Homicide The correlation between alcohol use and homicides is well known to police and judicial systems around the world. A meta-analysis of 23 published reports from nine countries revealed apparent variation across countries, but overall just about half of those who committed homicide were "under the influence" of alcohol at the time.[16] Previous studies have reported that a similar proportion of homicide victims had also been drinking just before they were killed. These data certainly imply that homicide is more likely to occur in situations in which drinking also occurs, but they leave open the question as to whether alcohol plays a causal role in homicides.

Assault and Other Crimes of Violence As with homicide, studies of assault, spousal abuse, and child abuse reveal correlations with drinking: Heavier drinkers are more likely to engage in such behaviors, and self-reports by offenders indicate a high likelihood that they had been consuming alcohol before the violent act. However, scientists are still cautious in trying to determine how much of a causal role alcohol plays in such activity. For example, if fights are likely to occur when men get together in groups at night and drinking is likely to occur when men get together in groups at night, how much of a role does alcohol itself play in increasing the chances of violence? Similarly, if both heavy drinking and violent arguments are characteristics of dysfunctional family situations, how much of the ensuing family violence can be blamed on the use of alcohol? Unfortunately, it has proven difficult to perform controlled experimental studies on these complex problems, so the answers remain unclear.

Date Rape In spite of widespread concern about drugs being slipped into someone's drink, by far the most significant date rape drug is and always has been alcohol. For most college women who report having been sexually assaulted by a date, the assault happened after the woman had consumed alcohol.[17]

That is why many college campuses now combine sexual assault prevention education with alcohol education.

Suicide Most studies show that alcohol is involved in about one-third of all suicides. Suicide *attempts* seem to have a different background than successful suicides, but alcohol abuse is second only to depression as the diagnosis in suicide attempters. The relationship between alcohol abuse and depression is a strong one and has been the subject of many studies. A study of almost 2,000 suicide attempts in Germany again found that acute alcohol consumption was present in about one-third of the cases, and in about one-sixth of the total cases the person could be diagnosed with an alcohol use disorder.[18]

Physiological Effects

Peripheral Circulation One effect of alcohol on the CNS is the dilation of peripheral blood vessels. This increases heat loss from the body but makes the drinker feel warm. The heat loss and cooling of the interior of the body are enough to cause a slowdown in some biochemical processes. This dilation of peripheral vessels argues against giving alcohol to individuals in shock or extreme cold. Under these conditions, blood is needed in the central parts of the body, and heat loss must be diminished if the person is to survive.

Fluid Balance One action of alcohol on the brain is to decrease the output of the antidiuretic hormone (ADH, also called vasopressin) responsible for retaining fluid in the body. It is this effect, rather than the actual fluid consumption, that increases the urine flow in response to alcohol. This diuretic effect can lower blood pressure in some individuals.

Hormonal Effects Even single doses of alcohol can produce measurable effects on a variety of hormonal systems: Adrenal corticosteroids are released, as are catecholamines from the adrenal medulla, and the production of the male sex hormone testosterone is suppressed. It is not known what significance, if any, these effects have for occasional, moderate drinkers. However, chronic abusers of alcohol can develop a variety of hormone-related disorders, including testicular atrophy and impotence in men and impaired reproductive functioning in women.

Alcohol Toxicity

Alcohol consumption can result in toxicity, both acute and chronic. We have already discussed the problem of alcohol-related traffic accidents, which we would consider to be examples of acute behavioral toxicity. In a similar vein are other alcohol-related accidents and adverse effects, such as falls, drowning, cycling and boating accidents, and accidents associated with operating machinery. Although we know that alcohol increases the risk of injury and death for all these types of accidents, we are less certain about how many of these problems are actually caused by alcohol intoxication.

Alcohol Poisoning

As the DAWN data in Chapter 2 revealed, many drug-related deaths include alcohol in combination with some other substance, so it is difficult to know exactly how many overdose deaths are primarily due to alcohol versus another drug, or to the specific combination. But people also die from acute alcohol poisoning alone, and the Centers for Disease Control estimates that about 2,200 people die each year simply from drinking too much alcohol.[19] Several well-publicized drinking deaths of young college students have occurred in recent years. These students had been drinking for many hours before their deaths, and as a result colleges and universities began reexamining their alcohol-use policies. Two pieces of advice are worth mentioning: (1) If one of your friends drinks enough to pass out, DO NOT simply leave her or him alone to sleep it off. The person should be placed on his or her side so that any vomit is less likely to be aspirated, and someone who is sober needs to monitor the person's breathing until he or she can be aroused and begins to move. If this is not possible, take the victim to the emergency room. Don't worry about getting in trouble for helping out a friend—the alternative can be much worse. (2) It is particularly dangerous to drink to the point of vomiting and then begin drinking again after vomiting. The vomiting reflex is triggered by rapidly rising BAC, usually above 0.12 percent. But the vomiting reflex is inhibited when the BAC rises above 0.20 or so, and it is then possible to continue drinking and reach lethal concentrations. See the Life Saver box on page 199 for more information on alcohol poisoning.

Hangover

The Germans call it "wailing of cats" *(Katzenjammer)*, the Italians "out of tune" *(stonato)*, the French "woody mouth" *(gueule de boise)*, the Norwegians "workmen in my head" *(jeg har tommeermenn)*, and the Swedes "pain in the roots of the hair" *(hont i haret)*. Hangovers aren't much fun. And they aren't very well understood, either. Even moderate drinkers who only occasionally overindulge are well acquainted with the symptoms: upset stomach, fatigue, headache, thirst, depression, anxiety, and general malaise.

Rapid consumption of alcohol can lead to acute toxicity.
©Brand X Pictures RF

Some authorities believe that the symptoms of a hangover are the symptoms of withdrawal from a short- or long-term dependence on alcohol. The pattern certainly fits. Some people report continuing to drink just to escape the pain of the hangover. This behavior is not unknown to moderate drinkers, either: Many believe that the only cure for a hangover is some of "the hair of the dog that bit you"—alcohol. And it might work to minimize symptoms, because it spreads them out over a longer time. There is no evidence that any of the "surefire-this'll-fix-you-up" remedies are effective. The only known cures are an analgesic for the headache, rest, and time.

Some hangover symptoms are probably reactions to congeners. Congeners are natural products of the fermentation and preparation process, some of which are quite toxic. Congeners make the various alcoholic beverages different in smell, taste, color, and, possibly, hangover potential.

Still other factors contribute to the trials and tribulations of the "morning after the night before." Thirst means that the body has excreted more fluid than was taken in with the alcoholic beverages. However, this does not seem to be the only basis for the thirst experienced the next day. Another cause might be that alcohol causes fluid inside cells to move outside the cells. This cellular dehydration, without a decrease in total body fluid, is known to be related to, and might be the basis of, an increase in thirst.

The nausea and upset stomach typically experienced can most likely be attributed to the fact that alcohol is a gastric irritant. Consuming even moderate amounts causes local irritation of the mucosa lining the stomach. It has been suggested that the accumulation of acetaldehyde, which is quite toxic even in small quantities, contributes to the nausea and headache.

The best way to avoid a hangover is still to drink in moderation, regardless of the beverage.

Chronic Disease States

The relationship of alcohol use to many diseases has been studied extensively. As a general rule, heavy alcohol use, either directly or indirectly, affects every organ system in the body. The alcohol or its primary metabolite, acetaldehyde, can irritate and damage tissue directly. Because alcohol provides empty calories, many heavy drinkers do not eat well, and chronic malnutrition leads to tissue damage. Separating the effects of alcohol exposure from those of malnutrition relies to a great extent on experiments with animals. Some animals can be fed adequate diets and exposed to high concentrations of alcohol, whereas other animals are fed diets deficient in certain vitamins or other nutrients.

Brain Damage Perhaps the biggest concern is the damage to brain tissue that is seen in chronic alcohol abusers. It has been reported for years that the brains of deceased heavy drinkers demonstrate an obvious overall loss of brain tissue: The ventricles (internal spaces) in the brain are enlarged, and the fissures (sulci) in the cortex are widened. Modern imaging techniques have revealed this tissue loss in living alcohol abusers as well. This generalized loss of brain tissue is probably a result of direct alcohol toxicity rather than malnutrition and is associated with *alcoholic dementia,* a global decline of intellect. Patients with this type of organic brain syndrome might have difficulty swallowing in addition to impaired problem solving, difficulty in manipulating objects, and abnormal electroencephalograms. Another classical alcohol-related organic brain syndrome has two parts, which so often go together that the disorder is referred to as **Wernicke-Korsakoff syndrome.** *Wernicke's disease* is associated with a deficiency of thiamine (vitamin B_1) and can sometimes be corrected nutritionally. The symptoms include confusion, ataxia (impaired coordination while walking), and abnormal eye movements. Most patients with Wernicke's disease also exhibit *Korsakoff's psychosis,* characterized by an inability to remember recent events or to learn new information. Korsakoff's psychosis

Wernicke-Korsakoff syndrome (*wer* nick ee *core* sa kof): chronic mental impairments produced by heavy alcohol use over a long period of time.

can appear by itself in patients who maintain adequate nutrition, and it appears to be mostly irreversible. There has been great controversy about the specific brain areas that are damaged in Wernicke-Korsakoff syndrome, as well as about the relationship between the two parts of the disorder.

Important practical questions include the following: Exactly how much alcohol exposure is required before behavioral and/or anatomical evidence can be found indicating brain damage? And how much of the cognitive deficit seen in alcoholic dementia can be reversed when drinking is stopped and adequate nutrition is given? Both questions have been the subject of several experiments. There is no definitive answer for the first question. Some of the studies on moderate drinkers have included individuals who consume up to 10 drinks per day! Most studies with lower cutoffs for moderate drinking have not found consistent evidence for anatomical changes in the brain. As for recovery, several studies have reported both behavioral improvement and apparent regrowth of brain size in chronic alcohol abusers after some months of abstinence. However, not all such studies find improvement, and some have found improvement in some types of mental tasks but not in others.

Liver Disorders Fatty acids are the usual fuel for the liver. When present, alcohol has higher priority and is used as fuel instead. As a result, fatty acids (lipids) accumulate in the liver and are stored as small droplets in liver cells. This condition is known as alcohol-related *fatty liver,* which for most drinkers is not a serious problem. If alcohol input ceases, the liver uses the stored fatty acids for energy. Sometimes the droplets increase in size until they rupture the cell membrane, causing death of the liver cells. Before the liver cells die, a fatty liver is completely reversible and usually of minor medical concern.

Sometimes, with prolonged or high-level alcohol intake, another phase of liver damage is observed. Alcoholic hepatitis is a serious disease and includes both inflammation and impairment of liver function. Usually this occurs in areas of the liver where cells are dead and dying, but it is not known if an increasingly fatty liver leads to alcoholic hepatitis. Alcoholic hepatitis does exist in the absence of a fatty liver, so this form of tissue damage might be due to direct toxic effects of alcohol.

Cirrhosis is the liver disease everyone knows is related to high and prolonged levels of alcohol consumption. It's not easy to get cirrhosis from drinking alcohol—you have to work at it. Usually it takes about 10 years of steady drinking of the equivalent of a pint or more of whiskey a day. Not all cirrhosis is alcohol related, but a high percentage is, and cirrhosis is the seventh leading cause of death in the United States. In large urban areas it is the fourth or fifth leading cause of death in men aged 25 to 65. In cirrhosis, liver cells are replaced by fibrous tissue (collagen), which changes the structure of the liver (see Figure 9.5). These changes

(a)

(b)

Figure 9.5 (a) Normal Liver; (b) Cirrhotic Liver ©Southern Illinois University/Science Source (a), ©Martin M. Rotker/Science Source (b)

decrease blood flow and, along with the loss of cells, result in a decreased ability of the liver to function. When the liver does not function properly, fluid accumulates in the body, jaundice develops, and other infections or cancers have a better opportunity to establish themselves in the liver. Cirrhosis is not reversible, but stopping the intake of alcohol will retard its development and decrease the serious medical effects.

In drinkers with severely damaged livers, liver transplants have been quite successful—a 64 percent survival rate after two years. Most of these recipients do not resume drinking after the transplant.

Heart Disease Another area of concern is the effect of alcohol on the heart and circulation. Heavy alcohol use is associated with increased mortality resulting from heart disease. Much of this is due to damage to the heart muscle (cardiomyopathy), but the risk of the more typical heart attack resulting from coronary artery disease also increases. Heavy drinkers are also more likely to suffer from high blood pressure and strokes. An interesting twist to this story is that several studies have found a *lower* incidence of heart attacks in moderate drinkers than in abstainers, and for several years this protective effect of moderate alcohol consumption and the possible mechanism for it have been discussed. It has been pointed out that the abstainers in such studies might include both abstaining alcohol abusers who once drank heavily and others who quit on their doctor's advice because of poor health. However, studies that separate those who never drank from the "quitters" still report fewer heart attacks and lower overall mortality in moderate drinkers, with increased mortality for both abstainers and heavy drinkers. It has been proposed that alcohol increases high-density lipoproteins (HDL, sometimes called "good cholesterol"), some of which seem to protect against high blood pressure. The reduced blood clotting produced by alcohol could also play a role. There has been speculation that red wine might have better effects than other forms of alcohol due to the presence of antioxidants in the grapes from which the wine is made. But the scientific evidence

supports only a beneficial effect of regular alcohol use, with an increased risk for those who "binge" drink (heavy use once a week or so).[20]

Cancer Alcohol use is associated with cancers of the mouth, tongue, pharynx, larynx, esophagus, stomach, liver, lung, pancreas, colon, and rectum. There are many possible mechanisms for this, from direct tissue irritation to nutritional deficiencies to the induction of enzymes that activate other carcinogens. A particularly nasty interaction with cigarette smoking increases the incidence of cancers of the oral cavity, pharynx, and larynx. Also, suppression of the immune system by alcohol, which occurs to some extent every time intoxicating doses are used, probably increases the rate of tumor growth.

The Immune System The immune deficits seen in chronic alcohol abusers are associated with at least some increase in the frequency of various infectious diseases, including tuberculosis, pneumonia, yellow fever, cholera, and hepatitis B. Alcohol use might be a factor in AIDS, for several reasons: Loss of behavioral inhibitions probably increases the likelihood of engaging in unprotected sex; alcohol could increase the risk of HIV infection in exposed individuals; and alcohol could suppress the immune system and therefore increase the chances of developing full-blown AIDS once an HIV infection is established. Although one epidemiological study did not find an acceleration of HIV-related disease in infected individuals who drank, heavy alcohol use is probably not a good idea for anyone who is HIV-positive.

There is no evidence that the occasional consumption of one or two drinks has overall negative effects on the physical health of most individuals. An important exception to this statement might be drinking during pregnancy.

cirrhosis (sir *oh* sis): an irreversible, frequently deadly liver disorder associated with heavy alcohol use.

Fetal Alcohol Syndrome

The unfortunate condition of infants born to alcohol-abusing mothers was noted in an 1834 report to the British Parliament: They have a "starved, shriveled, and imperfect look." Until fairly recently most scientists and physicians believed that any effects on the offspring of heavy alcohol users were the result of poor nutrition or poor prenatal care. Those beliefs changed, however, when a 1973 report described eight children who displayed a particular pattern of craniofacial and other defects. All of these children had been born to alcohol-dependent mothers. This article was the first to describe the symptoms of **fetal alcohol syndrome** (FAS), a collection of physical and behavioral abnormalities that seems to be caused by the presence of alcohol during development of the fetus (see related photo). There are three primary criteria for diagnosing FAS, at least one of which *must* be present:

1. Growth retardation occurring before and/or after birth.
2. A pattern of abnormal features of the face and head, including small head circumference, small eyes, or evidence of retarded formation of the midfacial area, including a flattened bridge and short length of the nose and flattening of the vertical groove between the nose and mouth (the philtrum).
3. Evidence of CNS abnormality, including abnormal neonatal behavior, mental retardation, or other evidence of abnormal neurobehavioral development.

Each of these features can be seen in the absence of alcohol exposure, and other features might also be present in FAS, such as eye and ear defects, heart murmurs, undescended testicles, birthmarks, and abnormal fingerprints or palmar creases. Research also found a high frequency of various abnormalities of the eyes, often associated with poor vision. Thus, the diagnosis of FAS is a matter of judgment, based on several symptoms and often on the physician's knowledge of the mother's drinking history.

Many animal studies have been done in a variety of species, and they indicate that FAS is related to peak BAC and to duration of alcohol exposure, even when malnutrition is not an issue. In mice and other animal models, increasing amounts of alcohol yield an increase in mortality, a decrease in infant weight, and increased frequency of soft-tissue malformation. The various components of the complete FAS reflect damage occurring at different developmental stages, so heavy alcohol exposure throughout pregnancy is the most damaging situation, followed by intermittent high-level exposure designed to imitate binge drinking.

Not all infants born to drinking mothers show abnormal development. If they did, it would not have taken so long to recognize FAS as a problem.

This boy shows typical features of fetal alcohol syndrome, including small eyes, flattened bridge of the nose, and flattening of the vertical groove between the nose and mouth.   Source: Amanda Mills/CDC

It is estimated that the overall rate of FAS in the general U.S. population is about 2 per 1,000 live births.[21] Estimating the prevalence among problem drinkers or alcohol abusers is more of a problem. There is the difficulty not only of diagnosing FAS but also of diagnosing alcohol abuse. If the physician knows that the mother is a heavy drinker, this can increase the probability of noticing or diagnosing FAS, thus inflating the prevalence statistics among drinking mothers. FAS seems to occur in as many as 2 or 3 percent of births when the mothers are known to be problem drinkers, or at 10 times the rate in the general population. If all alcohol-related birth defects (referred to as **fetal alcohol spectrum disorder,** or FASD) are counted, the rate among heavy-drinking women is higher, from 80 to a few hundred per 1,000. Maternal alcohol abuse might be the most frequent known environmental cause of mental retardation in the Western world.

In addition to the risk of FAS, the fetus of a mother who drinks heavily has a risk of not being born at all. Spontaneous abortion early in pregnancy is perhaps twice as likely among the 5 percent of women who are the heaviest drinkers. The data on later pregnancy loss (stillbirths) are not as clearly related to alcohol for either animals or humans.

An important question, and one that can never be answered in absolute terms, is whether there is an acceptable level of alcohol consumption for pregnant women (see the Taking Sides box). The data on drinking during pregnancy rely on self-reports by the mothers, who are assumed to be at least as likely as everyone else to underreport their drinking. In addition, almost every study has used different definitions of heavy drinking, alcohol abuse, and problem drinking. The heaviest drinkers in each study are the most at risk for alcohol-related problems with their children, but we don't really know if the large number of light or moderate drinkers are causing significant risks. Based on the dose-related nature of birth problems in animal studies, one might argue that any alcohol use at all produces some risk, but at low levels the increased risk is too small to be revealed except in a large-scale study. In 1981, the U.S. surgeon general recommended that "pregnant women should drink absolutely no alcohol because they may be endangering the health of their unborn children." Maybe that went a bit too far. The bottom line is this: Scientific data do not demonstrate that occasional consumption of one or two drinks definitely causes FAS or other alcohol-related birth defects. On the other hand, neither do the data prove that low-level alcohol use is safe, nor do they indicate a safe level of use. Remember from Chapter 5 that it is not within the realm of science to declare something totally safe, so it will be impossible to ever set a safe limit on alcohol use. Most women decrease their alcohol use once they have become pregnant, and many decrease it further as pregnancy progresses.

Alcohol Dependence

Withdrawal Syndrome

The physical dependence associated with prolonged heavy use of alcohol is revealed when alcohol intake is stopped. *The abstinence syndrome that develops is medically more severe and more likely to cause death than is withdrawal from opioid drugs.* In untreated advanced cases, the mortality rate can be as high as one in seven. For that reason it has long been recommended that the initial period of **detoxification** (allowing the body to rid itself of the alcohol) be carried out in an inpatient medical setting, especially for people who have been drinking very heavily or have other medical complications.

---

fetal alcohol syndrome: facial and developmental abnormalities associated with the mother's alcohol use during pregnancy.

fetal alcohol spectrum disorder: individual developmental abnormalities associated with the mother's alcohol use during pregnancy.

detoxification: an early treatment stage, in which the body eliminates the alcohol or other substance.

Taking Sides

Protecting the Unborn from Alcohol

Increased concern about fetal alcohol syndrome has led to some significant changes in the status of pregnant women, at least in certain instances and locations. Waiters have refused to serve wine to pregnant women, women have been arrested and charged with child abuse for being heavily intoxicated while pregnant, and others have been charged with endangerment for breastfeeding while drunk. These social interventions represent concerns for the welfare of the child. However, to women already concerned about their own rights because of the issue of government regulation of abortion, such actions seem to be yet another infringement, yet another signal that the woman's rights are secondary to the child's.

We know that heavy alcohol consumption during pregnancy does increase the risk to the child of permanent disfigurement and mental retardation. We also know that, even among the heaviest drinkers, the odds still favor a normal-appearing baby (less than 10 percent of the babies born to the heaviest-drinking 5 percent of mothers exhibit full-blown FAS).

Do you think that men are more likely than women to support limiting the rights of pregnant women to drink while they are pregnant? You might ask a group of both men and women to give you answers to the following questions.

How strongly do you agree (5 = strong agreement, 1 = strong disagreement) with the following statements?

1. Women who repeatedly get drunk while they are pregnant should be kept in jail if necessary until the baby is born.
2. All bartenders should be trained not to serve any drinks at all to a woman who is obviously pregnant.
3. If a man and a pregnant woman are drinking together and both become intoxicated, both the man and the woman should be arrested for child abuse.

Box icon credit: ©Nova Development RF

The progression of withdrawal, the abstinence syndrome, has been described in the following way:

- Stage 1: tremors, excessively rapid heartbeat, hypertension, heavy sweating, loss of appetite, and insomnia.

- Stage 2: hallucinations—auditory, visual, tactile, or a combination of these; and, rarely, olfactory signs.

- Stage 3: delusions, disorientation, delirium, sometimes intermittent and usually followed by amnesia.

- Stage 4: seizure activity.

Medical treatment is usually sought in stage 1 or 2, and rapid intervention with a sedative drug, such as diazepam, will prevent stage 3 or 4 from occurring. The old term **delirium tremens** is used to refer to severe cases including at least stage 3.

Tremors are one of the most common physical changes associated with alcohol withdrawal and can persist for a long period after alcohol intake has stopped. Anxiety, insomnia, feelings of unreality, nausea, vomiting, and many other symptoms can also occur.

The withdrawal symptoms do not develop all at the same time or immediately after abstinence begins. The initial signs (tremors, anxiety) might develop within a few hours, but the individual is relatively rational. Over the next day or two, hallucinations appear and gradually become more terrifying and real to the individual. One common feature of alcohol-withdrawal hallucinations includes the sensation of ants or snakes crawling on the skin. You might remember that this also occurs after high doses of stimulant drugs. In the context of alcohol withdrawal, it is an indication that the nervous system is rebounding from constant inhibition and is hyperexcitable.

Optimal treatment of patients during the early stages involves the administration of a benzodiazepine, such as chlordiazepoxide or diazepam (see Chapter 7). Because of the high degree of cross-dependence between alcohol and chlordiazepoxide, one drug can be substituted for the other and withdrawal continued at a safer rate.[22]

Some withdrawal symptoms can last for up to several weeks. Unstable blood pressure, irregular breathing, anxiety, panic attacks, insomnia, and depression are all reported during this period. These phenomena have been referred to as a protracted withdrawal syndrome, and they can trigger intense cravings for alcohol. Thus, some chronic drinkers might benefit from residential or inpatient treatment for up to six weeks, simply to prevent relapse during this critical period. Preventing relapse for longer periods is a more difficult task.

Alcohol Use Disorder

Probably the most significant influence on American attitudes about alcoholism was a 75-year-old book called *Alcoholics Anonymous*. This book described the experiences of a small group of people who formed a society whose "only requirement for membership is a desire to stop drinking." That society has now grown to include more than 2 million members in over a hundred countries. A central part of their belief system is that alcohol dependence is a progressive disease characterized by a loss of control over drinking and that the disease can never be cured. People who do not have the disease might drink and even become intoxicated, but they do not "lose control over alcohol." There is a suspicion that the dependent drinker is different even before the first drink is taken. The only treatment is to arrest the disease by abstaining from drinking. This *disease model* of alcohol dependence has received support from many medical practitioners and has been endorsed by the American Medical Association and other professional groups. In one sense, this description of alcohol dependence as a disease is a reaction against long-held notions that excessive drinking is only a symptom of some other underlying pathology, such as depression, or some type of personality defect. Traditional psychoanalysts practicing many years ago might have treated alcohol abusers by trying to discover the unconscious conflicts or personality deficiencies that caused the person to drink. One important consequence of defining alcohol dependence as a *primary* disease is to recognize that the drinking itself might be the problem and that treatment and prevention should be aimed directly at alcohol abuse/dependence.

However, there are many scientific critics of the disease concept. If alcohol dependence is a disease, what is its cause? How are alcohol abusers different from others, except that they tend to drink a lot and have many alcohol-related problems? Although sequential stages have been described for this "progressive disease," most individual drinkers don't seem to fit any single set of descriptors. Some don't drink alone, some don't drink in the morning, some don't go on binges, some don't drink every day, and some don't report strong cravings for alcohol. Experiments have shown that alcohol-dependent individuals do retain considerable control over their drinking, even while drinking—it's not that they completely lose control when they start drinking, but they might have either less ability or less desire to limit their drinking because they do drink excessively. Although an "alcoholic personality" has been defined that characterizes many drinkers who enter treatment, the current belief is that these personality factors (impulsive, anxious, depressed, passive, dependent) reflect the years of intoxication and the critical events that led to the decision to enter treatment rather than preexisting abnormalities that caused the problem drinking.

The American Psychiatric Association's *Diagnostic and Statistical Manual of Mental Disorders*[23] is the closest thing there is to a single official, widely accepted set of labels for behavioral disorders, including substance use disorders

---

delirium tremens (de *leer* ee um *tree* mens): an alcohol withdrawal syndrome that includes hallucinations and tremors.

Focus on Treatment

Treating Alcohol Use Disorder

Behavioral Treatments

For several decades, it was safe to say that most programs offering treatment for alcoholism were based mainly on the Alcoholics Anonymous (AA) 12-step model. Many were residential facilities to which people went for three weeks or more, separating them from the temptations of their regular lives. Following a detoxification period, the participants could focus all their time on learning about their disorder and the 12 steps to recovery. Both individual and group counseling sessions were provided, often on a daily basis, and when the residential phase ended the participant would be expected to continue attending AA meetings.

More recently there has been an effort to provide research-based behavioral treatments, often on an outpatient basis. The U.S. Substance Abuse and Mental Health Services Administration recognizes three primary behavioral approaches to treating alcohol use disorder, in addition to those programs that rely primarily on 12-step approaches:

- **Motivational enhancement,** also known as motivational interviewing, is based on helping people to accept the need for change and then develop strategies for implementing and maintaining their efforts to change their own behavior.
- **Cognitive-behavioral therapy** focuses on stopping and preventing negative thought patterns and learning to behave differently in the situations that have typically led to excessive drinking.

- **Contingency management** provides incentives when participants meet certain goals, such as remaining abstinent for a week.

Medications

Three medications have received FDA approval for treating alcohol use disorder:

- **Disulfiram (Antabuse)** is the oldest of these medical treatments, and it is acts by interfering with the metabolism of acetaldehyde (see p. 198). A person taking disulfiram will develop some very unpleasant symptoms (headache, nausea, flushing) if he or she drinks alcohol, because the alcohol will be metabolized to acetaldehyde, which will then build up and produce these toxic effects. The effectiveness of this approach depends on the patient's continuing to take the medication.
- **Naltrexone** is an opioid antagonist that blocks the effects of drugs like heroin, but it has also been demonstrated to reduce cravings for alcohol. When used as an adjunct to behavioral treatment, naltrexone increases the likelihood of maintaining abstinence.
- **Acamprosate** reduces symptoms of protracted withdrawal and has been shown to help individuals with alcohol use disorder who have achieved abstinence go on to maintain abstinence for several weeks to months.

For the latest official information on treatment approaches to alcohol use disorder, go to https://www.samhsa.gov/treatment/substance-use-disorders.

Box icon credit: ©dencg/Shutterstock.com RF

(see Chapter 2). The *DSM-5* lists 11 possible criteria for alcohol use disorder, including drinking more than intended, desire to cut down or stop, craving, drinking causing disruption of major life roles, social problems, giving up other activities, repeated hazardous use, tolerance, and withdrawal. The severity of the disorder is then ranked based on the number of these criteria, with six or

more of the symptoms indicating a severe alcohol use disorder.

Why are some people able to drink in moderation all their lives, whereas others repeatedly become intoxicated, suffer from alcohol-related problems, and continue to drink excessively? So far, no single factor and no combination of multiple factors has been presented that allows us to predict which individuals will become alcohol abusers. Multiple theories exist, including biochemical, psychoanalytic, and cultural approaches. At this period of scientific history, probably the most attention is being focused on understanding two types of factors: cognitive and genetic. Two important tools have been used in the cognitive research: the Alcohol Expectancy Questionnaire (asking people what effects they think alcohol has on people), and the balanced placebo design (p. 200).[24] Both alcohol-dependent drinkers and social drinkers report more intoxication and consume more drinks when they are told the drinks have alcohol, regardless of the actual alcohol content. It is important that alcohol-dependent people actually given small amounts of alcohol (equivalent to one or two drinks) do not report becoming intoxicated and do not increase their drinking if they are led to expect that the drink contains no alcohol. Therefore, it would seem that, if alcohol abusers do lose control when they begin drinking, it might be because they have come to *believe* that they will lose control if they drink (this is sometimes referred to as the *abstinence violation effect*). These balanced placebo experiments have been replicated several times by others. The most obvious interpretation of such results is that alcohol use provides a social excuse for behaving in ways that would otherwise be considered inappropriate, and it is enough for one to believe that one has drunk alcohol for such behaviors to be released.

Considerable evidence supports the idea that some degree of vulnerability to alcohol dependence might be inherited. Alcohol dependence does tend to run in families, but some of that could be due to similar expectancies developed through similar cultural influences and children learning from their parents. Studies on twins provide one way around this problem. Monozygotic (one-egg, or identical) twins share the same genetic material, whereas dizygotic (two-egg, or fraternal) twins are no more genetically related than any two nontwin siblings. Both types of twins are likely to share very similar cultural and family learning experiences. If one adult twin is diagnosed as alcohol dependent, what is the likelihood that the other twin will also receive that diagnosis (are the twins concordant for the trait of alcohol dependence)? Almost all such studies report the concordance rate for monozygotic twins is higher than that for dizygotic twins, and in some studies it is as high as 50 percent. These results imply that inheritance plays a strong role but is far from a complete determinant of alcohol dependence. Another important type of study looks at adopted sons whose biological fathers were alcohol dependent. These reports consistently find that such adoptees have a much greater than average chance of becoming alcohol dependent, even though they are raised by "normal" parents. Although these studies again provide clear evidence for a genetic influence, most children of alcohol abusers do not become alcohol dependent—they simply have a statistically greater risk of doing so. For example, in one study, 18 percent of the adopted-away sons of alcohol-dependent drinkers became dependent on alcohol, compared with 5 percent of the adopted-away sons whose parents had not received the diagnosis.

motivational enhancement: a treatment approach based on assisting the client to understand the need to make changes in behavior and to implement those changes.

cognitive-behavioral therapy: a widely-used form of psychotherapy that develops coping strategies for dealing with unhealthy patterns of thinking, feeling, and behaving.

contingency management: a form of applied behavior analysis that provides some form of positive reinforcement when clients behave in desired ways. For example, a client who provides a urine sample in which no illicit drug is detected might receive a prepaid debit card with a $10 value.

disulfiram (Antabuse): a drug that blocks the metabolism of acetaldehyde, so that consumption of alcohol leads to headaches and other unpleasant symptoms of acetaldehyde toxicity.

naltrexone: an opioid receptor blocker that has been shown to reduce urges for various substances.

acamprosate: a medication used along with counseling in the treatment of alcohol abuse.

Alcohol dependence is a complicated feature of human behavior, and even if genetic influences are critical, more than one genetic factor could be involved. Probably it is too much to hope that a single genetic marker will ever be found to be a reliable indicator of alcohol dependence in all individuals.

Summary

- Alcohol is made by yeasts in a process called fermentation. Distillation is used to increase the alcohol content of a beverage.

- Reformers first proposed temperate use of alcoholic beverages, and it was not until the late 1800s that alcohol sales were prohibited in several states.

- National Prohibition of alcohol was successful in reducing alcohol consumption and alcohol-related problems, but it also led to increased law-breaking and a loss of alcohol taxes.

- Alcohol use has decreased since 1980, and consumption varies widely among different cultural groups and in different regions of the United States.

- Men are more likely than women to be heavy drinkers, and college students are more likely to drink than others of the same age.

- Alcohol is metabolized by the liver at a constant rate, which is not much influenced by body size.

- The exact mechanism(s) by which alcohol exerts its effects in the central nervous system is not known, but its interactions with the GABA receptor are probably important.

- Knowing a person's weight, gender, and the amount of alcohol consumed, one can estimate the blood alcohol concentration (BAC), and from that the typical effects on behavior.

- The balanced placebo design has helped to separate the pharmacological effects of alcohol from the effects of alcohol expectancies.

- Alcohol tends to increase the user's focus on the "here and now," a kind of alcohol myopia.

- Alcohol-related traffic fatalities have decreased considerably since 1980, but there are still thousands every year in the United States.

- Alcohol appears to enhance interest in sex, but to impair physiological arousal in both sexes.

- Alcohol use is statistically associated with homicide, assault, family violence, and suicide.

- Chronic heavy drinking can lead to neurological damage, as well as damage to the heart and liver. However, moderate drinking has been associated with a decrease in heart attacks.

- Fetal alcohol syndrome is seen in less than 10 percent of babies whose mothers drink heavily.

- Withdrawal from heavy alcohol use can be life-threatening when seizures develop.

- The notion that alcohol dependence is a disease in its own right goes back at least to the 1700s but did not become popular until Alcoholics Anonymous began to have a major influence in the 1940s and 1950s.

- Although many studies have indicated a likely genetic influence on susceptibility to alcohol dependence, the exact nature and extent of this genetic link is not known.

Review Questions

1. What is the maximum percentage of alcohol obtainable through fermentation alone? What would that be in "proof"?
2. Did Prohibition reduce alcohol abuse?
3. In about what year did apparent consumption of alcohol reach its peak in the United States?
4. About how much more likely are men than women to engage in frequent heavy drinking?
5. About how many standard drinks can the typical human metabolize each hour?
6. For your own gender and weight, about how many standard drinks are required for you to reach the legal BAC limit for driving under the influence?
7. Alcohol enhances the action of which neurotransmitter at its receptors?

8. What is the typical behavior of a person with a BAC of 0.20 percent?

9. Describe the four groups in the balanced placebo design.

10. What term is used to describe the fact that drinkers tend to focus on the "here and now"?

11. About what proportion of U.S. traffic fatalities are considered to be alcohol related?

12. What is the role of expectancy in males' increased interest in sex after drinking?

13. If alcohol did not actually increase violent tendencies, how might we explain the statistical correlation between alcohol and such things as assault and homicide?

14. Why is it dangerous to drink alcohol to "stay warm" in the winter?

15. If someone you know has drunk enough alcohol to pass out, what are two things you can do to prevent a lethal outcome?

16. Can brain damage be reversed if someone has been drinking heavily for many years?

17. About what percentage of the heaviest-drinking women will have children diagnosed with FAS?

18. What is the most dangerous withdrawal symptom from alcohol?

19. Did the early founders of AA view alcohol dependence as a disease?

20. If one identical twin is diagnosed with alcohol dependence, what is the likelihood that the other twin will also receive this diagnosis?

References

1. Lender, M. E. *Drinking in America.* New York: The Free Press, 1987.

2. Koren, J. *Economic Aspects of the Liquor Problem.* New York: Houghton Mifflin, 1899.

3. Clark, N. H. *The Dry Years: Prohibition and Social Change in Washington.* Seattle: University of Washington Press, 1965.

4. "Culture Shapes Young People's Drinking Habits." *Science Daily,* September 23, 2008.

5. List of countries by beer consumption per capita. Retrieved from Wikipedia.com, February 8, 2017.

6. Haughwout, S.P, R. LaVallee, and I.-J. P. Castle. *NIAAA Surveillance Report #104.* Bethesda, MD: National Institute on Alcohol Abuse and Alcoholism, 2016.

7. "Mass. Alcohol Tax Cut Hurt Bottom Line at N. H. State-Owned Liquor Stores." *Concord Monitor,* February 26, 2013.

8. Substance Abuse and Mental Health Services Administration. (2016). *Results from the 2015 National Survey on Drug Use and Health.* Available at: http://www.samhsa.gov/data.

9. American College Health Association. ACHA-NCHA Reference Group Data Report. Hanover, MD. American College Health Association, Spring 2016.

10. Frezza, M., and others. "High Blood Alcohol Levels in Women: The Role of Decreased Gastric Alcohol Dehydrogenase Activity and First-Pass Metabolism." *New England Journal of Medicine* 322 (1990), p. 95.

11. Staples, J. M., W. H. George, C. A. Stappenbeck, K. C. Davis, J. Norris, and J. R. Heiman. "Alcohol Myopia and Sexual Abdication among Women: Examining the Moderating Effect of Child Sexual Abuse." *Addictive Behaviors* 41 (2015), pp. 72–77.

12. National Highway Traffic Safety Administration. (2016). *Traffic Safety Facts: Alcohol-Impaired Driving, 2015 Data.* NHTSA Publication DOT HS 812 350.

13. Yi, H. Y., and others. *NIAAA Surveillance Report #76: Trends in Alcohol-Related Traffic Fatalities in the United States, 1982–2004.* Bethesda, MD: USPHS, 2006.

14. George, W. H., and S. A. Stoner. "Understanding Acute Alcohol Effects on Sexual Behavior." *Annual Review of Sex Research* 11 (2000), pp. 1053–2528.

15. Crothers, T. D. "Alcoholic Trance." *Popular Science* 26 (1884), pp. 189, 191.

16. Kuhns, J. B., M. L. Exum, T. A. Clodfelter, and M. C. Bottia. "The Prevalence of Alcohol-Involved Homicide Offending: A Meta-Analytic Review." *Homicide Studies* 18 (2014), pp. 251–70.

17. Krebs, C. P., and others. "College Women's Experiences with Physically Forced, Alcohol- or Other Drug-Enabled, and Drug-Facilitated Sexual Assault before and since Entering College." *Journal of American College Health* 57 (2009), pp. 639–49.

18. Boenisch, S., and others. "The Role of Alcohol Use Disorder and Alcohol Consumption in Suicide Attempts–A Secondary Analysis of 1921 Suicide Attempts." *European Psychiatry* 25 (2010), pp. 414–20.

19. Centers for Disease Control and Prevention. "Vital Signs: Alcohol Poisoning Deaths." Available at: https://www.cdc.gov/vitalsigns/pdf/2015-01-vitalsigns.pdf

20. Britton, A. "Alcohol and Heart Disease." *British Medical Journal* 341 (2010), pp. 1114–5.

21. Popova, S., S. Lange, C. Probst, N. Parunashvili, and J. Rehm. "Prevalence of Alcohol Consumption during Pregnancy and Fetal Alcohol Spectrum Disorders among the General and Aboriginal Populations in Canada and the United States." *European Journal of Medical Genetics,* 60 (2017), pp. 32–48.

22. Sachdeva, A. "Alcohol Withdrawal Syndrome: Benzodiazepines and Beyond." *Journal of Clinical and Diagnostic Research,* 9 (2015), pp. 1–7.

23. American Psychiatric Association. *Diagnostic and Statistical Manual of Mental Disorders,* 5th ed. Washington, DC: American Psychiatric Association, 2013.

24. Kreusch, F., and others. "Assessing the Stimulant and Sedative Effects of Alcohol with Explicit and Implicit Measures in a Balanced Placebo Design." *Journal of Studies on Alcohol and Drugs* 74 (2013), pp. 923–30.

Check Yourself

Do You Have a Drinking Problem?

This assessment was designed to be a simple and rapid way for a physician to interview a patient and get an initial indication of whether to suggest a more thorough assessment of alcohol use disorder. You can ask the questions about your own drinking.

Rapid Alcohol Problems Screen (RAPS 4)

1. During the last year have you had a feeling of guilt or remorse after drinking? **[Remorse]**
2. During the last year has a friend or a family member ever told you about things you said or did while you were drinking that you could not remember? **[Amnesia]**
3. During the last year have you failed to do what was normally expected from you because of drinking? **[Perform]**
4. Do you sometimes take a drink when you first get up in the morning? **[Starter]**

A "yes" answer to any one of these should cause you to reflect seriously on whether your drinking behavior is already on a dangerous path. If you answered "yes" to two or more, we suggest that you visit a professional counselor, psychologist, or physician who specializes in substance abuse, to discuss your drinking and get a more in-depth assessment.

C. J. Cherpitel, "A Brief Screening Instrument for Alcohol Dependence in the Emergency Room: The RAPS 4," *Journal of Studies on Alcohol*, 61 (2000), pp. 447–49.

FIVE

Familiar Drugs

Some drugs are seen so often that they don't seem to be drugs at all, at least not in the same sense as cocaine or marijuana. However, tobacco and its ingredient nicotine, as well as caffeine in its various forms, are psychoactive drugs meeting any reasonable definition of the term *drug*. Certainly the drugs sold over the counter (OTC) in pharmacies are drugs, and many of them have their primary effects on the brain and behavior. In Section Five, we learn about the psychological effects of all these familiar drugs, partly because they are used so commonly. Also, they provide several interesting points for comparison with the less well-known, more frightening drugs.

10 Tobacco
Why do people smoke, and why do they have such a hard time quitting?

11 Caffeine
How much of an effect does caffeine really produce? What are the relative strengths of coffee, tea, and soft drinks?

12 Dietary Supplements and Over-the-Counter Drugs
Which of the common drugstore drugs are psychoactive?

10 Tobacco

©tevarak11/123RF RF

The selling and using of tobacco products has always generated controversy, but never greater than today. Tobacco is an interesting social dilemma—a product that is legal for adults to use, and that a significant proportion of adults enjoy using and expect to continue using, yet a substance that is responsible for more addiction, illness, and death than any other. This chapter examines how tobacco's current status came to be, and what changes lie on the horizon for this agricultural commodity, dependence-producing substance, and topic for policy discussions from local city councils to Congress.

Objectives

When you have finished this chapter, you should be able to:

- Describe how Europeans spread tobacco around the world.

- Explain the historical importance of tobacco to America.

- Describe the history of anti-tobacco efforts and the tobacco companies' responses.

- Explain the difficulties in marketing "safer" cigarettes as related to FDA regulation, and how this impacts regulation of electronic cigarettes.

- Describe the most important adverse health consequences of smoking and the total annual smoking-attributable mortality in the United States.

- Understand the controversy over secondhand smoke as both a social issue and a public health issue.

- Describe the effects of cigarette smoking on the developing fetus and the newborn.

- Explain why smoking is not immediately lethal, in spite of nicotine's powerful toxicity.

- Describe how nicotine affects cholinergic receptors in the brain and throughout the body.

- Describe the most common physiological and behavioral effects of nicotine.

- Describe the roles of counseling, nicotine replacement therapy, and other medications in smoking cessation.

Tobacco History

Tobacco was unknown to Europeans when Columbus arrived in the New World in 1492. In fact, one of the first things he was given by the people he met was some dried leaves with a pungent odor. Because no one knew what to do with the leaves, they were thrown away. Tobacco use was remarkably widespread in the Americas, and it had been cultivated for many hundreds of years. It had many names in the various languages of the natives, but the word *tab-aco* was adopted by the Spanish, either from an Arawak term they encountered in the Caribbean, or perhaps because the Arabic word *tabbaq* was already used in Spain in reference to medicinal herbs. Europeans discovered that Amerindians sometimes put tobacco into tubes made from reeds, started a fire at one end of the reed, and "drank" the smoke from the other end. Or, they did a similar thing with tobacco leaves rolled up like a cigar, or they "drank" smoke from stone or clay pipes. Powdered tobacco was sometimes put into the mouth, or sucked into the nose through a tube. Tobacco leaves were also used to treat wounds, and powdered tobacco was thought to have a variety of medicinal benefits.

Most Europeans who first encountered tobacco found both its taste and the smell of the smoke not only foreign, but disgusting. Furthermore, it was associated with cultural traditions that were rejected by the Church. In fact, it was a hundred years after Columbus's voyage before tobacco became popular anywhere in Europe. The assimilation of tobacco and chocolate into European culture is the subject of an interesting 2008 book.[1] The short form of the story is that merchants and members of the clergy who spent time in the Americas trading with natives, eating meals, and sharing ceremonial occasions, first adopted the use of both tobacco and chocolate. These people became wealthy and

Tobacco was in use by Native Americans long before it was introduced into Europe. Source: Bob Nichols/U.S. Department of Agriculture

powerful members of society back in Europe, and over the years the practices they brought back with them came to be associated with their status. They spread their new habits to their wealthy and powerful friends and family, and included gifts of tobacco and chocolate along with gold, silver, and other treasures they gave to royalty and to the pope. It was this association with respected members of society that eventually made tobacco a desired commodity for the masses. Commercial importation of tobacco into Europe in large quantities began around 1600.

Early Medical Uses

Travelers returning to Europe mentioned the potential medical uses of tobacco, but the medical establishment was leery at first. Beginning with a few trials by physicians, recognition of the potential of tobacco grew during the middle of the 1500s.

The French physician Jean Nicot became enamored with the medical uses of tobacco. He tried it on enough people to convince himself of its value and sent glowing reports of the herb's effectiveness to the French court. He was successful in "curing" the migraine headaches of Catherine de Medici, queen of Henry II of France, which made tobacco use very much "in." It was called the *herbe sainte,* "holy plant," and *the herbe à tous les maux,* "the plant against all evils." By 1565, the plant had been called nicotiane, after Nicot. In 1753, Linnaeus, the Swedish "father of taxonomy," named the plant genus *Nicotiana.* When a pair of French chemists isolated the active ingredient in 1828, they acted like true nationalists and called it nicotine.

In the 16th century, Sir Anthony Chute summarized much of the available information and said, "Anything that harms a man inwardly from his girdle upward might be removed by a moderate use of the herb." Others, however, felt differently: "If taken after meals the herb would infect the brain and liver," and "Tobacco should be avoided by (among others) women with child and husbands who desired to have children."[1]

Drugs in the Media

Tobacco Use in the Movies

In 1989, U.S. tobacco companies voluntarily agreed to halt a long-standing practice, directly paying film producers for what is known as "product placement" in popular films. All sorts of companies do this, and at times, the practice is fairly obvious once you know about it. For example, you might notice that in one movie a particular brand of new automobile appears with unusual frequency. In another, one type of soft drink can or billboard (and never a competing brand) might be seen in the background of several shots. Despite all the efforts to control more explicit advertising of cigarettes to young people, this practice is especially insidious because research indicates that tobacco use by an adolescent's favorite actor does influence the adolescent's smoking behavior. Thus, this type of product placement is likely to be a very potent form of advertising for cigarette manufacturers. Did the 1989 voluntary ban work?

Yes, but not completely, according to a study published in 2011.[2] The researchers studied the 10 top-grossing movies each week during 2010 and looked for instances of tobacco use (as opposed to having a cigarette pack or billboard in the background). Obviously, cigarette smoking might be considered important for dramatic effect in some films, especially those aimed at adults, so we should not expect no tobacco use at all. Although 70 percent of R-rated films and 30 percent of G, PG, and PG-13 rated films still contained some tobacco use, this represents a decrease from 2005 levels. Also, the number of incidents per film decreased considerably after 2005.

Box icon credit: ©Glow Images RF

In 1617, Dr. William Vaughn phrased the last thought a little more poetically:

> *Tobacco that outlandish weede*
> *It spends the braine and spoiles the seede*
> *It dulls the spirite, it dims the sight*
> *It robs a woman of her right.*[3]

Dr. Vaughn may have been ahead of his time: Current research verifies tobacco's adverse effects on reproductive functioning in both men and women (see pages 232–235).

The slow advance of medical science through the 18th and 19th centuries gradually removed tobacco from the doctor's black bag, and nicotine was dropped from *The United States Pharmacopoeia* in the 1890s.

The Spread of Tobacco Use

There are more than 60 species of *Nicotiana,* but only two major ones. ***Nicotiana tobacum,*** the major species grown today in more than a hundred countries, is a large-leaf species. *Tobacum* was indigenous only to South America, so the Spanish had a monopoly on its production for over a hundred years. ***Nicotiana rustica*** is a small-leaf species and was the plant existing in the West Indies and eastern North America when Columbus arrived.

The Spanish monopoly on tobacco sales to Europe was a thorn in the side of the British. When settlers returned to England in 1586 after failing to colonize Virginia, they took with them seeds of the *rustica* species and planted them in England, but this species never grew well. The English crown again attempted to establish a tobacco colony in Virginia in 1610, when John Rolfe arrived as leader of a group. From 1610 to 1612, Rolfe tried to cultivate *rustica,* but the small-leaf plant was weak and poor in flavor, and it had a sharp taste.

In 1612, Rolfe somehow got some seeds of the Spanish *tobacum* species. This species grew beautifully and sold well. The colony was saved, and every available plot of land was planted with *tobacum.* By 1619, as much Virginia tobacco as

Spanish tobacco was sold in London. That was also the year that King James prohibited the cultivation of any tobacco in England and declared the tobacco trade a royal monopoly.

Income from the sale of tobacco became so important to the English colonists that tobacco planting spread to Maryland, Massachusetts, and the other colonies. For a time there was concern that the Virginia colonists were neglecting both food crops and the maintenance of their buildings, they were so focused on tobacco planting. Because tobacco depleted the soil's nutrients, more and more land was cleared, leading to the first large-scale fighting between the Virginia colonists and the Native Americans in the period 1622–1640. Also, King James's special taxes and requirement that tobacco be sold only to England became the first source of discontent between the king and the English colonists, who began to meet and openly criticize the crown. Many resorted to smuggling or to bribing customs officials to avoid what they considered an unfair tax—all this more than 150 years before the more well-known "Boston Tea party"[4] (see Chapter 11).

Snuff

During the 18th century, smoking gradually diminished, but the use of tobacco did not. Snuff replaced the pipe in England. At the beginning of that century, the upper class was already committed to snuff. The middle and lower classes only gradually changed over, but by 1770 very few people were smoking. The reign of King George III (1760–1820) was the time of the big snuff. His wife, Charlotte, was such a heavy user of the powder that she was called "Snuffy Charlotte," although for obvious reasons not to her face. On the continent, Napoleon had tried smoking once, gagged horribly, and returned to his seven pounds of snuff per month.

Tobacco in Early America

Tobacco played an important role in the Revolutionary War; it was one of the major products for which France would lend the colonies money. Knowing the importance of tobacco to the colonies,

one of British general Cornwallis's major campaign goals in 1780 and 1781 was the destruction of the Virginia tobacco plantations.

After the war, ordinary Americans rejoiced and rejected snuff as well as tea and all other things British. The aristocrats who organized the republic were not as emotional, though, and installed a communal snuff box for members of Congress. However, to emphasize the fact that snuff was a nonessential, the new Congress put a luxury tax on it in 1794.

Chewing Tobacco

If you don't smoke and you don't snuff
How can you possibly get enough?

You can get enough by chewing, which gradually increased in the United States. Chewing was a suitable activity for a country on the go; it freed the hands, and the wide-open spaces made an adequate spittoon. There were also other considerations: Boston, for example, passed an ordinance in 1798 forbidding anyone from possessing a lighted pipe or "segar" in public streets. The original impetus was a concern for the fire hazard involved in smoking, not the individual's health, and the ordinance was finally repealed in 1880. Today it is difficult to appreciate how much of a chewing country we were in the 19th century. In 1860, only 7 of 348 tobacco factories in Virginia and North Carolina manufactured smoking tobacco. The amount of tobacco for smoking did not equal the amount for chewing until 1911 and did not surpass it until the 1920s.

The start of the 20th century was the approximate high point for chewing tobacco, the sales of

---

Nicotiana tobacum (ni co she *ann* a toe *back* um): the species of tobacco widely cultivated for smoking and chewing products.
Nicotiana rustica (*russ* tick a): the less desirable species of tobacco, which is not widely grown in the United States.

Most tobacco produced in the 19th century was chewing tobacco. Source: Library of Congress Prints and Photographs Division [LC-USZC4-4309]

which slowly declined through the early part of that century, as other tobacco products became more popular. In 1945, cuspidors were removed from all federal buildings.

Cigars

The transition from chewing to cigarettes had a middle point, a combination of both smoking and chewing: cigars. Cigarette smoking was coming, and the cigar manufacturers did their best to keep cigarettes under control. They suggested that cigarettes were drugged with opium, so one could not stop using them and that the paper was bleached with arsenic and, thus, was harmful. They had some help from Thomas Edison in 1914:

> The injurious agent in Cigarettes comes principally from the burning paper wrapper.... It has a violent action in the nerve centers, producing degeneration of the cells of the brain, which is quite rapid among boys. Unlike most narcotics, this degeneration is permanent and uncontrollable. I employ no person who smokes cigarettes.[4]

The efforts of the cigar manufacturers worked for a while, and cigar sales reached their highest level in 1920, when 8 billion were sold. As sales increased, though, so did the cost of the product. Lower cost

and changing styles led to the emergence of cigarettes as the leading form of tobacco use.

Cigarettes

Thin reeds filled with tobacco had been seen by the Spanish in Yucatan in 1518. In 1844, the French were using them, and the Crimean War circulated the cigarette habit throughout Europe. The first British cigarette factory was started in 1856 by a returning veteran of the Crimean War, and in the late 1850s an English tobacco merchant, Philip Morris, began producing handmade cigarettes.

In the United States, cigarettes were being produced during the same period (14 million in 1870), but their popularity increased rapidly in the 1880s. The date of the first patent on a cigarette-making machine was 1881, and by 1885 more than a billion cigarettes a year were being sold. Not even that great he-man, boxer John L. Sullivan, could stem the tide, though in 1905 his opinion of cigarette smokers was pretty clear:

> Smoke cigarettes? Not on your tut-tut.... You can't suck coffin-nails and be a ring-champion.... Who smokes 'em? Dudes and college stiffs— fellows who'd be wiped out by a single jab or a quick undercut....[4]

At the start of the 20th century, there was a preference for cigarettes with an aromatic component— that is, Turkish tobacco. Camels, a new cigarette in 1913, capitalized on the lure of the Near East while rejecting it in actuality. The Camel brand contained just a hint of Turkish tobacco. Eliminating most of the imported tobacco made the price lower. Low price was combined with a big advertising campaign: "The Camels are coming. Tomorrow there'll be more CAMELS in town than in all of Asia and Africa combined." In 1918, Camels had 40 percent of the market and stayed in front until after World War II.

The first ad showing a woman smoking appeared in 1919. To make the ad easier to accept, the woman was pictured as Asian and the ad was for a Turkish type of cigarette. King-size cigarettes appeared in 1939 in the form of Pall Mall, which became the top seller. Filter cigarettes as filter cigarettes, not cigarettes that happen to have filters along with a mouthpiece, appeared in 1954 with Winston, which rapidly took over the market and continued to be number one until the mid-1970s. Filter cigarettes captured an increasing share of the market and now constitute over 99 percent of all U.S. cigarette sales.

Tobacco under Attack

As with every other psychoactive substance, use by some raises concerns on the part of others, and many efforts have been made over the years to regulate tobacco use. In 1604, King James of England (the same one who had the Bible translated) wrote and published a strong anti-tobacco pamphlet stating that tobacco was "harmefull to the braine, dangerous to the lungs." Never one to let morality or health concerns interfere with business, he also supported the growing of tobacco in Virginia in 1610, and when the crop prospered, he declared the tobacco trade a royal monopoly.

Some early tobacco control efforts focused on women, who were considered to be physically more delicate than men. Source: Library of Congress Prints and Photographs Division [LC-USZ62-56425]

New York City made it illegal in 1908 for a woman to use tobacco in public, and in the Roaring Twenties women were expelled from schools and dismissed from jobs for smoking. These concerns were partly for society and partly to "protect women from themselves." Those sensitive to feminist issues will find an analogy to current reactions to drug and alcohol use by pregnant women in this quote from the 1920s:

> Smoking by women and even young girls must be considered from a far different standpoint than smoking by men, for not only is the female organism by virtue of its much more frail structure and its more delicate tissues much less able to resist the poisonous action of tobacco than that of men, and thus, like many a delicate flower, apt to fade and wither more quickly in consequence, but the fecundity of woman is greatly impaired by it. Authorities cannot be expected to look on unmoved while a generation of sterile women, rendered incapable of fulfilling their sublime function of motherhood, is being produced on account of the immoderate smoking of foolish young girls.[5]

And those familiar with the 1930s "Reefer Madness" arguments might find it interesting that earlier in the same decade a weed other than marijuana was blamed for various social ills:

> Fifty percent of our insanity is inherited from parents who were users of tobacco.... Thirty-three percent of insanity cases are caused direct from cigarette smoking and the use of tobacco....
>
> Judge Gimmill, of the court of Domestic Relations of Chicago, declared that, without exception, every boy appearing before him that had lost the faculty of blushing was a cigarette fiend. The poison in cigarettes has the same effect upon girls: it perverts the morals and deadens the sense of shame and refinement.[6]

The long and slowly developing attack on tobacco as a major health problem had its seeds in reports in the 1930s and 1940s indicating a possible link between smoking and cancer. A 1952 article in *Readers' Digest* called "Cancer by the Carton" drew public attention to the issue, and led to a temporary decline in cigarette sales. The major U.S. tobacco companies recognized the threat and responded vigorously in two important ways. One was the formation of the supposedly independent Council for Tobacco Research to look into the health claims (later investigations revealed this council was not independent of tobacco company influence and served largely to try to undermine any scientific evidence demonstrating the negative health consequences of tobacco use). The other response was the mass marketing of filter cigarettes and cigarettes with lowered tar and nicotine content. The public apparently had faith in these "less hazardous" cigarettes, because cigarette sales again began to climb. In the early 1960s, the U.S. Surgeon General's office formed an Advisory Committee on Smoking and Health. Its first official report, released in 1964, stated clearly that cigarette smoking was a cause for increased lung cancer in men (at the time, the evidence for women was less extensive). Per-capita sales of cigarettes began a decline that continued over the next 40 years (see Figure 10.1). In 1965, Congress required cigarette packages to include the surgeon general's warning. All television and radio advertising of cigarettes was banned in 1971, and smoking was banned on interstate buses and domestic airline flights in 1990.[7] The list of state and local laws prohibiting smoking in public buildings, offices, restaurants, and even bars grows every year. Clearly, momentum is behind efforts to restrict smoking and exposure to secondhand smoke.

Evidence about the health dangers of tobacco accumulated slowly over time. ©Universal Images Group/Getty Images

The original laws regulating drugs had specifically excluded tobacco products, reflecting their status as an agricultural commodity, their widespread use among the social elite, and the economic importance of tobacco to the U.S. economy. In 1995, the Food and Drug Administration announced plans to regulate tobacco. After a year of discussion, rules were proposed that further limited advertising on billboards and other public displays, sponsorship of sporting events, promotional giveaways of caps and T-shirts, and advertising in magazines with significant youth readership.

One important attack on tobacco came from lawsuits seeking compensation for the health consequences of smoking. For years the tobacco companies had succeeded in winning such lawsuits, based on the idea that smokers had a significant share of the responsibility for their smoking-related illnesses. But internal tobacco company documents were disclosed demonstrating both the companies' knowledge of the adverse health consequences of smoking and their efforts to hide that knowledge from customers. A group of attorneys representing individual clients joined with several state governments seeking compensation for increased Medicaid costs, and eventually 46 states reached a 1998 settlement with the major U.S. tobacco producers that included $205 billion in payments to the states as well as agreeing to the previously proposed FDA advertising regulations and a federally supported program to enforce laws prohibiting sales to minors. In exchange, the companies received a cap on certain aspects of their legal liability, which otherwise threatened to bankrupt the industry.[7]

The Quest for "Safer" Cigarettes

Nicotine appears to be the constituent in tobacco that keeps smokers coming back for more—if the nicotine content of cigarettes is varied, people tend to adjust their smoking behavior, taking more puffs and inhaling more deeply when given low-nicotine cigarettes, and reporting no satisfaction if all the nicotine is removed.[8] Another complex product of burning tobacco is something called tar, the sticky

Millions have been spent to promote antismoking messages, often using funds provided by tobacco companies to the states under the 1998 tobacco settlement. ©Matthew Simmons/ Getty Images

brown stuff that can be seen on the filter after a cigarette is smoked. Beginning in the mid-1950s with the mass marketing of filter cigarettes, the tobacco companies began to promote the idea of a "safer" cigarette, without actually admitting that there was anything unsafe about their older products. Because the companies were advertising their cigarettes as being lower in tar and nicotine, for many years the Federal Trade Commission (with industry support and cooperation) monitored the tar and nicotine yields of the various cigarette brands and made those results public. The U.S. Congress and the National Cancer Institute promoted research to develop safer cigarettes. The public listened to all this talk about safer cigarettes and bought in—sales of filter cigarettes took off, and by the 1980s low-tar and nicotine cigarettes dominated the market.

The problem with all this is that "safer" doesn't mean "safe," and it wasn't at all clear how much safer these low-tar and nicotine cigarettes actually are for people over a lifetime of smoking. Some early studies had indicated that those who had smoked lower-yield cigarettes for years were at less risk for cancer and heart disease than those who smoked high-yield brands. But other studies showed that if a smoker switched from a high-yield to a low-yield cigarette, changes in puff rate and depth of inhalation would compensate for the lower

yield per puff, and there might be no advantage to switching. The tobacco industry was caught in an ironic position, as evidenced by the plight of Liggett (former manufacturer of Chesterfield, L&M, and Lark, now selling Eve and other brands). During the 1960s, Liggett developed a cigarette that in the laboratory significantly reduced tumors in mice compared to the company's standard brand. Lawyers advised Liggett against reporting these results because the data would confirm that the standard brand was hazardous. Liggett suppressed the information and did not market the "safer" cigarette, a fact that was revealed in a lawsuit during the 1980s.[9]

A major blow to the "healthier cigarette" notion was dealt in 2006 when the U.S. government obtained a conviction against nine tobacco companies and two tobacco industry trade organizations for racketeering and fraud. The purposeful manipulation of nicotine levels to increase nicotine dependence was one charge, but another was that for years the tobacco companies promoted low-tar and nicotine cigarettes as safer alternatives, when their own research and other evidence showed these claims to be misleading.

Electronic Cigarettes

The "safer" cigarette controversy took a high-tech turn in 1988 when R. J. Reynolds attempted to market Premier, a sort of noncigarette cigarette. Although packaged like cigarettes and having the appearance of a plastic cigarette, the product contained catalytic crystals coated with a tobacco extract but no actual tobacco. When "lit" with a flame, these cigarettes produced no smoke, but inhaling through them allowed the user to absorb some nicotine. The FDA couldn't accept that this was the traditional agricultural product rather than a nicotine "delivery device," something it would have to regulate as a drug. Reynolds was unable to find a legal way to sell the product and was forced to drop it. But the company did not give up. In 2004, Reynolds marketed Eclipse, another high-tech "cigarette" that the company said "may present less risk," and produced up to 80 percent less smoke than a regular cigarette. This one did contain tobacco, so they could claim it was an agricultural product. Instead of burning the tobacco, a carbon element heated the tobacco to release nicotine vapors. In 2008, a Vermont judge ruled that Reynolds had not presented sufficient scientific evidence for their claim that Eclipse "may present less risk of cancer." Eclipse is no longer being marketed. However, several battery-powered electronic cigarettes began to be imported from China in 2004. These contain some form of nicotine liquid that is warmed by a small electric element inside the cigarette. These products were widely marketed as safer alternatives to regular cigarettes, but none of the companies involved had submitted them to the FDA for review. The FDA attempted to ban these products, but in early 2010 a federal judge ruled that they could not do so. A wide variety of electronic cigarettes and other devices are currently available, although they are now subject to new FDA rules.

Tobacco Products and the FDA

After the 1995 FDA proposals that cigarettes be regulated, it was not clear exactly how they could do this, since tobacco products had originally been excluded as neither food nor drug. And in 2000, the U.S. Supreme Court ruled that existing federal law did not give the FDA authority to regulate tobacco. Various members of Congress proposed legislation to allow the FDA to regulate tobacco products as drugs. In this book, we are considering tobacco as a drug because it delivers nicotine, a known psychoactive chemical. But the drugs that the FDA reviews and approves all claim to have therapeutic benefits of some kind. What is the intended use or health benefit of a tobacco cigarette? How could the FDA balance the benefits versus the risks without someone defining the benefits?

In June 2009, President Barack Obama signed the Family Smoking Prevention and Tobacco Control Act, authorizing the FDA to regulate tobacco products themselves in specific ways. The FDA began studying and proposing new regulations for a wide variety of products, and after input from industry and the public, final rules were published in 2016. One important rule is that claims for "modified health risk" are now prohibited until such claims can be clearly demonstrated—in other words, a seller cannot claim that e-cigarettes or hookahs are safer than regular cigarettes. Also, all tobacco products will be regulated in a manner similar to drugs, in that companies will have to apply to the FDA, describing their product and its intended uses. Current products will remain available until the application and review process is finished, expected to be around 2020 for most existing products. Also, any product containing nicotine intended for human consumption is included under this law. This aspect of the law is aimed primarily at e-cigarettes and pipes but also includes a nicotine gel that is "consumed" by rubbing it on the hands. These new rules are likely to have a major impact on the market for tobacco and nicotine products over the next few years.

Current Cigarette Use

Cigarette smoking is declining in the United States (Figure 10.1). Per-capita consumption has declined since 1963, when the surgeon general's report officially linked smoking and cancer. Total sales increased until 1981 due to the rise in the adult population, but there has been a continued decline for over 30 years. Large drops in sales occurred in

Despite antismoking education, one in five young people still becomes a regular smoker. ©McGraw-Hill Education/Christopher Kerrigan, photographer

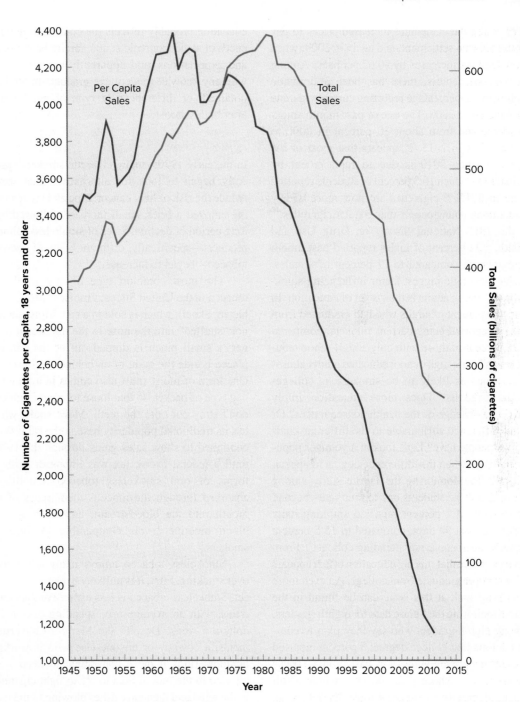

Figure 10.1   Trends in Cigarette Sales 1945–2013

SOURCE: USDA Economic Research Service, *Tobacco Outlook* (http://www.ers.usda.gov), and Federal Trade Commission, *Cigarette Report* (http://www.ftc.gov).

1999, when the companies increased prices to pay for the tobacco settlement, and again in 2009, when the federal tax increased by $0.62 per pack. Among high-school seniors, there has been a dramatic decline in the percentage reporting current cigarette smoking since 2000. The rate of past-month smoking decreased from about 30 percent in 2000 to 11.4 percent in 2015. It appears that most of the decrease since 2010 is due to replacement by e-cigarettes, which 16.3 percent of students reported using in 2015. E-cigarettes are now more widely used among young people than regular cigarettes.[10] In the 2015 National Survey on Drug Use and Health,[11] 22 percent of males reported past month cigarette use, compared to 17 percent of females. By far the single biggest factor influencing smoking rates among adults is their level of education. In 2015, 10 percent of adults who had graduated from college reported being current smokers, compared to 28 percent of those with only a high-school education. Why are high-school educated adults almost three times as likely to be smokers as college-educated adults? Does more education imply greater knowledge of the health consequences? Or is the difference attributable to the different kinds of jobs people have? Let's look at a younger population to see when this difference begins to appear. In the 2015 Monitoring the Future study among full-time college students one to four years beyond high school, 4.2 percent reported smoking daily within the past 30 days, compared to 15.5 percent for same-age people not attending college.[12] From this we can see that this big education effect appears before people graduate from college. An even more interesting look at this issue can be found in the 2015 Monitoring the Future data for eighth-graders. Among eighth-graders who say they plan to complete a four-year college degree, 3 percent reported smoking cigarettes within the past month. Those eighth-graders whose plans do not include a full college degree (no college, a trade school, or an associate's degree) are *four times* as likely to be current smokers: 12 percent report using cigarettes in the past month. Thus, we can see that this difference in cigarette smoking based on college

education probably reflects the considerable influences of socioeconomic status, family background, and expectations, and apparently has little to do with any knowledge a college graduate might have obtained, or differences in type of employment after high school.

Smokeless Tobacco

In the early 1970s, many cigarette smokers apparently began to look for alternatives that would reduce the risk of lung cancer. Pipe and cigar smoking enjoyed a brief, small increase, followed by a long period of decline. Sales of **smokeless tobacco** products—specifically, different kinds of chewing tobacco—began to increase.

The most common type of oral smokeless tobacco in the United States is **moist snuff** (Copenhagen, Skoal), which is sold in a can. Moist snuff is not "snuffed" into the nose in the traditional manner; a small pinch is dipped out of the can and placed beside the gum, often behind the lower lip. One form of moist snuff also comes in a little tea-bag type of packet, so that loose tobacco fragments don't stray out onto the teeth. Moist snuff, which has its traditional popularity base in the rural West, continued to show sales gains through the 1980s, until a federal excise tax was imposed. With all forms of oral smokeless tobacco, nicotine is absorbed through the mucous membranes of the mouth into the bloodstream, and users achieve blood nicotine levels comparable to those of smokers.

Smokeless tobacco enjoys many advantages over smoking. First, it is unlikely to cause lung cancer. Smokeless tobacco is less expensive than cigarettes, with an average user spending only a few dollars a week. Despite the Marlboro advertisements, a cowboy or anyone else who is working outdoors finds it more convenient to keep some tobacco in the mouth than to try to light cigarettes in the wind and then have ashes blowing in the face. And chewing might be more socially acceptable than smoking under most circumstances. After all, the user doesn't blow smoke all around, and most people don't even notice when someone is chewing, unless the chewer has a huge wad in the mouth or spits frequently. Many users can control the amount of tobacco they put in their mouths so that they don't have to spit very often. What they do with the leftover **quid** of tobacco is a different story and often not a pretty sight.

The use of chewing tobacco had never completely died out in rural areas, and its resurgence was strongest there. The high-school senior class of 2015 reported that 11 percent of the boys and about 2 percent of the girls were using smokeless tobacco in the past month, down from 19 percent of boys and 2 percent of girls in 1993.[10]

Chewing tobacco might not be as unhealthy as smoking it. However, smokeless tobacco is not without its hazards. Of most concern is the increased risk of cancer of the mouth, pharynx, and esophagus. Snuff and chewing tobacco do contain potent carcinogens, including high levels of tobacco-specific **nitrosamines.** Many users experience tissue changes in the mouth, with **leukoplakia** (a whitening, thickening, and hardening of the tissue) a relatively frequent finding. Leukoplakia is considered to be a precancerous lesion (a tissue change that can develop into cancer). The irritation of the gums can cause them to become inflamed or to recede, exposing the teeth to disease. The enamel of the teeth can also be worn down by the abrasive action of the tobacco. Dentists are also becoming more aware of the destructive effects of oral tobacco.

Concerns about these oral diseases led the surgeon general's office to sponsor a conference and produce a 1986 report, *The Health Consequences of Using Smokeless Tobacco.*[13] This report went into some depth in reviewing epidemiological, experimental, and clinical data and concluded "the oral use of smokeless tobacco represents a significant health risk. It is not a safe substitute for smoking cigarettes. It can cause cancer and a number of noncancerous oral conditions and can lead to nicotine addiction and dependence." Packages of smokeless tobacco now carry a series of rotating warning labels describing these dangers.

"Vaping" is increasing in popularity among young people.
©pixinoo/Shutterstock.com RF

Hookahs

In the early 2000s, an ancient form of tobacco use increased somewhat in popularity. *Hookahs* are large, ornate water pipes, imported to the United States from Egypt and other Arab countries where their use has never completely gone out of style. Burning charcoal is put into the pipe bowl, and a piece of prepared flavored tobacco *(shisha)* is placed on a screen over the charcoal. The smoke is drawn down through a tube into a water reservoir by drawing on mouthpieces connected to tubes that enter the hookah above the water. The water-filtered smoke is milder, and the social nature of smoking in this manner has led to some bars providing hookahs for their customers' use (in cities that do not outlaw smoking in bars). Hookahs and shisha are being sold over the Internet and in tobacco shops, but it is not clear how widespread the habit has become.

smokeless tobacco: a term used for chewing tobacco during the 1980s.

moist snuff: finely chopped tobacco, held in the mouth rather than snuffed into the nose.

quid: a piece of chewing tobacco.

nitrosamines (nye *troh* sa meens): a type of chemical that is carcinogenic; several are found in tobacco.

leukoplakia (luke o *plake* ee ah): a whitening and thickening of the mucous tissue in the mouth, considered to be a precancerous tissue change.

Causes for Concern

Although the first clear scientific evidence linking smoking and lung cancer appeared in the 1950s, acceptance of the evidence was slow to come. Each decade brought clearer evidence and more forceful warnings from the surgeon general. The tobacco industry fought back by establishing in 1954 the Council for Tobacco Research to provide funds to independent scientists to study the health effects of tobacco use. A 1993 exposé in *The Wall Street Journal*[14] detailed the manipulation of this "independent" research by tobacco industry lawyers, who arranged direct funding for research casting doubt on smoking-related health problems and who suppressed the publication of findings that threatened the industry. Despite tobacco industry efforts, it is abundantly clear that tobacco is America's true "killer weed" and is a bigger public health threat than all the other drug substances combined, including alcohol. It was not until the late 1990s, however, that a tobacco manufacturer finally admitted in public that cigarettes have seriously adverse effects on health.

Adverse Health Effects

Fifty years after the 1964 surgeon general's report first linked cigarette smoking to lung cancer, we now know that there are several other deadly diseases for which smoking significantly increases the risk. In the 2014 report, it was estimated that smoking was responsible for an additional 20 million early deaths over that 50-year period, and that millions more will die early unless smoking is further reduced. This is why: Although lung cancer is not common, over 80 percent of all lung cancers occur in smokers. Among deaths resulting from all types of cancer, smoking is estimated to be related to almost half, or about 160,000 premature deaths per year. However, cancer is only the second leading cause of death in the United States. It now appears that smoking is also related to about 30 percent of deaths from the leading killer, cardiovascular disease, or about 150,000 premature deaths per year. In addition, cigarette smoking is the cause of

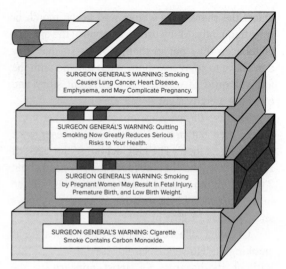

Figure 10.2   Cigarette Packages and Advertisements Are Required to Rotate among Different Warning Labels

80 percent of deaths resulting from chronic obstructive lung disease—another 100,000 cigarette-related premature deaths per year. The total "smoking attributable mortality" is more than 440,000 premature deaths per year in the United States, representing about 20 percent of all U.S. deaths.[15] No wonder these reports keep saying that "cigarette smoking is the chief, single, avoidable cause of death in our society and the most important public health issue of our time." In an effort to raise awareness about the potential harmful effects of smoking, many countries require tobacco companies to place warning labels on the packaging of their tobacco products (Figure 10.2).

Think of anything related to good physical health; the research says that cigarette smoking will impair it. The earlier the age at which you start smoking, the more smoking you do, and the longer you do it, the greater the impairment. Smoking doesn't do any part of the body any good, at any time, under any conditions.

Secondhand Smoke

A great deal has been said and written about **secondhand smoke**—that is, the inhaling of cigarette smoke from the environment by nonsmokers.

Breathing secondhand smoke subjects infants and children to dangerous carcinogens. ©Royalty-Free/Corbis RF

It is obvious that cigarette smoke can be irritating to others, but is it damaging? Besides the cases of individuals who have lung disorders or are allergic to smoke, is there evidence that cigarette smoke is harmful to exposed nonsmokers? Research is complicated; the smoke rising from the ash of the cigarette (**sidestream smoke**) is higher in many carcinogens than is the mainstream smoke delivered to the smoker's lungs. Of course, it is also more diluted. How many smokers are in the room? How much do they smoke? How good is the ventilation? How much time does the nonsmoker spend in this room? These variables have made definitive research difficult, but enough studies have produced consistent enough findings that the Environmental Protection Agency in 1993 declared secondhand smoke to be a known carcinogen and estimated that passive smoking is responsible for several thousand lung cancer deaths each year. The Centers for Disease Control now estimates that secondhand smoke is responsible for about 7,300 lung cancer deaths and 34,000 deaths from heart disease each year.[15]

Concerns about the effects of secondhand smoke have led to many more restrictions on smoking in the workplace and in public. Most states and municipalities now have laws prohibiting smoking in public conveyances and requiring the establishment of smoking and nonsmoking areas in public buildings and restaurants, and some communities have banned smoking in all restaurants. A few

employers have gone so far as to either encourage or attempt to force their employees to quit smoking both on the job and elsewhere, citing health statistics indicating more sick days and greater health insurance costs associated with smoking. This conflict between smoker and nonsmoker seems destined to get worse before it gets better. Although to some observers this battle might seem silly, it represents a very basic conflict between individual freedom and public health.

Smoking and Health in Other Countries

Cigarette smoking is a social and medical problem worldwide. A 2009 World Health Organization report estimated that, worldwide, smoking is killing 5 million people a year and that by the year 2030 the rate might be as high as 8 million per year.[16] In recent years, as sales declined in developed countries, advertising and promotions in Third World countries (touting cigarettes as delivering "the great taste of America") resulted in large increases in exports of American cigarettes. Asians, in particular, seemed to want American cigarettes, and one of the major efforts was to open Japanese, Taiwanese, Korean, and Chinese cigarette markets to U.S. imports.

Smoking and Pregnancy

The nicotine, hydrogen cyanide, and carbon monoxide in a smoking mother's blood also reach the developing fetus and have significant negative consequences there. On the average, infants born to smokers are about half a pound lighter than infants born to nonsmokers. This basic fact has been known for almost 30 years and has been confirmed in numerous studies. There is a dose-response relationship: The more the woman smokes during pregnancy, the greater the reduction in birth weight. Is

secondhand smoke: cigarette smoke inhaled from the environment by nonsmokers.

sidestream smoke: smoke arising from the ash of the cigarette or cigar.

Smoking during pregnancy is associated with miscarriage, low birth weight, smaller head circumference, and later effects on the physical and intellectual development of the child. ©vchalup/123RF RF

the reduced birth weight the result of an increased frequency of premature births or of retarded growth of the fetus? Smoking shortens the gestation period by an average of only two days, and when gestation length is accounted for, the smokers still have smaller infants. Ultrasonic measurements taken at various intervals during pregnancy show smaller fetuses in smoking women for at least the last two months of pregnancy. The infants of smokers are normally proportioned, are shorter and smaller than the infants of nonsmokers, and have smaller head circumference. The reduced birth weight of infants of women smokers is not related to how much weight the mother gains during pregnancy, and the consensus is that a reduced availability of oxygen is responsible for the diminished growth rate. Women who give up smoking early in pregnancy (by the

fourth month) have infants with weights similar to those of nonsmokers.

Besides the developmental effects evident at birth, several studies indicate small but consistent differences in body size, neurological problems, reading and mathematical skills, and hyperactivity at various ages. It therefore appears that smoking during pregnancy can have long-lasting effects on both the intellectual and physical development of the child. The increased perinatal (close to the time of birth) smoking-attributable mortality associated with sudden infant death syndrome (SIDS), low birth weight, and respiratory difficulties adds up to about 10,000 infant deaths per year in the United States.[15]

So far we have been talking about normal deliveries of babies. Spontaneous abortion (miscarriage) has also been studied many times in relation to smoking and with consistent results: Smokers have more spontaneous abortions than nonsmokers (perhaps 1.5 to 2 times as many). As for congenital malformations, the evidence for a relationship to maternal smoking is not as clear. If there is a small effect here, it could be either related to or obscured by the fact that many smokers also drink alcohol and coffee. One study indicated an increased risk of facial malformations associated with the father's smoking. Several studies have also found an increased risk of SIDS if the mother smokes, but it is not clear if this is related more to the mother's smoking during pregnancy or to passive smoking (the infant's breathing smoke) after birth.

Several studies have reported an increased risk for nicotine dependence in adolescents whose mothers smoked during pregnancy. One obvious question is whether this relationship is due entirely to cultural and social similarities between the mothers and their offspring, but a number of animal studies have demonstrated that prenatal nicotine exposure produces changes in brain chemistry in the offspring, as well as differences in behavioral response to nicotine and other drugs in adolescence.[17]

The overall message is very clear. Definite, serious risks are associated with smoking during pregnancy. In fact, the demonstrated effects of cigarette smoking on the developing child are of the same magnitude and type as those reported for "crack babies," and many more pregnant women are smoking cigarettes than using cocaine. If a woman smoker discovers she is pregnant, she should quit smoking.

Pharmacology of Nicotine

Nicotine is a naturally occurring liquid alkaloid that is colorless and volatile. On oxidation, it turns brown and smells much like burning tobacco. Tolerance to its effects develops, along with the dependency that led Mark Twain to remark how easy it was to stop smoking—he'd done it several times!

Nicotine was isolated in 1828 and has been studied extensively since then. The structure of nicotine is shown in Figure 10.3; there are both *d* and *l* forms, but they are equipotent. It is of some importance that nicotine in smoke has two forms, one with a positive charge and one that is electrically neutral. The neutral form is more easily absorbed through the mucous membranes of the mouth, nose, and lungs.

Absorption and Metabolism

Inhalation is a very effective drug-delivery system; 90 percent of inhaled nicotine is absorbed. The physiological effects of smoking one cigarette have been mimicked by injecting about 1 mg of nicotine intravenously.

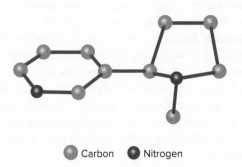

● Carbon   ● Nitrogen

Figure 10.3   Nicotine (1-methyl-2 [3-pyridyl] pyrrolidone)

Acting with almost as much speed as cyanide, nicotine is well established as one of the most toxic drugs known. In humans, 60 mg is a lethal dose, and death follows intake within a few minutes. A cigar contains enough nicotine for two lethal doses (who needs to take a second one?), but not all of the nicotine is delivered to the smoker or absorbed in a short enough time period to kill a person.

Nicotine is primarily deactivated in the liver, with 80 to 90 percent being modified before excretion through the kidneys. Part of the tolerance that develops to nicotine might result from the fact that either nicotine or the tars increase the activity of the liver microsomal enzymes that are responsible for the deactivation of drugs. These enzymes increase the rate of deactivation and thus decrease the clinical effects of the benzodiazepines and some antidepressants and analgesics. The final step in eliminating deactivated nicotine from the body may be somewhat slowed by nicotine itself, since it acts on the hypothalamus to cause a release of the hormone that acts to reduce the loss of body fluids.

Physiological Effects

The effect of nicotine on areas outside the central nervous system has been studietd extensively. Nicotine mimics acetylcholine by acting at several nicotinic subtypes of cholinergic receptor site. Nicotine is not rapidly deactivated, and continued occupation of the receptor prevents incoming impulses from having an effect, thereby blocking the transmission of information at the synapse. Thus, nicotine first stimulates and then blocks the receptor. These effects at cholinergic synapses are responsible for some of nicotine's effects, but others seem to be the result of an indirect action.

Nicotine also causes a release of adrenaline from the adrenal glands and other sympathetic sites and thus has, in part, a sympathomimetic action. Additionally, it stimulates and then blocks some sensory receptors, including the chemical receptors found in some large arteries and the thermal pain receptors found in the skin and tongue.

The symptoms of low-level nicotine poisoning are well known to beginning smokers and small children behind barns and in alleys: nausea, dizziness, and a general weakness. In acute poisoning, nicotine causes tremors, which develop into convulsions, terminated frequently by death. The cause of death is suffocation resulting from paralysis of the muscles used in respiration. This paralysis stems from the blocking effect of nicotine on the cholinergic system that normally activates the muscles. With lower doses, respiration rate actually increases because the nicotine stimulates oxygen-need receptors in the carotid artery. At these lower doses of 6 to 8 mg, there is also a considerable effect on the cardiovascular system as a result of the release of adrenaline. Such release leads to an increase in coronary blood flow, along with vasoconstriction in the skin and increased heart rate and blood pressure. The increased heart rate and blood pressure raise the oxygen need of the heart but not the oxygen supply. Another action of nicotine with negative health effects is that it increases platelet adhesiveness, which increases the tendency to clot. Within the central nervous system, nicotine seems to act at the level of the cortex to increase somewhat the frequency of the electrical activity, that is, to shift the electroencephalogram (EEG) toward an arousal pattern.

Many effects of nicotine are easily discernible in the smoking individual. The heat releases the nicotine from the tobacco into the smoke. Inhaling while smoking one cigarette has been shown to inhibit hunger contractions of the stomach for up to an hour. That finding, along with a very slight increase in blood sugar level and a deadening of the taste buds, might be the basis for a decrease in hunger after smoking.

In line with the last possibility, it has long been folklore that a person who stops smoking begins to nibble food and thus gains weight. Carbohydrate-rich snack foods appear to be even more appealing when smokers are deprived of nicotine.[18] In addition, there is evidence that smoking increases metabolism rate, so that a weight gain on quitting might be partially due to a decreasing metabolism rate or less energy utilization by the body.

In a regular smoker, smoking results in a constriction of the blood vessels in the skin, along with a decrease in skin temperature and an increase in blood pressure. The blood supply to the skeletal muscles does not change with smoking, but in regular smokers the amount of carboxyhemoglobin in the blood is usually abnormally high (up to 10 percent of all hemoglobin). All smoke contains carbon monoxide; cigarette smoke is about 1 percent carbon monoxide, pipe smoke 2 percent, and cigar smoke 6 percent. The carbon monoxide combines with the hemoglobin in the blood, so that it can no longer carry oxygen. This effect of smoking, a decrease in the oxygen-carrying ability of the blood, probably explains the shortness of breath smokers experience when they exert themselves.

The decrease in oxygen-carrying ability of the blood and the decrease in placental blood flow probably are related to the many results showing that pregnant women who smoke greatly endanger their unborn children.

Behavioral Effects

Despite all the protests and cautionary statements, the evidence is overwhelming that nicotine is the primary, if not the only, reinforcing substance in tobacco. Monkeys will work very hard when their only reward consists of regular intravenous injections of nicotine. The more nicotine in a cigarette, the lower the level of smoking. Intravenous injections and oral administration of nicotine will decrease smoking under some conditions—but not all.

Nicotine has the unusual ability to act as a mild stimulant, helping people to stay awake and to focus attention, as well as providing a sense of relaxation. Even initial smokers report both kinds of effects, with large individual differences based on the situation and several genetic factors.[19] Smokers report seeking both effects, and experimental results are heavily influenced by the smoker's history and the situation.

Most people smoke in a fairly consistent way, averaging one to two puffs per minute, with each puff

Nicotine is a dependence-producing substance, and users typically have a difficult time quitting. ©alexandre zveiger/Shutterstock.com RF

lasting about two seconds with a volume of 25 ml. This rate delivers to the individual about 1 to 2 μg of nicotine per kilogram of body weight with each puff. Smokers could increase the dose by increasing the volume of smoke with each puff or puffing more often, but this dose appears to be optimal for producing stimulation of the cerebral cortex.

Several studies have shown that smokers are able to sustain their attention to a task requiring rapid processing of information from a computer screen much better if they are allowed to smoke before beginning the task. This could be either because the nicotine produces a beneficial effect on

this performance or because when the smokers are not allowed to smoke they suffer from some sort of withdrawal symptom.

Nicotine Dependence

Evidence that nicotine is a reinforcing substance in nonhumans, that most people who smoke want to stop and can't, that when people do stop smoking they gain weight and exhibit other withdrawal signs, and that people who chew tobacco also have trouble stopping led to a need for a thorough look at the dependence-producing properties of nicotine. A 1988 surgeon general's report provided it, in the form of a 600-page tome.[20] This had been a traditionally difficult subject: Not many years ago, psychiatrists were arguing that smoking fulfilled unmet needs for oral gratification and therefore represented a personality defect. It has come to light that the cigarette manufacturing company Philip Morris obtained evidence of the dependence-producing nature of nicotine with rats in the early 1980s, but, instead of publishing the results, it fired the researchers and closed the laboratory.[21] Industry executives in 1994 congressional hearings unanimously testified that nicotine was not "addicting," still arguing that smoking was simply a matter of personal choice and that many people have been able to quit. One can theoretically choose to stop using a drug, but one has a very difficult time doing so because of the potent reinforcing properties of the substance. That is the case with nicotine. The following conclusions of the surgeon general's report were pretty strong:

1. Cigarettes and other forms of tobacco are addicting.
2. Nicotine is the drug in tobacco that causes addiction.
3. The pharmacological and behavioral processes that determine tobacco addiction are similar to those that determine addiction to drugs such as heroin and cocaine.

Recent research is focusing on the role of genetic differences in how people respond to their first smoking experience and whether they develop a rapid dependence or remain occasional smokers. Most of the focus has been on genes that are responsible for the structure of the various parts of the acetylcholine receptors in the brain. There are certainly wide individual differences in how easily people can stop smoking, and for those who have repeatedly failed to stop in spite of health consequences, the hope is that someday this genetic research will lead to a pharmacological treatment that can assist them in quitting.[22]

The past decade has seen a great deal of research into the different subtypes of nicotinic cholinergic receptors, and several companies are developing new drugs targeted more specifically to certain subtypes. The three main potential uses for these drugs would be in treating Alzheimer's disease and other cognitive disorders of aging, controlling pain, and possibly in treating ADHD. Although several such drugs are being tested in human trials, none is yet on the market.

How to Stop Smoking

When you're young and healthy, it's difficult, if not impossible, to imagine dying, being chronically ill, or having **emphysema** so that you can't get enough oxygen to walk across the room without having to stop to catch your breath. By the time you're old enough to worry about those things, it's difficult to change your health habits.

Many people want to stop smoking. A lot of people have already stopped. Are there ways to efficiently and effectively help those individuals who want to stop smoking to stop? With any form of pleasurable drug use, it is easier to keep people from starting to use the drug than it is to get them to stop once they have started. All the educational programs have had an effect on our society and on our behavior. There are now more than 40 million former smokers in the United States, and about 90 percent of them report that they quit smoking without formal treatment programs. There is some indication that those who have quit on their own do better than those who have been in a treatment program, but then those who quit on their own also

Drugs in Depth

Smoker's Face

Images of aging skin, wrinkles, and sores have been used in prevention advertisements for methamphetamine in recent years, with the idea that people would avoid using the drug if they knew that some users seem to age quickly and become unattractive. Would the same idea work for cigarette smoking?

There is plenty of research on the skin-aging effects of cigarette smoking. In various studies, as many as half the smokers have shown some signs of wrinkling, loss of elasticity, or other effects linked to the use of cigarettes. Combined with delayed wound healing, an increased risk of skin cancers, and lesions in the oral cavity, smoking clearly is not good for the body's largest organ. Would photographs showing what could happen be useful in preventing young people from starting to smoke, in your opinion? You can see one interesting photographic comparison of twins, in which one member of each pair is a smoker, at www.webmd.com/smoking-cessation/ss/slideshow-ways-smoking-affects-looks.

Box icon credit: ©Ingram Publishing/SuperStock RF

tend not to have been smoking as much or for as long.

One reason it is so hard for people to stop is that a pack-a-day smoker puffs at least 50,000 times a year. That's a lot of individual nicotine "hits" reinforcing the smoking behavior. A variety of behavioral treatment approaches are available to assist smokers who want to quit, and hundreds of research articles have been published on them. Although most of these programs are able to get almost everyone to quit for a few days, by six months 70 to 80 percent of participants are smoking again.

If nicotine is the critical thing, why not provide nicotine without the tars and carbon monoxide? Prescription nicotine chewing gum became available in 1984, after carefully controlled studies showed it to be a useful adjunct to smoking cessation programs. This gum is now available over the counter. In 1991,

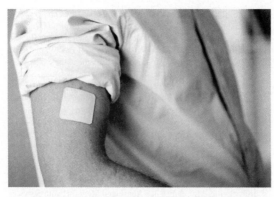

Nicotine replacement therapy—in the form of gum, patch, lozenge, inhaler, or nasal spray—helps some smokers quit.
©Stockdisc/PunchStock RF

several companies marketed nicotine skin patches that allow slow release of nicotine to be absorbed through the wearer's skin. Nicotine lozenges are now available over the counter, and smokers can also get a prescription for a nicotine inhaler or nasal spray. Also, the prescription drug bupropion (Zyban) has been shown to help many people.

In 2006, the FDA approved varenicline (Chantix), a nicotine partial-agonist drug. Then in 2009, the FDA required both Chantix and Zyban to include black box warnings about the chances of changes in behavior, depressed mood, hostility, and suicidal thoughts. While some have joked that these are possibly just the symptoms associated with quitting cigarettes, the number of serious complaints from users of these products is a real concern, and the FDA is requiring the companies to conduct careful clinical trials to determine how great these risks are.

There is money to be made helping people quit smoking, especially if it can apparently be done painlessly with a substitute. The controlled studies done to demonstrate the usefulness of gum or skin patches have been carried out under fairly strict conditions, with a prescribed quitting period, several visits to the clinic to assess progress, and the usual trappings of a clinical research study, often including the collection of saliva or other samples to detect tobacco use. That's a far cry from buying nicotine gum and a patch off the shelf, with no plan for quitting, no follow-up interviews, and no

monitoring. No wonder that some people have found themselves, despite warnings, wearing a nicotine patch and smoking at the same time.

Is there an effective nondrug program for quitting smoking? Yes and no. The effect of any program varies—some people do very well, some very poorly—and if one program won't work for an individual, maybe another one will. Combining counseling and pharmacological treatments increases the odds of quitting.[23] We don't yet know which program will be best for any particular individual. If you want to stop smoking, keep trying programs; odds are you'll find one that works—eventually.

Summary

- Tobacco was introduced to Europe and the East after Columbus's voyage to the Americas.

- As with most other "new" drugs, Europeans at first rejected tobacco, and then its use slowly spread.

- The predominant style of tobacco use went from pipes to snuff to chewing to cigars to cigarettes.

- The typical modern cigarette is about half as strong in tar and nicotine content as a cigarette of 50 years ago.

- Cigarette smoking has declined considerably since the 1960s, but about 20 percent of young people still become regular smokers.

- The use of smokeless tobacco increased during the 1980s, causing concerns about increases in oral cancer.

- Although tobacco continues to be an important economic factor in American society, it is also responsible for more annual deaths than all other drugs combined, including alcohol.

- Cigarette smoking is clearly linked to increased risk of heart disease, lung and other cancers, emphysema, and stroke.

emphysema (em fah *see* mah): a chronic lung disease characterized by difficulty breathing and shortness of breath.

- There is increased concern about the health consequences of secondhand smoke.

- Smoking cessation leads to immediate improvements in mortality statistics, and new products, including different types of nicotine replacement therapy, are being widely used by those who wish to quit.

Review Questions

1. Why was nicotine named after Jean Nicot?
2. Which was the desired species of tobacco that saved the English colonies in Virginia?
3. What techniques have been used to produce "safer" cigarettes?
4. About what proportion of 18- to 25-year-olds are smokers in the United States?
5. What is the significance of tobacco-specific nitrosamines?
6. What are the major causes of death associated with cigarette smoking?
7. What evidence is there that passive smoking can harm nonsmokers?
8. What are the effects of smoking during pregnancy?
9. Nicotine acts through which neurotransmitter in the brain? How does it interact with this neurotransmitter?
10. What is the evidence as to why cigarette smoking produces such strong dependence?

References

1. Norton, M. *Sacred Gifts, Profane Pleasures.* Ithaca, NY: Cornell University Press, 2008.
2. Centers for Disease Control and Prevention. "Smoking in Top-Grossing Movies—United States, 2010." *Morbidity and Mortality Weekly Report*, July 15, 2011.
3. Vaughn, W. Quoted in Dunphy, E. B. "Alcohol and Tobacco Amblyopia: A Historical Survey." *American Journal of Ophthalmology* 68 (1969), p. 573.
4. Burns, E. *The Smoke of the Gods.* Philadelphia: Temple University Press, 2007.
5. Lorand, A. *Life Shortening Habits and Rejuvenation.* Philadelphia: F. A. Davis, 1927.
6. Eaglin, J. *The CC Cough-fin Brand Cigarettes.* Cincinnati: Raisbeck, 1931.
7. U.S. Institute of Medicine. *Ending the Tobacco Problem.* Washington, DC: The National Academies Press, 2007.
8. Sherer, G. "Smoking Behavior and Compensation: A Review of the Literature." *Psychopharmacology* 145 (1999), pp. 1–20.
9. Fairchild, A., and J. Colgrove. "Out of the Ashes: The Life, Death, and Rebirth of the "Safer" Cigarette in the United States." *American Journal of Public Health* 94 (2004), pp. 192–205.
10. Miech, R. A., L. D. Johnston, P. M. O'Malley, J. G. Bachman, and J. E. Schulenberg. *Monitoring the Future National Survey Results on Drug Use, 1975–2015: Volume I, Secondary School Students.* Ann Arbor: Institute for Social Research, The University of Michigan, 2016. Available at http://monitoringthefuture.org/pubs.html#monographs
11. Center for Behavioral Health Statistics and Quality. *2015 National Survey on Drug Use and Health: Detailed Tables.* Rockville, MD: Substance Abuse and Mental Health Services Administration, 2016. Available at www.samhsa.gov/data
12. Johnston, L. D., P. M. O'Malley, J. G. Bachman, J. E. Schulenberg, and R. A. Miech. *Monitoring the Future National Survey Results on Drug Use, 1975–2015: Volume 2, College Students and Adults Ages 19–55.* Ann Arbor: Institute for Social Research, The University of Michigan, 2016. Available at http://monitoringthefuture.org/pubs.html#monographs
13. *The Health Consequences of Using Smokeless Tobacco: A Report of the Advisory Committee to the Surgeon General.* (NIH Pub. No. 86-2874). Washington, DC: U.S. Government Printing Office, 1986.
14. "Smoke and Mirrors: How Cigarette Makers Keep Health Question Open Year after Year." *Wall Street Journal,* February 11, 1993.
15. U.S. Department of Health and Human Services. *The Health Consequences of Smoking: 50 Years of Progress. A Report of the Surgeon General.* Atlanta, GA: U.S. Department of Health and Human Services, Centers for Disease Control and Prevention, National Center for Chronic Disease Prevention and Health Promotion, Office on Smoking and Health, 2014.
16. World Health Organization. *WHO Report on the Global Tobacco Epidemic.* Geneva, Switzerland: WHO, 2009.
17. Lacy, R. T., R. W. Brown, A. J. Morgan, C. F. Mactutus, and S. B. Harrod. "Intravenous Prenatal Nicotine Exposure Alters METH-Induced Hyperactivity, Conditioned Hyperactivity, and BDNF in Adult Rat Offspring." *Developmental Neuroscience* 38 (2016), pp. 171–85.
18. Geha, P. Y., and others. "Altered Hypothalamic Response to Food in Smokers." *American Journal of Clinical Nutrition* 97 (2013), pp. 15–22.
19. Haberstick, B. C., and others. "Dizziness and the Genetic Influences on Subjective Experiences to Initial Cigarette Use." *Addiction* 106 (2011), pp. 391–99.
20. U.S. Department of Health and Human Services. *The Health Consequences of Smoking: Nicotine Addiction, a Report of the Surgeon General.* DHHS Pub. No. (CDC) 88-8406. Washington, DC: U.S. Government Printing Office, 1988.
21. Kessler, D. *A Question of Intent.* New York: Public Affairs, 2001, pp. 113–39.
22. Whitten, L. "Studies Link Family of Genes to Nicotine Addiction." *NIDA Notes* 22 (2009). Available at http://www.drugabuse.gov/NIDA_notes.
23. Lamburg, L. "Patients Need More Help to Stop Smoking." *Journal of the American Medical Association* 292 (2004), p. 1286.

Check Yourself

Test Your Tobacco Awareness

Whether you smoke, chew, or don't use tobacco at all, tobacco is an important economic and political issue in virtually every community and in every country. See how well you do with these questions about tobacco's place in the United States and the world:

1. About what proportion of adults in the United States are smokers?
2. About how many Americans die each day from tobacco-related illnesses?
3. What two tobacco-related health problems account for most deaths among smokers?
4. Which country produces the most cigarettes?

Answers

1. About 25 percent (Most people tend to overestimate the proportion of smokers, which makes smoking seem to be a typical behavior, when in fact, it's not.)
2. About 1,200 per day, representing about 20 percent of all deaths in the United States.
3. Smoking-related heart disease kills about 140,000 in the United States each year, along with about 160,000 smoking-related lung cancer deaths.
4. China produces about 30 percent of the world's cigarettes, with the United States a distant second. Most of the cigarettes produced in China are consumed in China.

11 Caffeine

©Ingram Publishing/SuperStock RF

Caffeine: The World's Most Common Psychostimulant

On a daily basis, more people use caffeine than any other psychoactive drug. Many use it regularly, and there is evidence for dependence and some evidence that regular use can interfere with the very activities people believe that it helps them with. It is now so domesticated that most modern kitchens contain a specialized device for extracting the chemical from plant products (a coffeemaker), but Western societies were not always so accepting of this drug.

Coffee

The legends surrounding the origin of coffee are at least geographically correct. The best one concerns an Ethiopian goatherd named Kaldi who couldn't

Objectives

When you have finished this chapter, you should be able to:

- Describe the early history of coffee, tea, and chocolate use.

- Name the xanthines found in coffee, tea, and chocolate.

- Describe the methods for removing caffeine from coffee.

- Name the one plant from which hundreds of varieties of tea are produced.

- Distinguish among the terms cacao, cocoa, and coca.

- Describe the origin of Coca-Cola in relation to cocaine, caffeine, and FDA regulations.

- Explain the caffeine content of "energy drinks" in relation to colas and coffee.

- Describe the caffeine content of drugs like NoDoz and Vivarin.

- Explain how caffeine exerts its actions on the brain.

- Describe the time course of caffeine's effects after ingestion.

- Describe symptoms of caffeine withdrawal.

- Discuss the circumstances in which caffeine appears to enhance mental performance and those in which it does not.

- Describe the concerns about high caffeine consumption during pregnancy.

understand why his goats were bounding around the hillside so playfully. One day he followed them up the mountain and ate some of the red berries the goats were munching. "The results were amazing. Kaldi became a happy goatherd. Whenever his goats danced, he danced and whirled and leaped and rolled about on the ground." Kaldi had taken the first human coffee trip! A holy man took in the scene, and "that night he danced with Kaldi and the goats." Whatever the actual origin of human coffee use, the practice spread to Egypt and other Arabic countries by the 1400s, throughout the Middle East by the 1500s, and into Europe in the 1600s.

Coffeehouses began appearing in England (1650) and France (1671), and a new era began. Coffeehouses were all things to all people: a place to relax, to learn the news of the day, to seal bargains, and to plot. This last possibility made Charles II of England so nervous that he outlawed coffeehouses, labeling them "hotbeds of seditious talk and slanderous attacks upon persons in high stations." In only 11 days the ruling was withdrawn, and the coffeehouses developed into the "penny universities" of the early 18th century. For a penny a cup people could listen to and learn from most of the great literary and political figures of the period. Lloyds of London, an insurance house, started in Edward Lloyd's coffeehouse around 1700. Women in England argued against the use of coffee in a 1674 pamphlet titled "The Women's Petition Against Coffee, representing to public consideration the grand inconveniences accruing to their sex from the excessive use of the drying and enfeebling liquor." The women claimed men used too much coffee, and as a result the men were as "unfruitful as those *Desarts* whence that unhappy *Berry* is said to be brought." The women were *really* unhappy, and the pamphlet continued:

> Our Countrymens pallates are become as *Fanatical* as their Brains; how else is't possible they should *Apostatize* from the good old primitive way of Ale-drinking, to run a *Whoreing* after such variety of distructive Foreign Liquors, to trifle away their time, scald their *Chops,* and spend their *Money,* all for a little *base, black, thick, nasty bitter stinking, nauseous* Puddle water.[1]

Some men probably sat long hours in one of the many coffeehouses composing "The Men's Answer

Younger coffee drinkers are a growing customer base for espresso bars and coffeehouses. ©Ryan McVay/Getty Images RF

to the Women's Petition Against Coffee," which said in part:

> Why must innocent COFFEE be the object of your Spleen? That harmless and healing Liquor, which Indulgent Providence first sent amongst us.... Tis not this incomparable fettle Brain that shortens Natures standard, or makes us less Active in the Sports of Venus, and we wonder you should take these Exceptions.[1]

Across the Atlantic, coffee drinking increased in the English colonies, although tea was still preferred. Cheaper and more available than coffee, tea had everything, including, beginning in 1765, a 3-pence-a-pound tax on its importation.

The British Act that taxed tea helped fan the fire that lit the musket that fired the shot heard around the world. That story is better told in connection with tea, but the final outcome was that to be a tea drinker was to be a Tory, so coffee became the new country's national drink.

Coffee use expanded as the West was won, and per-capita consumption increased steadily in the early 1900s. Some experts became worried about the increase, which some believed was caused by the widespread prohibition of alcohol.

But even after Prohibition went away, coffee consumption continued to rise. In 1946, annual per-capita coffee consumption reached an all-time high of 20 pounds. Americans now drink about half that much coffee per year. The wide variety of soft

Drugs in Depth

Caffeine Shampoo for Hair Loss?

Caffeine has been added to a lot of products, but one of the strangest has to be shampoo. The idea is not to wake you up by absorbing caffeine through the scalp, but to stimulate hair growth for those people who are concerned about hair loss or who want thicker hair. A search on the Internet will find several caffeine-containing shampoos, most claiming to be a "hair-loss formula." But do they actually work?

The FDA has approved only two medications for hair loss: minoxidil (Rogaine) and finasteride (Propecia). But there is some evidence that caffeine might be helpful. If hair follicles are removed from the scalp and maintained in a test tube, the addition of caffeine directly into the test tube does increase several measures of hair growth.[2] However, that doesn't necessarily mean that including some amount of caffeine in a shampoo will have the same effect on the scalp itself. So, until further research provides a more definitive answer, we will have to be content with not knowing.

Box icon credit: ©Ingram Publishing/SuperStock RF

drinks, energy drinks, and bottled water have apparently replaced coffee as our most popular nonalcoholic beverages.

If the national drink is not as national as it once was, neither is it as simple. Kaldi and his friends were content to simply munch on the coffee beans or put them in hot water. Somewhere in the dark past, the Middle East discovered that roasting the green coffee bean improved the flavor, aroma, and color of the drink made from the bean. For years housewives, storekeepers, and coffeehouse owners bought the green bean, then roasted and ground it just before use. Commercial roasting started in 1790 in New York City, and the process gradually spread through the country. However, although the green bean can be stored indefinitely, the roasted bean deteriorates seriously within a month. Ground coffee can be maintained at its peak level in the home only for a week or two, and then only if it is in a closed container and refrigerated. Vacuum packing of ground coffee was introduced in 1900, a process that maintains the quality until the seal is broken.

Coffee growing spread worldwide when the Dutch began cultivation in the East Indies in 1696. Latin America had an ideal climate for coffee growing, and with the world's greatest coffee-drinking nation just several thousand miles up the road, it became the world's largest producer. Different varieties of the coffee tree and different growing and

processing conditions provide many opportunities for varying the characteristics of coffee.

Green coffee beans are roasted to improve the color and flavor of the drink made from the beans. ©Thanyani Srisombut/ 123RF RF *(top)*, ©Jules Frazier/Getty Images RF *(bottom)*

Although there are many bean-producing shrubs in the genus *caffea,* virtually all coffee is made from two species: *caffea Arabica* and *caffea robusta. Arabica* beans have a milder flavor, take longer to develop after planting, and require a near-tropical climate to grow properly. They are therefore more expensive and more desirable for most purposes. *Robusta* beans have a stronger and more bitter flavor and a higher caffeine content, and are used primarily in less-expensive blends and to make instant coffee. In some countries, such as Colombia, only *Arabica* beans are grown, whereas Brazil, the world's largest coffee producer, produces both kinds. According to the U.S. Department of Agriculture (USDA.gov), in 2016 Brazil produced twice as much coffee as Vietnam, the second-biggest coffee growing country. Colombia and Indonesia were next, followed by Mexico and Central America. You can see that coffee is now grown in tropical climates around the globe. As for the over 3 billion pounds of coffee imported to the United States in 2016, Brazil supplied the most, followed by Colombia and Vietnam.

Beginning in the early 1970s, health-conscious Americans began to drink more decaffeinated coffee and less regular coffee. There are several ways of removing caffeine from the coffee bean. In the process used by most American companies, the unroasted beans are soaked in an organic solvent, raising concerns about residues of the solvent remaining in the coffee. The most widely used solvent has been methylene chloride, and studies have shown that high doses of that solvent can cause cancer in laboratory mice. In 1985, the FDA banned the use of methylene chloride in hair sprays, which can be inhaled during use, but allowed the solvent to be used in decaffeination as long as residues did not exceed 10 parts per million. Because the solvent residue evaporates during roasting, decaffeinated coffees contain considerably lower amounts than that, so the assumption is that the risk is minimal. The Swiss water process, which is not used on a large commercial scale in the United States, removes more of the coffee's flavor. The caffeine that is taken out of the coffee is used mostly in soft drinks. One of the largest decaffeinating companies is owned by Coca-Cola.

Today's supermarket shelves are filled with an amazing variety of products derived from this simple bean—pure Colombian, French roast, decaf, half-caf, flavored coffees, instants, mixes, and even cold coffee beverages. The competition for the consumer's coffee dollar has never been greater, it seems. And Americans are lining up in record numbers at espresso bars to buy cappuccinos, lattes, and other exotic-sounding mixtures of strong coffee, milk, and flavorings. The number of these specialty coffee shops increased from fewer than 200 in 1989 to about 24,000 in 2016.[3] They are found in small towns, in shopping malls, and on practically every corner in cities.

Tea

Tea and coffee are not like day and night, but their differences are reflected in the legends surrounding their origins. The bouncing goatherd of Arabia suggests that coffee is a boisterous, blue-collar drink. Tea is a different story: much softer, quieter, more delicate. According to one legend, Daruma, the founder of Zen Buddhism, fell asleep one day while meditating. Resolving that it would never happen again, he cut off both eyelids. From the spot where his eyelids touched the earth grew a new plant. From its leaves a brew could be made that would keep a person awake. Appropriately, the tea tree,

Specialty coffee drinks are expected to continue to gain popularity. ©Limpido/Getty Images RF

Thea sinensis (now classed as *Camellia sinensis*), is an evergreen, and *sinensis* is the Latin word for "Chinese."

The first report of tea that seems reliable is in a Chinese manuscript from around AD 350, when it was primarily seen as a medicinal plant. The non-medical use of tea is suggested by an AD 780 book on the cultivation of tea, but the real proof that it was in wide use in China is that a tax was levied on it in the same year. Before this time, Buddhist monks had carried the cultivation and use of tea to Japan.

Europe had to wait eight centuries to savor the herb that was "good for tumors or abscesses that come from the head, or for ailments of the bladder... it quenches thirst. It lessens the desire for sleep. It gladdens and cheers the heart." The first European record of tea, in 1559, says, "One or two cups of this decoction taken on an empty stomach removes fever, headache, stomachache, pain in the side or in the joints...." Fifty years later, in 1610, the Dutch delivered the first tea to the continent of Europe.

An event that occurred 10 years before had tremendous impact on the history of the world and on present patterns of drug use. In 1600, the English East India Company was formed, and Queen Elizabeth gave the company a monopoly on everything

Most tea is grown in Sri Lanka, India, and Indonesia. The leaves are harvested by hand, with only the top few leaves of new growth harvested every 6–10 days. ©Chayapon Bootboonneam/123RF RF

from the east coast of Africa across the Pacific to the west coast of South America. The English East India Company concentrated on importing spices, so the first tea was taken to England by the Dutch. As the market for tea increased, the English East India Company expanded its imports of tea from China. Coffee had arrived first, so most tea was sold in coffeehouses. Even as tea's use as a popular social drink expanded in Europe, there were some prophets of doom. A 1635 publication by a physician claimed that, at the very least, using tea would speed the death of those over 40 years old. The use of tea was not slowed, however, and by 1657 tea was being sold to the public in England. This was no more than 10 years after the English had developed the present word for it: *tea.* Although spelled *tea,* it was pronounced tay until the 19th century. Before this period the Chinese name *ch'a* had been used, anglicized to either *chia* or *chaw.*

With the patrons of taverns off at coffeehouses living it up with tea, coffee, and chocolate, tax revenues from alcoholic beverages declined. To offset this loss, coffeehouses were licensed, and a tax of eight pence was levied on each gallon of tea and chocolate sold. Britain banned Dutch imports of tea in 1669, which gave the English East India Company a monopoly. Profit from the China tea trade colonized India, brought about the Opium Wars between China and Britain, and induced the English to switch from coffee to tea. In the last half of the 18th century, the East India Company conducted a "Drink Tea" campaign unlike anything ever seen. Advertising, low cost on tea, and high taxes on alcohol made Britain a nation of tea drinkers.

That same profit motive led to the American Revolution. Because the English East India Company had a monopoly on importing tea to England and thence to the American colonies, the British government imposed high duties on tea when it was taken from warehouses and offered for sale. But, as frequently happens, when taxes went up, smuggling increased. Eventually, more smuggled tea than legal tea was being consumed in Britain. The drop in legal tea sales filled the tea warehouses and put the East India Company in financial trouble.

The American colonies, ever loyal to the king, had become big tea drinkers, which helped the king and the East India Company stay solvent. The Stamp Act of 1765, which included a tax on tea, changed everything. Even though the Stamp Act was repealed in 1766, it was replaced by the Trade and Revenue Act of 1767, which did the same thing. These measures made the colonists unhappy over paying taxes they had not helped formulate (taxation without representation), and in 1767 this resulted in a general boycott on the consumption of English tea. Coffee use increased, but the primary increase was in the smuggling of tea. In 1773, Parliament gave the East India Company the right to sell tea in the American colonies without paying the tea taxes. The company was also allowed to sell the tea through its own agents, thus eliminating the profits of the merchants in the colonies.

Several boatloads of this tea, which would be sold cheaper than any before, sailed toward various ports in the colonies. The American merchants, who would not have made any profit on this tea, were the primary ones who rebelled at the cheap tea. Some ships were turned away from port, but the beginning of the end came with the 342 chests of tea that turned the Boston harbor into a teapot on the night of December 16, 1773.

The revolution in America and the colonists' rejection of tea helped tea sales in Great Britain— to be a tea drinker was to be loyal to the Crown. Although their use of coffee increases yearly and that of tea declines, the English are still tea drinkers. The annual per-capita consumption of tea in the United Kingdom is about 4.5 pounds, second in the world only to Turkey. In comparison, Americans consume about one-half pound of tea per person per year.

Tea starts its life on a four- to five-foot bush high in the mountains of China, Sri Lanka, India, or Indonesia. Unpruned, the bush would grow into a 15- to 30-foot tree, which would be difficult to pluck, as picking tea leaves is called. The pluckers select only the bud-leaf and the first two leaves at each new growth.

The Boston Tea Party contributed to the English preference for tea over coffee. Source: Library of Congress Prints and Photographs Division [LC-USZ62-24071]

In one day a plucker will pluck enough leaves to make 10 pounds of tea as sold in the grocery store. Plucking is done every 6 to 10 days in warm weather as new growth develops on the many branches. The leaves are dried, rolled to crush the cells in the leaf, and placed in a cool, damp place for fermentation (oxidation) to occur. This oxidation turns the green leaves to a bright copper color. Nonoxidized leaves are packaged and sold as green tea, sales of which have seen large increases in recent years. Oxidized tea is called black tea and accounts for about 84 percent of the tea Americans consume. Oolong tea is greenish-brown, consisting of partially oxidized leaves.

Until 1904, the only choices available were sugar, cream, and lemon with your hot tea. At the Louisiana Purchase Exposition in St. Louis in 1904, iced tea was sold for the first time. It now accounts for 85 percent of all tea consumed in America. Tea lovers found 1904 to be a very good year. Fifteen hundred miles east of the fair, a New York City tea merchant decided to send out his samples in hand-sewn silk bags rather than tin containers. Back came the orders—send us tea, and send it in the same little bags you used to send the samples. From that inauspicious beginning evolved the modern tea bag machinery, which cuts the filter paper, weighs the tea, and attaches the tag—all this at a rate of 150 to 180 tea bags per minute.

Pound for pound, loose black tea contains a higher concentration of caffeine than coffee beans. However, because about 200 cups of tea can be

A wide variety of tea products is available—black, oolong, green, flavored, and herbal teas. A pound of dry tea leaves makes about 200 cups of tea. ©Spike Mafford/Getty Images RF

Chocolate

Now we come to the third legend, concerning the origin of the third xanthine-containing plant. Long before Columbus landed on San Salvador, Quetzalcoatl, Aztec god of the air, gave humans a gift from paradise: the chocolate tree. Linnaeus was to remember this legend when he named the cocoa tree *Theobroma*, "food of the gods." The Aztecs treated it as such, and the cacao bean was an important part of their economy, with the cacao bush being cultivated widely. Montezuma, emperor of Mexico in the early 16th century, is said to have consumed nothing other than 50 goblets of *chocolatl* every day. The *chocolatl*—from the Mayan words *choco* ("warm") and *latl* ("beverage")—was flavored with vanilla but was far from the chocolate of today. It was a thick liquid, like honey, that was sometimes frothy and had to be eaten with a spoon.

Cortez introduced sugarcane plantations to Mexico in the early 1520s and supported the

made from each pound of dry tea leaves, compared with 50 or 60 cups of coffee per pound, a typical cup of tea has less caffeine than a typical cup of coffee. The caffeine content of teas varies widely, depending on brand and the strength of the brew. Most teas have 40 to 60 mg of caffeine per cup.

The market has been flooded with a variety of tea products. Most tea is sold in tea bags these days, but instant teas, some containing flavorings and sweeteners, are popular for convenience. Flavored teas—which contain mint, spices, or other substances along with tea—offer other options. The biggest boom in recent years has been in so-called herbal teas, which mostly contain no real "tea." These teas are made up of mixtures of other plant leaves and flowers for both flavor and color and have become quite popular among people who avoid caffeine.

Although tea contains another chemical that derived its name from the tea plant, **theophylline** ("divine leaf") is present only in very small, non-pharmacological amounts in the beverage. Theophylline is very effective at relaxing the bronchial passages and is prescribed for use by asthmatics.

The genus of the chocolate (cacao) tree, *Theobroma*, is Latin for "food of the gods." ©Stephen Goodwin/123RF RF

> **theophylline (thee *off* a lin):** a xanthine found in tea.

Chocolate candy is made by mixing cocoa butter, sugar, and chocolate powder. ©Pixelstock/Alamy Stock Photo

bush. When he returned to Spain in 1528, Cortez carried with him cakes of processed cocoa. The cakes were eaten, as well as being ground up and mixed with water for a drink. Although chocolate was introduced to Europe almost a century before coffee and tea, its use spread very slowly. Primarily this was because the Spanish kept the method of preparing chocolate from the cacao bean a secret until the early 17th century. When knowledge of the technique spread, so did the use of chocolate.

During the 17th century, chocolate drinking reached all parts of Europe, primarily among the wealthy. Maria Theresa, wife of France's Louis XIV, had a "thing" about chocolate, and this furthered its use among the wealthy and fashionable. Gradually it became more of a social drink, and by the 1650s chocolate houses were open in England, although usually chocolate was sold alongside coffee and tea in the established coffeehouses.

In the early 18th century, health warnings were issued in England against the use of chocolate, but use expanded. Its use and importance are well reflected in a 1783 proposal in the U.S. Congress that the United States raise revenue by taxing chocolate as well as coffee, tea, liquor, sugar, molasses, and pepper.

Although the cultivation of chocolate never became a matter to fight over, it, too, has spread around the world. The New World plantations were almost destroyed by disease at the beginning of the 18th century, but cultivation had already begun in Asia, and today a large part of the crop comes from Africa.

Until 1828, all chocolate sold was a relatively indigestible substance obtained by grinding the cacao kernels after processing. The preparation had become more refined over the years, but it still followed the Aztec procedure of letting the pods dry in the sun, then roasting them before removing the husks to get to the kernel of the plant. The result of grinding the kernels is a thick liquid called chocolate liquor. This is baking chocolate. In 1828, a Dutch patent was issued for the manufacture of "chocolate powder" by removing about two-thirds of the fat from the chocolate liquor.

The fat that was removed, cocoa butter, became important when someone found that, if it was mixed with sugar and some of the chocolate powder, it could easily be formed into slabs or bars. In 1847, the first chocolate bars appeared, but it was not until 1876 that the Swiss made their contribution to the chocolate industry by inventing milk chocolate, which was first sold under the Nestlé label. By FDA standards, milk chocolate today must contain at least 12 percent milk solids, although better grades contain almost twice that amount.

The unique xanthine in chocolate is **theobromine.** Its physiological actions closely parallel those of caffeine, but it is much less potent in its effects on the central nervous system. The average cup of cocoa contains about 200 mg of theobromine but only 4 mg of caffeine. Table 11.1 compares the caffeine contents of various forms of coffee, tea, and chocolate.

Other Sources of Caffeine

Soft Drinks

The early history of cola drinks is not shrouded in the mists that veil the origins of the other xanthine drinks, so there is no problem in selecting the correct legend.

Table 11.1
Caffeine in Coffee, Tea, and Chocolate

Coffee	Serving Size	Caffeine (mg)
Starbucks Coffee	venti, 20 oz.	425
Dunkin' Donuts Coffee with Turbo Shot	large, 20 oz.	398
Starbucks Coffee	tall, 12 oz.	235
Starbucks Latte or Cappuccino	grande, 16 oz.	150
Maxwell House Ground Coffee	12 oz.	100–160
Keurig Coffee K-cup	8 oz.	75–150
Dunkin' Donuts, Panera or Starbucks Decaf Coffee	16 oz.	10–25

Tea	Serving Size	Caffeine (mg)
Starbucks Chai Latte	grande, 16 oz.	95
Black tea, brewed for 3 min	8 oz.	47
Green tea, brewed for 3 min	8 oz.	29
Arizona Iced Tea, black, all varieties	16 oz.	30

Chocolate	Serving Size	Caffeine (mg)
Starbucks Hot Chocolate	grande, 16 oz.	25
Hershey's Special Dark Cocolate Bar	1.5 oz.	20
Hershey's Milk Chocolate Bar	1.6 oz.	9

Source: Center for Science in the Public Interest, http://www.cspinet.org/new/cafchart.htm.

And that's what the story of Coca-Cola is: a true legend in our time. From a green nerve tonic in 1886 in Atlanta, Georgia, that did not sell well at all, Coca-Cola has grown into "the real thing," providing "the pause that refreshes," selling almost 3 billion cases a year and operating in more than 200 countries.

Dr. J. C. Pemberton's green nerve tonic in the late 1800s contained caramel, fruit flavoring, phosphoric acid, caffeine, and a secret mixture called Merchandise No. 5. The unique character of Coca-Cola and its later imitators comes from a blend of fruit flavors that makes it impossible to identify any of its parts. An early ad for Coca-Cola suggested its varied uses:

The "INTELLECTUAL BEVERAGE" and TEMPERANCE DRINK contains the valuable TONIC and NERVE STIMULANT properties of the Coca plant and Cola (or Kola) nuts, and makes not only a delicious, exhilarating, refreshing and invigorating Beverage, (dispensed from the soda water fountain or in other carbonated beverages), but a valuable Brain Tonic, and a cure for all nervous affections—SICK HEADACHE, NEURALGIA, HYSTERIA, MELANCHOLY, &c.[4]

theobromine (thee oh *broh* meen): a xanthine found in chocolate.

When introduced in the late 1800s, Coca-Cola was marketed as a tonic and named for two flavoring ingredients with tonic properties—coca leaves and cola (kola) nuts. The coca leaves used in Coca-Cola today have had the cocaine extracted. Source: Library of Congress Prints and Photographs Division [LC-USZC4-12222]

Coca-Cola was touted as "the new and popular fountain drink, containing the tonic properties of the wonderful coca plant and the famous cola nut." In 1903, the company admitted its beverage contained small amounts of cocaine, but soon after that it quietly removed all the cocaine; a government analysis of Coca-Cola in 1906 did not find any.

The name *Coca-Cola* was originally conceived to indicate the nature of its two ingredients with tonic properties: coca leaves and cola (kola) nuts. In 1909, the FDA seized a supply of Coca-Cola syrup and made two charges against the company. One was that the syrup was misbranded because it contained "no coca and little if any cola" and, second, that it contained an "added poisonous ingredient," caffeine.

Before a 1911 trial in Chattanooga, Tennessee, the company paid for research into the physiological effects of caffeine and, when all the information was in, the company won. The government appealed the decision. In 1916, the U.S. Supreme Court upheld the lower court by rejecting the charge of misbranding, stating that the company had repeatedly said that "certain extracts from the leaves of the coca shrub and the nut kernels of the cola tree were used for the purpose of obtaining a flavor" and that "the ingredients containing these extracts," with the cocaine eliminated, was called Merchandise No. 5. Today, coca leaves are imported by a pharmaceutical company in New Jersey. The cocaine is extracted for medical use and the decocainized leaves are shipped to the Coca-Cola plant in Atlanta, where Merchandise No. 5 is produced. A 1931 report indicated that Merchandise No. 5 contained an extract of three parts coca leaves and one part cola nuts, but to this day it remains a secret formula.

In 1981, the FDA changed its rules, so that a cola no longer has to contain caffeine. If it does contain caffeine, it may not be more than 0.02 percent, which is 0.2 mg/ml, or a little less than 6 mg per ounce. Some consumer and scientist groups believe that all cola manufacturers should indicate on the label the amount of caffeine the beverage contains. This has not happened, even though soft drinks, as with other food products, must now list nutrition information, such as calories, fat, sodium, and protein content.

Table 11.2 lists the caffeine content in a 12-ounce serving of popular soft drinks. Diet soft drinks, most now sweetened with aspartame, and caffeine-free colas are commanding a larger share of the market, but regular colas are still the single most popular type of soft drink. As with beers and some other products, the modern marketing strategy seems to be for each company to try to offer products of every type, in order to cover the market. Also as with beers, the large companies are buying up their competitors: In 2012, the Coca-Cola and PepsiCo companies represented more than 65 percent of total shipments. Coca-Cola Classic remains the most popular single brand, with almost 20 percent of the total market. Although more soft drinks are consumed in the United States than in any other

Table 11.2
Caffeine in Popular Soft Drinks and Energy Drinks

Soft Drinks	Serving Size	Caffeine (mg)
Pepsi Zero Sugar	12 oz.	69
Mountain Dew, regular or diet	12 oz.	54
Diet Coke	12 oz.	46
Dr Pepper	12 oz.	41
Pepsi	12 oz.	38
Coca-Cola, Coke Zero, Diet Pepsi	12 oz.	34
Barq's Root Beer	12 oz.	22

Energy Drinks	Serving Size	Caffeine (mg)
Bang Energy Drink	16 oz.	357
5-hour Energy	1.9 oz.	200
Monster Energy	16 oz.	160
Rockstar	16 oz.	160
Red Bull	8.3 oz.	80

Source: Center for Science in the Public Interest, http://www.cspinet.org/new/cafchart.htm.

campaign links its product with heavy-metal music and extreme skiing, snowboarding, and similar high-energy activities. The parent company, PepsiCo, said on the Mountain Dew website that "Doing the 'Dew' is like no other soft drink experience because of its daring, high-energy, high-intensity, active, extreme citrus taste," but most of its users know its caffeine content is higher than the major brands of colas (but still not high compared with brewed coffee). Then along came the Austrian sensation in a small can, Red Bull. Touted as an "energy drink," the main active ingredient in this expensive drink is caffeine, at 80 mg per 8.3-ounce can (still less than a cup of coffee). The original marketers seemed to be aiming the product at people who exercise and want to "build" their bodies by including some ingredients found in dietary supplements sold to athletes, such as the amino acid taurine. Although rumors abound about Red Bull, the product does not appear to have any unique properties, and there is no evidence that the ingredients besides caffeine and sugar have any

The main active ingredient in so-called energy drinks is caffeine. ©McGraw-Hill Education/Jill Braaten, photographer

country, per-capita consumption of soft drinks has declined a bit from its maximum of 50 gallons per-capita to about 45, due to competition from energy drinks and bottled water.

Energy Drinks

Some consumers have always preferred to obtain their caffeine from soft drinks instead of from coffee. This led to the development and promotion of Jolt cola, which had the maximum allowable caffeine content per ounce, or almost 72 mg in a 12-ounce can. This might be a lot for a soft drink, but it isn't a great deal when compared to 235 mg in a 12-ounce cup of Starbucks coffee. Mountain Dew's hugely successful television marketing

particular effect, either psychologically or in helping one to gain strength. Studies on combining energy drinks with alcohol indicate that any important interaction between the two is based on combining caffeine and alcohol.[5]

Much of the explosion in soft drink varieties has been aimed at this "high-energy" market. (The hype has been pretty high energy, even if the products are nothing special, urging consumers to "feed the rush," or "blow your mind" using the drink.) The list of Mountain Dew competitors includes Kick and Surge, while Red Bull imitators have names like Stallion, Whoopass, Adrenaline Rush, Monster, and Rockstar.

Over-the-Counter Drugs

Few people realize that many nonprescription drugs also include caffeine, some in quite large amounts. Table 11.3 lists the caffeine content of some of these drugs. Presumably many people who

buy "alertness tablets," such as NoDoz, are aware that they are buying caffeine. But many buyers of such things as Excedrin might not realize how much caffeine they are getting. Imagine the condition of someone who took a nonprescription water-loss pill and a headache tablet containing caffeine, who then drank a couple of cups of coffee.

Considering all the various sources of caffeine, it is estimated that 80 percent of Americans regularly use caffeine in some form, and that the average intake is 200 to 250 mg per day.[6] As with other psychoactive substances, this "average" takes in a wide range, with some users regularly consuming 1,000 mg or more each day.

Caffeine Pharmacology

Xanthines are the oldest stimulants known. *Xanthine* is a Greek word meaning "yellow," the color of the residue that remains after xanthines are heated with nitric acid until dry. The three xanthines of primary importance are caffeine, theophylline, and theobromine. These three chemicals are methylated xanthines and are closely related alkaloids. Most alkaloids are insoluble in water, but these are unique, because they are slightly water soluble.

These three xanthines have similar effects on the body. Caffeine has the greatest effect. Theobromine has almost no stimulant effect on the central nervous system and the skeletal muscles. Theophylline is the most potent, and caffeine the least potent, agent on the cardiovascular system. Caffeine, so named because it was isolated from coffee in 1820, has been the most extensively studied and, unless otherwise indicated, is the drug under discussion here.

Time Course

In humans, the absorption of caffeine is rapid after oral intake; peak blood levels are reached 30 minutes after ingestion. Although maximal CNS effects are not reached for about two hours, the onset of effects can begin within half an hour after intake. The half-life of caffeine in humans is about three hours, and no more than 10 percent is excreted unchanged.

Table 11.3
Caffeine in Nonprescription Drugs and Dietary Supplements

Stimulants	Dose	Caffeine (mg)
NoDoz	1 caplet	200
Vivarin	1 caplet	200

Analgesics	Dose	Caffeine (mg)
Exedrine Migraine	2 tablets	130
Midol Complete	2 caplets	120
Bayer Back & Body	2 caplets	65
Anacin	2 caplets	64

Weight Loss Supplement	Dose	Caffeine (mg)
Zantrex-3	2 capsules	300

Source: Center for Science in the Public Interest, http://www.cspinet.org/new/cafchart.htm.

Taking Sides

Caffeine Use Disorder?

As reviewed in Chapter 2, the American Psychiatric Association's DSM-5 lists the criteria for substance use disorder. During its development, the question arose as to whether caffeine should be included as one of these substances. In 1994, a group of researchers reported the cases of 16 individuals who they considered to meet the criteria for substance disorder under the previous version on the manual.[9]

Of 99 subjects who responded to newspaper notices asking for volunteers who believed they were psychologically or physically dependent on caffeine, 27 were asked to undergo further testing, which included a psychiatric interview to assess caffeine dependence. Sixteen of the 27 were diagnosed as having caffeine dependence. Of those 16, 11 agreed to participate in a double-blind caffeine withdrawal experiment. All were placed on a restricted diet during two two-day study periods and were given capsules to take at various times of the day to match their normal caffeine intake. During one of the two sessions, each volunteer was given caffeine, and during the other session the capsules contained a placebo. Neither the participants nor the interviewers were told on which session they were getting the caffeine. Withdrawal symptoms found during the placebo session included headaches, fatigue, decreased vigor, and increased depression scores. Several of the subjects were unable to go to or stay at work, went to bed several hours early, or needed their spouse to take over child-care responsibilities.

The DSM-5, published in 2013, includes this statement: "DSM-5 will not include caffeine use disorder, although research shows that as little as two or three cups of coffee can trigger a withdrawal marked by tiredness or sleepiness. There is sufficient evidence to support this as a condition, however, it is not yet clear to what extent it is a clinically significant disorder." This perhaps reflects the belief that in most cases a dependence on caffeine does not interfere greatly with one's ability to work, go to school, or maintain normal social relationships.

Box icon credit: ©Nova Development RF

Cross-tolerance exists among the methylated xanthines; loss of tolerance can take more than two months of abstinence. The tolerance, however, is low grade, and by increasing the dose two to four times an effect can be obtained even in the tolerant individual. There is less tolerance to the CNS stimulation effect of caffeine than to most of its other effects. The direct action on the kidneys, to increase urine output, and the increase of salivary flow do show tolerance.

Dependence on caffeine is real (see the Taking Sides box). People who are not coffee drinkers or who have been drinking only decaffeinated coffee often report unpleasant effects (nervousness, anxiety) after being given caffeinated coffee, but those who regularly consume caffeine report mostly pleasant mood states after drinking coffee. Various experiments have reported on the reinforcing properties of caffeine in regular coffee drinkers; one of the most clear-cut studies allowed patients on a research ward to choose between two coded instant coffees, identical except that one contained caffeine. Participants had to choose at the beginning of each day which coffee they would drink for the rest of that day. People who had been drinking caffeine-containing coffee before this experiment almost always chose the caffeine-containing coffee.[7] Thus, the reinforcing effect of caffeine probably contributes to psychological dependence.

There has long been clear evidence of physical dependence on caffeine as well. The most reliable withdrawal sign is a headache, which occurs an average of 18 to 19 hours after the most recent caffeine intake. Other symptoms include increased fatigue and decreased sense of vigor. These withdrawal symptoms are strongest during the first two

xanthines (*zan* theens): the class of chemicals to which caffeine belongs.

Drugs in Depth

The Caffeine Craze: Buying a Dream

Considerable mythology surrounds the supposed ability of caffeine to support sustained, high-level mental effort. For example, the famous mathematician Paul Erdos once said, "A mathematician is a device for turning coffee into theorems." This mythology of caffeine as brain fuel has been widely adopted by Americans. One result has been the proliferation of products containing caffeine. Besides coffee, tea, and energy drinks, it is now possible to buy caffeinated ice cream, gum, jelly beans, potato chips, jerky, Wired Waffles, and even a candy called Crackheads2, which enhances chocolate-covered espresso beans with added caffeine for a total of 600 mg per box.

One has to ask whether those people who believe they can't work effectively without their coffee are more dependent on the caffeine or on the idea that caffeine helps them work harder or smarter. The evidence reviewed in this textbook indicates that once a person has developed a tolerance to higher levels of daily caffeine consumption, the caffeine probably does little good. However, stopping use at that point will likely lead to a lack of energy and headaches, interfering with work production.

In this competitive world, we'd all like to think that there's a magic substance that could give us "smarts" and energy, and it's that mythical dream that helps sell everything from 5-Hour Energy to Crackheads2.

---

days of withdrawal, then decline over the next five or six days.[8]

Mechanism of Action

For years no one really knew the mechanism whereby the methylxanthines had their effects on the CNS. In the early 1980s, evidence was presented that caffeine and the other xanthines block the brain's receptors for a substance known as **adenosine,** which is a neurotransmitter or neuromodulator. Adenosine normally acts in several areas of the brain to produce behavioral sedation by inhibiting the release of other neurotransmitters. Caffeine's stimulant action results from blocking the receptors for this inhibitory effect. One possible therapeutic use of caffeine or other adenosine blockers could be in slowing neural degeneration in diseases such as Alzheimer's.[10]

Physiological Effects

The pharmacological effects on the CNS and the skeletal muscles are probably the basis for the wide use of caffeine-containing beverages. With two cups of coffee taken close together (about 200 mg of caffeine), the cortex is activated, the EEG shows an arousal pattern, and drowsiness and fatigue decrease. This CNS stimulation is also the basis for "coffee nerves," which can occur at low doses in sensitive individuals and in others when they have consumed large amounts of caffeine. In the absence of tolerance, even 200 mg will increase the time it takes to fall asleep and will cause sleep disturbances. There is a strong relationship between the mood-elevating effect of caffeine and the extent to which it will keep the individual awake.

Higher dose levels (about 500 mg) are needed to affect the autonomic centers of the brain, and heart rate and respiration can increase at this dose. The direct effect on the cardiovascular system is in opposition to the effects mediated by the autonomic centers. Caffeine acts directly on the vascular muscles to cause dilation, whereas stimulation of the autonomic centers results in constriction of blood vessels. Usually dilation occurs, but in the brain the blood vessels are constricted, and this constriction might be the basis for caffeine's ability to reduce migraine headaches.

People can develop dependence on caffeine and experience withdrawal symptoms such as headaches if they discontinue caffeine intake. ©Wavebreak Media Ltd/123RF RF

The opposing effects of caffeine, directly on the heart and indirectly through effects on the medulla, make it very difficult to predict the results of normal (i.e., less than 500 mg) caffeine intake. At higher levels, the heart rate increases, and continued use of large amounts of caffeine can produce an irregular heartbeat in some individuals.

The basal metabolic rate might be increased slightly (10 percent) in chronic caffeine users, because 500 mg has frequently been shown to have this effect. This action probably combines with the stimulant effects on skeletal muscles to increase physical work output and decrease fatigue after the use of caffeine.

Behavioral Effects

Stimulation A hundred years ago, French essayist Balzac spoke with feeling when describing the effects of coffee:

> It causes an admirable fever. It enters the brain like a bacchante. Upon its attack, imagination runs wild, bares itself, twists like a pythoness and in this paroxysm a poet enjoys the supreme possession of his faculties; but this is a drunkenness of thought as wine brings about a drunkenness of the body.[11]

The research data are not so uniformly positive—the effects of caffeine depend on the difficulty of the task, the time of day, and to a great extent how much caffeine the subject typically consumes. When regular users of high amounts of caffeine (more than 300 mg/day, the equivalent of three cups of brewed coffee) were tested on a variety of study-related mental tasks without caffeine, they performed more poorly than did users of low amounts, perhaps because of withdrawal effects. Although their performance was improved after being given caffeine, they still performed more poorly on several of the tasks than did users of low amounts. It seems as though the beneficial short-term effects can be offset by the effects of tolerance and dependence in regular users.[12] High consumption of either coffee or energy drinks among college students has been associated with lower academic performance.[13] It is not clear from these studies if students who are struggling use more caffeine to compensate, or if more caffeine use actually interferes with overall performance.

There is considerable evidence that 200 to 300 mg of caffeine will partially offset fatigue-induced decrement in the performance of motor tasks. Like the amphetamines, but to a much smaller degree, caffeine prolongs the amount of time an individual can perform physically exhausting work.

The primary behavioral effect of caffeine is stimulation, although high levels of caffeine consumption among college students have been associated with lower academic performance. ©Ryan McVay/Getty Images RF

adenosine (a _den_ o sen): an inhibitory neurotransmitter through which caffeine acts.

Drugs in Depth

Caffeine and Panic Attacks

Caffeine can precipitate full-blown *panic attacks* in some people. Panic attacks are not common but can be very debilitating for those who suffer them. They consist of sudden, irrational feelings of doom, sometimes accompanied by choking, sweating, heart palpitations, and other symptoms.

In one recent experiment, 61 percent of patients with a history of panic disorder experienced a panic attack after being given 480 mg of caffeine orally. Among the control subjects, none of whom had a history of panic or anxiety disorder, there were no panic attacks after the same dose of caffeine, and the placebo did not produce panic attacks in either group.[14]

The results are interesting from a scientific point of view because they reveal individual differences in susceptibility to panic. It is not clear whether the sensitivity to panic attacks reveals some biochemical differences among individuals that also renders them more susceptible to caffeine-induced panic, or whether people who have experienced panic attacks before more easily become panicky when they are stimulated by caffeine. The experiment may also have more immediate and practical implications in that, if a person does experience a panic attack, caffeine consumption should be looked at as a possible trigger.

Headache Caffeine's vasoconstrictive effects are considered to be responsible for the drug's ability to relieve migraine headaches. However, a study of nonmigraine headache pain found that caffeine reduced headache pain, even in individuals who normally consumed little or no caffeine (in other words, not only headaches resulting from caffeine withdrawal).[15] As for migraine headaches, in 1998, the FDA allowed the relabeling of extra-strength Excedrine, which contains 65 mg caffeine, for over-the-counter use as "Excedrine Migraine."

Hyperactivity Many studies have looked at the effect of caffeine on the behavior of children

diagnosed with attention-deficit/hyperactivity disorder, and the results have been inconsistent. There is some indication that relatively high doses of caffeine may decrease hyperactivity, though not as well as methylphenidate[16] (see Chapter 6).

Sobering Up It has long been thought that coffee can help a drinker to "sober up," but little evidence supports the value of this. Caffeine will not lower blood alcohol concentration, but it might arouse the drinker. As they say—put coffee in a sleepy drunk and you get a more awake drunk. However, that awake drunk will still be uncoordinated, have slowed reaction times, and should not be driving a car or engaging in any other dangerous activity.

Causes for Concern

Because caffeine is probably the most widely used psychoactive drug in the world (it's acceptable to those in most Judeo-Christian as well as Islamic traditions), it is understandable that it would elicit both good and bad reports. Although there is not yet clear evidence that moderate caffeine consumption is dangerous, the scientific literature has investigated the possible effects of caffeine in cancer, benign breast disease, reproduction, and heart disease. Part of the problem in knowing for certain about some of these things is that epidemiological research on caffeine consumption is difficult to do well, because of the many sources of caffeine and the variability of caffeine content in coffee. Coffee drinkers also tend to smoke more, for example, so the statistics have to correct for smoking behavior.

Cancer

In the early 1980s, an increased risk of pancreatic cancers was reported among coffee drinkers. However, studies since then have criticized procedural flaws in that report and have found no evidence of such a link. The 1984 American Cancer Society nutritional guidelines indicated there is no reason to consider caffeine a risk factor in human cancer.

Reproductive Effects

Although studies in pregnant mice have indicated that large doses of caffeine can produce skeletal abnormalities in the pups, studies on humans have not found a relationship between caffeine and birth defects. However, studies do strongly suggest that consumption of more than 300 mg of caffeine per day by a woman can reduce her chances of becoming pregnant, increase the chances of spontaneous abortion (miscarriage), and slow the growth of the fetus so that the baby weighs less than normal at birth.[17] The most controversial of these findings has been the reported increase in spontaneous abortion, which is found in some studies, but not in others. The best advice for a woman who wants to become pregnant, stay pregnant, and produce a strong, healthy baby is to avoid caffeine, alcohol, tobacco, and any other drug that is not absolutely necessary for her health.

Heart Disease

There are many reasons for believing that caffeine might increase the risk of heart attacks, including the fact that it increases heart rate and blood pressure. Until recently, about as many studies found no relationship between caffeine use and heart attacks as did studies that found such a relationship. One interesting report used an unusual approach. Rather than ask people who had just had heart attacks about their prior caffeine consumption and compare them with people who were hospitalized for another ailment (the typical retrospective study), this study began in 1948 to track male medical students enrolled in the Johns Hopkins Medical School.[18] More than 1,000 of these students were followed for 20 years or more after graduation and were periodically asked about various habits, including drinking, smoking, and coffee consumption. Thus, this was a prospective study, to see which of these habits might predict future health problems. Those who drank five or more cups per day were about 2.5 times as likely as nondrinkers to suffer from coronary heart disease. However, there is also some evidence that consuming small amounts of coffee can actually reduce the risk of heart attack. Therefore, as with alcohol, the relationship between coffee drinking and this important health risk is complex. A recent review indicated that moderate caffeine intake (two to three cups per day) may reduce the risk of type 2 diabetes and obesity, which increase cardiovascular risk. Overall, such moderate use seems to have neutral or even slightly beneficial effects on overall cardiac health.[19]

The latest research, then, says that two or three cups of coffee per day is OK, but four or five (or more!) increases the risk of heart attack. This is of special concern to those with other risk factors (e.g., smoking, family history of heart disease, obesity, high blood pressure, and high cholesterol levels).

Caffeinism

Caffeine is not terribly toxic, and overdose deaths are extremely rare. An estimated 10 g (equivalent to 100 cups of coffee) would be required to cause death from caffeine taken by mouth. Death is produced by convulsions, which lead to respiratory arrest.

However, **caffeinism** (excessive use of caffeine) can cause a variety of unpleasant symptoms, and because of caffeine's domesticated social status it might be overlooked as the cause. For example, nervousness, irritability, tremulousness, muscle twitching, insomnia, flushed appearance, and elevated temperature can all result from excessive caffeine use. There can also be palpitations, heart arrhythmias, and gastrointestinal disturbances. In several cases in which serious disease has been suspected, the symptoms have miraculously improved when coffee was restricted.

caffeinism: excessive use of caffeine.

Summary

- The ancient plants coffee, tea, and cacao contain caffeine and two related xanthines.

- Caffeine is also contained in soft drinks and nonprescription medicines.

- Caffeine has a longer-lasting effect than many people realize.

- Caffeine exerts a stimulating action in several brain regions by blocking inhibitory receptors for adenosine.

- In regular caffeine users, headache, fatigue, or depression can develop if caffeine use is stopped.

- Caffeine is capable of reversing the effects of fatigue on both mental and physical tasks, but it might not be able to improve the performance of a well-rested individual, particularly on complex tasks.

- Heavy caffeine use during pregnancy is not advisable.

- Daily use of large amounts of caffeine increases the risk of heart attack.

- Excessive caffeine consumption, referred to as caffeinism, can produce a panic reaction.

Review Questions

1. What role did the American Revolution and alcohol prohibition play in influencing American coffee consumption?
2. What are the differences among black tea, green tea, and oolong?
3. What are the two xanthines contained in tea and chocolate, besides caffeine?
4. Rank the caffeine content of a cup of brewed coffee, a cup of tea, a chocolate bar, and a 12-ounce serving of Coca-Cola.
5. How does caffeine interact with adenosine receptors?
6. What are some of the behavioral and physiological effects of excessive caffeine consumption?
7. Describe the effects of caffeine on migraine headaches, caffeine-withdrawal headaches, and other headaches.
8. What are the typical symptoms associated with caffeine withdrawal?
9. What are three possible ways in which caffeine use by a woman might interfere with reproduction?
10. What is the relationship between caffeine and panic attacks?

References

1. Meyer, H. *Old English Coffee Houses.* Emmaus, PA: Rodale Press, 1954.
2. Fischer, T. W., E. Herczeg-Liztes, W. Funk, D. Zillikens, T. Biro, and R. Paus. "Differential Effects of Caffeine on Hair Shaft Elongation, Matrix and Outer Root Sheath Keratinocyte Proliferation, and Transforming Growth Factor-β/Insulin-like Growth Factor-1-Mediated Regulation of the Hair Cycle in Male and Female Human Hair Follicle." *British Journal of Pharmacology,* 171 (2014), pp. 1031–43.
3. First Research Industry Profile: Coffee Shops. http://www.firstresearch.com/industry-research/Coffee-Shops.html.
4. Huisking, C. L. *Herbs to Hormones.* Essex, CT: Pequot Press, 1968.
5. Ferré, S., and M. C. O'Brien. "Alcohol and Caffeine: The Perfect Storm." *Journal of Caffeine Research* 1 (2011), pp. 153–62.
6. Patton, C., and D. Beer. "Caffeine: The Forgotten Variable." *International Journal of Psychiatry in Clinical Practice* 5 (2001), pp. 231–36.
7. Griffiths, R. R., and others. "Human Coffee Drinking: Reinforcing and Physical Dependence Producing Effects of Caffeine." *Journal of Pharmacology and Experimental Therapeutics* 239 (1986), pp. 416–25.
8. Juliano, L. M., and others. "Development of the Caffeine Withdrawal Symptom Questionnaire: Caffeine Withdrawal Symptoms Cluster into Seven Factors." *Drug and Alcohol Dependence* 124 (2012), pp. 229–34.
9. Juliano, L. M., and R. R. Griffiths. "A Critical Review of Caffeine Withdrawal: Empirical Validation of Symptoms and Signs, Incidence, Severity, and Associated Features." *Psychopharmacology* 176 (2004), pp. 1–29.
10. Ribeiro, J. A. and A. M. Sebastiao. "Caffeine and Adenosine." *Journal of Alzheimer's Disease* 20 suppl. (2013) pp. 3–15.
11. Mickel, E. J. *The Artificial Paradises in French Literature.* Chapel Hill, NC: University of North Carolina Press, 1969.
12. Mitchell, P. J., and J. R. Redman. "Effects of Caffeine, Time of Day, and User History on Study-Related Performance." *Psychopharmacology (Berl)* 109 (1992), p. 121.
13. Champlin, S. E., K. E. Pasch, and C. L. Perry. "Is the Consumption of Energy Drinks Associated with Academic

Achievement among College Students?" *Journal of Primary Prevention* 37 (2016), pp. 345–59.

14. Nardi, A. E., and others. "Panic Disorder and Social Anxiety Disorder Subtypes in a Caffeine Challenge Test." *Psychiatry Research* 169 (2008), pp. 149–53.

15. Ward, N., and others. "The Analgesic Effects of Caffeine in Headache." *Pain* 44 (1991), pp. 151–55.

16. Leon, M. R. "Effects of Caffeine on Cognitive, Psychomotor, and Affective Performance of Children with Attention Deficit/ Hyperactivity Disorder." *Journal of Attention Disorders* 4 (2000), pp. 27–47.

17. "Statement on the Reproductive Effects of Caffeine." UK Food Standards Agency, 2001. Retrieved from www.food.gov. uk/science/ouradvisors/toxicity/statements/cotstatements 2001/caffeine.

18. LaCroix, A. Z., and others. "Coffee Consumption and the Incidence of Coronary Heart Disease." *New England Journal of Medicine* 315 (1986), pp. 977–82.

19. O'Keefe, J. H., and others. "Effects of Habitual Coffee Consumption on Cardiometabolic Disease, Cardiovascular Health, and All-Cause Mortality. *Journal of American College of Cardiology* 62 (2013), pp. 1043–51.

Check Yourself

How Much Caffeine Do You Consume?

How many different products do you use that contain caffeine? (Review Tables 11.1 to 11.3.) Keep a complete record of your own intake of coffee, tea, soft drinks, and so on for a typical three-day period (72 hours). From that record, estimate as closely as you can your total caffeine intake in milligrams. If you regularly consume 300 mg or more per day, you might ask yourself if caffeine is interfering with your sleep, work, or studying.

12

Dietary Supplements and Over-the-Counter Drugs

©Colin Anderson/Getty Images RF

Dietary Supplements

When does "food" become a "drug"? When we think of typical food items, such as a loaf of bread or an apple, it seems unlikely that we would confuse those with drugs, such as a prescription antibiotic or illicit heroin. Both contain chemicals that interact with the body's ongoing physiology, in one case to provide nutrients, in the other to alter functioning in some way desired by the user. But a huge class of pills, capsules, liquids, and powders that look like drugs, and that many consumers think of and use in the same way as drugs, is legally classified as food products. This is very important to the consumer because of substantial differences in the way foods and drugs are regulated by the Food and Drug Administration (FDA). This distinction has been at the heart of an ongoing conflict between the FDA

Objectives

When you have finished this chapter, you should be able to:

- Explain the legal distinction between drugs and dietary supplements, particularly with regard to health-related claims.

- Understand the implications of the 1994 Dietary Supplement Health and Education Act.

- Recognize Saint John's wort, SAMe, and *Ginkgo biloba* as dietary supplements intended to have psychoactive effects.

- Explain the concepts behind the terms GRAS and GRAE.

- Name the only active ingredient allowed in OTC stimulants.

- Explain the risks of PPA and *ephedra* and describe how their removal from the market impacted OTC products promoted for weight loss.

- Name the primary ingredient in OTC sleep aids.

- Describe the benefits and dangers of aspirin.

- Explain what is meant by NSAID and give some examples.

- Name the four types of ingredients found in many OTC cold and allergy drugs and give a common example of each type.

and various manufacturers of these "dietary supplements" over health-related claims.

To make the food versus drug issue more concrete, let's think about Saint John's wort (*Hypericum*). The plant is a perennial shrub with yellow flowers and, like many plants, a history of use as a folk remedy. An Internet search will find numerous references to Saint John's wort as a "natural remedy for depression," or "nature's Prozac," and suggestions that it can improve mood, reduce anxiety, and aid sleep. Many people take tablets or capsules containing Saint John's wort for these purposes. Food or drug? Sure sounds like a drug, right? But both the manufacturers of these products and the FDA have agreed that these products are not drugs, but foods, even though people take them not when they're hungry, but when they're seeking relief from depression, anxiety, or insomnia.

The Food, Drug and Cosmetic Act under which the FDA operates says a product "intended for use in the diagnosis, cure, mitigation, treatment or prevention of disease in man" is a drug. So, if the users and sellers of Saint John's wort intend it to be used to mitigate or treat depression, shouldn't it be considered a drug? Chapter 3 reported that when this whole process of regulating patent medicines began in 1906, the FDA was concerned about purity of the products and accurate *labeling* so that consumers would know what they were buying. Later, when issues of the accuracy of health claims arose, the FDA's primary focus was on the claims made on the label affixed to the product. A bottle of Saint-John's-wort tablets may look like a drug bottle, and the tablets may say "300 mg" and look like drug tablets, but if it was sold in the United States its label will include terms you don't expect to see on a drug product, such as "nutrition information" and "serving size," the kind of information you see on breakfast cereal packages. Also, the label will not claim that the product is good for treating depression or insomnia. If it did, it would legally be a drug and subject to FDA regulation.

Remember also from Chapter 3 that drug manufacturers have to demonstrate to the FDA, before marketing the drug, that the drug is (1) *safe* when used as intended, and (2) *effective* for its intended use. Since 1906, the FDA has also been concerned about the purity and safety of food products and ingredients, but not with efficacy. Food products contain some ingredients with known nutritional value, but other ingredients that may enhance flavor or simply provide bulk. Processed foods also contain ingredients that are simply preservatives— included to keep the product from going bad, but having no nutritional value. For many years, people have also taken "dietary supplements," such as vitamins and minerals, meant to ensure sufficient intake of these important chemicals in case they are insufficient in the diet. Ongoing controversy about how much of each vitamin is needed and how much is too much has led to the establishment of "recommended daily allowances," which are sometimes adjusted in response to industry pressure to raise them or medical research suggesting a need to limit them. Saint John's wort and a wide variety of other products are now sold as dietary supplements. Under this category, they need to be pure and they need to be safe, but the manufacturer doesn't have to show to the FDA or to anyone else that they provide any benefit, either nutritionally or as a treatment for disease.

If the "300 mg" tablet of Saint John's wort contains some amount of the plant, then it's accurately labeled. With a drug, we'd expect to know exactly how much of the active ingredient it contains, but with a dietary supplement derived from a plant (an "herbal" supplement), we might not even know what the active ingredient is, let alone how much is in the 300-mg tablet. It's possible that no amount of Saint John's wort is really effective (the research evidence on this is mixed; see the following page), and also possible that the amount contained in a given pill is too small in any case. That's legal because the seller isn't directly making a health claim, so it doesn't have to demonstrate effectiveness.

In the early 1990s, the FDA had become concerned about two things. One was claims such as "heart healthy" being put on food products, and the other was the rapidly growing market in dietary supplements, fueled partly by Americans interested in healthful nutrition to prevent disease and partly by the emergence of several aggressive multilevel marketing organizations that recruited individuals to become distributors, offering both "wholesale" prices for their own products and the potential of high profits on sales to their friends and neighbors. In 1993, the FDA took two important actions. One was the approval, after careful study, of seven health claims that food manufacturers could use if

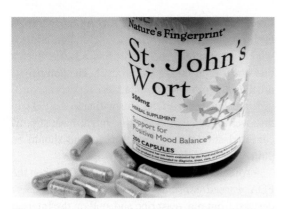

Dietary supplements such as St. John's wort are not regulated as over-the-counter drugs. They do not have to be shown to be effective, and the amount of presumed active ingredient varies widely. ©McGraw-Hill Education/Jill Braaten, photographer

their products met certain requirements (e.g., foods high in calcium can say they reduce the risk of osteoporosis, and foods low in sodium can say they reduce the risk of high blood pressure). In doing so, the FDA also made it clear it was not going to allow other unapproved health claims on foods. The second important action in 1993 was the release of the publication "Unsubstantiated Claims and Documented Health Hazards in the Dietary Supplement Marketplace." This document, as well as specific enforcement actions against products the FDA considered to be violating the existing law, led to a rapid and strong reaction on the part of the nutritional supplement industry. Raising fears among customers that the federal government would soon require them to get a doctor's prescription before they could purchase nutritional supplements, and using the multilevel marketing networks to generate a widespread grassroots campaign, the dietary supplement industry pressured Congress to limit the FDA's role. In 1994, both houses of Congress unanimously passed the Dietary Supplement Health and Education Act (DSHEA).

The DSHEA made several important changes. First, it redefined dietary supplements to include a variety of substances such as herbs, amino acids, and concentrates and extracts of herbs. Previously, the FDA had only allowed "essential nutrients," such as vitamins and minerals that were known to be required in a healthy diet, to be sold as dietary supplements in tablet, capsule, or liquid form. Second, the definition of safety was altered so that the FDA could declare a product to be "adulterated" only if it presents "a significant or unreasonable risk of illness or injury." Any ingredient being sold at the time the DSHEA was passed was presumed to be okay unless the FDA could demonstrate its risk. Any new ingredient introduced after 1994 would need to be accompanied by some evidence that it would not present a significant or unreasonable risk. Previously, an ingredient was not supposed to be sold until after the FDA reviewed it and allowed it to be included on the "generally recognized as safe" list. Third, while a dietary supplement still cannot claim to be a cure or treatment for a disorder, statements can be made indicating the supplement has a beneficial effect on some structure or function of the body, or on "well being." The sellers do not have to prove these claims, as they would for a drug, but they have to provide supporting evidence that the claims are not false or misleading. In other words, if there is some indication that the statement is possibly true, and some that it might not be true, then the information can be included because the evidence does not indicate the statement is clearly false and misleading. Finally, products running such statements must also include the following: "This statement has not been evaluated by the Food and Drug Administration. This product is not intended to diagnose, treat, cure, or prevent any disease."

The result of this 1994 law was that dietary supplement manufacturers were now free to market a wide variety of products without fear that the FDA would consider them to be drugs, requiring solid premarketing evidence of both safety and effectiveness. The already growing dietary supplement market expanded rapidly from an estimated total of $3.5 billion in 1992 to $11 billion in 1995, and by 2015 it was estimated at $36.7 billion, greater than the market for over-the-counter (OTC) drugs such as aspirin and cough and cold remedies.[1]

Was the DSHEA a boon or a threat to consumers? On one hand, consumers now had available a wider variety of products. However, critics say more regulation is needed. In 1994, the FDA first publicized serious concerns about products containing *ephedra* (see Chapter 6). Many of these products were used by people seeking to control their weight. Ten years later, in 2004, after the widely publicized death of baseball pitcher Steve Bechler, the FDA declared that products containing *ephedra* did pose significant and unreasonable risk and therefore were not to be sold. That it took 10 years to accomplish this action and that it was up to the FDA to compile evidence supporting the risks are indicators that the burden of proof might have swung too far away from the sellers and onto the FDA. In 2003, Senate hearings were held on whether the FDA needed more authority or simply needed more resources to implement the authority allowed it under the DSHEA. The answer appeared to be some of each. The FDA has the authority to establish "Good Manufacturing Practices" regulations, requiring food makers to establish procedures to ensure that their products contain what they say they contain, and that they are not "adulterated" with unwanted contaminants. With additional resources, the urging of Congress, and the cooperation of many of the larger supplement manufacturers, the FDA announced its Good Manufacturing Practices rules for dietary supplements in June 2007. Each manufacturer will decide what procedures to follow so that pesticides, fertilizers, and so on do not get mixed in, and that the proper ingredients are included in the appropriate amounts. FDA inspectors will spot check to see that these practices are in place. As with most regulations, it is expected that some of the bigger manufacturers will welcome these rules because they will increase public confidence in their products, whereas other manufacturers will have a difficult time meeting the requirements and may be forced out of the business.

Congress also granted additional authority to the FDA in 2006, to set up an "Adverse Events Reporting" process. The rules for that were finalized at the end of 2007. Among other things, each product label now has to include an address where a consumer can report any adverse events that occur after taking the product. The companies are then supposed to compile these reports and provide the data to the FDA. This will help the FDA to discover types of products that might have significant and unreasonable health risks and should be pulled from the market.

An interesting case occurred in 2007, when the FDA warned consumers to avoid certain products derived from red yeast rice and sold on the Internet as treatments for high cholesterol. It turns out that some of the prescription drugs used to treat high cholesterol ("statin" drugs) were originally derived from a type of red yeast rice. The products the FDA was concerned about were made from strains that produce a higher level of the chemical lovastatin. This chemical does work to lower cholesterol, but when it is sold as a prescription drug it comes with warnings about possible kidney impairment, and also with warnings about dangerous interactions with several other types of drugs. These particular products were pulled off the market by their suppliers. However, other red yeast rice products containing lower amounts of lovastatin are still available, and should be used with caution.

Consumer Reports magazine has published a list of dietary supplement ingredients that it considers to be potentially dangerous to consumers (see Table 12.1). The FDA has taken regulatory action against some of these (shown in the table), but most remain on the market unless or until the FDA can develop clear evidence that they present "a significant or unreasonable risk of illness or injury."

Following a report from the U.S. Government Accountability Office that proposed greater authority for the FDA to regulate dietary supplements,[1] Senator John McCain introduced the "Dietary Supplement Safety Act" in February 2010. The proposed law would have required all manufacturers of dietary supplements to register with the FDA and to provide complete lists of ingredients. It also gave the FDA authority to issue a mandatory recall of any ingredients it found to be unsafe. The dietary

Table 12.1
15 Supplement Ingredients to Avoid

Ingredient	Claimed Benefits	Risks
Aconite Also called: Aconiti tuber, aconitum, angustifolium, monkshood, radix aconti, wolfsbane	Reduces inflammation, joint pain, gout	Nausea, vomiting, weakness, paralysis, breathing and heart problems, possibly death
Caffeine Powder Also called: 1,3,7-trimethylxanthine	Improves attention, enhances athletic performance, weight loss	Seizures, heart arrhythmia, cardiac arrest, possibly death; particularly dangerous when combined with other stimulants
Chaparral Also called: Creosote bush, greasewood, larrea divaricata, larrea tridentata, larreastat	Weight loss; improves inflammation; treats colds, infections, skin rashes, cancer	Kidney problems, liver damage, possibly death
Coltsfoot Also called: Coughwort, farfarae folium leaf, foalswort, tussilago farfara	Relieves cough, sore throat, laryngitis, bronchitis, asthma	Liver damage, possible carcinogen
Comfrey Also called: Blackwort, bruisewort, slippery root, symphytum officinale	Relieves cough, heavy menstrual periods, stomach problems, chest pain; treats cancer	Liver damage, cancer, possibly death
Germander Also called: Teucrium chamaedrys, viscidum	Weight loss; alleviates fever, arthritis, gout, stomach problems	Liver damage, hepatitis, possibly death
Greater Celandine Also called: Celandine, chelidonium majus, chelidonii herba	Alleviates stomachache	Liver damage
Green Tea Extract Powder Also called: Camellia sinensis	Weight loss	Dizziness, ringing in the ears, reduced absorption of iron; exacerbates anemia and glaucoma; elevates blood pressure and heart rate; liver damage; possibly death
Kava Also called: Ava pepper, kava kava, piper methysticum	Reduces anxiety, improves insomnia	Liver damage, exacerbates Parkinson's and depression, impairs driving, possibly death
Lobelia Also called: Asthma weed, lobelia inflata, vomit wort, wild tobacco	Improves respiratory problems, aids smoking cessation	Nausea, vomiting, diarrhea, tremors, rapid heartbeat, confusion, seizures, hypothermia, coma, possibly death
Methylsynephrine Also called: Oxilofrine, p-hydroxyephedrine, oxyephedrine, 4-HMP	Weight loss, increases energy, improves athletic performance	Causes heart rate and rhythm abnormalities, cardiac arrest; particularly risky when taken with other stimulants

continued

Table 12.1

15 Supplement Ingredients to Avoid—*continued*

Ingredient	Claimed Benefits	Risks
Pennyroyal Oil Also called: Hedeoma pulegioides, mentha pulegium	Improves breathing problems, digestive disorders	Liver and kidney failure, nerve damage, convulsions, possibly death
Red Yeast Rice Also called: Monascus purpureus	Lowers LDL ("bad") cholesterol, prevents heart disease	Kidney and muscle problems, liver problems, hair loss; can magnify effect of cholesterol-lowering statin drugs, increasing the risk of side effects
Usnic Acid Also called: Beard moss, tree moss, usnea	Weight loss, pain relief	Liver injury
Yohimbe Also called: Johimbi, pausinystalia yohimbe, yohimbine, corynanthe johimbi	Treats low libido and erectile dysfunction, depression, obesity	Raises blood pressure; causes rapid heart rate, headaches, seizures, liver and kidney problems, heart problems, panic attacks, possibly death

Source: "15 Ingredients to Always Avoid," Consumer Reports, September 2016. Available at: http://www.consumerreports.org/vitamins-supplements/15-supplement-ingredients-to-always-avoid/

supplement industry mounted an immediate campaign against this increased regulation, and a month later Senator McCain withdrew the bill.

Some Psychoactive Dietary Supplements

Saint John's Wort

Saint John's wort (botanical name *Hypericum perforatum*) has been used for centuries and was once known as "the devil's scourge" because it was supposed to prevent possession by demons. In recent years its psychoactive uses have included the treatment of both anxiety and depression. There is limited evidence on the effectiveness of Saint John's wort in the treatment of anxiety, but several studies have indicated some usefulness in treating depression. One systematic review of 35 controlled clinical trials with Saint John's Wort in major depressive disorder found

moderate evidence that it was superior to a placebo and about as effective as antidepressants.[2]

The FDA has raised concerns about Saint John's wort interacting with various prescription drugs (see Chapter 5), so people using it should notify their physicians.

SAMe

S-adenosyl-L-methionine is a naturally occurring substance found in the body. It is an active form of the amino acid methionine, and it acts as a "methyl donor" in a variety of biochemical pathways. (A methyl group consists of one carbon and three hydrogen atoms.) As long ago as the 1970s, SAMe was tested in Italy for its effectiveness as an antidepressant. Several studies have reported that SAMe is approximately as effective as prescription antidepressant medications, although many of the studies have not been well controlled.

Drugs in the Media

Natural Male Enhancement?

A few years ago there were frequent late-night television ads for Enzyte, one of many dietary supplements that claim to enhance a man's sex life. The problem is, the claims are not backed up by either scientific fact or by lots of people's experience after using them. After thousands of complaints to the Better Business Bureau about Enzyte, a widely advertised product, the federal government raided the company and arrested the CEO, who was sentenced to prison for fraud. That hasn't stopped another company from continuing to sell Enzyte, and many other products can also be found on the Internet, with suggestive names like Oxysurge, Virmax, and Zytenz. There's apparently a pretty big market for dietary supplements that claim to improve a man's sex life. An Internet search using the term "male enhancement pills" will result in advertisements for several of these products, most promising several benefits such as stronger erections, larger penis size, and greater partner satisfaction. These pills contain small amounts of several plant extracts, most notably *Tribulus terrestris, Panax ginseng,* and *Ginkgo biloba.* Controlled clinical studies provide limited evidence that *ginseng* (widely available in many products) might be helpful in treating erectile dysfunction,[3] though it is not clear what value this would have for men with otherwise normal penile function. The clinical results for *ginkgo* have been mixed, but the only controlled study showed no effect. One controlled study has been reported on a combination product including *Tribulus terrestris,* again reporting improved

function in some men with moderate erectile dysfunction.[4] Many offerings also include *Avena sativa* extract. This is the common oat plant from which oatmeal is made. The extract has been promoted as an aphrodisiac in several products, but without scientific evidence. Finally, there is some *Epimedium sagittatum,* called "horny goat weed." This has been used to enhance male sexual energy in traditional Chinese herbal medicine. It appears to dilate blood vessels, possibly lowering blood pressure. Some of the products also list yohimbe and/or "tongkat ali." Yohimbe bark contains yohimbine, which in high enough doses does seem to improve erectile function but also causes heart palpitations and other unpleasant side effects. Tongkat ali is the Malaysian name for *Eurocoma logifolia,* which in high enough doses can increase testosterone production. The issue with both of these possible effective ingredients is that most of the dietary supplements appear to contain miniscule amounts, if any, of the active ingredient.

This is just one example of the kinds of products sold as *dietary supplements.* These tablets and capsules are treated by the FDA more like foods than drugs, and as such there is no requirement that the manufacturer demonstrate the effectiveness of the products. The labels for all of these products include the standard disclaimer that "these statements have not been evaluated by the Food and Drug Administration."

Box icon credit: ©Glow Images RF

Researchers continue to investigate the possibility that, by combining SAMe with approved antidepressants, a more rapid remission of symptoms can be achieved.[5]

Ginkgo biloba

Extracts from the leaves of the *Ginkgo biloba* tree have a long history of medical use in China. It is not clear which of the identified ingredients in ginkgo are the active agents, and it is not completely clear how effective it is for a variety of uses for which it has been proposed. The substance does reduce

blood clotting, so it has been proposed as a blood thinner, which improves circulation. However, combining ginkgo with aspirin, which also reduces clotting, could be dangerous. The most interesting suggestion is that *Ginkgo biloba* extract might improve memory in Alzheimer's patients, due to its presumed ability to increase blood circulation in the brain. Several studies have tested ginkgo in both normal and memory-impaired older adults. Overall, the results have found slight improvements for some people, but not a reliable effect that would be really useful.[6]

Evidence suggests that a compound in ginkgo acts as a blood thinner; it may be dangerous for people to take ginkgo supplements in combination with aspirin or other drugs that also reduce clotting. ©Mitch Hrdlicka/Getty Images RF

Weight-Control Products

People hoping to lose weight are probably the biggest market for dietary supplements. This story can best be told by reference to Herbalife, still one of the largest marketers of dietary weight-loss products. Founded out of the trunk of a car in 1980, many of the original products contained the herb *ma huang* (see Chapter 6), which contains *ephedra*, an amphetamine-like stimulant. Sales of these products exploded, thanks partly to an aggressive multilevel marketing scheme. By the 1990s, the financial resources of this company, combined with the thousands of distributors in its marketing system, provided a major political push behind passage of the 1996 DSHEA. None of Herbalife's products contain *ephedra*, which has been banned by the FDA. Their weight-loss products now include a variety of protein drinks, plus several products they say are designed to promote fat-burning or appetite control. At least some of those products rely on large doses of caffeine to produce the stimulant effect formerly obtained from *ephedra*. However, as with other nutritional supplements, no scientific evidence of effectiveness is required. Herbalife reported $3.5 billion in worldwide sales in 2011.

Herbalife is far from the only company making lots of money selling nutritional supplements to people who want to lose weight. Many of the products also have significant amounts of caffeine in them. Before buying a product based on a list of botanical names, ask yourself these questions: If a pill says it contains green tea, for example, how much powdered green tea can you even fit in the capsule? If it's an extract of green tea, what are they extracting, and how much of that is in the pill? Is there supposed to be an active ingredient, and if so, is it present in enough quantity to do anything? The makers of these nutritional supplement products typically reveal none of these answers.

Over-the-Counter Drugs

Over-the-counter drugs are those that are self-prescribed and self-administered for the relief of symptoms of self-diagnosed illnesses. The FDA estimates that consumers self-treat four times more health problems than doctors treat, often using OTC drugs.

Americans spend over $18 billion a year on OTC products. That's not as much as we spend on prescription drugs, alcohol, cigarettes, or illicit cocaine, but it's enough to keep several OTC drug manufacturers locked in fierce competition for those sales. The two biggest markets are for aspirin-like analgesics and for the collection of cough, cold, and flu products. Do we really need all these nonprescription tablets, capsules, liquids, and creams? How much of what we buy is based on advertising hype, and how much is based on sound decisions about our health? How are we as consumers to know the difference? The FDA is trying to help us with these decisions.

FDA Regulation of OTC Products

The 1962 Kefauver-Harris Amendment required that all drugs be evaluated for both safety and efficacy. The FDA was to set up criteria for new drugs entering the market and establish a procedure for

A shopper reads the label on an OTC medication.
©McGraw-Hill Education/Ken Karp, photographer

reviewing all the OTC drugs already on the market. At first glance this seemed an impossible task, because there were between 250,000 and 300,000 products already being sold (no one knew for sure how many). In addition, each product was likely to change its ingredients without warning. The FDA made the decision not to study individual products but to review each active ingredient. Many competing brands contain the same ingredients, so there are many fewer ingredients than products. The FDA divided OTC products into 26 classes and appointed an advisory panel for each class. Each panel was to look at the active ingredients contained in the products in its class, decide whether evidence indicated each ingredient was safe and effective for its purpose, and determine what claims could be made for that ingredient on the label.

Several of the 26 classes of OTC drugs to be reviewed by the FDA included psychoactive ingredients: sedatives and sleep aids, analgesics, cold remedies and antitussives, antihistamines and allergy products, and stimulants.

Before the panel could begin work, some rules had to be laid down about what was meant by such terms as *safe* and *effective,* keeping in mind that no drug is entirely safe and that many might have only limited effectiveness. The FDA uses the acronym **GRAS** ("generally recognized as safe") to mean that, given the currently available information, people who are informed and qualified would agree that the ingredient should be considered safe. "Safe" means "a low incidence of adverse reactions or significant side effects under adequate directions for use and warnings against unsafe use as well as low potential for harm which may result from abuse."

Similar acronyms are used for two other important concepts: GRAE ("generally recognized as effective") and GRAHL ("generally recognized as honestly labeled"). "Effective" means that there is "a reasonable expectation that, in a significant proportion of the target population, the pharmacological effect of the drug, when used under adequate directions for use and warnings against unsafe use, will provide clinically significant relief of the type claimed." The advisory panel was to rule on each active ingredient and decide whether the evidence indicates that the ingredient is both GRAS and GRAE, or failed on one or both criteria, or if further information was needed.

The overall result of this procedure can be seen by taking a trip to your neighborhood drugstore and looking at the lists of ingredients on medications of a given type. All the competing brands contain much the same few ingredients. In some classes, there might be only one approved active ingredient, meaning that all competing brands are essentially identical. The differences among them often are in the long list of other (inactive) ingredients (colorings, flavorings, etc.). The exact number

GRAS: "generally recognized as safe."

of OTC products on the market is not known because they still come and go and change, but we do know that there are more than 300,000, and they contain fewer than 1,000 total active ingredients now reviewed in over 80 therapeutic classes.

Simplifying Labels

Both the safety and effectiveness of OTC drugs depend greatly on consumers using them according to the directions and warnings on the label. To reduce confusion and make it more likely that consumers will be able to understand the labels, the FDA moved in 1997 to create uniform standards for labels, with minimum print size, topics in a consistent order (active ingredients, directions for use, warnings), and bold, bulleted headings. One important change was to make the language clearer and more concise, avoiding medical terminology (e.g., "pulmonary" replaced by "lung"). This new, consistent approach to labeling has made it easier to compare products and their ingredients.

Over-the-Counter versus Prescription Drugs

The 1938 Food, Drug, and Cosmetic Act established a classification of drugs that would be available only by prescription. A drug is supposed to be

Should some over-the-counter drugs be kept behind the counter, where they can be dispensed only after a pharmacist has advised the consumer about safe use? ©Royalty-Free/Getty Images RF

permitted for OTC sale unless, because of potential toxicity or for other reasons (e.g., if it must be injected), it may be safely sold and used only under a prescription.

Sometimes the only difference between an OTC product and a prescription product is the greater amount of active ingredient in each prescription dose. More often, however, prescription drugs are chemicals that are unavailable OTC. Until the FDA began its OTC Drug Review process, once a new drug was approved for prescription sale it almost never became available OTC. Neither the FDA nor the manufacturers seemed to have much interest in switching drugs to OTC status. However, the FDA advisory panels that reviewed products in a given OTC category sometimes did more than was required of them. In some cases, they recommended that higher doses be allowed in OTC preparations—and as a result we can now buy higher-strength OTC antihistamines. And in several cases the suggestion was that previous prescription-only ingredients, such as ibuprofen, be sold OTC.

Between 1972 and 1992, 20 ingredients were switched to OTC status. Then the FDA established the Nonprescription Drug Advisory Committee, which has an advisory role regarding all the drug categories and has helped move many more drugs from prescription to OTC. Drugs recently switched to OTC status include the heartburn drug esomeprazole (Nexium) and the two intranasal steroids for allergies, fluticasone (Flonase) and budesonide (Rhinocort).[7]

Behind-the-Counter Drugs?

In 2006, the revised USA PATRIOT Act included a federal requirement that OTC products containing pseudoephedrine be removed from shelves that are accessible to the public and be kept "behind the counter." This step was taken because pseudoephedrine was being used as a precursor in the illicit manufacture of methamphetamine. Literally hundreds of products in the cough and cold and allergy categories were affected by this new law. Many of the manufacturers reformulated their products to include phenylephrine instead of pseudoephedrine (see Treatment of Cold Symptoms, page 281). Others, including Sudafed (obviously named for its main ingredient) made the old formula available behind the counter and also made a reformulated product that could be out on the shelves. Under the current regulations, people who do ask for and purchase the pseudoephedrine-containing products are limited in the quantities they can buy, and they must show identification and sign for the purchase.

Some Psychoactive OTC Products

Stimulants

Stimulants, one of the original FDA categories, is one of the simplest categories. The FDA allows stimulants to be sold to "help restore mental alertness or wakefulness when experiencing fatigue or drowsiness." If it sounds like caffeine could do this, you're right! NoDoz, a well-known product that has been around for years, has the tried-and-true formula: 100 mg of caffeine (about the equivalent of an average cup of brewed coffee). The recommended dose is two tablets initially, then one every three hours. Another well-known product, Vivarin, contains 200 mg of caffeine, and the initial dose is one tablet. Thus, although the packages look different and different companies make them, a smart consumer would choose between these two based on the price per milligram of caffeine. Or he or she could choose a less expensive store brand, or buy coffee (usually more expensive), or just get enough rest and save money. The labels warn against using these caffeine tablets with coffee, tea, or cola drinks. The only active ingredient the FDA allows in OTC stimulants is caffeine.[8]

There is a reasonably brisk business in the semilegal field of selling caffeine tablets or capsules resembling prescription stimulants, such as the amphetamines. Many street purchases of speed turn out to contain caffeine as their major ingredient. It is, however, a violation of the controlled substances act to sell something that is represented to

be a controlled substance. The FDA has ruled that products labeled as stimulants that contain anything other than caffeine as an active ingredient cannot be sold OTC. The FDA also outlawed OTC products, labeled for any purpose, that contained combinations of caffeine and ephedrine and has taken legal action against several mail-order distributors of such combination products.

Weight-Control Products

The original FDA list of OTC drug categories did not include appetite suppressants or a similar term. Apparently the FDA didn't think it would be dealing with such a product, because, at the time, the use of the prescription amphetamines for this purpose was under widespread attack. However, data were presented indicating that **phenylpropanolamine (PPA)** was safe and effective, and by the late 1970s several products were being sold that contained PPA as their only active ingredient. Some studies indicated caffeine could potentiate the appetite-suppressing effect of PPA, and for a brief period during the early 1980s several of the products included both PPA and caffeine. After the 1983 FDA ruling prohibiting such combinations on the grounds that they might not be safe, all products returned to PPA only. The recommended dose for appetite suppression was 75 mg per day. There was some concern about the safety even of 75-mg doses, with the threat being increased blood pressure resulting from sympathetic stimulation. There was also some controversy about the effectiveness of PPA, given that its effect, as with most appetite suppressant drugs, is small and rather short-lived.

In November 2000, the FDA issued a Public Health Advisory on the safety of PPA, based on a new study showing that women taking PPA had an increased risk of hemorrhagic stroke (bleeding into the brain, usually a result of elevated blood pressure). The FDA requested that all drug

phenylpropanolamine (PPA) (fen il pro pa *nole* a meen): until 2000, an active ingredient in OTC weight-control products.

companies discontinue marketing products containing PPA and that consumers not use any products containing PPA. Manufacturers and retailers responded quickly, and by early 2001 no remaining weight-control products contained PPA. Dexatrim, one of the most widely sold products previously based on PPA, was marketing a "natural" (dietary supplement) version containing various herbal products, including a small amount of *ma huang* (*ephedra*). *Ephedra* was found in several weight-control products until its ban in 2004. The current Dexatrim formula relies on "green tea extract" and is sold as a dietary supplement rather than as an OTC drug. Until 2007, there was no FDA-approved OTC weight-control ingredient available to consumers. Orlistat, which had been a prescription-only medicine called Xenical, was switched to OTC status and is being sold under the brand name alli. Orlistat does its work in the intestine, inhibiting an enzyme that breaks down dietary fats. Therefore, some of the fat that would have been absorbed is instead retained in the intestine and passed out in the feces. When given in conjunction with a restricted diet, orlistat has been shown to help people lose weight, but once the drug is stopped there is a tendency to gain back some of the lost weight. The major problem with using this drug is that the fats and oils that remain in the bowel can lead to loose, oily stools; frequent, urgent bowel movements that sometimes are hard to control; and flatulence. The manufacturer recommends a low-fat diet to avoid as many of these side effects as possible.

The market for weight-control products has shifted largely from OTC drugs to the less well regulated dietary supplement category (page 270).

Sedatives and Sleep Aids

A few years ago the shelves contained a number of OTC sedative, or "calmative," preparations, including Quiet World and Compoz, which contained very small amounts of the acetylcholine receptor blocker *scopolamine* combined with the **antihistamine** methapyrilene. At the same time, sleep aids, such as Sleep-Eze and Sominex, contained just a bit

more of the same two ingredients. The rationale for the scopolamine, particularly at these low doses, was under FDA investigation, but scopolamine had traditionally been included in many such medications in the past. Some antihistamines do produce a kind of sedated state and might produce drowsiness. The FDA advisory panel accepted methapyrilene but eventually rejected scopolamine. For a while all of these medications contained only methapyrilene. Then in 1979, it was reported that methapyrilene caused cancer in laboratory animals, so it was no longer GRAS. Next came pyrilamine maleate, then doxylamine succinate, and then *diphenhydramine,* all antihistamines. If you bought the same brand from one year to the next, you would get a different formulation each time. But if you bought several different brands at the same time, you stood a good chance of getting the same formulation in all of them.

The sedative category no longer exists for OTC products. One product, Miles Nervine, which went from being a sedative containing bromide salts to a calmative containing whatever they all contained each year, is now Miles Nervine Nighttime Sleep-Aid, containing 25 mg of diphenhydramine. Nytol is also a nighttime sleep aid containing the same ingredient. Sominex and Sleep-Eze are still around, and both contain diphenhydramine.

As we saw in Chapter 7, insomnia is perceived to be a bigger problem than it actually is for most people, and it is rare that medication is really required. Antihistamines can induce drowsiness, but not very quickly. If you do feel the need to use these to get you to sleep more rapidly, take them at least 20 minutes before retiring. Their sedative effects are potentiated by alcohol, so it is not a good idea to take them after drinking.

Analgesics

People and Pain

Pain is such a little word for such a big experience. Most people have experienced pain of varying intensities, from mild to moderate to severe to excruciating. Two major classes of drugs are used to reduce pain or the awareness of pain, anesthetics and analgesics. Anesthetics (meaning "without sensibility") have this effect by reducing all types of sensation or by blocking consciousness completely. The local anesthetics used in dentistry and the general anesthetics used in major surgery are examples of this class of agent. The other major class, the analgesics (meaning "without pain"), are compounds that reduce pain selectively without causing a loss of other sensations. The analgesics are divided into two groups. Opioids (see Chapter 13) are one group of analgesics, but this chapter primarily discusses the OTC internal analgesics, such as aspirin, acetaminophen, and ibuprofen.

Although pain itself is a complex psychological phenomenon, there have been attempts to classify different types of pain to develop a rational approach to its treatment. One classification divides pain into two types, depending on its place of origin. Visceral pain, such as intestinal cramps, arises from nonskeletal portions of the body; opioids are effective in reducing pain of this type. Somatic pain, arising from muscle or bone and typified by sprains, headaches, and arthritis, is reduced by salicylates (aspirin) and related products.

Pain is unlike other sensations in many ways, mostly because of nonspecific factors. The experience of pain varies with personality, gender, and time of day and is increased with fatigue, anxiety, fear, boredom, and anticipation of more pain. Because pain is very susceptible to nonspecific factors, studies have shown that about 35 percent of patients will receive satisfactory pain relief from a placebo.

Aspirin

More than 2,400 years ago, the Greeks used extracts of willow and poplar bark in the treatment of pain, gout, and other illnesses. Aristotle commented on some of the clinical effects of similar preparations, and Galen made good use of these formulations. These remedies fell into disrepute, however, when St. Augustine declared that all diseases of Christians were the work of demons and thus a punishment from God. American Indians, unhampered by this attitude, used a tea brewed from willow bark to reduce fever. This remedy was not rediscovered in Europe until about 200 years ago, when an Englishman, the Reverend Edward Stone, prepared an extract of the bark and gave the same dose to 50 patients with varying illnesses and found the results to be "uniformly excellent." In the 19th century, the active ingredient in these preparations was isolated and identified as salicylic acid. In 1838, salicylic acid was synthesized, and in 1859 procedures were developed that made bulk production feasible. Salicylic acid and sodium salicylate were then used for many ills, especially arthritis.

In the giant Bayer Laboratories in Germany in the 1890s worked a chemist named Hoffmann. His father had a severe case of rheumatoid arthritis, and only salicylic acid seemed to help. The major difficulty then, as today, was that the drug caused great gastric discomfort. So great was the stomach upset and nausea that Hoffmann's father frequently preferred the pain of the arthritis. Hoffmann studied the salicylates to see if he could find one with the same therapeutic effect as salicylic acid but without the side effects.

In 1898, he synthesized **acetylsalicylic acid** and tried it on his father, who reported relief from pain without stomach upset. The compound was tested, patented, and released for sale in 1899 as *Aspirin*. Aspirin was a trademark name derived from the name *acetyl* and *spiralic acid* (the old name for salicylic acid).

Aspirin, either in the gastrointestinal tract or in the bloodstream, is converted to salicylic acid. Taken orally, aspirin is a more potent analgesic than salicylic acid, because aspirin irritates the stomach less and is thus absorbed more rapidly.

antihistamine: the active ingredient in OTC sleep aids and cough/cold products.

acetylsalicylic acid (a *see* till sal i *sill* ick): the chemical known as aspirin.

Life Saver

Acetaminophen and Liver Damage

Acetaminophen, the pain-relieving ingredient in Tylenol and many other OTC drugs, is considered safe and effective when used in the proper dose. But we have known for many years that taking larger doses can cause severe liver problems. The package labels warn people not to exceed the recommended dose, but still thousands of people come to emergency rooms every year and a few hundred people have died in the past five years as a result of acetaminophen-induced liver damage. There seem to be several problems: People don't read labels carefully, and there seems to be an assumption that if a drug is sold OTC it must be pretty safe. Someone with a really bad headache wants quick and sure relief, and so there is a tendency to take an extra pill. Then there is confusion over the fact that for many years the maximum adult dose of aspirin or acetaminophen was delivered by taking two tablets. When you buy "maximum strength" acetaminophen tablets, should you still take two? Acetaminophen is included in many OTC cold medications, and people might not even realize that if they take pain pills in addition

to a cold pill they are exceeding the recommended dose. Finally, acetaminophen is included in a great many prescription pain pills in combination with an opioid (e.g., Percocet or Vicodin). As the abuse of these opioid pain pills has increased in recent years, the most serious medical complication has often been the liver damage caused by the acetaminophen that some users don't realize is included.

In 2009, an FDA advisory panel voted to make some changes in the doses available OTC, and to require a "black box" warning on all prescription medications that include acetaminophen. But they voted not to outlaw OTC combination products, such as cold medications, that include acetaminophen.

Were you aware of this danger before reading this chapter? Did the FDA panel go far enough or too far? What else can we do to reduce the accidental liver damage caused by the use of this common OTC drug?

Box icon credit: ©McGraw-Hill Education

Aspirin was marketed for physicians and sold as a white powder in individual dosage packets, available only by prescription. It was immediately popular worldwide, and the U.S. market became large enough that it was very soon manufactured in this country. In 1915, the 5-grain (325-mg) white tablet stamped "Bayer" first appeared, and, for the first time, aspirin became a nonprescription item. The Bayer Company was on its way. It had an effective drug that could be sold to the public and was known by one name—Aspirin—and the name was trademarked. Before February 1917, when the patent on Aspirin was to expire, Bayer started an advertising campaign to make it clear that there was only one Aspirin, and its first name was Bayer. Several companies started manufacturing and selling Aspirin as aspirin, and Bayer sued. What happened after this is a long story, but Bayer obviously lost, and aspirin is now a generic name.

Therapeutic Use Aspirin is truly a magnificent drug. It is also a drug with some serious side effects. Aspirin has three effects that are the primary basis for its clinical use. It is an analgesic that effectively blocks somatic pain in the mild-to-moderate range. Aspirin is also an **antipyretic:** It reduces fever. Last but not least, aspirin is an **anti-inflammatory** agent: It reduces the swelling, inflammation, and soreness in an injured area. Its anti-inflammatory action is the basis for its extensive use in treating arthritis. It is difficult to find another drug that has this span of effects coupled with a relatively low toxicity. It does, however, have side effects that pose problems for some people.

Aspirin is readily absorbed from the stomach but even faster from the intestine. Thus, anything that delays movement of the aspirin from the stomach should affect absorption time. The evidence is mixed on whether taking aspirin with a meal, which delays emptying of the stomach, increases the time before onset of action. It should, however, reduce the stomach irritation that sometimes accompanies aspirin use.

The *therapeutic* dose for aspirin is generally considered to be in the range of 600 to 1,000 mg. Most reports suggest that 300 mg is usually more effective than a placebo, whereas 600 mg is clearly even more effective. Many studies indicate that increasing the dose above that level does not increase aspirin's analgesic action, but some research indicates that 1,200 mg of aspirin provides greater relief than 600 mg. The maximum pain relief is experienced about one hour after taking aspirin, and the effect lasts for up to four hours.

At therapeutic doses, aspirin has analgesic actions that are fairly specific. First, and in marked contrast to narcotic analgesics, aspirin does not affect the impact of the anticipation of pain. It seems probable also that aspirin has its primary effect on the ability to withstand continuing pain. This, no doubt, is the basis for much of the self-medication with aspirin, because moderate, protracted pain is fairly common. Aspirin is especially effective against headache and musculoskeletal aches and pains, less effective for toothache and sore throat, and only slightly better than placebo in visceral pain, as well as in traumatic (acute) pain.

The antipyretic (fever-reducing) action of aspirin does not lower temperature in an individual with normal body temperature. It has this effect only if the person has a fever. The mechanism by which aspirin decreases body temperature is fairly well understood. It acts on the temperature-regulating area of the hypothalamus to increase heat loss through peripheral mechanisms. Heat loss is primarily increased by vasodilation of peripheral blood vessels and by increased perspiration. Heat production is not changed, but heat loss is facilitated so that body temperature can go down.

More aspirin has probably been used for its third major therapeutic use than for either of the other two. The anti-inflammatory action of the salicylates is the major basis for its use after muscle strains and in treating rheumatoid arthritis.

Effects: Adverse and Otherwise *Aspirin increases bleeding time by inhibiting blood platelet aggregation.* This is not an insignificant effect. Two or three aspirins can double bleeding time, the time it takes for blood to clot, and the effect can last four to seven days. There's good and bad in the anticoagulant effect of aspirin. Its use before surgery can help prevent blood clots from appearing in patients at high risk for clot formation. For many surgical patients, however, facilitation of blood clotting is desirable, and the general rule is no aspirin for 7 to 10 days before surgery.

Aspirin will induce gastrointestinal bleeding in about 70 percent of normal subjects. In most cases, this is only about 5 ml per day, but that is five times the normal loss. In some people the blood loss can be great enough to cause anemia. The basis for this effect is not clear but is believed to be a direct eroding by the aspirin tablets of the gastric mucosa. Aspirin can be deadly with severe stomach ulcers. For the rest of us, the rule is clear: Drink lots of water when you take aspirin or, better yet, crush the tablets and drink them in orange juice or other liquid.

The anticoagulant effect of aspirin has a potentially beneficial effect in preventing heart attacks and strokes. Either can be brought on by a blood clot becoming lodged in a narrowed or hardened blood vessel. Several studies demonstrated that patients who are at high risk for these problems can help to prevent both strokes and heart attacks by taking a small dose of aspirin daily. Many patients over a certain age are taking low-dose aspirin (82 mg is typical) regularly, even though the available research doesn't provide clear evidence for any benefit for low-risk patients.[9]

---

antipyretic (an tee pie *reh* tick): fever-reducing.
anti-inflammatory: reducing swelling and inflammation.

In the early 1980s, concern increased about the relationship of aspirin use to *Reye's syndrome,* a rare disease (fewer than 200 cases per year in the United States). Almost all of the cases occur in people under the age of 20, usually after they have had a viral infection, such as influenza or chicken pox. The children begin vomiting continuously; then they might become disoriented, undergo personality changes, shout, or become lethargic. Some enter comas, and some of those either die or suffer permanent brain damage. The overall mortality rate from Reye's syndrome is about 25 percent.

No one knows what causes Reye's, and it isn't believed to be caused by aspirin. However, data suggest the disease is more likely to occur in children who have been given aspirin during a preceding illness. In late 1984, the results of a Centers for Disease Control and Prevention pilot study were released, indicating that the use of aspirin can increase the risk of Reye's syndrome as much as 25 times. In 1985, makers of all aspirin products were asked to put warning labels on their packages. These labels recommend that you consult a physician before giving aspirin to children or teenagers with chicken pox or flu.

In early 1986, it was reported that fewer parents in Michigan were giving aspirin to children for colds and influenza, and the incidence of Reye's syndrome had also decreased in Michigan. The Michigan study lends further strength to the relationship between aspirin use and Reye's syndrome. No one under the age of 20 should use aspirin in treating chicken pox, influenza, or even what might be suspected to be a common cold.

Aspirin has long been associated with a large number of accidental poisonings of children, as well as with suicide attempts. It has now been joined on the DAWN lists (see Chapter 2) by its relatives acetaminophen and ibuprofen. Together, these drugs received about 100,000 mentions in the most recent DAWN emergency room data.

Mechanism of Action   *Prostaglandins* are local hormones that are manufactured and released when cell membranes are distorted or damaged—that is, injured. The prostaglandins then act on the endings of the neurons that mediate pain in the injured areas. The prostaglandins sensitize the neurons to mechanical stimulation and to stimulation by two other local hormones, histamine and bradykinin, which are released more slowly from the damaged tissue. Aspirin blocks the synthesis of the prostaglandins by inhibiting two forms of the cyclo-oxygenase enzyme (COX-1 and COX-2).

The antipyretic action has also been spelled out: A specific prostaglandin acts on the anterior hypothalamus to decrease heat dissipation through the normal procedures of sweating and dilation of peripheral blood vessels. Aspirin blocks the synthesis of this prostaglandin in the anterior hypothalamus, and this is followed by increased heat loss.

Acetaminophen

There are two related analgesic compounds: *phenacetin* and **acetaminophen.** Phenacetin was sold for many years in combination with aspirin and caffeine in the "APC" tablets that fought headache pain "three ways." Phenacetin has been around since 1887 and had long been suspected of causing kidney lesions and dysfunction. In 1964, the FDA required a warning on all products containing phenacetin, which limited their use to 10 days because the phenacetin might damage the kidneys. In 1983, it was removed from the market entirely.

Acetaminophen has been marketed as an OTC analgesic since 1955, but it was the big advertising pushes in the 1970s for two brand-name products, Tylenol and Datril, that brought acetaminophen into the big time. Acetaminophen was advertised as having most of the good points of "that other pain reliever" and many fewer disadvantages. To a degree this is probably true: If only analgesia and fever reduction are desired, acetaminophen might be safer than aspirin *as long as dosage limits are carefully observed.* Overuse of acetaminophen can cause serious liver disorders. Acetaminophen has now far surpassed aspirin for both drug-related emergency room visits and drug-related deaths, according to the DAWN statistics (see Chapter 2).

Life Saver

Hidden Ingredients

The FDA has its hands full regulating all the various OTC drugs and dietary supplements. It's one thing when the manufacturers are honest and provide an accurate list of the ingredients, as they are legally required to do. But with the increasing number of products that are being imported from various countries, it is especially tough when the product includes undisclosed, or "hidden" ingredients.

In 2013, the FDA advised consumers not to purchase two products: Perfect Body Solutions and Burn 7. These weight-loss products were being promoted on the Internet and in some retail stores. Although their labels listed ingredients such as green tea and other herbal products, they were in fact found to include a drug called sibutramine. Sibutramine had been available as a prescription weight-loss product in the United States under the brand name Meridia (Chapter 6) until 2010. It was withdrawn from the market that year because of increased risk of heart attack and stroke. It is also a controlled substance.

The FDA noted that this use of "hidden" drugs and chemicals represents an increasing trend, and that they are unable to test and identify all the dietary supplements that are being sold. U.S. companies can be shut down or fined for such practices, but the FDA is more limited in its ability to punish foreign manufacturers.

The FDA doesn't want to advertise on the package that acetaminophen can be lethal, for fear of attracting suicide attempts. So it requires a warning against overdose and includes the statement "Prompt medical attention is critical for adults as well as for children even if you do not notice any signs or symptoms." This statement reflects the fact that damage to the liver might not be noticed until 24 to 48 hours later, when the symptoms of impaired liver function finally emerge. You should remember that acetaminophen is not necessarily safer than aspirin, especially if the recommended dose is

exceeded. As of 2009, the FDA limited the maximum amount contained in a single capsule to 650 mg for OTC products.

Ibuprofen and Other NSAIDs

Since the discovery that aspirin and similar drugs work by inhibiting the two COX enzymes, the drug companies have used that information to design new and sometimes more potent analgesics, which were introduced as prescription products. **Ibuprofen,** which originally was available only by prescription, is now found in several OTC analgesics. In addition to its analgesic potency, ibuprofen is a potent anti-inflammatory and has received wide use in the treatment of arthritis. The most common side effects of ibuprofen are gastrointestinal: nausea, stomach pain, and cramping. There have been reports of fatal liver damage with overdoses of ibuprofen, so again it is wise not to exceed the recommended dose.

Ibuprofen was the first of several new drugs that are now collectively referred to as "nonsteroidal anti-inflammatory drugs" (**NSAIDs**). Naproxen is also available OTC.

One product that luckily did not make the switch to OTC was rofecoxib (Vioxx), which was pulled from the market in 2004 after it was clear that it increased the risk of heart attacks.

Table 12.2 lists several OTC analgesics along with the amounts of each ingredient they contain. The FDA has been discussing whether to exclude products that contain both aspirin and acetaminophen. Products containing ibuprofen warn against combining them with aspirin, because that mixture hasn't been thoroughly studied.

acetaminophen (a seet a *min* o fen): an aspirinlike analgesic and antipyretic.
ibuprofen (eye bu *pro* fen): an aspirinlike analgesic and anti-inflammatory.
NSAIDs: nonsteroidal anti-inflammatory drugs, such as ibuprofen.

Table 12.2
Ingredients in OTC Analgesics (mg)

Brand	Aspirin	Acetaminophen	Ibuprofen	Naproxen	Caffeine	Other
Aleve	—	—	—	220	—	—
Anacin	500	—	—	—	32	—
Advil	—	—	200	—	—	—
Bufferin	325	—	—	—	—	Magnesium carbonate, calcium carbonate, magnesium oxide
Empirin	325	—	—	—	—	—
Excedrin	250	250	—	—	65	—
Mediprin	300	—	—	—	—	—
Nuprin	—	—	200	—	—	—
Vanquish	227	194	—	—	33	Magnesium hydroxide, aluminum hydroxide gel

Cold and Allergy Products

The All-Too-Common Cold

There has to be something good about an illness that Charles Dickens could be lyrical about:

> *I am at this moment*
> *Deaf in the ears,*
> *Hoarse in the throat,*
> *Red in the nose,*
> *Green in the gills,*
> *Damp in the eyes,*
> *Twitchy in the joints,*
> *And fractious in temper*
> *From a most intolerable*
> *And oppressive cold.*[10]

The common cold is caused by viruses: More than a hundred have been identified. But in 40 to 60 percent of individuals with colds, researchers cannot connect the infection to a specific virus. That makes it tough to find a cure. Two groups of viruses are known to be associated with colds—the *rhinoviruses* and the more recently identified *coronaviruses*. These viruses are clearly distinct from those that cause influenza, measles, and pneumonia. Success in developing vaccines against other diseases has made some experts optimistic about finding a vaccine for the common cold. Others are pessimistic because of the great variety of viruses and the fact that the rhinoviruses can apparently change their immunologic reactivity very readily.

Viruses damage or kill the cells they attack. The rhinoviruses zero in on the upper respiratory tract, at first causing irritation, which can lead to reflex coughing and sneezing. Increased irritation inflames the tissue and is followed by soreness and swelling of the mucous membranes. As a defense against infection, the mucous membranes release considerable fluid, which causes the runny nose and the postnasal drip that irritates the throat.

Although the incubation period for a cold can be a week in some cases, the more common interval between infection and respiratory tract symptoms is two to four days. Before the onset of respiratory symptoms, the individual might just feel bad and develop joint aches and headaches. When fever does occur, it almost always develops early in the cold.

Most of us grew up believing that colds are passed by airborne particles jet-propelled usually through unobstructed sneezing. ("Cover your mouth! Cover your face!") The old folklore—and the scientists—were wrong. You need to know four things so that you can avoid the cold viruses of others—and avoid reinfecting yourself:

1. Up to 100 times as many viruses are produced and shed from the nasal mucosa as from the throat.
2. There are few viruses in the saliva of a person with a cold, probably no viruses at all in about half of these individuals.
3. Dried viruses survive on dry skin and nonporous surfaces—plastic, wood, and so on—for over three hours.
4. Most cold viruses enter the body through the nostrils and eyes.

Usually colds start by the fingers picking up viruses, either from hand-to-hand contact or from surfaces that have been contaminated within the past few hours. The hands are then used to rub the eyes or pick the nose, and the virus has found its new host.[11] The moral of the story is clear. To avoid colds, wash your hands frequently, and you may kiss but not hold hands with your cold-infected sweetheart. You don't have to worry about your pets—only humans and some apes are susceptible to colds.

The experimental animal of choice for studying colds has to be the human. In many studies with human volunteers, three types of findings seem to

recur. First, not all who are directly exposed to a cold virus develop cold symptoms. In fact, only about 50 percent do. Second, in individuals with already existing antibodies to the virus, there might be only preliminary signs of a developing cold. These signs might last for a brief period (12 to 24 hours) and then disappear. Finally, it doesn't seem to matter whether people are subjected to "chilling" treatment (e.g., sitting in a draft in a wet bathing suit). *Being* cold has nothing to do with *catching* a cold.

Treatment of Cold Symptoms

There's no practical way to prevent colds and no way to cure the infection once it starts. So why do Americans spend billions each year on cold "remedies"? Apparently, it's in an effort to reduce those miserable symptoms described by Dickens. Cold symptoms are fairly complex, so most cold remedies have traditionally included several active ingredients, each aimed at a particular type of symptom. In some ways, the FDA's Cold, Cough, Allergy, Bronchodilator, and Antiasthmatic Advisory Review Panel probably had the most difficult job: multiple symptoms, many ingredients for each symptom, and rapid changes in scientific evidence during the time it studied these products. In the preliminary report, issued in 1976, the panel approved less than half of the 119 ingredients it reviewed. Modern cold remedies contain three common types of ingredients: *antihistamines,* for the temporary relief of runny nose and sneezing; *sympathomimetic nasal decongestants,* for the temporary relief of swollen membranes in the nasal passages; and *analgesic-antipyretics,* for the temporary relief of aches and pains and fever reduction. The most common antihistamine to be found in cold remedies is **chlorpheniramine maleate;** the most common nasal decongestant in cold remedies is now phenylephrine. The analgesic-antipyretic is usually acetaminophen.

Frequent handwashing is a good strategy to reduce the risk of contracting a cold. ©McGraw-Hill Education/Christopher Kerrigan, photographer

chlorpheniramine maleate (clor fen *eer* a meen mal i ate): a common antihistamine in cold products.

Table 12.3

Ingredients* in Selected Brand-Name OTC Cold and Allergy Products

Brand	Sympathomimetic	Antihistamine	Analgesic	Cough Suppressant
Night Comtrex	30 phenylephrine HCl	2 chlorpheniramine maleate	500 acetaminophen	15 dextromethorphan
Dristan	5 phenylephrine HCl	2 chlorpheniramine maleate	325 acetaminophen	—
Tylenol Cold	5 phenylephrine HCl	2 chlorpheniramine maleate	325 acetaminophen	10 dextromethorphan
Theraflu Severe Cold	10 phenylephrine HCl	25 diphenhydramine HCl	650 acetaminophen	—

*mg/tablet

Table 12.3 gives recent formulations for five popular OTC cold remedies. Note that two of them also contain the cough suppressant **dextromethorphan,** which is the most common active ingredient in OTC cough medicines.

It is ironic that the one type of ingredient found in almost every cold remedy before the FDA began its review continues to be under attack. The FDA advisory panel had serious questions about the data supporting the effectiveness of antihistamines in treating colds. Although some studies have since reported that chlorpheniramine maleate is better than placebo at reducing runny noses, prompting the FDA to approve several antihistamines, more recent controlled experiments have not found any benefit. A 1987 symposium of specialists concluded that "antihistamines do not have a place in the management of upper respiratory infection, though they continue to be useful for allergy." Still more studies have been done that question the effectiveness of antihistamines, and congressional hearings were held in 1992, asking why the FDA still allowed antihistamines in cough and cold remedies. They're still there.

In 2008, the FDA issued a Public Health Advisory warning parents not to give OTC cough and cold products to children under 2 years of age, because of serious and potentially life-threatening effects that are relatively rare but more likely to occur in these very young children. The same announcement recommended that parents or caregivers also use caution if they choose to give cough and cold products to older children up to the age of 11. The most critical parts of this include a reminder that these products do not cure nor shorten the duration of the cold and a caution to read the labels and follow the dosing directions carefully.

Allergy and Sinus Medications

There are other related products on your pharmacy shelves. In addition to the cough medicines, there are *allergy* relief pills, which rely mainly on an antihistamine, to slow down the runny nose. Sinus medicines use one of the sympathomimetic nasal decongestants (phenylephrine), often combined with an analgesic, to reduce swollen sinus passages and to treat sinus headache.

Drugs in Depth

Abuse of OTC Dextromethorphan

High school and college students have been "getting high" with large doses of OTC cough suppressants containing dextromethorphan (DM). Possibly, students first came on the effects of DM by drinking large quantities of Robitussin or similar cough syrups containing alcohol. However, the effects reported by those using 4 to 8 ounces of Robitussin (up to 720 mg DM) could not be due to the less than one-half ounce of alcohol in them and include visual and auditory hallucinations.[12] The altered psychological state may last for several hours. The few cases reported in the literature and individual reports from college students indicate that habitual use (e.g., twice per week or more) is common.

DM has been the standard ingredient in OTC cough suppressants for many years and was originally developed as a nonopiate relative to codeine. DM is not an opioidlike narcotic, produces no pain relief, and does not produce an opioidlike abstinence syndrome. More recent evidence indicates that it may interact with a specific receptor from the opioid family known as the sigma receptor. This apparently safe and simple drug, which is contained in more than 50 OTC products, has more complicated effects when taken in the large doses by recreational users.

It's not clear how recent this phenomenon really is. The Swedish government restricted DM to prescription-only use in 1986 as a result of abuse of OTC preparations, and there were two later reports of DM-caused fatalities in Sweden. In the United States, this has remained a mostly underground activity, apparently spread by word of mouth.

A posting to the alt.psychoactives newsgroup on the Internet described a user's first DM experience, after taking 20 capsules of an OTC cough remedy (600 mg DM):

> 45 minutes worth of itching and for ten seconds it stopped. During one of the most weirdest and stupidest visions, I flew quickly over a mountain. As I did this in that second the itching seemed to go away and it seemed like I wasn't in my body anymore. I flew from one side of a rainbow to another. Then I was flying quickly towards the head of an ostrich and when I got close it only showed the silhouette of the head and I flew into the black nothingness. All that craziness in ten seconds made me laugh out loud as I tried to look at it all soberly. Then the itching came back into my body. No matter how hard I tried the itching never went away.

The itching feeling has been reported by others, along with nausea and other unpleasant side effects. Despite such unpleasantness, some users find it difficult to stop using DM once they have tried it a few times.

The 2016 Monitoring the Future study (see Chapter 1) found that 4 percent of 12th graders reported nonmedical use of over-the-counter cough medicines within the previous year, a decrease from 7 percent in 2006.

Box icon credit: ©Ingram Publishing/SuperStock RF

Choosing an OTC Product

By now you should be getting the idea that, thanks to the FDA's decision to review ingredients rather than individual formulations, you as a consumer can now review and choose from among the great variety of products by knowing just a few ingredients and what they are intended to accomplish. Table 12.4 lists only seven ingredients. Those seven are the major active ingredients to be found in different combinations in OTC stimulants; sleep aids; weight-control products; analgesics; and cold, cough, allergy, and sinus medications.

Do you want to treat your cold without buying a combination cold remedy? If you have aches and pains, take your favorite analgesic. For the vast majority of colds, the slight elevation in temperature should probably not be treated, because it is not dangerous

dextromethorphan (dex tro meh *thor* fan): an OTC antitussive (cough control) ingredient.

Table 12.4
Common OTC Ingredients

Ingredient	Action	Source
Acetylsalicylic acid (ASA; aspirin)	Analgesic-antipyretic	Headache remedies, arthritis formulas, cold and sinus remedies
Acetaminophen	Analgesic-antipyretic	Headache remedies, cold and sinus remedies
Caffeine	Stimulant	"Alertness" medications
Chlorpheniramine maleate	Antihistamine	Cold remedies, allergy products
Dextromethorphan	Antitussive	Cough suppressants, cold remedies
Diphenhydramine	Antihistamine	Sleep aids, some cold remedies
Phenylephrine	Sympathomimetic	Cold and sinus remedies

and can even help fight the infection. Unless body temperature remains at 103°F or above or reaches 105°F, fever is not considered dangerous. If you have a runny nose, you might or might not get relief from an antihistamine. Generic chlorpheniramine maleate or a store-brand allergy tablet is an inexpensive source. These will probably give you a dry mouth and might produce some sedation or drowsiness (which, of course, is why some of the more sedating antihistamines are used in sleep aids). Do you have a stuffed-up nose? Pseudoephedrine nose drops will shrink swollen membranes for a time. Although oral sympathomimetics will work, nose drops are more effective. You can find these ingredients in sinus and allergy preparations. However, these sympathomimetics should be used cautiously. There is a rapid tolerance to their effects, and, if they are used repeatedly, a rebound stuffiness can develop when they are stopped. Do you have a cough? Dextromethorphan can be obtained in cough medications.

Why not buy all this in one tablet or capsule? That's a common approach. But why treat symptoms you don't have? During the course of a cold, a runny nose might occur at one time, congestion at another, and coughing not at all. By using just the ingredients you need, when you need them, you might save money, and you would have the satisfaction of being a connoisseur of colds. Then again, given the state of research on the effectiveness of these "remedies," why buy them at all? It's easy for a skeptic to conclude that there's little or no real value in cold remedies. The experts say to rest and drink fluids. But when they actually have a cold, most people are less inclined to be skeptical and more inclined to be hopeful that something will help.

Summary

- In contrast to FDA-approved OTC drugs, dietary supplements do not have to be proven effective. Also, the burden of proof for safety concerns is on the FDA as opposed to the manufacturer.

- Saint John's wort and SAMe have been proposed to treat depression, but the effectiveness of either is not clear from the available research.

- A drug can be sold over the counter only if a panel of experts agrees it can be used safely when following the label directions.

- For a given category of OTC drug, most of the various brands all contain the same few ingredients.

- OTC stimulants are based on caffeine.

- OTC sleep aids are based on antihistamines.

- Orlistat (alli) is the only FDA-approved weight-control medicine available to consumers.

- Aspirin has analgesic, antipyretic, and anti-inflammatory actions. Acetaminophen, ibuprofen, and other NSAIDs have related effects.

- Cold remedies usually contain an antihistamine, an analgesic, an antitussive, and a decongestant.

- An informed consumer can understand a large fraction of OTC medicines by knowing only seven ingredients.

Review Questions

1. What is the main difference between OTC drugs and dietary supplements?

2. What do the acronyms GRAS and GRAE stand for?

3. What are the criteria for deciding whether a drug should be sold OTC or by prescription?

4. What is the main ingredient found in OTC stimulants?

5. How safe and effective are OTC weight-control products, according to the FDA?

6. Diphenhydramine is found in what three brand-name sleep aids?

7. What effect of aspirin might be involved in its use to prevent strokes and heart attacks?

8. What are the differences in the therapeutic effects of acetaminophen and ibuprofen?

9. What is the most common route for a cold virus to enter a person's system?

10. Which cold symptoms are supposed to be relieved by chlorpheniramine maleate and which by phenylephrine?

References

1. NBJ Supplement Business Report. *National Business Journal,* 2015. Available at: http://www.transchem.com.au/wp-content/uploads/2015/09/NBJ_2015_Supplement_Report.pdf.

2. Apaydin, E. A., A. R. Maher, R. Shanman, M. S. Booth, J. N. V. Miles, M. E. Sorbero, and S. Hempel. "A Systematic Review of St. John's Wort for Major Depressive Disorder." *Systematic Reviews* 5 (2016), pp. 1–25.

3. Jang, D. J., and others. "Red Ginseng for Treating Erectile Dysfunction: A Systematic Review." *British Journal of Clinical Pharmacology* 66 (2008), pp. 444–50.

4. Shah, G. R., M. V. Chaudhari, S. B. Patankar, S. V. Pensalwar, V. P. Sabale, and N. A. Sonawane. "Evaluation of a Multi-Herb Supplement for Erectile Dysfunction: A Randomized Double-Blind, Placebo-Controlled Study." *BMC Complementary and Alternative Medicine* 12 (2012), pp. 1–9.

5. Sarris J., N. Schoendorfer, and D. J. Kavanaugh. "Major Depressive Disorder and Nutritional Medicine: A Review of Monotherapies and Adjuvant Treatments." *Nutrition Reviews* 67 (2009), pp. 125–31.

6. Evans, J. G., and others. "Evidence-Based Pharmacotherapy of Alzheimer's Disease." *International Journal of Neuropsychopharmacology* 3 (2004), pp. 351–69.

7. Consumer Healthcare Products Association. "Ingredients and Dosages Transferred from Rx to OTC Status by the Food and Drug Administration." Retrieved from www.chpa-info.org, January 2017.

8. FDA. "OTC Stimulant Drug Products, Final Monograph." *Federal Register,* February 29, 1988.

9. Lei, H., Q. Gao, S.-R. Liu, and J. Xu. "The Benefit and Safety of Aspirin for Primary Prevention of Ischemic Stroke: A Meta-Analysis of Randomized Trials." *Frontiers in Pharmacology* 7 (2016), pp. 1–10.

10. Dickens, C. *The Collected Letters of Charles Dickens.* Chapman & Hall, 1880.

11. Eccles, R., and O. Weber (Eds.). *Common Cold.* Basel, Switzerland: Birkhauser-Verlag, 2009.

12. Banken, J. A., and H. Foster. "Dextromethorphan." *Annals of the New York Academy of Sciences* 1139 (2008), pp. 402–11.

Name _____   **Date** _____

Can You Guess What These OTC Products Are Used For?

The following mock product labels include the actual list of ingredients from some OTC products. Your job is to figure out what each product is used for.

(Hint: none of them is a laxative, an acne medication, or a contraceptive.)

Use for _____

Use for _____

Use for _____

Use for _____

Use for _____

Use for _____

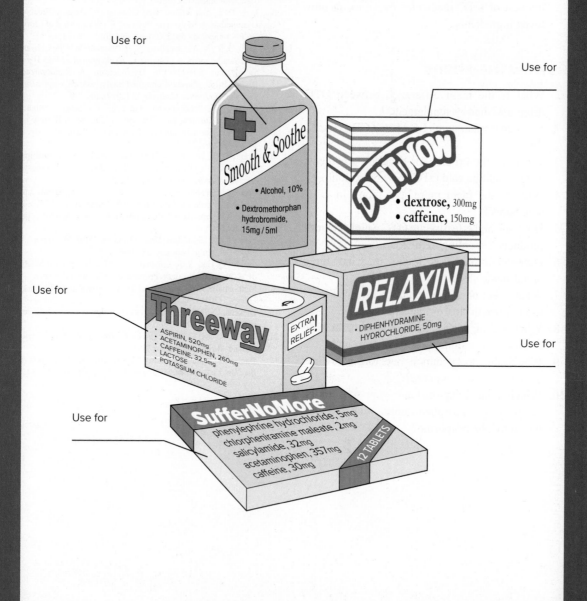

Smooth & Soothe
- Alcohol, 10%
- Dextromethorphan hydrobromide, 15mg / 5ml

QUIT NOW
- dextrose, 300mg
- caffeine, 150mg

RELAXIN
- DIPHENHYDRAMINE HYDROCHLORIDE, 50mg

Threeway EXTRA! RELIEF!
- ASPIRIN, 520mg
- ACETAMINOPHEN, 260mg
- CAFFEINE, 32.5mg
- LACTOSE
- POTASSIUM CHLORIDE

SufferNoMore
phenylephrine hydrochloride, 5mg
chlorpheniramine maleate, 2mg
salicylamide, 32mg
acetaminophen, 357mg
caffeine, 30mg
12 TABLETS

Restricted Drugs

In contrast to the everyday drugs such as nicotine and caffeine, the drugs discussed in this section include some of the least familiar and most feared substances: heroin, LSD, and marijuana. Anabolic steroids (and other performing-enhancing drugs), when used by some athletes, reliably evoke the concern of the public, most of whom have no direct contact with the drugs. Along with the stimulants, cocaine, and amphetamines, these substances are commonly viewed as evil, "devil drugs."

13 Opioids

The opioids, or narcotics, include some of the oldest useful medicines. Why did they also become the most important illicit drugs?

14 Psychedelics

Are some drugs really capable of enhancing intellectual experiences? Of producing madness?

15 Marijuana

Why has a lowly and common weed become such an important symbol of the struggle between lifestyles?

16 Performance-Enhancing Drugs

What improvements can athletes obtain by resorting to drugs? What are the associated dangers?

13

Opioids

©Botonica/JupiterImages/Getty Images

Objectives

When you have finished this chapter, you should be able to:

- Describe how opium is obtained from poppies.

- List several historical uses for opium and describe early recreational uses of opium and its derivatives.

- Explain the role of the opium trade in the wars between Great Britain and China in the 1800s.

- Describe the relationship of morphine and codeine to opium and the relationship of heroin to morphine.

- Explain how the "typical" opioid abuser has changed from the early 1900s to the present.

- Describe how sources of supply for heroin have changed over the past 30 years and list the current major source countries.

- Explain how opioid antagonists block the effects of opioid drugs.

- Recognize that endorphins and enkephalins are endogenous opioids (and explain what is meant by "endogenous").

- Describe three current medical uses for opioids.

- Describe the typical opioid withdrawal syndrome.

- Explain how people die from opioid overdose.

- Describe the typical method of preparing and injecting illicit heroin.

And soon they found themselves in the midst of a great meadow of poppies. Now it is well known that when there are many of these flowers together their odor is so powerful that anyone who breathes it falls asleep, and if the sleeper is not carried away from the scent of the flowers he sleeps on and on forever. But Dorothy did not know this, nor could she get away from the bright red flowers that were everywhere about; so presently her eyes grew heavy and she felt she must sit down to rest and to sleep. . . . Her eyes closed in spite of herself and she forgot where she was and fell among the poppies, fast asleep. . . . They carried the sleeping girl to a pretty spot beside the river, far enough from the poppy field to prevent her breathing any more of the poison of the flowers, and here they laid her gently on the soft grass and waited for the fresh breeze to waken her.[1]

From the land of Oz to the streets of San Francisco to the mountains of West Virginia, the poppy has caused much grief—and much joy. **Opium** is a unique substance. This juice from the plant *Papaver somniferum* has a history of medical use perhaps 6,000 years long. Except for the past century and a half, opium has stood alone as the one agent from which physicians could obtain sure results. Compounds containing opium solved several of the recurring problems for medical science wherever used. Opium relieved pain and suffering magnificently. Just as important in the years gone by was its ability to reduce the diarrhea and subsequent dehydration caused by **dysentery,** which is still a major cause of death in some underdeveloped countries.

Parallel with the medical use of opium was its use as a deliverer of pleasure and relief from anxiety. Because of these effects, extensive unsanctioned use of opium has also occurred throughout history. Through all those years, many of its users experienced addiction.

History of Opioids

Opium

Early History of Opium The most likely origin of opium is in a hot, dry, Middle Eastern country several millennia ago, when someone discovered that for 7 to 10 days of its yearlong life *Papaver somniferum* produced a substance that, when eaten, eased pain and suffering. The opium poppy is an annual plant that grows three to four feet high with large flowers four to five inches in diameter. The flowers can be white, pink, red, purple, or violet.

Opium is produced and available for collection for only a few days of the plant's life, between the time the petals drop and the seedpod matures. Today, as before, opium harvesters move through the fields in the early evening and use a sharp, clawed tool to make shallow cuts into, but not through, the unripe seedpods. During the night a white substance oozes from the cuts, oxidizes to a red-brown color, and becomes gummy. In the morning the resinous substance is carefully scraped from the pod and collected in small balls. This raw opium forms the basis for the opium medicines that

have been used throughout history and is the substance from which morphine is extracted and then heroin is derived.

The importance and extent of use of the opium poppy in the early Egyptian and Greek cultures are still under debate, but in the Ebers papyrus (circa 1500 BC) a remedy is mentioned "to prevent the excessive crying of children." Because a later Egyptian remedy for the same purpose clearly contained opium (as well as fly excrement), many writers report the first specific medical use of opium as dating from the Ebers papyrus.

Opium was important in Greek medicine. Galen, the last of the great Greek physicians, emphasized caution in the use of opium but felt that it was almost a cure-all, saying that it

> resists poison and venomous bites, cures chronic headache, vertigo, deafness, epilepsy, apoplexy, dimness of sight, loss of voice, asthma, coughs of all kinds, spitting of blood, tightness of breath, colic, the iliac poison, jaundice, hardness of the spleen, stone, urinary complaints, fevers, dropsies, leprosies, the troubles to which women are subject, melancholy and all pestilences.[2]

Greek and Roman knowledge of opium use in medicine languished during the Dark Ages and thus had little influence on the world's use of opium for the next thousand years. The Arabic world, however, clutched opium to its breast. Because the Koran forbade the use of alcohol in any form, opium and hashish became the primary social drugs wherever the Islamic culture moved, and it did move. While Europe rested through the Dark Ages, the Arabian world reached out and made contact with India and China. Opium was one of the products they traded, but they also sold the seeds of the opium poppy, and cultivation began in these countries. By the 10th century AD, opium had been referred to in Chinese medical writings.

opium: a raw plant substance containing morphine and codeine.

dysentery: an intestinal inflammation that can lead to severe diarrhea with mucus or blood in the feces.

Drugs in the Media

If There Isn't a Heroin Epidemic, Why Do the Media Keep Saying There Is?

For several years now in this book we have been skeptical of news reports warning of an impending "heroin epidemic." These reports were usually triggered by an apparent heroin-related death of a celebrity; use of heroin by young, white suburban dwellers (seen as evidence that a new generation is being affected); or the spectacular seizure of a large drug shipment. Despite these scary news accounts, filled with lurid details and predictions of doom, the predicted epidemic never seems to materialize and fades from memory. Once the "epidemic" has been forgotten, television and newspaper reporters are primed to alarm us about the next epidemic a few years later.

A few years have passed, and the most recent apparent heroin epidemic is upon us. But now there is an additional opioid that we have been made to fear—fentanyl. Fentanyl produces a heroin-like high but is considerably more potent, meaning that less of the drug is required to produce an effect, including overdose. To make matters worse, some media reports suggest that illicit heroin is often adulterated with fentanyl. This, of course, can be problematic, and even fatal, for unsuspecting heroin users who ingest too much of the substance thinking that it's heroin alone. Given these observations, it is not difficult to understand public fear about epidemic use of heroin and/or fentanyl.

But questions remain regarding whether use of these substances has indeed reached epidemic proportions. It might be helpful for us to first define the term *epidemic*. This will aid us in our effort to determine whether we are in the midst of a heroin (or fentanyl) use epidemic. *Drug epidemic* usually refers to a sudden increase in the number of users of a particular drug. Has there been a sudden increase in heroin use? Probably not. Heroin use has always been less common than use of other illicit drugs such as marijuana and cocaine, and its use has also been restricted to a very small proportion of the U.S. population. An examination of both past-month and past-year heroin use shows that use has remained stable from 2014 to 2015.[3] Even if we go back further in time to 2006 and compare the number of past-month heroin users with

the number of users in 2015, we will see that about 300,000 Americans reported heroin use in both years. But, when we examine the number of past-year heroin users from 2006 to 2015, we see that the number of users increased gradually from about 600,000 to 800,000. The increase in past-year users, while past-month use remained stable, suggest that we should continue to monitor heroin for additional signs of rising use. It would be far more concerning, for example, if both past-month and past-year heroin use increased during the same period.

What about the prevalence of fentanyl use, whether used intentionally or not? Intentional recreational use of fentanyl is even more rare than heroin use. Indeed, the numbers are so low that use of this drug rarely shows up in our typical survey. Fentanyl, however, has been reported as one of the contributing causes of death in an increasing number of cases involving fatal opioid overdoses. The precise role of fentanyl in these cases is difficult to disentangle because often multiple drugs, including alcohol and benzodiazepines, are involved.

Media reports that blare headlines warning about drug epidemics are good at attracting attention—and increasing sales and advertising revenue—so there's always a market for such stories. But they are often misleading and simply inaccurate, which does little to focus on issues that will help keep drug users safe, such as providing information about overdose prevention or discussing strategies to test illicit drugs to ensure they do not contain potential dangerous adulterants.

Keep your eyes and ears open, and it won't be long before you read or hear a news report about an epidemic of heroin use in a part of the United States or in another country. Ask yourself whether the report cites formal studies that help quantify the problem, or does it vaguely point to "ominous signs" of increasing drug use? Also, ask yourself whether the report provides a discussion of solutions designed to help keep users safe.

Box icon credit: ©Glow Images RF

During this period, two Arabic physicians made substantial contributions to medicine and to the history of opium. Shortly after AD 1000, Biruni composed a pharmacology book. His descriptions of opium contained what some believe to be the first written description of **opioid** addiction.[4] In the same period the best-known Arabic physician, Avicenna, was using opium preparations very effectively and extensively in his medical practice. His writings, along with those of Galen, formed the basis of medical education in Europe as the Renaissance dawned, and thus the glories of opium were advanced. (Avicenna, a knowledgeable physician and a believer in the tenets of Islam, died as a result of drinking too much of a mixture of opium and wine.)

Early in the 16th century, Paracelsus was a successful clinician and accomplished some wondrous cures for the day. One of his secrets was an opium extract called laudanum. Paracelsus was one of the early Renaissance supporters of opium as a panacea and referred to it as the "stone of immortality."

Due to Paracelsus and his followers, awareness of the broad effectiveness of opium increased, and new opium preparations were developed in the 16th, 17th, and 18th centuries. One of these was laudanum as prepared by Dr. Thomas Sydenham, the father of English clinical medicine. Sydenham's general contributions to English medicine are so great that he has been called the English Hippocrates. He spoke more highly of opium than did Paracelsus, saying that "without opium the healing art would cease to exist." His laudanum contained two ounces of strained opium, one ounce of saffron, a dram of cinnamon, and a dram of cloves dissolved in one pint of Canary wine, taken in small quantities.

Writers and Opium: The Keys to Paradise Several famous English authors wrote about the joys of opium, including Elizabeth Barrett Browning and Samuel Taylor Coleridge. Coleridge's beautiful "Kubla Khan" is believed to have been conceived and partially composed in an opium reverie. But, perhaps the author who most enthusiastically articulated the powers of opium was Thomas De Quincey. In his 1821 book, *Confessions of an English Opium-Eater,* De Quincey meticulously describes both the pleasures and the pains of regular opium use. Of the pleasures, he wrote:

> . . . my pains had vanished . . . here was the secret of happiness, about which philosophers had disputed for so many ages, at once discovered: happiness now might be bought for a penny, and carried in a waistcoat pocket: portable ecstasies might be had corked up in a pint-bottle . . .[5]

The effects of most psychoactive agents are not unidimensional. De Quincey discovered that opium was no exception. He detailed the pains of opium withdrawal and reported not being able to write for long periods of time due to his dependence on the drug. Even in the early 19th century, a period that many contemporary observers tend to regard as one with few drug use moral strictures, De Quincey felt compelled to provide justification for his daily use of opium:

> True it is, that for nearly ten years I did occasionally take opium for the sake of the exquisite pleasure it gave me . . . It was not for the purpose of creating pleasure, but of mitigating pain in the severest degree, that I first began to use opium as an article of daily diet. In the twenty-eighth year of my age, a most painful affection of the stomach, which I had first experienced about ten years before, attached me in great strength.[5]

It seems that regular use of opium has a long history of being viewed unfavorably by certain members of society, and this view was prevalent even when De Quincey wrote about his opium experiences.

The Opium Wars Although opium and the opium poppy had been introduced to China well before the year AD 1000, there was only a moderate level of use there by a select, elite group. Tobacco smoking

---

opioid: a drug derived from opium (e.g., morphine and codeine) or a synthetic drug with opiumlike effects (e.g., oxycodone).

Smoking opium results in more rapid effects than taking the drug orally. ©SOE ZEYA TUN/Alamy Stock Photo

spread much more rapidly after its introduction. It is not clear when tobacco was introduced to the Chinese, but its use had spread and become so offensive that in 1644 the emperor forbade tobacco smoking in China. The edict did not last long (as is to be expected), but it was in part responsible for the increase in opium smoking.

Up to this period the smoking of tobacco and the eating of opium had existed side by side. The restriction on the use of tobacco and the population's appreciation of the pleasures of smoking led to the combining of opium and tobacco for smoking. Presumably the addition of opium took the edge off the craving for tobacco. The amount of tobacco used was gradually reduced and soon omitted. Although opium eating had never been very attractive to most Chinese, opium smoking spread rapidly, perhaps in part because smoking opium results in a rapid effect, compared with oral use.

In 1729, China's first law against opium smoking mandated that opium shop owners be strangled. Once opium for nonmedical purposes was outlawed, it was necessary for the drug to be smuggled in from India, where poppy plantations were abundant. Smuggling opium was so profitable for everyone—the growers, the shippers, and the customs officers—that unofficial rules were gradually developed for the "game."[2] The background to the Opium Wars is lengthy and complex, but the following can help explain why the British went to war so that they could continue pouring opium into China against the wishes of the Chinese national government.

Since before 1557, when the Portuguese were allowed to develop the small trading post of Macao, pressure had been increasing on the Chinese emperors to open up the country to trade with the "barbarians from the West." Not only the Portuguese but also the Dutch and the English repeatedly knocked on the closed door of China. Near the end of the 17th century the port of Canton was opened under very strict rules to foreigners. Tea was the major export, and the British shipped out huge amounts. There was little that the Chinese were interested in importing from the "barbarians," but opium could be smuggled so profitably that it soon became the primary import. The profit the British made from selling opium paid for the tea they shipped back to England.[6] In the early 19th century the government of India was actually the British East India Company. As such, it had a monopoly on opium, which was legal in India. However, smuggling it into China was not. The East India Company auctioned chests of opium cakes to private merchants, who gave the chests to selected British firms, which sold them for a commission to Chinese merchants. In this way the British were able to have the Chinese "smuggle" the opium into China. The number of chests of opium, each with about 120 pounds of smokable opium, imported annually by China increased from 200 in 1729 to about 5,000 at the century's end to 25,000 chests in 1838.

In 1839, the emperor of China made a fatal mistake—he sent an honest man to Canton to suppress the opium smuggling. Commissioner Lin demanded that the barbarians deliver all their opium supplies to him and subjected the dealers to confinement in their houses. After some haggling, the representative of the British government ordered the merchants to deliver the opium—20,000 chests worth about $6 million—which was then destroyed, and everyone was set free. Pressures mounted, however, and an incident involving drunken American and British sailors killing a Chinese citizen started the Opium Wars in 1839. The British army arrived 10 months later, and in two years, largely by avoiding land battles and by using the superior artillery of the royal navy ships, they won a victory over a country of more than 350 million citizens. As victors, the British were given the island of Hong Kong, broad trading rights, and $6 million to reimburse the merchants whose opium had been destroyed.

The Chinese opium trade posed a great moral dilemma for Britain. The East India Company protested until its end that it was not smuggling opium into China, and technically it was not. From 1870 to 1893, motions in Parliament to end the extremely profitable opium commerce failed to pass but did cause a decline in the opium trade. In 1893, a moral protest against the trade was supported, but not until 1906 did the government support and pass a bill that eventually ended the opium trade in 1913.

Morphine

In 1806, Frederich Sertürner published a report of more than 50 experiments, which clearly showed that he had isolated the primary active ingredient in opium. The active agent was 10 times as potent as opium. Sertürner named it *morphium* after Morpheus, the god of dreams. Use of the new agent developed slowly, but by 1831 the implications of his chemical work and the medical value of **morphine** had become so overwhelming that this pharmacist's assistant was given the French equivalent of the Nobel Prize. Later work into the mysteries of opium found more than 30 different alkaloids, with the second most important one being isolated in 1832 and named **codeine,** the Greek word for "poppy head."

The availability of a clinically useful, pure chemical of known potency is always capitalized on in medicine. The major increase in the use of morphine came as a result of two nondrug developments, one technological and one political. The technological development was the perfection of the hypodermic syringe in 1853 by Dr. Alexander Wood. This made it possible to deliver morphine directly into the blood or tissue rather than by the much slower process of eating opium or

Raw opium is the substance from which morphine is extracted and then heroin is derived.
Source: Drug Enforcement Administration

morphine and waiting for absorption to occur from the gastrointestinal tract. A further advantage of injecting morphine was thought to exist. Originally it was felt that morphine by injection would not produce the same degree of craving (hunger) for the drug as with oral use. This belief was later found to be false.

The political events that sped the drug of sleep and dreams into the veins of people worldwide were the American Civil War (1861–1865), the Prussian-Austrian War (1866), and the Franco-Prussian War (1870). Military medicine was, and to some extent still is, characterized by the dictum "first provide relief." Morphine given by injection worked rapidly and well, and it was administered regularly in large doses to many soldiers for the reduction of pain and relief from dysentery. The percentage of veterans returning from these wars who were dependent on morphine was high enough that the illness was later called "soldier's disease" or the "army disease."

Heroin

Toward the end of the 19th century, a small but important chemical transformation was made to the morphine molecule. In 1874, two acetyl groups

> **morphine:** the primary active agent in opium.
>
> **codeine:** the secondary active agent in opium.

were attached to morphine, yielding diacetylmorphine, which was given the brand name Heroin and placed on the market in 1898 by Bayer Laboratories. The chemical change was important because **heroin** is about three times as potent as morphine. The pharmacology of heroin and morphine is identical, except that the two acetyl groups increase the lipid solubility of the heroin molecule, and thus the molecule enters the brain more rapidly. The additional groups are then detached, yielding morphine. Therefore, the effects of morphine and heroin are identical, except that heroin is believed to be more potent and acts faster.

Heroin was originally marketed as a nonaddictive cough suppressant that would replace morphine and codeine.[7] It seemed to be the perfect drug, more potent yet less harmful. Although not introduced commercially until 1898, heroin had been studied, and many of its pharmacological actions had been reported in 1890.[8] In January 1900, a comprehensive review article concluded that tolerance and dependence on heroin were only minor problems:

> Habituation has been noted in a small percentage . . . of the cases. . . . All observers are agreed, however, that none of the patients suffer in any way from this habituation, and that none of the symptoms which are so characteristic of chronic morphinism have ever been observed. On the other hand, a large number of the reports refer to the fact that the same dose may be used for a long time without any habituation.[9]

The basis for the failure to find dependence probably was the fact that heroin was initially used as a substitute for codeine, which meant oral doses of 3 to 5 mg used for brief periods of time. Slowly the situation changed, and a 1905 text, *Pharmacology and Therapeutics,* took a middle ground on heroin by saying that it "is stated not to give rise to habituation. A more extended knowledge of the drug, however, would seem to indicate that the latter assertion is not entirely correct."[10] In a few more years, everyone knew that heroin could produce a powerful dependence when injected in higher doses.

Opioid Abuse before the Harrison Act

In the second half of the 19th century, three forms of opioid addiction were developing in the United States. The long-useful oral intake of opium, and then morphine, increased greatly as patent medicines became a standard form of self-medication. After 1850, Chinese laborers were imported in large numbers to the West Coast, and they introduced opium smoking to this country. The last form, medically the most dangerous and ultimately the most disruptive socially, was the injection of morphine.

Around the start of the 20th century, the percentage (and perhaps the absolute number) of Americans addicted to one of the opioids was probably greater than at any other time before or since. Several authorities, both then and more recently, agree that no less than 1 percent of the population was addicted to opioids, although accurate statistics are not available. The opium smoking the Chinese brought to this country never became widely popular, although about one-fourth of the opium imported was smoking opium at the start of the 20th century. Perhaps it was because the smoking itself occupies only about a minute and is then followed by a state of reverie that can last two or three hours—hardly conducive to a continuation of daily activities or consonant with the outward, active orientation of most Americans in that period. Another reason that opium smoking did not spread was that it originated with Asians, who were scorned by whites.

The growth of the patent medicine industry after the Civil War has been well documented. Everything seemed to be favorable for the industry, and it took advantage of each opportunity. There were few government regulations on the industry, and as a result, drugs with a high abuse potential were an important part of many tonics and remedies, although this fact did not have to be indicated on the label.

Patent medicines promised, and in part delivered, the perfect self-medication. They were easily available, not too expensive, socially acceptable, and they worked. The amount of alcohol and/or opioids in many of the nostrums was certain to relieve the user's aches, pains, and anxieties.

Gradually some medical concern developed over the number of people who were dependent on opioids, and this concern was a part of the motivation that led to the passage of the 1906 Pure Food and Drugs Act. In 1910, a government expert in this area made clear that this law was only a beginning:

> The thoughtful and foremost medical men have been and are cautioning against the free use of morphine and opium, particularly in recurring pain. The amount they are using is decreasing yearly. Notwithstanding this fact, and the fact that legislation, federal, state and territorial, adverse to the indiscriminate use and sale of opium and morphine, their derivatives and preparations, has been enacted during the past few decades, the amount of opium per capita imported and consumed in the United States has doubled during the last forty years. . . . It is well known that there are many factors at work tending to drug enslavement, among them being the host of soothing syrups, medicated soft drinks containing cocaine, asthma remedies, catarrh remedies, consumption remedies, cough and cold remedies, and the more notorious so-called "drug addiction cures." It is often stated that medical men are frequently the chief factors in causing drug addiction.[11]

Data presented in this paper tended to support the belief that medical use of opioids initiated by a physician was one, if not the, major cause of addiction in this country at that time. A 1918 government report clearly indicted the physician as the major cause of addiction in individuals of "good social standing."

That physicians widely used opioid medications is understandable in light of articles that had been published, such as one in 1889 titled "Advantages of Substituting the Morphia Habit for the Incurably Alcoholic." The author stated:

> In this way I have been able to bring peacefulness and quiet to many disturbed and distracted homes, to keep the head of a family out of the gutter and out of the lock-up, to keep him from scandalous misbehavior and neglect of his affairs, to keep him from the verges and actualities of delirium tremens horrors, and above all, to save him from committing, as I veritably believe, some terrible crime.[12]

Besides all those good things, a morphine habit was cheap: By one estimate it was 10 times as expensive

to be a heavy drinker—costing 25 cents a day. The article concluded:

> I might, had I time and space, enlarge by statistics to prove the law-abiding qualities of opium-eating peoples, but of this any one can perceive somewhat for himself, if he carefully watches and reflects on the quiet, introspective gaze of the morphine habitue, and compares it to the riotous, devil-may-care leer of the drunkard.[12]

In the late 19th century, regular opioid use was viewed as a "vice of middle life." The typical opioid user of this period was a 30- to 50-year-old white woman who functioned well and was adjusted to her life as a wife and mother. She bought opium or morphine legally at the local store, used it orally, and caused few, if any, social problems. She might have ordered her "family remedy" through the mail from Sears, Roebuck—two ounces of laudanum for 18 cents or 1½ pints for $2. Of course, there were problems associated with addiction during this period. There are always individuals who are unable to control their drug intake, whether the drug is used for self-medication or recreation. Nonetheless, because of the high opioid content of patent medicines and the ready availability of dependence-producing drugs for drinking and/or injecting, very high levels of drug were frequently used. As a result, the symptoms of withdrawal were severe and the most expedient relief was obtained by taking more of the drug.

Abuse after the Harrison Act

The complex reasons for the passage of the 1914 Harrison Act were discussed in detail in Chapter 3. Remember that this was a fairly simple revenue measure. However, as is true of most laws, it is not the law itself that becomes important in the ensuing years, but the court decisions and enforcement practices that evolve as the law interacts with the people it affects.

> The passing of the Harrison Act in 1914 left the status of the addict almost completely indeterminate. The act did not make addiction illegal and it neither

heroin: diacetylmorphine, a potent derivative of morphine.

authorized nor forbade doctors to prescribe drugs regularly for addicts. All that it clearly and unequivocally did require was that whatever drugs addicts obtained were to be secured from physicians registered under the act and that the fact of securing drugs be made a matter of record. While some drug users had obtained supplies from physicians before 1914, it was not necessary for them to do so since drugs were available for purchase in pharmacies and even from mail-order houses.[13]

In 1915, the U.S. Supreme Court decided that possession of smuggled opioids was a crime, and thus users not obtaining the drug from a physician became criminals with the stroke of a pen. Addicted users could still obtain their supply of drugs on a prescription from a physician, until this avenue was removed by Supreme Court decisions in 1919 and 1922 (see Chapter 3). Even though the *Lindner* case in 1925 reversed these earlier decisions and stated that a physician could prescribe drugs to nonhospitalized users just to maintain their dependence, the

doctors had been harassed and arrested enough. Few physicians would do so. Clinics for the treatment of opioid addictions were closed during the 1920s under pressure from federal officials.

The number of oral opioid users began to decline in response to these pressures, and the primary remaining group were those who injected morphine or heroin. By 1922, about the only source of opioids for a nonhospitalized abuser was an illegal dealer. Because heroin was the most potent opioid available, it was the easiest to conceal and therefore became the illegal dealer's choice. The cost through this source was 30 to 50 times the price of the same drug through legitimate sources, which no longer were available to people who suffered from opioid addiction. Because of this cost, users wanted to be certain to get the most "bang for their buck," so intravenous injection became more common. To maintain a supply of the drug in this way was expensive. A minority of users resorted to

---

Taking Sides

Should Naloxone Be Made Available to Opioid Users?

Each year, in major U.S. cities, hundreds of opioid users die from overdose. Most of these deaths occur in the presence of a drug-using mate, who may be reluctant to contact emergency medical services for fear of prosecution. Naloxone, a fast-acting opioid antagonist, can reverse opioid-induced respiratory depression and prevent death if given within minutes of an overdose. While naloxone has been used in hospital emergency departments for decades, it is not readily available to opioid users because, in the United States, it can be obtained only via a prescription in most cities. However, concern regarding the increased number of opioid related overdose deaths has prompted health officials around the country, to initiate programs that would provide naloxone and rescue-breathing training to illicit opioid users and their partners, friends, and/or family members.

Despite reported reductions in the number of overdose deaths in areas where these programs exist, critics argue that by making illicit opioid use less dangerous it sends a message that drug use is condoned

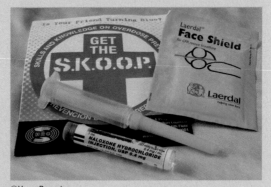

©Harry Peronius

and will decrease the likelihood of opioid users seeking treatment even if they need it. Proponents, however, view such programs as a form of harm reduction—that is, the prioritizing of preventing harms associated with drug use rather than focusing solely on preventing drug use. What do you think?

Box icon credit: ©Nova Development RF

criminal activity, primarily burglary and other crimes against property, to finance their addiction.

During this period, law enforcement agencies and the popular press brought about a change in the attitudes of society toward the illicit opioid users. Thus, sometime during the 1920s, the general public became even less tolerant of people with drug addictions (some of the reasons for this shift are discussed below). Instead of being viewed as unfortunate victims deserving sympathy and medical assistance, illicit opioid users were now viewed as degenerates and criminals. As such, the law enforcement approach became the primary means of addressing drug dependence.

The Changing Population of Opioid Users After the Harrison Act, the number of white middle-aged people using opioids orally declined. In the early years after World War II, heroin use slowly increased in the lower-class areas of the large cities. Heroin was inexpensive in this period; a dollar would buy enough for a good high for three to six people; $2-a-day habits were not uncommon. As the 1950s passed, heroin use spread. As demand increased, so did both the price and the amount of adulteration.

The 1960s and onward In the 1960s, the use of various drugs skyrocketed. Flower children, hippies, Tim Leary, and LSD received most of the media attention, but within the central core of the large American cities the number of regular and irregular heroin users also increased. Mainstream USA became concerned with the heroin problem of the large cities. As the drug became more demonized—through print and electronic media, the most visible users were black or Latino. The white majority expressed little patience or tolerance toward people who were addicted to or who sold heroin. In fact, this view fueled the passage of New York State's infamous Rockefeller Drug Laws in 1973. These laws created mandatory minimum prison sentences of 15 years to life for possession of four ounces of drugs such as heroin, and earned New York the distinction of having the strictest drug laws in the nation. More than 90 percent of the individuals convicted under these laws were either black or

Latino, prompting calls for reform because of selective enforcement and prosecution. After 36 years with no appreciable changes to the Rockefeller Laws, in April 2009, Governor David Patterson signed into law sweeping reforms, which eliminated the harsh sentences that the laws mandated by returning the discretion to judges who could now divert individuals with drug addictions to treatment.

Vietnam The attitude of people in the street toward the relevance of heroin use to their personal lives changed rapidly with the reports that began to filter out of Southeast Asia toward the end of the 1960s. Public anxiety increased dramatically with the possibility that the Vietnam conflict might produce thousands of drug users among the military personnel stationed there.

Heroin was about 95 percent pure and sold almost openly in South Vietnam, whereas purity in the United States was about 5 percent in 1969. Not only was the Southeast Asia heroin undiluted, but it also was inexpensive. Ten dollars would buy about 250 mg, enough for 5 to 10 injections and an amount that would cost more than $500 in the United States. The high purity of the heroin made it possible to obtain psychological effects by smoking or sniffing the drug. This fact, coupled with the fallacious belief that addiction occurs only when the drug is used intravenously, resulted in about 40 percent of the users sniffing, about half smoking, and only 10 percent injecting their heroin.[14]

Some early 1971 reports estimated that 10 to 15 percent of the American troops in Vietnam were addicted to heroin. As a result of the increased magnitude and visibility of the heroin problem, the U.S. government took several rapid steps in mid-1971. One step was to initiate Operation Golden Flow, a urine-testing program to detect opioids in service personnel ready to leave Vietnam.

In October 1971, the Pentagon released figures for the first three months of testing, which showed that 5.1 percent of the 100,000 personnel tested showed traces of opioids in their urine. Most of the opioid users were in the lower ranks.

In retrospect, the Vietnam drug-use situation was "making a mountain out of a molehill," but much was learned. An excellent follow-up study of veterans who returned from Vietnam in September 1971 showed that most of the Vietnam heroin users did not continue heroin use in this country.[15] Only 1 to 2 percent were using opioids 8 to 12 months after returning from Vietnam and being released from the service, approximately the same percentage of individuals found to be using opioids when examined for induction into the service.

One of the important things learned from this experience is that heroin addiction and compulsive use are not inevitable among occasional users. (By the way, today most users of opioid drugs are not addicted, compulsive users.) The pattern of drug use in Vietnam also supports the belief that under certain conditions—availability and low cost of the drug, limited sanctions, stress—a relatively high percentage of individuals will use opioids recreationally.

Production and Purity In 1972, the major source of U.S. heroin was opium grown in Turkey and converted into heroin in southern French port cities, such as Marseilles. This "French connection" accounted for as much as 80 percent of U.S. heroin before 1973. In 1972, Turkey banned all opium cultivation and production in return for $35 million the United States provided to make up for the financial losses to farmers and to help them develop new cash crops. This action, combined with a cooperative effort with the French (also partially funded by the United States), did lead to a reduction in the supply of heroin on the streets of New York in 1973.

This relative shortage did not last for long. In Mexico, opium is processed into morphine by a different process, and the resulting pure heroin has a brown or black color. In 1975, the Drug Enforcement Administration (DEA) estimated that 80 percent or more of all U.S. heroin was from Mexico (depending on its appearance, either called *Mexican brown* or **black tar**). The supply was plentiful, the price low, and the purity high. In 1974, the United States began to finance opium eradication programs in Mexico. Although it is hopeless to try to eliminate all such production, these monumental and expensive efforts did slow the importation

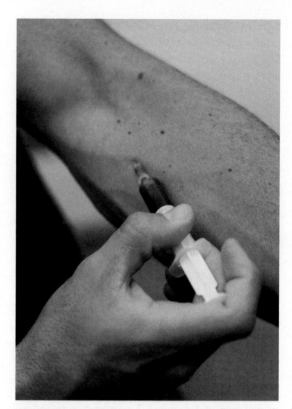

Although heroin dependence is often associated with intravenous use, dependence can occur via any route that produces behavioral or physiological effects.
©Medioimages/PictureQuest RF

from Mexico to some extent, and the "epidemic" of the 1970s began to decline.

In the late 20th century, about half of the U.S. heroin supply apparently originated in Southwest Asia (Afghanistan, Pakistan, Iran). Mexico was the next biggest contributor, with the Golden Triangle area of Southeast Asia (Myanmar, Laos, and Thailand) producing about 15 to 20 percent of the total. Today, the world's supply of heroin has shifted dramatically, with more than 90 percent originating in Afghanistan. While the overwhelming majority of heroin in Europe, Russia, the Middle East, and Asia is supplied by Afghanistan, most of the heroin used in the United States is derived from poppies grown in Mexico.[16] To a much lesser extent, heroin in the United States is also produced in Colombia.

Increased production in Mexico and South America has resulted in both greater availability

Life Saver

Opioids: Less Hysteria and More Useful Information

A major problem with the current media coverage that exaggerates opioid use is that useful information is rarely transmitted. One of our goals within these pages is to provide education that helps to keep people safe whether they use drugs or not. Most of us have loved ones who do use drugs. Thinking about potential problems associated with opioid use within this frame, it is important for you to know that the major concerns related to opioid use are (1) opioid-sedative combination deaths, (2) acetaminophen toxicity, and (3) addiction. It is possible to die from an overdose involving a single opioid drug, but this accounts for a relatively small percentage of opioid-related deaths each year.

1. Combining an opioid with another sedative, such as alcohol or a benzodiazepine (like Xanax or Klonopin), accounts for most opioid-related deaths. Rather than cast fear and uncertainty on opioids across the board, public health education campaigns would be more effective at saving lives if they advised opioid users to avoid combining opioids with other sedatives.
2. The latest data from the National Survey on Drug Use and Health show that just over 300,000 people reported using heroin at least once in the past 30 days. (Note that this number is substantially lower than the number of individuals who reported use of marijuana, at about 22 million; prescription opioids, at about 4 million; and cocaine, at 2 million, over the same period). Instead, most individuals seeking a heroin-like high use prescription opioids recreationally. On the one hand, this is a good thing, because the purity of street heroin is sometimes poor due to adulterants added to increase the quantity of the product. Prescription opioids

are usually a higher quality, as they are pharmaceutical grade.

But popular prescription medications like Percocet, Vicodin, and Tylenol 3 contain a relatively low dose of an opioid in combination with a considerably larger dose of acetaminophen—and excessive acetaminophen exposure is the number-one cause of liver damage in the United States. Some users may unwittingly risk liver damage by taking too many of these pills. It would be far more helpful to inform people not to overdo it on opioids containing acetaminophen because it can be more fatal than the low doses of opioids contained in these formulations.

3. The overwhelming majority of opioid users do not become addicts. One review of the research put the rate of addiction among people prescribed opioids for pain at less than 1 percent.[17] We recognize that this finding may not conform with the popular view. But the quicker we can dispel myths surrounding drug use, the better our focus on real concerns becomes.

In our view, far less emphasis should be placed on hyping the dangers of opioids. Opioids have been used safely for centuries and are important instruments in the physician's toolbox. As we are learning in this chapter, they are used medically to treat pain and suppress cough. Exaggerating the harms of opioids, or any other drug, does little to ensure the safety of users. It merely diverts attention and resources away from the real concerns and decreases our ability to take the most appropriate steps to keep people healthy and safe.

Box icon credit: ©McGraw-Hill Education

---

and greater purity in the U.S. market. From the mid-1970s through the mid-1980s the average purity varied from 4 to 6 percent heroin (more than 90 percent was something else the dealers used to cut the heroin). However, in the late 1980s, increased shipments of increasingly pure heroin began to arrive, and in 1989 the average street purity was estimated to be 25 percent, at least four

times as strong as in years past. Today, heroin purity ranges between 50 and 75 percent. The price of a "bag" has not changed much, so the price per milligram of actual heroin was down.

black tar: a type of illicit heroin usually imported from Mexico.

Heroin use has for many years been restricted to a small fraction of any population studied. For example, in the 2015 National Survey on Drug Use and Health described in Chapter 1, only about 1 percent of U.S. adults reported ever having used heroin in their lifetimes, with 0.3 percent reporting use in the past year. These numbers have remained relatively stable for at least a decade, but this has not tempered periodic press reports indicating that the country is experiencing a heroin epidemic (see Drugs in the Media box, page 290).

Abuse of Prescription Opioids

The most popular prescription opioids are various brands of hydrocodone (e.g., Vicodin and Lortab) and oxycodone (OxyContin and Percocet). These are mostly taken orally, but when used recreationally they are sometimes snorted or injected. In 2015,

1.4 percent of Americans aged 12 and older reported nonmedical use of a prescription pain reliever within the past month. Recently, you may have seen or read news reports contending that prescription pain reliever use has now reached epidemic rates. Without any context, however, it can be difficult to determine whether past month use of these drugs warrants our concern. When making this determination, you should know that over the past several years the prevalence of prescription opioids has remained relatively stable. For example, in 2002, 2 percent of Americans reported past month nonmedical use—a figure that is slightly higher than the current one. Keep in mind also that past month use could range from using only once to using on multiple occasions. Another question that you should probably ask is how do the rates of illicit prescription opioid use compare with other illicit drugs? In 2015, 8.3 percent and 0.7 percent of

---

Drugs in Depth

Prescribing Pain Medications: Damned If You Do and Damned If You Don't

Chronic pain is a condition that can negatively impact an individual's quality of life, by disrupting sleep, employment, social functioning, and many other routine daily activities. Approximately one-third of the U.S. population (or more than 90 million Americans) has symptoms of chronic pain. Opioids are the most effective medications in the treatment of chronic pain. But, periodic high-profile deaths of celebrities and reports of drugstore robberies reignited concerns about physicians overprescribing opioid pain medications. Many believe that physicians are too quick to distribute opioid medications to patients. Indeed, occasionally media headlines blare with stories about rogue physicians arrested for "pushing pills," that is, dispensing pain medications indiscriminately for quick cash. There are also periodic stories of cunning patients who "doctor shop," deceiving physicians in order to obtain large amounts of opioid medications. The fact that most physicians want to do the right thing and are judicious in their prescribing of pain medications is frequently omitted from sensational accounts of the "drug pusher doctor."

This situation, coupled with the fact that pain is a subjective experience that can be difficult to rate externally, has placed pain management physicians in an awkward position. What's more, some patients may have developed tolerance to the medications and may require larger doses to alleviate their symptoms. Many responsible physicians attempting to adequately treat chronic pain patients have come under suspicion for running "pill mills." Some have even been prosecuted and convicted. The message seems clear: "Don't prescribe opioid pain medications but, if you absolutely have to, do so only in small doses." Of course, this could lead to charges of "grossly undertreating" patients' pain symptoms. In 1999, the Oregon Board of Medical Examiners disciplined Dr. Paul Bilder for precisely this reason. In several cases, Dr. Bilder was reluctant to give patients opioid medications, even though their symptoms clearly indicated that these medications were the most prudent course of action. As a result of physicians being sanctioned for both over- and underprescribing opioids, some feel that they are damned if they do and damned if they don't.

Box icon credit: ©Ingram Publishing/SuperStock RF

Americans reported past-month use of marijuana and cocaine, respectively. Clearly, prescription opioid use (1.4 percent) exceeds cocaine use but is markedly lower than marijuana use. What about toxicity? It is important to note that most opioid overdoses occur in combination with a sedative such as alcohol (see Life Saver box, page 299). Nonetheless, concern about the relatively high rates of nonmedical use of opioids and their potential for toxic consequences when misused has led the FDA and drug manufacturers to take preventive measures. For example, the FDA now requires opioid manufacturers to prepare educational materials that physicians or prescribers can use when counseling patients about the risks and benefits of opioid use, while some opioid manufacturers have developed "abuse deterrent" formulations of their drugs (e.g., the drug can't be dissolved in water and injected). The bottom line is that the use of prescription pain relievers has not increased dramatically in recent years, but there appears to be a real concern about the potential for toxicity when the drugs are misused. As is the case with many controlled substances, this situation requires balancing the need for continued access to these medications with measures to reduce their risks.

Pharmacology of Opioids

Chemical Characteristics

Raw opium contains about 10 percent morphine by weight and a smaller amount of codeine. The addition of two acetyl groups to the morphine molecule results in diacetylmorphine, or heroin (Figure 13.1). The acetyl groups allow heroin to penetrate the blood-brain barrier more readily, and heroin is therefore two to three times more potent than morphine.

Medicinal chemists have worked hard over the decades to produce compounds that would be effective painkillers, trying to separate the analgesic effect of the opioids from their dependence-producing effects. Although the two effects could not be separated, the research has resulted in a variety of opioids that are sold as pain relievers (see Table 13.1). Especially interesting among these is fentanyl, which is approximately a hundred times as potent as morphine. Fentanyl is used primarily in conjunction with surgical anesthesia, although both fentanyl and some of its derivatives have also been manufactured illegally and sold on the streets.

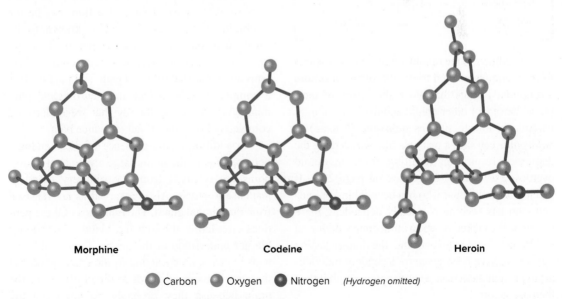

Morphine   Codeine   Heroin

● Carbon   ● Oxygen   ● Nitrogen   *(Hydrogen omitted)*

Figure 13.1   Narcotic Agents Isolated or Derived from Opium

Table 13.1
Some Prescription Narcotic Analgesics

Generic Name	Trade Name
Natural Products	
morphine	Morphabond, Arymo
codeine	
Semisynthetics	
heroin, diamorph	(Not medically available in the United States)
Synthetics	
methadone	Dolophine
meperidine	Demerol
oxycodone	Percodan, Oxycontin, Percocet, Xtampza
oxymorphone	Numorphan, Opana
hydrocodone	Vicodin, Lortab, Hysingla, Zohydro, Vantrela
hydromorphone	Dilaudid
dihydrocodeine	
propoxyphene	Darvon
pentazocine	Talwin
fentanyl	Sublimaze, Actiq

In addition to the opioid analgesics, this search for new compounds led to the discovery of **opioid antagonists,** drugs that block the action of morphine, heroin, or other opioid agonists. The administration of a drug such as **naloxone** (Narcan) or *nalorphine* can save a person's life by reversing the depressed respiration resulting from an opioid overdose (see Taking Sides box on page 296). If given to an individual who has been taking opioids and who has become physically dependent, these antagonists can precipitate an immediate withdrawal syndrome. Both naloxone and the longer-lasting *naltrexone* have been given to dependent individuals to prevent them from experiencing a high if they then use heroin.

Mechanism of Action

The finding that opioid receptors exist in the membrane of some neurons led to an obvious question: What are opioid receptors doing in the synapses of the brain—waiting for someone to extract the juice from a poppy? Scientists all over the world went to work, looking for a substance in the brain that could serve as the natural activator of these opioid receptors. Groups in England and Sweden succeeded in 1974: A pair of molecules, leu-enkephalin and met-enkephalin, were isolated from brain extracts. These **enkephalins** acted like morphine and were many times more potent. Next came the discovery of a group of **endorphins** (endogenous morphinelike substances) that are also found in brain tissue and have potent opioid effects. In addition to these two major types of endogenous opioids, dynorphins and other substances have some actions similar to those of morphine. These substances, as well as the natural and synthetic opioid drugs, have actions on at least three types of opioid receptors, the structures of which were discovered in the 1990s. All three opioid receptors—mu, kappa, and delta—play a role in pain perception, although it appears that the role of delta receptors is limited to chronic pain.[18] One of the most important sites of action may be the midbrain central gray, a region known to be involved in pain perception. However, there are many other sites of interaction between these systems and areas that relate to pain, and pain itself is a complex psychological and neurological phenomenon, so we cannot say that we understand completely how opioids act to reduce pain.

In addition to the presence of these endogenous opioids in the brain, large amounts of endorphins are released from the pituitary gland in response to stress. Also, enkephalins are released from the adrenal gland. The functions of these peptides circulating through the blood as hormones are not understood at this point. They could perhaps reduce pain by acting in the spinal cord, but they are unlikely to produce direct effects in the brain because they probably do not cross the blood-brain barrier. It has been speculated that long-distance runners experience a release of endorphins that might be responsible for the so-called runner's high. Unfortunately, the only evidence in support of this notion was measurements of blood levels of endorphins that seemed to be elevated in some, but not all, runners. These endorphins are presumably from the pituitary and might not be capable of producing a high. It is not known whether exercise alters *brain* levels of these substances.

Beneficial Uses

Pain Relief

The major therapeutic indication for morphine and the other opioids is the reduction of pain. After the administration of an analgesic dose of morphine, some patients report that they are still aware of pain but that the pain is no longer aversive. The opioids seem to have their effect in part by diminishing the patient's awareness of and response to the aversive stimulus. Morphine primarily reduces the emotional response to pain (the suffering) and to some extent the knowledge of the pain stimulus.

The effect of opioids is relatively specific to pain. Fewer effects on mental and motor ability accompany analgesic doses of these agents than accompany equipotent doses of other analgesic and depressant drugs. Although one of the characteristics of these drugs is their ability to reduce pain without inducing sleep, drowsiness is not uncommon after a therapeutic dose. (In the user's vernacular, the patient is "on the nod.") The patient is readily awakened if sleeping, and dreams during the sleep period are frequent.

Intestinal Disorders

Opioids have long been valued for their effects on the gastrointestinal system. They quiet colic and save lives by counteracting diarrhea. In years past and today in many underdeveloped countries, contaminated food and water have resulted in severe intestinal infections (dysentery). Particularly in the young and the elderly, diarrhea and resulting dehydration can be a major cause of death.

Opioid drugs decrease the number of peristaltic contractions, which is the type of contraction responsible for moving food through the intestines. Considerable water is absorbed from the intestinal material; this fact, plus the decrease in peristaltic contractions, often results in constipation in patients taking the drugs for pain relief. This side effect is what has saved the lives of many dysentery victims. Although modern synthetic opioids are now sold for this purpose, old-fashioned paregoric, an opium solution, is still available for the symptomatic relief of diarrhea.

Cough Suppressants

The opioids also have the effect of decreasing activity in what the advertisers refer to as the cough control center in the medulla. Although coughing is often a useful way of clearing unwanted material from the respiratory passages, at times nonproductive coughing can itself become a problem. Since it was first purified from opium, codeine has been widely used for its **antitussive** properties and is still available in a number of prescription cough remedies. Nonprescription cough remedies contain dextromethorphan, an opioid analogue that is somewhat more selective in its antitussive effects. At high doses, dextromethorphan produces hallucinogenic effects through a different mechanism, by blocking the N-methyl-D-aspartate (NMDA) glutamate receptor.

---

opioid antagonists: drugs that can block the actions of opioids.

naloxone (nal *ox* own): an opioid antagonist.

enkephalins (en *kef* a lins): morphinelike neurotransmitters found in the brain and adrenals.

endorphins (en *dor* fins): morphinelike neurotransmitters found in the brain and pituitary gland.

antitussive: a medication used to suppress or relieve coughing.

Causes for Concern

Dependence Potential

Tolerance Tolerance develops to most of the effects of the opioids, although with different effects tolerance can occur at different rates. If the drug is used chronically for pain relief, for example, it will probably be necessary to increase the dose to maintain a constant effect. The same is true for the euphoria sought by recreational users: Repeated use results in a decreased effect, which can be overcome by increasing the dose or simply by abstaining for several days. Cross-tolerance exists among all the opioids.

The development of tolerance to opioid-related effects is usually discussed as a negative consequence of drug use. In fact, tolerance is one of the symptoms listed in the *DSM-5* and used to determine whether an individual meets criteria for a substance use disorder. There is, however, a potential benefit of developing tolerance to opioids. Regular opioid users who have developed tolerance are less likely to experience opioid-induced respiratory depression at doses that may be harmful to infrequent users of opioids.

Physical Dependence Concomitant with the development of tolerance is the establishment of physical dependence: In a person who has used the drug chronically and at high doses, as each dose begins to wear off, certain withdrawal symptoms begin to appear. These symptoms and their approximate timing after opioid use are listed in Table 13.2. This list of symptoms might have more personal meaning for you if you compare it to a case of the 24-hour, or intestinal, flu. Combine nausea and vomiting with diarrhea, aches, pains, and a general sense of misery, and you have a pretty good idea of what a moderate case of opioid withdrawal is like— rarely life-threatening, but most unpleasant. If an individual has been taking a large amount of the drug, then these symptoms can be much worse than those caused by 24-hour flu and can last at least twice as long. Note that **methadone,** a long-lasting synthetic opioid, produces withdrawal symptoms that are usually less severe and that appear later than with heroin but may last longer. Cross-dependence is seen among the opioids. No matter which of them was responsible for producing the initial dependence, withdrawal symptoms can be prevented by an appropriate dose of any opioid

Table 13.2
Sequence of Appearance of Some of the Abstinence Syndrome Symptoms

Signs	APPROXIMATE HOURS AFTER PREVIOUS DOSE	
	Heroin and/or Morphine	Methadone
Craving for drugs, anxiety	6	24
Yawning, perspiration, running nose, teary eyes	14	34–48
Increase in above signs plus pupil dilation, goose bumps (pilorection), tremors (muscle twitches), hot and cold flashes, aching bones and muscles, loss of appetite	16	48–72
Increased intensity of above, plus insomnia; raised blood pressure; increased temperature, pulse rate, respiratory rate and depth; restlessness; nausea	24–36	
Increased intensity of above, plus curled-up position, vomiting, diarrhea, weight loss, spontaneous ejaculation or orgasm, hemoconcentration, increased blood sugar	36–48	

agonist. This is the basis for the use of methadone in treating heroin dependence, because substituting legal methadone prevents withdrawal symptoms for as much as a day.

An interesting clue to the biochemical mechanism of withdrawal symptoms has been the finding that *clonidine,* an alpha-adrenergic agonist that is used to treat high blood pressure, can diminish the severity of withdrawal symptoms. Studies on brain tissue reveal that opioid receptors and alpha-adrenergic receptors are found together in some brain areas, including the norepinephrine-containing cells of the locus ceruleus.

Toxicity Potential

Acute Toxicity   One specific effect of the opioids is to depress the respiratory centers in the brain, so that respiration slows and becomes shallow. This is perhaps the major side effect of the opioids and one of the most dangerous, because death resulting from respiratory depression can follow an excessive dose of these drugs. The basis for this effect is that the respiratory centers become less responsive to carbon dioxide levels in the blood. It is this effect that keeps opioids near the top of the list of drugs mentioned in overdose deaths. As discussed earlier, this respiratory depression is additive with the effects of alcohol or other sedative-hypnotics, and a large fraction of those who die from heroin overdose have elevated blood alcohol concentrations and might better be described as dying from a combination of heroin (or another opioid) and alcohol. Opioid overdose can be diagnosed on the basis of the *opioid triad:* coma, depressed respiration, and pinpoint pupils. Emergency medical treatment calls for the use of naloxone (Narcan), which antagonizes the opioid effects within a few minutes (see Taking Sides box on page 296).

The behavioral consequences of having morphinelike drugs in the brain are probably less dangerous. Those who inject heroin might nod off into a dream-filled sleep for a few minutes, and opium smokers are famous for their "pipe dreams." It is perhaps not surprising that individuals under the influence of opioids are likely to be less active and less

alert than they otherwise would be. A clouding of consciousness makes mental work more difficult.

Opioid agonists also stimulate the brain area controlling nausea and vomiting, which are other frequent side effects. Nausea occurs in about half of ambulatory patients given a 15 mg dose of morphine. Also, nausea and vomiting are a common reaction to heroin among street users. Another common, and perhaps more bothersome, side effect associated with opioid use is constipation. Activation of mu receptors within the **gastrointestinal tract** slows the motility of the affected organs and interferes with muscle contraction in the small intestines and colon, which leads to constipation.

Chronic Toxicity   Although early in the 20th century many medical authorities believed that chronic opioid use weakened the user both mentally and physically, there is no scientific evidence that exposure to opioid drugs per se causes long-term damage to any tissue or organ system. Some street users do suffer from sores and abscesses at injection sites, but these can be attributed to the lack of sterile technique. Also, the practice of sharing needles can result in the spread of such blood-borne diseases as serum hepatitis and HIV. Again, this is a result not of the drug but of the technique used to inject it.

Misconceptions and Preconceptions

Most people have strongly held beliefs about heroin, derived from television, magazines, movies, and conversations. These individuals, including many professionals, have major misconceptions about nonmedical use and misuse of opioids.

One of the most common misconceptions is that injecting heroin or morphine induces in everyone an intense pleasure unequaled by any other

methadone (*meth* **a doan):** a long-lasting synthetic opioid.
gastrointestinal tract: an organ system within the body that takes in food, digests it to extract and absorb energy and nutrients, and expels the remaining waste as feces and urine.

Focus on Treatment

Medication Treatments

Most users of opioids do not become addicted and, therefore, do not need treatment. But each year a substantial minority of users seek treatment for opioid addiction. Most of these individuals are prescribed medications as part of their treatment plan, in large part because abrupt discontinuation of long-term opioid use leads to unpleasant withdrawal symptoms. Opioid agonists effectively relieve these symptoms and are usually the first-line of treatment. Currently, there are two FDA-approved medications for this purpose: methadone and buprenorphine. Methadone is a full agonist, meaning that it fully stimulates the opioid receptor; buprenorphine, by contrast, is a partial agonist and cannot stimulate the receptor to full capacity regardless of the dose administered. Nonetheless, both medications are effective in treating withdrawal symptoms.

Once withdrawal symptoms are no longer present, other strategies may be implemented. For example, the patient may be continued on daily doses of either methadone or buprenorphine in an effort to help the individual avoid returning to problematic or illicit drug use. Another approach is to use the opioid antagonist naltrexone as a maintenance medication. Naltrexone prevents opioid agonists such as heroin from binding to opioid receptors. Even if the patient takes heroin, for example, while being maintained on naltrexone, the effects of heroin would not be felt. Although naltrexone therapy has been shown to be effective in the treatment of opioid dependence, this therapy appears to be appropriate only for highly motivated individuals because most individuals enrolled in naltrexone therapy simply discontinue treatment in order to experience the effects of an opioid agonist. To summarize, methadone or buprenorphine are the predominant form of therapy used to treat opioid use disorders. Most experts agree, however, that medications should be used in conjunction with behavioral therapy in order to achieve best results.

Box icon credit: ©dencg/Shutterstock.com RF

Supplies for shooting up heroin. ©Don Mason/Getty Images RF

experience. Often it is described as similar to a whole-body orgasm that persists up to five or more minutes. Some users report that they try with every injection to reexperience the extreme euphoria of the first injection, but always have a lesser effect. However, studies, as well as clinical and street reports, show that many people experience nausea and discomfort after administration of morphine or heroin, especially if large doses are administered. Despite this, some of these users persist and the discomfort decreases—that is, it shows tolerance more rapidly than the euphoric effects. Under these conditions, opioid administration soon results primarily in pleasant effects. To maintain these pleasurable feelings, though, the dose level must gradually be increased if the drug is used on a regular basis.

Another misconception has to do with the development of withdrawal symptoms. The heroin user undergoing withdrawal without medication is always portrayed as being in excruciating pain, truly suffering. It depends. With a large habit, withdrawal without medication can be extremely difficult. The opioid abuse scene is changing too rapidly to be definite about today's user, but many street users use a low daily drug dose. For many such users, the withdrawal symptoms resemble a mild case of intestinal flu (cramps, diarrhea, headache, lethargy).

Perhaps the most common misconception about heroin is that, after one shot, you are hooked for life. None of the opioids, or any other drug, fits into that fantasized category. Becoming dependent takes time, perhaps weeks, and persistence on the part of the beginner. Regular use of the drug seems to be more important in establishing physical dependence than the size of the dose used. Becoming physically dependent is possible on a weekend, but it frequently requires a longer period, with three or four injections a day.

There are probably about one million opioid-dependent individuals in the United States. There may be two to three times as many heroin *chippers*—occasional users. Several reports have appeared on the characteristics of these occasional users, but no consistent differences, compared with opioid-dependent persons, have yet been found, other than the pattern of use.

Summary

- Opium was used in its raw form for centuries, both medicinally and for pleasure.

- Opium had significant influences on medicine, literature, and world politics through the 1800s.

- Opioid addiction has been recognized for a long time, but no concerted effort to control addiction was tried until the patent medicine era of the late 1800s, combined with opium smoking by Chinese Americans, led to federal regulations in the early 1900s.

- The stereotypical opioid user changed from being a middle-aged, middle-class woman using patent medicines by mouth to being a young, lower-class man using heroin by intravenous injection.

- Various synthetic opioids are now available along with the natural products of the opium poppy. These drugs all act at opioid receptors in the brain.

- Opioid receptors are normally acted on by the naturally occurring opioidlike products of the nervous system and endocrine glands, endorphins and enkephalins.

- The opioid overdose triad consists of coma, depressed respiration, and pinpoint pupils. Death occurs because breathing ceases.

- Illicit heroin comes primarily from South America, Mexico, Southeast Asia, and Southwest Asia.

- Combining opioids with sedatives can increase the likelihood of respiratory depression.

Review Questions

1. What two chemicals are extracted from the opium poppy?
2. What was the significance of De Quincey's writing about opium eating?
3. What were the approximate dates and who were the combatants in the Opium Wars?
4. How is it possible that heroin was at first sold as a nonaddicting pain reliever?
5. How did the stereotypical opioid abuse change from the early 1900s to the 1920s?
6. Why and when did private physicians and public clinics stop maintaining dependent individuals with morphine and other opioids?
7. What were some of the lessons learned about heroin addiction as a result of the Vietnam experience?
8. What is the effect of a narcotic antagonist on someone who has developed a physical dependence on opioids?
9. What are the enkephalins and endorphins, and how do they relate to plant-derived opioids such as morphine?
10. Explain why taking opioids in combination with sedatives is not advised.

References

1. Baum, L. F. *The New Wizard of Oz.* New York: Grosset & Dunlap, 1944.
2. Scott, J. M. *The White Poppy: A History of Opium.* New York: Funk & Wagnalls, 1969.
3. Center for Behavioral Health Statistics and Quality. (2016). *Key Substance Use and Mental Health Indicators in the United*

States: Results from the 2015 National Survey on Drug Use and Health (HHS Publication No. SMA 16-4984, NSDUH Series H-51). Retrieved from http://www.samhsa.gov/data/

4. Hamarneh, S. "Sources and Development of Arabic Medical Therapy and Pharmacology." *Sudhoffs Archiv fur Geschichte der Medizin und der Naturwissenschaften* 54 (1970), p. 34.

5. De Quincey, T. *Confessions of an English Opium-Eater.* London; New York: W. Scott Pub. Co., 1886.

6. Kramer, J. C. "Opium Rampant: Medical Use, Misuse and Abuse in Britain and the West in the 17th and 18th Centuries." *British Journal of Addiction,* 1979, p. 377.

7. Kramer, J. C. "Heroin in the Treatment of Morphine Addiction." *Journal of Psychedelic Drugs* 9, no. 3 (1977), pp. 193–97.

8. Dott, D. B., and R. Stockman. *Proceedings of the Royal Society of Edinburgh,* 1890, p. 321.

9. Manges, M. "A Second Report on the Therapeutics of Heroin." *New York Medical Journal* 71 (1900), pp. 51, 82–83.

10. Wilcox, R. W. *Pharmacology and Therapeutics,* 6th ed. Philadelphia: P. Blakiston's Son, 1905.

11. Kebler, L. F. "The Present Status of Drug Addiction in the United States." In *Transactions of the American Therapeutic Society.* Philadelphia: FA Davis, 1910.

12. Black, J. R. "Advantages of Substituting the Morphia Habit for the Incurably Alcoholic." *The Cincinnati Lancet—Clinic* 22 (1889), pp. 538–41.

13. Lindesmith, A. R. *The Addict and the Law.* Bloomington: Indiana University Press, 1965.

14. *The World Heroin Problem.* Committee Print, House of Representatives, Committee on Foreign Affairs, Ninety-Second Congress, First Session, May 27, 1971. Washington, DC: U.S. Government Printing Office, 1971.

15. Robins, L. N. *The Vietnam Drug User Returns.* Special Action Office for Drug Abuse Prevention Monograph, Series A, No. 2, May 1974, Contract No. HSM-42-72-75; Robins, L. N., Helzer, J. E., Hesselbrock, M., and Wish, E. "Vietnam Veterans Three Years after Vietnam: How Our Study Changed Our View of Heroin." *American Journal on Addictions* 19 (2010), pp. 203–11.

16. U.S. Department of Justice National Drug Intelligence Center. *National Drug Threat Assessment 2016.* Product No. DEA-DCT-DIR-001-17. https://www.hsdl.org/?view&did=797265

17. Noble, M., and others. "Long-Term Opioid Management for Chronic Noncancer Pain." *Cochrane Database Systematic Review* 20 (2010), CD006605.

18. Vicente-Sanchez, A., Segura, L., and Pradhan, A. A. "The Delta Opioid Receptor Tool Box." *Neuroscience* 338 (2016), pp. 145–159.

14 Psychedelics

Source: Drug Enforcement Administration

Objectives

When you have finished this chapter, you should be able to:

- Explain why plants with psychoactive effects have been used in religious practices all over the world.

- Recognize several examples of indole and catechol psychedelics.

- Describe the relationship of LSD to the ergot fungus.

- Discuss the early research and evidence on LSD for use in interrogation and in psychotherapy.

- Understand what is meant by "hallucinogen persisting perception disorder."

- Describe the major active ingredient and some history of use of psilocybe, morning glories, ayahuasca, peyote, San Pedro cactus, *Amanita,* and *Salvia divinorum.*

- Understand the chemical relationship among DOM, MDA, and MDMA.

- Compare and contrast PCP effects with those of LSD.

- Explain how anticholinergic psychedelics act in the brain.

- Compare stories about medieval witches using belladonna to contemporary stories about people using marijuana, LSD, or cocaine.

From the soft, quiet beauty of the sacred *Psilocybe* mushroom to the angry, mottled appearance of the toxic *Amanita,* from the mountains of Mexico to the streets of Anytown, USA, from before history to the 21st century, humans have searched for the perfect aphrodisiac, spiritual experiences, and other worlds. The plants have been there to help; plants have evolved to produce chemicals that alter the biochemistry of animals. If they make us feel sick, we are unlikely to eat them again, and if they kill us, we are certainly not going to eat them again. But humans long ago learned to "tame" some of these plants, to use them in just the right ways and in just the right amounts to alter perceptions and emotions without too many unpleasant consequences.

Animism and Religion

Animism, the belief that animals, plants, rocks, streams, and so on derive their special characteristics from a spirit contained within the object, is a common theme in most of the world's religions.

Plants that are able to alter our perception of the world and of ourselves fit right into such a view. If the plant contains a spirit, then eating the plant transfers that spirit to the person who eats it, and the spirit of the plant can speak to the consumer, make her feel the plant's joy or provide her with special powers or insights.

In early hunter-gatherer societies, certain individuals became specialists in the ways of these plants, learning when to harvest them and how much to use under what circumstances. These traditions were passed down from one generation to another, and colorful stories were used to teach the principles to apprentices. Our modern term for these individuals is **shaman** because of their knowledge of drug-containing plants. But because they also were the experts on obtaining power from the spirit world, their function in hunter-gatherer societies had as much to do with the origins of religion as with the origins of modern medicine. These plants and their psychoactive effects were probably important reasons for the development of spiritual and religious traditions and folklore in many societies all over the world.[1]

Terminology and Types

There has been some controversy about what to call this group of drugs. Because the drugs are capable of producing hallucinations and some altered sense of reality, a state that could be called psychotic, they have been referred to as **psychotomimetic** drugs. This term implies that the drugs produce dangerous effects and a form of mental disorder, which is also a controversial conclusion.

More recently, proponents have popularized newer terms, such as **entheogen** and **entactogen**, to describe these substances. For example, *entheogen* is used to describe substances (e.g., sacred mushrooms) that are thought to create spiritual or religious experiences, whereas *entactogen*, meaning "to produce a touching within," is used to describe substances, such as MDMA, that are said to enhance feelings of empathy.

Is there a descriptive and unbiased term that will allow us to categorize the drugs and then to examine their effects without prejudice? Probably not. As a matter of convention, however, we have chosen to refer to this class of drugs as psychedelics in this chapter.

Although we will call all of these drugs psychedelics, there are important differences among them. They can be classified according to their chemical structures, their known pharmacological properties, how much loss of awareness occurs under their influence, and how dangerous they can be. The first types we will review are the classical psychedelics: They are capable of altering perceptions while allowing the person to remain in communication with the present world. The individual under the influence of these drugs will often be aware of both the "fantasy" world and the real world at the same time, might talk avidly about what is being experienced, and will be able to remember much of it later. Many of these drugs can produce psychedelic effects without much acute physiological toxicity—that is, there is relatively little danger of dying from an overdose of LSD, psilocybin, or mescaline. The two major classes of psychedelics, the indoles and catechols are grouped according to their chemical structures.

Indoles

The basic structure of the neurotransmitter serotonin is referred to as an **indole** nucleus. Figure 14.1 illustrates that the psychedelics LSD and psilocybin also contain this structure. For that reason and the fact that some other chemicals with this structure have similar psychedelic effects, we refer to one group of psychedelics as the indoles.

d-Lysergic Acid Diethylamide (LSD)   The most potent of the psychedelics, and the one that brought these drugs into the public eye in the 1960s, is not found in nature. Although there are naturally occurring compounds that resemble the indole d-lysergic acid diethylamide (LSD), their identity as psychedelics was not known until after the discovery of LSD. It

Drugs in the Media

Psychedelics: Back in Mainstream Medical Research?

A few years ago, a headline in *Time* magazine read "LSD May Help Treat Alcoholism." Other mainstream publications have printed similar enthusiastic pieces. The reason for the resurgent optimism about LSD therapy are the findings of a 2012 study published in the *Journal of Psychpharmacology*.[2] Researchers from Norway conducted a retrospective analysis of studies published in the late 1960s and early 1970s in order to assess the utility of LSD as a treatment for excessive drinking. Data from six randomized, double-blind trials involving 536 participants were evaluated. The researchers found that a single dose of LSD decreased problem drinking to a greater extent than a control drug (ephedrine, amphetamine, or placebo). These findings add to a growing number of studies showing beneficial effects of psychedelics in the treatment of psychiatric conditions, following nearly four decades of limited interest in these compounds for medical purposes.

In the 1950s and 1960s, psychedelics were promoted by physicians as treatments for several medical conditions ranging from anxiety to schizophrenia. Excitement about the potential medical benefits of this class of drug abruptly ended, as nonmedical use became more widespread and associated problems increased. In addition, some researcher investigating the effects of psychedelics began using less than rigorous methodology in their studies, which increased the likelihood of adverse drug effects. For example,

appropriate medical supervision was not included in some studies. Together, these concerns led policy makers to impose greater restrictions on access to psychedelics, and effectively ended their role in research and medical treatment.

In the last decade or so, however, a new generation of researchers has been investigating the potential therapeutic benefits of psychedelics. For example, studies have shown that 3,4-methylenedioxymethamphetamine (MDMA) decreases symptoms of posttraumatic stress disorder (PTSD),[3] ayahuasca reduces symptoms of depression,[4] and psilocybin facilitates tobacco smoking cessation[5] and decreases depression and anxiety in patients with life-threatening cancer. [6]

Researchers in this area today emphasize that psychedelic therapies should be thought of as adjuncts, or add-ons, to psychotherapies and not stand-alone treatments. The idea that this class of drugs comprised "magic bullets" probably contributed to the backlash against their use in research and medicine in the 1960s. In an effort to move psychedelics back into mainstream medical research, researchers are avoiding mistakes of the past by remaining cautious about the role of psychedelics in medicine and stressing the importance of proper education for professionals using these drugs in research and treatment.

Box icon credit: ©Glow Images RF

---

was originally synthesized from ergot alkaloids extracted from the ergot fungus *Claviceps purpurea*. This mold occasionally grows on grain, especially rye, and eating infected grain results in an illness called **ergotism**, which can cause headaches, vomiting, diarrhea, and gangrene of the fingers and toes.

LSD Discovery and Early Research Dr. Albert Hofmann first synthesized LSD in 1938 when he was working as a scientist at Sandoz Laboratories in Basel, Switzerland. It was not until 1943, however, that LSD entered the world of psychopharmacology, when Hofmann recorded his LSD-induced experiences.

animism: the belief that objects attain certain characteristics because of spirits.

shaman: a person having access to, and influence in, the world of spirits, especially among certain tribal societies. Also known as medicine men/women.

psychotomimetic (sy cot o mim *et* ick): mimicking psychosis.

entheogen (en thee o gen): generating the divine within.

entactogen (en tac to gen): generating empathy and openness.

indole (*in* dole): a particular chemical structure found in serotonin and LSD.

ergotism: a condition caused by fungal contamination of grains resulting in headache, vomiting, diarrhea, and gangrene of the fingers and toes.

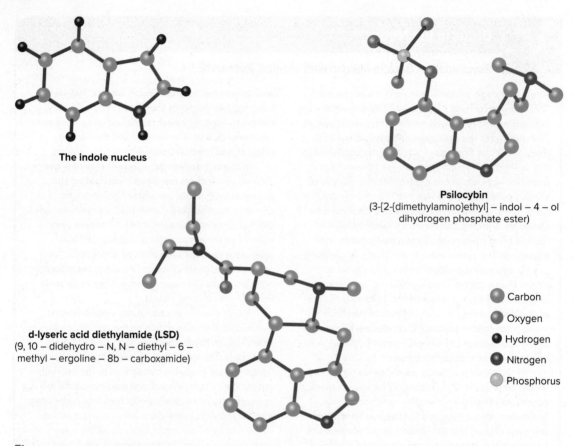

The indole nucleus

Psilocybin
(3-[2-{dimethylamino}ethyl] – indol – 4 – ol
dihydrogen phosphate ester)

d-lyseric acid diethylamide (LSD)
(9, 10 – didehydro – N, N – diethyl – 6 –
methyl – ergoline – 8b – carboxamide)

Carbon
Oxygen
Hydrogen
Nitrogen
Phosphorus

Figure 14.1   Indole Hallucinogens

He wrote, "The first experience was a very weak one, consisting of rather small changes. It had a pleasant, fairy tale—magic theater quality."[7] He was sure that the experience resulted from the accidental absorption, through the skin of his fingers, of the compound with which he was working. The next Monday morning Hofmann prepared what he thought was a very small amount of LSD, 0.25 mg, and made the following record in his notebook:

April 19, 1943: Preparation of an 0.5% aqueous solution of d-lysergic acid diethylamide tartrate.
    4:20 P.M.: 0.5 cc (0.25 mg LSD) ingested orally. The solution is tasteless.
    4:50 P.M.: no trace of any effect.
    5:00 P.M.: slight dizziness, unrest, difficulty in concentration, visual disturbances, marked desire to laugh.

At this point the laboratory notes were discontinued and were continued on a subsequent day:

The last words could only be written with great difficulty. I asked my laboratory assistant to accompany me home as I believed that my condition would be a repetition of the disturbance of the previous Friday. While we were still cycling home, however, it became clear that the symptoms were much stronger than the first time. I had great difficulty in speaking coherently, my field of vision swayed before me, and objects appeared distorted like images in curved mirrors. I had the impression of being unable to move from the spot, although my assistant told me afterwards that we had cycled at a good pace.. . .
    A remarkable feature was the manner in which all acoustic perceptions (e.g., the noise of a passing car) were transformed into optical effects, every

sound causing a corresponding colored hallucination constantly changing in shape and color like pictures in a kaleidoscope. At about 1 o'clock I fell asleep and awakened the next morning somewhat tired but otherwise feeling perfectly well.[7]

The dose that Hofmann had taken was quite large for someone who had not developed tolerance; the potency of the drug attracted attention. Mescaline had long been known to cause strange experiences, alter consciousness, and lead to a particularly vivid kaleidoscope of colors, but it takes 4,000 times as much mescaline as LSD to produce that effect. LSD is usually active when only 0.05 mg (50 µg) is taken, and in some people a dose of 0.03 mg is enough to produce psychoactive effects.

Hofmann's discovery of LSD and his advocacy for its responsible use made him a cult hero among psychedelic enthusiasts. He remained steadfast in his view that LSD is a valuable psychotherapeutic tool and could be used to enhance humans' understanding of their place in nature until his death in April 2008 at age 102. Hofmann's discovery also spurred a tremendous amount of research on LSD between the early 1950s and 1970s.

A fair amount of research in this area centered on developing a model of psychoses and accessing the "subconscious mind." The focus on the subconscious mind probably derived from the dreamlike quality of the reports of LSD experiences and the long-held psychoanalytic view that dreams represent subconscious thoughts trying to express themselves. Thus, LSD was widely used as an adjunct to psychotherapy. When a psychiatrist felt that a patient had reached a roadblock and was unable to dredge up repressed memories and motives, LSD might be used for its "mind-viewing" properties. Thus, LSD took over as a modern truth serum, replacing sodium pentothal, scopolamine, and amphetamines. Whether LSD actually helped these patients in the long run or only seemed helpful to the psychiatrists who believed in it is still being debated.

Scientific study of LSD and other psychedelics declined in the 1970s. A 1974 report by a National Institute of Mental Health (NIMH) research task force on hallucinogenic research stated:

> Virtually every psychological test has been used to study persons under the influence of LSD or other such hallucinogens, but the research has contributed little to our understanding of the bizarre and potent effects of this drug.[8]

This conclusion, along with the growing public perception that this class of drug produced unpredictable effects, led to a virtual moratorium on government funding to support LSD research in humans.

Secret Army/CIA Research with LSD As had happened with amphetamines earlier, various militaries, including the U.S. military, experimented with LSD and other psychedelics. Between the 1950s and 1960s, hundreds of soldiers and civilians were unwittingly administered doses of these drugs. The vast majority of these unsuspecting individuals did not have previous experience with this class of drug. As a result, drug effects were sometimes toxic. Many of the unsuspecting victims believed they were losing their minds. Some suffered long-term psychiatric disturbances and others had difficulties adjusting to their usual lives. Even by the standards of the day, this practice was unethical; once knowledge of these activities became public, the U.S. government was required to pay reparations exceeding hundreds of thousands of dollars to some victims and their families.

Remember back in Chapters 1 and 5 when we explained that drug effects are not determined by pharmacology alone (drug-receptor interactions)? Other factors, including the situation in which drug use occurs and the user's level of experience with the drug, can greatly influence the effects experienced. The U.S. Army–LSD experimentations highlight this point. Imagine being given a powerful mind-altering drug without your knowledge prior to taking your final examination. Also, imagine not having any experience with the drug you were administered. The effects could be horrifying, and you too might think that you were going insane.

The important point here is that administering any psychoactive drug to individuals without their knowledge is not only unethical, but it can also be extremely dangerous.

Recreational Use of LSD Psychologist Timothy Leary was another popular advocate for LSD use. In the early 1960s, he conducted research investigating the psychological effects of LSD and psilocybin at Harvard University. Leary's research came under increasing criticism due to charges that his methods were not rigorous and were unethical. For example, proper controls, such as carefully screening subjects prior to administering drugs, were sometimes omitted, as was proper medical supervision. These concerns may have contributed to Leary's dismissal from Harvard and the world of research, but he was instrumental in popularizing LSD use among the general public.

Dr. Albert Hofmann was known as the father of LSD because he was the first person to synthesize the drug.
©Keystone/Getty Images

LSD use is thought to have peaked in the late 1960s but has always remained relatively low. In 2015, about 350,000 people aged 12 or older reported using LSD in the past month, which corresponds to about 0.1 percent of the population aged 12 or older. LSD can also be monitored by examining past-year use. For past-year use, 0.6 percent of people aged 12 or older in 2015 had used LSD, which represents about 1.5 million people.

LSD Pharmacology LSD is usually taken by mouth and is rapidly absorbed from the gastrointestinal tract. Following ingestion, the brain contains less LSD than any of the other organs in the body, so it is not selectively taken up by the brain. Half of the LSD in the blood is metabolized every three hours, so blood levels decrease fairly rapidly. LSD is metabolized in the liver and excreted as 2-oxy-lysergic acid diethylamide, which is inactive.

Tolerance develops rapidly, usually within 3–4 days if the drug is taken daily on multiple occasions. Cross-tolerance has been shown among LSD, mescaline, and psilocybin. Physical dependence to LSD or to any psychedelics has not been demonstrated.

LSD is a sympathomimetic agent, and the autonomic signs are some of the first to appear after LSD is taken. Typical symptoms are dilated pupils, elevated temperature and blood pressure, and an increase in salivation.

The fact that the LSD molecule resembles the chemical structure of serotonin provided a clue that

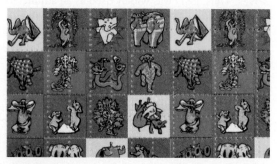

A very small dose of LSD has powerful effects. Liquid LSD solution may be taken orally; it is often applied to blotter paper divided into squares containing single doses. Source: Drug Enforcement Administration

the drug might act on serotonin receptors to produce its effects. The best evidence seems to indicate that LSD and several other psychedelics, including mescaline and psilocybin, act by stimulating the serotonin-2A subtype of receptors. Among a large group of psychedelic chemicals, there is a high correlation between their potency in binding to this type of receptor in rat brains and their potency in producing psychedelic effects in humans.[9]

The LSD Experience   In the past 40 years, hundreds of studies investigating the direct effects of marijuana, opioids, sedatives, and stimulants on human behavior have been published in the scientific literature. Far fewer empirical investigations of psychedelics have taken place in this same period, in part because of previous research abuses involving these agents. As a result, much of our knowledge about the effects of LSD and other psychedelics in humans is anecdotal. Fortunately, this situation is changing, and an increasing number of LSD studies are being conducted using human subjects.

One of the most prominent LSD-related effects is the modification of perception, particularly of visual images. Other commonly reported effects include an altered sense of time, changes in the perception of one's own body, and some alterations of auditory input. A particularly interesting phenomenon is that of **synesthesia,** a "mixing of senses," in which sounds might appear as visual images (as reported by Hofmann on the first-ever LSD trip), or the visual picture might alter in rhythm with music.

Adverse Reactions   The adverse reactions to LSD ingestion have been repeatedly emphasized in the popular press. Because there is no way of knowing how much illegal LSD is being used or how pure the LSD is that people are taking, there is no possibility of determining the true incidence of adverse reactions to LSD. Adverse reactions to the street use of what is thought to be LSD can result from many factors. Drugs obtained on the street frequently are not what they are claimed to be—in purity, chemical composition, or quantity.

The primary active ingredient in so-called magic mushrooms is psilocybin, an indole psychedelic. ©IT Stock/age fotostock RF

Flashbacks have been widely discussed in the popular press as a common adverse effect of psychedelics. Unfortunately, the term *flashback* has multiple meanings, making it difficult to investigate its occurrence with any precision. As a result, the term *flashback* has been replaced in the *DSM-5* by the phrase "hallucinogen persisting perception disorder." An individual diagnosed with this disorder has not used the drug recently, but has re-experienced one or more of the perceptual symptoms experienced while intoxicated, such as geometric hallucinations, false perceptions of movement, intensified colors, and so on. In general, although psychedelics are reported to have been consumed by millions, few cases of flashbacks have been reported. This

synesthesia (sin ess *thees* ya): the blending of different senses, such as "seeing" sounds.
flashbacks: in a nondrug state, reexperiencing of one or more of the perceptual alterations that occurred during psychedelic intoxication.

number is even lower when individuals who were administered psychedelics under carefully controlled laboratory conditions are assessed.[10]

A more common adverse effect that can occur while under the influence of LSD (or other psychedelics) is the panic reaction. The intensity of these reactions can range from a mild case of increased anxiety to a full-blown panic attack. In general, they are not life threatening and, in less severe cases, can be dealt with by calmly talking the person through the experience. In more severe cases, the individual might require medical attention, and benzodiazepines or another sedative might be indicated.

Beliefs About LSD   One of the most widely occurring beliefs is that these psychedelics increase creativity or release creativity that our inhibitions keep bottled inside us. Several experiments have attempted to study the effects of LSD on creativity, but there is no good evidence that the drug increases it.

Another belief is that LSD has therapeutic usefulness, particularly in the treatment of alcohol dependence. The publication of a study that reanalyzed data published in the 1960s and 1970s suggest that LSD is effective at decreasing problem drinking.[2] This has reignited interest in the therapeutic potential of LSD in the treatment of psychiatric disorders. LSD has also been reported to reduce the number of cluster headaches in those who suffer from this disorder and decrease anxiety associated with life-threatening illnesses.[11,12] These findings are preliminary and need to be replicated in larger controlled studies. More recently, the author Ayelet Waldman published a memoir detailing her apparent successful use of LSD to treat a debilitating mood disorder.[13] Waldman took 10 micrograms of LSD every 3 days for 30 days. This dose is about one-tenth of the typical dose taken by a recreational user seeking notable LSD-induced mood and perceptual alterations. Ten micrograms taken regularly, observes Waldman, did not produce noticeable **acute** perceptual changes but was transformative in treating her mood disorder. Of course, Waldman's experience is but one anecdotal

case and needs to be confirmed using rigorous experimental procedures.

Psilocybin   The magic mushrooms of Mexico have a long history of religious and ceremonial use. These plants, as well as peyote, dropped from Western sight (but not from native use) for 300 years after the Spanish conquered the Aztecs and systematically destroyed their writings and teachings. Use of the mushrooms was particularly suppressed.

In the late 1930s, it was clearly shown that these mushrooms were still being used by natives in southern Mexico and the first of many species was identified. The real breakthrough came in 1955. During that year a New York banker turned ethnobotanist and his wife established rapport with a native group still using mushrooms in religious ceremonies. Gordon Wasson became the first outsider to participate in the ceremony and to eat of the magic mushroom. He wrote of his experiences in a 1957 *Life* magazine article, spreading knowledge of the mushrooms and their psychoactive properties and religious uses.

The most well-known psychoactive mushroom is *Psilocybe mexicana.* The primary active agent in this mushroom is **psilocybin,** an indole that the discoverer of LSD, Albert Hofmann, isolated in 1958 and later synthesized.

Another psilocybin-containing mushroom, *Psilocybe cubensis,* grows on cow dung along the U.S. Gulf Coast. Aside from the obvious questions about eating something found on manure, identifying the correct psilocybin-containing mushrooms in the field can be tricky. Most *Psilocybe* species are described as "little brown mushrooms," and there are several toxic look-alikes.

The dried mushrooms are 0.2 to 0.5 percent psilocybin. The psychedelic effects of psilocybin are quite similar to those of LSD and the catechol psychedelic mescaline, and cross-tolerance exists among these three agents.

Acute and Long-Term Subjective Effects   Over the past decade or so, a growing number of studies have examined the effects of psilocybin on research volunteers. Following acute administration of oral doses ranging from 0.045 to 0.315 mg/kg, psilocybin dose dependently induces intense changes in mood, perception, and thought. Most individuals describe the experience as pleasurable, enriching, and nonthreatening. The most frequently reported acute negative drug reactions are strong feelings of dysphoria and anxiety. These effects are more likely when the drug dose is increased but occur only in a relatively small proportion of individuals. Another common adverse effect reported after taking larger doses of psilocybin is headache. The onset is about seven hours after drug administration; they are transient, lasting no more than a day after psilocybin administration.[14,15]

Less information is available regarding the long-term effects of psilocybin, although at least one literature review has been published. Studerus and colleagues (2012) analyzed pooled data from eight double-blind placebo-controlled experimental studies conducted between 1999 and 2008.[14] A major focus of the literature review was the examination of data collected from a follow-up questionnaire. The questionnaire probed subjective experiences and psychological functioning 8–16 months after participants had received 1–4 oral doses of psilocybin in a study. The data indicated no subsequent drug abuse, persisting perception disorders, prolonged psychosis, or other long-term impairment of functioning in any of the participants. Together, the growing body of evidence suggests that psilocybin produces predictable effects when the drug is administered to healthy individuals in carefully monitored research environments.

Psilocybin and Mystical Experiences In 1963, as part of his Ph.D. requirements, Walter Pahnke conducted the classic "Good Friday Experiment," in which the ability of psilocybin to induce meaningful religious experiences was investigated.[16] Twenty Christian theological seminary students were assigned to two groups: one group received psilocybin (30 mg); the other, nicotinic acid (200 mg) as a "placebo." Following drug administration, the students attended a Good Friday religious service.

Psilocybin occasioned a mystical experience, whereas nicotinic acid did not. However, an important methodological concern associated with the Pahnke study was that participants were explicitly told that they would receive psilocybin, and it was conducted in a group setting. These features compromised blinding procedures and undoubtedly influenced the findings.

In a series of follow-up studies, Roland Griffiths and colleagues used rigorous double-blind clinical pharmacology methods to investigate both the acute and longer-term psychological effects of psilocybin.[17,18] They found that psilocybin acutely increased mystical experience. One and two months after drug administration sessions, participants rated the psilocybin experience as having substantial personal and spiritual significance, and attributed to the experience sustained positive changes in attitudes, mood, and behavior. These effects were undiminished 14 months later. Findings from the Griffiths study replicated and extended Pahnke's results, and raised questions about why so few studies evaluating the effects of psychedelics in human volunteers have appeared in the literature in the past half century (see the Taking Sides box).

Morning Glories and Hawaiian Baby Woodroses Of the psychoactive agents used freely in Mexico in the 16th century, *ololiuqui,* seeds of the morning glory plant *Rivea corymbosa,* perhaps had the greatest religious significance. These seeds tie America to Europe even today. When Albert Hofmann analyzed the seeds of the morning glory, he found several active alkaloids as well as d-lysergic acid amide, which is about one-tenth as active as LSD. The presence of d-lysergic acid amide is quite amazing (to botany majors) because before this discovery in 1960, lysergic acid had

---

acute: abrupt or immediate onset of effects.

psilocybin (sill o sy bin): the active chemical in *Psilocybe* mushrooms.

been found only in much more primitive groups of plants, such as the ergot fungus.[19]

The recreational use of seeds from *Argyreia nervosa,* commonly known as Hawaiian baby woodrose, has also been reported.[20] These seeds contain higher levels of d-lysergic acid amide than morning glories. However, recreational use of these seeds often has adverse effects, probably because

the fuzzy outer coating contains toxic cyanogenic glycosides (which can make one sick).

DMT Dimethyltryptamine (DMT) has never been widely used in the United States, although it has a long, if not noble, history. On a worldwide basis, DMT is one of the most important naturally occurring psychedelic compounds, and it occurs in many

---

Taking Sides

Do You Think the Federal Government Should Fund Psychedelic Research?

Findings from a 2006 study indicate that psilocybin produces positive mystical experiences, which may last at least two months.[17] This may not be a surprise to anyone who remembers the 1960s, but the study by Roland Griffiths and colleagues at Johns Hopkins University represented one of the few rigorous investigations in the past 40 years. In response to widespread psychedelic misuse and poorly conducted studies of these compounds, laws were enacted and federal funding was terminated, virtually ending clinical research on this class of drugs for more than four decades. As a result, from a modern clinical scientific perspective, relatively little was known about psilocybin and other psychedelics.

Proponents of this type of research argue that understanding how psilocybin-induced mystical and altered consciousness states arise in the brain might inform us about basic neurobiology and could have therapeutic implications such as ameliorating pain and suffering of the terminally ill. In an unprecedented editorial in the journal *Psychopharmacology,* where the Griffiths et al. study was published, Dr. Harriet de Wit remarked, "It is time for psychopharmacologists . . . to consider the entire scope of human experience and behavior as legitimate targets for systematic and ethical scientific investigation. Griffiths et al. set an excellent example for such a venture."[21]

Critics are less enthusiastic about the study and its results. They point out that the positive findings might increase experimentation with these drugs by young people. In response to the Griffiths et al. study, Dr. Nora Volkow, Director of the U.S. National Institute on Drug Abuse (NIDA), released a statement underscoring the risks of psychedelic use.

Roland Griffiths, of Johns Hopkins University, lead author on the landmark study evaluating the effects of psilocybin in humans. ©Carl Hart

Dr. Volkow noted, "Psilocybin can trigger psychosis in susceptible individuals and . . . its adverse effects are well known."[22] Some have interpreted this as an indication that NIDA will not fund clinical research investigating the effects of psychedelics, although the institute currently spends nearly a billion dollars each year supporting research on other psychoactive drugs, including cocaine, heroin, marijuana, and methamphetamine. Do you think the federal government should fund this type of research?

Box icon credit: ©Nova Development RF

plants. DMT is the active agent in cohoba snuff, which is used by some South American and Caribbean indigenous people in hunting rituals. Although DMT was synthesized in the 1930s, its discovery as the active ingredient in cohoba first led to human examination of its psychoactive properties in 1956.

DMT is normally ineffective when taken orally because it is metabolized by monoamine oxidase (MAO) before reaching the brain. As a result, the drug is usually snuffed, smoked, or injected. The effective intramuscular dose is about 1 mg/kg body weight. Intravenously, psychedelic effects are seen within two minutes after doses of 0.2 mg/kg or more and last for less than 30 minutes. Classic psychedelic effects are observed following acute administration. DMT produces alterations of visual, auditory, and tactile perception. At larger doses, auditory (e.g., music, whispering voices) and visual (e.g., complex geometric patterns on walls) hallucinations may occur. Mood can vary from anxious to expansive and euphoric. Data from at least one controlled study suggest that DMT is unique among classic psychedelics in that tolerance to its psychological effects does not develop.[23]

Ayahuasca Ayahuasca is a psychoactive tea that was originally used by indigenous cultures in South America for shamanic, religious, and medicinal purposes. It is now used worldwide for a variety of reasons ranging from ceremonial to medicinal to recreational. The main psychoactive component of the tea is DMT and it is usually prepared by combining the vine *Banisteriopsis caapi* with leaves of *Psychotria viridis,* which contains DMT. Recall that we stated that MAO metabolizes oral DMT rapidly before the drug reaches the brain. So, how does ayahuasca produce psychoactive effects? The vine *Banisteriopsis caapi* contains harmaline, an MAO inhibitor. The monoamine-oxidase-inhibiting properties of harmaline prevent the degradation of oral DMT, thereby allowing DMT to reach the brain, where it produces psychoactive effects.

Other Tryptamines There seems to be an endless list of indole psychedelics, but many are infrequently used. Two that have received some attention recently are 5-methoxy DIPT (known as "foxy methoxy") and alpha-methyltryptamine (AMT). The prevalence of their use remains limited, but they are usually taken orally.

Catechols

The second group of psychedelics, although having psychological effects quite similar to those of the indole types, is based on a different structure, that of the catechol nucleus. That nucleus forms the basic structure of the catecholamine neurotransmitters, norepinephrine and dopamine. Figure 14.2 shows the catechol structure and the structures of some catechol psychedelics. Look for the catechol nucleus in each of the psychedelics, and then compare these structures with the structure of the amphetamines and other stimulants shown in Chapter 6.

Mescaline Peyote (from the Aztec *peyotl*) is a small, spineless, carrot-shaped cactus, *Lophophora williamsii*—Lemaire, which grows wild in the Rio Grande Valley and the Southwest. It is mostly subterranean, and only the grayish-green pincushion-like top appears above ground. In pre-Columbian times, the Aztec, Huichol, and other Mexican indigenous people ate the plant ceremonially either in the dried or green state, producing psychological effects lasting an entire day.

Only the top of the peyote cactus appears above ground, but the entire plant is psychoactive. Source: US Fish & Wildlife

peyote (pay *oh* tee): a type of psychedelic cactus.

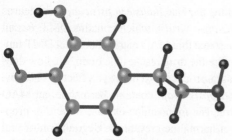

The basic catecholamine structure (dopamine)

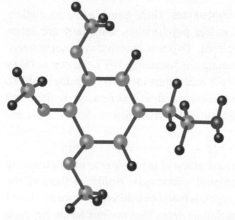

3, 4, 5 trimethoxyphenylethylamine (mescaline)

Carbon
Oxygen
Hydrogen
Nitrogen

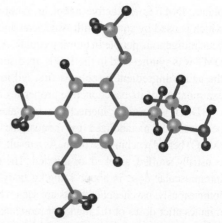

2', 5' dimethoxy −4' − methylamphetamine (DOM)

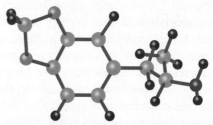

3, 4 methylenedioxy amphetamine (MDA)

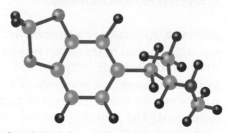

3, 4 methylenedioxy methamphetamine (MDMA)

Figure 14.2   Catechol Hallucinogens

Near the end of the 19th century, Arthur Heffter isolated several alkaloids from peyote and showed that **mescaline** was the primary psychoactive agent found in peyote. Mescaline was synthesized in 1918, and most experiments on the psychoactive effects since then have used synthesized mescaline. More than 30 psychoactive compounds have now been identified in peyote, but mescaline is believed to be the agent responsible for the vivid colors and other visual effects.

Several writers have written about their peyote experiences, good and bad. William James had been told about the unique visions that the cactus could inspire, but as can be seen from the letter he wrote to his brother, Henry, one must sometimes rely on faith:

> I ate one but three days ago, was violently sick for twenty-four hours, and had no other symptoms whatever except that and the Katzenjammer the following day. I will take the visions on trust.

Aldous Huxley's 1954 *The Doors of Perception* details his experiences with peyote.[24] He too warned that peyote's effects were mixed:

> Along with the happily transfigured majority of mescaline takers there is a minority that finds in the drug only hell and purgatory.

There was evidence that the use of peyote had moved north into the United States as early as 1760. In the late 19th century, a group of Native Americans in the Plains became known for its use of peyote during religious ceremonies. From that time to the present, Native American missionaries have spread the peyote religion to almost a quarter of a million Native Americans, some as far north as Canada. The *Native American Church* of the United States was first chartered in Oklahoma in 1918. It is an amalgamation of Christianity and traditional beliefs, incorporating peyote use into its ceremonies. This is sometimes referred to as Peyotism.

Peyotism continues to be an important religious practice among Native Americans between the Rocky Mountains and the Mississippi. Peyote is also used in other ways because the Native Americans attribute spiritual power to the peyote plant. As such, peyote is believed to be helpful, along with prayers and modern medicines, in curing illnesses. It is also worn as an amulet, much as some Christians wear a Saint Christopher's medal, to protect the wearer from harm.

Peyotism remains an important religious practice among Native Americans in certain areas of the United States. ©Hemis/Alamy Stock Photo

For many years the use of peyote as a sacrament by the Native American Church was protected by the constitutional guarantee of freedom of religion. However, in 1990 the Supreme Court ruled that the State of Oregon could prosecute its citizens for using peyote, and the freedom of religion argument was not allowed. In response, the U.S. Congress passed an amendment to the American Indian Religious Act of 1978 (i.e., the American Indian Religious Freedom Act Amendments of 1994), which in essence reversed the Supreme Court's ruling. The relevant portion of the amended Act stated: *"the use, possession, or transportation of peyote by an Indian for bona fide traditional ceremonial purposes in connection with the practice of a traditional Indian religion is lawful, and shall not be prohibited by the United States or any State. No Indian shall be penalized or discriminated against on the basis of such use, possession or transportation, including, but not limited to, denial of otherwise applicable benefits under public assistance programs."*

San Pedro Cactus Another mescaline-containing cactus, *Trichocereus pachanoi*, whose common name is the San Pedro cactus, is native to the Andes Mountains of Peru and Ecuador and has been used for thousands of years as a religious sacrament.[25] The San Pedro is a large, multibranched cactus, often growing to heights of 10 to 15 feet. Its mescaline content is less than that of peyote, and its recreational use more often results in adverse effects rather than in the desired psychedelic experience.

Pharmacology of Mescaline Mescaline is readily absorbed if taken orally but does not readily pass the blood-brain barrier (which explains the high doses required). There is a maximal concentration of the drug in the brain after 30 to 120 minutes. About half of it is removed from the body in six hours, and

mescaline (*mess* ka lin): the active chemical in the peyote cactus.

there is evidence that some mescaline persists in the brain for up to 10 hours. Similar to the indole psychedelics, the effects obtained with low doses, about 3 mg/kg body weight, are primarily euphoric, whereas doses in the range of 5 mg/kg give rise to a full set of hallucinations. Most of the mescaline is excreted unchanged in the urine, and the metabolites identified thus far are not psychoactive.

A dose that is psychoactive in humans causes pupil dilation, pulse rate and blood pressure increases, and an elevation in body temperature. All of these effects are similar to those induced by LSD, psilocybin, and most other alkaloid psychedelics. There are other signs of central stimulation, such as EEG arousal, after mescaline intake. In rats the LD_{50} is about 370 mg/kg body weight, 10 to 30 times the dose that causes behavioral effects. Death results from convulsions and respiratory arrest. Tolerance develops more slowly to mescaline than to LSD, but there is cross-tolerance between the two drugs.

Although mescaline and the other catechol psychedelics have a structure that resembles the catecholamine neurotransmitters, they act indirectly on the serotonin 2A receptor.

Amphetamine Derivatives A large group of synthetic psychedelics is chemically related to the amphetamines. Anecdotally, it has been said that the effects produced by this class of agents were more similar to those produced by mescaline. This view was probably motivated by the observation that the molecular structures of MDMA, MDA, DOM, and mescaline are similar.

MDMA and MDA Perhaps the best known of these agents is MDMA (sometimes referred to as Ecstasy or molly). Prior to July 1985, the drug could be used legally in the United States. Some psychiatrists used it as a therapeutic aide, arguing that it facilitated communication by increasing the patient's openness and empathy. Data supporting such arguments, however, are limited. Studies that have evaluated the effects of MDMA in young adults indicate that its effects are more similar to those of

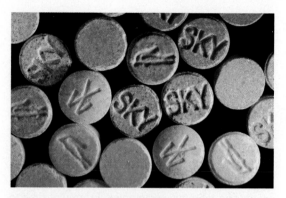

Some evidence suggests that Ecstasy may be neurotoxic, affecting serotonin neurons in the brain.
Source: Drug Enforcement Administration

amphetamine and methamphetamine than those of classical psychedelics. From a psychological perspective, the drug increases sociability and euphoria. Physiologically, it increases blood pressure, pulse, and body temperature but decreases appetite and sleep. There are also reports of the drug causing teeth grinding (bruxism), but this effect has been less well studied.

Anecdotal reports suggest that MDMA users report substantially more negative or depressed mood states in the days immediately following MDMA administration. Colloquially, this phenomenon is frequently referred to as "Suicide Tuesday." Some have speculated that initially MDMA administration causes a substantial release of serotonin, followed by a marked reduction of the neurotransmitter, lasting several hours to days after the last dose. Because serotonin plays a major role in mood regulation, it is thought that this "reduction" in serotonin produces the depressed mood state reported by MDMA users in the days following drug use. But there are no empirical evidence to support this position. In fact, unpublished data collected in our laboratory at Columbia University do not indicate the emergence of depressed mood states in the days after MDMA use, even when the drug is given repeatedly.

Another frequently mentioned potential negative consequence of MDMA is damage to brain cells. Several investigators have shown that large

Drugs in Depth

Extrapolating Findings from Animals to Humans: What You Need to Know

"The amount of the drug Ecstasy that some recreational users take in a single night may cause permanent brain damage and lead to symptoms like those of Parkinson's disease," read an article published in *The New York Times* on September 27, 2002. This and similar statements were based on assertions made in a scientific paper that appeared in the journal *Science*.[26] George Ricaurte and colleagues gave nonhuman primates three doses of MDMA over the course of six hours and, then, a couple of weeks later evaluated neuroanatomical and neurochemical changes. They found damage to dopamine and serotonin neurons as well as reduced levels of these neurotransmitters in the brain.

What made these results intriguing was that the doses of MDMA used and the pattern of drug administration were claimed to be comparable to those used by recreational human users. The researchers injected MDMA at a dosage of 2 mg/kg, three times, at three-hour intervals, for a total dose of 6 mg/kg. This dosing regimen does not correspond with those typically used by humans: (1) Most people do not take three large doses in one evening; and (2) most people do not inject MDMA. Recall from Chapter 5 that drugs administered by injection result in greater brain concentrations of the drug and increase the potential for toxicity, especially in naive users. Potential toxicity is decreased, by contrast, when a drug is self-administered compared to experimenter-administered.[27] Thus, these factors increased the likelihood of observing toxicity in the Ricaurte study.

The study's findings generated a wave of controversy. But in an embarrassing turn of events, Ricaurte and colleagues were forced to retract their paper one year after its publication because they discovered that larger doses of methamphetamine had been mistakenly given, rather than MDMA.[28] This was deduced after several unsuccessful attempts by the researchers to replicate their original findings. It is noteworthy that the studies that failed to replicate the neurotoxic findings were never published. This highlights another important point: There is a bias toward publishing results that show drug-induced neurotoxicity. Together, these observations raise questions about the relevancy of drug-induced neurotoxicity findings collected in laboratory animals.

As a student trying to evaluate drug-related data, which sources are credible? In your attempt to evaluate the research, you should ask a few simple questions: (1) What was the drug dosing regimen used, and is it similar to regimens used by humans? (2) What was the route of drug administration used, and do humans use the drug in this manner? (3) Was the drug self-administered or administered by the experimenter? (4) Were the animals administered escalating doses prior to receiving a larger dose? All of these factors potentially impact neurochemical findings and should be considered when making extrapolations about data collected in laboratory animals to humans.

Box icon credit: ©Ingram Publishing/SuperStock RF

doses of MDMA given to laboratory animals can destroy serotonin neurons, but the relevance of this and related findings for human recreational use is unclear (see the Drugs in Depth box). Recreational MDMA users do not typically use doses as large as those used in animal experiments, and when the cognitive abilities of these users is compared with education- and age-matched counterparts, they perform equally well. These observations raise serious questions about the relevance of data collected in laboratory animals demonstrating MDMA-induced

toxicity. This does not, however, suggest that illicit MDMA use is safe. As is the case with most illicit drugs, there is the potential for contamination with adulterants, which are sometimes more toxic than the compound of interest.

MDA, known on the street as the love drug, has received considerably less research attention. From what little is known, the drug appears to produce effects similar to those seen with MDMA, although there has yet to be a human study that directly compares the two drugs.

DOM (STP) DOM is 2,5-dimethoxy-4-methylamphetamine. In the 1960s and 1970s, DOM was called STP, and street talk was that the initials stood for serenity, tranquility, and peace. Its actions and effects are similar to those of mescaline and LSD, with a total dose of 1 to 3 mg yielding euphoria and 3 to 5 mg a six- to eight-hour psychedelic period. This makes DOM about a hundred times as potent as mescaline but only one-thirtieth as potent as LSD.

2-CB and 2-C-T7 It's happened before and it will happen again: As federal and state agencies work to limit access to one drug, another arrives to fill the gap. In this case, two drugs have arrived to share the rave scene with MDMA: 4-bromo-2, 5-dimethoxyphenethylamine (known as 2-CB) and 4-propylthio-2, 5-dimethoxyphenethylamine (2-C-T7). As phenylethylamines, both are chemical cousins to the amphetamine series of psychedelics. Along with the recently popularized tryptamine derivatives AMT and "foxy methoxy" (see page 319), a confusing array of chemicals is being made available to "ravers," who may find themselves trying unknown amounts of unfamiliar drugs more often than they'd like.

N-Methyl-DL-Aspartate (NMDA) Antagonists

PCP

In the 1950s, Parke, Davis & Company investigated a series of drugs in the search for an efficient intravenous anesthetic. On the basis of animal studies, the company selected 1-(1-phenylcyclohexyl) piperidine hydrochloride (**PCP,** generic name *phencyclidine*) for testing in humans. The studies on monkeys had indicated that PCP was a good analgesic but did not produce good muscle relaxation or sleep. Instead, the animals showed a sort of "dissociation" from what was happening. In 1958, the first report was published on the use of PCP (Sernyl) for surgical anesthesia in humans. Sernyl produced good analgesia without depressing blood

circulation or respiration and did not produce irregularities in heartbeat. Loss of sensation occurred within two or three minutes of beginning the intravenous infusion, after about 10 mg of the drug had been delivered. The patients later had no memory of the procedure, did not remember being spoken to, and remembered no pain. Compared with existing anesthetics, which tend to depress both respiration and circulation through general depression of the CNS, this type of "dissociative" anesthetic seemed to be quite safe. However, the psychological reactions to the drug were unpredictable.

Thus, by 1960, PCP had been characterized as an excellent anesthetic for monkeys, a medically safe but psychologically troublesome anesthetic for humans, and a psychedelic different from LSD and mescaline, with profound effects on body perception. Parke, Davis withdrew Sernyl as an investigational drug for humans in 1965 and in 1967 licensed another company to sell Sernylan as an animal anesthetic. It was primarily used with primates, in both research laboratories and zoos. Also, because of its rapid action and wide safety margin, Sernylan was used in syringe bullets to immobilize stray, wild, or dangerous zoo animals. Because of the popular term *tranquilizer gun* for this use, PCP became popularly, and inaccurately, known as an animal "tranquilizer."

Recreational Use of PCP In the early 1970s, it was said that PCP crystals were sometimes sprinkled onto oregano, parsley, or alfalfa and sold to unsuspecting youngsters as marijuana. In this form, it became known as **angel dust.** Because PCP can be made inexpensively and relatively easily by amateur chemists, when it is available it usually doesn't cost much. Eventually, the rapid and potent effects of angel dust made it a desired substance in its own right. Joints made with PCP sometimes contained marijuana, sometimes another plant substance, and were known as "killer joints" or "sherms" (because they hit the user like a Sherman tank).

At some point in the 1970s, it was reported that PCP users became violent when under the influence of the drug. Police narratives claiming to experience great difficulties subduing PCP-intoxicated individuals further cemented the association of PCP and violence. One frequently reported police story is about the PCP user who was so violent, had such superhuman strength, and was so insensitive to pain that he was shot 28 times (or a similarly large number of times) before he fell. Although there is no evidence that this actually happened, the story continues to live and is repeated as if factual. What's worse is that this and similar stories may contribute to the notion that extraordinary use of force is justified when apprehending a suspected PCP user. One such example occurred in March 1991 when Los Angeles police officers were videotaped beating Rodney King. During their trial, the officers said that they used such force because they believed King might have been "dusted"—under the influence of PCP. He wasn't. Alcohol was the only drug found in his system. And regarding the science and PCP-induced violence, a comprehensive clinical literature review concluded that assumptions about PCP and violence are simply not warranted.[29]

PCP produces many of its effects by selectively blocking the NMDA subtype of glutamate receptor. In other words, PCP is a selective NMDA receptor antagonist. Ketamine, memantine, and dextromethorphan also act as NMDA receptor antagonists, but their effects at the NMDA receptor are less selective than PCP's. One of the most recent exciting lines of research investigates the ability of ketamine to treat major depressive disorders. A growing body of evidence indicates that the drug not only is effective but also produces antidepressive effects at a much more rapid rate than traditional antidepressant drugs.[30] The therapeutic effects of ketamine are observed within 24 hours, whereas the beneficial effects of traditional antidepressants are not seen for 7–14 days.

Anticholinergic Psychedelics

The potato family contains all the naturally occurring agents to be discussed in this section. Three of the genera—*Atropa, Hyoscyamus,* and *Mandragora* —have a single species of importance and were primarily restricted to Europe. The fourth genus, *Datura,* is worldwide and has many species containing the active agents.

The family of plants in which all these genera are found is *Solanaceae,* "herbs of consolation," and three pharmacologically active alkaloids are responsible for the effects of these plants. *Atropine,* which is dl-hyoscyamine, scopolamine, or l-hyoscine, and l-hyoscyamine are all potent central and peripheral cholinergic blocking agents. These drugs occupy the acetylcholine receptor site but do not activate it; thus, their effect is primarily to block muscarinic cholinergic neurons, including the parasympathetic system.

These agents have potent peripheral and central effects, and some of the psychological responses to these drugs are probably a reaction to peripheral changes. These alkaloids block the production of mucus in the nose and throat. They also prevent salivation, so the mouth becomes uncommonly dry, and perspiration stops. Temperature can increase to fever levels (109°F has been reported in infants

Belladonna, or deadly nightshade, is a poisonous plant that contains an anticholinergic psychedelic. ©Steven P. Lynch RF

PCP: phencyclidine; originally developed as an anesthetic; has psychedelic properties.
angel dust: the street name for PCP sprinkled on plant material.

with atropine poisoning), and heart rate can show a 50-beat-per-minute increase with atropine. Even at moderate doses these chemicals cause considerable dilation of the pupils of the eyes, with a resulting inability to focus on nearby objects. With large enough doses, a behavioral pattern develops that resembles toxic psychosis; there is delirium, mental confusion, loss of attention, drowsiness, and loss of memory for recent events. These two characteristics—a clouding of consciousness and no memory for the period of intoxication—plus the absence of vivid sensory effects separate these drugs from the indole and catechol psychedelics. The anticholinergics are the original *deliriants*.

Belladonna Atropine, which was isolated in 1831, is the active ingredient in the deadly nightshade, *Atropa belladonna*. The name of the plant reflects two of its major uses in the Middle Ages and before. The genus name reflects its use as a poison. Deadly nightshade was one of the plants used extensively by both professional and amateur poisoners; 14 of its berries contain enough of the alkaloid to cause death.

Belladonna, the species name, meaning "beautiful woman," comes from the use of the extract of this plant to dilate the pupils of the eyes. Interestingly, ancient Roman and Egyptian women knew something that science did not learn until more recently. In the 1950s, it was demonstrated, by using pairs of photographs identical except for the amount of pupil dilation, that most people judge the girl with the more dilated eyes to be prettier.

Of more interest here than pretty girls or poisoned men is the sensation of flying reported by some users of belladonna. The origin of this story goes back at least to the Middle Ages in Europe, and in particular to descriptions of witches and witchcraft. Every early society for which we have any history has a tradition of people with special knowledge of useful plants. In Europe, the people who were consulted for their special arcane knowledge of plant potions were most often women, and their traditions are kept alive in our modern concept of "witches." Among the rich folklore about witches are several accounts from the 1400s describing

"flying ointments" (e.g., *The Book of the Sacred Magic of Abremelin the Mage,* 1458), and one ingredient often included in these ointments was deadly nightshade. The idea is that this ointment was spread upon the body and/or on a stick, or "staffe," which was straddled. This is certainly the origin of our notion that witches flew about on broomsticks, though in many accounts it seems that the sticks were used more as phallic symbols and were perhaps ridden in a different manner. What is actually known about witches and witchcraft of this era is confused considerably by what was written about witches by Catholic priests during the Inquisition.

During the Middle Ages, all such pagan rituals were considered to be heresy, and practitioners were tortured and killed. Admissions by witches that they "flew" long distances to celebrate Black Mass were extracted during torture and were likely to have reflected the beliefs of the inquisitors more than the history of the person being tortured. Some incredibly lurid accounts of the practices of witches associated drugs, sex, and human sacrifice. Similar lurid accounts linking other drugs (marijuana, LSD, cocaine) to sexual abandon and criminal violence have appeared during more recent years, also promoted by those protecting the established order. The facts are usually not so exciting. Anticholinergics can make people feel light-headed, and in conjunction with the power of suggestion one might get the *sensation* of floating, or flying, but it's not a realistic way to get from New York to Laramie.

Mandrake The *mandrake* plant (*Mandragora officinarum*) contains all three alkaloids. Although many drugs can be traced to the Bible, it is particularly important to do so with mandrake because its close association with love and lovemaking has persisted from Genesis to recent times:

> In the time of wheat-harvest Reuben went out and found some mandrakes in the open country and brought them to his mother Leah. Then Rachel asked Leah for some of her son's mandrakes, but Leah said, "Is it so small a thing to have taken away my husband, that you should take my son's mandrakes as

well?" But Rachel said, "Very well, let him sleep with you tonight in exchange for your son's mandrakes." So when Jacob came in from the country in the evening, Leah went out to meet him and said, "You are to sleep with me tonight; I have hired you with my son's mandrakes." That night he slept with her.[31]

The mandrake root is forked and, if you have a vivid imagination, resembles a human body. The root contains the psychoactive agents and was endowed with all sorts of magical and medical properties. The association with the human form is alluded to in Shakespeare's Juliet's farewell speech: "And shrieks like mandrakes torn out of the earth, That living mortals hearing them run mad."

Henbane Compared with deadly nightshade and mandrake, *Hyoscyamus niger* has had a most uninteresting life. This is strange, because it is pharmacologically quite active and contains both scopolamine and l-hyoscyamine. Other plants of this genus contain effective levels of the alkaloids, but it is *Hyoscyamus niger* that appears throughout history as *henbane,* a highly poisonous substance and truly the bane of hens, as well as other animals.

Pliny in AD 60 said, "For this is certainly known, that, if one takes it in drink more than four leaves, it will put him beside himself." Shakespeare's Hamlet's father must have had more than four leaves because it was henbane that was used to poison him.

Datura The distribution of the many *Datura* species is worldwide, but they all contain the three alkaloids under discussion—tropine, scopolamine, and hyoscyamine—in varying amounts. Almost as extensive as the distribution are its uses and its history. Although it is not clear when the Chinese first used *Datura metel* as a medicine to treat colds and nervous disorders, the plant was important enough to become associated with Buddha:

The Chinese valued this drug far back into ancient times. A comparatively recent Chinese medical text, published in 1590, reported that "when Buddha

preaches a sermon, the heavens bedew the petals of this plant with rain drops."[32]

Halfway around the world, 2,500 years before the Chinese text, virgins sat in the temple to Apollo in Delphi and, probably under the influence of *Datura,* mumbled sounds that holy men interpreted as predictions that always came true. Engraved on the temple at Delphi were the words "Know thyself."

Datura is associated with the worship of Shiva in India, where it has long been recognized as an ingredient in love potions and has been known as "deceiver" and "foolmaker." In Asia the practice of mixing the crushed seeds of *Datura metel* in tobacco, cannabis, and food persists even today.

One interesting use of *Datura stramonium,* which is native and grows wild in the eastern United States, was devised by the Algonquin Indians. They used the plant to solve the problem of the adolescent search for identity, allowing male youths to consume only concoctions of the plant for a period of two to three weeks, during which time it was believed that these youths would forget their former lives and leave boyhood behind.[32] The same plant is

The red- and white-speckled mushroom *Amanita muscaria* played a major role in the early history of Indo-European and Central American religions. ©Ingram Publishing RF

now called Jamestown weed, or jimsonweed, as a result of an incident in the 17th century, recorded in the book *The History and Present State of Virginia,* during which soldiers ate the plant and "turn'd natural fools upon it for several Days."[33]

Although there has been some recent abuse of jimsonweed, the unpleasant and dangerous side effects of this plant limit its recreational use.

Synthetic Anticholinergics Anticholinergic drugs were once used to treat Parkinson's disease (before the introduction of L-DOPA) and are still widely used to treat the pseudoparkinsonism produced by antipsychotic drugs (see Chapter 8). Particularly in older people, there is concern about inadvertently producing an "anticholinergic syndrome," characterized by excessive dry mouth, elevated temperature, delusions, and hallucinations. Anticholinergic drugs such as trihexyphenidyl (Artane) and benztropine (Cogentin) have rarely been abused for their delirium-producing properties.

Amanita Muscaria

The *Amanita muscaria* mushroom is also called "fly agaric," probably because of what it does to flies. It doesn't kill them, but when they suck its juice, it puts them into a stupor for two to three hours. It is one of the common poisonous mushrooms found in forests in many parts of the world. The older literature suggests that eating 5 to 10 *Amanita* mushrooms results in severe effects of intoxication, such as muscular twitching, leading to twitches of limbs and raving drunkenness, with agitation and vivid hallucinations. Later follow many hours of partial paralysis with sleep and dreams.

When the ancient Aryan invaders swept down from the north into India 3,500 years ago, they took soma, itself considered a deity. The cult of Soma ruled India's religion and culture for many years— the poems of the Rig Veda celebrate the sacramental use of this substance. It has only been within the past 30 years that scholars have discovered and agreed on the identity of soma as *Amanita.*[1]

The suggestion has been made that the ambrosia ("food of the gods") mentioned in the secret rites of the god Dionysius in Greece was a solution of the *Amanita* mushroom. And based on paintings representing the "tree of life" found in ancient European cave paintings, it has been suggested that *Amanita muscaria* use formed a basis for the cult that originated about 2,000 years ago and today calls itself Christianity.[34]

Until the Russians introduced them to alcohol, many of the isolated nomadic tribes of Siberia had no intoxicant but *Amanita.*

In the frozen northland, these mushrooms are expensive; sometimes several reindeer are exchanged for an effective number of the mushrooms. During the long winter months they might be worth the price. While the mushrooms themselves are not reusable (once eaten, they're gone), the psychedelic is excreted unchanged in the urine.

There is evidence that *Amanita* was also used as a holy plant by several tribal groups in the Americas, ranging from Alaska and the Great Lakes to Mexico and Central America. In several of the legends, its origin is associated with thunder and lightning.[1]

For many years the active agent in this mushroom was thought to be *muscarine* (for which the muscarinic cholinergic receptors were named). This substance activates the same type of acetylcholine receptor that is blocked by the anticholinergics. However, pharmacological studies with other cholinergic agonists did not produce similar psychoactive effects. Next, attention focused on *bufotenin,* an indole that is found in high concentrations in the skins of toads. However, the psychedelic properties of bufotenin have been in doubt, and *Amanita* species contain only small amounts of it. In the mid-1960s, meaningful amounts of two chemicals were found: ibotenic acid and muscimol.

The effects of *Amanita* ingestion are not similar to those of other psychedelics, and that helped confuse the picture with regard to the mechanism. Muscimol can act as an agonist at GABA receptors, which are inhibitory and found throughout the central nervous system. Muscimol is more potent than ibotenic acid, and drying of the mushroom, which is usually done by those who use it, promotes the transformation of ibotenic acid to muscimol. Muscimol has been given to humans, resulting in confusion, disorientation in time and place, sensory disturbances, muscle twitching, weariness, fatigue, and sleep.[19]

Amanita muscaria and other related poisonous mushrooms are found in North America, and they are a particularly dangerous type of plant with which to experiment.

Salvia Divinorum

This member of the mint family is known by its botanical name, which is translated as "diviner's sage." It has been used for centuries by the Mazatec people of Oaxaca, Mexico, in religious ceremonies. The traditional methods of using the plant include chewing the leaves, drinking a tea made from the crushed leaves, or smoking the dried leaves. Recreational users in the United States and in Europe have cultivated the plant for the past several years and use it via the smoking route. The U.S. government does not list *Salvia divinorum* as a controlled substance, but multiple states have taken matters into their own hands by banning the substance.

The plant was identified in 1962 by Wasson and Hoffman, and the active agent, salvinorin A, was identified in 1982. Salvinorin A is a kappa opioid receptor agonist. The drug produces no effect on the serotonin-2A receptor, the main target for classic psychedelics such as LSD, mescaline, and DMT.[35]

Given its pharmacological profile, one might predict that the drug would produce effects different from the classical psychedelics. At least two studies have been published investigating the effects of salvinorin A in human users: the first by Matthew Johnson and colleagues and the second by Peter Addy.[36,37] In both studies, the drug was inhaled and doses ranged from 0 to 21 µg/kg. Salvinorin A produced dose-dependent effects on participant ratings of drug strength. The drug also increased ratings of euphoria and did not increase dysphoric ratings. At the larger doses, salvinorin A produced a profile of effects similar to DMT and psilocybin on the Hallucinogen Rating Scale, a

measure that consists of six subscales assessing various aspects of psychedelic effects. In addition, salvinorin A occasioned mystical-type effects similar in magnitude to those seen with psilocybin. These results were replicated and extended, demonstrating that there was no evidence of persisting adverse effects one month following drug administration.[38]

The findings from these studies markedly differ from the uncontrolled effects seen in online videos of *Salvia divinorum* use. This observation underscores the importance of the user's history and the setting in which drug use occurs. As is the case with all psychoactive drugs, adverse consequences are more likely when inexperienced users take drugs in chaotic and uncontrolled settings compared with use by experienced users in carefully controlled settings.

Summary

- Psychedelic plants have been used for many centuries, not only as medicines but for spiritual and recreational purposes as well.

- LSD, a synthetic psychedelic, alters perceptual processes and enhances emotionality, so that the real world is seen differently and is responded to with great emotion.

- Other chemicals that contain the indole nucleus, such as psilocybin (from the Mexican mushroom), have effects similar to those of LSD.

- Mescaline, from the peyote cactus, and synthetic derivatives of the amphetamines represent the catechol psychedelics. They have psychological effects quite similar to those of the indole types.

- PCP, or angel dust, produces more changes in body perception and fewer visual effects than LSD.

- Anticholinergics are found in many plants throughout the world and have been used not only recreationally, medically, and spiritually but also as poisons.

Review Questions

1. Why was LSD used in psychoanalysis in the 1950s and 1960s? How does this relate to its proposed use by the Army and the CIA?

2. Describe the dependence potential of LSD in terms of tolerance, physical dependence, and psychological dependence.

3. What is the diagnostic term for *flashbacks?*

4. What is the active agent in the "magic mushrooms" of Mexico, and is it an indole or a catechol?

5. Besides the psychological effects, what other effects are reliably produced by peyote?

6. Contrast MDMA and PCP in terms of how they appear to make people feel about being close to others.

7. Which of the psychedelic plants was most associated with witchcraft?

8. What can be concluded from the evidence regarding the neurotoxic effects of MDMA?

9. Which psychedelic acts as an agonist at kappa opiate receptors?

References

1. Schultes, R. E., and A. Hofmann. *Plants of the Gods.* New York: McGraw-Hill, 1979.

2. Krebs, T. S., and P. O. Johansen "Lysergic Acid Diethylamide (LSD) for Alcoholism: Meta-analysis of Randomized Controlled Trials." *Journal of Psychopharmacology,* 26 (2012), pp. 994–1002.

3. Mithoefer, M. C., and others. "The Safety and Efficacy of (+/–)3,4-methylenedioxymethamphetamine-Assisted Psychotherapy in Subjects with Chronic, Treatment-Resistant Posttraumatic Stress Disorder: The First Randomized Controlled Pilot Study." *Journal of Psychopharmacology,* 25 (2011), pp. 439–52.

4. Sanches, R.F., and others. "Antidepressant Effects of a Single Dose of Ayahuasca in Patients with Recurrent Depression: A SPECT Study." *Journal of Clinical Psychopharmacology* 36 (2016), pp. 77–81.

5. Johnson, M.W., A. Garcia-Romeu, and R. R. Griffiths. "Long-Term Follow-Up of Psilocybin-Facilitated Smoking Cessation. *American Journal of Drug and Alcohol Abuse* 43 (2017), pp. 55–60.

6. Griffiths, R.R., and others. "Psilocybin Produces Substantial and Sustained Decreases in Depression and Anxiety in Patients with Life-Threatening Cancer: A Randomized Double-Blind Trial." *Journal of Psychopharmacology* 30 (2016), pp. 1181–97.

7. Hofmann, A. "Psychotomimetic Agents." In A. Burger, ed. *Drugs Affecting the Central Nervous System* (Vol. 2). New York: Marcel Dekker, 1968.

8. Segal, J., ed. *Research in the Service of Mental Health, Research on Drug Abuse.* National Institute on Mental Health, Pub. No. (ADM) 75–236, U.S. Department of Health, Education, and Welfare. Washington, DC: U.S. Government Printing Office, 1975.

9. Julien, R. M. *A Primer of Drug Action,* 10th ed. New York: Worth, 2005.

10. Halpern, J. H., and others. "Hallucinogen Persisting Perceptual Disorder: What Do We Know after 50 Years?" *Drug & Alcohol Dependence* 69 (2003), pp. 109–19.

11. Sewell, R. A., J. H. Halpern, and H. G. Pope, Jr. "Response of Cluster Headache to Psilocybin and LSD." *Neurology* 66 (2006), pp. 1920–22.

12. Gasser, P., K. Kirchner, and T. Passie. "LSD-Assisted Psychotherapy for Anxiety Associated with a Life-Threatening Disease: A Qualitative Study of Acute and Sustained Subjective Effects." *Journal of Psychopharmacolqlgy* 29 (2015), pp. 57–68.

13. Waldman, A. *A Really Good Day: How Microdosing Made a Mega Difference in My Mood, My Marriage, and My Life.* New York: Knopf, 2017.

14. Studerus, E., and others. "Acute, Subacute and Long-Term Subjective Effects of Psilocybin in Healthy Humans: A Pooled Analysis of Experimental Studies." *Journal of Psychopharmacology* 25 (2011), pp. 1434–52.

15. Johnson, M. W., and others. "Psilocybin Dose-Dependently Causes Delayed, Transient Headaches in Healthy Volunteers." *Drug and Alcohol Dependence,* 123 (2012), pp. 132–40.

16. Pahnke, W. "Drugs and Mysticism: An Analysis of the Relationship between Psychedelic Drugs and the Mystical Consciousness." Ph.D. thesis, Harvard University, 1963.

17. Griffiths, R. R., W. A. Richards, U. McCann, and R. Jesse. "Psilocybin Can Occasion Mystical-Type Experiences Having Substantial and Sustained Personal Meaning and Spiritual Significance." *Psychopharmacology* 187 (2006), pp. 268–83.

18. Griffiths, R. R., and others. "Psilocybin Occasioned Mystical-Type Experiences: Immediate and Persisting Dose-Related Effects." *Psychopharmacology* 218 (2011), pp. 649–65.

19. Schultes, R. E., and A. Hofmann. *The Botany and Chemistry of Psychedelics.* Springfield, IL: Charles C. Thomas, 1980.

20. Al-Assmar, S. E. "The Seeds of the Hawaiian Baby Woodrose Are a Powerful Hallucinogen [letter]." *Archives of Internal Medicine* 159 (1999), p. 2090.

21. de Wit H. (2006) Towards a science of spiritual experience. Volume 187, Issue 3, pp 267–267.

22. Volkow V (2006) Statement by NIDA Director Nora D. Volkow, M.D., in response to a study published in the Journal Psychopharmacology on July 11, 2006. Study authors: R.R. Griffiths, et al. Johns Hopkins University School of Medicine. https://www.drugabuse.gov/about-nida/directors-page/messages-director/2006/07/statement-by-nida-director-nora-d-volkow-md-in-response-to-study-publisher.

23. Strassman, R. J., and others. "Differential Tolerance to Biological and Subjective Effects of Four Closely-Spaced Doses of N, N-dimethyltryptamine in Humans." *Biological Psychiatry* 39 (1996), pp. 784–95.

24. Huxley, A. *The Doors of Perception.* New York: Harper & Row, 1954.

25. Dobkin de Rios, M., and M. Cardenas. "Plant Psychedelics, Shamanism, and Nazca Ceramics." *Journal of Ethnopharmacology* 2 (1980), pp. 233–46.

26. Ricaurte, G. A., J. Yuan, G. Hatzidimitriou, B. J. Cord, and U. D. McCann. "Severe Dopaminergic Neurotoxicity in Primates after a Common Recreational Dose Regimen of MDMA (Ecstasy)." *Science* 297 (2002), pp. 2260–63.

27. Dworkin, S. I., S. Mirkis, and J. E. Smith. "Response-Dependent versus Response-Independent Presentation of Cocaine: Differences in the Lethal Effects of the Drug." *Psychopharmacology* 117 (1995), pp. 262–66.

28. Ricaurte, G. A., J. Yuan, G. Hatzidimitriou, B. J. Cord, and U. D. McCann. "Retraction." *Science* 301 (2003), p. 1479.

29. Brecher, M., and others. "Phencyclidine and Violence: Clinical and Legal Issues." *Journal of Clinical Psychopharmacology* 8 (1988), pp. 397–401.

30. Han, Y., and others. "Efficacy of Ketamine in the Rapid Treatment of Major Depressive Disorder: A Meta-analysis of Randomized, Double-Blind, Placebo-Controlled Studies." *Neuropsychiatric Disease and Treatment* 12 (2016), pp. 2859–67.

31. Genesis 30:14–16. *The New English Bible.* Oxford University Press and Cambridge University Press, 1970.

32. Schultes, R. E. "The Plant Kingdom and Hallucinogens (Part III)." *Bulletin on Narcotics* 22, no. 1 (1970), pp. 43–46.

33. Beverly, R. *The History and Present State of Virginia,* 1705. Chapel Hill: University of North Carolina Press, 1947.

34. Allegro, J. M. *The Sacred Mushroom and the Cross.* New York: Doubleday, 1970.

35. Sheffler, D. J., B. L. Roth, and A. Salvinorin. "The 'Magic Mint' Hallucinogen Finds a Molecular Target in the Kappa Opioid Receptor." *Trends in Pharmacological Sciences* 24 (2003), pp. 107–09.

36. Johnson, M. W., and others. "Human Psychopharmacology and Dose-Effects of Salvinorin A, a Kappa Opioid Agonist Hallucinogen Present in the Plant *Salvia divinorum.*" *Drug and Alcohol Dependence,* 115 (2011), pp. 150–55.

37. Addy, P. H. "Acute and Post-Acute Behavioral and Psychological Effects of Salvinorin A in Humans." *Psychopharmacology,* 220 (2012), pp. 195–204.

38. MacLean, K. A., and others. "Dose-Related Effects of Salvinorin A in Humans: Dissociative, Hallucinogenic, and Memory Effects." *Psychopharmacology* 226 (2013), pp. 381–92.

Cannabis

Objectives

When you have finished this chapter, you should be able to:

- **Describe the relationship among *Cannabis*, marijuana, and THC and discuss different preparations of cannabis.**

- **Describe how Europeans became exposed to the psychological effects of *Cannabis*.**

- **Explain how marijuana was described in the years leading up to the 1937 Marijuana Tax Act.**

- **Discuss the legal status of marijuana in the United States since 1937, including current debates.**

- **Draw parallels among the various scientific and medical studies on marijuana.**

- **Describe the type of receptor THC acts on in the brain and compare the time course of smoked vs. oral THC.**

- **List the two most consistent physiological effects of marijuana.**

- **Discuss evidence for the abuse potential of marijuana and influences on the psychological effects of marijuana.**

- **Describe the effects of marijuana use on driving ability, the lungs, sperm motility, and the immune system.**

- **Describe the range of evidence relating to whether marijuana smoking leads to brain damage in humans.**

Source: Drug Enforcement Administration

Cannabis, the Plant

As with other psychoactive plants discussed in previous chapters, the psychological effects produced by *Cannabis* have been experienced by humans for many hundreds of years. In fact, *Cannabis* has such a long and complex human history that scholars still do not agree on such basic questions as the number and names of species. A thorough review of *Cannabis* botanical and cultural history proposes that we can trace three categories of human use: for fiber used in making ropes and cloth, nonpsychoactive medical use, and use focused mainly on its psychological effects.[1] In fact, it is not unreasonable to speculate that a well-read American living in the early part of the 20th century would have known the term *hemp* as a crop from which ropes were made, *cannabis* as

a little-used pharmaceutical product, and *marijuana* as a type of intoxicating cigarette, without realizing that all these would soon be legally classified as a single species, *Cannabis sativa*. This single-species classification has been controversial, because there is a long tradition of distinguishing two main types of *Cannabis*. Traditionally, *C. sativa* was cultivated primarily for hemp fiber and seeds. It grew as a lanky plant up to 18 feet high and was relatively low in potency in terms of psychoactive effects. *C. indica* was cultivated in China and India, not only for fiber and seeds but also for its psychoactive potency, as a more compact plant, usually only two or three feet tall. Currently, both *C. sativa* and *C. indica* are widely grown in such a way as to maximize their psychoactive effects, and many hybrids have been generated. Both users and commercial producers promote the notion that *C. sativa* is more mentally "uplifting" (stimulating) and *C. indica* is more sedating, although there is little scientific backing for these proposed distinctions.

Preparations from *Cannabis*

The primary psychoactive agent, delta-9-tetrahydrocannabinol (**THC**), is concentrated in a resin, with different amounts of the resin produced by different parts of the plant. The highest concentration is found in tiny hairs called *trichomes*, which are most abundant on the flowers of the female plant (photograph). Therefore, various products made from the plant will vary widely in their psychoactive potency. The seeds, which contain oil rich in essential amino acids, have at times been used as food for both humans and domestic animals, and they have no psychoactive potency. Marijuana cigarettes made from leaves may have as little as 1% THC, whereas cigarettes made from the flowering tops ("buds") of some strains may contain up to around 20% THC. By scraping or breaking off the tiny hairlike trichomes and packing them together, a more concentrated product called **hashish** can be made, with up to 65% THC by weight. Growers have become expert at selecting particular strains and removing the male plants prior to pollination so that the female plants produce more flowers and no seeds (**sinsemilla**). Artificial lighting cycles also encourage flowering, thus increasing the yield of the most psychoactive parts of the plant.

The widespread commercialization of first medical and later recreational cannabis in several U.S. states has led to a proliferation of products.

A female Cannabis plant containing trichomes. ©Canna Obscura/Shutterstock.com RF

An Internet search of any of the large commercial marijuana dispensaries will provide insight into a mind-boggling array of cannabis products, as well as claims regarding the potential benefits of each. In addition to various strains of *C. sativa* and *C. indica*, plus hybrid strains, various extracts and edible products are made from these plants.

Extracts

THC does not dissolve well in water, so over the years people have used a variety of organic solvents to extract THC from the plant material. A traditional method involved soaking the plant material in ethanol, which could then be filtered and evaporated, leaving behind a concentrated substance referred to as "hash oil." Liquid butane allows a faster and more efficient extraction, but this is a dangerous method due to the explosiveness of butane as it is evaporating. Most commercial extraction facilities these days use liquid carbon dioxide (CO_2) to produce oils or other forms known as "budder," "wax," or "shatter," with THC concentrations as high as 70–80 percent. These concentrated forms are mostly used by heating them in specially designed pipes and inhaling the vapors. Solutions are also available for use in "vape" pens (e-cigarettes, see Chapter 10).

Hashish, concentrated resin from the *Cannabis* plant, is relatively rare in the United States.   Source: Drug Enforcement Administration

Edibles

Plant material may be included in baked **edibles**, such as cookies or brownies, to allow oral consumption of cannabis. Also, extracts can be incorporated into hard or chewy sugar candies, chocolate candy, sodas, and many other edible products.

History

Early History

The earliest reference to *Cannabis* is in a pharmacy book written in 2737 BC by Chinese emperor Shen Nung. Referring to the euphoriant effects of *Cannabis,* he called it the "Liberator of Sin." He recommended it for some medical uses, including "female weakness, gout, rheumatism, malaria, beriberi, constipation and absent-mindedness." Social use of the plant had spread to the Middle East and North Africa by AD 1000. In this period in the eastern Mediterranean area, a legend developed around a religious group that committed murder for political reasons. The group was called "hashishiyya," from which our word *assassin* developed. In 1299, Marco Polo told the story he had heard of this group and its leader. It was a marvelous tale and had all the ingredients necessary for a tale to survive through the ages: intrigue, murder, sex, the use of drugs, and mysterious lands. The story of this group and its activities was told in many ways over the years, and Boccaccio's *Decameron* contained one story based on it. Stories of this group, combined with the frequent reference to the power and wonderment of hashish in *The Arabian Nights,* were widely circulated in Europe over the years.

Harry Anslinger's Case against Marijuana

At the beginning of the 20th century, there was limited public interest in cannabis or use of the drug. In the early 1920s, a few references in the mass media reported the use by Mexican Americans of something the newspapers called marijuana, but public concern was not aroused. In the late 1920s, however, a series of articles associating marijuana and crime appeared in southern newspapers. As a result, the public began to take an interest in this "new" drug.

By the mid 1930s, perhaps no one was more interested in marijuana than Harry Anslinger. From 1930 to 1962, Anslinger served as the commissioner of the U.S. Bureau of Narcotics, an agency located within the Department of the Treasury. The Department of the Treasury was responsible for coordinating enforcement efforts around several major drug laws, including the 1914 Harrison Act and the 18th Amendment, which instituted Prohibition. After the 18th Amendment was repealed in December 1933, marijuana became a main target of drug law enforcement efforts. This meant that Anslinger's bureau would now take center stage. In an effort to convince the American public that he

Cannabis (can a biss): the genus of plant known as marijuana.

THC: delta-9-tetrahydrocannabinol, the most psychoactive chemical in cannabis.

hashish (hash *eesh* or *hash* eesh): concentrated resin from the *Cannabis* plant.

sinsemilla (sin se *mee* ya): "without seeds"; a method of growing more potent marijuana.

edible: any edible product that contains THC, usually brownies, cookies, and candies.

Drugs in the Media

From Crack Babies to Marijuana Babies: Here We Go Again

Recently, two much-discussed articles on marijuana use during pregnancy appeared in the scientific and popular presses. In January 2017, Ira Chasnoff—the same Ira Chasnoff who wrote about the so-called crack babies in the 1980s (see Chapter 6)—published a piece in the *American Journal of Obstetrics and Gynecology*, entitled "Medical Marijuana Laws and Pregnancy: Implications for Public Health Policy."[2] A month later, Catherine S. Louis authored "Pregnant Women Turn to Marijuana, Perhaps Harming Infants," which appeared in *The New York Times*.[3]

Both authors argued that the number of pregnant women using marijuana has increased as a result of legislation in some states that allow patients to use marijuana on the advice of their physicians and as a result of eight states now allowing adults to legally purchase and use the substance for recreational purposes. Moreover, these women may be subjecting their fetuses, the authors explained, to subsequent cognitive impairments. Chasnoff further concluded that physicians should be educated about the negative effects of marijuana use during pregnancy and should discourage its use by pregnant women and women considering becoming pregnant. In our view, because the arguments put forth in these pieces appear, at least on the surface, helpful, it might be instructive to take a closer look at the evidence on which the claims are based.

Regarding the assertion that increasing numbers of expectant mothers are using marijuana, the percentage of pregnant women who report having used the drug within the past month ranges from 1 percent to 5 percent.[4] These percentages have remained consistent for decades. In addition, it is important to note that illicit substance use, including marijuana, substantially decreases during pregnancy, especially as pregnancy progresses.[5]

An extremely concerning feature of the article by Chasnoff is that it misinterprets several previous findings in order to draw its conclusion. For example, in referring to research by van Gelder and colleagues,[6] Chasnoff states there is "a significant increased risk for **anencephaly** when the fetus is exposed to marijuana." The original paper, however, revealed no such statistically significant difference. Importantly, the overwhelming majority of individuals exposed to marijuana were not afflicted with anencephaly. This, combined with the fact that there are multiple causes for anencephaly,

highlights the inappropriateness of the author's singling out marijuana as the causal agent.

Chasnoff's and Louis's articles suffer from over-interpretation of animal data. Multiple caveats suggest that caution should be exercised when extrapolating findings from laboratory animals to humans. Typical dosing regimens used in these studies exceed doses taken by humans for medical or recreational purposes. Humans usually escalate their doses gradually, preventing potential toxic effects. This is pertinent because the harmful effects of larger drug doses can be prevented with previous exposure to escalating doses.[7] In these animal studies, doses were not administered in gradually escalating fashion, mimicking typical human consumption patterns. Therefore, the relevance of the animal data—discussed in both articles—to humans is, at best, unclear.

The articles overstate data on cognition as well. For example, based on findings from Goldschmidt and coworkers,[8] Chasnoff states that "a consistent pattern of deficits" has been observed in prenatally marijuana-exposed children. In reality, evidence from the entire literature shows that cognitive performance of marijuana-exposed children does not differ from control subjects on the overwhelming majority of measures.[9] Furthermore, even when there is an observed statistical difference, it would be inappropriate to conclude that the difference has an impact on the daily functioning of the marijuana-exposed individual. That is why it is paramount to determine whether scores are within the normal population range.[10] If scientists (as well as nonscientists) are not cognizant of this potential pitfall, they run the risk of inappropriately labeling children as impaired, just as was the case during the "crack baby epidemic."

To be clear, in our view, women already receive sound advice related to proper nutrition, environmental hazards, and substance use. This is quite appropriate. However, the suggestions by Chasnoff and Louis exaggerate the potential negative consequences of prenatal marijuana exposure and put women and their children at greater risk for stigmatization and punitive legal consequences. Clearly, we support the goal of increased education, but it is critically important to ensure that the education is accurate, comprehensive, and not biased. This objective approach will decrease unintended consequences and, ultimately, enhance public health.

Box icon credit: ©Glow Images RF

was up for the task, Anslinger used his position to tout the dangers of marijuana and to lobby for federal legislation banning the use, sale, and trafficking of the drug.

In 1937, Anslinger wrote an influential editorial entitled "Marijuana—Assassin of Youth."[11] He claimed that marijuana caused some troubled teenaged girls to commit suicide and others to run away from home and become "slaves of the narcotic." But the primary purpose of the article was to convince readers that marijuana directly caused dozens of murders. In one particularly gruesome account, Anslinger described the murder of an entire family: "[P]olice found a youth staggering about in a human slaughterhouse. With an ax he had killed his father, mother, two brothers, and a sister. He had no recollection of having committed this multiple crime. Ordinarily a sane, rather quiet young man, he had become crazed from smoking marijuana." The fact that there was a paucity evidence to support the claims put forth by Anslinger did not deter him from publishing essentially the same editorial, with the same title, in multiple popular outlets.

With such poor evidence supporting a relationship between marijuana use and crime, it seems strange that the true story was never told. There are probably several reasons for this. One might have had something to do with the fact that most people had never heard of marijuana prior to the exaggerated claims made by Anslinger and the press. They were familiar with *Cannabis* and its effects, but marijuana was being publicized as a "new" drug. Of course, it wasn't. You might recall that a similar thing happened in the mid-1980s with "crack" and in the late 1990s with "meth." Most people thought these were new drugs as well and didn't realize they were just cocaine and methamphetamine—two drugs that were medically legal and that had been used recreationally for decades.

A second reason was the Great Depression, which made everyone acutely sensitive to, and wary of, any new and particularly foreign influences. The fact that it was Mexican Americans and African Americans who were associated with use of the drug made the drug doubly stigmatized for white Americans.

The Marijuana Tax Act of 1937

Passage of the Marijuana Tax Act was a foregone conclusion. Few witnesses testified other than law enforcement officials. The birdseed industry had the act modified so they could import sterilized *Cannabis* seed for use in their product. An official of the American Medical Association (AMA) testified on his own behalf, not representing the AMA, against the bill. In general, physicians resented being monitored by the Bureau of Narcotics and some wanted to preserve access to marijuana for medical purposes. Other physicians did not want to associate the old remedies based on *Cannabis* with this new, foreign-sounding drug marijuana. The bill was passed in August and became effective on October 1, 1937.

The general characteristics of the law followed the regulation-by-taxation theme of the Harrison Act of 1914. The federal law did not outlaw *Cannabis* or its preparations; it just taxed the grower, distributor, seller, and buyer and made it, administratively, almost impossible for anyone to have anything to do with *Cannabis*. In addition, the Bureau of Narcotics prepared a uniform law that many states adopted. The uniform law on marijuana specifically named *C. sativa* as the species of plant whose leafy material is illegal. In later years, the defense in some court cases argued that the material confiscated by the police had come from *C. indica* and thus was not illegal. In the usual specimens obtained by police or presented in court, all distinguishing characteristics between species are either not present or are obliterated by drying and crushing. Because the cannabinoids are present in all species, there is no way of telling what species most confiscated marijuana belongs to. The current federal and uniform laws refer only to *Cannabis*.

anencephaly (an, en ′sefalē): a condition, at birth, in which major portions of the brain, skull, and scalp are absent.

The state laws made possession and use of *Cannabis* illegal per se. In May 1969, 32 years later, the U.S. Supreme Court declared the Marijuana Tax Act unconstitutional and overturned the conviction of Timothy Leary because there was

> in the Federal anti-marijuana law—a section that requires the suspect to pay a tax on the drug, thus incriminating himself, in violation of the Fifth Amendment: and a section that assumes (rather than requiring proof) that a person with foreign-grown marijuana in his possession knows it is smuggled.[12]

After the Marijuana Tax Act

Passage of the Marijuana Tax Act had an amazing effect. Almost immediately there was a sharp reduction in the reports of heinous crimes committed under the influence of marijuana. The price of the drug increased rapidly (the war came along, too), so that five years after passage of the act the cost of a marijuana cigarette—a reefer—had increased 6 to 12 times and cost about a dollar.

The year after the law was enacted, 1938, Mayor Fiorello LaGuardia of New York City asked the New York Academy of Medicine to study the effects of marijuana to determine whether the drug caused long-term damage to its users. The report, issued in 1944, was extensive and drew conclusions that were not popular:

> Those who have been smoking marihuana for a period of years showed no mental or physical deterioration which may be attributed to the drug.[13]

Reactions from authorities were swift and pejorative. An editorial published in the influential *JAMA* shortly after the report was released provides an indication of how it was viewed by many in the medical community:

> A recent tragedy, the case of the hotel bell boy who killed a federal guard in Oklahoma City while under the influence of marihuana, is more eloquent testimony concerning the dangers of the drug.... Public officials will do well to disregard this unscientific, uncritical study, and continue to regard marihuana as a menace wherever it is purveyed."[14]

As is the case with many reports and criticisms of them, there is little dispute over the data. Most of the concerns deal with the interpretations of the data. In general, data from the LaGuardia Report are consistent with reports before and after its publication, including the Hemp Commission Report of the 1890s, the Panama Canal Zone reports of the 1930s, and reports in the 1970s by the governments of New Zealand, Canada, the United Kingdom, and the United States. The findings of the LaGuardia Report are also in agreement with those of the Institute of Medicine's comprehensive 1999 study entitled *Marijuana and Medicine: Assessing the Science.*[15] Thus, it seems as though the strong negative reactions by some authorities were motivated by factors other than the actual data.

The 1950s and 1960s were a unique period in the history of marijuana. There was a hiatus in scientific research on *Cannabis,* but experimentation in the streets increased. With the arrival of the "psychedelic '60s," the popular press emphasized the more sensational hallucinogens. Marijuana, however, became the most common symbol of youthful rejection of authority and identification with a new era of personal freedom. According to the Monitoring the Future survey and the National Survey on Drug Use and Health (see Chapter 1), marijuana use apparently peaked in popularity in the United States in the late 1970s.

During the mid-1980s and early 1990s, marijuana use became much less popular than it had been in the 1970s, but the mid-1990s saw a significant rise in the number of young people using marijuana. This number peaked in the late 1990s and around 2012, although it never reached the levels observed in the 1970s.

Pharmacology

Cannabinoid Chemicals

The chemistry of *Cannabis* is quite complex, and the isolation and extraction of the active ingredient are difficult even today. There are more than 400 chemicals in marijuana, but only about 70 of them are unique to the *Cannabis* plant—these are called cannabinoids. One of them, delta-9-tetrahydrocannabinol (THC), was isolated and synthesized in 1964 and is clearly the most pharmacologically active. However, other cannabinoids may also contribute to the overall effects. In particular, cannabidiol (**CBD**) has received a great deal of attention as a nonpsychoactive cannabinoid that has been tested as an antiseizure medication and seems to limit some of the effects of THC when administered concurrently. Although most of the research has been aimed at THC and CBD, an Internet search using the term "cannabinoid" will reveal claims and speculations about the potential medical benefits of at least eight other plant-derived cannabinoids (*phytocannabinoids*). Medical marijuana proponents also argue that the benefits of using the plant itself might not be captured in any single pure chemical, such as THC, due to *entourage* effects, that is, effects produced by a combination of not only cannabinoids but also the *terpenes* (oils produced by several types of plants). The terpenes in cannabis are primarily responsible for the particular odors of the plants.

Absorption, Distribution, and Elimination

When smoked, THC is rapidly absorbed into the blood and distributed first to the brain, then redistributed to the rest of the body, so that within 30 minutes much is gone from the brain. The peak mood-altering and cardiovascular effects occur together, usually within 5 to 10 minutes. When taken in the form of an edible, THC is slowly and poorly absorbed and less than 20 percent reaches the brain due to extensive metabolism in the liver. This means that the peak effects following this route of administration do not occur before 60 to 90 minutes after ingesting the drug. THC has a half-life of about 19 hours, but metabolites (of which there are at least 45), primarily 11-hydroxy-delta-9-THC, are formed in the liver and have a half-life of 50 hours. After one week, 25 to 30 percent of the THC and its metabolites might still remain in the body. Complete elimination of a large dose of THC and its metabolites might take two or three weeks.

The high lipid solubility of THC means that it (like its metabolites) is selectively taken up and stored in fatty tissue to be released slowly. Excretion is primarily through the feces. All of this has two important implications: (1) There is no easy way to monitor (in urine or blood) THC/metabolite levels and relate them to behavioral and/or physiological effects, as can be done with alcohol, and (2) the long-lasting, steady, low concentration of THC and its metabolites on the brain and other organs might have effects not yet determined.

Mechanism of Action

Scientists searched for years for a key to help them unlock the mystery of marijuana's action on the central nervous system. The identification and purification of THC was a necessary step. A significant breakthrough was made in 1988 by researchers who developed a technique to identify and measure highly specific and selective binding sites for THC and related compounds in rat brains. One result was the development and testing of more potent marijuana analogues. Another result was the 1992 discovery of a natural substance produced in the body that has marijuana-like effects when administered to animals. This endogenous substance (see Figure 15.1) is called **anandamide** (*ananda* is sanskrit for "bliss").

THC and other cannabinoids are known to bind to two receptors, designated CB1 and CB2.[16] There are substantial differences in the structures of these two receptors and their anatomical distribution in the body. CB2 receptors are found mainly outside the brain in immune cells, suggesting that cannabinoids may play a role in the modulation of the immune response. CB1 receptors are found throughout the body, but primarily in the brain. These receptors are much more abundant than receptors for morphine and heroin,[16] suggesting that the potential actions of cannabinoids are widespread. The locations of CB1 receptors in the brain also may provide some clues about their functions. For example, the highest density of CB1 receptors has been found in cells of the basal ganglia; its primary components include the caudate nucleus, putamen, and globus pallidus. Cells of the basal

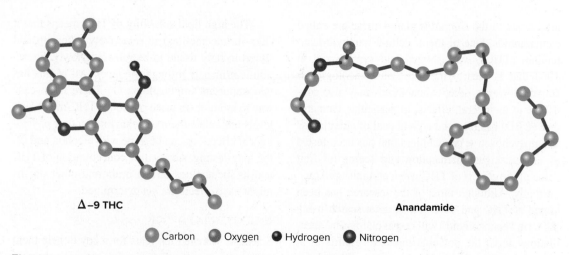

Figure 15.1 Delta-9 THC, The Most Active Substance Found in *Cannabis*, and Anandamide, Isolated from Brain Tissue

ganglia are involved in coordinating body movements. Other regions that also contain a larger number of CB1 receptors include the *cerebellum,* which coordinates fine body movements; *hippocampus,* which is involved in aspects of memory storage; *cerebral cortex,* which regulates the integration of higher cognitive functions; and *nucleus accumbens,* which is involved in reward.

Physiological Effects

Cardiovascular One of the most consistent physiological effects observed after smoking marijuana or ingesting THC in the form of an edible is an increase in heart rate. Figure 15.2 shows that both smoked marijuana and oral THC increase heart rate in a dose-dependent fashion (i.e., larger THC doses produced larger heart rate elevations).[17,18] While peak effects produced by smoking marijuana containing 4 percent THC are similar to 20 mg oral THC, the drug's time course of action is different. Peak heart-rate elevations produced by smoked marijuana occur within 10 minutes and return to baseline levels after about 90 minutes, whereas peak heart-rate elevations produced by oral THC do not occur until 90 minutes following ingestion and remain elevated for at least four hours after drug administration. The effect of cannabis-based drugs on blood pressure is more variable, with

some studies reporting slight increases and others reporting no effect. Concern has been raised that smoking marijuana might have permanent adverse effects on the cardiovascular system, but there is no evidence to indicate that marijuana-related cardiovascular effects are associated with serious health problems for most young, healthy users. Individuals with hypertension, cerebrovascular disease, and coronary atherosclerosis, however, should probably avoid smoking marijuana or ingesting THC because of the drug's effects on heart rate.

Other Effects Other consistent acute effects of smoked marijuana are reddening of the eyes and dryness of the mouth and throat. Except for bronchodilation, acute exposure to marijuana has little effect on breathing as measured by conventional pulmonary tests. Heavy marijuana smoking over a much longer period could lead to clinically significant and less readily reversible impairment of pulmonary function.

Behavioral Effects

Abuse Potential Less than 10 percent of marijuana users will become addicted to the drug at some point. This number may seem small or large depending on your perspective or preconceived beliefs about marijuana. Perhaps it would be helpful

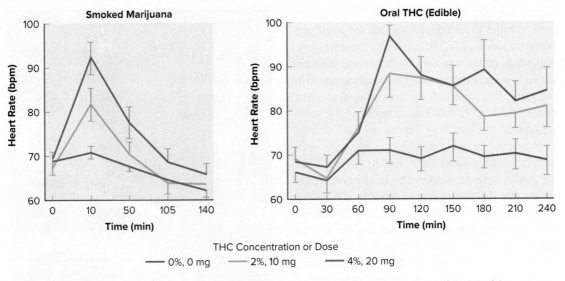

Figure 15.2   The Time Course for Heart Rate after Smoking Marijuana (*left*) and Ingesting Oral THC (*right*)

to know that about 15 percent of alcohol drinkers and a third of tobacco smokers will become addicted over their lifetime.[19] Comparatively speaking, marijuana has a lower abuse potential than the other two legally available psychoactive drugs. THC is the main component of marijuana that is thought to be responsible for consumption of the drug. In other words, if THC was removed from marijuana, far fewer people would consume the substance. Indeed, data from laboratory studies show that marijuana is robustly self-administered by young adults and that marijuana self-administration is THC concentration-dependent. That is, marijuana cigarettes containing a higher concentration of THC are preferred to those containing a lower THC concentration.[20] These findings not only confirm the importance of THC in the maintenance of marijuana self-administration, but they also suggest that THC administered alone (e.g., oral administration of THC capsules) might be rewarding or reinforcing. In one study, experienced marijuana smokers were given repeated opportunities to self-administer oral THC capsules or to receive $2. Several important findings from that study are worth mentioning. Participants selected (1) money on more occasions than the capsules, (2) more

drug-containing capsules than placebo, and (3) more THC capsules during social/recreational periods compared to non–social/recreational periods. These observations indicate that the abuse potential of oral THC is modest at best, experienced marijuana smokers can readily distinguish THC-related effects, and cannabis self-administration is influenced by social factors.[18]

Subjective Effects Some have argued that before novice marijuana smokers are able to experience marijuana-associated positive subjective effects (e.g., euphoria, feeling stoned), they must go through a process by which they learn to recognize and interpret the psychoactive effects produced by smoked marijuana.[21] Although this position remains open for debate, marijuana-related effects in experienced users have been well characterized. In general, experienced smokers report increased ratings of euphoria, high, mellowness, hunger, and

CBD: cannabidiol, a nonpsychoactive cannabinoid that is being tested to treat several illnesses, including epilepsy.

anandamide (an *and* a mide): a chemical isolated from brain tissue that has marijuana-like properties.

stimulation after smoking marijuana. These effects peak within 5 to 10 minutes and last for about two hours; they are usually THC concentration-dependent. Subjective effects reported by infrequent smokers are similar but more intense because these individuals are less tolerant to marijuana-associated effects. Also, at higher THC concentrations some infrequent smokers may report negative effects such as mild paranoia and hallucination. As seen with heart rate, peak subjective effects of oral THC are similar to those produced by smoked marijuana except that the time course of the effects is different. Peak subjective effects occur about 90 minutes following oral ingestion and can last for several hours. According to the dominant view in drug abuse research, an important factor in determining whether a drug is likely to be abused is the rapidity of the onset of its effects. The more rapidly a drug's effects are experienced, the more likely it will be abused. This might be why the abuse potential of oral THC is limited.

Although an earlier study demonstrated that relatively less-experienced marijuana smokers reported being intoxicated after smoking a placebo cigarette, more recent studies demonstrate that regular marijuana smokers are not so readily duped. Placebo cigarettes were made by extracting the THC and other cannabinoids from marijuana—the cigarettes looked and smelled like regular marijuana cigarettes. In these studies, participants "sampled" marijuana cigarettes (containing placebo or different THC concentrations) and alternative reinforcers (e.g., money or snack food), and subsequently were given an option to choose. Participants selected cigarettes containing THC on more than 75 percent of choice opportunities compared to only about 40 percent when placebo cigarettes were available.[22] Furthermore, subjective effects produced by the placebo cigarette were identical to baseline levels, whereas subjective effects produced by cigarettes containing THC were significantly elevated.

Cognitive Effects   The effect of marijuana on cognitive performance has received a great deal of attention in the popular press and the scientific literature

Experienced marijuana smokers report euphoria, "high," hunger, and mellowness after smoking; the magnitude of the effects depends on the THC concentration.   ©Doug Menuez/ Getty Images RF

for many years with little consensus. Unfortunately, many discussions on this topic add to the confusion because they fail to differentiate between the direct (acute) effects and long-term (chronic) effects of marijuana. They also fail to consider the marijuana use history of the user. Following acute administration of smoked marijuana, infrequent users display temporary disruptions in several domains: The amount of time that is required to complete cognitive tasks is increased (*slowed cognitive processing*); performance on immediate recall tasks is decreased (*disrupted short-term memory*); premature responding is increased (*disrupted inhibitory control*); performance on tracking tasks is decreased (*loss of sustained concentration or vigilance*); and performance on tasks requiring participants to reproduce computer-generated patterns is disrupted (*disrupted visuospatial processing*). The acute effects of marijuana on the performance of frequent smokers are less dramatic, owing to tolerance.[17] Some negative cognitive effects, however, have been reported. For example, slowing of cognitive performance is a consistent finding, even in regular users. This effect may have significant behavioral consequences under circumstances requiring complex operations that must be accomplished in a limited time frame, such as certain workplace tasks and the operation of machinery and automobiles.

It is also difficult to make definitive statements about *long-term* cognitive effects of marijuana use because of divergent findings and interpretations. More general conclusions, however, are possible. Based on the available evidence, it appears that following a sufficient period of abstinence (greater than one month), regular marijuana use produces minimal effects on cognition as measured by standard neuropsychological tests.[23] The reader is cautioned, though, because as the number of better controlled studies increases the current conclusions about the long-term effects of marijuana on cognition may change.

Today, it is almost impossible to review the cognitive effects of marijuana without a discussion of brain-imaging findings. Recent studies have combined cognitive testing and brain-imaging techniques to examine differences in cognitive performance and brain activation between marijuana users and nonusers. One study used positron emission tomography (PET) and an executive function task to investigate brain activation and cognition in a group of control subjects and frequent marijuana smokers who had been abstinent for 25 days.[24] The researchers found increased activity in the hippocampus and decreased activity in the left anterior cingulate and left lateral prefrontal cortex among marijuana users compared to control subjects. Despite these differential brain activations, there were no differences between marijuana users and nonusers on cognitive performance. Others have reported similar findings.[25,26] These observations highlight at least two important points: (1) Subtle brain activation differences may have little impact on behavior; and (2) the major behavior of interest—cognitive performance—should be examined carefully first. Otherwise, researchers may conduct neuroimaging studies with limited or no behavioral correlates, and they (and the public) may be enticed to draw inappropriate conclusions about the neural basis of cognition. The take-home message is that there has been no scientific study demonstrating meaningful brain differences between marijuana users and controls.

Appetite We've all heard about someone smoking marijuana and then getting a case of the "munchies," a marked increase in food intake. Data from a large number of studies clearly demonstrate that marijuana and oral THC significantly increase food intake. These findings provided the basis for at least one clinical use of cannabis-based drugs—appetite stimulation (see "Medical Uses of *Cannabis*"). A related question that has received less scientific attention is: Why aren't most chronic marijuana users overweight? Some have speculated that tolerance develops to the food-intake-enhancing effect of cannabis-based drugs, but no empirical data support this view. The bottom line is that the average weight of chronic marijuana users is not known because there have been no studies addressing this issue. So, the average chronic marijuana user may indeed be overweight. Or it could be that most marijuana use occurs during youth (this is certainly supported by data from national surveys), when people and their metabolisms are most active. This would possibly offset weight gain caused by marijuana use.

Talking Another consistent behavioral effect of marijuana is on verbal behavior (talking). Stimulant drugs such as amphetamines have been shown to increase verbal interactions, as have moderate doses of alcohol. Marijuana appears to be different. Several researchers have reported that whereas nonverbal social interactions are increased following marijuana smoking, verbal exchanges are dramatically decreased.[27]

Medical Uses of *Cannabis*

By the early 1900s, a variety of *Cannabis* preparations were available for medical use. Passage of the Marijuana Tax Act of 1937 resulted cannabis-based medicines being withdrawn from the market, and in 1941 *Cannabis* was dropped from *The National Formulary and The U.S. Pharmacopoeia.* The decline in the medical use of *Cannabis* occurred long before 1937, and the law did not eliminate an actively used therapeutic agent. Four factors, however, contributed to the declining prescription rate of this plant. One was the development of new and better drugs for most illnesses. Second was the variability of the available medicinal preparations of *Cannabis*. Third, the active ingredient is insoluble in water and thus not amenable to injectable preparations. Last, taken orally it has an unusually long latency to onset of action.

But in 1971, a time when even President Richard Nixon was calling on the medical community to conduct rigorous research investigating the potential medical utility of marijuana, a letter published in the widely read *Journal of the American Medical Association* (JAMA) spurred tremendous renewed interest in medical marijuana.[28] The letter described the cases of 11 glaucoma patients who had their **intraocular pressure** measured before and after smoking marijuana cigarettes. Marijuana dramatically reduced the fluid pressure of the eye in 10 of the 11 patients. The *JAMA* letter became a cause célèbre in 1975, when Robert Randall, a glaucoma patient, was arrested for growing marijuana plants on his back porch for medical purposes. Fifteen months later, he (1) saw the charges against him dropped, (2) had his physician certify that the only way for him to avoid blindness was to smoke five joints a day, and (3) had these marijuana joints legally supplied to him by the U.S. government.[29] This began a limited program in which the federal government provided marijuana cigarettes to patients with the FDA's approval of a "compassionate use" protocol. This federal program remains open today but has always enrolled only a small number of patients.

The potential medical benefits of marijuana is an issue with a long and controversial history. ©Lars A. Niki RF

At the same time, other researchers were assessing the effects of oral THC and smoked marijuana for nausea and vomiting caused by certain drugs used to treat cancer. Results from the studies consistently showed that cannabis-based treatments were superior to placebo and other **antiemetic** medications.[30] In 1985, the FDA approved oral THC for treating nausea during cancer chemotherapy. The drug is referred to by the generic name **dronabinol** and the brand name **Marinol.** In 1993, dronabinol, oral THC, was also approved as an appetite-stimulant in patients with AIDS. Thus, oral THC is FDA approved for two indications: (1) nausea and vomiting associated with cancer chemotherapy and (2) appetite stimulation in patients with AIDS.

Smoked marijuana has not received FDA approval for any indications, even though it has been shown to be more, or as, effective as oral THC in treating conditions for which oral THC is approved. As you may know, this situation has led to heated

Table 15.1
29 States and Washington, D.C., Have Passed Laws Legalizing Medical Marijuana

States	Year Passed	Possession Limits
Alaska	1998	1 oz; 6 plants
Arkansas	2016	3 oz
Arizona	2010	2.5 oz; 12 plants
California	1996	8 oz; 18 plants
Colorado	2000	2 oz; 6 plants
Connecticut	2012	2.5 oz
Delaware	2011	6 oz
District of Columbia	2010	2 oz; to be determined
Florida	2016	Amount to be determined
Hawaii	2000	3 oz; 7 plants
Illinois	2013	2.5 oz
Maine	1999	2.5 oz; 6 plants
Maryland	2014	30-day supply
Massachusetts	2012	60-day supply
Michigan	2008	2.5 oz; 12 plants
Minnesota	2014	30-day supply
Montana	2004	1 oz; 6 plants
Nevada	2000	1 oz; 7 plants
New Hampshire	2013	2 oz
New Jersey	2010	2 oz
New Mexico	2007	6 oz; 16 plants
New York	2014	30-day supply
North Dakota	2016	3 oz
Ohio	2016	90-day supply
Oregon	1998	24 oz; 24 plants
Pennsylvania	2016	30-day supply
Rhode Island	2006	2.5 oz; 12 plants
Vermont	2004	2 oz; 9 plants
Washington	1998	24 oz; 15 plants
West Virginia	2017	30-day Supply

debates about whether the smoked version of the drug should be approved by the FDA. Proponents of smoked marijuana for medical purposes argue that the drug should be made legally available because it has several advantages relative to oral THC, including a more rapid onset of effects and greater ability of the patient to control therapeutic effects. It is also possible that marijuana plant constituents other than THC may contribute to the drug's therapeutic effects, that is, the combination and/or balance of the chemicals contained in the plant may be an important factor for beneficial effects.

Such arguments, however, have not been successful in terms of reclassifying marijuana under the U.S. Controlled Substance Act. Opponents of smoked medical marijuana argue that there are already approved effective drugs for the proposed conditions that marijuana would treat and that the abuse potential of marijuana is too high. Marijuana remains a Schedule I drug, which means, from a federal government perspective, it cannot be legally prescribed because it has no acceptable medical use.

As a result of a growing scientific database showing smoked marijuana to be efficacious in treating some medical conditions, including anorexia associated with weight loss in patients with AIDS and **neuropathic pain**, and anecdotal reports indicating the therapeutic potential of marijuana for a variety of other conditions ranging from posttraumatic stress disorder to seizure control, citizens in individual states have passed ballot initiatives allowing for the medical use of marijuana.

As can be seen in Table 15.1, a total of 28 states and Washington, D.C., have passed legislation allowing patients, with a physician's authorization,

intraocular pressure: the fluid pressure inside the eye.
antiemetic: a drug used to reduce nausea and vomiting.
dronabinol (dro *nab* i noll): the generic name for prescription THC in oil in a gelatin capsule.
Marinol (*mare* i noll): the brand name for dronabinol.
neuropathic pain: a chronic condition that leads to persistent pain symptoms.

Taking Sides

Federal Medical Cannabis Law Is Inconsistent with State Laws

In August 2016, the Drug Enforcement Agency (DEA) rejected a petition that would have reclassified marijuana under the federal Controlled Substance Act. The drug is currently listed on Schedule I, meaning that it is viewed as having "no acceptable medical use in treatment," and is therefore banned in the United States. The proposed change would have moved marijuana to Schedule II, making it available by prescription nationwide. Such a change would have represented a major step toward resolving the confusion that characterizes our current laws on marijuana.

Despite many peoples' assumptions to the contrary, the current law does not ban scientific investigation into the harms and benefits of the drug, so moving marijuana to Schedule II won't lead to major changes in research activity. It's true that scientists studying marijuana must jump through multiple bureaucratic and regulatory hoops. But the same requirements apply to many other Schedule II substances. Nevertheless, dozens of scientists have been engaged in such research for decades. That is how we know, for example, that the drug stimulates appetite in HIV-positive patients, which could be a lifesaver for someone suffering from AIDS wasting syndrome, and that marijuana is useful in the treatment of neuropathic pain, chronic pain, and spasticity due to multiple sclerosis.

It is therapeutic benefits such as these that have compelled citizens to vote repeatedly over the past two decades to legalize medical marijuana at the state level. Today, 28 states and the District of Columbia allow patients to use marijuana for specific medical conditions. Yet federal law still technically forbids the use of medical marijuana. The inconsistency of federal laws with these other programs and initiatives, and with the increasing number of studies demonstrating the medical usefulness of the substance, makes marijuana's Schedule I status seem like medical and/or governmental hypocrisy, undermining peoples' trust in the relevant federal agencies.

In fact, there is now a general sentiment among scientists that the failed war on drugs has biased the DEA against acknowledging *any* therapeutic potential of marijuana. Many scientists and educators have expressed concerns about losing credibility with many young people and with those seeking treatments for a variety of medical conditions because our current scheduling of marijuana ignores the scientific and medical evidence. The scheduling of marijuana appears to be based on factors other than the available empirical evidence.

As a result, health care professionals should be concerned that individuals most in need of help and objective advice might reject other drug-related information from "official" sources, even when the information is accurate. This can contribute to patients being more susceptible to seeking quackery in lieu of proven medicine, which can put them at unnecessary risk. This raises the question of whether a law enforcement agency should have the final word on medical decisions. What do you think? Which federal agency should determine whether marijuana can be used medically?

Box icon credit: ©Nova Development RF

to use marijuana for medical purposes. You may have noticed that some medical marijuana advocates overreach when extolling the virtues of marijuana, claiming that the drug is a cure for everything from heartache to cancer. Clearly, many of these claims are exaggerations. This does not, however, mean we should dismiss all claims of the drug's potential medical utility. Indeed, results from controlled studies show that marijuana is effective at providing short-term relief in patients suffering from neuropathic pain,[31] as well as in decreasing spasticity and pain in patients with multiple sclerosis.[32] Better evidence is still needed for many other conditions for which marijuana is recommended. As such we can expect the number of controlled studies assessing the drug's potential medical utility to grow. We can also expect the number of medical marijuana states will continue to increase with each election, as has been the case for the two decades.

Causes for Concern

Abuse and Dependence

Can regular marijuana use produce a withdrawal syndrome? Data from a variety of human laboratory and clinical studies demonstrate that an abstinence syndrome can be observed following abrupt cessation of several days of smoked marijuana administration or oral delta-9-THC administration.[33] Cannabinoid withdrawal is not life threatening, but symptoms can be unpleasant. Marijuana withdrawal syndrome in regular users may include negative mood states (e.g., anxiety, restlessness, depression, and irritability), disrupted sleep, decreased food intake, and in some cases, aggressive behavior. These symptoms have been reported to begin 1 day after cannabinoid cessation and persist from 4 to 12 days, depending on an individual's level of marijuana dependence. The majority of marijuana users do not experience withdrawal symptoms nor do they meet *DSM-5* criteria for cannabis use disorder. But these findings remind us that regular use of marijuana (or any psychoactive substance) can produce a variety of effects, both positive and negative.[34]

The evidence now suggests that if high levels of marijuana are used regularly over a sustained period, tolerance can develop to many marijuana-related effects, including the cognitive-impairing, physiological, and subjective effects. However, tolerance may not develop uniformly across each of these variables. For example, it has been demonstrated that heavy marijuana smokers exhibit minimal cognitive disruptions during marijuana intoxication, while showing dramatic heart rate increases and reporting significant levels of euphoria. These findings suggest that tolerance may develop more readily to marijuana-related cognitive effects than to heart rate responses and subjective effects.[17]

Toxicity Potential

Acute Physiological Effects   The acute physiological effects of marijuana, primarily an increase in heart rate, have not been thought to be a threat to health. However, as the marijuana-using population ages, there is concern that individuals with high blood pressure, heart disease, or hardening of the arteries might be harmed by smoking marijuana.[34] The lethal dose of THC has not been extensively studied in animals, and no human deaths have been reported from "overdoses" of marijuana. Thus, marijuana overdose does not appear to be an important public health issue.

Chronic Lung Exposure   There has been a great deal of concern about the possible long-term effects of chronic marijuana use on lung function or risk of lung diseases such as cancer and emphysema. Most studies that have evaluated the association of marijuana smoking with chronic respiratory symptoms (cough, phlegm, wheezing, and breathlessness) have found a positive correlation of smoking with symptoms of chronic bronchitis (mainly cough and phlegm), but not with shortness of breath.[34] Shortness of breath is the most serious and debilitating symptom of progressive lung disease. In addition, most individuals who smoke marijuana also smoke tobacco cigarettes, and when tobacco use is accounted for, the positive correlation between marijuana smoking and symptoms of chronic bronchitis is no longer statistically significant. This suggest that marijuana smoking alone does not present a significant risk for developing lung disease.

Nonetheless, marijuana smoke has been compared with tobacco smoke. Some of the constituents differ (there is no nicotine in marijuana smoke and no THC in tobacco), but many of the dangerous components are found in both. Total tar levels, carbon monoxide, hydrogen cyanide, and nitrosamines are found in similar amounts (except for tobacco-specific nitrosamines, which are carcinogens). Another potent carcinogen, *benzopyrene,* is found in greater amounts in marijuana than in tobacco. Everyone suspects that marijuana smoking will eventually be shown to cause cancer, but how much of a problem this will be compared with tobacco is hard to say. On the one hand, few marijuana smokers smoke 20 marijuana cigarettes every day, whereas tobacco smokers regularly smoke this much. On the other hand, the marijuana cigarette is not filtered and the user generally gets as much concentrated smoke as possible as far down in the lungs as possible and holds it there. When compared with tobacco smoking, the accumulated evidence suggests far lower risks for lung dysfunctions of even regular heavy use of marijuana compared with the grave lung consequences of tobacco smoking.[35]

Vaping to Decrease Toxicity In an effort to decrease potential lung toxicity associated with smoking marijuana, some individuals have begun **vaping** the drug. Vaping refers to the vaporization of substances (e.g., cannabis products) whereby liquid, oil, or plant material is heated to a temperature that releases an aerosolized mixture of water vapor and active ingredients (e.g., THC or CBD), which is then inhaled. This method of administration avoids combustion of the substance and the inhaling of smoke, which contains carbon monoxide and other potentially dangerous by-products of combustion. Preliminary evidence suggest that vaping cannabis is associated with fewer reports of respiratory symptoms,[36] but there have been no well-controlled studies that experimentally investigated this issue using cannabis smokers.

Anxiety Another behavioral problem associated with cannabis intoxication is the potential for increased anxiety or panic reaction. Much like many of the bad trips with hallucinogens, the reaction is usually fear of loss of control and fear that things will not return to normal. Although many people do seek emergency medical treatment for cannabis-induced anxiety and are sometimes given sedatives or tranquilizers, the best treatment is probably "talking down," or reminding the person of who and where they are, that the reaction is temporary, and that everything will be all right. And the best way to avoid such reactions after ingesting cannabis, in any form, is to ingest lower doses, especially if the user has limited experience with cannabis-based products.

Immune System Effects There have also been reports that marijuana smoking impairs some measures of the functioning of the immune system.[37] Animal studies have found that THC injections can reduce immunity to infection, but at doses well above those obtainable by smoking marijuana. Some studies of marijuana smokers have suggested reduced immunity, but most have not. If the effect were real, it could result in marijuana smokers' being more susceptible to infections, cancer, and other diseases, such as genital herpes. One might suspect that such problems would eventually be reflected in the overall death rate of marijuana users. However, a report examining 10 years of mortality data for more than 65,000 people found no relationship between marijuana use and overall death rates.[38]

Marijuana Madness The 1936 cult classic film *Reefer Madness* depicted how smoking marijuana could turn nice middle-class youth into psychotic killers. Today, this cautionary tale is mocked and spoofed for its outrageous assertions. At the same time, however, some researchers are collecting data that they claim show that marijuana indeed causes psychosis. Were the statements made in the 1930s about the dangers of marijuana accurate? The connection between marijuana use and psychosis was one of the main arguments for outlawing the drug. It seems that the marijuana-psychosis link is similar to other emotionally arousing drug issues in the past—they return in slightly different forms periodically. Given this situation, we feel that it might be useful to discuss this topic in some detail.

In our attempt to understand the relationship between marijuana use and psychosis, we must first know something about how studies investigating this issue are conducted. Typically, a few thousand adults are separated into groups based on their reported use of marijuana: marijuana users in one group and nonusers in the other. Then, researchers see if the groups differ on the outcome measure of interest—psychosis. An important question that you should ask is: How do they define psychosis in these studies? Remember from Chapter 8 that psychosis is a mental disorder involving a loss of contact with reality and is characterized by hallucinations, irrational beliefs, and disorganization of speech and behaviors. We typically think of psychosis in association with schizophrenia, but it can also be present in other disorders. For a person to be given a diagnosis of psychosis, he or she must be evaluated by a psychiatrist or psychologist. This can be a rather involved and time-consuming evaluation. As such, participants in the overwhelming majority of these studies are not assessed for a psychosis disorder. Instead, they are asked to complete a questionnaire, containing about 20 items, that probes psychotic symptoms.

Some studies have found a correlation between marijuana use and psychotic symptoms. That is, participants in the marijuana group were more likely to admit to having experienced at least one psychotic symptom. This type of finding has fueled sensational media headlines such as "Even infrequent use of marijuana increases risk of psychosis." Here, we'd like to make two important points that will better help you evaluate the veracity of these claims and of research in this area in general. First, you should know that someone could endorse psychotic symptoms without meeting criteria for a disorder. Indeed, in some of these studies, marijuana users reported an average of fewer than five symptoms; the specific symptoms endorsed are usually not made clear by researchers. This makes it impossible to determine whether the marijuana users reported symptoms that were clinically meaningful (e.g., I hear voices that others do not) or those that were not (e.g., I sometimes feel uncomfortable in public). In addition, many of the symptoms contained on these questionnaires can be experienced only for a brief period and are not necessarily an indication of a permanent disorder.

Our second point deals with the question of how we determine causation in science. In general, the conclusion drawn from these studies is that marijuana causes psychosis. Is this the case? It could be that psychosis causes people to smoke marijuana. It is difficult to determine what came first, because research participants' psychotic symptoms are not usually assessed before the initiation of marijuana use. So, it is possible that psychotic individuals may have exhibited symptoms prior to using marijuana. Furthermore, because marijuana users typically use other psychoactive drugs at higher rates than nonmarijuana users, it is extremely difficult to disentangle the influence of other drug use on psychotic symptoms. Finally, we recently reviewed the scientific literature in this area and found evidence that bipolar disorder, anxiety disorder, and mood disorder have all been correlated with cannabis use; in addition, psychosis has been correlated with heavy tobacco smoking, heavy alcohol use, stimulant misuse, and sedative misuse.[39] In other words, the correlation between cannabis use and psychosis is not specific, either with regard to the chemicals found in cannabis or to psychosis as opposed to other disorders. Together, these issues lead us to conclude that there is no clear evidence for a causal relationship between cannabis and psychosis.

Driving Ability Drugged driving is a safety concern of increasing importance in the United States, especially as more states pass legislation that relaxes

Inhaling marijuana smoke. ©Gary He RF

vaping: the use of electricity to heat cannabis products, causing a release of cannabis resin as a vapor that is inhaled.

restrictions on marijuana use. Even before these legislative movements, marijuana was one of the most commonly detected substances in American drivers. This is not surprising because, as noted in Chapter 1, it is the most widely used illicit drug in the United States; in addition, its metabolites can remain in a person's urine for two to three weeks after the last use. Other drugs leave the urine within days. This situation raises at least two relevant questions: (1) Does marijuana intoxication impair driving performance; and (2) are there standard urine or blood levels that indicate marijuana intoxication?

Data from laboratory studies of computer-controlled driving simulators indicate that marijuana can produce significant impairments.[40] Most of the laboratory studies have employed relatively infrequent marijuana users as participants, a group that would be expected to show marked disruptions. Because tolerance can develop to many of the cognitive-impairing effects of marijuana, one would predict that the performance of frequent and heavy users would be altered less than infrequent users.

The task of determining standardized urine and/or blood levels for marijuana intoxication has proven to be difficult, if not impossible. As you know, the rate of THC absorption into the bloodstream is determined by the route of drug administration. The onset and intensities of effects differ depending on whether the drug is smoked or eaten. Importantly, levels of THC in the blood or urine do not consistently predict levels of intoxication. The route of administration and the user's level of tolerance undoubtedly complicates this situation. The bottom line is that field sobriety tests based on performance remain the best way for determining marijuana intoxication.

Marijuana and American Society

Twenty-five years ago, there were no state laws allowing the medical use of marijuana, and presidential candidate Bill Clinton was being hounded about allegations centering on whether he had ever smoked marijuana. Today, 28 states and Washington, D.C., have legalized medical marijuana, and this number continues to grow with each successive election. The two immediate subsequent U.S. presidents—George W. Bush and Barack Obama—both admitted to previously smoking marijuana as adults, and Obama also acknowledged his previous cocaine use; unlike their predecessor, Bush's and Obama's admitted drug use never threatened their bids for the White

Focus on Treatment

Medication Treatments for Cannabis Use Disorder

Most users of cannabis consume the drug infrequently without apparent negative consequences. A small proportion, however, experience problems related to frequent cannabis use. An estimated 1 in 11 cannabis users will become dependent.[41] Many individuals seeking treatment for cannabis use disorder reported experiencing withdrawal symptoms and that these symptoms made it more difficult to maintain abstinence. As a result, efforts to develop treatments have focused primarily on relieving withdrawal symptoms. Cannabis withdrawal is characterized by symptoms of irritability, anxiety, sleep disruptions, and

aches.[33] A growing number of medications have been tested for efficacy in relieving these symptoms, but only one has been demonstrated to be effective—oral delta-9-THC (dronabinol). Dronabinol has been shown to reduce symptoms associated with cannabis. Despite these findings, to date, no medications are approved for the treatment of cannabis use disorder. As is the case with the treatment of other substance use disorders, medications should be used in combination with behavioral therapy for better results.

Box icon credit: ©dencg/Shutterstock.com RF

House. Clearly, attitudes about marijuana use have changed over the past three decades.

A similar shift in attitudes occurred during the late 1960s and 1970s. The period before this, young people were told that marijuana would make them insane, enslave them in drug addiction, and lead to violence and perverted sexual acts. These stories, however, did not square with their own observations or experiences. Marijuana, more than anything else, convinced many young people that the government and so-called drug experts had been lying about drugs, and this led to broad rejections of government information on a range of issues, including drugs. Indeed, data from the annual Monitoring the Future survey show that the number of seniors who had ever smoked marijuana peaked at about 60 percent in the late 1970s.

Marijuana Legalization In 1970, the grassroots group National Organization for the Reform of Marijuana Laws (NORML) was started, and its major mission was to repeal marijuana prohibition so that adults could legally consume marijuana just as they could alcohol or tobacco. Throughout the 1970s, several states changed possession of a small amount of marijuana from a criminal offense to only a civil one, known as decriminalization, but there was never really a serious movement to legalize the drug for recreational purposes. Most Americans did not support marijuana legalization. In 1978, when marijuana use was at its peak, only about 30 percent of Americans supported legalizing the drug.

Figure 15.3 shows that attitudes about marijuana legalization have changed dramatically in recent years. Today, support for legalizing marijuana is at its highest, with nearly 60 percent of Americans indicating that they think "the use of marijuana should be legal" in 2017. As can be seen in Table 15.2, this is consistent with the fact that citizens in eight states have voted to legalize recreational use of marijuana by adults 21 years and older. In 2012, voters in Colorado and Washington made these states the first to pass laws allowing adults to use marijuana recreationally. Nearly a year

Federal and state laws and penalties related to marijuana possession tend to reflect other social trends, becoming more severe in periods of social and political conservatism. ©Doug Menuez/Forrester Images RF

later, Uruguay became the first nation to do the same. We should point out that despite these developments, marijuana use remains a schedule I drug in the United States, meaning individuals caught possessing or ingesting the substance can still be subject to federal prosecution. Given concerns about **states' rights**, however, federal actions seem unlikely.

You may be asking what is driving the current movement to liberalize marijuana laws. Is it an increase in marijuana use? In 2016, 45 percent of high-school seniors reported having ever smoked marijuana, compared to 60 percent of seniors in 1979. So, it seems unlikely that marijuana use is driving the legalization trend.

states' rights: the rights and powers held by individual U.S. states rather than by the federal government.

Response: Legal
Breakdown: Total

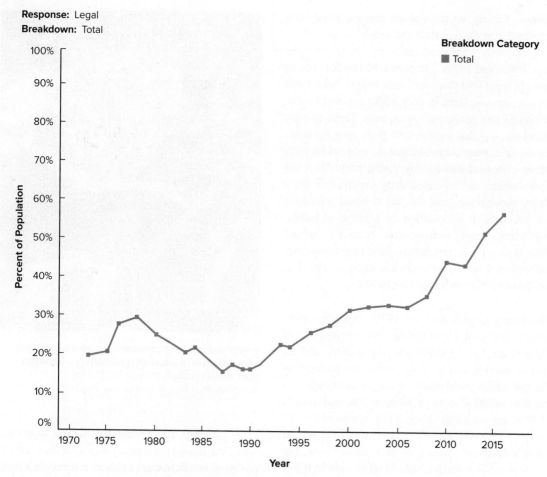

Figure 15.3   Civil Liberties: Should Marijuana Be Made Legal?

SOURCE: Smith, Tom W., Peter Marsden, Michael Hout, and Jibum Kim. General Social Surveys, 1972–2014 [machine-readable data file]/ Principal Investigator, Tom W. Smith; Co-Principal Investigator, Peter V. Marsden; Co-Principal Investigator, Michael Hout; Sponsored by National Science Foundation. NORC, ed. Chicago: NORC at the University of Chicago [producer and distributor]. Data accessed from the GSS Data Explorer website at gssdataexplorer.norc.org.

If we can't point to an increase in marijuana use as the cause for this attitude shift, how can we explain it? We think that at least four other factors are at play. First, an increasing amount of scientific evidence shows that marijuana is not as toxic as was thought when it was banned in 1937. Second, beginning in late 2007, the economy of the United States plummeted into a crisis from which some experts warned it might take years to recover. At the same time, billions of dollars were being spent yearly in an effort to stop illicit drug use. For example, more than 700,000 Americans are arrested each year for marijuana-related violations, most for minor possession infractions. In the face of limited funds, many believe that arresting people for simple possession of marijuana is not the most prudent use of public resources. This perspective forms the basis for our third factor. A growing number of Americans have suggested that if recreational marijuana use were legal, states could tax its cultivation, transportation, and sale in order to generate additional income. It has been estimated that the legal marijuana industry in the United States could reach nearly $22 billion in total annual sales by 2020.[42] This would surpass the

Unintended Consequences

Synthetic Cannabis: The Devil You Know or the One You Don't

Over the past several decades, our knowledge about marijuana's effects on human behavior has increased dramatically. Such knowledge affords us the ability to maximize beneficial effects while minimizing deleterious ones. Recently, a new generation of synthetic cannabinoid agonists has been reported to be used recreationally, especially by teens and young adults. The products are marketed as natural herbal incense or potpourri under various brand names such as "Spice" or "K2," and have been sold legally in "head shops," convenience stores, and through the Internet to those seeking the "marijuana-like high." The poorly labeled contents have been found to include a mixture of psychoactive herbs and aromatic extracts sprayed with synthetic cannabinoid compounds. The ingredient that has generated the most interest is JWH-018, a synthetic cannabinoid developed by chemist John W. Huffman (JWH). Anecdotal reports indicate that when one of these products is inhaled, it produces psychoactive effects similar to those produced by marijuana. While the truthfulness of such claims is difficult to confirm because there are no published studies investigating this product in humans, the fact that many young people around the country readily pay about $40 per gram to obtain such products suggest that they do something. There is real concern, however, that synthetic cannabinoids may cause negative effects on human health. Relative to delta-9-THC, the synthetic compounds are more potent and efficacious agonists, which could lead to greater toxicity. Marijuana, the most frequently used cannabis agent, contains over 60 identified cannabinoids that may modulate delta-9-THC-related effects, including negative ones. Anecdotal case reports and increasing calls to poison control centers suggest potential adverse effects of synthetic cannabinoid exposure such as anxiety, rapid heart rate and psychosis, coupled with the abuse potential of the substances, recently led to DEA control of several synthetic cannabinoids under the Controlled Substances Act. In addition, lawmakers in several states, alarmed by growing concerns about synthetic cannabinoids, have banned these products. At present, the long-term effects of inhaling synthetic cannabinoids on brain functioning and behavior is unknown. Thus, it seems less than wise to consume these products when so little is known about their potential harmful effects.

Box icon credit: ©Adam Gault/age fotostock RF

Table 15.2
Eight States and Washington, D.C., Have Passed Laws Legalizing Recreational Marijuana

States	Year Passed
Alaska	2014
California	2016
Colorado	2012
District of Columbia	2014
Maine	2016
Massachusetts	2016
Nevada	2016
Oregon	2014
Washington	2012

$12 billion revenues generated by the National Football League in 2016. You can be certain that citizens from other states are closely watching these figures as they consider the legal status of marijuana locally. A final reason we think attitudes about marijuana's legal status have changed deals with the almost weekly media reports of the violence, especially in Mexico, related to the illicit drug trade. A popular view suggests that legalizing marijuana would take the profits out of the illicit drug markets and, thereby, decrease much of the violence. We still don't know for certain which, if any, of these factors are most important for the observed recent attitude change toward marijuana. What is clear, however, is that we are in the midst of a paradigm shift, in which this generation views marijuana as being more benign than did the generation immediately preceding it.

Summary

- *Cannabis* has a rich history relating both to its medicinal use and to its recreational uses.

- Marijuana became famous as the "Assassin of Youth" in the 1930s and was outlawed in 1937.

- *Cannabis* contains many active chemicals, but the most active is delta-9-THC.

- THC is absorbed rapidly by smoking but slowly and incompletely when taken by mouth.

- THC has a long half-life of elimination, and its metabolites can be found in the body for up to several weeks after THC enters the body.

- Selective THC receptors exist in brain tissue, leading to the discovery of a naturally occurring brain cannabinoid, anandamide.

- Marijuana causes an increase in the heart rate and reddening of the eyes as its main physiological effects.

- Marijuana is useful in the treatment of glaucoma, the reduction of nausea in patients undergoing cancer chemotherapy, and the increase of appetite in AIDS patients. A legal form of THC is available by prescription.

- Although high addiction rates are not common, addiction does occur in some individuals.

- Marijuana can impair driving skills, but it is not clear that smoking marijuana leads to an increased frequency of accidents.

Review Questions

1. What are the major differences between *C. sativa* and *C. indica?*
2. How are hashish and sinsemilla produced?
3. When and where was the earliest recorded medical use of cannabis?
4. What were the general conclusions of the 1944 LaGuardia Commission?
5. What is meant by "cannabinoid," and about how many are there in *Cannabis?* What is the cannabinoid found in brain tissue?
6. How is the action of THC in the brain terminated after about 30 minutes, when the half-life of metabolism is much longer than that?
7. What are the two most consistent physiological effects of smoking marijuana?
8. What two medical uses have been approved by the FDA for dronabinol?
9. What evidence suggests that attitudes about the regulation of marijuana have changed?

References

1. Schultes, R. E., and A. Hofmann. *The Botany and Chemistry of Hallucinogens.* Springfield, IL: Charles C Thomas, 1980.
2. Chasnoff, I. J. "Medical Marijuana Laws and Pregnancy: Implications for Public Health Policy." *American Journal of Obstetrics and Gynecology* 216 (2017), pp. 27–30.
3. Louis, C. S. "Pregnant Women Turn to Marijuana, Perhaps Harming Infants." *New York Times,* February 2, 2017.
4. Ko, J. Y., and others. "Prevalence and Patterns of Marijuana Use among Pregnant and Nonpregnant Women of Reproductive Age." *American Journal of Obstetrics and Gynecology* 213 (2015), pp. 201.e201–201.e210.
5. Substance Abuse and Mental Health Services Administration. *Results from the 2013 National Survey on Drug Use and Health: Summary of National Findings,* NSDUH Series H-48, HHS Publication No. (SMA) 14-4863. Rockville, MD: Substance Abuse and Mental Health Services Administration, 2014.
6. van Gelder, M. M., and others. "National Birth Defects Prevention Study. Maternal Periconceptional Illicit Drug Use and the Risk of Congenital Malformations." *Epidemiology* 20 (2009), pp. 60–66.
7. Segal, D. S., and others. "Escalating Dose Methamphetamine Pretreatment Alters the Behavioral and Neurochemical Profiles Associated with Exposure to a High-Dose Methamphetamine Binge." *Neuropsychopharmacology* 28 (2003), pp. 1730–40.
8. Goldschmidt, L., and others. "Prenatal Marijuana Exposure and Intelligence Test Performance at Age 6." *Journal of the American Academy of Child and Adolescent Psychiatry* 47 (2008), pp. 254–63.
9. Torres, C. A., J. P. Curley, and C. L. Hart. "Prenatal Cannabis Exposure and Cognitive Functioning: A Systematic and Critical Review." *Drug and Alcohol Dependence* (under consideration).
10. Hart, C. L., and others. "Is Cognitive Functioning Impaired in Methamphetamine Users? A Critical Review." *Neuropsychopharmacology* 37 (2012), pp. 586–608.
11. Anslinger, H. J., and C. R. Cooper. "Marijuana: Assassin of Youth." *The American Magazine* 124 (1937), pp. 19, 153.
12. Fort, J. "Pot: A Rational Approach." *Playboy,* October 1969, pp. 131, 154.
13. "Mayor LaGuardia's Committee on Marijuana." In D. Solomon, ed. *The Marihuana Papers.* New York: New American Library, 1966.

14. "Marijuana Problems." *Journal of the American Medical Association* 127 (1945), p. 1129.

15. Joy, J. E., S. J. Watson, Jr., and J. A. Benson, Jr., eds. *Marijuana and Medicine: Assessing the Science Base.* Washington, DC: Institute of Medicine, National Academies Press, 1999.

16. Sim, L. I., and others. "Differences in G-protein Activation by Mu- and Delta-Opioid, and Cannabinoid, Receptors in Rat Striatum." *European Journal of Pharmacology* 307 (1996), pp. 97–105.

17. Hart, C. L., and others. "Effects of Acute Smoked Marijuana on Complex Cognitive Performance." *Neuropsychopharmacology* 25 (2001), pp. 757–65.

18. Hart, C. L., and others. "Reinforcing Effects of Oral delta-9-THC in Male Marijuana Smokers in a Laboratory Choice Procedure." *Psychopharmacology,* 181 (2005) pp. 237–43.

19. Anthony, J. C., L. A. Warner, and R. C. Kessler. "Comparative Epidemiology of Dependence on Tobacco, Alcohol, Controlled Substances, and Inhalants: Basic Findings from the National Comorbidity Survey." *Experimental and Clinical Psychopharmacology* 2 (1994), pp. 244–68.

20. Kelly, T. H., and others. "Effects of D⁹-THC on Marijuana Smoking, Dose Choice, and Verbal Report of Drug Liking." *Journal of the Experimental Analysis of Behavior* 61 (1994), pp. 203–11.

21. Becker, H. S. "Becoming a Marijuana User." *American Journal of Sociology* 59 (1953), pp. 235–43.

22. Ward, A. S., and others. "The Effects of a Monetary Alternative on Marijuana Self-Administration." *Behavioural Pharmacology* 8 (1997), pp. 275–86.

23. Pope, H. G., and others. "Neuropsychological Performance in Long-Term Cannabis Users." *Archives of General Psychiatry* 58 (2001), pp. 909–15.

24. Eldreth, D. A., J. A. Matochik, J. L. Cadet, and K. I. Bolla. "Abnormal Brain Activity in Prefrontal Brain Regions in Abstinent Marijuana Users." *NeuroImage* 23 (2004), pp. 914–20.

25. Kanayama, G., J. Rogowska, H. G. Pope, S. A. Gruber, and D. A. Yugelun-Todd. "Spatial Working Memory in Heavy Cannabis Users: A Functional Magnetic Resonance Imaging Study." *Psychopharmacology* 176 (2004), pp. 239–47.

26. Jager, G., R. S. Kahn, W. Van Den Brink, J. M. Van Ree, and N. F. Ramsey. "Long-Term Effects of Frequent Cannabis Use on Working Memory and Attention: An fMRI Study." *Psychopharmacology* 185 (2006), pp. 358–68.

27. Foltin, R. W., and M. W. Fischman. "Effects of Smoked Marijuana on Human Social Behavior in Small Groups." *Pharmacology, Biochemistry, and Behavior* 30 (1988), pp. 539–41.

28. Hepler, R. S., and I. R. Frank, "Marijuana Smoking and Intra-ocular Pressure." *Journal of the American Medical Association* 217 (1971), p. 1392.

29. "Medical Therapy, Legalization Issues Debated at Marijuana Reform Conference." *National Drug Reporter* 7, no. 1 (1977), pp. 3–5.

30. Sallan, S. E., and C. M. Cronin. "Is THC an Effective Antiemetic for Cancer Patients? Opinion 2." *CA: A Cancer Journal for Clinicians* 30 (1980), pp. 283–85.

31. Andreae, M. H., and others. "Inhaled Cannabis for Chronic Neuropathic Pain: A Meta-analysis of Individual Patient Data." *Journal of Pain* 16 (2015), pp. 1221–32.

32. Corey-Bloom, J., and others. "Smoked Cannabis for Spasticity in Multiple Sclerosis: A Randomized, Placebo-Controlled Trial." *Canadian Medical Association Journal* 184 (2012), pp. 1143–50.

33. Hart, C. L. "Increasing Treatment Options for Cannabis Dependence: A Review of Potential Pharmacotherapies." *Drug and Alcohol Dependence* 80 (2005), pp. 147–59.

34. Hancox R. J., and others. "Effects of quitting cannabis on respiratory symptoms." European Respiratory Journal 46 (2015) pp. 80–87.

35. Tashkin, D. P. "Effects of Marijuana Smoking on the Lung." *Annals of the American Thoracic Society* 12 (2015), pp. 235–36.

36. Earleywine, M., and S. S. Barnwell. "Decreased Respiratory Symptoms in Cannabis Users Who Vaporize." *Harm Reduction Journal* 4 (2007), p. 11.

37. Shay, A. H., and others. "Impairment of Antimicrobial Activity and Nitric Oxide Production in Alveolar Macrophages from Smokers of Marijuana and Cocaine." *Journal of Infectious Diseases* 187 (2003), pp. 700–04.

38. Sidney, S., J. E. Beck, and G. D. Friedman. "Marijuana Use and Mortality." *American Journal of Public Health* 87 (1997), pp. 585–90.

39. Ksir, C., and C. L. Hart. "Cannabis and Psychosis: A Critical Overview of the Relationship." *Current Psychiatry Reports* 18 (2016), p. 12.

40. Ramaekers, J. G., and others. "Dose-Related Risk of Motor Vehicle Crashes after Cannabis Use." *Drug and Alcohol Dependence* 73 (2004), pp. 109–19.

41. Anthony, J. C., L. A. Warner, and R. C. Kessler. "Comparative Epidemiology of Dependence on Tobacco, Alcohol, Controlled Substances, and Inhalants: Basic Findings from the National Comorbidity Survey." *Experimental and Clinical Psychopharmacology* 2 (1994), pp. 244–68.

42. Arcview Market Research. *The State of Legal Marijuana Markets,* 5th ed., 2017. Retrieved from http://arcviewgroup.com/documents/report/5thedition/es/executive-summary_the-state-of-legal-marijuana-markets_5th-edition_22qxqm-RQPyp7R.pdf.

Performance-Enhancing Drugs

©Stockbyte/Getty Images RF

Objectives

When you have finished this chapter, you should be able to:

- **Relate historical uses of performance-enhancing drugs by athletes.**

- **Describe the history of use of stimulants to enhance performance.**

- **Describe the development and current state of drug testing in sports.**

- **Explain why the BALCO scandal received so much publicity.**

- **Describe the performance-enhancing effects and primary dangers of stimulant drugs.**

- **Distinguish between androgenic and anabolic effects of testosterone and other related steroid hormones.**

- **Describe the desired effects and undesirable side effects of steroids in men, women, and adolescents.**

- **Explain the effects of human growth hormone as well as its dangers.**

- **Explain the effects of creatine.**

- **Discuss the usefulness of dietary supplements in relation to their label claims.**

Why is there so much concern over drug use by athletes? Why not focus on drug use by clarinet players or muffler repair people? There are several answers to this question, some more compelling than others. First, well-known athletes are seen as role models for young people, portraying youth, strength, and health. When a famous athlete is reported to be using steroids or some other illicit substance, there is concern that impressionable young people will see drug use in a more positive light. This perspective acknowledges that it may be unfair to hold certain athletes to higher standards than those imposed on other members of our society.

Second, some of the drugs used by athletes are intended to give the user an advantage over the competition, an advantage that is clearly viewed as being unfair. Of course, wealthier athletes may have access to better training instruction, facilities, and equipment, which could give them an advantage over less well-off competitors. Yet, this is rarely considered in discussions of fairness in sports. Nonetheless, an unfair advantage is viewed as inconsistent with our tradition of fair play in sports.

Third, there is a concern that both the famous and the not-so-famous athletes who use drugs are endangering their health and perhaps their lives for the sake of a temporary burst of power or speed.

There are risks associated with the use of these drugs, especially when they are obtained through illicit channels. Mind you, there are also health hazards with many sports. It seems hypocritical to ignore these risks as we consider potential harms caused by performing-enhancing drugs.

Historical Use of Drugs in Athletics

Ancient Times

Although we tend to think of drug use by athletes as a recent phenomenon, the use of chemicals to enhance performance might be as old as sport itself. As with many early drugs, some of these concoctions seemed to make sense at the time but probably had only placebo value. We no longer think that the powdered hooves of an ass will make our feet fly as fast as that animal's, but perhaps it was a belief in that powder that helped the ancient Egyptian competitor's self-confidence. Also, if all the others are using it, why take chances?

The early Greek Olympians used various herbs and mushrooms that might have had some pharmacological actions as stimulants, and Aztec athletes used a cactus-based stimulant resembling strychnine. Athletic competitions probably developed in tribal societies as a means of training and preparing for war or for hunting, and various psychoactive plants were used by tribal peoples during battles and hunts, so it is not surprising that the drugs were also used in athletic contests from the beginning.

Early Use of Stimulants

During the 1800s and early 1900s, three types of stimulants were reported to be in use by athletes. *Strychnine,* which became famous as a rat poison, can at low doses act as a central nervous system stimulant. However, if the dose is too high, seizure activity will be produced in the brain. The resulting convulsions can paralyze respiration, leading to death. At least some boxers were reported to have used strychnine tablets. This might have made

One of the major concerns over the use of performance-enhancing drugs is that they violate the tradition of fair play in sports. ©David Madison/Digital Vision/Getty Images RF

them more aggressive and kept them from tiring very quickly, but it was a dangerous way to do it. We'll never know how many of those rugged heroes were killed in this way, but there must have been a few. Thomas Hicks won the marathon in the 1904 St. Louis Olympics, then collapsed and had to be revived. His race was partly fueled by a mixture of brandy and strychnine.[1] Although the availability of amphetamines later made highly dangerous drugs such as strychnine less attractive, some evidence indicates the occasional use of strychnine continued at the level of world competition into the 1960s.

Cocaine was also available in the 1800s, at first in the form of Mariani's Coca Wine (used by the French cycling team), which was referred to in some advertisements as "wine for athletes."[2] When pure cocaine became available, athletes quickly adopted this more potent form. Many athletes used coffee as a mild stimulant, and some added pure *caffeine* to their coffee or took caffeine tablets. There were numerous reports of the suspected doping of swimmers, cyclists, boxers, runners, and other athletes during this period. Then, as now, some of the suspicions were raised by the losers, who might or might not have had any evidence of doping. Our use of the word *dope* for illicit drugs is derived from a Dutch word used in South Africa to refer to a cheap brandy, which was sometimes given

Drugs in the Media

Marijuana Legalization Presents a Unique Challenge for the NFL

In 2013, the National Football League announced that Denver Broncos star linebacker Von Miller would serve a six-game suspension for violating its substance-abuse policy. The violation resulted from Miller submitting spilled and diluted urine samples. And although the name of the substance responsible for triggering the suspension has not been released, many suspect marijuana because in 2011 Miller tested positive for that drug on multiple occasions.

This case raises interesting questions for collegiate and professional athletes and governing boards in states that allow adults to use marijuana recreationally. For example, what's the purpose of testing for marijuana in adult athletes in states where recreational use of the drug is protected by the law? Perhaps NFL officials are operating under the assumption that a positive urine result provides information about the individual's level of intoxication and marijuana intoxication would jeopardize player safety. Like alcohol, marijuana-induced intoxication is relatively short-lived: two to four hours. But tetrahydrocannabinol, or THC,

can remain in the body for as long as two to four weeks. Thus, a marijuana-positive urine test does not provide any information about the user's current level of intoxication or her or his ability to function. In essence, it would be analogous to testing for alcohol use several days after consumption.

The NFL's current detection limit of 15 ng/ml of THC is perhaps lower than necessary. These levels are observed in sober individuals who have not smoked marijuana for a day or more. Indeed, recently the World Anti-Doping Agency announced that they have increased the detection limit from 15 to 150 ng/ml of THC, saying that they are only interested in detecting use that could produce effects at the time of the performance. This seems to be a rational approach; further, it will significantly reduce the number of athletes who are disqualified or banned from competing owing to out-of-competition recreational marijuana use.

Box icon credit: ©Glow Images RF

to racing dogs or horses to slow them down. From this came the term for doping horses and then people, more often in an effort to improve rather than impair performance. Dogs and horses received all the substances used by humans, including coca wine and cocaine, before the days of testing for drugs.

Amphetamines

It isn't clear when athletes first started using amphetamines for their stimulant effects, but it was probably not long after the drugs were introduced in the 1930s. Amphetamines were widely used throughout the world during World War II, and in the 1940s and 1950s there were reports of the use of these pep pills by professional soccer players in England and Italy. Boxers and cyclists also relied on this new synthetic energy source. More potent than caffeine, longer-lasting than cocaine, and safer than strychnine, it seemed for a while to be the ideal

ergogenic (energy-producing) drug for both training and competition.

In 1952, the presence of syringes and broken ampules in the speed-skating locker room at the Oslo Winter Olympics indicated the presence of amphetamines in international competition. There were other reports from the 1952 summer games in Helsinki and the 1956 Melbourne Olympics. Several deaths during this period were attributed to overdoses of amphetamines or other drugs. By the time of the 1960 Rome games, amphetamine use had spread around the world and to most sports. On opening day a Danish cyclist died during time trials. An autopsy revealed that his death resulting from "sunstroke" was aided by the presence of

---

ergogenic (er go *gen* ic): producing work or energy; a general term for performance enhancement.

amphetamines, which reduce blood flow to the skin, making it more difficult for the body to cool itself. Three other cyclists collapsed that day, and two were hospitalized.[1] This and other examples of amphetamine abuse led to investigations and to antidoping laws in France and Belgium. Other nations, including the United States, seemed less concerned.

International Drug Testing

Some sports, especially cycling, began to test competitors for drugs on a sporadic basis. Throughout the 1960s, some athletes refused to submit to tests or failed tests and were disqualified. These early testing efforts were not enough to prevent the death of cyclist Tommy Simpson, an ex-world champion, who died during the 1967 Tour de France. His death was seen on television, and weeks later it was reported that his body contained two types of amphetamines and that drugs had been found in his luggage. This caused the International Olympic Committee in 1968 to establish rules requiring the disqualification of any competitor who refuses to take a drug test or who is found guilty of using banned drugs. Beginning with fewer than 700 urine tests at the 1968 Mexico City Olympics, each subsequent international competition has had more testing, more disqualifications, and more controversy. More than 5,000 urine tests were performed at the 2012 London Olympics, but there were fewer disqualifications due to a drug-positive urine test than at the three previous games.

American Football

Most Americans did not seem to be very concerned about drug use by athletes until reports surfaced in the late 1960s and early 1970s that professional football players were using amphetamines during games. Before that, people might not have been very concerned about it even if they had known. Remember from Chapter 6 that the amphetamines underwent a major status change in the United States during the 1960s. For years an increasing

number of Americans had used amphetamines to keep them awake, to provide extra energy, or to lose weight. They were seen by most people as legal, harmless pep pills. It was in that context that the physicians for professional football teams ordered large quantities of the drugs as a routine part of their supplies, and trainers dispensed them liberally.

At the end of the 1960s, amphetamines were widely considered to be drugs of abuse, dangerous drugs that could lead to violent behavior. In this context, revelations that many professionals were playing high made for sensational headlines. Several National Football League (NFL) players sued their teams for injuries received while playing under the influence of drugs, and the NFL officially banned the distribution of amphetamines by team physicians and trainers in 1971. Although the drugs were no longer condoned by the league, the NFL did little at that time to enforce the ban, except to request copies of each team's orders for medical supplies. Athletes who wanted amphetamines still obtained and used them, often through a legal prescription from their own physicians. The attitude seemed to be that, if the players wanted to use pep pills and obtained them on their own, that was their business, but team physicians and trainers shouldn't be using medications to push the athletes beyond their normal endurance. The current NFL policy, of course, restricts all use of amphetamines, as well as many other drugs, no matter where they are obtained.

Steroids

During and after World War II, it was found that malnourished people could gain weight and build themselves up more rapidly if they were given the male hormone testosterone. The Soviets were the first to put this hormone to use on a wide scale to build up their athletes. An American team physician at the 1956 Olympics reported that the Soviet athletes were using straight testosterone, sometimes in excessive doses and with unfortunate side effects. Testosterone helps both men and women become more muscular, but its masculinizing effects on women and enlargement of the prostate gland in men are definite drawbacks. The American physician at the 1956 Olympics returned to the United States and helped develop and test **anabolic** steroids, which were quickly adopted by American weight lifters and bodybuilders.[3]

American and British athletes in events such as discus and shotput were the first to acknowledge publicly that they had used steroids, and there was evidence that steroid use was widespread during the 1960s in most track and field events. These drugs were not officially banned, nor were they tested for in international competition until the early 1970s, mainly because a sensitive urine test was not available until then. Of the 2,000 urine samples taken during the 1976 Olympics, fewer than 300 were tested for the presence of steroids, and 8 of those were positive.[1] The first international athletes to be found guilty of taking steroids were a Bulgarian discus thrower, a Romanian shotputter, a Polish discus thrower, and weight lifters from several countries. By that time, individual Western athletes might have chosen to use steroids, but some of the Eastern European countries seemed to have adopted their use almost as a matter of official policy. When the East German swimming coach was asked during the 1976 Olympics why so many of their women swimmers had deep voices, the answer was, "We have come here to swim, not sing."[4]

The BALCO Scandal

For years, rumors had circulated around professional baseball that certain players were using steroids, but Major League Baseball did not test for them. When Barry Bonds came into the 2001 season looking bigger and stronger, and went on to hit a record 79 home runs, some speculated that he might have used steroids, but the rumors were always denied. In 2002, former player Ken Caminiti admitted to using steroids and claimed that "half" the Major League players were doing so. Major League Baseball did institute a limited testing program that was generally considered to be too weak to have much effect.

In June 2003, an unidentified track coach delivered to the U.S. Anti-Doping Agency a syringe containing an "undetectable" steroid, naming the source as Victor Conte, founder of BALCO Laboratories. Analysis determined that the syringe contained tetrahydrogestrinone (THG), a steroid previously unknown to the agency that did not show up in agency tests. The BALCO investigation led to a raid on the laboratory and the discovery of other steroids and human growth hormone.[5] Conte testified before a grand jury in San Francisco after being given immunity from prosecution and named a long list of Olympic and professional athletes who had been his clients, including Barry Bonds and many other professional baseball players. Bonds admitted to unknowingly taking steroids but has steadfastly denied intentionally using these drugs to enhance performance.

As a result of this and other developments, at the start of the 2006 season, Major League Baseball instituted more frequent testing and toughened penalties for drug policy violations. In addition, testing for amphetamines was included as part of the new policy for the first time (see the Myth Buster box). Under the current policy, each player is tested at least twice: once during the preseason and once during the regular season. All players are also subjected to additional random tests throughout the season. Table 16.1 summarizes the penalties associated with violations. Note that steroid violations are treated more harshly than amphetamine violations. For example, the first steroid infraction results in an 80-game suspension, whereas a similar amphetamine infraction does not trigger a suspension.

anabolic (an a *ball* ick): promoting constructive metabolism; building tissue.

Myth Buster

Amphetamine: Baseball's Real Performance-Enhancing Drug

Although discussions about performance-enhancing drugs in Major League Baseball have focused primarily on strength-inducing substances, such as steroids and human growth hormone, data collected since implementation of the League's 2006 drug policy suggest that amphetamine is the preferred performance enhancer for many. This is not surprising for those familiar with the demands of professional baseball and the immediate and reliable effects of amphetamine.

The Major League Baseball season is a grueling endurance test, comprised of seven weeks of spring training followed by 162 games in six months. There are also double-headers (two games in one day), rain delays, cross-country flights, and the expectation that players perform at their peak each game. Amphetamine increases alertness and improves attention, focus, reaction time, vigilance, and mood. The drug also reverses decrements caused by fatigue and sleep deprivation. Given this situation, it is not difficult to see why amphetamine use became and remains common in baseball.

Under baseball's current drug policy, however, amphetamine use is banned. While penalties associated with amphetamine infractions are not as severe as penalties for steroid violations, players consistently testing positive for the substance run the risk of being permanently banned from the game. Despite this potential consequence, each year since the new policy went into effect, considerably more players violate the amphetamine ban than the steroid ban. Another indication of amphetamine's prominent role in baseball can be gleaned from information regarding the number of players granted therapeutic-use exemptions for attention-deficit/hyperactivity disorder (ADHD). As discussed in Chapter 6, stimulants, including amphetamine, are used to treat this disorder, and its diagnosis provides a legal avenue through which a player could obtain amphetamine. In 2006, of the roughly 1,300 Major League Baseball players, only 28 were granted therapeutic-use exemptions for ADHD. The following year, 103 players were granted such exemptions; in 2015, this number was 113, putting baseball's ADHD rate at about 10 percent. It is worth noting that the prevalence rate for ADHD in all U.S. adults is half the rate in baseball. These observations lead us to speculate that amphetamine is baseball's real performance enhancer.

Box icon credit: ©McGraw-Hill Education

The Battle over Testing

During the 1980s, public revelations of drug use by athletes became common and cocaine was often mentioned. Professional basketball, baseball, and football players in the United States were being sent into treatment centers for cocaine dependence, and several either dropped out or were kicked out of professional sports. Most amateur and professional sports organizations adopted longer and more complicated lists of banned substances and rules providing for more and more participants to be tested. For example, in 1986, the National Collegiate Athletic Association (NCAA) adopted a list of more than 3,000 brand-name drugs containing banned substances. All participants are to be tested during the championship contest and after all postseason football games. In many events around the world, all contestants must now be subjected to urine tests as a matter of routine.

Because of both the expense and the inconvenience, some have questioned the wisdom of trying to test every athlete for everything. Despite the enormous expense to which sports organizations have gone, the use of steroids, stimulants, and other performance-enhancing substances seems to be as great as ever. Both the extent of testing and the ingenuity of athletes trying to beat the tests continue to escalate. The BALCO scandal demonstrates that chemists will keep coming up with new ways to help the athletes avoid detection.

Table 16.1
Penalties for Violating Major League Baseball Drug Policy Since 2015

	Penalty
Steroid	
First positive test	80-game suspension
Second positive test	162-game suspension
Third positive test	Lifetime suspension—may seek reinstatement after two years
Amphetamine	
First positive test	Mandatory follow-up testing
Second positive test	25-game suspension
Third positive test	80-game suspension
Fourth positive test	Commissioner's discretion

Stimulants as Performance Enhancers

The first question to be answered about the use of a drug to increase energy or otherwise enhance athletic performance is, Does it work? We might not worry so much about unfair competition if we didn't feel that the use of a drug would really help the person using it. Also, if we could prove that these drugs were ineffective, then we could presumably convince young people not to take the risk of using drugs because there would be no gain to be had. But experiments can never prove that a drug has no effect—you might have done a hundred experiments and not used the right dose or the right test (peak output? endurance? accuracy?). The possibility always exists that someone will come along later with the right combination to demonstrate a beneficial effect. Therefore, be wary when someone tries to use scientific evidence to argue that a drug doesn't work, has no effect, is not toxic, or is otherwise inactive.

We've had a pretty good idea of the effectiveness of the amphetamines since 1959, when Smith and Beecher published the results of a double-blind study comparing amphetamines and placebos in runners, swimmers, and weight throwers.[6] They concluded that most of the athletes performed better under amphetamines, but the improvement was small (a few percentage points' improvement). Several subsequent studies reported no differences or very small differences in performance, and some medical experts in the 1960s argued that amphetamines were essentially ineffective and there was no reason for people to use them. An excellent 1981 review of the existing literature put it all into perspective. The authors pointed out that it had been taking athletes an average of about seven years for each 1 percent improvement in the world record speed for the mile run. If amphetamines produced even a 1 percent improvement, they could make an important difference at that level of competition. The study concluded that there is an amphetamine margin. It is usually small, amounting to a few percent under most circumstances. But even when that tiny, it can spell the difference between a gold medal and sixth place.[7]

Whether amphetamines or other stimulants increase physical ability (provide pep or energy) or produce their actions only through effects on the brain is an interesting question, which might not be answerable. Surely a person who feels more confident will train harder, compete with a winning attitude, try harder, and keep trying longer. With

Stimulants have been shown to improve endurance.
©epicstockmedia/123RF RF

Taking Sides

Using Stimulants as Cognitive Enhancers: Where Do You Stand?

We have known for many years that low doses of stimulant drugs (e.g., amphetamines, methylphenidate) can improve performance that has been disrupted by fatigue or sleep deprivation. Recently, there has been renewed interest, however, in using stimulants as nootropics or cognitive enhancers. Healthy college students are using these drugs to get better grades, and some aspiring writers claim that the drugs aid them in their quests to write that great American novel. It seems that weekly there are stories on television news shows or in local newspapers about college students popping pills in an effort to boost their brainpower or to "give them an edge." Many of these stories imply that stimulant use for this purpose is rampant and that the majority of college students take these drugs to enhance their performance. Of course, this is not true. The best available data indicate that 4 to 7 percent of college students have taken stimulants in this manner. Another misconception is that the practice of using stimulants to enhance the performance of healthy individuals is a new phenomenon. It isn't. As is illustrated in this chapter, the use of stimulant-like drugs to enhance performance is as old as human performance itself. Nonetheless, the practice of using stimulants as cognitive enhancers raises a number of questions that warrant our attention.

Do they work? Can stimulants make healthy people smarter? To some, such claims might be reminiscent of those made about certain artists and the influence that drug use had on their genius. For example, it has been suggested that were it not for Miles Davis's heroin use, he might not have become the accomplished trumpeter that we celebrate. While heroin might cause individuals to be slightly less inhibited and allow them to take certain risks (including musically), there is no evidence that heroin enhances one's ability to play the trumpet or any other instrument. Indeed, several budding trumpeters and admirers of Davis used heroin but did not become accomplished musicians. In the case of stimulants, there is good evidence showing that these drugs can improve endurance and simple cognitive performance such as reaction time, attention, and vigilance. The impact of stimulants on more complicated cognitive operations (e.g., flexibility and reasoning), however, is, at best, less clear and, at worst, disruptive. In short, the drugs may be useful in increasing alertness and assisting one to work and/or study for longer periods of time, but they won't improve critical thinking skills or enhance creativity.

What are the health risks associated with nootropics? The main stimulants used for this purpose are amphetamines (e.g., Adderall), methylphenidate (Ritalin), and modafinil (Provigil). All of these drugs increase cardiovascular activity, which can, at large doses, increase the likelihood of a heart attack or stroke, although these effects are less likely in healthy individuals taking low to moderate oral doses. Another concern is that these drugs can disrupt sleep; excessive sleep loss can lead to the development of physical and mental health problems, including heart disease and psychosis. However, these effects are minimized when the medications are prescribed and monitored by a responsible physician.

What about issues of fairness? Some students, for example, may not have access to a physician to prescribe stimulant medications, while others do. Or some students may not want to take stimulants because of the potential health risks but feel compelled to do so in order to remain competitive in the classroom. Of course, similar issues of unfairness already exist. For example, some students have access to private tutors and preparatory courses for entrance examinations, while others do not. Clearly, there are multiple ways in which some students may gain advantages over others. As a result of these issues, where do you stand? Should we allow for some regulated form of stimulant medication use to enhance cognitive performance of healthy students? Or should we discourage use of these drugs for that purpose?

Box icon credit: ©Nova Development RF

amphetamines, improvements have been seen both in events requiring brief, explosive power (shotput) and in events requiring endurance, such as distance running. In laboratory studies, increases have been found in isometric strength and in work output during endurance testing on a stationary bicycle (the subjects rode longer under amphetamine conditions). This endurance improvement could be due to the masking of fatigue effects, allowing a person to compete to utter exhaustion.

Caffeine has also been shown to improve endurance performance under laboratory conditions. In one experiment, 330 mg of caffeine (approximately equivalent to three cups of brewed coffee) increased the length of a stationary bicycle ride by almost 20 percent. In another experiment, when subjects rode for two hours, their total energy output was 7 percent higher after 500 mg caffeine than in the control condition.[8] The effectiveness of caffeine might depend on other factors: For example, one study reported no benefit from caffeine when athletes ran long distances (12 miles) in hot, humid conditions.[9] Small amounts of caffeine are acceptable in most sports, but a urine level above 12 µg/mL will lead to disqualification in many competitions. The doses needed to produce large performance increases produce much higher levels than that, but there could still be a slight improvement even at legal levels.

Apparently no controlled laboratory or field experiments have tested the performance-enhancing capabilities of cocaine, but especially during the 1980s many athletes believed in its power. Cocaine's stimulant properties are generally similar to those of the amphetamines, so we can assume that cocaine would be effective under some circumstances. Given cocaine's shorter duration of action, it would not be expected to improve endurance over a several-hour period as well as either amphetamines or caffeine.

For years, athletes had another readily available stimulant in the form of ephedrine, either as a drug or in the form of ephedra extract. Ephedra (ma huang) was introduced in Chapter 6 as the herbal source of ephedrine, and it was the ephedrine molecule that was modified in the 1920s to produce amphetamine. When Olympic and NCAA officials developed lists of banned substances, ephedrine soon made its way onto the lists (except for people whose physicians said they suffered from asthma—ephedrine relaxes bronchial passages and is an ingredient in asthma medications). Professional sports organizations were at first less concerned about ephedrine, but eventually the NFL also banned it. Major League Baseball did not, and baseball players used it to provide extra energy, or in some cases to reduce weight, since ephedra was also found in many weight-control dietary supplements (Chapter 12). In 2003, Baltimore Orioles pitcher Steve Bechler died after collapsing during practice—his temperature rose to 108 degrees in the hospital before his death, which was attributed to heat stroke due to the ingestion of "significant amounts" of ephedrine from a dietary supplement.[10] This widely publicized death finally gave the FDA enough political backing to go along with the years of evidence it had been accumulating, leading to the 2004 ban on ephedra and ephedrine in dietary supplements.

With all these and several other CNS stimulants banned by most sports associations, some athletes have continued to use them during training, to allow them to run, ride, or swim harder. They then do not use the drug for several days before the competition or during the competition, hoping that traces of the substance will not appear in the urine test. This might make sense, but no one knows whether training under one drug condition has an effect on competition under another condition. Also, overexertion under the influence of a fatigue-masking drug might be most dangerous during training, leading to muscle injury, a fall or another accident, or heat exhaustion.

Athletes and others who use amphetamines or cocaine regularly run the risk of becoming addicted to the drug, developing paranoia, and suffering from the loss of energy and psychological depression that could occur as the drugs wear off (see Chapter 6).

Steroids

The male sex hormone testosterone has two major types of effects on the developing man. **Androgenic** effects are masculinizing actions: Initial growth of the penis and other male sex glands, deepening of the voice, and increased facial hair are examples. This steroid hormone also has anabolic effects. These include increased muscle mass, increases in the size of various internal organs, control of the distribution of body fat, increased protein synthesis, and increased calcium in the bones. In the 1950s, drug companies began to synthesize various steroids that have fewer of the androgenic effects and more of the anabolic effects than testosterone. These are referred to as *anabolic steroids,* although none of them is entirely free of some masculinizing effect.

Steroids are known to enhance the natural process of muscle building. Key elements in building muscles are protein synthesis and cellular repair. Skeletal muscle is composed of long fiber chains containing proteins. Bundles of thousands of fibers make up the muscle itself. This structure is damaged when a person engages in a vigorous workout, causing microtrauma in the muscle fiber. The body naturally repairs this damage by healing the fibers. The result is a muscle that is larger and stronger than before, and with each additional workout the person adds bulk and strength. Steroids speed up the muscle repair and recovery process. Normally, it takes about 48 hours for muscles to repair themselves following a heavy workout. Steroids can shorten the repair and recovery process to only 24 hours, allowing the athlete to returning to heavy training more quickly.

Whether these drugs are effective in improving athletic performance was once controversial: For many years the medical position was that they were not, whereas the lore around the locker room was that they would make anyone bigger, stronger, and more masculine-looking. A lot of people must have had more faith in the locker-room lore than in the official word. The 1992 *Physician's Desk Reference* contained the following statement in boldface type: **"Anabolic Steroids Have Not Been Shown to Enhance Athletic Ability."** Try telling that to any current Major League Baseball player, sports writer, or fan. That disclaimer is no longer required by the FDA.

There is no doubt that testosterone has a tremendous effect on muscle mass and strength during puberty, and experiments on castrated animals clearly show the muscle-developing ability of the synthetic anabolics.[11] What is not so clear is the effect of adding additional anabolic stimulation to adolescent or adult males who already have normal circulating levels of testosterone.

Laboratory research on healthy men who are engaged in weight training and are maintained on a proper diet has often found that anabolic steroids produce small increases in lean muscle mass and sometimes small increases in muscular strength. There is no evidence for an overall increase in aerobic capacity or endurance in those studies. However, it might never be possible to conduct experiments demonstrating the effectiveness of the high doses used by some athletes. Many athletes report that they take 10 or more times the dose of a steroid that has been tested and recommended for treatment of a deficiency disorder.[12] It is also common for athletes to take more than one steroid at a time (both an oral and an injectable form, for example). This practice is known as "stacking." To expose research subjects to such massive doses would clearly be unethical.

Another impediment to doing careful research on this topic is that these steroids produce detectable psychological effects. When double-blind experiments have been attempted, almost always the subjects have known when they were on steroids, thus destroying the blind control.[13] This is important because steroid users report that they feel they can lift more or work harder when they are on the steroids. This may be due to CNS effects of the steroids leading to a stimulant-like feeling of energy and loss of fatigue or to increased aggressiveness expressed as more aggressive training. There is a further possibility of what is known as an *active placebo effect,* with a belief in the power of steroids, enhanced by the clear sensation that the drug is doing something because one can "feel" it. Until recently, many of the scientists studying steroid hormones believed that their main effects were psychological, combined with a "bloating" effect on the muscle, in which the muscle retains more fluids, is larger, weighs more, but has no more physical strength.[1]

Psychological Effects of Steroids

The reported psychological effects of steroids, including a stimulant-like high and increased aggressiveness, might be beneficial for increasing the amount of work done during training and for increasing the intensity of effort during competition. However, there are also concerns that these psychological effects might produce great problems, especially at high doses. One concern is that a psychological dependence seems to develop in some users, who feel great when they are on the steroids but become depressed when they are off them. Many users take the drugs in cycles, and their mood swings can interfere with their social relationships and other life functions.

There has been a great deal of discussion about "roid rage," a kind of manic rage that has been reported by some steroid users.[14] We should be careful about attributing instances of violence to a drug on the basis of uncontrolled retrospective reports, especially when the perpetrator of a violent crime might be looking for an excuse.[15]

Adverse Effects on the Body

There are many concerns about the effects of steroid use on the body. In young users who have not attained their full height, steroids can cause premature closing of the growth plates of the long bones, thus limiting their adult height. For all users, the risk of peliosis hepatitis (bloody cysts in the liver) and the changes in blood lipids possibly leading to atherosclerosis, high blood pressure, and heart disease are potentially serious concerns. Acne and baldness are reported, as are atrophy of the testes and breast enlargement in men using anabolic steroids.

There are also considerations for women who use anabolic steroids. Because women usually have only trace amounts of testosterone produced by the adrenals, the addition of even relatively small doses of anabolic steroids can have dramatic effects, in terms of both muscle growth and masculinization. Some of the side effects, such as mild acne, decreased breast size, and fluid retention, are reversible. The enlargement of the clitoris might be reversible if steroid use is stopped soon after it is noticed. Other effects, such as increased facial hair and deepening of the voice, might be irreversible.[13]

Regulation

As we found in Chapter 2, when a drug produces dependence, violent behavior, and toxic side effects, society may feel justified in trying to restrict the drug's availability. In 1988, congressional hearings were held on the notion of placing anabolic steroids on the list of controlled substances. Evidence was presented that a large black market had developed for these drugs, amounting to perhaps $100 million per year. In addition, there was concern that adolescent boys, many of whom were not athletic at all, had begun to use steroids in the belief that they would quickly become more muscular and "macho" looking. As part of the Omnibus Crime Control Act of 1990, anabolic steroids became listed as a Schedule III controlled substance, requiring more record-keeping and limited prescription refills.[16]

Other Hormonal Manipulations

Whereas the anabolic steroids have been in wide use, other treatments have been experimented with on a more limited basis. Female sex hormones have been used to feminize men, so that they could compete in women's events. The women's gold medal sprinter in the 1964 Olympics was shown by chromosome testing to have been a man, and he had to

androgenic (an drow *gen* ick): masculinizing.

Drugs in Depth

Nutritional Ergogenic Aids

If athletes can't get or refuse to use pharmacological aids in athletic competition, most believe that certain foods or nutritional supplements are a "natural" way to enhance their performance. Following is a very abbreviated description of a more complete review of this topic.[7]

Amino acids are the natural building blocks of the protein required to build muscle, and one certainly requires a basic minimum intake. There is some evidence that very active people can benefit from a somewhat increased intake of dietary protein, slightly above the recommended daily allowances, but there is no demonstrated need to purchase expensive amino acid supplements to achieve this. Marketers of these "muscle-building" dietary supplements walk a fine line by avoiding making specific claims on the product labels, so they do not fall under the FDA's rules for demonstrating effectiveness. Usually nearby posters or pamphlets link amino acids to the idea of muscle growth. These supplements are probably of little or no value to an athlete who is receiving proper nutrition.

Carbohydrates are burned as fuels, especially during prolonged aerobic exercise. Carbohydrates taken two to four hours before an endurance performance lasting for more than an hour may enhance the performance by maintaining blood glucose levels and preventing the depletion of muscle stores of glycogen. Carbohydrate loading before marathon runs consists of resting for the last day or two while ingesting extra carbohydrates, increasing both muscle and liver stores of carbohydrates. In either case, there is not much evidence to support the value of carbohydrate supplements for athletic performances lasting less than an hour.

Fats, in experiments with fat supplements, have not been found to be a useful ergogenic aid.

Vitamins, especially the water-soluble B vitamins, are necessary for normal utilization of food energy. Deficiencies in these vitamins, such as might result when a wrestler is dieting to meet a weight limit, can clearly impair physical performance. However, once the necessary minimum amount is available for metabolic purposes, further supplements are of no value. Many experiments have been done with supplements of C, E, and B-complex vitamins or with multivitamin supplements, the so-called vitamin B_{15}, and with bee pollen, and there is no evidence for enhanced performance or faster recovery after workouts. Again, these supplements are probably of no value to an athlete who is receiving proper nutrition.

Minerals, in the form of various mineral supplements, are widely used by athletes. Once again, most are probably not needed or useful, but there may be some exceptions. Electrolyte drinks are designed to replace both fluids and electrolytes, such as sodium and chloride that are lost in sweat. Actually, sweat contains a lower concentration of these electrolytes than does blood, so it is more important to replace the fluids than the electrolytes under most circumstances. Sodium supplementation may be useful for those engaged in ultraendurance events, such as 100-mile runs.

Iron supplements are helpful in athletes who are iron-deficient, as may occur especially in female distance runners. However, if iron status is normal, there is probably no value in iron supplements.

The jury is still out on whether "buffering" the blood pH with sodium bicarbonate (baking soda) enhances performance in anaerobic events, such as 400- to 800-meter runs. Some studies indicate improvements, whereas others do not.

Water is needed by endurance athletes to keep their body temperatures down, especially in a warm environment. Drinking water both before and during prolonged exercise can deter dehydration and improve performance. Visit the Online Learning Center for links to more information on supplements.

Box icon credit: ©Ingram Publishing/SuperStock RF

return the medal. Hormone receptor–blocking drugs have probably been used to delay puberty in female gymnasts. In women, puberty shifts the center of gravity lower in the body and changes body proportions in ways that adversely affect performance in some gymnastic events. Smaller women appear to be more graceful, spin faster on the uneven bars, and generally have the advantage, which is why top female gymnasts are usually in their teens. However, the Soviets were suspected of tampering with nature: Their top three international gymnasts in 1978 were all 17 or 18 years old, but the following were their heights and weights: 53 inches, 63 pounds; 60 inches, 90 pounds; and 57 inches, 79 pounds.

We have certainly not seen the end of growth-promoting hormonal treatments. **Human growth hormone,** which is released from the pituitary gland, can potentially increase the height and weight of an individual to gigantic proportions, especially if administered during childhood and adolescence. In rare instances, the excessive production of this hormone creates giants well over 7 feet tall. These pituitary giants usually die at an early age because their internal organs continue to grow. However, administration of a few doses of this hormone at the right time might produce a more controlled increase in body size. Likewise, the growth-hormone-releasing hormone, and some of the cellular intermediary hormones by which growth hormone exerts its effects, might work to enhance growth. It is difficult to test for the presence of these substances. Despite the possible dangers, the lure of an otherwise capable basketball player growing a couple of inches taller or of a football player being 30 pounds heavier has no doubt caused many young athletes to experiment with these substances. Studies have shown that growth hormone increases lean body mass but may not improve strength.[18] The 1990 legislation that placed anabolic steroids on the list of controlled substances also made it a crime to distribute human growth hormone for nonmedical purposes.

Beta-2 Agonists

At the beginning of the 1992 Olympics, the leader of the British team was disqualified because of the detection of a new drug. Clenbuterol was developed as a treatment for asthma and is a relative of several other bronchodilators that are found in prescription inhalers. These drugs have sympathomimetic effects on the bronchi of the lungs but are designed to be more specific than older sympathomimetics, such as ephedrine or the amphetamines (see Chapter 6). Their specificity comes from a selective stimulation of the beta-2 subtype of adrenergic receptors. Research with cows had revealed an increase in muscle mass, and speculation was beginning that this might represent a new type of nonsteroidal anabolic agent. Apparently someone in Great Britain was keeping an eye on the animal research literature and decided to try the anabolic actions on at least one Olympic athlete. Presumably it was hoped that such a new drug would not be tested for, but the Olympic officials were also well informed and ready, at least for clenbuterol. Human studies have shown some increases in strength of selected muscle types with clenbuterol or a similar drug, but there is no evidence that beta-2 agonists improve athletic performance.[19]

Creatine

One widely used substance among bodybuilders has been creatine, a natural substance found in meat and fish. This legal product is sold as a food supplement. There is clear evidence that creatine helps regenerate ATP, which provides the energy for muscle contractions. Users of creatine tend to gain some weight, some of which is water weight. There is considerable evidence that the use of creatine can improve strength and short-term speed in sprinting. However, studies of longer-distance running, cycling, and swimming often find no effect, and in one case a significant slowing was reported, probably due to weight gain.[4]

Getting "Cut"

If getting "cut," "ripped," and "shredded" sounds like something you'd want to avoid, then you're probably not into bodybuilding. These terms refer to the appearance of someone who is both muscular

human growth hormone: a pituitary hormone responsible for some types of giantism.

Bodybuilders and other athletes have used steroids or other supplements to develop a lean, strong, muscular body—to become "cut" or "ripped." ©McGraw-Hill Education/Jill Braaten, photographer

and lean. Because amateur wrestlers compete in weight classes and they need to be strong, they have always had the problem of eating well to build strength and train hard, but then needing to "cut" weight before the weigh-ins for matches. Jockeys have had a similar problem. Over the years, some of these athletes have engaged in fairly extreme methods to achieve short-term weight reduction, such as purging, taking diuretic drugs to lose water weight, and exercising in a heated environment or wearing nonporous clothing to maximize sweating. The entire list of weight-control drugs mentioned in Chapters 6 and 12 have been used as well, ranging from amphetamine to ephedrine to caffeine.

Increasingly, bodybuilders are seeking the look of someone who is both strong and lean, with lots of muscle definition. That appearance is referred to as looking "cut," probably derived from the idea of cutting weight or cutting fat, but perhaps also carrying the connotation of "sculpted." A more extreme version of looking cut is looking "ripped," or sometimes "shredded." These are the men and women whose every muscle fiber and vein can be seen through the skin, perhaps with a body fat

percentage down to an unhealthy 6 to 9 percent (14 to 20 percent is considered ideal for a healthy male). They also are using drugs and nutritional supplements to help achieve this appearance. Steroids increase muscle mass, but they don't produce this kind of lean definition. A brisk market has developed in dietary supplements containing the word *ripped* in their name, such as "Ripped Fuel" and "Ripped Fast." For many years these products relied mainly on ephedra as the main active ingredient. Once ephedra was banned, these profitable products did not go away. They simply changed their formulas and kept making the same claims about being "fat burners" and promising incredible results. They contain a bewildering variety of plant extracts, many of which contain caffeine in unknown amounts (e.g., guarana extract, green tea extract, and coffee bean extract).

Remember that these dietary supplements do not have to be demonstrated to be effective, and the beneficial claims have not been evaluated by the FDA (or anyone else). If an included ingredient should turn out to be dangerous, it might take a long time for this to come to the attention of the FDA, and it would then take a long time for the agency to build a case to remove the ingredient from the market (it took 10 years for ephedra). No such product has ever been shown to actually be a "fat burner," so it's unlikely that these are either. If you buy them, the closest you'll get to being "ripped" as a result is probably feeling "ripped off" when the magic pill doesn't deliver what you hoped.

Summary

- Performance-enhancing drugs have been used by athletes throughout history.

- Athletic use of stimulants appears to have increased and spread to most sports with the use of amphetamines during the 1950s and 1960s.

- Amphetamines and caffeine have both been shown to increase work output and to mask the effects of fatigue.

- Some athletes continue to use stimulants for training, despite the dangers of injury and overexertion.

- Anabolic steroids are capable of increasing muscle mass and probably strength, although it has been difficult to separate the psychological stimulant-like effect of these drugs from the physical effects on the muscles themselves.

- Anabolic steroids can also produce a variety of dangerous and sometimes irreversible side effects.

- It is difficult to do ethical and well-controlled research on the effects of steroids.

- Misuse of human growth hormone and related substances might be the next problem to arise.

- Creatine is a legally available nutritional supplement that can increase strength but might slow distance runners because of resultant weight gain.

Review Questions

1. What was the first type of stimulant drug reported to be used by boxers and other athletes in the 1800s?

2. What was the first type of drug known to be widely used in international competition and that led to the first Olympic urine-testing programs?

3. When and in what country were the selective anabolic steroids first developed?

4. Do amphetamines and caffeine actually enhance athletic performance? If so, how much?

5. How was ephedrine used by athletes, and what happened to it?

6. What muscle effect do we know for certain that anabolic steroids can produce in healthy men?

7. What is meant by "roid rage," and what double-blind studies have been done on this phenomenon?

8. What specific effect of anabolic steroids might be of concern to young users? to females?

9. Why do "pituitary giants" often die at an early age?

10. How does creatine increase strength?

References

1. Donohue, T., and N. Johnson. *Foul Play: Drug Abuse in Sports.* Oxford, England: Basil Blackwell, 1986.

2. Asken, M. J. *Dying to Win: The Athlete's Guide to Safe and Unsafe Drugs in Sports.* Washington, DC: Acropolis, 1988.

3. Eichner, E. R. "Ergogenic Aids: What Athletes Are Using—and Why." *Physician and Sportsmedicine* 25 (1997), pp. 70–83.

4. Goldman, B. *Death in the Locker Room.* South Bend, IN: Icarus Press, 1984.

5. Fainaru-Wada, F., and L. Williams. "Sports and Drugs: How the Doping Scandal Unfolded. Fallout from BALCO Probe Could Taint Olympics, Pro Sports." *San Francisco Chronicle,* December 21, 2003.

6. Smith, G. M., and H. K. Beecher. "Amphetamine Sulfate and Athletic Performance." *Journal of the American Medical Association* 170 (1959), pp. 542–57.

7. Laties, V. G., and B. Weiss. "The Amphetamine Margin in Sports." *Federation Proceedings* 40 (1981), pp. 2689–92.

8. Noble, B. J. *Physiology of Exercise and Sport.* St Louis: Mosby, 1986.

9. Cohen, B. S., and others. "Effects of Caffeine Ingestion on Endurance Racing in Heat and Humidity." *European Journal of Applied Physiology* 73 (1996), pp. 358–63.

10. Bodley, H. "Medical Examiner: Ephedra a Factor in Bechler Death." *USA Today,* March 13, 2003.

11. Williams, M. H. *Ergogenic Aids in Sports.* Champaign, IL: Human Kinetics, 1983.

12. Marshall, E. "The Drug of Champions." *Science* 242 (1983), pp. 183–84.

13. Taylor, W. N. *Hormonal Manipulation: A New Era of Monstrous Athletes.* Jefferson, NC: McFarland & Co., 1985.

14. Pope, H. G., and D. L. Katz. "Affective and Psychotic Symptoms Associated with Anabolic Steroid Use." *American Journal of Psychiatry* 145 (1988), pp. 487–90.

15. Lubell, A. "Does Steroid Abuse Cause—or Excuse—Violence? *Physician and Sportsmedicine* 17 (1989), pp. 176–85.

16. Nightingale, S. L. "Anabolic Steroids as Controlled Substances." *Journal of the American Medical Association* 265 (1991), p. 1229.

17. Burke, L., and others. "Supplements and Sports Foods." *Clinical Sports Nutrition,* 3rd ed. Edited by L. Burke and V. Deakin. Sydney: McGraw-Hill, 2006, pp. 485–579. Available at http://www.ais.org.au/nutrition/documents/16Complete.pdf

18. Liu, H., and others. "Systematic Review: The Effects of Growth Hormone on Athletic Performance." *Annals of Internal Medicine* (2008) [March 17 Epub ahead of print].

19. Spann, S. "Effect of Clenbuterol on Athletic Performance." *Annals of Pharmacotherapy* 29 (1995), p. 75.

Prevention and Harm Reduction

This final section on prevention and harm reduction comes at the end of the book for a reason. Now that you're more familiar with a wide spectrum of substances and their effects, we are better able to talk about what we're trying to prevent, and how to reduce substance-related harms. As a result, we discuss various policies and strategies implemented by some countries in order to prevent substance abuse and potential related harms.

Preventing Substance Abuse

- Distinguish between education and propaganda programs based on their goals and approaches.

- Describe two systems for classifying prevention programs: one based on stages of involvement, the other based on target populations defined by risk for drug use.

- Describe the historical shifts in substance abuse prevention programs from the knowledge-attitudes-behavior model to affective education to antidrug norms.

- Explain how the social influence model for smoking prevention led to the development of DARE and similar programs.

- Describe the outcome of research on DARE's effectiveness and how DARE America has responded.

- List some examples of effective prevention programs that have been adopted as model programs by SAMHSA.

- Give some examples of peer, family, and community approaches to prevention.

- Describe the most consistent feature of workplace prevention programs.

©Simon Marcus Taplin/Getty Images RF

When speaking about drug prevention, one of the most important questions is rarely asked: What are we trying to prevent? Is our aim to prevent *all* drug use, including alcohol use? Or is our aim to prevent drug *abuse* and its associated harms? We would like to make this point absolutely clear: A major goal of this entire book is to decrease drug *abuse* and related harms. In 2016, half of all high-school seniors had used an illicit drug at least once in their life and more than 60 percent reported drinking alcohol at some point. These numbers suggest that the goal of preventing all drug use might be somewhat unrealistic. Drugs have always been and will continue to be a part of our society, so we should try to teach people to live in a world that includes them. Our society has taken this approach with tobacco and alcohol, despite the fact that some people are harmed by them. The relative number of people who have alcohol- or tobacco-related problems is small, in part, because prevention efforts are focused primarily on teaching people how to coexist with these substances and to live in such a way that their lives and health are not impaired by them. Can we do the same for illegal substances? We think so.

Defining Goals and Evaluating Outcomes

Think about the process you are engaged in while reading and studying this book. The text is aimed at teaching its readers about drugs: their effects, how they are used, and how they relate to society. The goal of the authors is *education*. A person who understands all this information about all these drugs will perhaps be better prepared to make decisions about personal drug use, more able to understand drug use by others, and better prepared to participate in social decisions about drug use and abuse. We hope that a person who knew all this would be in a position to act more rationally, neither glorifying a drug and expecting miraculous changes from using it nor condemning it as the essence of evil. But our ultimate goal is not to change readers' behavior in a particular direction. For example, the chapter on alcohol, although pointing out the potential dangers of its use and the problems it can cause, does not attempt to influence readers to avoid all alcohol use. The success of this book is measured by how much a person knows about sedatives, psychedelics, cannabis, opioids, stimulants, and tobacco, not whether he or she is convinced never to use any of these substances.

On the other hand, a tradition exists, going back to the "demon rum" programs of the late 1800s, of presenting negative information about alcohol and other drugs in the public schools with the clear goal of *prevention* of use. Some of these early programs presented information that was so clearly one-sided that they should have been classified as propaganda rather than education. We would not measure the success of such a program by how much objective information the students gained about the pharmacology of cocaine, for example. A more appropriate index might be how many of the students did subsequently experiment with the drugs against which the program was aimed. Until the early 1970s, it was simply assumed that these programs would have the desired effect, and few attempts were made to evaluate them.

Types of Prevention

The goals and methods of a prevention program also depend on the drug-using status of those served by the program. The programs designed to prevent young people from starting smoking might be different from those used to try to prevent relapse in smokers who have quit, for example. Until recently, drug-abuse prevention programs have been classified according to a public health model:

- **Primary prevention** programs are those aimed mainly at young people who have not yet tried the substances in question or who may have tried tobacco or alcohol a few times. As discussed in the section "Defining Goals and Evaluating Outcomes," such programs might encourage abstinence from specific drugs or might have the broader goal of teaching people how to view drugs and the potential influences of drugs on their lives, emotions, and social relationships. Because those programs are presented to people with little personal experience with drugs, they might be expected to be especially effective. But, there is the danger of introducing large numbers of children to information about drugs that they might otherwise never have heard of, thus arousing their curiosity.

- **Secondary prevention** programs can be thought of as designed for people who have tried the drug in question or a variety of other substances. The goals of such programs are usually the prevention of the use of other, more dangerous substances and the prevention of the development of more dangerous forms of use of the substances they are already experimenting with. We might describe the clientele here as more "sophisticated" substance users who have not suffered seriously from their drug experiences and who are not obvious candidates for treatment. Many college students

Drugs in the Media

Are Antidrug Media Campaigns Effective?

In 1998, Congress created the Office of National Drug Control Policy's National Youth Anti-Drug Media Campaign. The campaign promotes antidrug messages targeting teens and young adults through advertisements, with the goal of preventing and reducing drug use. A major component is the "Above the Influence" campaign, which targets young people ages 12–17. These advertisements are intended to provide listeners and viewers with information about the dangers of drug use and ways to avoid being pressured to use drugs. For the most part, the messaging does not overstate or exaggerate the effects of drug use. A major focus is providing young people with examples of alternatives to drug use.

The current advertisement campaign is quite a departure from previous government-sponsored campaigns. Some may recall that these are folks who, in the late 1980s, brought us the public service announcement: "This is your brain on drugs." During the original spot, a man holds up an egg and says, "This is your brain." Then, he picks up a frying pan and says, "This is drugs." Then, he cracks open the egg, fries the contents, and says, "This is your brain on drugs." Finally, he asks, "Any questions?" While this is perhaps the most memorable antidrug use advertisement, it is frequently ridiculed because it overstates the potential harmful effects of drugs used by its target audience, namely young people. Indeed, a major concern of drug educators is that these types of embellishments decrease their credibility and may lead some young people to reject all drug-related information from so-called informed sources.

Does the current advertisement campaign avoid past mistakes? More important, is it effective? Information from surveys indicates that teens who were aware of or interacted with Above the Influence had significantly stronger antidrug beliefs than teens who were not aware of or did not interact with Above the Influence. While this is important information, it doesn't tell us about the drug-using behavior of these teens. Nor does it provide us with information about whether teens exposed to Above the Influence are better equipped to deal with drug use if and when it occurs. Perhaps the current advertisement campaign is less likely to alienate its target audience, but questions about its effectiveness remain.

Box icon credit: ©Glow Images RF

---

fall into this category, and programs aimed at encouraging responsible use of alcohol among college students are good examples of this stage of prevention.

- **Tertiary prevention,** in our scheme, is relapse prevention, or follow-up programs. For individuals who meet criteria for a substance use disorder, treatment programs are the first order of priority. However, once a person has been treated or has stopped the substance use without assistance, we enter another stage of prevention.

The Institute of Medicine has proposed a classification of the "continuum of care," which includes prevention, treatment, and maintenance.[1] Prevention efforts are categorized according to the intended target population, but the targets are not defined only by prior drug use:

- **Universal prevention** programs are de-signed for delivery to an entire population—for example, all schoolchildren or an entire community.
- **Selective prevention** strategies are designed for groups within the general population that are deemed to be at high risk—for example, students who are not doing well academically or the poorest neighborhoods in a community.
- **Indicated prevention** strategies are targeted at individuals who show signs of developing problems, such as a child who began smoking cigarettes at a young age or an adult arrested for a first offense of driving under the influence of alcohol.

Life Saver

Targeting the Pain

Good prevention programs should move the focus from the drug that is used to the person who is using it and the circumstances under which drug use occurs. No drug is inherently more evil than the other and the overwhelming majority of drug users do not become addicted. This shows that the drugs themselves are not the problem.

People become addicted for a variety of reasons ranging from psychiatric disorders to economic desperation. That is why it is, first, critically important to determine the reasons underlying each person's addiction before intervening with half-baked solutions. For example, if a person is using heroin to deal with anxiety or trauma, effective treatment of the psychiatric illness should alleviate the need to use heroin. Similarly, providing destitute addicts with specific skills and viable economic opportunities will go a long way in helping them to overcome their drug addiction. A lesson here is that one shoe doesn't fit all and that careful assessment is an important component in helping addicts.

If more people were aware of these simple points, it would help our society deal with drug users in a more ethical and decent manner. When a society defers to the evidence and not hysteria, compassion can be extended to all of its citizens alike, regardless of whether they use alcohol, marijuana, tobacco, or heroin.

Box icon credit: ©McGraw-Hill Education

Prevention Programs in the Schools

The Knowledge-Attitudes-Behavior Model

After the increase in the use of illicit drugs by young middle-class people in the 1960s, there was a general sense that society was not doing an adequate job of drug education, and most school systems increased their efforts. However, there was confusion over the methods to be used. Traditional antidrug programs had relied heavily on representatives of the local police, who went into schools and told a few horror stories, describing the legal trouble due anyone who got caught with illicit drugs. Sometimes the officers showed what the drugs looked like or demonstrated the smell of burning marijuana, so that the kids would know what to avoid. Sometimes, especially in larger cities, a former user described how easy it was to get "hooked," the horrible life of the junkie, and the horror of withdrawal symptoms. The 1960s saw more of that, plus the production of a large number of scary antidrug films.

Teachers and counselors knew little about these substances, and many teachers attended courses taught by experts. Some of the experts were enforcement-oriented and presented the traditional scare-tactics information, whereas others were pharmacologists who presented the "dry facts" about the classification and effects of various drugs. The teachers then brought many of these facts into their classrooms. It was later pointed out that the programs of this era were based on an assumed model: that providing information about drugs would increase the students' *knowledge* of drugs and their effects, that this increased knowledge would lead to changes in *attitudes* about drug use, and that these changed attitudes would be reflected in decreased drug-using *behavior.*[2]

In the early 1970s, this model began to be questioned. A 1971 study indicated that students who had more knowledge about drugs tended to have a more positive attitude toward drug use.[3] Of course, it may have been that pro-drug students were more interested in learning about drugs, so this was not an actual assessment of the value of drug education programs. A 1973 report by the same group indicated that four different types of drug education programs were equally effective in producing increased knowledge about drugs and equally ineffective in altering attitudes or behavior.[4] Nationwide, drug use had increased even with the greater emphasis on drug education. Concern arose about the possibility that drug education may even have contributed to increased drug use. Before the 1960s, the use of marijuana and LSD was rare among school-age youngsters. Most of them didn't know much about these things, had given them little thought, and had probably never considered using them. Telling them over and over not to use drugs was a bit like telling a young boy not to put beans in his nose. He probably hadn't thought of it before, and your warning gives him the idea. These concerns led the federal government in 1973 to stop supporting the production of drug-abuse films and educational materials until it could determine what kinds of approaches would be effective.

The question of effectiveness depended greatly on the goals of the program. Did we want all students *never to experiment* with cigarettes, alcohol, marijuana, or other drugs? Or did we want students to be prepared to *make rational decisions* about drugs? For example, a 1976 report indicated that students in drug education programs did increase their use of drugs over the two years after the program, but they were less likely to show drastic escalation of the amount or type of drug use over that period, when compared with a control group.[5] Perhaps by giving the students information about drugs, we make them more likely to try them, but we also make them more aware of the dangers of excessive use. For a time in the 1970s, it seemed as though teaching students to make rational decisions about their own drug use with the goal of reducing the overall harm produced by misuse and abuse could be a possible goal of prevention programs.

Affective Education

Educators have been talking for several years about education as including both a "cognitive domain" and an "*affective* domain," the domain of emotions and attitudes. One reason that young people might use psychoactive drugs is to produce certain feelings: of excitement, of relaxation, of power, of being in control. Or perhaps a child might not really want to take drugs but does so after being influenced by others. Helping children know their own

Helping young people learn to deal with emotions in healthy ways and giving them successful experiences may reduce their rates of smoking, drinking, and drug use. ©Image Source/Getty Images RF

feelings and express them, helping them achieve altered emotional states without drugs, and teaching them to feel valued, accepted, and wanted are all presumed to be ways of reducing drug use.

Values Clarification The **values clarification** approach makes the assumption that what is lacking in drug-using adolescents is not factual information about drugs but, rather, the ability to make appropriate decisions based on that information.[6] Perhaps drug use should not be "flagged" for the students by having special curricula designed just for drugs but, instead, emphasis should be placed on teaching generic decision-making skills. Teaching students to analyze and clarify their own values in life is accomplished by having them discuss their reactions to various situations that pose moral and ethical dilemmas. Groups of parents or other citizens who are concerned about drug abuse sometimes have great difficulty understanding and accepting these approaches because they do not take a direct antidrug approach. In the 1970s, when these programs were developed, it seemed important that the schools not try to impose a particular set of values but, rather, allow for differences in religion, family background, and so on. For this reason, the programs were often said to be *value-free*. To many parents, the purpose of values clarification training is not immediately clear, and teaching young children to decide moral issues for themselves may run contrary to the particular set of values the parents want their children to learn.

Alternatives to Drugs Along with values clarification, another aspect of affective education involves the teaching of **alternatives** to drug use. Under the assumption that students might take drugs for the experience, for the altered states of consciousness that a drug might produce, students are taught so-called natural highs, or altered states, that can be produced through relaxation exercises, meditation, vigorous exercise, or an exciting sport. Students are encouraged to try these things and to focus on the psychological changes that occur. These alternatives should be discussed with some degree of sensitivity to the audience; for example, it would make little sense to suggest to many inner-city 13-year-olds that expensive activities such as scuba diving and snow skiing would be good alternatives to drugs.

Personal and Social Skills Several studies indicate that adolescents who smoke, drink, or use marijuana also get lower grades and are less involved in organized sports or school clubs. One view of this is that students might take up substance use in response to personal or social failure. Therefore, teaching students how to communicate with others and giving them success experiences is another component of affective education approaches. For example, one exercise that has been used is having the students operate a school store. This is done as a group effort with frequent group meetings. The involved students are expected to develop a sense of social and personal competence without using drugs. Another approach is to have older students tutor younger students, which is designed to give the older students a sense of competence. An experiment carried out in Napa, California, combined these approaches with a drug education course, small-group discussions led by teachers, and classroom management techniques designed to teach discipline and communication skills and to

enhance the students' self-concepts.[7] Although a small effect on alcohol, marijuana, and cigarette use was found among the girls, the effects were gone by the one-year follow-up.

Antidrug Norms

In the mid-1980s, there were growing concerns that affective education approaches placed too little emphasis on the acquisition of skills needed to resist the interpersonal pressures to begin using drugs.

Refusal Skills In response, the next efforts at preventing drug use focused on teaching students to recognize peer pressure to use drugs and on teaching specific ways to respond to such pressures without using drugs. This is sometimes referred to as psychological inoculation. In addition to the focus on substance use, "refusal skills" and "pressure resistance" strategies are taught in a broader context of self-assertion and social skills training. The first successful application of this technique was a film in which young actors acted out situations in which one person was being pressured to smoke cigarettes. The film then demonstrated effective ways of responding to the pressure gracefully without smoking. After the film, students discuss alternative strategies and practice the coping techniques presented in the film. This approach has been demonstrated to be successful in reducing cigarette smoking in adolescent populations. It has been adapted for use with groups of various ages and for a wider variety of drugs and other behaviors, and students are taught from kindergarten on to "just say no" when someone is trying to get them to do something they know is wrong.

Drug-Free Schools In 1986 the federal government launched a massive program to support "drug-free schools and communities." Among other things,

---

values clarification: teaching students to recognize and express their own feelings and beliefs.
alternatives: alternative nondrug activities, such as relaxation or dancing.

Taking Sides

Montana Meth Project: Popular but Doesn't Decrease Drug Use

Over the past two decades, methamphetamine abuse has become a major global concern, especially in many rural communities in the western portion of the United States. In an effort to stop young people from experimenting with methamphetamine, in 2005, the state of Montana adopted a graphic advertising campaign called the Montana Meth Project. In general, the advertisements show in horrifying details a young person who uses methamphetamine for the first time, and then ends up engaging in some unthinkable act such as prostitution or assaulting strangers for money to buy methamphetamine. At the end of the advertisement, printed on the screen is the message: "Meth, not even once."

A year after its inception, the Montana Meth Project was recognized by the White House for its innovative approach to drug prevention. Indeed, preliminary findings from a report by the Montana Department of Justice suggested that the campaign was successful at decreasing methamphetamine use among teens. This apparent success led seven other states to join the "Meth Project" and adopt identical advertising strategies.

Is it true that negative advertisement campaigns decrease drug use? A critical review of the impact of the Montana Meth Project on methamphetamine use indicated that the advertisement campaign had no effect when preexisting downward trends in methamphetamine use were taken into account.[8] One potential reason for the lack of success is that the individuals who are most likely to use methamphetamine find the advertisements laughable because they exaggerate methamphetamine-related harmful effects. These individuals most likely know people who have used the drug, and the information presented in the advertisements are inconsistent with their own knowledge.

What are the potential negative consequences of presenting exaggerated or misleading information about drugs to young people? Some educators and health care professionals have expressed concern that the types of embellishment used by the Montana Meth Project decrease their credibility and relevance and lead many young people to reject other drug-related information from "official" sources, even when the information is accurate. What are your thoughts? Should drug prevention efforts exaggerate the effects of the targeted drug in order to discourage its use? Or could such misinformation undermine the trust young people have in official sources?

Box icon credit: ©Nova Development RF

---

the government provided millions of dollars' worth of direct aid to local school districts to implement or enhance drug-prevention activities. Along with this, the Department of Education produced a small book called *What Works: Schools without Drugs*,[9] which made specific recommendations for schools to follow. This book did not recommend a specific curriculum; its most significant feature was the emphasis on factors other than curriculum, such as school policies on drug and alcohol use. It suggested policies regarding locker searches, suspension, and expulsion of students. The purpose was not so much to take a punitive approach to alcohol or drug use as to point out through example and official policy that the school and community were opposed to drug and alcohol use by minors. Following this general drug-free lead, schools adopted "tobacco-free" policies, stating that not only the students but also teachers and other staff people were not to use tobacco products at school or on school-sponsored trips or activities.

According to this approach, the curriculum should include teaching about the laws against drugs, as well as about the school policies. In other words, as opposed to the 1970s values clarification approach of teaching students how to make responsible decisions for themselves, this approach wants to make it clear to the students that the society at large, the community in which they live, and the school in which they study have already made the decision not to condone drug use or underage alcohol use. This seems to be part of a more general educational trend away from "value-free" schools toward teaching values that are generally accepted in our society. For schools to be eligible for federal Drug-Free Schools funding, they must certify that their program teaches that "illicit drug use is wrong and harmful." Many of these policies remain in place today, even though the goal of a "drug-free society" is probably unrealistic.

Development of the Social Influence Model

Some of the most sophisticated prevention research in recent years has been focused directly on cigarette smoking in adolescents. This problem has two major advantages over other types of drug use, as far as prevention research is concerned. First, a large enough fraction of adolescents do smoke cigarettes so that measurable behavior change is possible in a group of reasonable size. In contrast, one would have to perform an intervention with tens of thousands of people before significant alterations in the proportion of heroin users would be statistically evident. Second, the health consequences of smoking are so clear with respect to cancer and heart disease that there is a fairly good consensus over goals: We'd like to prevent adolescents from becoming smokers. One research advantage is the relatively simple verification available for self-reported use of tobacco: Saliva samples can be measured for cotinine, a nicotine metabolite.

Virtually all the various approaches to drug-abuse prevention have been tried with smoking behavior; in fact, Evans's 1976 smoking prevention paper introduced the use of the psychological inoculation approach based on the **social influence model.**[10] Out of all this research, certain consistencies appear. The most important of these is that it *is* possible to design smoking prevention programs that are effective in reducing the number of adolescents who begin smoking. Some practical lessons about the components of those programs have also emerged.[11] For example, presenting information about the delayed consequences of smoking (possible lung cancer many years later) is relatively

ineffective. Information about the immediate physiological effects (increased heart rate, shortness of breath) is included instead. Some of the most important key elements that were shown to be effective were the following:

- *Training refusal skills* (e.g., eight ways to say no). This was originally based on films demonstrating the kinds of social pressures that peers might use to encourage smoking and modeling a variety of appropriate responses. Then the students engage in role-playing exercises in which they practice these refusal skills. By using such techniques as changing the subject or having a good excuse handy, students learn to refuse to "cooperate" without being negative. When all else fails, however, they are taught to be assertive and insist on their right to refuse.

- *Public commitment.* Researchers found that having each child stand before his or her peers and promise not to start smoking and sign a pledge not to smoke are effective prevention techniques.

- *Countering advertising.* Students are shown examples of cigarette advertising, and then the "hidden messages" are discussed (young, attractive, healthy, active models are typically used; cigarette smoking might be associated with dating or with sports). Then the logical inconsistencies between these hidden messages and the actual effects of cigarette smoking (e.g., bad breath, yellow teeth, shortness of breath) are pointed out. The purpose of this is to "inoculate" the children against cigarette advertising by teaching them to question its messages.

- *Normative education.* Adolescents tend to overestimate the proportion of their peers who smoke. Presenting factual information about the smoking practices of adolescents

social influence model: a prevention model adopted from successful smoking programs.

Training in refusal skills, including role-playing exercises, is a key component of the social influence model. ©Diego Cervo/ Shutterstock.com RF

provides students with a more realistic picture of the true social norms regarding smoking and reduces the "everybody is doing it" attitude. When possible, statistics on smoking from the specific school or community should be used in presenting this information.

- *Use of teen leaders.* Presenting dry facts about the actual proportion of smokers should ideally be reinforced by example. If you're presenting the program to junior high students, it's one thing to *say* that fewer than one-fifth of the high school students in that community smoke, but it's another to bring a few high school students into the room and have them discuss the fact that neither they nor their friends smoke, their attitudes about smokers, and ways they have dealt with others' attempts to get them to smoke.

Possible improvements to those approaches are offered by the *cognitive developmental* approach to smoking behavior. McCarthy criticized the social influence/social skills training

model for assuming that all students should be taught social skills or refusal skills without regard to whether they need such training.[12] The model "is that of a defenseless teenager who, for lack of general social skills or refusal skills, passively accedes to social pressures to smoke." Alternative models have been proposed in which the individual makes active, conscious decisions in preparation for trying cigarettes, trying smoking and becoming an occasional or regular user. The decision-making processes, and thus the appropriate prevention strategy, might be different at each of these "stages of cognitive development" as a smoker. Furthermore, smokers who begin smoking very young behave differently than smokers who begin as older adolescents (e.g., those who start young show more unanimity in selecting the most popular brand). Unfortunately, adolescents continue to initiate smoking every year, and the risk and protective factors reviewed in Chapter 1 have more influence on smoking behavior (and on alcohol and other drug use) than any information or education programs yet devised.[13]

DARE

Perhaps the most amazing educational phenomenon in a long time had fairly modest beginnings in 1983 as a joint project of the Los Angeles police department and school district. Those who are familiar with the Drug Abuse Resistance Education (**DARE**) program will have recognized its components described under the social influence model of smoking cessation. The difference here is that the educational program with DARE is delivered by police officers, originally in fifth- and sixth-grade classrooms. By basing the curriculum on sound educational research, by maintaining strict training standards for the officers who were to present the curriculum, and by encouraging the classroom teacher to participate, some of the old barriers to having nonteachers responsible for curriculum were overcome. The officers are in uniform, and they use interactive techniques as described for the social influence

Drugs in Depth

Are We Better Off for Exaggerating the Horrors of Methamphetamine?

Over the past decade, concerns about illicit methamphetamine use have further intensified. Most media portrayals of methamphetamine use emphasized unrealistic effects and exaggerated the harms associated with the drug. For example, in January 2010, National Public Radio (NPR) ran a story entitled, "This Is Your Face on Meth, Kids." The story described a California sheriff who was trying to stop young people from experimenting with methamphetamine. With the help of a programmer, he developed a computer program that digitally altered teenagers' faces to show them what they would look like after using methamphetamine for 6, 12, and 36 months. These young people watched their images change from those of healthy, vibrant individuals to faces marred by open scabs, droopy skin, and hair loss. They were told that these were the direct physiological effects of using methamphetamine. Ninety percent of individuals who tried methamphetamine once, they were also told, would become "addicted."

There is no empirical evidence to support the claim that methamphetamine causes physical deformities. And the evidence shows that less than 15 percent of those who have ever used the drug will become addicted.

Veracity aside, the anti-methamphetamine media campaign and incredible statements made about the drug has led to considerable concern by the general public, which, in turn, inspired policy makers to pass new legislation. These laws focus on both methamphetamine and compounds used to make the drug illicitly (i.e., precursors). Amphetamine tablets were available over the counter in the United States until the early 1950s. In 1970, in response to perceived abuses of the drug in the 1960s, amphetamine was placed under Schedule II of the newly passed Controlled Substances Act. This meant that all amphetamines were classified under the most restrictive category for drugs available by prescription. More recently, the Comprehensive Methamphetamine Control Act of 1996 increased criminal penalties for trafficking and producing methamphetamines, and a 2005 law restricted access to the methamphetamine precursor pseudoephedrine, which is a key ingredient in over-the-counter cold medicines. Pharmacists and sellers of medications containing pseudoephedrine were required to place these medications behind the counter, and buyers were required to show a state-issued identification card and sign a log that could be used to track their purchases. Fearing that this inconvenience would decrease sales, many pharmaceutical companies simply replaced pseudoephedrine with phenylephrine. Unfortunately, compared with pseudophrine, phenylephrine is a less effective nasal decongestant, the condition for which these medications are most often used. This important unintended consequence is rarely discussed among supporters of these laws.

Have these actions decreased the availability of illicit methamphetamine? Yes and no. Initially, the supply of methamphetamine was substantially disrupted, but this effect was only temporary. Within 18 months, the methamphetamine market had returned to pre-intervention levels. This suggests that legislation aimed at restricting precursors such as pseudoephedrine may have only short-term effects on illicit drug markets, while it permanently reduces the ability of the whole population to obtain effective cold medications.

Box icon credit: ©Ingram Publishing/SuperStock RF

model. Most of the components are there: refusal skills, teen leaders, and a public commitment not to use illicit drugs. In addition, some of the affective education components are included: self-esteem building, alternatives to drug use, and decision making. The component on consequences of drug abuse is, no doubt, enhanced by the presence of a uniformed officer who can serve as an information source and symbol for concerns over gang activity and violence and can discuss

DARE: Drug Abuse Resistance Education, the most popular prevention program in schools.

arrest and incarceration. The 17-week program is capped by a commencement assembly at which certificates are awarded.

This program happened to be in place at just the right time, both financially and politically. With the assistance of drug-free schools money and with nationwide enthusiasm for new drug-prevention activities in the 1980s, the program spread rapidly across the United States. By the early 1990s, DARE programs were found in every state.

This program was accepted quickly by many schools, and endorsed enthusiastically by educators, students, parents, and police participants, even though its effectiveness in preventing drug use was not evaluated extensively until 1994.

In 1994, two important, large-scale studies of the effects of DARE were reported. One was based on a longitudinal study in rural, suburban, and urban schools in Illinois, comparing students exposed to DARE with students who were not.[14] Although the program had some effects on reported self-esteem, there was no evidence for long-term reductions in self-reported use of drugs. The other report was based on a review of eight smaller outcome evaluations of DARE, selected from 18 evaluations based on whether the reports had a control group, a pretest-posttest design, and reliable outcome measures.[15] The overall impact of these eight programs was to increase drug knowledge and knowledge about social skills, but the effects on drug use were marginal at best. There was a very small but statistically significant reduction of tobacco use and no reliable effect on alcohol or marijuana use.

A more recent review of 20 studies on DARE published in peer-reviewed journals found an average effect size that was small and not statistically significant.[16] The repeated failures to demonstrate a significant impact of the DARE program on drug use remain a dilemma in light of its widespread popularity. Communities have not abandoned the program. Instead, DARE America has developed additional programs, including DARE 1 PLUS (Play and Learn Under Supervision) as an extension to the elementary program, and curriculum for middle school and high school DARE programs designed to follow up with these older adolescents. We cannot yet evaluate the effectiveness of these additional programs.

Programs That Work

Several school-based drug-use prevention programs have been modeled after the successful social influence model and have components similar to those of DARE. A few of these programs have been demonstrated to have beneficial effects on actual drug use:

Project ALERT was first tested in 30 junior high schools in California and Oregon.[17] The program targeted cigarette smoking, alcohol use, and marijuana use. Before the program, each student was surveyed and classified as a nonuser, an experimenter, or a user for each of the three substances. The curriculum was taught either by health educators or by educators with the assistance of trained teen leaders. Control schools simply continued whatever health or drug curriculum they had been using. The program was delivered in the seventh grade, and follow-up surveys were done 3, 12, and 15 months later. Three "booster" lessons were given in the eighth grade.

Some school-based drug-use prevention programs have been shown to reduce initiation and levels of drug use.
©Stockbyte/Getty Images RF

The program surprisingly had no measurable effect on initiation of smoking by nonusers. However, those who were cigarette experimenters before the program began were more likely to quit or to maintain low rates of smoking than the control group. The group with teen leader support showed the largest reduction: 50 percent fewer students were weekly smokers at the 15-month follow-up.

The experimental groups drank less alcohol soon after the program was presented, for previous alcohol nonusers, experimenters, and users. However, this effect diminished over time and disappeared by the end of the study.

The most consistent results were in reducing initiation of marijuana smoking and reducing levels of marijuana smoking. For example, among those who were not marijuana users at the beginning, about 12 percent of the control-group students had begun using marijuana by the 15-month follow-up. In the treatment groups, only 8 percent began using during that time period, representing a one-third decrease in initiation to marijuana use.

Another program, the Life Skills Training program, has been subjected to several tests and has shown long-term positive results. This three-year program is based on the social influence model and teaches resistance skills, normative education, and media influences. Self-management skills and general social skills are also included. One study of this program found significantly lower use of marijuana, alcohol, and tobacco after six years. A subsequent application of this program among ethnic minority youth (Latino and African American) in New York City found reduced use on a two-year follow-up.[18]

Peers, Parents, and the Community

Our nation's public schools clearly are the most convenient conduit for attempts to achieve widespread social changes among young people, and that is why most efforts at drug-abuse prevention have been carried out there. However, peers, parents, and the community at large also exert powerful social influences on young people. Because these groups are less accessible than the schools, fewer prevention programs have been based on using parent and community influences. Nevertheless, important efforts have been made in all these areas.

Peer Programs

Most peer programs have occurred in the school setting, but some have used youth-oriented community service programs (such as YMCA, YWCA, and recreation centers) or have focused on "street" youth by using them in group community service projects.

- *Peer influence* approaches start with the assumption that the opinions of an adolescent's peers are significant influences on the adolescent's behavior. Often using an adult group facilitator/coordinator, the program's emphasis is on open discussion among a group of children or adolescents. These discussions might focus on drugs, with the peer group discussing dangers and alternatives, or they might simply have the more general goal of building positive group cohesiveness, a sense of belonging, and communication skills.

- *Peer participation* programs often focus on groups of youth in high-risk areas. The idea here is that young people participate in making important decisions and in doing significant work, either as "peers" with cooperating adults or in programs managed almost entirely by the youth themselves. Sometimes participants are paid for community service work, in other cases they engage in money-making businesses, and sometimes they provide youth-oriented information services. These groups almost never focus on drug use in any significant way; rather, the idea is to help people become participating members of society.

The benefits of these "extracurricular" peer approaches are measurable in terms of acquired skills, improved academic success, higher self-esteem, and a more positive attitude toward peers and school. As to whether they alter drug use significantly, the data either are not available or are inconclusive for the most part.

Parent and Family Programs

The various programs that have worked with parents have been described as taking at least one of four approaches.[19] Most of the programs include more than one of these approaches.

- *Informational* programs provide parents with basic information about alcohol and drugs, as well as information about their use and effects. Although the parents often want to know simply what to look for, how to tell if their child is using drugs, and what the consequences of drug abuse are, the best programs provide additional information. One important piece of information is the actual extent of the use of various types of drugs among young people. Another goal might be to make parents aware of their own alcohol and drug use to gain a broader perspective of the issue. A basic rationale is that well-informed parents will be able to teach appropriate attitudes about drugs, beginning when their child is young, and will be better able to recognize potential problems relating to drug or alcohol use.
- *Parenting skills* might be taught through practical training programs. Communication with children, decision-making skills, how to set goals and limits, and when and how to say no to your child can be learned in the abstract and then practiced in role-playing exercises. One risk factor for adolescent drug and alcohol use is poor family relationships, and improving family interaction and strengthening communication can help prevent alcohol and drug abuse.
- *Parent support groups* can be important adjuncts to skills training or in planning community efforts. Groups of parents meet regularly to discuss problem solving, parenting skills, their perceptions of the problem, actions to be taken, and so on.

- *Family interaction* approaches call for families to work as a unit to examine, discuss, and confront issues relating to alcohol and drug use. Other exercises might include more general problem solving or response to emergencies. Not only do these programs attempt to improve family communication, but also the parents are placed in the roles of teacher of drug facts and coordinator of family action, thus strengthening their knowledge and skills.

One selective prevention program, called the Strengthening Families program, targets children of parents who are substance abusers. This program has been successfully implemented several times within diverse populations. It has three major goals: improving parenting skills, increasing children's skills (such as communication skills, refusal skills, awareness of feelings, and emotion expression skills), and improving family relationships (decreasing conflict, improving communication, increasing parent-child time together, and increasing the planning and organizational skills of the family). Children and parents attend evening sessions weekly for 14 weeks to learn and practice these skills. Evaluations of this program indicate that it reduces tobacco and alcohol use in the children as well as reduces substance abuse and other problems in the parents.[20]

Community Programs

Two basic reasons exist for organizing prevention programs at the community level. The first is that a coordinated approach using schools, parent and peer groups, civic organizations, police, newspapers, radio, and television can have a much greater impact than an isolated program that occurs only in the school, for example. Another reason is that drug-abuse prevention and drug education are controversial and emotional topics. Parents might question the need for or the methods used in drug education programs in the schools. Jealousy and mistrust about approaches can separate schools, police, church, and parent groups. A program that starts by involving all

Unintended Consequences

With a Girlfriend Like Her, You Don't Need Enemies

In May 2011, Palm Beach County School District police announced the arrest of 30 students for selling primarily small amounts of marijuana. It was the culmination of "Operation D-minus," during which undercover officers posed as students at three local high schools for an entire school year. They did all the things that students do, including taking classes, becoming Facebook friends, and flirting with other students; they also bought drugs from their classmates. At the schools, only the principals knew which "students" were officers.

Justin Laboy, an 18-year-old honor student, was one of people arrested during the sting operation. He fell in love with one of the undercover officers after several weeks of sharing personal information, flirting, and texting multiple times per day. She is an attractive 25-year-old Hispanic woman, who claimed to have moved to Florida from Queens, New York. Justin too is Hispanic and had moved from the Bronx, New York.

After about three months of flirting, one day the officer asked Justin if he could get her some marijuana. After several days of failed attempts, Justin was able to get her marijuana. He brought it to class and slipped it in her purse; she insisted on giving him $25 for the drug. He said, "No thanks, it's my gift to you." After several minutes of such discussion, Justin eventually took the money. In Florida, it's a felony to sell marijuana and the penalty is even harsher for selling it on school property.

Justin was arrested and spent more than a week in jail. Ultimately, he accepted a plea deal, which made him a convicted felon and gave him three years of probation. As a result of his conviction, Justin has lost many of his civil rights, including the right to vote or serve as a juror. He is also ineligible for federal or state aid and certain employment; he had planned on joining the U.S. Air Force after high-school graduation. This is no longer an option. He cannot obtain state licenses or hold public office. In other words, he can now be legally discriminated against.

While some argue that this is precisely the type of drug-use deterrence we need in our schools, many concerns have been raised about the fairness and effectiveness of this approach. Inducing a love-struck 18-year-old to purchase and sell a drug that she or he would not otherwise have sold seems unfair. It seems like entrapment. How many public resources are used to get the small amounts of marijuana (or other drugs) confiscated in these operations? Is it worth tarnishing young people's reputations and retarding their ability to make meaningful contributions to the society? We think not.

Box icon credit: ©Adam Gault/age fotostock RF

these groups in the planning stages is more likely to receive widespread community support. Clearly, the spread of the DARE program in the schools is based partly on the fact that it demonstrates and encourages cooperation between the police and the schools, as well as encourages parental involvement.

Community-based programs can bring other resources to bear. For example, the city council and local businesses can be involved in sponsoring alcohol-free parties, developing recreational facilities, and arranging field trips so that, when the school-based program talks about alternatives, the alternatives are available. The public media can be enlisted not only to publicize public meetings and programs but also to present drug- and alcohol-related information that reinforces what is learned in the other programs.

Communities Mobilizing for Change on Alcohol is one of SAMHSA's model prevention programs (see Table 17.1). The program works for change in alcohol ordinances in the community and alcohol policies of schools, universities, and civic organizations. It encourages parents, faith organizations, the police, city government, and all businesses and organizations within the community to promote the idea of limiting alcohol availability for 13- to 18-year-olds. The program was studied in 15 communities over a five-year period and resulted in decreased alcohol sales to minors, decreases in friends providing alcohol to minors, and decreases in self-reported drinking in the targeted age group.

Table 17.1
Effective Prevention Programs

Model Programs

- Across Ages
- Lions Quest Skills for Adolescence
- Alcohol: True Stories Hosted by Matt Damon
- The Michigan Model for Health
- All Stars
- ModerateDrinking.com and Moderation Management
- Athletes Training and Learning to Avoid Steroids (ATLAS)
- Nurse-Family Partnership
- Brief Alcohol Screening and Intervention for College Students (BASICS)
- Project ALERT
- Brief Strategic Family Therapy
- Project EX
- CARE
- Project Northland
- Caring School Community
- Project SUCCESS
- CAST
- Project Towards No Drug Abuse
- Class Action
- Project Towards No Tobacco Use
- Coping with Work and Family Stress

- Protecting You/Protecting Me
- The Curriculum-Based Support Group
- SPORT
- Drugs: True Stories
- Start Taking Alcohol Risks Seriously (STARS) for Families
- Familias Unidas
- Storytelling for Empowerment
- Good Behavior Game
- The Strengthening Families Program: For Parents and Youth 10–14
- Guiding Good Choices
- Strong African American Families
- Healthy Workplace
- Team Awareness
- Hip-Hop 2 Prevent Substance Abuse and HIV
- Too Good for Drugs
- Keep a Clear Mind (KACM)
- Training for Intervention ProcedureS (TIPS) for the University
- Keepin' It REAL
- Wellness Outreach at Work
- LifeSkills Training (LST)
- Lions Quest Skills for Adolescence

Prevention in the Workplace

As a part of its efforts to reduce the demand for drugs, the federal government has encouraged private employers, especially those who do business with the government, to adopt policies to prevent drug use by their employees. The most consistent feature of these programs is random urine screens. In 1989, rules went into effect requiring all companies and organizations that obtain grants or contracts from the federal government to adopt a "drug-free workplace" plan. The exact nature of the plan is up to the company, but guidelines were produced by the Department of Labor. Modeled after the Education Department's *What Works* book, the Labor Department's is called *What Works: Workplaces without Drugs.*[21] At a minimum, the Labor Department expects employers to state clearly that drug use on the job is unacceptable and to notify employees of the consequences of violating company policy regarding drug use. The ultimate goal is not to catch drug users and fire them but to prevent drug use by making it clear that it is not condoned.

What Should We Be Doing?

By now you have picked up some ideas for things to do to reduce drug use, as well as some things to avoid doing. But the answer as to what needs to be done in a particular situation depends on the motivations for doing it. Most states require drug- and alcohol-abuse prevention education as part of a health curriculum, for example. If that is the primary motive for doing something, and if there doesn't seem to be a particular problem with substance abuse in the schools, then the best thing would be to adopt one of the modern school-based programs that have been developed for this purpose, to make sure the teachers and other participants are properly trained in it, and to go ahead. In selecting from among the curricula, a sensible, balanced approach that combines some factual information with social skills training, perhaps integrated into the more general themes of health, personal values, and decision making, would be appropriate. The ones mentioned in the section "Programs That Work" fit this general description, and each deserves a careful look. Above all, avoid sensational scare stories, preachy approaches from the teacher to the student, and untrained personnel developing their own curricula. Another good thing to avoid is the inadvertent demonstration of how to do things you don't want students to do.

If, on the other hand, there is a public outcry about the "epidemic" of drugs and alcohol abuse in the community, speakers have inflamed passions, and there is a widespread fervor to do something about it, this presents both a danger and an opportunity. The danger is that this passionate group might attack and undermine the efforts already being made in the schools, substituting scary, preachy, negative approaches, which can have negative consequences. The opportunity lies in the possibility that this energy can be organized into a community planning effort, out of which could develop cooperation, increased parent understanding, a focus on family communication, interest in the lives of the community's young people, and increased recreational and creative opportunities.

The key to making this happen is convincing the aroused citizenry of the possibly negative consequences of doing what seems obvious and selling them on the idea of studying what needs to be done. A good place to start is by visiting the website of the Center for Substance Abuse Prevention (www.samhsa.gov/csap). This agency produces updated materials for groups interested in developing drug- and alcohol-abuse prevention programs, provides technical assistance and training to communities interested in developing programs, and offers Community Partnership Grants. (A list of CSAP model programs is shown in Table 17.1.)

Summary

- We can distinguish between education programs with the goal of imparting knowledge and prevention programs aimed at modifying drug-using behavior.

- Most of the research over the past 40 years has failed to demonstrate that prevention programs can produce clear, meaningful, long-lasting effects on drug-using behavior.

- The affective education programs of the 1970s have been criticized for being too value-free.

- Based on the success of the social influence model in reducing cigarette smoking, a variety of school-based prevention programs have used the same techniques with illicit drugs.

- The DARE program has been adopted rapidly and widely, despite research showing limited impact on drug-using behavior.

- Current school-based approaches use refusal skills, countering advertising, public commitments, and teen leaders. Several of these programs have been demonstrated to be effective.

- Other nonschool programs are peer-based through after-school groups or activities, parent-based through parent and family training, or community-based.

Review Questions

1. What is the distinction between secondary and tertiary prevention?
2. What is the knowledge-attitudes-behavior model, and what information first called it into question?
3. Explain what is meant by "value-free" values clarification programs, and why they fell out of favor in the 1980s.
4. When the Drug-Free Schools programs began in 1986, the emphasis shifted away from curriculum to what?
5. What were the five successful components of the social influence model for smoking prevention?
6. In Project ALERT, what was the impact of using teen leaders to assist the instructors?
7. What distinguishes DARE from other similar programs based on the social influence model?
8. What do ALERT and Life Skills Training have in common, besides their effectiveness?
9. What are some of the "parenting" skills that might be taught and practiced in a prevention program?
10. What is the most common component of "drug-free workplace" plans?

References

1. National Institute on Drug Abuse. *Drug Abuse Prevention for the General Population*. Washington, DC: U. S. Department of Health and Human Services, 1997.
2. Goodstadt, M. S. "School-Based Drug Education in North America: What Is Wrong? What Can Be Done?" *Journal of School Health* 56 (1986), pp. 278–81.
3. Swisher, J. D., and others. "Drug Education: Pushing or Preventing?" *Peabody Journal of Education* 49 (1971), pp. 68–75.
4. Swisher, J. D., and others. "A Comparison of Four Approaches to Drug Abuse Prevention at the College Level." *Journal of College Student Personnel* 14 (1973), pp. 231–35.
5. Blum, R. H., E. Blum, and E. Garfield. *Drug Education: Results and Recommendations*. Lexington, MA: D. C. Heath, 1976.
6. Swisher, J. D. "Prevention Issues." In R. I. DuPont, A. Goldstein, J. O'Donnell, eds. *Handbook on Drug Abuse*. Washington, DC: NIDA, U.S. Government Printing Office, 1979.
7. Schaps, E., and others. *The Napa Drug Abuse Prevention Project: Research Findings*. Washington, DC: DHHS Publication No. (ADM) 84-1339, U.S. Government Printing Office, 1984.
8. D. M. "Does Information Matter? The Effect of the Meth Project on Meth Use Among Youths." *Journal of Health Economics* 29 (2010), pp. 732–42.
9. U.S. Department of Education. *What Works: Schools without Drugs*. Washington, DC: 1987.
10. Evans, R. I. "Smoking in Children: Developing a Social Psychological Strategy of Deterrence." *Preventive Medicine* 5 (1976), pp. 122–27.
11. Flay, B. R. "What We Know about the Social Influences Approach to Smoking Prevention: Review and Recommendations." In C. S. Bell, and R. Battjes, eds. *Prevention Research: Deterring Drug Abuse Among Children and Adolescents*. Washington, DC: NIDA Research Monograph 63, DHHS Publication No. (ADM) 85-1334, U.S. Government Printing Office, 1985.
12. McCarthy, W. J. "The Cognitive Developmental Model and Other Alternatives to the Social Skills Deficit Model of Smoking Onset." In C. S. Bell, and R. Battjes, eds. *Prevention Research: Deterring Drug Abuse Among Children and Adolescents*. Washington, DC: NIDA Research Monograph 63, DHHS Publication No. (ADM) 85-1334, U.S. Government Printing Office, 1985.
13. Albaum, G., and others. "Smoking Behavior, Information Sources, and Consumption Value of Teenagers: Implications for Public Policy and Other Intervention Failures." *Journal of Consumer Affairs* 36 (2002), pp. 50–76.
14. Ennett, S. T., and others. "Long-Term Evaluation of Drug Abuse Resistance Education." *Addictive Behaviors* 19 (1994), p. 113.
15. Ennett, S. T., and others. "How Effective Is Drug Abuse Resistance Education? A Meta-Analysis of Project DARE Outcome Evaluations." *American Journal of Public Health* 84 (1994), p. 1394.
16. Pan, W., and H. Bai. "A Multivariate Approach to a Meta-analytic Review of the Effectiveness of the D.A.R.E. Program." *International Journal of Environmental Research and Public Health* 6 (2010), pp. 267–77.
17. Ellickson, P. L., and R. M. Bell. "Drug Prevention in Junior High: A Multi-site Longitudinal Test." *Science* 247 (1990), pp. 1299–1305.
18. Botvin, G. J., and S. P. Schinke. "Effectiveness of Culturally Focused and Generic Skills Training Approaches to Alcohol and Drug Abuse Prevention among Minority Adolescents: Two-Year Follow-Up Results." *Psychology of Addictive Behaviors* 9 (1995), p. 183.
19. "Parent Education." In *Prevention Plus: Involving Schools, Parents, and the Community in Alcohol and Drug Education*. Washington, DC: DHHS Publication No. (ADM) 84-1256, U.S. Government Printing Office, 1984.
20. National Institute on Drug Abuse. *Drug Abuse Prevention for At-Risk Groups*. Washington, DC: U.S. Department of Health and Human Services, 1997.
21. U.S. Department of Labor. *What Works: Workplaces without Drugs*. Washington, DC: 1989.

Check Yourself

Do Your Goals and Behaviors Match?

If you are a parent, think about your own family for a moment. Several of the risk and protective factors mentioned in Chapter 2 are related to family, and some of the effective prevention strategies target family activities. Consider the following questions (they can be answered either from the perspective of a child or a parent).

1. Is the interaction between the parent(s) and child generally positive?
2. Do the parents provide attention and praise to the child?
3. Is discipline consistent and usually effective and never involves physical punishment?
4. Is the child able to communicate his or her feelings to the parent(s)?
5. Does the child feel comfortable discussing rules and consequences, especially when it comes to the use of substances or other inappropriate behavior?
6. Does the family spend time together doing things every week?
7. Is the family capable of planning and organizing family activities?

If the answer to most of these questions is yes, then your family is probably functioning pretty well. If the answer to most of them is no, then think about what steps you can take to change this situation. That might include scheduling some time with a family therapist or counselor.

Rethinking Drug Policy: What Works, What's Possible, and What's Feasible

©Darryl Dyck/AP Images

Objectives

When you have finished this chapter, you should be able to:

- **Understand the goals of effective drug policy.**

- **Distinguish among drug legalization, drug prohibition, and drug decriminalization.**

- **Explain how relying on anecdotal information can lead to inappropriate drug policy.**

- **Understand how employers can legally discriminate against certain individuals.**

- **Give examples of countries that have decriminalized all illegal drugs.**

- **List specific strategies used to reduce harms associated with illegal drugs.**

Throughout this book, we have attempted to present a balanced perspective on the wide range of issues related to psychoactive substance use. We examined several types of substances and the biology underlying their effects. We also reviewed psychological and societal factors that influence drug effects and drug use. These are some of the important elements that governments consider when developing approaches to regulate the use of certain substances. Of course, effective drug policy attempts to strike a balance between individual freedom and public health and safety. When it comes to recreational drugs, such as the ones covered in this book, some countries strike a better balance than others. In this final chapter, we present a few successful strategies employed around the globe in an effort to help you understand what works, what's possible, and what's feasible.

Impetus for Change

As we have seen, the development of drug policy usually occurs in response to some crisis, during which there is considerable hyping of anecdotal reports and extensive misinterpretation of the scientific evidence when it is even considered. This situation has not only wrongly stigmatized specific individuals who are identified as users of certain drugs, but it has also led to inappropriate drug policies. We have documented the racial discrimination that flourishes under these conditions and how this discrimination has been especially devastating for black males. Selective targeting and racial discrimination in the application of drug laws contributes to some horrifying statistics. In the United States, nearly one-third of those arrested for drug law violations are black,[1] although drug use rates do not differ by race. Black males comprise about 6 percent of the general population but make up nearly 40 percent of the incarcerated population.[2] We have also pointed out that deaths caused by drug overdoses continue to be a major public health concern. The majority of these deaths are caused by ingesting a combination of various sedating drugs. Rarely are overdose deaths caused by a single drug. This suggests a need for better drug education in the public domain. These are just a few observations that have spurred many people to reconsider how drugs should be regulated.

Drug Decriminalization

Many individuals are uncomfortable with the idea of legalizing all drugs. But **drug legalization** is not the only option available to societies that reconsider what drug policies should be in place. **Drug prohibition**, the most prevalent current form of drug policy in the United States, and drug legalization are on opposite ends of the drug policy continuum. There are multiple options in between. One such option is **drug decriminalization**.

Decriminalization is often confused with legalization. They are not the same thing. The major difference is that under legalization, the sale, acquisition, use, and possession of recreational drugs are legal for adults. Current federal policies regulating alcohol and tobacco are examples of drug legalization. Under decriminalization, by contrast, the acquisition, use, and possession of drugs can be punished by a citation much like for traffic violations, for example, with fines or warnings. Bear in mind that the drugs still are *not* legal, but infractions do not lead to criminal convictions—an important component that has contributed to large incarceration rates in the United States and egregious human rights violations around the world.

Criminal convictions have also led to *de facto* and legal discrimination. For example, employers often discriminate against people who have been criminally convicted by choosing not to hire them. In addition, those with criminal records may find themselves in similar predicaments when seeking housing, government benefits, or drug treatment, and they often lose the right to vote. The major feature under decriminalization is that individuals are not arrested for simple drug possession, which

becomes even more important when one considers these facts: (1) drug offenses are the single most common cause of arrests,[3] and (2) each year, more than 80 percent of arrests in the United States for drug offenses involve only simple *possession*.[4] In simpler terms, drug decriminalization would dramatically decrease the number of arrests and allow law enforcement to focus on more serious crimes. We should note that the *selling* of all illicit drugs, however, remains a criminal offense under decriminalization laws.

Drug decriminalization is not a new concept. In fact, a handful of states, including California, Massachusetts, and New York, have decriminalized marijuana. Although the specifics vary from state to state, in general the laws stipulate that being caught with less than an ounce of marijuana or smoking the drug in public is punishable by a civil fine of $100. No state has decriminalized other recreational drugs, in part, because of the perceived dangers associated with drugs such as cocaine or heroin. Within these pages, we have shown that many of the harmful effects associated with certain drugs have been exaggerated.

Around the globe, a handful of countries have decriminalized all illegal drugs. In Spain, for example, possession of drugs for personal use has never been a criminal offense, and in the Czech Republic, drug decriminalization became the law in the 1990s. But the country that has received the most attention for decriminalizing drugs is Portugal. In late 2000, Portugal decriminalized all illegal drugs, including, cocaine, heroin, methamphetamine, 3,4-methylenedioxymethamphetamine (MDMA, or ecstasy)—in short, everything.

It might be instructive to explain how the Portuguese system works. Acquisition, possession, and use of recreational drugs for personal use—defined as quantities up to a 10-day supply—are no longer criminal offenses. Individuals stopped by police and found to have drugs may be given a verbal warning or the equivalent of a traffic ticket. They are not arrested and stigmatized with a criminal record. If given a ticket, they may be required to appear before a local panel called (in translation) the "Commission for Dissuasion of Drug Addiction," typically consisting of a social worker, a medical professional like a psychologist or a psychiatrist, and a lawyer. Note that police officers are not included, in part, because they do not have training in assessing substance use disorders and, in part, because this is not a criminal proceeding.

The panel is set up to address drug use as a potential health problem. The idea is to encourage those who use drugs to discuss their drug use in an open and honest manner with people who will serve as health experts and advisors, not adversaries. The person sits at a table with the panel. If he or she is not thought to have a drug problem, nothing further is usually required, other than payment of a fine, if determined. Treatment is recommended for those who are found to have drug problems—and referral for appropriate care is made. Still, treatment attendance is not mandatory. Repeat offenders, however—fewer than 10 percent of those seen every year—can receive noncriminal punishments like suspension of their driver's license or being banned from a specific neighborhood known for drug sales.

The Portuguese seem to be happy with their drug regulation system. Overall, they have increased spending on prevention and treatment, and decreased spending for criminal prosecution and imprisonment. The number of drug-induced deaths has dropped, as have overall rates of drug use, especially among young people (15–24 years old). In general, drug use rates in Portugal are similar, or slightly better, than those in other European Union countries.[5] From the perspective of many global observers as well as the Portuguese, Portugal's experiment with decriminalization has been successful. No, it did not stop all drug use. That would have been an unrealistic expectation. The Portuguese continue to alter their consciousness with psychoactive substances, just as their contemporaries and all human societies have before them. But they do not seem to have the problem of wide-scale discrimination in the enforcement of drug laws; nor do they have the problems of stigmatizing, marginalizing, and incarcerating substantial proportions of

their citizens for minor drug violations. Together, these are some of the reasons more countries are seriously considering drug decriminalization as a potential option.

Uncommon Strategies to Enhance Public Health and Safety

It is important for you to understand that drug decriminalization does not address other important concerns related to illegal drug use, for instance, drug quality control and violence in drug trafficking. Sometimes illegal drug sellers may cut or spike their drugs with other substances that may be more dangerous than the drug that customers are seeking. For example, recent media reports suggest that illicit heroin is frequently adulterated with fentanyl. Fentanyl produces a high similar to that of heroin but is far more potent, meaning that less fentanyl is required to produce an effect, including overdose. This, of course, can be fatal for unsuspecting heroin users who ingest too much of the substance thinking that it is heroin alone.

Under drug legalization, of course, drug quality control is regulated by the government. Today, the risk of alcohol drinkers dying from contaminated alcoholic beverages is considerably lower than the situation during alcohol prohibition when bootleggers were the only source through which the drug could be obtained. The point is that although decriminalization is ineffective for dealing with adulterated drugs, drug legalization is certainly one strategy to minimize the availability of adulterated

---

drug legalization: when the sale, acquisition, use, and possession of recreational drugs are legal for adults. Alcohol and tobacco are examples.

drug prohibition: when the sale, acquisition, use, and possession of drugs are banned.

drug decriminalization: when the possession of illegal drugs for personal use is not a criminal offense.

drugs and to decrease potential drug-related toxicity experienced by individuals who use drugs.

Drug trafficking, especially in new drug markets, is sometimes associated with violence and murder because drug supply organizations compete for greater shares of these illicit markets. Drug legalization has been suggested as one strategy to decrease violence associated with drug trafficking. Theoretically, this seems reasonable, but you should know that this specific conflict resolution tactic has yet to be embraced by any nation.

Given that many governments are not prepared to legalize drugs such as MDMA or heroin, are there alternative strategies to help users of illegal drugs to avoid ingesting dangerous adulterants? At least two approaches address this issue: free drug-purity testing services and administering of the illegal drug used as part of the addicted individual's treatment plan.

Drug Purity-Testing

In 1999, a Spanish nongovernmental organization, Energy Control, began offering anonymous and confidential drug-testing services. People who use illegal drugs submit their drug samples for testing in order to understand the composition and purity of the sample and to identify adulterants. The service is provided free of charge to Spanish citizens and is credited with decreasing many harms associated with illegal drug use. Following the lead of Energy Control, smaller organizations in a select number of countries have instituted limited forms of drug-testing services at music festivals and other events where psychoactive substance use is pervasive. Unfortunately, outside of Spain, for the most part, providers of drug-testing services are breaking the law by offering such services and run the risk of being prosecuted, even though these services clearly decrease harms associated with illegal drug use and potentially save lives.

Heroin-Assisted Treatment

In the late 1980s and early 1990s, Swiss public health officials were faced with increasing rates of HIV infections exacerbated by intravenous heroin use and needle sharing. In 1994, in an effort to address this crisis, Swiss authorities approved a program of heroin-assisted treatment, during which individuals meeting criteria for a heroin use disorder are eligible to receive a prescription for pharmaceutical-grade heroin as part of their treatment. This decreases the likelihood that individuals enrolled in the program will use street heroin and be exposed to adulterants commonly found in heroin obtained via illicit markets. Heroin administration is just one part of this approach (albeit an important one). In addition to receiving two daily injections of heroin, individuals selected for this program are assigned a nurse, physician, psychologist, and social worker to aid in their care and to address the multiple issues that accompany heroin addiction.

Switzerland's heroin-assisted treatment programs are credited with decreasing the number of Swiss who contracted the HIV virus and the number of these individuals who died from AIDS-related illnesses in the 1990s.[6] These programs have also reduced the public use of heroin (e.g., in "needle parks," which had become an embarrassment for Swiss politicians and public health officials). As a result of more than 20 years of successful implementation of heroin-assisted treatment programs in Switzerland, similar programs have been initiated by several other countries, including Belgium, Canada, Denmark, Germany, the Netherlands, and the United Kingdom.

Safe Drug Consumption Sites

The availability of safe consumption sites is another approach taken by some countries to combat drug overdoses and to decrease the spread of blood-borne illness, including HIV and hepatitis C. Consumption sites are usually designed to be accessible to drug users who may not be well connected to other health care services. Therefore, many people view these facilities as part of a continuum of care for people with addiction, mental illness, HIV/AIDS, and hepatitis.

In these clean, safe, and protective facilities, people who use drugs are permitted to consume their substance of choice under medical supervision, although the supervision is not overbearing or intrusive. Nonetheless, this component can be crucial if a client experiences a drug overdose, which sometimes occurs in these facilities. Trained medical personnel are prepared to reverse these overdoses. Clients of consumption sites are also provided with clean drug kits, such as needles, syringes, pipes, and the like, to lessen harms associated with contaminated drug equipment. Safe consumption facilities are located in multiple countries around the globe (e.g., Canada, Switzerland, and the United States) and are increasing in popularity.

Concluding Remarks

Given the successes associated with drug decriminalization in countries such as the Czech Republic, Portugal, Spain, and Switzerland, it is striking that more countries have not implemented similar policies. It seems that many of those in positions to influence drug policy still remain uninformed about the findings from countries other than their own. And several nations' drug policies are based largely on misinformation and not evidence. Pharmacology—or actual drug effects—plays less of a role when policies are devised. As such, members of our society are frequently misled to believe that cocaine, heroin, methamphetamine, or some other drug fad is so dangerous that any possession or use of it should not be tolerated and deserves to be severely punished. Decriminalization, or any other policy perceived to be permissive, is inconsistent with this misguided perspective.

To begin a serious national discussion about drug policy, first, large segments of the public will have to be reeducated about drugs, separating the real potential dangers from exaggerations. We hope this book is a step in that direction, but we recognize that this is only the beginning of a long journey to obtain accurate and objective information about drugs and drug policy. As you begin this journey, you are now armed with the knowledge that scientists have studied nearly all of the popular recreational drugs used by people. We have learned a great deal about the conditions under which either positive or negative effects are more likely to occur. It is our responsibility to share this information with individuals who use drugs and with those in positions to help keep them safe. And as more people are exposed to the broad range of evidence from around the world, perhaps more rational drug policy will follow.

Summary

- Ideal drug policy strikes a balance between individual freedom and public health and safety.

- A drug-related crisis is usually the impetus for developing new drug policies.

- Developing drug policies based on anecdotal information often leads to inappropriate policies, which can have unintended consequences such as racial discrimination.

- Drug legalization, drug prohibition, and drug decriminalization are three different forms of drug policies.

- Drug decriminalization is the removal of criminal penalties for drug possession in amounts consistent with personal use.

- Employers are allowed to discriminate against people who have been convicted of drug-related felony crimes.

- Drug-related offenses are the single most common cause of arrests.

- Multiple countries have decriminalized all drugs.

- Under drug legalization, the number of impurities and adulterants in drugs, and violence associated with drug trafficking would decrease.

- Drug purity-testing services help to decrease many of the harms associated with illegal drug use.

- Switzerland's heroin-assisted treatment programs helped to decrease the number of people who contracted the HIV virus.

- In safe drug consumption facilities, individuals are allowed to consume their substance of choice under medical supervision.

Review Questions

1. What are two important factors that should be considered when developing effective drug policy?
2. What are some events that may lead to the development of new drug policy?
3. Give an example of an unintended consequence associated with inappropriate drug policy?
4. Compare and contrast drug legalization and drug decriminalization.
5. How might employers discriminate against someone who has been convicted of a drug-related crime?
6. Explain how one might decrease the number of impurities found in illegal drugs through effective drug policy.
7. What are safe drug consumption facilities?

References

1. U.S. Department of Justice. "Arrests by Race 2013." In *Crime in the United States: 2013*. Retrieved from http://www.fbi.gov/about-us/cjis/ucr/crime-in-the-u.s/2013/crime-in-the-u.s.-2013/tables/table-43
2. Carson, E. A. *Prisoners in 2013*. Washington, DC: U.S. Bureau of Justice Statistics, 2014. Retrieved from http://www.bjs.gov/content/pub/pdf/p13.pdf
3. U.S. Department of Justice. "Persons Arrested." In *Crime in the United States: 2012*. Retrieved from https://ucr.fbi.gov/crime-in-the-u.s/2012/crime-in-the-u.s.-2012/persons-arrested/persons-arrested
4. U.S. Department of Justice. "Persons Arrested." In *Crime in the United States: 2014*. Retrieved from https://ucr.fbi.gov/crime-in-the-u.s/2014/crime-in-the-u.s.-2014/persons-arrested/main
5. Hughes, C. E., and A. Stevens. "A Resounding Success or a Disastrous Failure: Re-examining the Interpretation of Evidence on the Portuguese Decriminalisation of Illicit Drugs," *Drug & Alcohol Review* 31 (2012): 101–113.
6. Csete, J. *From the Mountaintops: Drug Policy Change in Switzerland*. New York: Global Drug Policy Program, Open Society Foundations, 2010.

A

Abilify: aripiprazole. A typical antipsychotic.

acamprosate: Campral. Treatment for alcohol dependence.

acetaminophen: OTC analgesic. Similar to aspirin in its effects.

acetophenazine: Tindal. Antipsychotic.

acetylsalicylic acid: aspirin. OTC analgesic.

alprazolam: Xanax. Benzodiazepine sedative.

Amanita muscaria: hallucinogenic mushroom.

Ambien: zolpidem. Non-benzodiazepine sedative-hypnotic.

amitriptyline: Elavil, Endep. Tricyclic antidepressant.

amobarbital: Amytal. Barbiturate sedative-hypnotic.

amoxapine: Asendin. Tricyclic antidepressant.

amphetamine: Benzedrine. CNS stimulant and sympathomimetic.

Amytal: amobarbital. Barbiturate sedative-hypnotic.

Anavar: oxandrolone. Anabolic steroid.

angel dust: street name for PCP.

Antabuse: disulfiram. Alters metabolism of alcohol; used to treat alcohol dependence.

aprobarbital: Alurate. Barbiturate sedative-hypnotic.

Aripiprazole: Abilify. A typical antipsychotic.

Artane: trihexyphenidyl. Anticholinergic used to control extrapyramidal symptoms.

Asendin: amoxapine. Tricyclic antidepressant.

aspirin: acetylsalicylic acid. OTC analgesic.

Ativan: lorazepam. Benzodiazepine sedative.

atropine: anticholinergic.

Aventyl: nortriptyline. Tricyclic antidepressant.

ayahuasca: a combination of two plants, one of which contains DMT. Hallucinogen.

B

belladonna: poisonous anticholinergic plant.

Benzedrine: amphetamine. CNS stimulant and sympathomimetic. Brand name no longer used.

benzodiazepines: class of sedative-hypnotics that includes diazepam (Valium).

benztropine: Cogentin. Anticholinergic used to control extrapyramidal symptoms.

black tar: a type of illicit heroin.

bromide: group of salts with sedative properties.

buprenorphine: Subutex. Opioid used as a maintenance treatment for heroin users.

bupropion: Wellbutrin. Atypical antidepressant. Also Zyban, to reduce craving during tobacco cessation.

butabarbital: Butisol. Barbiturate sedative-hypnotic.

Butisol: butabarbital. Barbiturate sedative-hypnotic.

C

caffeine: mild stimulant found in coffee and in OTC preparations.

Campral: acamprosate. Treatment for alcohol dependence.

cannabis: the marijuana plant.

carbamazepine: Tegretol. Anticonvulsant also used as a mood stabilizer in bipolar disorder.

Catapres: clonidine. Antihypertensive drug shown to reduce narcotic withdrawal symptoms.

Celexa: citalopram. Atypical antidepressant.

Chantix: varenicline. Partial nicotine agonist used to reduce nicotine intake and craving during tobacco cessation.

chloral hydrate: Noctec. Nonbarbiturate sedative-hypnotic.

chlordiazepoxide: Librium. Benzodiazepine sedative.

chlorpheniramine maleate: OTC antihistamine.

chlorpromazine: Thorazine. Antipsychotic.

chlorprothixene: Taractan. Antipsychotic.

Cibalith: lithium citrate. Salt used in treating mania and bipolar affective disorders.

Citalopram: Celexa. Atypical antidepressant.

clenbuterol: an alpha-2 adrenergic agonist developed to treat asthma, but used by athletes to build muscle.

clonidine: Catapres. Antihypertensive drug shown to reduce narcotic withdrawal symptoms.

clorazepate: Tranxene. Benzodiazepine sedative.

clozapine: Clozaril. Atypical antipsychotic.

Clozaril: clozapine. Atypical antipsychotic.

cocaine: CNS stimulant and local anesthetic.

codeine: opioid analgesic found in opium.

Cogentin: benztropine. Anticholinergic used to control extrapyramidal symptoms.

Compazine: prochlorperazine. Antipsychotic.

creatine: natural substance found in meat and fish that might have anabolic properties and is used by athletes.

Cylert: pemoline. Stimulant used to treat ADD with hyperactivity.

D

Dalmane: flurazepam. Benzodiazepine hypnotic.

Darvon: propoxyphene. Opioid analgesic.

Datura: genus of plants, many of which are anticholinergic.

Demerol: meperidine. Opioid analgesic.

Depakene: valproic acid. Anticonvulsant also used as a mood stabilizer in bipolar disorder.

desipramine: Norpramin, Pertofrane. Tricyclic antidepressant.

Desoxyn: methamphetamine. CNS stimulant and sympathomimetic.

Desyrel: trazodone. Atypical antidepressant.

Dexedrine: dextroamphetamine. CNS stimulant and sympathomimetic.

dexfenfluramine: Redux. Appetite suppressant, removed from the market in 1997.

dextroamphetamine: Dexedrine. CNS stimulant and sympathomimetic.

dextromethorphan: OTC cough suppressant.

diazepam: Valium. Benzodiazepine sedative.

diethylpropion: Tenuate, Tepanil. Amphetamine-like appetite suppressant.

dihydrocodeine: opioid analgesic.

Dilaudid: hydromorphone. Opioid analgesic.

diphenhydramine: antihistamine.

disulfiram: Antabuse. Alters metabolism of alcohol; used to treat alcoholism.

DMT: dimethyltryptamine. Hallucinogen.

Dolophine: methadone. Opioid analgesic.

DOM: hallucinogen.

doxepin: Sinequan. Tricyclic antidepressant.

dronabinol: Marinol. Prescription form of delta-9-tetrahydrocannabinol.

E

Effexor: venlafaxine. Antidepressant (SSRI).

Elavil: amitriptyline. Tricyclic antidepressant.

Endep: amitriptyline. Tricyclic antidepressant.

endorphin: endogenous substance with effects similar to those of the opioid analgesics.

enkephalin: endogenous substance with effects similar to those of the opioid analgesics.

ephedrine: sympathomimetic used to treat asthma.

Equanil: meprobamate. Nonbarbiturate sedative-hypnotic.

Eskalith: lithium carbonate. Salt used in treating mania and bipolar affective disorders.

eszopiclone: Lunesta. Non-benzodiazepine sedative-hypnotic.

F

fenfluramine: Pondimin. Appetite suppressant, removed from the market in 1997.

fentanyl: Sublimaze. Potent synthetic analgesic.

flunitrazepam: Rohypnol. Benzodiazepine hypnotic, not sold in the U.S. Known as a "date-rape" drug.

fluoxetine: Prozac. Antidepressant (SSRI).

fluphenazine: Permitil, Prolixin. Antipsychotic.

flurazepam: Dalmane. Benzodiazepine hypnotic.

G

GEOdon: Ziprasidone. Atypical antipsychotic.

GHB: gamma hydroxybutyrate. CNS depressant, produced naturally in small amounts in the human brain. Has been used recreationally and, in combination with alcohol, has some reputation as a "date-rape" drug.

Ginkgo biloba: a dietary supplement believed by some to increase blood circulation.

H

Halcion: triazolam. Benzodiazepine hypnotic.

Haldol: haloperidol. Antipsychotic.

haloperidol: Haldol. Antipsychotic.

henbane: poisonous anticholinergic plant.

heroin: Diacetylmorphine. Narcotic analgesic.

hydrocodone: Opioid analgesic.

hydromorphone: Dilaudid. Opioid analgesic.

I

ibogaine: hallucinogen, also proposed to reduce craving in drug addicts.

ibuprofen: analgesic and anti-inflammatory.

imipramine: Janimine, Tofranil. Tricyclic antidepressant.

isocarboxazid: Marplan. MAO inhibitor used as antidepressant.

J

Janimine: imipramine. Tricyclic antidepressant.

K

Ketalar: ketamine. Dissociative anesthetic.

ketamine: Ketalar. Dissociative anesthetic.

Klonopin: Clonazepam. Benzodiazepine sedative-hypnotic, also used as an anticonvulsant.

L

LAAM: L-alpha-acetyl-methadol. Long-lasting synthetic opioid used in maintenance treatment of narcotic addicts.

Lamictal: lamotrigine. Anticonvulsant also used as a mood stabilizer in bipolar disorder.

lamotrigine: Lamictal. Anticonvulsant also used as a mood stabilizer in bipolar disorder.

laudanum: tincture (alcohol solution) of opium.

Lexapro: escitalopram. Atypical antidepressant.

Librium: chlordiazepoxide. Benzodiazepine sedative.

Lithane: lithium carbonate.

lithium carbonate, lithium citrate: salts used in treating mania and bipolar affective disorders.

Lithobid: lithium carbonate.

lorazepam: Ativan. Benzodiazepine sedative.

Lortab: acetaminophen-hydrocodone combination. Analgesic.

loxapine: Loxitane. Antipsychotic.

Loxitane: loxapine. Antipsychotic.

LSD: lysergic acid diethylamide. Hallucinogen.

Ludiomil: maprotiline. Tricyclic antidepressant.

Luminal: phenobarbital. Barbiturate sedative-hypnotic.

Lunesta: eszopiclone. Non-benzodiazepine sedative-hypnotic.

M

mandrake: anticholinergic plant.

maprotiline: Ludiomil. Tricyclic antidepressant.

marijuana: Common name for the cannabis plant and for its dried leaves.

Marinol: dronabinol. Prescription form of delta-9-tetrahydrocannabinol.

Marplan: isocarboxazid. MAO inhibitor used as antidepressant.

Mazanor: mazindol. Appetite suppressant.

mazinodol: Mazanor, Sanorex. Appetite suppressant.

MDA: stimulant-hallucinogen.

MDMA: stimulant-hallucinogen.

Mebaral: mephobarbital. Barbiturate sedative-hypnotic.

Mellaril: thioridazine. Antipsychotic.

meperidine: Demerol. Opioid analgesic.

mephobarbital: Mebaral. Barbiturate sedative-hypnotic.

meprobamate: Equanil, Miltown. Nonbarbiturate sedative-hypnotic.

mescaline: hallucinogen found in peyote cactus.

mesoridazine: Serentil. Antipsychotic.

methadone: Dolophine. Narcotic analgesic.

methamphetamine: Desoxyn, Methedrine. CNS stimulant and sympathomimetic.

methaqualone: Quaalude, Sopor. Nonbarbiturate sedative-hypnotic.

methylphenidate: Ritalin. Stimulant used to treat ADD with hyperactivity.

Metrazol: pentylenetetrazol. Convulsant formerly used in convulsive therapy.

Miltown: meprobamate. Nonbarbiturate sedative-hypnotic.

mirtazapine: Remeron. Atypical antidepressant.

Moban: molindone. Antipsychotic.

modafinil: Provigil. Atypical CNS stimulant.

molindone: Moban. Antipsychotic.

morphine: opioid analgesic.

N

naloxone: Narcan. Opioid antagonist.

naltrexone: Trexan, reVIA. Opioid antagonist. Used in treating alcoholism.

Nardil: phenelzine. MAO inhibitor used as antidepressant.

Navane: thiothixene. Antipsychotic.

Nembutal: pentobarbital. Barbiturate sedative-hypnotic.

Norpramin: desipramine. Tricyclic antidepressant.

nortriptyline: Aventyl, Pamelor. Tricyclic antidepressant.

Novocain: Procaine. Local anesthetic.

Numorphan: oxymorphone. Opioid analgesic.

O

olanzepine: Zyprex. Atypical antipsychotic.

opium: opioid analgesic.

oxandrolone: Anavar. Anabolic steroid.

oxazepam: Serax. Benzodiazepine sedative.

oxycodone: Percodan. Opioid analgesic.

OxyContin: continuous-release form of oxycodone.

oxymorphone: Numorphan. Opioid analgesic.

P

Pamelor: nortriptyline. Tricyclic antidepressant.

paraldehyde: nonbarbiturate sedative-hypnotic.

paregoric: tincture (alcohol solution) of opium.

Parnate: tranylcypromine. MAO inhibitor used as antidepressant.

paroxetine: Paxil. Antidepressant (SSRI).

Paxil: paroxetine. Antidepressant (SSRI).

PCP: phencyclidine, angel dust. Hallucinogen.

pemoline: Cylert. Stimulant used to treat ADD with hyperactivity.

pentazocine: Talwin. Opioid analgesic.

pentobarbital: Nembutal. Barbiturate sedative-hypnotic.

pentylenetetrazol: Metrazol. Convulsant formerly used in convulsive therapy.

Percodan: oxycodone. Opioid analgesic.

Permitil: fluphenazine. Antipsychotic.

perphenazine: Trilafon. Antipsychotic.

Pertofrane: desipramine. Tricyclic antidepressant.

peyote: cactus containing mescaline (hallucinogenic).

phencyclidine: PCP, angel dust. Hallucinogen.

phendimetrazine: amphetamine-like appetite suppressant.

phenelzine: Nardil. MAO inhibitor used as antidepressant.

phenmetrazine: Preludin. Amphetamine-like appetite suppressant.

phenobarbital: Luminal. Barbiturate sedative-hypnotic.

phentermine: Amphetamine-like appetite suppressant.

phenylpropanolamine (PPA): OTC appetite suppressant.

Pondimin: fenfluramine. Appetite suppressant, removed from the market in 1997.

Preludin: phenmetrazine. Amphetamine-like appetite suppressant.

prochlorperazine: Compazine. Antipsychotic.

Prolixin: fluphenazine. Antipsychotic.

propoxyphene: Darvon. Narcotic analgesic.

protriptyline: Vivactil. Tricyclic antidepressant.

Prozac: fluoxetine. Antidepressant (SSRI).

pseudoephedrine: OTC sympathomimetic.

psilocybin: hallucinogen from the Mexican psilocybe mushroom.

Q

Quaalude: methaqualone. Non-barbiturate sedative-hypnotic.

R

Redux: dexfenfluramine. Appetite suppressant, removed from the market in 1997.

Remeron: mirtazapine. Atypical antidepressant.

Restoril: temazepam. Benzodiazepine hypnotic.

reVIA: naltrexone. Opioid antagonist used in treating alcohol dependence.

Risperdal: risperidone. Atypical antipsychotic.

risperidone: Risperdal. Atypical antipsychotic.

Ritalin: methylphenidate. Stimulant used to treat ADHD.

Rohypnol: flunitrazepam. Benzodiazepine hypnotic, not sold in the U.S., known as a "date-rape" drug.

S

Saint John's wort: a dietary supplement used by some to treat depression.

SAMe: S-adenosyl-L-methionine. Dietary supplement proposed as a possible treatment for depression.

Sanorex: mazindol. Appetite suppressant.

scopolamine: anticholinergic.

secobarbital: Seconal. Barbiturate sedative-hypnotic.

Seconal: secobarbital. Barbiturate sedative-hypnotic.

Serax: oxazepam. Benzodiazepine sedative.

Serentil: mesoridazine. Antipsychotic.

Sernyl: former brand name for PCP.

sertraline: Zoloft. Antidepressant (SSRI).

Sinequan: doxepin. Tricyclic antidepressant.

Sonata: zaleplon. Non-benzodiazepine sedative-hypnotic.

Sopor: methaqualone. Non-barbiturate sedative-hypnotic.

Steroids: Various important hormones and their chemical derivatives. Usually refers to the anabolic steroids used by athletes and body builders.

stanozolol: Winstrol. Anabolic steroid.

Stelazine: trufluoperazine. Antipsychotic.

Sublimaze: fentanyl. Potent synthetic analgesic.

Subutex: buprenorphine. Opioid used as a maintenance treatment for heroin users.

T

Talwin: pentazocine. Opioid analgesic.

Taractan: chlorprothixene. Antipsychotic.

Tegretol: carbamazepine. Anticonvulsant also used as a mood stabilizer in bipolar disorder.

temazepam: Restoril. Benzodiazepine hypnotic.

Tenuate: diethylpropion. Amphetamine-like appetite suppressant.

Tepanil: diethylpropion. Amphetamine-like appetite suppressant.

Teslac: testolactone. Anabolic steroid.

testolactone: Teslac. Anabolic steroid.

theophylline: mild stimulant found in tea; used to treat asthma.

thioridazine: Mellaril. Antipsychotic.

thiothixene: Navane. Antipsychotic.

Thorazine: chlorpromazine. Antipsychotic.

Tindal: acetophenazine. Antipsychotic.

TMA: indole hallucinogen.

Tofranil: imipramine. Tricyclic antidepressant.

Tranxene: clorazepate. Benzodiazepine sedative.

tranylcypromine: Parnate. MAO inhibitor used as an antidepressant.

trazodone: Desyrel. Atypical antidepressant.

Trexan: naltrexone. Opioid antagonist.

triazolam: Halcion. Benzodiazepine hypnotic.

trifluoperazine: Stelazine. Antipsychotic.

trihexyphenidyl: Artane. Anticholinergic used to control extrapyramidal symptoms.

Trilafon: perphenazine. Antipsychotic.

2-CB: catechol hallucinogen.

V

Valium: diazepam. Benzodiazepine sedative.

valproic acid: Depakene. Anticonvulsant also used as a mood stabilizer in bipolar disorder.

Varenicline: Chantix. Partial nicotine agonist used to reduce nicotine intake and craving during tobacco cessation.

venlafaxine: Effexor. Antidepressant (SSRI).

Vesprin: triflupromazine. Antipsychotic.

Vicodin: Hydrocodone-acetaminophen conbination. Analgesic.

Vivactil: protriptyline. Tricyclic antidepressant.

W

Wellbutrin: bupropion. Atypical antidepressant.

Winstrol: stanozolol. Anabolic steroid.

X

Xanax: alprazolam. Benzodiazepine sedative.

Z

zaleplon: Sonata. Non-benzodiazepine sedative-hypnotic.

Ziprasidone: Gedon. Atypical antipsychotic.

Zoloft: Sertraline. Antidepressant (SSRI).

Zyban: bupropion. Atypical antidepressant used to reduce craving during tobacco cessation.

zolpidem: Ambien. Non-benzodiazepine sedative-hypnotic.

Zyprexa: olanzepine. Atypical antipsychotic.

B

Resources for Information and Assistance

Federal Government Agencies

National Clearinghouse for Alcohol and Drug
Information
https://www.addiction.com/a-z/samhsas-national-
clearinghouse-for-alcohol-and-drug-information/

Drugs & Crime Data Center
Bureau of Justice Statistics
https://www.bjs.gov/index.cfm?ty=tp&tid=35#pubs

The National Institute on Alcohol Abuse and
Alcoholism (NIAAA)
https://www.niaaa.nih.gov/

The National Institute on Drug Abuse (NIDA)
https://www.drugabuse.gov/drugs-abuse/alcohol

Alcohol

Alcoholics Anonymous
http://www.aa.org/

MADD (Mothers Against Drunk Driving)
www.madd.org

National Council on Alcoholism and Drug Dependence
www.ncadd.org

Smoking

Tobacco Institute
www.tobaccoinstitute.com

Drugs

Drug Policy Alliance Network
www.drugpolicy.org

Harm Reduction Coalition
http://harmreduction.org/

National Families in Action
www.nationalfamilies.org

Families Against Mandatory Minimums (FAMM)
http://famm.org/

NORML (National Organization for the Reform of
Marijuana Laws)
www.norml.org

Multidisciplinary Association for Psychedelic Studies
(MAPS)
http://www.maps.org/

Glossary

A

abstinence Refraining completely from the use of alcohol or another drug. Complete abstinence from alcohol means no drinking at all.

abstinence syndrome See withdrawal syndrome.

abstinence violation effect The tendency of a person who has been abstaining (as from alcohol), and "slips," to go on and indulge fully, because the rule of abstinence has been broken.

acamprosate A medication used along with counseling in the treatment of alcohol abuse.

acetaldehyde The chemical product of the first step in the liver's metabolism of alcohol. It is normally present only in small amounts because it is rapidly converted to acetic acid.

acetaminophen An aspirinlike analgesic and antipyretic.

acetylcholine A neurotransmitter found in the parasympathetic branch and in the cerebral cortex.

acetylsalicylic acid The chemical known as aspirin; an over-the-counter drug that relieves pain and reduces fever and inflammation.

action potential A brief electrical signal transmitted along a neuron's axon.

active metabolites Pharmacologically active chemicals formed when enzymes in the body act on a drug.

acute In general, "sharp." In medicine, "rapid." Referring to drugs, the short-term effects or effects of a single administration, as opposed to *chronic*, or long-term, effects of administration.

Adderall (combination of amphetamine and dextroamphetamine) A medication used to treat ADHD and narcolepsy.

additive effects When the effects of two different drugs add up to produce a greater effect than either drug alone. As contrasted with *antagonistic* effects, in which one drug reduces the effect of another, or *synergistic* effects, in which one drug greatly amplifies the effect of another.

adenosine A chemical believed to be a neurotransmitter in the CNS, primarily at inhibitory receptors. Caffeine might act by antagonizing the normal action of adenosine on its receptors.

ADHD Attention-deficit/hyperactivity disorder, a learning disability. Terminology of the *DSM-5*.

adjunctive therapy A treatment used together with the primary treatment. Its purpose is to assist the primary treatment.

adulterated To make something poorer in quality by adding another substance. With regard to street drugs, also known as "cut" or "stepped on."

affective education In general, education that focuses on emotional content or emotional reactions, in contrast to *cognitive* content. In drug education, one example is learning how to achieve certain "feelings" (of excitement or belonging to a group) without using drugs.

agonist A substance that facilitates or mimics the effects of a neurotransmitter on the postsynaptic cell.

AIDS Acquired immunodeficiency syndrome, a disease in which the body's immune system breaks down, leading eventually to death. Because the disease is spread through the mixing of body fluids, it is more prevalent in intravenous drug users who share needles. The infectious agent is the human immunodeficiency virus (HIV).

alcohol Generally refers to grain alcohol, or ethanol, as opposed to other types of alcohol (e.g., wood or isopropyl alcohol), which are too toxic to be drinkable.

alcohol dehydrogenase The enzyme that metabolizes almost all of the alcohol consumed by an individual. It is found primarily in the liver.

alcohol use disorder In the *DSM-5*, defined as a pattern of pathological alcohol use that causes impairment of social or occupational functioning. This disorder may include tolerance and/or withdrawal symptoms.

Alcoholics Anonymous (AA) A worldwide organization of self-help groups based on alcoholics helping each other achieve and maintain sobriety.

alcoholism The word has many definitions and therefore is not a precise term. Definitions might refer to pathological drinking behavior (e.g., remaining drunk for two days), to impaired functioning (e.g., frequently missing work), or to physical dependence. See also *alcohol use disorder*.

alternatives (to drugs) Assuming that there are motives for drug use, such as the need to be accepted by a group, many prevention and treatment programs teach alternative methods for satisfying these motives; may include activities such as relaxation or dancing.

Alzheimer's disease A progressive neurological disease that occurs primarily in the elderly. It causes loss of memory and then progressively impairs more aspects of intellectual and social functioning. Large acetylcholine-containing neurons of the brain are damaged in this disease.

Amanita muscaria The fly agaric mushroom, widely used in ancient times for its hallucinogenic properties.

amotivational syndrome A hypothesized loss of motivation that has been attributed to chronic marijuana use.

amphetamine A synthetic CNS stimulant and sympathomimetic.

anabolic Promoting constructive metabolism; building tissue.

anabolic steroids Substances that increase anabolic (constructive) metabolism, one of the functions of male sex hormones. The result is increased muscle mass.

analgesic Pain-relieving. An analgesic drug produces a selective reduction of pain, whereas an *anesthetic* reduces all sensation.

anandamide A naturally occurring brain chemical with marijuana-like properties.

androgenic Masculinizing.

anencephaly A condition, at birth, in which major portions of the brain, skull, and scalp are absent.

anesthetic Sense-deadening. An anesthetic drug reduces all sensation, whereas an *analgesic* drug reduces pain.

angel dust A street name for phencyclidine (PCP) when sprinkled on plant material.

anhedonia Lack of emotional response; especially an inability to experience joy or pleasure.

animism The belief that objects and plants contain spirits that move and direct them.

Antabuse Brand name for disulfiram, a drug that interferes with the normal metabolism of alcohol, so that a person who drinks alcohol after taking disulfiram will become quite ill. Antabuse interferes with the enzyme aldehyde dehydrogenase, so that there is a buildup of acetaldehyde, the first metabolic product of alcohol.

antagonist A substance that prevents the effects of a neurotransmitter on the postsynaptic cell.

antecedents In the context of Chapter 1, behaviors or individual characteristics that can be measured before drug use and might therefore be somewhat predictive of drug use. These are not necessarily causes of the subsequent drug use.

anticonvulsant A drug that prevents or reduces epileptic seizures.

antidepressant A group of drugs used in treating depressive disorders. The MAO inhibitors, the tricyclics, and the SSRIs are the major examples.

antidiuretic The suppression of urine production.

antiemetic A drug used to reduce nausea and vomiting.

antihistamines A group of drugs that act by antagonizing the actions of histamine at its receptors. Used in cold and sinus remedies and in over-the-counter sedatives and sleep aids.

anti-inflammatory Reducing the local swelling, inflammation, and soreness caused by injury or infection. Aspirin has anti-inflammatory properties.

antipsychotics A group of drugs used to treat psychotic disorders, such as schizophrenia. Also called neuroleptics or major tranquilizers.

antipyretic Fever-reducing. Aspirin is a commonly used antipyretic.

antitussive Cough-reducing. Narcotics have this effect. Over-the-counter antitussives generally contain dextromethorphan.

anxiety disorders Mental disorders characterized by excessive worry, fears, avoidance, or a sense of impending danger. At pathological levels, these disorders can be debilitating.

anxiolytics Drugs, such as Valium, used in the treatment of anxiety disorders. Literally, "anxiety-dissolving."

aphrodisiac Any substance that is said to promote sexual desire.

area postrema A region of the brain stem, located in the medulla oblongata, that is important for triggering nausea and vomiting.

aspirin Originally Bayer's brand name for acetylsalicylic acid, now a generic name for that chemical.

ataxia Loss of coordinated movement; for example, the staggering gait of someone who has consumed a large amount of alcohol.

attention-deficit/hyperactivity disorder A learning disability accompanied by hyperactivity. More common in male children. This *DSM-5* diagnostic category replaces *hyperkinetic syndrome* and *minimal brain dysfunction*.

autoimmune disease A condition that occurs when the immune system mistakenly attacks and destroys healthy body tissue.

autonomic nervous system The branch of the peripheral nervous system that regulates the visceral, or automatic ("involuntary") functions of the body, such as heart rate and intestinal motility. In contrast to the *somatic*, or voluntary, nervous system.

axon A region of a neuron that extends from the cell body and is responsible for conducting the electrical signal to the presynaptic terminals.

axon terminals The end region of the axon.

B

BAC Blood alcohol concentration, also called blood alcohol level (BAL). The proportion of blood that consists of alcohol. For example, a person with a BAC of 0.10 percent has alcohol constituting one-tenth of 1 percent of the blood and is legally intoxicated in all states.

balanced placebo A research design in which alcohol is compared with a placebo beverage, and subjects either believe they are drinking alcohol or believe they are not.

barbiturate A major class of sedative-hypnotic drugs, including amobarbital and sodium pentothal.

basal ganglia A subcortical brain structure containing large numbers of dopamine synapses. Responsible for maintaining proper muscle tone as a part of the *extrapyramidal motor system*. Damage to the basal ganglia, as in Parkinson's disease, produces muscular rigidity and tremors.

bath salts When referring to drugs, this term has been used for any of several synthetic drugs similar to cathinone, a stimulant derived from khat.

behavioral tolerance Repeated use of a drug can lead to a diminished effect of the drug (tolerance). When the diminished effect occurs because the individual has learned to compensate for the effect of the drug, it is called behavioral tolerance. For example, a novice drinker might be unable to walk with a BAC of 0.20 percent, whereas someone who has practiced walking while intoxicated would be able to walk fairly well at the same BAC.

behavioral toxicity Refers to the fact that a drug can be toxic because it impairs behavior and amplifies the danger level of many activities. The effect of alcohol on driving is an example.

benzodiazepine The group of drugs that includes Valium (diazepam) and Librium (chlordiazepoxide). They are used as *anxiolytics* or *sedatives*, and some types are used as sleeping pills.

bhang A preparation of cannabis (marijuana) that consists of the whole plant, dried and powdered. The weakest of the forms commonly used in India.

binding The interaction between a molecule and a receptor for that molecule. Although the molecules float onto and off the receptor, there are chemical and electrical attractions between a specific molecule and its receptor, so that there is a much higher probability that the receptor will be occupied by its proper molecule than by other molecules.

biopsychosocial A theory or perspective that relies on the interaction of biological, individual psychological, and social variables.

bipolar disorder One of the major mood disorders. Periods of mania and periods of depression have occurred in the same individual. Also called *manic-depressive illness*.

black tar A type of illicit heroin usually imported from Mexico.

blackout A period of time during which a person was behaving, but of which the person has no memory. The most common cause of this phenomenon is excessive alcohol consumption, and blackouts are considered to indicate pathological drinking.

blood alcohol concentration A measure of the concentration of alcohol in the blood, expressed in grams per 100 ml (percentage).

blood-brain barrier Refers to the fact that many substances, including drugs, that can circulate freely in the blood do not readily enter the brain tissue. The major structural feature of this barrier is the tightly jointed epithelial cells lining blood capillaries in the brain. Drug molecules cannot pass between the cells but must instead go through their membranes. Small molecules and molecules that are lipid (fat) soluble cross the barrier easily. Obviously, all psychoactive drugs must be capable of crossing the blood-brain barrier.

brain stem The medulla oblongata, pons, and midbrain. Located between the spinal cord and the forebrain, and generally considered to contain the "oldest" (in an evolutionary sense) and most primitive control centers for such basic functions as breathing, swallowing, and so on.

brand name The name given to a drug by a particular manufacturer and licensed only to that manufacturer. For example, *Valium* is a brand name for diazepam. Other companies may sell diazepam, but Hoffman-LaRoche, Inc., owns the name *Valium*.

C

caffeinism Excessive use of caffeine.

Camellia sinesis The plant from which tea is made.

Cannabis Genus of plants known as marijuana or hemp. Includes *C. indica* and *C. sativa*.

carbon monoxide A poisonous gas found in cigarette smoke.

catheter A piece of plastic or rubber tubing that is inserted or implanted into a vein or other structure.

CBD Cannabidiol, a nonpsychoactive cannabinoid that is being tested to treat several illnesses, including epilepsy.

cell body The central region of a neuron, which is the control center.

central nervous system Brain and spinal cord.

cerebral cortex The outermost layer of the brain.

charas A preparation of cannabis, or marijuana, that is similar to hashish. The most potent form of marijuana commonly used in India.

chemical name For a drug, the name that is descriptive of its chemical structure. For example, the chemical name *sodium chloride* is associated with the *generic* name *table salt*, of which there may be several *brand* names, such as *Morton's*.

chipper An individual who uses heroin occasionally.

chlorpheniramine maleate A common over-the-counter antihistamine found in cold products.

chronic Occurring over time. Chronic drug use is long-term use; chronic drug effects are persistent effects produced by long-term use.

chronic obstructive lung disease A group of disorders that includes emphysema and chronic bronchitis. Cigarette smoking is a major cause of these disorders.

cirrhosis A serious, largely irreversible, and frequently deadly disease of the liver. Usually caused by chronic heavy alcohol use.

coca The plant *Erythroxylon coca*, from which cocaine is derived. Also refers to the leaves of this plant.

coca paste A crude, smokable extract derived from the coca leaf in the process of making cocaine.

cocaethylene A potent stimulant formed when cocaine and alcohol are used together.

cocaine A CNS stimulant and local anesthetic; the primary active chemical in coca.

cocaine hydrochloride The most common form of pure cocaine; it is stable and water soluble.

codeine A narcotic chemical present in opium.

cognitive-behavioral therapy A widely used form of psychotherapy that develops coping strategies for dealing with unhealthy patterns of thinking, feeling, and behaving.

comatose A state of unconsciousness from which the individual cannot be aroused.

congeners In general, members of the same group. With respect to alcohol, the term refers to other chemicals (alcohols and oils) that are produced in the process of making a particular alcoholic beverage.

contingency management A form of applied behavior analysis that provides some form of positive reinforcement when clients behave in desired ways. For example, a client who provides a urine sample in which no illicit drug is detected might receive a prepaid debit card with a $10 value.

controlled drinking The concept that individuals who have been drinking pathologically can be taught to drink in a controlled, nonpathological manner.

controlled substance A term coined for the 1970 federal law that revised previous laws regulating *narcotics and dangerous drugs*. Heroin and cocaine are examples of controlled substances.

correlate A variable that is statistically related to some other variable, such as drug use.

crack Street name for a smokable form of cocaine. Also called rock.

crank Street name for illicitly manufactured methamphetamine.

crystal meth Street term for a form of methamphetamine crystals, also called *ice*.

cumulative effects Drug effects that increase with repeated administrations, usually due to the buildup of the drug in the body.

CYP450 Cytochrome P450 refers to a group of enzymes found in the liver that are responsible for metabolizing foreign chemicals, including most drugs.

D

DARE Drug Abuse Resistance Education, the most popular prevention program in schools.

date-rape drug A substance given to someone without her knowledge to cause unconsciousness in order to have nonconsensual sex. Rohypnol and GHB have become known for such use. A 1996 U.S. law provides serious penalties for using drugs in this manner.

Datura A plant genus that includes many species used for their hallucinogenic properties. These plants contain anticholinergic chemicals.

DAWN Drug Abuse Warning Network, a federal government system for reporting drug-related medical emergencies and deaths.

DEA United States Drug Enforcement Administration, a branch of the Department of Justice.

delirium tremens Alcohol withdrawal symptoms, including tremors and hallucinations.

demand reduction Efforts to control drug use by reducing the demand for drugs, as opposed to efforts aimed at reducing the supply of drugs. Demand reduction efforts include education and prevention programs, as well as increased punishments for drug users.

dendrite A treelike region of a neuron that extends from the cell body and contains in its membrane receptors that recognize and respond to specific chemical signals.

depolarized When the membrane potential is less polarized.

depressant Any of a large group of drugs that generally slow activity in the CNS and at high doses induce sleep. Includes alcohol, the barbiturates, and other sedative-hypnotic drugs.

depression A major type of mood disorder.

detoxification The process of allowing the body to rid itself of a large amount of alcohol or another drug. Often the first step in a treatment program.

deviance Behavior that is different from established social norms and that social groups take steps to change.

dextromethorphan An over-the-counter cough control ingredient.

diagnosis The process of identifying the nature of an illness. A subject of great controversy for mental disorders.

distillation The process by which alcohol is separated from a weak alcohol solution to form more concentrated distilled spirits. The weak solution is heated, and the alcohol vapors are collected and condensed to a liquid form.

dopamine A neurotransmitter found in the basal ganglia and other regions of the brain.

dose-response curve A graph showing the relationship between the size of a drug dose and the size of the response (or the proportion of subjects showing the response).

double-blind procedure A type of experiment in which the patients and those evaluating them do not know which patients are receiving a placebo and which are receiving the test drug.

dronabinol The generic name for prescription THC in oil in a gelatin capsule.

drug Any substance, natural or artificial, other than food, that by its chemical nature alters structure or function in the living organism.

drug abuse The use of a drug in such a manner or in such amounts or in situations such that the drug use causes problems or greatly increases the chance of problems occurring.

drug decriminalization When the possession of illegal drugs for personal use is not a criminal offense.

drug dependence A state in which a person uses a drug so frequently and consistently that the individual appears to need the drug to function. This may take the form of *physical dependence*, or behavioral signs may predominate (e.g., unsuccessful attempts to stop or reduce drug use).

drug disposition tolerance The reduced effect of a drug, which can result from more rapid metabolism or excretion of the drug.

drug legalization When the sale, acquisition, use, and possession of recreational drugs are legal for adults. Alcohol and tobacco are examples of drugs that have been legalized.

drug misuse The use of prescribed drugs in greater amounts than, or for purposes other than, those prescribed by a physician or dentist.

drug prohibition When the sale, acquisition, use, and possession of drugs are banned.

drug recognition expert (DRE) A police officer trained to examine intoxicated individuals to determine which of several classes of drugs caused the intoxication.

DSM-5 *Diagnostic and Statistical Manual of Mental Disorders*, fifth edition, published by the American Psychiatric Association. It has become a standard for naming and distinguishing among mental disorders.

duration of action How long a drug's effects last.

dysentery An intestinal inflammation that can lead to severe diarrhea with mucus or blood in the feces.

E

Ecstasy Street name for the hallucinogen MDMA. Also called "XTC."

ECT Electroconvulsive therapy, or electroconvulsive shock treatment. A procedure in which an electrical current is passed through the head, resulting in an epileptic-like seizure. Although this treatment is now used infrequently, it is still considered to be the most effective and rapid treatment for severe depression.

ED$_{50}$ The effective dose for half the subjects in a drug test.

edible Any edible product that contains THC; usually brownies, cookies, and candies.

effective dose The dose of a drug that produces a certain effect in some percentage of the subjects. For example, an ED_{50} produces the effect in 50 percent of the subjects. Note that the dose will depend on the effect that is monitored.

emphysema A chronic lung disease in which tissue deterioration results in increased air retention and reduced exchange of gases. The result is difficulty breathing and shortness of breath. An example of a *chronic obstructive lung disease*, often caused by smoking.

endocannabinoids Cannabis-like chemicals that occur naturally in the brains of humans and other animals.

endorphins Morphine-like chemicals that occur naturally in the brains and pituitary glands of humans and other animals. There are several proper endorphins, and the term is also used generically to refer to both the endorphins and the enkephalins.

enkephalins Morphine-like chemicals that occur naturally in the brains and adrenal glands of humans and other animals. The enkephalins are smaller molecules than the endorphins.

entactogen (en tac to gen) Generating empathy and openness.

entheogen (en thee o gen) Generating the divine within.

enzyme A large, organic molecule that works to speed up or help along a specific chemical reaction. Enzymes are found in brain cells, where they are needed for most steps in the synthesis of neurotransmitter molecules. They are also found in the liver, where they are needed for the metabolism of many drug molecules.

ephedrine A drug derived from the Chinese medicinal herb *ma huang* and used to relieve breathing difficulty in asthma. A sympathomimetic from which amphetamine was derived.

epilepsy A disorder of the nervous system in which recurring periods of abnormal electrical activity in the brain produce temporary malfunction. There might or might not be loss of consciousness or uncontrolled motor movements (seizures).

ergogenic Energy-producing. Refers to drugs or other methods (e.g., blood doping) designed to enhance an athlete's performance.

ergotism A disease caused by eating grain infected with the ergot fungus. There are both psychological and physical manifestations.

F

FAS Fetal alcohol syndrome.

FDA United States Food and Drug Administration.

fen-phen A combination of two prescription weight-control medications, fenfluramine and phentermine. No longer prescribed due to concerns with toxicity to heart valves.

fermentation The process by which sugars are converted into grain alcohol through the action of yeasts.

fetal alcohol effect Individual developmental abnormalities associated with the mother's alcohol use during pregnancy.

fetal alcohol spectrum disorder Individual developmental abnormalities associated with the mother's alcohol use during pregnancy.

fetal alcohol syndrome Facial and developmental abnormalities associated with the mother's alcohol use during pregnancy.

flashback An experience reported by some users of LSD in which portions of the LSD experience recur at a later time without the use of the drug.

fly agaric mushroom *Amanita muscaria*, a hallucinogenic mushroom that is also considered poisonous.

free base In general, when a chemical salt is separated into its basic and acidic components, the basic component is referred to as the free base. Most psychoactive drugs are bases that normally exist in a salt form. Specifically, the salt cocaine hydrochloride can be chemically extracted to form the cocaine free base, which is volatile and can therefore be smoked.

functional disorder A mental disorder for which there is no known organic cause. Schizophrenia is a form of psychosis that is considered to be a functional disorder.

G

GABA An inhibitory neurotransmitter found in most brain regions; gamma-aminobutyric acid.

gamma hydroxybutyrate (GHB) A CNS depressant, produced naturally in small amounts in the human brain; has been used recreationally and, in combination with alcohol, has some reputation as a date-rape drug; chemically related to GABA.

ganja A preparation of *cannabis* (marijuana) in which the most potent parts of the plant are used.

gastrointestinal tract An organ system within the body that takes in food, digests it to extract and absorb energy and nutrients, and expels the remaining waste as feces and urine.

gateway substances Substances, such as alcohol, tobacco, and sometimes marijuana, that most users of illicit substances will have tried before their first use of cocaine, heroin, or other less widely used illicit drugs.

generic name For drugs, a name that specifies a particular chemical without being chemically descriptive or referring to a brand name. As an example, the *chemical name* sodium chloride is associated with the *generic name* table salt, of which there may be several *brand names*, such as Morton's.

glia Brain cells that provide firmness and structure to the brain, get nutrients into the system, eliminate waste, form myelin, and create the blood-brain barrier.

glutamate An excitatory neurotransmitter found in most brain regions.

GRAE "Generally recognized as effective"; a term defined by the FDA with reference to the ingredients found in over-the-counter drugs (see also *GRAS*).

GRAHL "Generally recognized as honestly labeled" (see also *GRAE* and *GRAS*).

grain neutral spirits Ethyl alcohol distilled to a purity of 190 proof (95 percent).

grand mal An epileptic seizure that results in convulsive motor movements and loss of consciousness.

GRAS "Generally recognized as safe"; a term defined by the FDA with reference to food additives and the ingredients found in over-the-counter drugs.

H

hallucinogen A drug, such as LSD or mescaline, that produces profound alterations in perception.

hash oil A slang term for oil of cannabis, a liquid extract from the marijuana plant.

hashish A potent preparation of concentrated resin from the *Cannabis* plant.

henbane A poisonous plant containing anticholinergic chemicals and sometimes used for its hallucinogenic properties. *Hyoscyamus niger*.

heroin Originally Bayer's name for diacetylmorphine, a potent narcotic analgesic synthesized from morphine.

HIV Human immunodeficiency virus. The infectious agent responsible for AIDS.

homeostasis A state of physiological balance maintained by various regulatory mechanisms; body functions such as blood pressure and temperature must be maintained within a certain range.

hookah A water pipe, often with more than one mouthpiece. Used to smoke tobacco or marijuana.

human growth hormone A pituitary hormone responsible for some types of giantism.

hyperactive Refers to a disorder characterized by short attention span and a high level of motor activity. The *DSM-5* term is *attention-deficit/hyperactivity disorder*.

hyperpolarized When the membrane potential is more negative.

hypnotic Sleep-inducing. For drugs, refers to sleeping preparations.

hypodermic syringe A device to which a hollow needle can be attached, so that solutions can be injected through the skin.

hypothalamus A group of nuclei found at the base of the brain, just above the pituitary gland.

I

ibogaine A hallucinogen that has been shown to reduce self-administration of cocaine and morphine in rats and is proposed to reduce craving in drug addicts.

ibuprofen An aspirinlike analgesic and anti-inflammatory.

ice The street name for crystals of methamphetamine hydrochloride.

illicit drug A drug that is unlawful to possess or use.

IND Approval to conduct clinical investigations on a new drug, filed with the FDA after animal tests are complete.

indole A type of chemical structure. The neurotransmitter serotonin and the hallucinogen LSD both contain an indole nucleus.

inhalants Any of a variety of volatile solvents or other products that can be inhaled to produce intoxication.

insomnia Inability to sleep. The most common complaint is difficulty falling asleep. Often treated with a hypnotic drug.

insufflation To take a drug through the nose.

intramuscular A type of injection in which the drug is administered into a muscle.

intraocular pressure The fluid pressure inside the eye.

intravenous (IV) A type of injection in which the drug is administered into a vein.

ion An atom or molecule that has a net electrical charge because of a difference in the number of electrons and protons.

ion channels Pores formed by proteins in the cell membrane, allowing the passage of ions from one side of the membrane to the other.

L

laissez-faire A theory that government should not interfere with business or other activities.

LD$_{50}$ The lethal dose for half the animals in a test.

lethal dose The dose of a drug that produces a lethal effect in some percentage of the animals on which it is tested. For example, LD$_{50}$ is the dose that would kill 50 percent of the animals to which it was given.

leukoplakia A whitening and thickening of the mucous tissues of the mouth. The use of chewing tobacco is associated with an increase in leukoplakia, considered to be a "precancerous" tissue change.

limbic system A system of various brain structures that are involved in emotional responses.

lipid solubility The tendency of a chemical to dissolve in oils or fats, as opposed to in water.

lipophilic The extent to which chemicals can be dissolved in oils and fats.

lithium A highly reactive metallic element, atomic number 3. Its salts are used in the treatment of mania and bipolar disorder.

longitudinal study A study done over a period of time (months or years).

look-alikes Drugs sold legally, usually through the mail, that are made to look like controlled, prescription-only drugs. The most common types contain caffeine and resemble amphetamine capsules or tablets.

M

ma huang A Chinese herb containing ephedrine, which is a sympathomimetic drug from which amphetamine was derived.

major depressive disorder A serious mental disorder characterized by a depressed mood. A specific diagnostic term in the *DSM-5*.

malting The process of wetting a grain and allowing it to sprout, to maximize its sugar content before fermentation to produce an alcoholic beverage.

mandrake *Mandragora officinarum*, a plant having a branched root that contains anticholinergic chemicals. Now classed among the other anticholinergic hallucinogens, this plant was widely believed to have aphrodisiac properties.

marijuana Also spelled marihuana; dried leaves of the *Cannabis* plant.

Marinol The brand name for prescription THC in oil in a gelatin capsule.

MDMA Methylenedioxy methamphetamine, a catechol hallucinogen related to MDA. Called "Ecstasy" or "XTC" on the street.

medial forebrain bundle A group of neuron fibers that projects from the midbrain to the forebrain, passing near the hypothalamus. Now known to contain several chemically and anatomically distinct pathways, including dopamine and norepinephrine pathways.

medical model With reference to mental disorders, a model that assumes that abnormal behaviors are symptoms resulting from a disease.

membrane A thin, limiting covering of a cell.

mental illness A term that, to some theorists, implies acceptance of a medical model of mental disorders.

mescaline The active hallucinogenic chemical in the peyote cactus.

mesolimbic dopamine pathway A group of dopamine-containing neurons that have their cell bodies in the midbrain and their terminals in the forebrain, on various structures associated with the limbic system. Believed by some theorists to be important in explaining the therapeutic effects of antipsychotic medications. Also believed by some theorists to be important for many types of behavioral reinforcers.

metabolism (of drugs) The breakdown or inactivation of drug molecules by enzymes, often in the liver.

metabolite A product of enzyme action on a drug.

metabolize To break down or inactivate a neurotransmitter (or a drug) through enzymatic action.

methadone A long-lasting synthetic opioid; commonly used in the long-term treatment for opioid dependence.

methadone maintenance A program for treatment of narcotic addicts in which the synthetic drug methadone is provided to the addicts in an oral dosage form, so that they can maintain their addiction legally.

methylphenidate A stimulant used in treating ADHD; brand name Ritalin.

Mexican brown A form of heroin that first appeared on American streets in the mid-1970s. Because the heroin is made from the hydrochloride salt of morphine, it is brown in its pure form.

moist snuff A type of oral smokeless tobacco that is popular among young American men. A "pinch" of this finely chopped, moistened, flavored tobacco is held in the mouth, often between the lower lip and the gum.

monoamine A class of chemicals characterized by a single amine group; monoamine transmitters include dopamine, norepinephrine, and serotonin.

monoamine oxidase (MAO) inhibitor A drug that acts by inhibiting the enzyme monoamine oxidase (MAO). Used as an antidepressant.

mood disorder Mental disorders characterized by depressed or manic symptoms.

morphine A narcotic; the primary active chemical in opium. Heroin is made from morphine.

morphinism An older term used to describe dependence on the use of morphine.

motivational interviewing A technique for encouraging alcoholics or addicts to seek treatment by first assessing their degree of dependence and then discussing the assessment results. Direct confrontation is avoided.

multiple sclerosis An autoimmune illness caused by damage to the myelin sheath that wrap axons. A wide range of symptoms can accompany this disorder including muscle spasms, vision loss, severe pain, dizziness, fatigue, and intestinal problems.

myelin A fatty white substance that is wrapped around portions of the axons.

N

naloxone An opioid antagonist used in treating alcoholism.

naltrexone An opioid receptor blocker that has been shown to reduce urges for various substances.

narcolepsy A form of sleep disorder characterized by bouts of muscular weakness and falling asleep suddenly and involuntarily. The most common treatment employs stimulant drugs such as amphetamine to maintain wakefulness during the day.

narcotic Opioid (in pharmacology terms), or a drug that is produced or sold illegally (in legal terms); in the United States, a "controlled substance."

narcotic antagonists Drugs that can block the actions of narcotics.

Native American Church A religious organization active among American Indians, in which the hallucinogenic peyote cactus is used in conjunction with Christian religious themes.

NDA In FDA procedures, a New Drug Application. This application, demonstrating both safety and effectiveness of a new drug in both animal and human experiments, must be submitted by a drug company to the FDA before a new drug can be marketed.

neuroleptic A general term for the antipsychotic drugs (also called *major tranquilizers*).

neuron A brain cell that analyzes and transmits information via chemical and electrical signals.

neuropathic pain A chronic condition that leads to persistent pain symptoms.

neuropeptides Small proteinaceous substances produced and released by neurons that act on neural targets.

neurotransmission The process of transferring information from one neuron to another at a synapse.

neurotransmitter A chemical messenger that is released by one neuron and that alters the electrical activity in another neuron; its effects are brief and local.

Nicotiana Any of several types of tobacco plant, including *N. tobacum* and *N. rustica*.

Nicotiana rustica (*russ* **tick a**) The less desirable species of tobacco, which is not widely grown in the United States.

Nicotiana tobacum (**ni co she** *ann* **a toe** *back* **um**) The species of tobacco widely cultivated for smoking and chewing products.

nicotine The chemical contained in tobacco that is responsible for its psychoactive effects and for tobacco dependence.

nigrostriatal dopamine pathway A group of dopamine-containing neurons that have their cell bodies in the substantia nigra of the midbrain and their terminals in the corpus striatum (basal ganglia), which is part of the extrapyramidal motor system. It is this pathway that deteriorates in Parkinson's disease and on which antipsychotic drugs act to produce side effects resembling Parkinson's disease.

nitrosamines A group of organic chemicals, many of which are highly carcinogenic. At least four are found only in tobacco, and these might account for much of the cancer-causing property of tobacco.

nonspecific effects Effects of a drug that are not changed by changing the chemical makeup of the drug. Also referred to as placebo effects.

norepinephrine A neurotransmitter that might be important for regulating waking and appetite.

NORML National Organization for the Reform of Marijuana Laws.

NSAIDs Nonsteroidal anti-inflammatory drugs, such as ibuprofen and naproxen.

nucleus accumbens A collection of neurons in the forebrain thought to play an important role in emotional reactions to events.

nucleus basalis A group of large cell bodies found just below the basal ganglia and containing acetylcholine. These cells send terminations widely to the cerebral cortex. In Alzheimer's disease, there is a loss of these neurons and a reduction in the amount of acetylcholine in the cortex.

O

off-label Use of a prescription drug to treat a condition for which the drug has not received U.S. FDA approval.

opioid One of a group of drugs similar to morphine, used medically primarily for their analgesic effects. Opioids include drugs derived from opium and synthetic drugs with opium-like effects.

opioid antagonist Any of several drugs that are capable of blocking the effects of opioids. Used in emergency medicine to treat overdose and in some addiction treatment programs to block the effect of any illicit opioid that might be taken. Nalorphine and naltrexone are examples.

opium A sticky raw substance obtained from the seed pods of the opium poppy and containing the narcotic chemicals morphine and codeine.

organic disorder For mental disorders, those with a known physical cause (e.g., psychosis caused by long-term alcohol use).

OTC Over-the-counter. OTC drugs are those drugs that can be purchased without a prescription.

P

Papaver somniferum The opium poppy.

paraphernalia In general, the equipment used in some activity. Drug paraphernalia include such items as syringes, pipes, scales, or mirrors.

parasympathetic The branch of the autonomic nervous system that has acetylcholine as its neurotransmitter and, for example, slows the heart rate and activates the intestine.

Parkinson's disease A degenerative disease of the extrapyramidal motor system, specifically involving damage to the nigrostriatal dopamine system. Early symptoms include muscular rigidity, tremors, a shuffling gait, and a masklike face. Occurs primarily in the elderly.

passive smoking The inhalation of tobacco smoke from the air by nonsmokers.

patent medicines Proprietary medicines. Originally referred to medicines that were, in fact, treated as inventions and patented in Great Britain. In America, the term came to refer to medicines sold directly to the public.

PCP Phenycyclidine; 1-(1-phenylcyclohexl) piperidine. A drug with hallucinogenic properties that was originally

developed as an anesthetic; it is not legally available for human use. This hallucinogen is often referred to as angel dust.

PDR *Physician's Desk Reference*, a book listing all prescription drugs and giving prescribing information about each. Updated yearly.

pekoe A grade of tea.

peptide A class of chemicals made up of sequences of amino acids. Enkephalins are small peptides containing only five amino acids, whereas large proteins may contain hundreds.

peyote A hallucinogenic cactus containing the chemical mescaline.

phantastica Hallucinogens that create a world of fantasy.

pharmacodynamic tolerance Reduced effectiveness of a drug resulting from altered nervous system sensitivity.

phenothiazines A group of chemicals that includes several antipsychotic medications.

phenylpropanolamine (PPA) Until 2000, an active ingredient in over-the-counter weight-control products.

physical dependence Defined by the presence of a consistent set of symptoms when use of a drug is stopped. These withdrawal symptoms imply that homeostatic mechanisms of the body had made adjustments to counteract the drug's effects and without the drug the system is thrown out of balance.

placebo An inactive drug, often used in experiments to control for nonspecific effects of drug administration.

postsynaptic Refers to structures associated with the neural membrane on the receiving side of a synapse.

potency Measured by the amount of a drug required to produce a given effect.

precursor Something that precedes something else. In biochemistry, a precursor molecule may be acted upon by an enzyme and changed into a different molecule. For example, the dietary amino acid tryptophan is the precursor for the neurotransmitter serotonin.

prodrugs Drugs that are administered in an inactive form and become effective after they are chemically modified in the body by enzymes.

Prohibition The period 1920–1933, during which the sale of alcoholic beverages was prohibited in the United States.

proof A measure of a beverage's alcohol content; twice the alcohol percentage.

proprietary A medicine that is marketed directly to the public. Also called *OTC (over-the-counter), patent,* or *nonprescription* medicines.

prostaglandins Local hormones, some of which are synthesized in response to cell injury and are important for initiating pain signals. Aspirin and similar drugs inhibit the formation of prostaglandins.

protective factors Behaviors, attitudes, or situations that correlate with low rates of deviant behavior, including use of illicit drugs. Examples include commitment to school, religiosity, and having parents who communicate opposition to drug use.

protein binding The combining of drug molecules with blood proteins.

psilocybin The active hallucinogenic chemical in *Psilocybe* mushrooms.

psychedelic Another name for hallucinogenic drugs. Has a somewhat positive connotation of mind viewing or mind clearing.

psychoactive A term used to describe drugs that have their principal effect on the CNS.

psychological dependence Behavioral dependence, indicated by a high rate of drug use, craving for the drug, and a tendency to relapse after stopping use.

psychopharmacology The science that studies the behavioral effects of drugs.

psychosis A type of mental disorder characterized by a loss of contact with reality and by deterioration in social and intellectual functioning.

psychotomimetic Another name for hallucinogenic drugs. Has a negative connotation of mimicking psychosis.

Q

quid A piece of something to be chewed, such as a wad of chewing tobacco.

R

racial discrimination An action that results in unjust or unfair treatment of persons from a specific racial group.

raphe nuclei A group of serotonin-containing neurons found in the brain stem and project widely throughout the brain.

receptors Specialized cell structures that recognize and respond to signals from specific chemicals (neurotransmitters or drugs).

reinforcement The process of strengthening a behavioral tendency by presenting a stimulus contingent on the behavior. For example, the tendency to obtain and take a drug might be strengthened by the stimulus properties of the drug that occur after it is taken, thus leading to psychological dependence.

resting potential The voltage maintained by a cell when it is not generating action potentials. The resting potential of neurons is about -65 mV.

reuptake One process by which neurotransmitter chemicals are removed from synapses. The chemical is taken back up into the cell from which it was released.

Reye's syndrome A rare brain infection that occurs almost exclusively in children and adolescents. There is some evidence that it is more likely to occur in children who have been given aspirin during a bout of flu or chicken pox.

risk factors Behaviors, attitudes, or situations that correlate with, and might indicate the development of, a deviance-prone lifestyle that includes drug or alcohol abuse. Examples are early alcohol intoxification, absence from school, and perceived peer approval of drug use.

rock Another street name for *crack,* a smokable form of cocaine.

Rohypnol (flunitrazepam) A benzodiazepine hypnotic; not sold legally in the United States and known as the "date-rape drug."

S

safety margin The dose range between an acceptable level of effectiveness and the lowest toxic dose.

salicylate A class of chemicals that includes aspirin.

schizophrenia A chronic psychotic disorder for which the cause is unknown.

secondhand smoke Cigarette smoke inhaled from the environment by nonsmokers.

sedative A drug used to relax, tranquilize, or calm a person, reducing stress and excitement.

semipermeable Allowing some, but not all, chemicals to pass.

serotonin A neurotransmitter found in the raphe nuclei that might be important for impulsivity and depression.

shaman A person having access to, and influence in, the world of spirits, especially among certain tribal societies. Also known as medicine men/women.

shisha Sweetened, flavored tobacco for use in a hookah.

side effects Unintended drug effects that accompany the desired therapeutic effect.

sidestream smoke Smoke that comes from the ash of a cigarette or cigar.

sinsemilla A process for growing marijuana that is especially potent in its psychological effects because of a high THC content; from the Spanish for "without seeds."

smokeless tobacco Various forms of chewing tobacco and snuff.

social influence model A prevention model adapted from successful smoking-prevention programs.

somatic system The part of the nervous system that controls the voluntary, skeletal muscles, such as the large muscles of the arms and legs.

specific effects Those effects of a drug that depend on the amount and type of chemical contained in the drug.

speed A street term used at one time for cocaine, then for injectable amphetamine, and later for all types of amphetamine. Probably shortened from *speedball*.

SSRI Selective serotonin reuptake inhibitor; a class of antidepressants that includes Prozac.

stages of change Theoretical description of the cognitive stages through which an addict would go in moving from active use to treatment and abstinence: precontemplation, contemplation, preparation, action, and maintenance.

states' rights The rights and powers held by individual U.S. states rather than by the federal government.

stimulant Any of a group of drugs that has the effect of reversing mental and physical fatigue.

striatum A term used to describe the caudate nucleus and putamen. Located in the forebrain, it is involved in the initiation of body movements and procedural memory.

subcutaneous Under the skin. A form of injection in which the needle penetrates through the skin (about 3/8 inch) but does not enter a muscle or vein.

substantia nigra A dopamine-rich midbrain structure that projects to the striatum.

sympathetic nervous system The branch of the autonomic nervous system that contains norepinephrine as its neurotransmitter and, for example, increases heart rate and blood pressure.

sympathomimetic Any drug that stimulates the sympathetic branch of the autonomic nervous system for example, amphetamine.

symptom In medical terms, an abnormality that indicates a disease. When applied to abnormal behavior, seems to imply a medical model in which an unseen disease causes the abnormal behavior.

synapse The space between neurons.

synaptic vesicles Small bubbles of membrane that store neurotransmitters.

synesthesia A phenomenon in which the different senses become blended or mixed for example, a sound is "seen." Might be reported by a person taking hallucinogens.

synthesis The formation of a chemical compound. For example, some neurotransmitter chemicals must be synthesized within the neuron by the action of enzymes on precursors.

T

tachyphylaxis A rapid form of tolerance in which a second dose of a drug has a smaller effect than a first dose taken only a short time before.

tar With regard to tobacco, a complex mixture of chemicals found in cigarette smoke. After water, gases, and nicotine are removed from the smoke, the remaining residue is considered to be tar.

tardive dyskinesia A movement disorder that appears after several weeks or months of treatment with antipsychotic drugs and that usually becomes worse if use of the drug is discontinued.

temperance With reference to alcohol, temperance originally meant avoiding hard liquor and consuming beer and wine in moderation. Eventually the temperance movement adopted complete abstinence as its goal and prohibition as the means.

tetrahydrocannabinol The most active of the many chemicals found in cannabis (marijuana).

THC Tetrahydrocannabinol.

theobromine A mild stimulant similar to caffeine and found in chocolate; a xanthine.

theophylline A mild stimulant similar to caffeine and found in tea; a xanthine.

therapeutic index (TI) Ratio of the lethal dose to the effective dose for half the animals in an experiment (LD_{50}/ED_{50}).

time course Timing of the onset, duration, and termination of a drug's effect in the body.

tolerance The reduced effectiveness of a drug after repeated administration.

toxic Poisonous, dangerous.

transporter Mechanism in the nerve terminal membrane responsible for removing neurotransmitter molecules from the synapse by taking them back into the neuron.

tricyclics A group of chemicals used in treating depression.

truth serum Any drugs used to "loosen the tongue," in association with either psychotherapy or interrogation. Although people might speak more freely after receiving some drugs, there is no guarantee that anything they say is true.

U

uptake The process by which a cell expends energy to concentrate certain chemicals within itself. For example, precursor substances to be synthesized into neurotransmitters must be taken up by the neuron.

V

values clarification A type of affective education that avoids reference to drugs but focuses on helping students recognize and express their own feelings and beliefs.

vaping The use of electricity to heat cannabis products, causing a release of cannabis resin as a vapor that is inhaled.

ventral tegmental area A group of dopamine-containing neurons located in the midbrain whose axons project to the forebrain, especially the nucleus accumbens and cortex.

Vyvanse (lisdexamfetamine dimesylate) A slightly different version of Adderall, approved to treat ADHD.

W

Wernicke-Korsakoff syndrome Chronic mental impairments produced by heavy alcohol use over a long period of time.

withdrawal syndrome The set of symptoms that occur reliably when someone stops taking a drug; also called abstinence syndrome.

X

xanthine The chemical class that includes caffeine, theobromine, and theophylline.

Index